CHRISTIAN
PETERSEN
SCULPTOR

This book is published on the occasion of the exhibition

CHRISTIAN PETERSEN, SCULPTOR

At the Brunnier Art Museum
University Museums
Iowa State University, Ames
22 August–31 December 2000

CHRISTIAN PETERSEN

SCULPTOR

LEA ROSSON DELONG

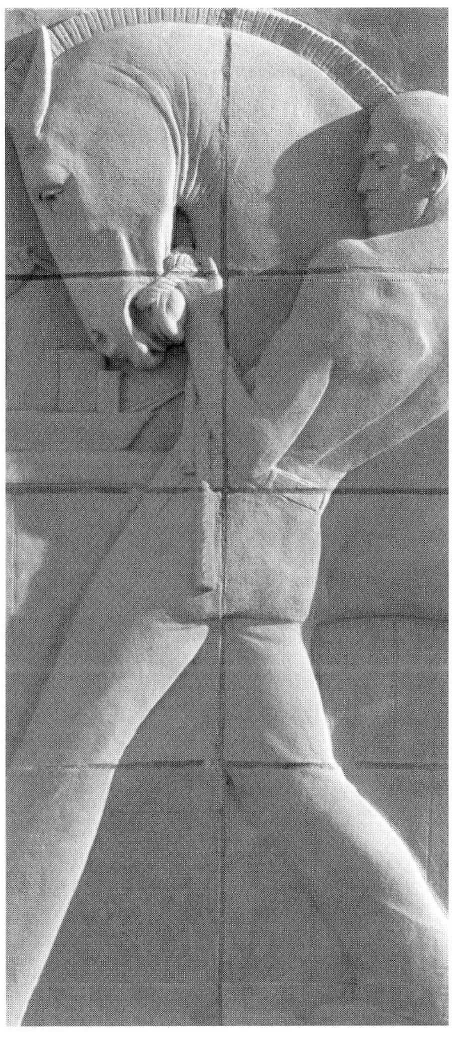

With contributions by
PATRICIA LOUNSBURY BLISS · CHARLES C. ELDREDGE · LINDA MERK-GOULD · DANA L. MICHELS · LYNETTE L. POHLMAN

IOWA STATE UNIVERSITY PRESS
In association with the Brunnier Art Museum, University Museums, Iowa State University, Ames, Iowa

Patricia Lounsbury Bliss is the author of *Christian Petersen Remembered* (ISU Press, 1986). She was the first to identify and organize Petersen's photographs and sketches, and she successfully nominated Petersen's dairy industry murals to the National Register of Historic Places.

Lea Rosson DeLong received her B.A. from the University of Oklahoma and her master's and Ph.D. from the University of Kansas. She is currently research curator at the Des Moines Art Center.

Dr. Charles C. Eldredge, presently the Hall Distinguished Professor of American Art and Culture at the University of Kansas, was formerly director of the Smithsonian Institution's National Museum of American Art.

Linda Merk-Gould is a Fellow of the American Institute for Conservation and a Fellow of the International Institute for Conservation. In 1982 she started Fine Objects Conservation, Inc., which was re-incorporated in Connecticut in 1995 as Conservation Technical Associates LLC.

Dana L. Michels received a B.A. from Drake University, and an M.A. with a focus on twentieth-century American art from the University of Iowa. She is currently curatorial assistant for the Brunnier Art Museum, University Museums, Iowa State University.

Lynette L. Pohlman is the director of the University Museums at Iowa State University. She administers and is chief curator of the Brunnier Art Museum and the Farm House Museum, and she heads the Art on Campus Program at ISU.

Iowa State University Press
2121 South State Avenue, Ames, Iowa 50014
Orders: 1-800-862-6657
Office: 1-515-292-0140
Fax: 1-515-292-3348
Web site: www.isupress.edu

∞ Printed on acid-free paper in the United State of America

First edition, 2000

Library of Congress Cataloging-in-Publication Data
Delong, Lea Rosson.
  Christian Petersen, sculptor / Lea Rosson DeLong;
  with contributions by Patricia Lounsbury Bliss ... [et al.] — 1st ed.
  p. cm.
  Exhibition catalogs.
  Includes bibliographical references and index.
  ISBN 0-8138-2946-1 (alk. paper)
  1. Petersen, Christian, 1884 or 5-1961— Exhibitions. I. Bliss, Patricia Lounsbury. II. Title.

NB237.P4 A4 2000
730'.92-dc21   00-033463

The last digit is the print number: 9 8 7 6 5 4 3 2 1

TABLE OF CONTENTS

*Create an American art, here in the rich soil of
the middlewest, where America has its roots. Here
shall be the soul and the seed and the strength of art.*

*Christian Petersen, unpublished writings
Special Collections Department
Iowa State University Library*

The relationship between Christian Petersen and Iowa State University is one of the most enduring in the history of this university, and one of the most meaningful in terms of defining its role in our society.

Christian Petersen loved Iowa, especially its people. All it took for him to fall in love with this state was one visit in the 1920s. In his words, "The country and the people so impressed me that I longed to return to the Midwest. And eventually, I came back, with the feeling that here was the place, in the very heart of America, where American art might flourish."

Petersen must have sensed in the people of Iowa the same quality that led this state to become first in the nation to embrace the land-grant movement — the movement that created Iowa State University and that forever changed higher education in the United States.

The marriage of practical and liberal education — agriculture and literature, engineering and philosophy, chemistry and art — is the unique and fundamental academic premise upon which the land-grant institutions were founded. Iowans understand this ideal, and I'm sure this is part of what attracted Petersen to Iowa and to Iowa State. Through his more than two decades of intense artistic labor here, he strengthened this marriage by portraying real life — people, animals, settings, and purposes — in images sculpted by perceptive eyes and gifted hands.

His sculptures are among our most beloved symbols, not only of this university, but of agriculture, veterinary medicine, and our national culture and heritage. More importantly, they provide a permanent visual representation and inspirational reminder of the importance of educating students for success in all aspects of life — professionally and as citizens and leaders in society — and the central role that art plays in that kind of education.

We are very fortunate that Petersen chose to come to Iowa State, and even more fortunate that he chose to make the campus his personal, professional and artistic home. With the largest public collection of works of art by Petersen and more than three hundred other works of art by scores of other artists, the Iowa State University campus has become an artistic, cultural, and educational treasure for all the people of Iowa to enjoy.

Iowa State has pledged to preserve this treasure so that it can continue to serve as an inspiration to future generations of Iowa State University students and Iowans — so that they, too, can be uplifted by its beauty and inspired by the creative and artistic genius of Christian Petersen. Indeed, over the past six years, all of the major works of art by Petersen in Iowa State's collection that were in need of conservation have been conserved.

The preservation of Petersen's works of art and the creation of this exhibit and accompanying book serve another important purpose. That purpose is to raise public awareness of this gifted artist and to place his contributions in the larger context of American art history. Petersen's works of art are among the best of the regionalist art of the 1930s and 1940s, yet, because he never sought public acclaim or recognition — some say that when he adopted Iowa as his home state, he also adopted its humility — his work is not well known outside Iowa.

We want to change that, both because the quality of his creations deserves broader recognition and because we believe it's important that others know the role that Iowa, Iowa State University, and individuals such as Christian Petersen played in the birth and development of the land-grant movement. For not only was Iowa the first state to adopt the Morrill Act that began the land-grant movement; not only was Iowa State University the first chartered land-grant institution in the nation; but Christian Petersen was also the first artist-in-residence at any college or university — public or private — in the nation.

Iowans should be proud of their leadership in the land-grant movement. Iowa State University is pleased to organize and curate this book and exhibition to document one of the major contributions to this leadership — the artistic contributions of Christian Petersen.

*Martin C. Jischke
President, Iowa State University*

As with many museum projects, the concept for an exhibition and book dedicated to Christian Petersen originated long ago and underwent an extended process of germination. I was a student in the 1970s when I happened to meet Christian's widow, Charlotte, in the courtyard of Iowa State University's Dairy Industry Building (now the Food Sciences Building). She was enjoying Christian's first bas-relief, the *History of Dairying Mural* that he created for Iowa State in 1934. I was struggling with an assignment to draw the mural. At the time, I did not know who Christian Petersen was, let alone his impact on Iowa State. Charlotte made quick note of my drawing deficiencies and gently offered her humorously sage council for an improved sketch. During our conversation that warm spring day, I learned about this helpful stranger and her credentials for offering advice on my drawing of Christian's mural. I was captivated as Charlotte spoke of her husband and his love for sculpture. In the Dairy Industry Courtyard, by the glistening pool, near the Jersey cows, my eyes, mind, and heart opened to the legacy of Christian Petersen. The seed was planted, and it took nearly twenty years to blossom.

It is quite appropriate that the Brunnier Art Museum of University Museums at Iowa State University undertake an assessment of Christian Petersen and his place in American art. Commissioned to do sculptural work, Petersen visited Iowa often in the 1920s and early 1930s, then returned to stay in 1934. He arrived at Iowa State College in 1934 with the intention of staying only a few months to complete a campus sculpture project. He subsequently remained for twenty-one years as sculptor-in-residence and as a member of the art faculty. He was the first collegiate sculptor-in-residence in the United States. Until this exhibition and publication, the honor of being this country's first university artist-in-residence went to John Steuart Curry, who received his appointment in 1936 at the University of Wisconsin in Madison. Christian Petersen now publicly holds this honor. His legacy at Iowa State literally changed the face of the campus, adding beauty as well as promoting social, cultural, and intellectual campus discourse.

This book and exhibition also celebrate the conservation of Petersen's major public works of art on the Iowa State campus. Due to Iowa's extreme weather patterns, several of Petersen's campus sculptures had experienced damage over time and were in danger of being lost. Of the twelve sculptures, ten have been conserved in the last six years, ensuring their preservation for the future.

This comprehensive retrospective brings together a cross section of Petersen's finest sculptures, preparatory models, and drawings. While thousands of people view his sculptures on the Iowa State campus each year, it has been more than forty years since the public has seen many of Petersen's studio sculptures. In addition, many private commissions are being seen publicly for the first time in this exhibition. Collectively, the works of art presented provide both a broad overview and an intimate insight into the rich oeuvre of a man whose influence is still passionately felt, most especially by the Iowa State family of students, alumni, and friends. We hope that through this book and exhibition the national public may become aware and appreciative of this most influential sculptor.

Petersen's sculptures were created with passion and intensity. Often times, inspiration came to him through his wife and her passion, the literary arts. It was words, phrases, and stories that truly delighted Charlotte, and she shared many of her favorite readings with Christian, who, in turn, found his own motivation from them. Some of those words are inscribed in his terra cotta and stone. They are also included in this book and began a legacy that continues today at Iowa State. They inspired today's Art on Campus Collection that has grown to include more than three hundred major works of art created by nationally and internationally significant visual artists. These works of art are located across campus in courtyards, lobbies, and other public spaces. Poets are regularly commissioned to contribute to the Art on Campus Poetry Collection, excerpts from which are printed in this book.

The Petersens arrived in Iowa during a tumultuous decade. The Spanish Civil War raged; Hitler and Mussolini rose to power; and World War II broke out in Europe. During the Great Depression, economic survival was a common concern for most Americans. The Gross National Product fell, imports dropped, and net income shrank, while unemployment steadily mounted. In the spring of 1933, with unprecedented speed, Franklin Delano Roosevelt's administration created a number of programs designed to relieve the plight of the nation's unemployed, one of whom was Petersen. The principal relief agency, the Works Progress Administration (WPA) was responsible for building roads, schools, and parks. It also had a mandate to decorate its new constructions, so in addition to construction workers, the WPA employed visual artists.

Petersen came to Iowa State College in the midst of national and international crisis. It was a time when the college was undertaking a progressive plan to promote the economic, intellectual, and moral development of the people of the state as part of the land-grant mission. Invited by President Raymond Hughes, Petersen fit into Hughes' campus vision of imparting solid science and technology education and providing students with an understanding of the humanities. Hughes initiated many interdisciplinary programs, as well as the first Iowa State courses in visual, performing, and literary arts appreciation. Petersen's sculptor-in-residency project was a continuation of his commitment to the arts.

In Petersen, Hughes found a kindred spirit. Also of Danish descent, Raymond M. Hughes (1873–1958, president 1927–1936) was Iowa State's first Iowa-born president. He grew up in Ohio and graduated from Ohio University in Miami with a degree in chemistry. Hughes guided the College through the difficult Depression years. He brought Iowa State into a more harmonious relationship with her sister institutions in the state through projects such as partnering with the University of Iowa in commissioning Grant Wood to create the first Public Works of Art Project (PWAP) and WPA projects for Iowa. This resulted in the creation of two murals at the Iowa State Library, *When Tillage Begins, Other Arts Follow* (1934) and *Breaking the Prairie* (1936–1937). The commission ultimately led to Grant Wood inviting Christian Petersen to Iowa to work on the terra cotta murals for the Dairy Industry Building. Hughes also promoted the enrichment of technical curricula at the College and teamed Petersen with Paul E. Cox, professor of ceramic engineering. It was Cox who taught Petersen the technical processes of using and kiln-firing terra cotta that Petersen ultimately used on seven major sculptures at Iowa State. This artistic partnership with scientific and technological overtones was a perfect match for Iowa State and Petersen. Hughes broadened campus research to focus on problems involving interdisciplinary efforts. Christian responded to this by creating public works of art representing a variety of campus departments, including agriculture, veterinary medicine, residence halls, athletics, and home economics. Hughes and Petersen were equally devoted to young people. Hughes instituted the development of placement and student counseling services, and Petersen, who had a reputation as a caring and patient teacher, immortalized students in his sculptures.

While Hughes provided Petersen the opportunity to work on campus, searched for funds to pay for his creative endeavors during the Depression, and set him on his artistic course at Iowa State, it was President Friley with whom Petersen spent most of his sculptor-in-residence career at Iowa State. Charles Friley (1887–1958, president 1936–1953) was a Louisiana native who graduated from Texas A&M, Columbia University, and the University of Chicago. The artistic relationship between Friley and Petersen was never as close and collaborative as that between Hughes and Petersen.

The late 1930s to 1950s spanned higher education's most turbulent era from the closing phase of the Depression through World War II and into the post-war period. Extension and research played vital roles in Iowa's recovery from the Depression, while Iowa State engaged in intensive academic self-appraisal, modernizing its curriculum with a shift from a practical emphasis toward a scientific one. As a college with highly developed programs in technology instruction and research, Iowa State became strategically vital as a World War II training center for more than 16,000 navy, air force and army personnel (1942–1944). After the recruitment of his young students to the war effort, Petersen dramatically portrayed these losses in *Men of Two Wars* and *Price of Victory*. Iowa State Extension conducted massive statewide programs to maximize Iowa's home-front contribution to the war effort, particularly in food production, preservation, and conservation. These themes had earlier been found in Petersen's campus sculptures such as *History of Dairying* and the *Fountain of the Four Seasons*.

Between 1933 and 1943, artists from across the United States created thousands of murals, sculptures, paintings, and silk-screened posters under New Deal art programs. The sheer volume of new art inspired other artists such as Christian Petersen, working outside the federal programs, to adopt themes of work and progress.

Petersen was one of the artists during this period who sought to establish a native style that would convey a renewed belief in the promise of America. These artists turned to the Midwest, where the folkways, customs, and ideals of farmers and workers provided reassuring, nostalgic images. Petersen was one artist who returned to the Midwest to live and work his artistic ideology. Petersen and other artists depicted the everyday heroism of life on farms, in small towns, and on campuses with straightforward naturalism. Their focus on local subjects and narrative themes earned them the label of *regionalists*. Many of Petersen's works were regionalist in subject matter, although he was not included in the pantheon of regionalists: Grant Wood, John Steuart Curry, and Thomas Hart Benton.

Prior to the scholarship presented in these pages, Christian Petersen has not been defined as a significant figure in the annals of American art history. Petersen provided a visual, intellectual, and emotional legacy at Iowa State. Through his art he paid tribute to the heroic accomplishments of students and the common person. He is an exemplar of an important artist of this region, and for that we must recognize his contribution to American art.

Lynette L. Pohlman
Director of University Museums
Iowa State University

Charlotte and Christian Petersen sought a life of art and to share art with campus students, family, and friends. Never seeking public acclaim, Christian's desire was to create and teach art, and his efforts produced a campus legacy. This exhibition and book is Iowa State's expression of gratitude and recognition for that legacy. It took many dedicated people to see these projects through to their fruition. I am pleased and honored to acknowledge their gracious help, commitment, and expertise.

I would like to thank Mary Petersen who over the years has made possible the museum's acquisition of more than 400 drawings by her father. These drawings provide an invaluable resource to understanding Christian Petersen's artistic development. She also generously gifted several of his sculptures to the permanent collection. These museum acquisitions vastly expanded the large holdings of over 550 works of art now forming the Christian Petersen Collection at the Brunnier Art Museum and as part of the Art on Campus Collection of the University Museums at Iowa State University.

One of the primary goals in undertaking this exhibition and book was to provide an understanding of Christian Petersen in American art. Dr. Lea Rosson DeLong and Dr. Charles C. Eldredge wonderfully fulfilled this primary task. I would like to especially thank Dr. DeLong for her scholarship and the diligent development of her essay for this publication and exhibition. Her essay elucidates and provides new insights into Christian's art. As guest curator, she selected the works of art for the exhibition and assisted in developing Petersen's catalogue raisonné, exhibition checklist, annotated chronology, and installation design. Her scholarly perspectives meaningfully united Petersen's career and are her legacy to the artist, the University Museums, and Iowa State. Noted scholar Dr. Charles C. Eldredge also contributed to this publication and provided vision and validation of Petersen's place in American art history, and I warmly thank him.

A special thank-you is extended to Patricia Lounsbury Bliss, who reflected and contributed on Charlotte as Christian's inspired muse in this book. Pat also wrote *Christian Petersen Remembered,* published by the Iowa State University Press in 1986. Her scholarship formed a pivotal publication, preserving the direct oral history of Charlotte Petersen. For this project, her advice, recollections, and perspectives were sought and enthusiastically given.

Linda Merk-Gould and the staff at Conservation Technical Associates, Westport, Connecticut, performed the valuable service of conserving, stabilizing, and preserving many of Petersen's sculptures for the future. She exhaustively researched Petersen's artistic style and applied her considerable expertise to conserving Petersen's sculptures in a way true to his vision. In all, Conservation Technical Associates conserved ten campus works of art and more than thirty small studio sculptures. Key conservators included Linda Merk-Gould, Joe Sembrat, Francis Miller, and Patty Miller. I thank them for helping us preserve Petersen's legacy. In summarizing for this book the conservation methods and treatments used on Petersen's art, Linda Merk-Gould has also preserved the documentation for future reference, and I thank her for this contribution of the conservation chapter.

Over the last eight years, with generous financial support from private and public donations, Iowa State has accomplished the monumental task of conserving Petersen's major public works of art on campus. I would like thank Mary Atherly of University Museums, Cathy Brown of the ISU Facilities, Planning, and Management Department, and Ivan Hanthorn, associate professor in ISU's Special Collections Department at Iowa State University Library, for their remarkable efforts in accessing, recording, and organizing conservation efforts.

Christian Petersen never kept a listing of any of the works of art he made. The task of locating his art and creating a catalogue raisonné is probably not over, and with the publication of this book and the presentation of the exhibition, we expect additional works of art will come to light. We began the listing with 450 of Petersen's works of art and ended with over 1,150 sculptures, drawings, and paintings. *Visions Magazine*, published by the Iowa State Alumni Association, helped us reach more than 30,000 ISU alumni and friends. The response was overwhelming, and I sincerely appreciate the hundreds of people from across the country who responded to the Museum's request for information about Petersen and his art. I would like to thank Carole Gieseke, Karol Crosbie, and the *Visions Magazine* staff for promoting the search for Christian's art.

The expertise and support of our museum staff were essential to mounting the exhibition *Christian Petersen, Sculptor* and preparing this book. I would like to recognize Mary Atherly for assistance with the checklist compilation, stewardship of the loans to the exhibit, and accompanying shipping arrangements. Dana Michels, curatorial assistant, led the efforts in compiling the catalogue raisonné, exhibition checklist, annotated chronology, and myriad details associated with presentation of the exhibition, and I sincerely thank her. Terri Hasselman, director of development, secured public and private funding for the entire project, and her detective work in locating works of art was invaluable. Marilyn Vaughan, public relations coordinator, shepherded this publication through development and compiled the publication's photographs. Stacy Brothers, administrative assistant, provided administrative editing and organizational support; Matthew DeLay, curator of education, developed interpretive programs; and Reneé Senter, former curator of education, assisted with concept development of the project and authored the school curriculum guide.

I am very grateful to the public and private lenders to this exhibition, all of whom are listed at the back of this volume (see Lenders and Donors to the Exhibition). Without their cooperation, *Christian Petersen, Sculptor* would not have had the depth and comprehensiveness that so clearly distinguishes it.

To Gretchen Van Houten, Anne Bolen, and Sherry Johnson at Iowa State University Press, I offer our appreciation for the masterful production of this book. I also wish to thank copy editor, Bonnie Harmon, for the careful reading and shaping of the manuscript and Nita Upchurch for the book design.

In an institution, we all walk in the shadows and inspirations of those who came before us. Certainly I am grateful to Charlotte and Christian Petersen, for they gave a life's creative work to Iowa State. There are others who have been fundamentally instrumental to the development of this project. Paul E. Cox, head of ceramic engineering from 1920 to 1939, taught Christian Petersen how to use and kiln-fire terra cotta. Without this partnership of art and science, Petersen would have never created the large public sculptures for the Iowa State campus. President Raymond Hughes advanced the arts and humanities early in Iowa State's history and had the courage and vision to commission public works of art during an era of great national strife and world turmoil. Joanne M. Hanson and Marjorie Garfield were chairs of the applied arts department during Petersen's tenure. They supported Christian and his work, and have not publicly received credit for the behind-the-scenes administrative support. Neva Petersen, professor emeritus, applied art department, inspired me about Christian Petersen and his art. Carl Hamilton, former vice president of information, allowed for the administrative joining of the Brunnier Art Museum, Farm House Museum, and the Art on Campus Collection into the University Museums in 1980. This allowed us to holistically approach the visual arts collections on the campus of Iowa State, conserve Petersen's campus sculptures, and ultimately present *Christian Petersen, Sculptor*.

Finally, it gives me great pleasure to thank our major sponsors. If I were a poet like Charlotte Petersen, I would craft a verse that would express how thankful and appreciative I am of Roberta and Robert Boeke. Through the years they have been so supportive of the University Museums, from attending museum events, to providing financial support, to always cheering us on. My deepest appreciation goes for their help in conserving the *Fountain of the Four Seasons* and for providing major funding for the publication of this book.

Campus partnerships are vital, and the College of Veterinary Medicine has been an ardent arts supporter for years. Charlotte and Christian Petersen had a special love of the vets, and they of the Petersens. The College of Veterinary Medicine funded the complete conservation of the *Veterinary Medicine Mural* and *The Gentle Doctor*, and also provided funds for the exhibition, *Christian Petersen, Sculptor*. I am deeply grateful to Dean Richard Ross and the many veterinarians, both faculty and alumni, who contributed to the conservation and exhibition. Many thanks also to the Coppola Family in honor of Joseph M. Coppola, Sr.; Iowa State University Foundation; National Endowment for the Arts, a federal agency; Mary Petersen; Mary Alice and Bill Reinhardt; Helen Sebek; John and Doris Salsbury, Stockman Family Foundation; Target Stores, Inc.; and the estate of William R. Merrill. Taken together, their support truly made this landmark project possible.

Lynette L. Pohlman
Director of University Museums
Iowa State University

Working on the career of Christian Petersen has been both enlightening and challenging. The chance to explore, research, and place into context this overlooked figure has been enlightening, as has the opportunity to examine and present his considerable sculptural achievement. It has been challenging because of the need to reconstruct parts of his life with relatively few documents. Petersen was a notoriously reticent man who apparently never attempted to market himself as an artist or to trumpet his accomplishments. He wrote little himself and, after his move to the Midwest, was written about even less in the mainstream art literature of the period. Those documents we do have reflect to a good extent the efforts of his wife, Charlotte, who served as his earliest archivist. It was undoubtedly she, as well, who acted as editor and advisor for his letters and lectures. Finally, it was her recollections which, though naturally biased but mainly accurate, formed the basis for Petersen's first biography, *Christian Petersen Remembered* by Patricia Lounsbury Bliss. No one who studies Petersen or wishes to understand his place at Iowa State University can do so successfully without reference to this foundational work.

Petersen struggled to become a sculptor and to earn his living as an artist, even after he had a secure position on the Iowa State faculty. His training was in die-cutting and other industrial arts, and as a man with a family to support, his formal training in the "fine arts" was acquired in a sporadic fashion. But he persevered, adding to his education and beginning a sculpture career as his professional and personal obligations permitted. Still, this lack of education and the delay in establishing himself as a professional artist proved a hardship for him and may, with his natural modesty, have contributed to his self-effacing posture. But that quality could only be said to apply to his self-advertising. It certainly did not apply when it came to his demands for his sculpture and also, importantly, for its installation. In these cases, he was willing to go up against any obstacle to finish and present his work exactly as he wanted. He frequently declined to comment directly on his sculpture, saying that the work should stand for itself, and in the end, perhaps that is exactly his great strength as an artist. Most people who encounter his major works, including the students at Iowa State University, do not necessarily know anything about him or about the history of American sculpture. Yet his sculpture continues to make its appeal and to endure as a thoughtful and — to use a word he would have embraced — beautiful part of whatever environment it finds itself in today.

One of the primary factors in the survival and good condition of much of Petersen's work is the devotion and attention of the director of the Brunnier Art Museum at Iowa State University, Lynette Pohlman. She has been tireless and highly effective in her efforts to make certain the legacy of this artist remains intact and is advanced. I would like to thank her for asking me to participate in this project and especially for her kind patience and her diligence in seeing this demanding project through. Others on the staff at the Brunnier were essential to this project and not only helped, but actually accomplished, much of the work. Dana Michels, Mary Atherly, Stacy Brothers, Terri Hasselman, and Marilyn Vaughan are all recipients of my most sincere gratitude. The Special Collections Department of the Iowa State University Library, where the Christian Petersen Papers are deposited, was especially helpful in the research and preparation of this project.

A Smithsonian Short-Term Visitor grant at the National Museum of American Art enabled me to conduct some of the research on this project. I thank senior curators Virginia Mecklenburg and George Gurney for their assistance in the grant and their encouragement of my work on Petersen.

Finally, and as always, a great debt is owed to my husband, Tim DeLong, who, despite his own considerable obligations, facilitates my productivity in a pleasant, reliable way.

Lea Rosson DeLong
Guest Curator

I would like to thank Lynette Pohlman, director of the University Museums at ISU, and the deans of the colleges with whom we consulted on this project, particularly Dean Ross, for their understanding of the value of technical studies prior to undertaking treatments. I have been grateful to come to understand the importance of preserving Christian Petersen's art for this community. It has made meeting the challenges inherent in preservation that much more rewarding.

Projects of this scope are most fruitful when undertaken by a committed team. I would like to thank my staff at Conservation Technical Associates for their thoughtful contributions to the projects and associated hard work: Chris Blum, Francis Miller, Patricia Miller, Nancy Persell, Joe Sembrat, and Steve Scrvis.

Linda Merk-Gould
Conservationist
Conservation Technical Associates LLC

INTRODUCTION: CONSIDERING
CHRISTIAN PETERSEN

CHARLES C. ELDREDGE

INTRODUCTION: CONSIDERING CHRISTIAN PETERSEN

The sculpture of Christian Petersen has been long admired by visitors to Iowa State University, with which he began his long association as sculptor-in-residence in 1934. Yet, his art remains unfamiliar to many other Americans today, even to specialists in the subject. His career, well documented by Lea Rosson DeLong elsewhere in this publication, warrants greater attention, both for his own achievements and as the epitome of the concerns and the fates of many American artists of his mid-twentieth-century date.

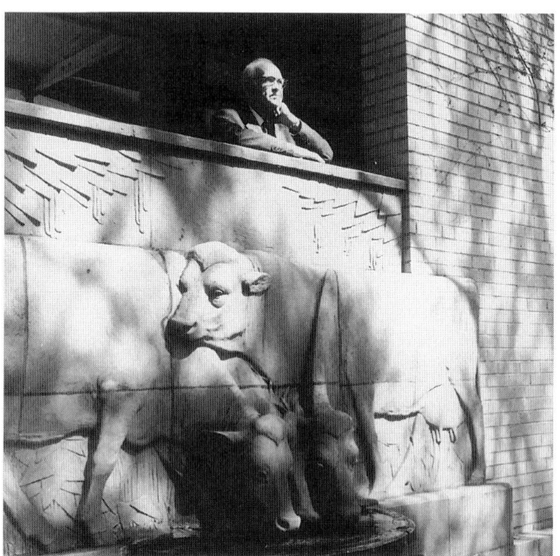

Figure I.1 Christian Petersen (1885-1961) overlooking the fountain of the *History of Dairying Mural*.

REGIONALISM

"Bunk!"

Christian Petersen had a ready response for a journalist's inquiry about his credentials as a regionalist. "Regionalism is the bunk," he replied. The sculptor quickly clarified his jocular response, distinguishing between the mannered styles of certain regionalist painters, such as Thomas Hart Benton or Grant Wood, then much in vogue, and the choice of motifs available to the artist. Separating himself from the former, he explained, "Of course my own work is regional in that it uses the material of the lives of Iowa and middlewestern people. It is natural that the artist uses the material around him. But I do not use a different style or work on eccentric principles because of the regional subject matter."[1] In his proclivity for midwestern motifs, the sculptor conformed to the principles enunciated decades earlier by another Iowan, author-and-critic Hamlin Garland, who advised American artists that "art, to be vital, must be local in its subject."[2]

Like Garland, Petersen envisioned the flourishing of "an American art, here in the Midwest, where America has its roots. Here," he predicted in 1934, "shall be the soil, and the seed, and the strength of art."[3] During the difficult years of the Depression, the agricultural college in Ames provided not only salary (albeit meager), but also inspiration. "I figured I could reach people here that I couldn't get to in a university with art courses," he confessed; "I have always found the keenest appreciation of my efforts has been by men and women whose work calls for some use of the hands."[4]

The issue of regionalism pervaded much of the commentary on American art during the period between world wars. In a review of contemporary American art on display at the 1939 World's Fair in New York, Holger Cahill remarked on the issues of style and subject. "It is interesting to see how regional differences come into play in this exhibition. The most striking distinction is that of subject matter. ... In all of these [regional] sections the artists are concerned with local subject matter." However, even as the artist focused on specifics peculiar to his region — perhaps lumbering in the Northwest, or Yankee fishermen, or, most familiarly, the Midwest's agrarian society — Cahill also recognized that individual artists were coping with formal and technical issues that transcended place: "they are interested too in problems of technique and expression — with the way the artist must use his media to attain the greatest possible coherence, depth and intensity."[5]

Petersen eschewed the exaggerated mannerisms favored by some of his contemporaries, regionalist or otherwise, which he thought could result in "some terrible monstrosities," attention grabbing performances that were "best ignored."[6] Yet many of his Iowa subjects were handled in a manner reflecting stylistic trends then broadly in vogue, suggesting a formal interest that transcended the merely local. If the much bruited regionalist mannerisms of Wood or Benton were not to his liking, he nevertheless brought to his local motifs a stylistic sophistication that betrays a familiarity with and aspiration toward artistic standards shared nationally.

Cahill's recognition of the individual artist's concerns for technique and materials reflected another sculptural preoccupation of the period. "What a wealth and variety of material, plastic or glyptic, now lie within the reach of our sculptors!" exclaimed critic Adeline Adams in 1929. "Monumental works still content themselves with stone and bronze, the good bread and wine of sculptural production, but lesser creations often delight in matter more exotic." For instance, she cited Malvina Hoffman's works in tinted wax, in alabaster, in black Belgian marble, and others in "simili-pierre," in wood, in animated brick, in sublimated coal — "the material in every instance being chosen for artistic fitness."[7]

For Petersen, however, working in such exotic and beautiful materials was out of the question. He might have preferred fine stone or bronze, or yet rarer stuff; but, during the Depression, his precarious financial situation and that of Iowa State College precluded such luxuries. Instead, Petersen worked in humbler materials, generally carved limestone or modelling plaster or terra cotta fired from local clays. Paul Cox, head of the Iowa State ceramics engineering department, who collaborated with Petersen on several campus projects, once reported to the school's president on the values of his laboratory. Not only did it provide student employment and educational benefits, advertise the college's work, and promise industrial development value, but it also, he proudly noted, "Uses Iowa clay rather than Indiana clay."[8] Professor Cox's boast seems a bid for presidential reward for his frugality; but it also conveys a patriotic pride in the resort to local materials for the fabrication of local motifs. In this it echoed the interests of other artists elsewhere during the 1930s. For instance, in San Antonio Octavio Medellin sometimes purposely chose local Texas stones for his carved figures inspired by traditions from his native Mexico, while in California Carroll Barnes carved a figure of John Bunyan for Sequoia National Park from an immense redwood tree, and Glen Lukens developed rough textured glazes from Death Valley minerals for ceramic works that were admired for their "characteristically Southwest feeling."[9] Whether out of regional pride or economic necessity, Petersen joined their ranks in using regional materials to convey a "characteristic feeling" of his Midwest.

FIGURES

Christian Petersen admired artists who combined keenness of observation with habits of introspection. He praised Gutzon Borglum's works, for instance, for their "recordings of American life and thought," which provided one of the "high spots of sculpture, not only of this country, but of the world."[10] His ability to create a likeness earned Petersen multiple commissions for portraits of Iowa's business and government luminaries. Despite his success with such projects, Petersen believed that sculpture should provide more than a likeness, that it "should give one the feeling of force. ... It should be the symbol of life itself."[11] In Iowa, he largely abandoned the classically inspired subjects of his youth, such as the *Spanish-American War Memorial* (1923) in Newport, Rhode Island, in which a robed and armed figure of Liberty tramples the severed head of Medusa. "While we admit the beauty of Greek myths, we no longer believe them, and, as a result, when we try to use them as symbols, we cannot be sincere. If we can get the lesson of sincerity from them and apply it to art, instead of trying to imitate, we can have great art."[12] By the 1930s, Petersen dismissed such classicizing works — including his own — as "those atrocities called 'soldier's' monuments [which were] dumped about the country ... by the ton."[13]

In their stead, he drew inspiration from his observations of rural life and newsworthy events of the day. These led to embodiments of "symbols of life" in contemporary guise, including figures as diverse as a champion cornhusker, a 4-H Club boy showing his calf, and victims of the Ohio River floods of 1938. Some of the most affective of his works are the small studio pieces that dealt with topical issues, such as *Drought* (1938), which personifies the environmental ravages of the Dust Bowl through a Pieta-like composition of a mother whose withered dugs offer no sustenance to the stricken child on her lap. More than the historicizing themes popular among many sculptors of his generation, these images drawn from his own time and place appealed to the artist and to his hard-working Iowa neighbors.

ANIMALS

Given the campus location of his studio in the veterinary quadrangle, animals not surprisingly entered his repertoire of subjects. His former students recalled their teacher sending them from the studio out to the vet barns to draw from the live (animal) models. Their availability and their significance to the school's agricultural curriculum, as well as to the state's economy, made them ready motifs; in this, he was similar to the regionalist painter John Steuart Curry, who, while appointed artist-in-residence at the University of Wisconsin, often depicted the prize livestock of its School of Agriculture (Figure I.2). But Petersen's animal subjects were more than the product of easy access to his models.

During the nineteenth century, animals had emerged as a favorite motif for sculptors in this country and abroad. The Age of Reason's emphasis on human capacities and achievements had often obscured animals' role in art; but in the Romantic era, and continuing through the nineteenth century, they reappeared as the specialty of *animaliers*, the first instance of a "school" focusing entirely on such subjects in an independent manner. In the twentieth century, especially during the years between world wars, animal motifs again gained currency internationally. The subject, which was readily accepted by the public, allowed a new generation of specialists to experiment with emotional and formal expression in works of great stylistic variety. For some of the new *animaliers*, such as San Francisco's Beniamino Bufano, modern form was the primary concern in his work. As he explained, "Some people think of a bear as a bear. I am concerned with the bear only in form."[14] While form is important to any sculptor, for Petersen it was necessarily combined with human associations and artistic empathy. In this, he seemingly followed the advice of Walter Winans, a prominent *animalier* of the early twentieth century, who advised that, "To be able to ... model an animal, one must be in perfect sympathy with that animal. ... The reason why the Danish china-animals are so lifelike, is this — the sculptor sees into the soul of the animal, and understands its feelings and wishes."[15]

In Petersen's work, animals did not often replace man, but were often depicted in combination with him. As his widow recalled, Petersen was "a very religious man ... [with] a reverence toward everything, toward humanity, toward animals, toward growing things around us." For her, Petersen's early panels for the Iowa State veterinary school were a reflection of the artist's thought: "man's contribution to animals, and the contribution of animals to man. One without the other is nothing."[16]

Human associations with animals were also the subject of Petersen's first undertaking at Ames, the ambitious series of terra cotta panels depicting the history of dairying. Agricultural themes figured prominently in the iconography of painted murals that decorated many post offices and other federal buildings during the Roosevelt administration. Such motifs, however, were rarer for sculptors; when the farmer or his environs were depicted three-dimensionally, it was often in allegorical terms, as in Concetta Scaravaglione's limestone relief of *Agriculture* (1937–38) over an entrance to the Federal Trade Commission Building in Washington; elsewhere, similar subjects might evoke not a universal theme but a particular locale, such as Allie Victoria Tennant's WPA relief, *Cattle, Oil and Wheat*, for the post office at Electra, Texas. Petersen's large relief is at once similar to both of these, yet different, too. In the personification of the dairy industry it parallels Scaravaglione's generalized treatment; insofar as that industry was important to his local audience, the reliefs, which were fired from clays gathered in Fort Dodge, Iowa, anticipate Tennant's geographical specificity. Yet, at the same time, his Dairy Industry murals suggest a documentary intent that distinguishes the project from its contemporaries, as Petersen presents a historical tableau of dairying's evolution over time throughout the United States.

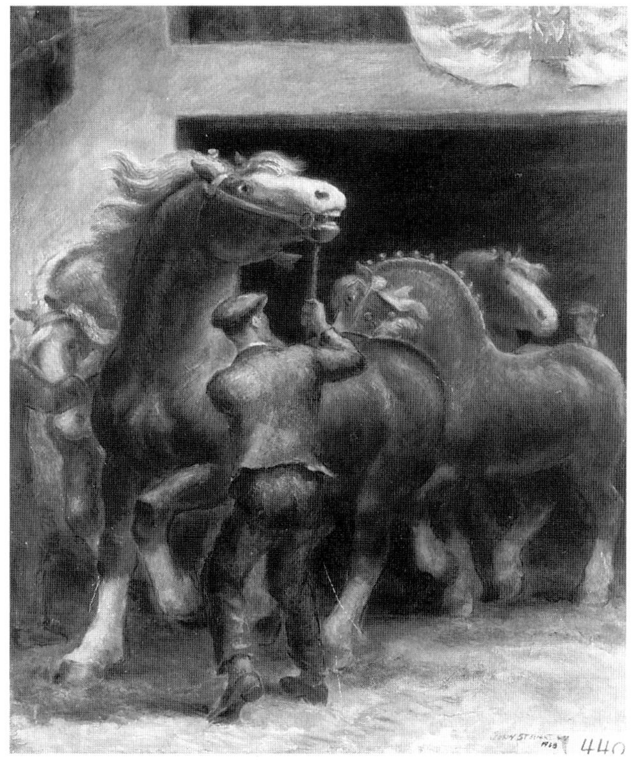

Figure I.2 *The Belgian Stallion*, 1938

John Steuart Curry; National Academy of Design, New York

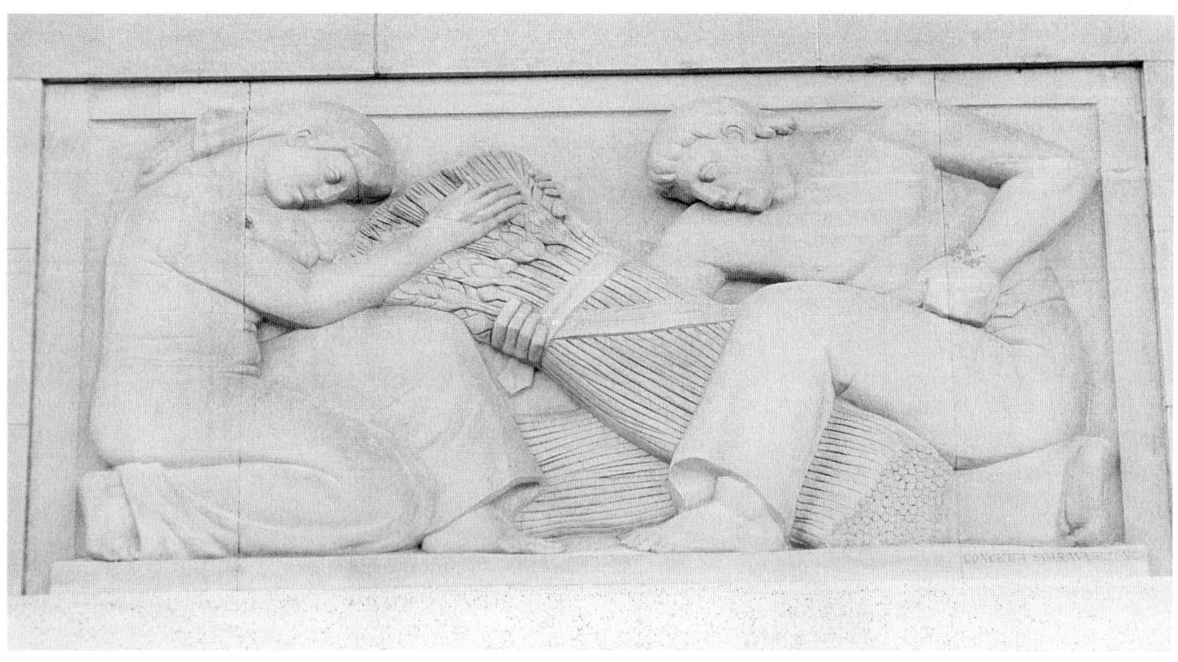

Figure I.3 *Agriculture,* 1937–38

Concetta Scaravaglione; Federal Trade Commission Building, Washington, D.C.

STYLE

Close examination of his models was important to Petersen, be the subject human or animal. Realistic effects were prized by many viewers, such as the critic who wrote approvingly of Marcel Loyau's *Buckingham Fountain* (1927) in Chicago's Grant Park, admiring his creatures for being "anatomically scientific. ... could they be touched to life, [they] would live and move coherently. The esthetic, in other words, is based on the organic."[17] But other factors might also shape the sculptor's aesthetic.

In 1932, critic Walter Agard advised designers of architectural sculpture that their work "must emerge naturally from the building rather than seem gouged out of it." In particular, he recommended "designs of a geometric character in low relief, or even incised in the stone, [which] are better suited to the flat surfaces of modern buildings than the high reliefs of the classical and baroque style." Agard singled out for praise the work of Lee Lawrie, who was then garnering many prominent public commissions across the country, in particular citing his use of the flat "Egyptian relief" technique.[18]

In Petersen's use of profiled figures, human and bovine, and in his masterful low relief, he achieved in the Dairy Industry reliefs an effect that echoed Agard's prescription. The flatness of the simplified forms of man and beast, only slightly relieved from the planar backgrounds, lends his panels an air of modernity suggestive of the stylization favored by other sculptors in the 1930s, such as Lawrie or Jacques Schnier. In the mid-1930s, the Californian Schnier also turned to agricultural themes for a group of panels rendered in similarly shallow, planar reliefs (Figure I.4). His works, with their repetitive decorative patterns, have often been cited as outstanding examples of the Art Deco aesthetic, the modernist impulse that flourished in American art and design in the interwar years.[19]

Petersen's Dairy panels suggest parallels in their agricultural subject with the work of Grant Wood, an artist to whom Petersen owed his initial appointment in Iowa, but to whom the sculptor never felt particularly close.[20] In formal aspects, too, the reliefs suggest inspiration that might have been drawn from the painter; for instance, the isolation of the subjects against blank grounds parallels Wood's treatment of the *Fruits of Iowa* (1932), the artist's humorous, schematic rendering of iconic farm types. Wood's series even included a dairy subject, *Boy Milking Cow* (Figure I.5), whose rump's-eye view presents what Wanda Corn called "a perfection of nature."[21] Petersen's silhouetted bovines, trios of which frame the lengthy composition at each end, are rendered with a similarly striking simplicity. Their overlapping silhouettes seem hinged from a common point at the shoulders, rhymed forms of geometric perfection worthy of Lawrie or Schnier. Indeed, in these terra cotta panels Petersen created for Iowa State a "Deco dairy," a conflation of carefully observed historical motifs and modern style.

Regional or universal? Traditional or modern? In his monuments for the Iowa State University campus, as well as in his independent studio works, Christian Petersen left a legacy that documents his own personal vision; but more than that, this body of work also illustrates the competing forces that flourished in American sculpture during an important transitional period, and it deserves an audience and a (re)consideration beyond its Iowa home.

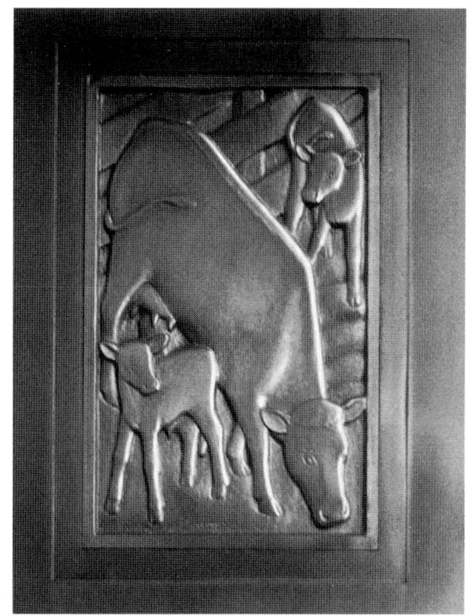

Figure I.4 Bronze Relief for Elevator Doors, 1936

Jacques Schnier; Helm Buildings, Fresno, California

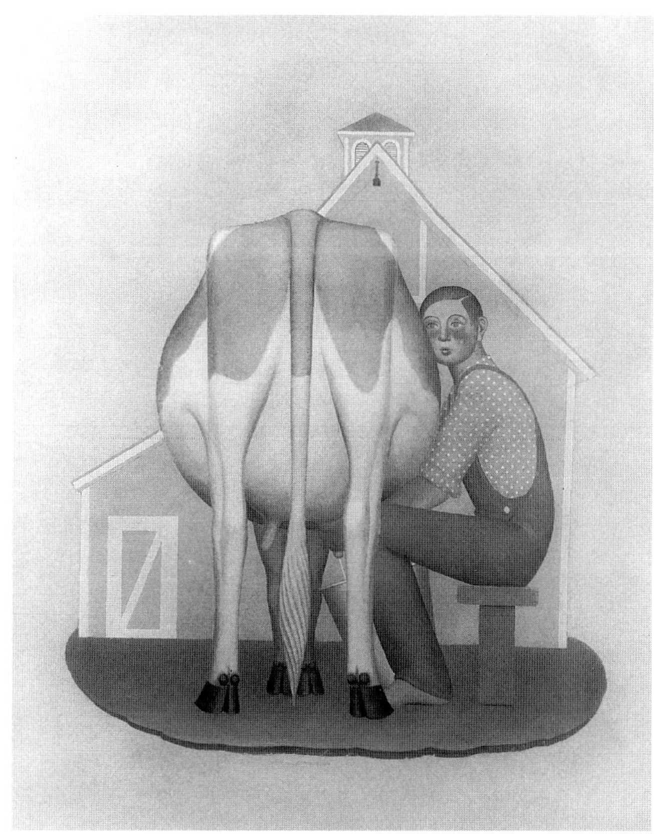

Figure I.5 *Boy Milking Cow*, 1932

Grant Wood, Coe College, Cedar Rapids, Iowa

NOTES

1. Petersen quoted in Virginia Cook, "Petersen in Discussion of Sculpture," *Ames Daily Tribune and Times*, 1 January 1938, 1, 3.

2. Hamlin Garland, "Impressionism," in *Crumbling Idols* (1894); reprinted in John McCoubrey, ed., *American Art 1700–1960: Sources and Documents,* Englewood Cliffs, New Jersey, Prentice-Hall, 1965, 171.

3. Petersen, First faculty lecture, Iowa State College, 1934; in Patricia Lounsbury Bliss, *Christian Petersen Remembered,* Ames, Iowa State University Press, 1986, 190.

4. Petersen, "Comments on quality in art," in Bliss, 189.

5. Holger Cahill, "American Art Today and in the World of Tomorrow: National Panorama of the WPA Projects," *Art News,* Annual Supplement 1940 ("Art at the Fair"), 50.

6. "Some of this has been done with the sole purpose of attracting attention, but then a person walking down main street in his B.V.D.'s with the temperature at zero would also attract attention." Petersen, "Comments on quality in art," in Bliss, 188.

7. Adeline Adams, "The Spirit of American Sculpture Today," *The American Magazine of Art* 20(5) May 1929, 249.

8. Paul E. Cox, to President Raymond E. Hughes, 12 June 1934; quoted in Bliss, 40–41.

9. Virginia Stewart, "Southern California," *Art News*, June 1946, 60.

10. Petersen, "Excerpts from Lectures on Art, 1934–1935," in Bliss, 177.

11. Ibid.

12. Petersen, "Comments on quality in art," in Bliss, 188.

13. Petersen, "Excerpts from Lectures on Art, 1934–1935," in Bliss, 181.

14. Beniamino Bufano, quoted in H. Wilkening and Sonia Brown, *Bufano, An Intimate Biography,* Berkeley, California, Howell-North Books, 1972, 129.

15. Walter Winans, *Animal Sculpture,* New York, G.P. Putnam's Sons, 1913, 1–2. The "Danish china-animals" are likely a reference to the realistically decorated porcelain figurines popularized by the Royal Copenhagen Porcelain Manufactory and other European firms of the nineteenth century. This popular tradition from his homeland might have added to the Danish-born Petersen's interest in animal subjects.

16. Charlotte Petersen, quoted in Bliss, 147, 63.

17. Commentary in *Chicago Tribune*, 4 September 1927; quoted in James L. Riedy, *Chicago Sculpture,* Urbana, University of Illinois Press, 1981, 51.

18. Walter R. Agard, "American Architectural Sculpture," *The American Magazine of Art*, March 1932, 210, 212.

19. See Ilene Susan Fort, *Jacques Schnier, Art Deco and Beyond: 60 Years of Sculpture,* Oakland, Mills College Art Museum, 1998.

20. Charlotte Petersen recalled that she and her husband were not part of Wood's coterie of fun-loving creative types in Iowa City. "We ranked right along with the young painters, at the bottom of the heap." Bliss, 30.

21. Wanda Corn, *Grant Wood, The Regionalist Vision,* New Haven, Yale University Press, 1983, 94.

A LIFE IN
SCULPTURE

LEA ROSSON DELONG

Chapter 1
Beginning a Career in Sculpture

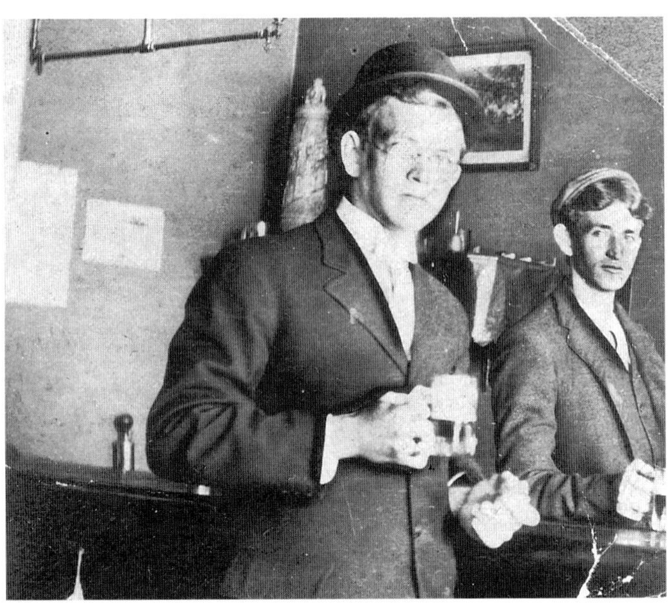

Figure 1.1 Petersen and George Nerney in New York saloon, ca. 1907.

The man who would spend most of his sculptural career in Iowa emigrated from Denmark with his family when he was nine years old. On February 25, 1885, he was born,[1] as his father had been, near Dybbol Molle on the eastern coast of southern Jutland, an area separated from the island of Als by the narrow Als Sound. His father, Peter(t) Petersen, was a farmer, and photographs of the Danish family farm in the Christian Petersen Papers at Iowa State University show a comfortable looking two-story house with a large barn nearby. Many years later, when asked to recall how he became interested in sculpture, he remembered,

I believe the first tool I ever used was a chisel — even before using a pencil. I could not have been more than five or six when I began using the tools in my grandfather's workshop. This was in Denmark, after my grandfather retired from active work as a carpenter and pattern maker. In this shop no tools fascinated me more than the chisels. I did not think of them as sculptor's tools. I did not know then what sculpture was — but I secured pieces of wood, and made boat after boat, then took them down to the seashore, which came right up to our farm. ... The love of carving has been with me ever since.[2]

The reason for the family's emigration was not, apparently, primarily economic but political. According to August L. Bang, a Danish-American writer and magazine editor, "they came here because they did not want to live under the Prussian regime."[3] Leaving their 160-acre farm in Denmark, they traveled at first to the Midwest, near Paxton, Illinois,[4] but the family (Petersen's mother, Helene, especially) felt that the land was too different from the Danish homeland. According to Bang, "They settled as farmers in New Jersey, near the sea. Once they went inland — all the way to Illinois — but no, even if Peter and the sons could have acquired land to till, it was too far inland. Helene would and must be near the sea."[5] The family maintained strong ties to their Danish origins, as did Christian Petersen throughout his life.[6]

The immigrants left Illinois and returned east first to a farm on Long Island, then to another near Orange, New Jersey, where Petersen completed his childhood.[7] He began his art education at the Newark Technical School where he learned the craft of steel engraving or die-cutting.[8] This practice involves sculpting small-scale designs into metal, often steel, which then serve as a model for reproductions on other objects, such as silverware or medals (Figure 1.2). Petersen quickly found success as a die-cutter, and his secure, profitable career in that profession could have been permanent had he been willing to give up his interest in sculpture. Over the next twenty years, during which he supported himself and his family as a die-cutter, he attended a series of short courses and night classes through which he prepared to eventually leave his commercial engraving and work exclusively as an artist.[9] He attended the Fawcett School of Design in Newark[10] after graduating from Newark Technical School, and by 1907, he was in Attleboro, Massachusetts, beginning his career as a die-cutter for the Robbins Company while continuing to further his education as he could in his spare time. While living in Attleboro, he began a lifelong friendship with George Nerney who was employed as a designer for the company and who encouraged Petersen to pursue sculpture.[11] Regarding Petersen as a person of "unusual skill," Nerney praised his carving of designs for silverware, medals, jewelry and seals as "exquisite" and "unrivaled in that field for excellence of artistic craftsmanship."[12]

For a short time in the fall of 1910, he attended the Art Students League in New York, where he was enrolled in George Bridgman's evening Antique class,[13] and in 1911–12 he was enrolled for a class at the Rhode Island School of Design.[14] Probably around 1920, Petersen succeeded in obtaining an apprenticeship with the Boston sculptor Henry Hudson Kitson (1865–1947), with whom he worked for about one year. Kitson was a prolific and popular

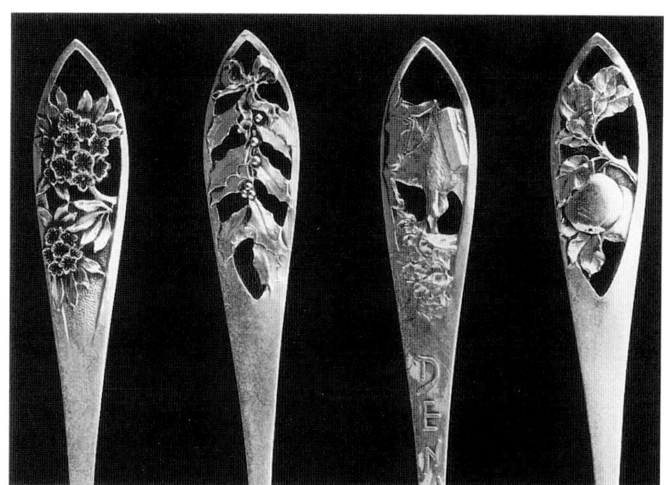

Figure 1.2 Metal design for spoons, 1920s.

creator of monuments and portrait busts whose best-known sculpture is probably *The Minuteman* of Lexington (Figure 1.3).[15] From him Petersen absorbed a firm grounding in the Beaux Arts style of the late nineteenth century. In contrast to an earlier American sculptural style that has been characterized as Naturalism (in which the sculptor seeks primarily to achieve an unvarnished, accurate likeness of the subject), the Beaux Arts style was exported from the studios of Paris in the second half of the century. It is derived from classicism, with its generalized and regular features, but blends idealism with a refined surface treatment that satisfied the nineteenth century taste for precision of detail. The subjects of Beaux Arts work are usually narrative, based on commonly recognized stories from literature and myth, often combined with elements of an easily deciphered symbolism. Although the French sculptor Auguste Rodin (1844–1916) was transforming the concept of sculpture during this period, his expressionism and frank treatment of emotion and sensuality were not reflected in the dominant style of the Beaux Arts, nor were his personal interpretations of subjects or his interest in focusing only on aspects or fragments of the figure. The Beaux Arts style was the one applied to the thousands of sculptural commissions for statues honoring Civil War, Spanish-American War and other American heroes and embodying civic and national virtues (such as "Progress" or "Commerce").

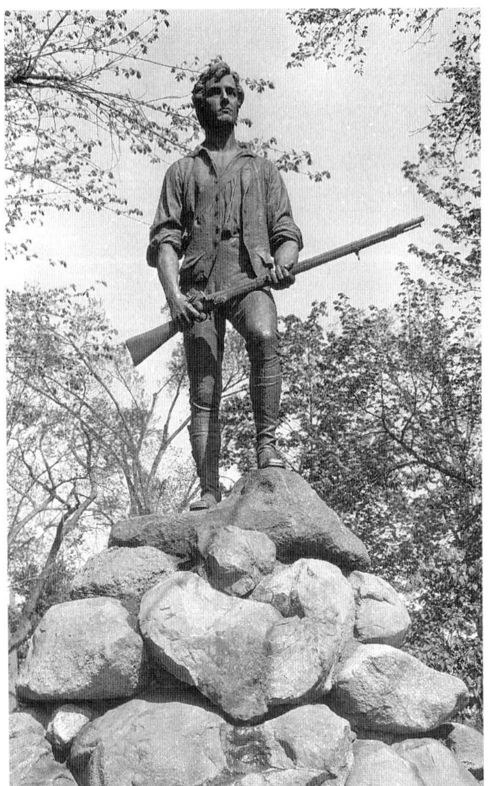

Figure 1.3 *The Minuteman*

Henry Hudson Kitson

In his association with Kitson's busy studio in Boston, Petersen might have encountered assistants and former assistants of Kitson's such as Gaston Lachaise (1882–1935), as well as other sculptors. One whose work he would surely have been aware of, if he did not actually know her, was Kitson's wife, Theo Alice Ruggles Kitson (1871–1932).[16] Although younger than they were, he might also have noted the work of Anna Vaughn Hyatt Huntington (1876–1973), who studied with Kitson briefly, and Janet Scudder (1873–1940), especially her garden sculpture. Kitson maintained an active studio to help carry out his many portrait and monument commissions, and some of Petersen's earliest opportunities may have come his way through the overflow at Kitson's studio. Among these early commissions were portrait busts of Governors Beeckman and Sans Souci of Rhode Island; John Cotton Dana, director of the Newark Art Museum; and Dean Peter C. Lutkin of the Northwestern University School of Music, all dating from the early 1920s. It is also possible that through Kitson's studio Petersen established the contacts in Iowa that eventually led to his move back to the Midwest. Kitson's own Iowa connection was made through the large commission for the Iowa Civil War monument in the National Military Park at Vicksburg, Mississippi, on which he worked, with considerable assistance, from 1904 until its installation in 1912. Kitson's wife also received important work at Vicksburg, including the Massachusetts State Monument and a great many busts and reliefs, on which she worked from 1904 to 1918.[17] Although Lachaise left Kitson's studio in 1912 to work for Paul Manship, it is possible that Petersen knew both sculptors, who were roughly his contemporaries.[18]

At the time Petersen sought to establish himself as a professional sculptor, there was still an active and profitable market in sculpted portraiture (both in relief plaques and freestanding busts) and public monuments. This market was little affected by the rumblings of modernism, which became more prominent as the nineteenth passed into the twentieth century. One of the earliest known commissions carried out by Petersen was a memorial plaque to Janie Flynn (Figure 1.4), a nurse who had died during the influenza epidemic of World War I,[19] which clearly revealed the important influence on Petersen's early sculpture of Augustus Saint-Gaudens (1848–1907). Considered the most innovative and significant American sculptor of the late nineteenth century, Saint-Gaudens introduced a relief style noted for its low but sensitive modeling and a spontaneous-looking effect of naturalism. A great many of Petersen's relief portraits from throughout his career show that he seldom varied the approach he had absorbed from the older sculptor. Saint-Gaudens' inscriptions in thin, block letters, which were an integral part of the design of the overall work, were also a characteristic Petersen maintained for the rest of his life.[20] He seems to have known Saint-Gaudens' monuments as well, especially his *Adams Memorial* (Figure 1.5) of 1886–91 in Washington, D.C. The restrained, concentrated simplicity shown in this figure may have influenced Petersen more than the pared-down style of early modernism.

Petersen's memorial to Janie Flynn presents a frontal view of Flynn dressed in her nurse's clothes, head lifted, with eyes focused above her while her right hand moves slightly out from her side, and the left is raised to her breast. The gesture and pose suggest alertness and readiness with a tone of surprise or perhaps some alarm. In one of the earliest critical notices of Petersen, the author deemed it "simplicity itself but somehow revealing in pose and expression."[21] The figure stands to one side of the plaque so that nearly a third of the piece (the entire upper right area) is given over to an inscription honoring her sacrifice.[22] The light-handed, almost flickering touch of the sculptor relates closely to Saint-Gaudens' relief carvings, which Petersen could have seen in numerous public monuments and collections. Petersen's admiration for Saint-Gaudens was such that even in his lectures at Iowa State College in the 1930s, Petersen still showed slides of Saint-Gaudens' work as examples of the best that the art of sculpture had to offer.[23] Although the effect of the older sculptor is unmistakable, Petersen nevertheless infused his own work here with a liveliness and animation that suggests his eagerness to move beyond the commercial work that made his living.

The years of World War I and afterward brought Petersen a number of opportunities for sculpture, both large and small. Some of Petersen's work from this period expresses both horror and outrage at the devastation of World War I, feelings shared by many Americans. A 1918 article on his strengthening career as a sculptor reproduces *War*, a composition described as "Spirited, and With Promise of a Budding Power in the Idiot Frenzy of the Principal Figure."[24] The principal figure is a rampaging, open-mouthed brute who drags a struggling, nude woman by her neck. At his feet appears to lie a stilled figure. In his treatment of the war as a new sculptural subject, the author declared Petersen as one of the more interesting younger artists dealing with it.

One of the newest of American artists, who has the truth and the power that are equal to portraying war, has also made it his subject both in direct symbolism and in the more common way of visualizing ... humanity ... in the effects of war. ... This man is Christian Petersen. His work runs from the naive simplicity that makes interesting the strings of a child's bib ... to the terrible power with which it invests the Prussian figure of 'War' that chokes a woman and leaves man prostrate as it goes unheeding on its bestial way.[25]

In a small bronze relief (Figure 1.6), Petersen produced an unusual concept of the subject that relates to his later sculptures on the themes of both war and religion. In a circular format, an American doughboy bayonets a screaming dragon whose clawed foot rests at the neck of a partially clad female figure whom it has slaughtered. Standing behind the twentieth century warrior is an angry-faced, robed figure who extends a hand that blesses,

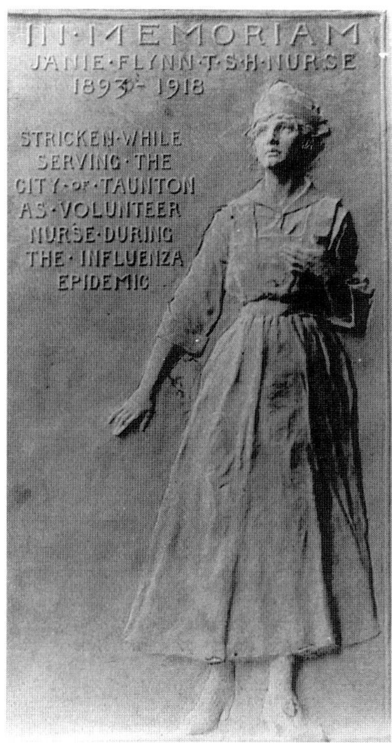

Figure 1.4 *Janie Flynn Memorial,* 1920.

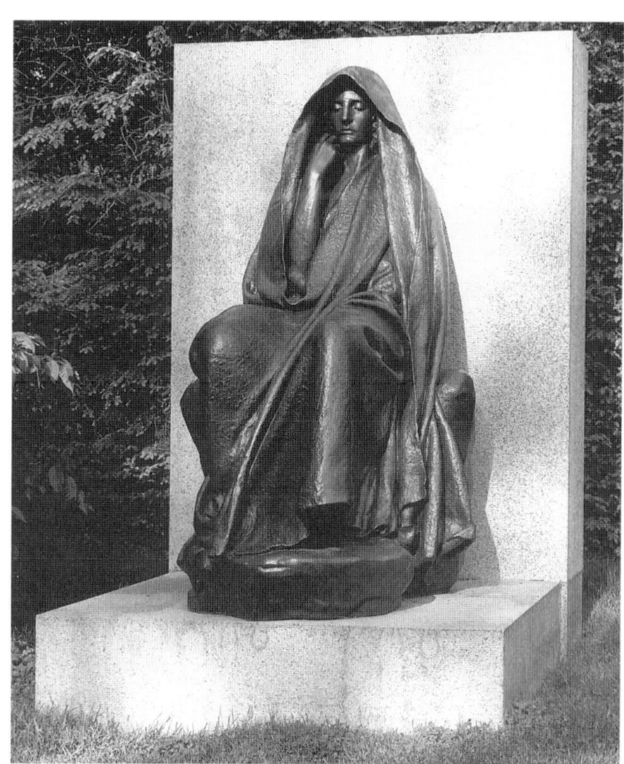

Figure 1.5 *Adams Memorial,*
bronze reproduction cast in 1968 from original mold.

Augustus Saint-Gaudens

if it does not actually guide, the killing of the monster. Rays of light radiate from the figure, who can only be identified as Christ or God the Father. Petersen's interpretation of the war is clear: the resolute and righteous American soldier ends the rampage of the German predator against Belgium and the rest of western Europe with the benediction of God himself. There could hardly be a more forceful image of America's view of its role in the war to "make the world safe for democracy," as President Woodrow Wilson had termed it. His symbol of Germany may also relate to the motivation for his parents' emigration from Denmark in the 1890s: according to Petersen's first biographer, Patricia L. Bliss, they left the German dominated area partly out of fear that their two sons would eventually be drafted into the Prussian army.[26]

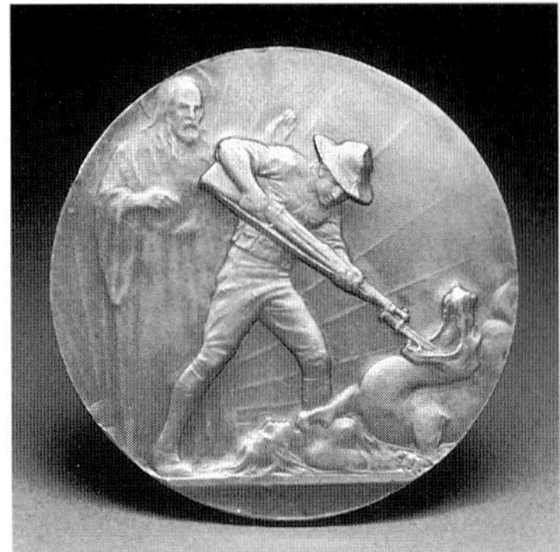

Figure 1.6 *Doughboy of World War I,* ca. 1920s.

An equally moving but more contemporary and graphic image from his World War I work is a relief, currently unlocated: the *Albert E. Scott Memorial* or the *Newsboys Memorial* of circa 1920.[27] In a thick wood that might suggest notorious American battlefields such as the Argonne Forest, four doughboys come upon the body of a fellow American soldier crumpled at the base of a tree. Their discovery has stopped them in their tracks as all stand in a silent circle around the dead figure. Three soldiers still hold their rifles as they look down in stunned focus at their comrade. A fourth soldier leans his arm against the tree as he turns away from the fallen figure toward the background where more bodies are just barely discernable through the thickening forest. Such a "memorial" that memorializes not the victorious heroism of war but its sorrow and loss is evidence that Petersen, for all his stylistic influences from traditional, academic sculpture, had left the nineteenth century behind to reflect a twentieth century shock and despair in the face of modern warfare. In sculptures Petersen created during World War II, he would again concentrate on the human costs of war.

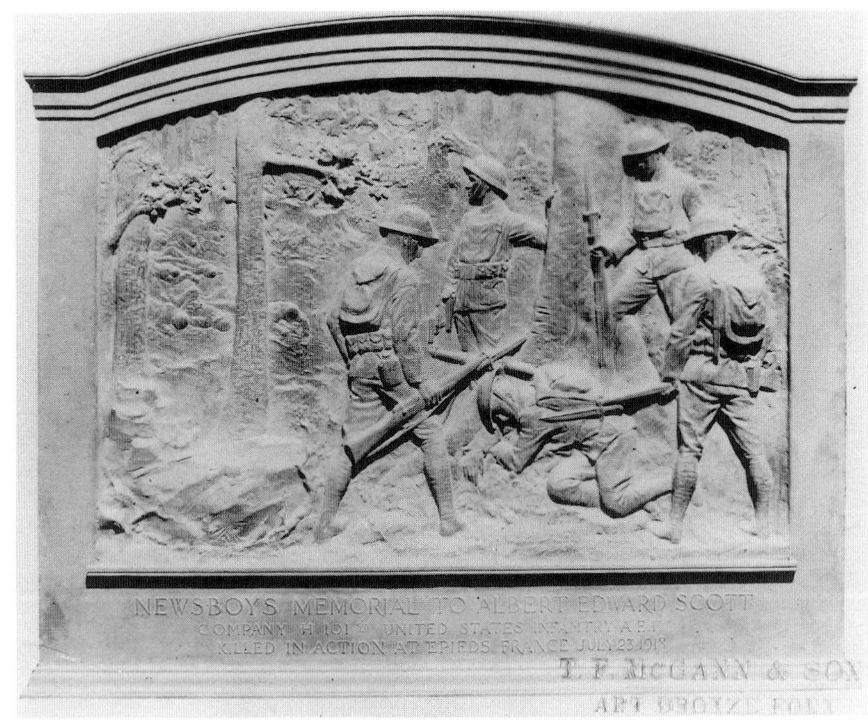

Figure 1.7 *Albert E. Scott Memorial,* ca. 1920.

Petersen's work on this theme continued in an early major commission from New Bedford, Massachusetts, for a memorial to the twenty-two soldiers of Battery D, 102 Field Artillery, 26th (Yankee) Division, who had been killed or died of their injuries in field hospitals in France.[28] Petersen's sculpture commemorating the men of New Bedford (Figure 1.8) was a large figure of a common soldier preparing to load a shell into a 75 mm gun. This concept surely arose at least in part from accounts of the speed with which the men of Battery D fired their artillery, as described during the dedication ceremonies on May 31, 1924, by Major General Clarence R. Edwards of the Yankee Division. General Edwards recalled a service of nine months on the front and one incident in which a mortally wounded German officer asked to see their automatic gun only to be told that there was no automatic gun, only the men of Battery D.[29] The sculpture breaks significantly from many earlier memorials in that it does not suggest in the slightest a glorious victory, but rather the grim, almost mechanized reality of the battles of attrition across northern France. The soldier is a solid, plain-faced worker who, despite his monumentality, fails to exhibit any trace of traditional heroism. He moves with vigor and purpose, suggesting a space, perhaps an entire situation, beyond the figure itself. The lack of any flamboyance or symbolism about the statue became a trademark of much of Petersen's work, as he concentrated on conveying the person or the situation in the sim-

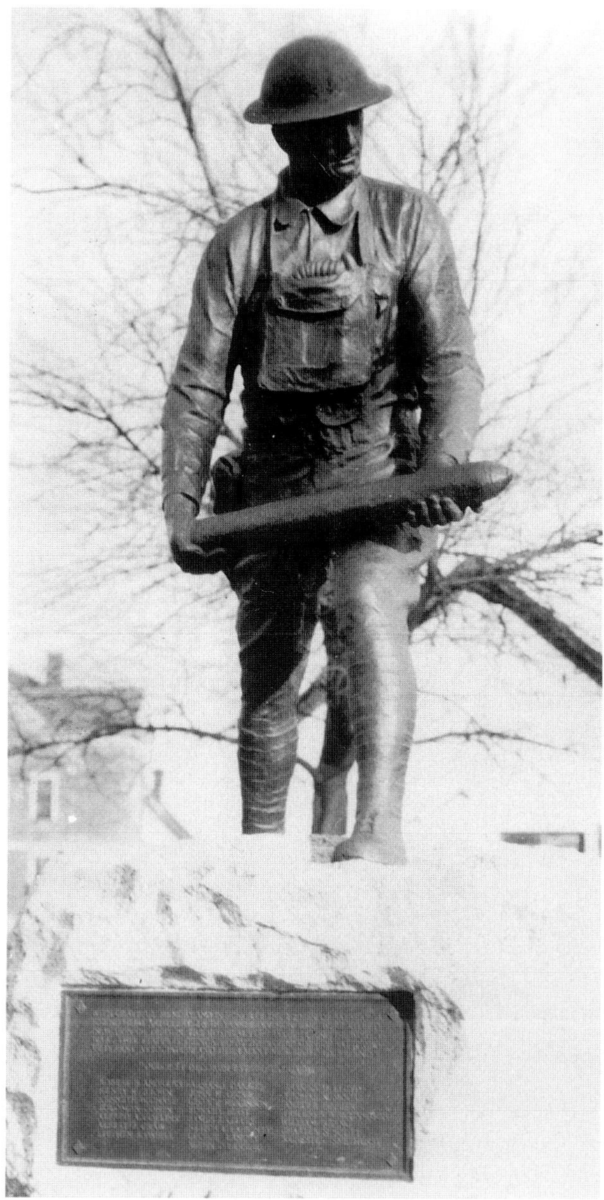

Figure 1.8 *Battery D Memorial,* Taunton, Massachusetts, 1924.

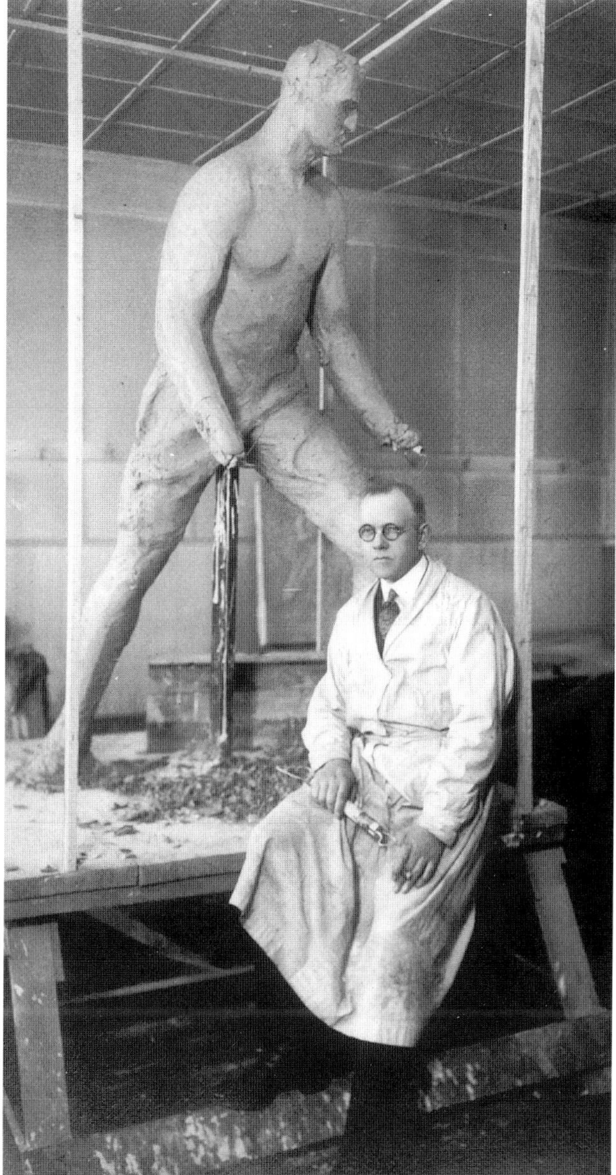

Figure 1.9 Petersen with *Battery D Memorial.*

plest terms possible. Throughout his career, Petersen made few comments about specific pieces (he felt his sculpture should speak for itself), but he did respond to a question about the *Battery D Memorial* for a newspaper article of around 1924: "There is art in interpreting the spirit as well as the features of the sitter, but copying the actual is the largest part of the work. Mr. Petersen feels that there is nothing symbolic about the figure of the gunner chosen for the Battery D memorial. It represents a typical soldier in a characteristic pose; no deeper significance is sought."[30]

A studio photograph (Figure 1.9) of the sculpture in process shows a large, powerful, almost crude form. The figure is partly nude, as if Petersen were grounding his work in a clear understanding of the anatomy beneath the uniform. His concern, however, does not seem to be the detailed articulation of muscles and joints (which are only generally indicated), but rather a grasp of the rhythm of energetic, wide-legged movement. The finished sculpture is remarkably simple, with an almost geometric composition of cylinders and planes which suggests Petersen may have been responding to the modernism that was flooding the post-war art world. In his effect of physical strength and endurance without pretension or overt emotion, the soldier is the predecessor of the farmers and veterinarians Petersen would later create in his Regionalist works at Iowa State.

Only one year before, in 1923, Petersen had dedicated another war memorial that, in contrast to the simplicity and innovation of the New Bedford memorial, exhibited some of the conventions he rejected for *Battery D*. The *Spanish-American War Memorial*[31] (Figure 1.10) for the city of Newport, Rhode Island, recalls the "Victory" figures of many Civil War commemorations, particularly that found in Augustus Saint-Gaudens' *General William Tecumseh Sherman* (Figure 1.11) of 1903 in New York City. In fact, the city of Newport records its actual title as "Victory," although it is popularly known as the "Liberty Memorial."[32] Garbed in classical drapery, the female figure lifts a laurel sprig in her left hand and holds a sword in her right.[33] At her feet is a Medusa head, a common symbol of good triumphing over evil. Although the sculpture is within the stylistic confines of the Beaux Arts style, it nevertheless shows a plainness and restraint in parts of the modeling (the neck and arms are almost cylindrical) that would become typical of Petersen's public works of the 1930s and later. The bronze figure is in the round, but it is displayed against an undecorated slab of stone (referred to as a die) that sets it apart from its surroundings and encourages a concentration on the figure itself. The base contains plaques on which are inscribed the major campaigns of the war, describing it as "a brief war, but one where results were many[,] startling and of worldwide meaning."[34] This background of the stone along with the low base and the occasional simplicity of the modeling recall Saint-Gaudens' *Adams Memorial* of 1886–91.

Petersen received the *Spanish-American War Memorial* commission in July of 1922 as part of the proposal of the Tilden-Thurber Company of Providence, a commercial producer of bronze works and monuments.[35] The model for the statue was placed in the window of a local store, "where the public in general may study it," and the newspaper ran a photograph of it, reporting that

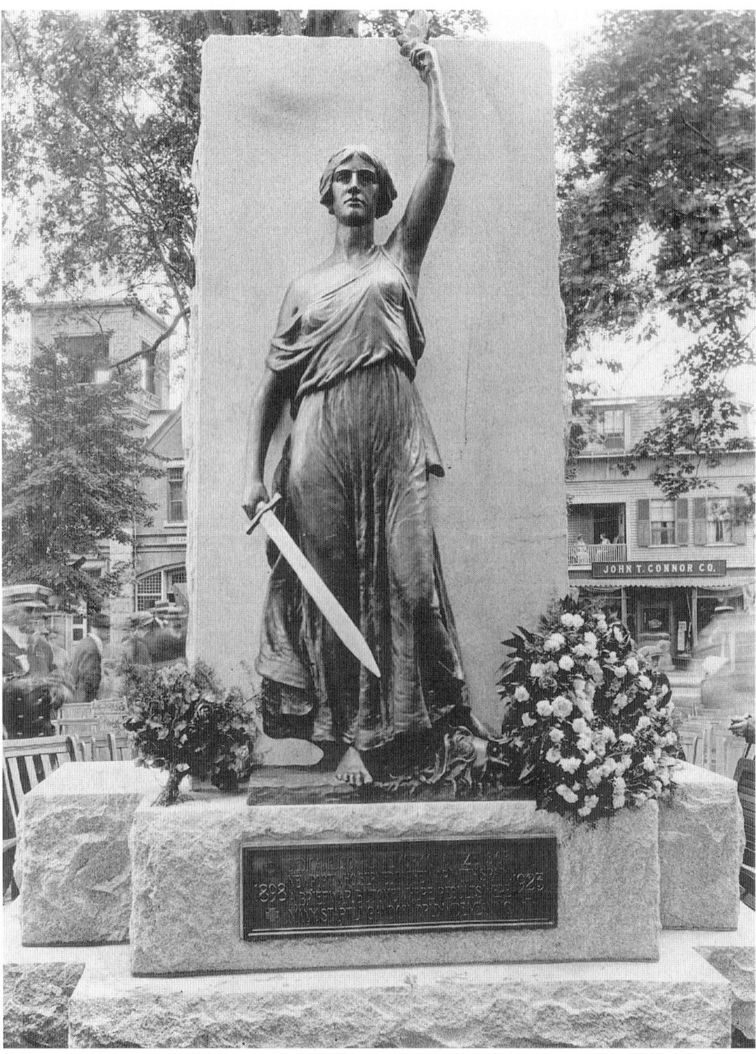

Figure 1.10 *Spanish-American War Memorial,* Newport, Rhode Island, 1923.

Petersen's design "has met favorable comment wherever seen."[36] It explained that "the design is the work of sculptor Christian Petersen of Providence, who has allegorically worked out the thought of victory over oppression which has always been a marked reason for the entry of this country into war."[37]

Victory is represented by a strongly modeled female figure, holding aloft a spray of laurel in the left hand, while in the right is a sword dropped to the ground, signifying rest. The left foot is firmly planted upon the Greek god of oppression, Medusa, the firmness of the pressure of the foot being plainly evident from the distortion of the face of the head. The face of Victory, on the other hand, while pleasing to look upon, is determination in every line. ... The stone chosen for the base and the die is of Barre, Vermont, granite which is used for the better class of work.[38]

After receiving the commission, Petersen traveled in May of 1923 to Newport, where he apparently was quite selective about the site and asked that the Park Commission make some changes to it.

Sculptor Petersen inspected various sites which [he] has been studying. He was not at all favorably impressed with the north lawn at the City Hall, did not care for the background at Vanderbilt Circle, and after considerable study found what he considered a favorable site in the park, despite the fact that some of the background was not what it might be.

According to his decision ... the grade of the park will be raised about a foot, for the proper poise of the monument, which will probably be surrounded by an iron fence.[39]

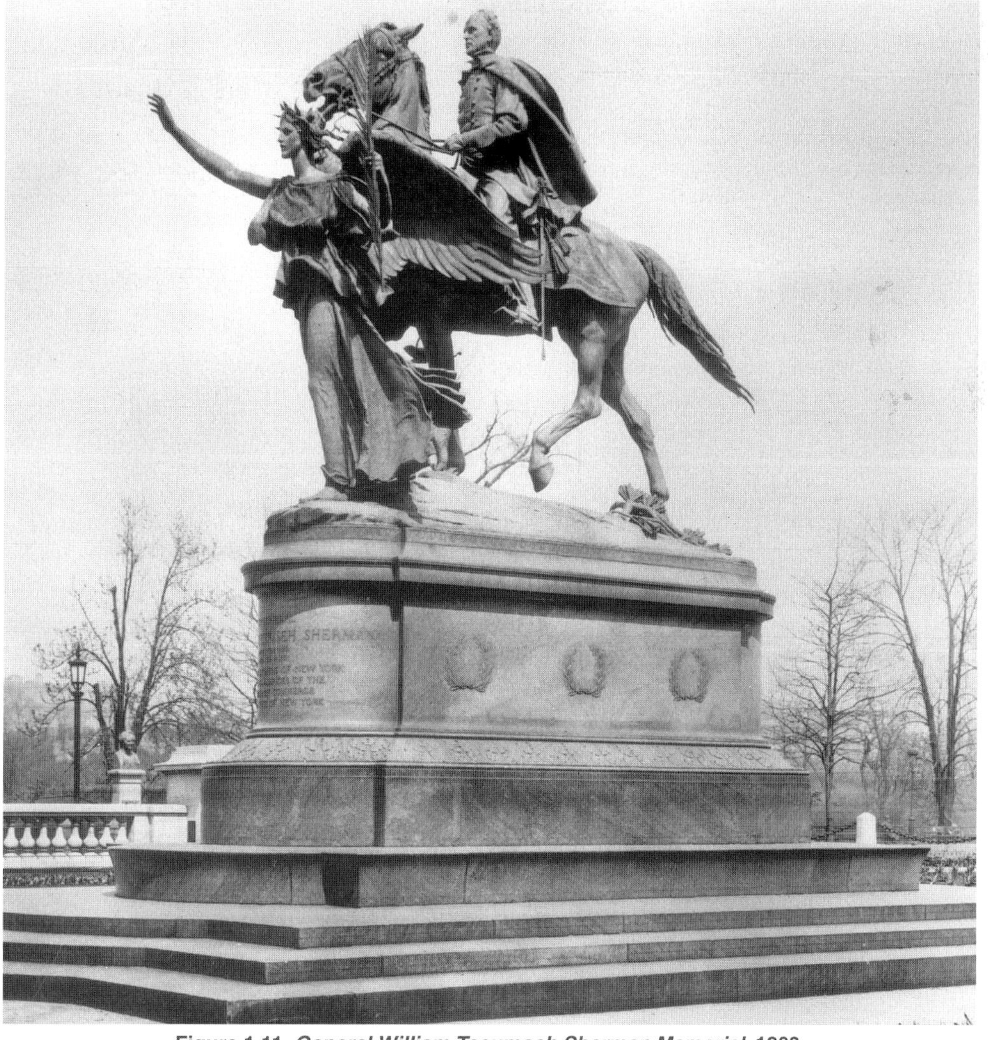

Figure 1.11 *General William Tecumseh Sherman Memorial,* 1903.

Augustus Saint-Gaudens

Petersen's careful judgments about his sculpture's relationship to its landscape surroundings would continue and develop in his work for Iowa State in the 1930s and 1940s. Much of the work the university commissioned from him was to be placed outside, and Petersen expended a good deal of effort to ensure that the environment for his work would be exactly as he planned it.

When the Memorial was finished, a day-long celebration was held on Sunday, July 15, 1923, complete with veterans, generals, widows, the mayor and prominent citizens, the governor, and a congressman. In the dedicatory oration, the Adjutant General of Rhode Island stated that the "classic memorial victory ... cannot fail to be an inspiration to all who in time to come may see her face."[40]

Throughout the 1910s and 1920s, Petersen continued his employment as a die-cutter while creating a substantial body of work in sculpture. Major public commissions such as those at Newport and New Bedford were only sporadic, however, and much of his production was portrait busts and plaques, such as those of New England governors, many of which likely came through contacts made from the Kitson studio. Some of the reliefs were actually medals such as that of the Prince and Princess Bibescu of Romania (Figure 1.12).[41] The portraits were placed in public and private collections in New York, New Jersey, and New England as Petersen's reputation as a sculptor increased. In the 1920s, he began to receive commissions from patrons in Iowa, (Figure 1.13)[42] as he recalled when asked to write about himself for a schoolbook on Iowa history.

My first visit to Iowa was sometime in the early twenties. ... I went there at that time to do a portrait for a medal — the subject being the then president of Bankers Life, George Kuhn. This led to other commissions — among them relief portraits of Frederick M. Hubbell and Henry Nollen as well as some others. This visit was all I needed. The country and the people so impressed me that I longed to return to the Midwest. And eventually I came back — with the feeling that probably here was the place, in the very heart of America, where an American Art might flourish.[43]

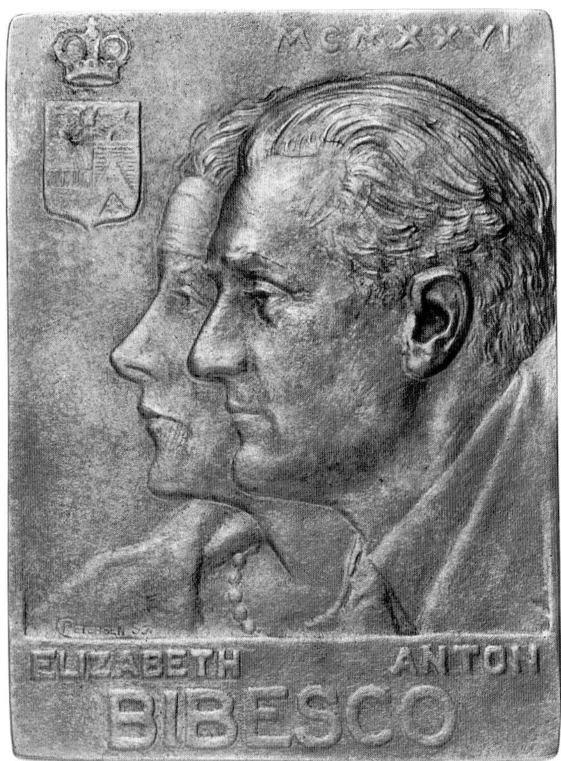

Figure 1.12 Medal of Prince and Princess Bibescu, 1926.

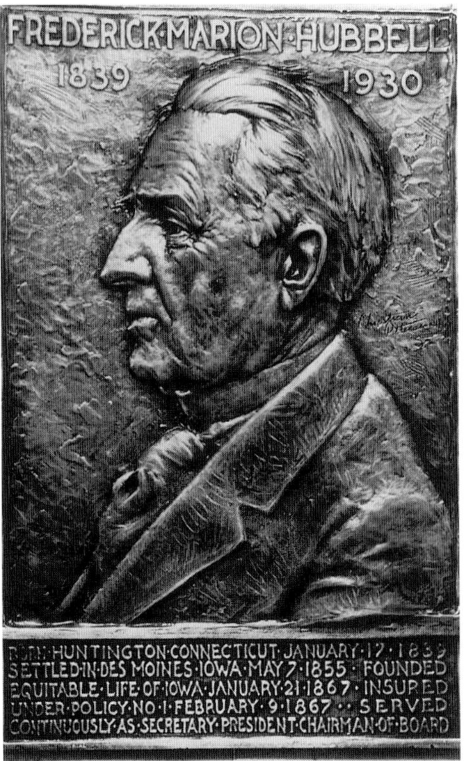

Figure 1.13 F.M. Hubbell relief portrait, 1933.

For the State Historical, Memorial, and Art Department, he modeled portraits of Meskwaki chiefs Young Bear and Pushetonequa, work that led to the encouragement of his Iowa career by the head of that department, Edgar R. Harlan. Petersen traveled to Des Moines to model many of his subjects, thus becoming acquainted with such city powers as Henry C. Wallace, E.T. Meredith, and Reece Stuart and Jay N. "Ding" Darling, both of the *Des Moines Register*. These and other citizens of the state befriended Petersen and were instrumental in his employment by Grant Wood in the Public Works of Art Project and later by Iowa State College in the 1930s.

Although Petersen continued working commercially as a steel engraver and die cutter, his reputation as a sculptor was steadily growing, and he was written about in the art press of his region. The earliest major notice of his sculpture appeared in the *Boston Transcript* in 1918. It included the kind of commentary that followed him throughout his career: "One of the very impressive facts about this man's work is its grasp of the reality with which we are all acquainted, its expression of life in terms that we instantly understand." It went on to describe how he struggled to produce serious sculpture at the same time that he maintained a demanding career as a craftsman in Attleboro. Describing Petersen as "individual and self-contained," the author discussed his determination as an artist.

He has his own shop, to which come orders for work from the great factories. Here, when he has fulfilled those orders, his time is his own for sculpture. It seems that there is no limit to the amount of it that he gives to work. He has no hours. He is not chiefly concerned over whether he will eat on time or when he will sleep. Met for the first time, say in the city, he may be excessively silent, exceedingly formal, entirely unsmiling. Met again in his workshop he smokes a seasoned pipe, develops a sense of humor and by his manner adds to the impression of strength that his height and bulk give to his physical aspect. He works and thinks and does not keep the two separate.

Perhaps this accounts for the freshness of his sculpture. He is trying to express what he thinks and sees in the directest way, without mannerisms. His mind tells him what subjects interest him and what particular qualities should be emphasized and his technique enables him to set these things down in exactly they way they appeal to him.[44]

Subsequent articles continued to emphasize his balancing of commercial and "fine" art as well as his "self-contained manner."[45]

"Die-cutting was too mechanical. I wanted to do something more — well, more inspirational. That's why I started to model a bit."

In this simple way, Christian Petersen, once an unlettered immigrant boy, now a coming figure in the field of sculpture, explains his progress from die-cutting to creative work.

A big, silent, almost brooding figure, Mr. Petersen points to the models he has worked over, wishing them to be his means of expression. When he does speak, it is slowly, choosing his words with utmost care.

Yet the big, barn-like studio in Attleboro is a pleasant place with its busts and plaques and piles of clay awaiting the touch of sensitive fingers.[46]

Another theme that emerges in the early commentary is Petersen's steadiness of purpose and his patience as he built his career as a fine artist.

In art ... patience is the one enduring, indispensable factor. ... To Christian Petersen, sculptor, time is precious indeed. ... He is an artist who has not been able to sculpt when his fancy decreed, however great his desire. A die-cutter by trade ... Mr. Petersen ... expounds the value of patience.

All in all, Mr. Petersen's artistic efforts are the result of a great deal more patience and conscientious work than academic training.[47]

Petersen seems to have confirmed that characteristic in a later article, which spoke directly about the work then ongoing in his studio.

Sometimes the work goes well. More often, one tries for a long time before getting just the expression wanted. I am dissatisfied more times than I am gratified.

A love for the work is not sufficient to make one successful. He must work hard and have much patience.[48]

He did work hard, but apparently his patience was at last exhausted, not only with the conflicts between his commercial work and his sculpture, but with other matters too. Near the end of the 1920s, Petersen was approaching middle age. He had married Emma L.

Hoenicke in 1908, and together they had raised three children: Helene (born 1909), Lawrence (born 1912), and Ruth (born 1915). In 1928, the couple was divorced, and he soon left for Chicago. For the rest of his life, he would explain the move in purely artistic terms, describing how he had come to feel that "the West and Middle West would be eventually the center of culture. The East has so much conscious culture that sometimes it suffers from indigestion."[49] His feeling coincided with the growing "American Wave," a sentiment that declared the United States tired of its apprenticeship to Europe and ready to create a distinctive culture of its own, especially in the visual arts. In fact, in articles from the mid-1920s about his developing sculpture career, Petersen stated his belief in the future of American art. "No man need go abroad to study, he says. ... He feels that American art is evolving an individuality and spirit of its own which is a new and encouraging development. Not many years ago there was everywhere here a spirit of dependence upon Europe, but that has gone. What the essence of the American school is Mr. Petersen feels it would be difficult to put into words, but it is there and can be sensed."[50] In another article from about the same time, he declared, "No longer is America so dependent upon Europe for its art. This country is achieving a new and encouraging development."[51] If his move was actually inspired by the belief that a true American culture would arise in the heartland, he was possibly the first artist to act on that expectation and actually leave the East for the Midwest and its anticipated artistic flowering. Even Grant Wood, the formulator of much of the Regionalist philosophy, was in Europe in the final years of the decade before the Depression, while Thomas Hart Benton and John Steuart Curry would not move westward until the 1930s. In his radical (for the time) alteration of his life, Petersen not only left behind family and the East, but also would soon find himself participating in a new art movement.

NOTES

1. Iowa State College (ISC) Faculty Personnel Information form, August 4, 1954, handwritten by Petersen. There is some discrepancy in regard to the year of Petersen's birth, but the college's form would appear to be a reliable source. Here, he also listed the spelling of his father's name as Petert" and his occupation as farmer. He gave his mother's name as Helene Lorensen Petersen, born at Rennberg. Christian Petersen Papers. The Christian Petersen Papers are deposited in the Special Collections Department of the Iowa State University Library.

2. Dwelle, Jessie Merrill, *Iowa Beautiful Land; A History of Iowa*, as revised by Ruth H. Wagner, Mason City: Klipto Loose Leaf Co., 1958, 183. He also remembered: "My first memory of a piece of sculpture was when I was about six. We, my brother and sister and myself, were taken to a photographer to sit for our portraits — new suits, shoes and all. What stands out in my memory of that occasion most of all was the bust of a woman, (probably a copy of a Greek or Roman bust) and the thing that bothered me most was the fact that the poor thing had her arms cut off near the shoulders. Whether that had any bearing on my becoming a sculptor, I doubt." 183.

3. Bang, August L., *Sculptor, Christian Petersen*. Typescript in Christian Petersen Papers.

4. Minser, Earl R., and Murray, Ray, "He Has Carved a Heritage," *The Iowan*, March 1954, 18.

5. Bang, typescript.

6. The friendship of Peter(t) Petersen and August L. Bang was continued by Christian. Bang often asked him to contribute to his Danish-language magazine, *Julegranen*, and his other publications and was a promoter of the artist's career whenever he saw an opportunity. Bang attributed many of Petersen's qualities, such as his love of nature, to his Danish origins. His typescript, *Sculptor, Christian Petersen*, discusses his fellow Dane, his family, and his art extensively, finding much evidence of the benefit of his Danish heritage. Throughout the Christian Petersen Papers, there is a good deal of material related to Petersen's connection to Denmark and to the Danish-American community.

7. There is little information about Petersen's youth before he began his training in technical school. An undated, hand-written script by Professor J.C. Cunningham, a close friend of Petersen's at Iowa State University, notes under "Early Life" that he "worked on a truck farm on Long Island pulling weeds and counting onions." Cunningham states that Petersen had "only a grade school education."

8. The Newark Technical School (1881–1920) became the Newark College of Engineering and is now the New Jersey Institute of Technology. Letter from Robert Blackwell, The Newark Public Library, to author, July 23, 1999.

9. Although it is clear that Petersen did not wish to make a career of die-cutting, he did recognize the technical skill it imparted to his work. In his account of his beginnings as a sculptor, he recalled, "After coming toAmerica and going to school here I was apprenticed to learn the trade of die cutter, probably because after coming here I had always shown a desire to draw, which I did whenever I had the chance (sometimes when I should be doing something else) and on whatever kind of paper was handy. While learning this trade I attended the evening classes of the Art Schools of Newark, N.J. Here, of course I was put through the regular art education — even two years of architectural drawing. But eventually I was introduced into the clay modeling class where I was put to modeling leaves, ears, hands, etc., from plaster casts. So I earned my living as a die cutter and studied sculpture from that time on — until I finally gave up die cutting and devoted my whole time to sculpture. Nevertheless, my work as a die cutter taught me the further use of chisels. And when a chisel finally fits your hand it is just a matter of learning the nature of the different materials — and using them to put forth your ideas." Dwelle, 183–4.

10. The school is now closed. Letter from Blackwell.

11. In 1942, Nerney was the guest speaker at a banquet in honor of Petersen at Iowa State. He recalled that the friendship was formed because "we found some very interesting common bonds of art, largely through mutual friends and in the influence of Truman Bartlett, the father of Paul Bartlett, one of America's greatest sculptors." Typescript of program broadcast on WOI radio, Iowa State College, November 5, 1942. Nerney had given up a career in art to work in the family business, the Bay State Optical Company of Attleboro, Massachusetts, but maintained with Petersen an active although somewhat one-sided correspondence. Truman Howe Bartlett (1835–1923) taught modeling at the Massachusetts Institute of Technology and was the author of books on Abraham Lincoln (a frequent subject in Petersen's work) and the American sculptor William Rimmer. His son, Paul Wayland Bartlett (1865–1925), was considered one of the leading sculptors of his day, using a rather informal version of a basic Beaux Arts style learned in France. He is best known for his sculptures for the Senate building of the U.S. Capitol.

12. Ibid.

13. His dates of enrollment are October 3 to November 3, 1910. The address given on his enrollment card is 291 Avon Avenue in Newark, New Jersey. Letter from Stephanie Cassidy, Archivist, Art Students League to author, July 14, 1999.

14. Telephone conversation with author and Steve Bailey, Assistant Registrar, Rhode Island School of Design, July 26,1999.

15. Casts of *The Minuteman* were placed in other cities as well, including Cedar Rapids. As of this writing, however, city officials can find no trace of the sculpture.

16. Theo A.R. Kitson began as a student in Kitson's studio in 1886, then studied in Paris and married Kitson in 1893. She was the first woman admitted to the American Sculpture Society (1895) and the first American woman to win a medal at the Paris Salon (1889).

NOTES

Her best known piece is her Spanish-American War memorial of 1906, popularly known as *The Hiker* (about fifty casts were made and dispersed throughout the country). See Rubinstein, Charlotte Streifer, *American Women Sculptors: A History of Women Working in Three Dimensions*, Boston: G.K. Hall and Co., 1990.

17. Rubinstein, 103.

18. Nordland, Gerald, *Gaston Lachaise: The Man and His Work*, New York: George Braziller, 1974, 15.

19. Unlocated for many years, the sculpture has been found at the Taunton (Massachusetts) State Hospital, a psychiatric facility since its founding in 1854.

20. This practice can still be seen in one of the latest of his portrait plaques, *Dimitri Mitroupoulos*, of 1946 (Hegstrom Collection).

21. Littmann, Minna, "From a Die Cutter ... (lost); Interesting Story Is That of Evolution of Christian Petersen ... He Is the Man Who Is to Do the Battery D. Memorial Statue;" no publication, no date; likely from circa 1924. Christian Petersen Papers.

22. The inscription reads "IN MEMORIAM / JANIE FLYNN. T.S.H. NURSE / 1893–1918" along the top. Below and to the left: "STRICKEN WHILE SERVING THE CITY OF TAUNTON AS VOLUNTEER NURSE DURING THE INFLUENZA EPIDEMIC."

23. "My first lecture at Iowa State College," mms. in Christian Petersen Papers at ISU. In the slide list for this lecture, Petersen also included *The Sun Vow*, 1898, by Herman Atkins MacNeil (1866–1947) and *Wisdom* (Appellate Court Building, New York) by Frederic Wellington Ruckstull (1853–1942; in his list, Petersen used the original spelling of the sculptor's name: Ruckstuhl). The work of these two conventional Beaux Arts sculptors was interspersed with slides of Michelangelo's work. In his lecture notes or other commentary, Petersen never mentioned H.H. Kitson as a sculptor whom he admired. Perhaps he shared Lachaise's low opinion of him. In fact, he rarely referred to his association with the older sculptor at all and records nothing of what he might have worked on for Kitson.

24. Macdonald William A., "The Rise of a New Paul Revere," *Boston Transcript*, January 23, 1918. The article reproduces two other early works which, like *War*, are unlocated: *Paul Revere* and *Private Jack*.

25. Ibid. In discussing his Danish heritage, the article accounts for Petersen's feelings about the World War: "He has a heritage of hate for the Prussian system which overran Schleswig as it overran Alsace-Lorraine. And in some of his bitterest work touching on this war he has expressed that hate."

26. Bliss, Patricia L., *Christian Petersen Remembered*, Ames: Iowa State University Press, 1986, 3.

27. A check by The Newark Museum in 1988 found no mention of this work in any inventories of city sculpture. Letter to author, June 20, 1988. In 1999, there was still no trace of the sculpture. The Newark Public Library to author, July 23, 1999.

28. *The Battery D Memorial* remains in its original location on Kempton and Watson Streets and is in good condition. Letter from Joan E. Barney, Free Public Library, City of New Bedford, to author, August 18, 1999.

29. "Thousands Honor Dead Veterans of New Bedford's Own Battery D," *The New Bedford Evening Standard*, May 31, 1924, 10. Also *Mercury Morning*, same date. The long article includes the speeches given that day and several photographs of the sculpture and the ceremonies. A similar, though shorter, article is "New Bedford Pays Tribute to Hero Dead," *New Bedford Daily Sun*, May 31, 1924. In a series on New Bedford Memorials, a newspaper article of 1949 states that on Memorial Day annually since the sculpture was dedicated in 1924, "survivors of Battery D wend their way to Battery D Park and Square and once more pay silent tribute to their departed comrades." "Battery D Park and Square Were Dedicated 25 Years Ago," *The Standard-Times*, July 11, 1949, 5. When Petersen died, *The Standard-Times* ran a notice: "Sculptor of City Statue Is Dead," April 6, 1961.

30. Littmann.

31. According to the Smithsonian Institution's Inventory of American Sculpture, the sculpture was dedicated July 15, 1923. The figure measures 92 x 35 x 10 1/2 inches with a base approximately 126 x 102 x 64 inches. Originally, four Spanish crosses were affixed to the plaques, but two are missing and two are replacements. One cross contains a scene of an American soldier and sailor capturing a Spaniard.

32. The sculpture remains on its original site in Equality Park although it is in need of restoration. (Letter from Nancy Grinnell, Curator, Newport Art Museum, to author, July 21, 1999.) The Art Committee of the Newport Cultural Commission has obtained a Save Outdoor Sculpture grant toward the conservation of this and other works in Newport. (Synnott, Terrence, "Art committee launches campaign to restore two statues on Broadway," Newport *Daily News*, November 13, 1998; includes contemporary photograph of portion of sculpture.)

According to the Outdoor Sculpture Assessment Report prepared for the Newport Cultural Commission by the Conservation Technology Group, "the statue is a multi-sectional, most likely cast using the lost wax process." (p.5) The report describes the figure as "somewhat stiff ... with mixed classical motif. The figure is rendered in a powerful and dramatic pose with left arm upraised; the placement of the head on the elongated neck and heavy arms are [*sic*] naive and far from being in classical scale, however." (p.4) No signature or founder's mark is present. Letter from Linda Gordon, Chair, Art Committee, Newport Cultural Commission, to author, August 9, 1999.

NOTES

33. The sword is a continual target of vandalism and is currently broken. Synnott, "Art committee ..."

34. According to the Smithsonian Institution's Inventory of American Sculpture, two plaques are found on the base. A plaque on the front of the base reads: "Dedicated to the memory of Citizens of / Newport who served in the War with Spain / A brief war, but one where results were / Many startling and of world-wide meaning / 1898 - 1923." A plaque on the back reads: "U.S.A. / Philippine Islands / Cuba / Porto Rico /Spanish. War. Veterans. 1898. 1902" The Conservation Technology Group reports that the date on front or north inscription is 1925, not 1923, and that the phrase on the back inscription is "Spanish War Victims," not "Veterans." (p.3).

35. When the Memorial was dedicated, Tilden-Thurber ran an advertisement with a photograph, entitling it "Memorial to Spanish War Veterans of Newport" with the caption: "Designed and Erected by the House of Tilden Thurber." The ad then described the nature of the business: "Monumental Work, Bronze Tablets, Bar-Relief [sic], Stained Glass Windows, Memorials of all kinds. Sculpture for the Home and Garden. Designs and Quotations gladly furnished." *The [Newport Daily] News*, July 16, 1923. A check of city directories in both Newport and Providence of the period confirmed that Petersen was a resident of neither city. (Letter from Robin Flynn, The Rhode Island Historical Society to author, August 6, 1999).

36. "Design for Memorial; Model Adopted for Monument of Spanish War Veterans; Thought of Victory Over Oppression, Reason for Country Entry Into Conflict, Worked Out," *The [Newport Daily] News*, July 31, 1922. The author is indebted to Linda Gordon of the Newport Cultural Commission for providing this and other clippings from Newport newspapers.

37. Ibid.

38. Ibid.

39. "Equality Park Selected; Site Chosen for Spanish War Monument," *The [Newport Daily] News*, May 21, 1923. The memorial was a joint project of the city and the veterans organization, the Rear Admiral Charles M. Thomas Camp, United Spanish War Veterans: "The city is to pay for the monument, but ... the ... Camp must put in the foundation and if necessary erect a fence."

40. "Memorial Unveiled; General Abbot Delivers Oration and Others Make Addresses," *The [Newport Daily] News*, July 16, 1923. There was also a small book commemorating the dedication, but Petersen's name is not mentioned there. (Letter from Robin Flynn, The Rhode Island Historical Society, to author, August 6, 1999).

41. The 4 x 3 inch medal is now in the collection of The Newark Museum, 29.2138. It was struck by the firm of Hoag and Whitehead. It seems especially likely that a connection to Kitson exists for this commission since he had produced busts of Elizabeth, Queen of Romania (Carmen Sylva), and Carol, King of Romania, and been decorated by the King. Fielding, Mantle, *Dictionary of American Painters, Sculptors and Engravers*, Poughkeepsie: Apollo Books, 1986. Though different from that on Petersen's medal, the spelling of the family name "Bibescu" is current Romanian usuage.

42. Bliss attributes these commissions to the influence of Kitson, largely because of his work on the Iowa memorial at Vicksburg; 5–6.

43. Dwelle, 183.

44. Macdonald.

45. *National Magazine*, January 1922. Typescript in Christian Petersen Papers.

46. *Boston Traveler*, 1924. Typescript in Christian Petersen Papers.

47. *National Magazine*, 1922.

48. *Boston Traveler*, 1924.

49. Petersen, Christian, "Bringing Sculpture to You." Undated typescript in Christian Petersen Papers.

50. Littmann. He added that Daniel Chester French was a good representative of the American school.

51. *Boston Traveler*, 1924.

Chapter 2
A New Start in Iowa

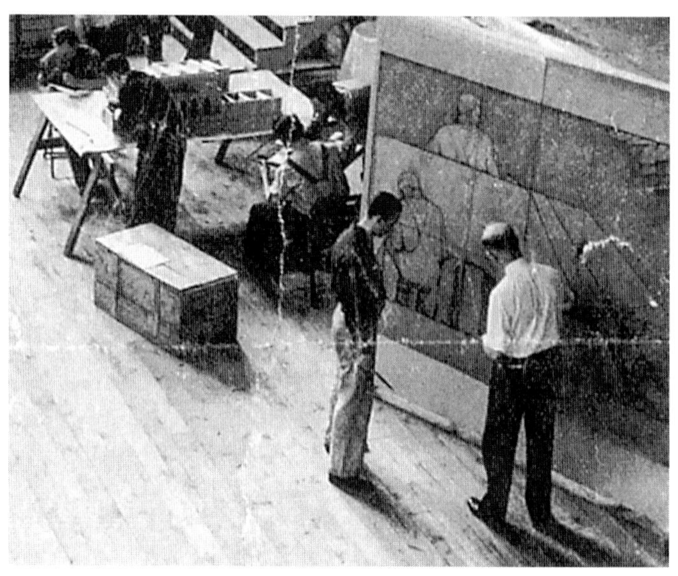

Petersen (right) working with colleague at
the Public Works of Art Project studio, Iowa City.

When Christian Petersen left his home in the East and traveled to Chicago, he hoped to begin a renewed career entirely devoted to sculpture. He immediately sought opportunities for exhibitions in Chicago galleries[1] while he continued work on a commission he had received while still in the East for a fountain sculpture *(Fountain of the Blue Herons)* for the A.E. Staley Company in Decatur, Illinois. But his plans for a career as a fine artist were ill timed, for within a year of his arrival in Chicago, the Stock Market crashed, money dried up, and the long years of the Great Depression began. In an informal biography, Petersen's friend Professor J.C. Cunningham wrote of this period as one of despair in the artist's life. "We find him in the city of Chicago with one hundred dollars in his pocket. His family [was] against him because he gave up a good paying job ... to become a poor artist."[2]

By November of 1929, it must have been clear that he could not support himself as an artist, and Petersen sought employment with a jewelry manufacturer in Chicago, the Dodge and Ascher Company. According to Cunningham, the artist was asked "what he could do with no sales ability," whereupon he drew a sketch on a pad and was hired immediately. It is also possible that once Dodge and Ascher realized who he was, they recognized his reputation as a die-cutter[3] and, even with unemployment statistics skyrocketing all over the country, his skill was valued. On December 15, 1931, he married Charlotte Garvey, the secretary who had greeted him at his job interview at Dodge and Ascher, and early the following year he was able to rent a studio in Chicago to continue his work in sculpture. Despite the security provided by his employment at the jewelry company, Petersen gave up his job in mid-1932 and once more attempted to work full time on his sculpture. He and his wife moved to Belvidere, a small town in north central Illinois less than a hundred miles from Chicago, where a friend of Mrs. Petersen's had offered to share her large house with them.[4]

Although Petersen had carried out a number of portrait commissions for Iowans, it was not until the early 1930s that he began to regularly visit the state. Among his earliest works with a firm Iowa connection seems to have been a large relief plaque of two brothers, Franz J. and Robert L. Wood of Des Moines, who owned the Wood Brothers Thresher Company from 1890 to 1947. The sculpture displays little variation either in figuration or lettering from the style established by Saint-Gaudens and practiced as well by Kitson.[5] Over the next years, he produced portraits of Henry C. Wallace, Sr. (1926), James D. Edmundson (1930), and local businessmen at the Bankers Life Company and the Equitable Life Insurance Company. In addition, he was commissioned by the History, Memorial, and Art Department of the State of Iowa to create portrait busts of two Native Americans, Pushetonequa and Young Bear (1930) of the Meskwaki tribe. The chief curator of this department, Edgar R. Harlan, became one of Petersen's most industrious supporters and was instrumental in his eventual move to Iowa.[6]

By 1932, Petersen was well enough known in Des Moines for his portrait sculptures that they had become a reliable, if not large, source of income. In the summer of 1932, he lived in Des Moines while he carried out some of those commissions, notably one of Governor George Clarke (Figure 2.1).[7] Despite this patronage, the Petersens led a precarious existence in 1932, waiting to be paid for the portraits.[8] Back in Belvidere, Petersen struggled to work and obtain commissions for sculpture, but 1933 brought few projects other than portrait busts and plaques of Des Moines citizens as well as plaster reliefs of the children of well-to-do families. Since there was no art museum in Des Moines at the time, an exhibition of over sixty-five of Petersen's works, mostly portraiture of locals, was held at the Tea Room of Younkers Department Store that year.[9] Nevertheless, the proceeds from this work were insufficient to support Petersen and his wife, and their savings drained away until, at the end of the year, they were nearly penniless.

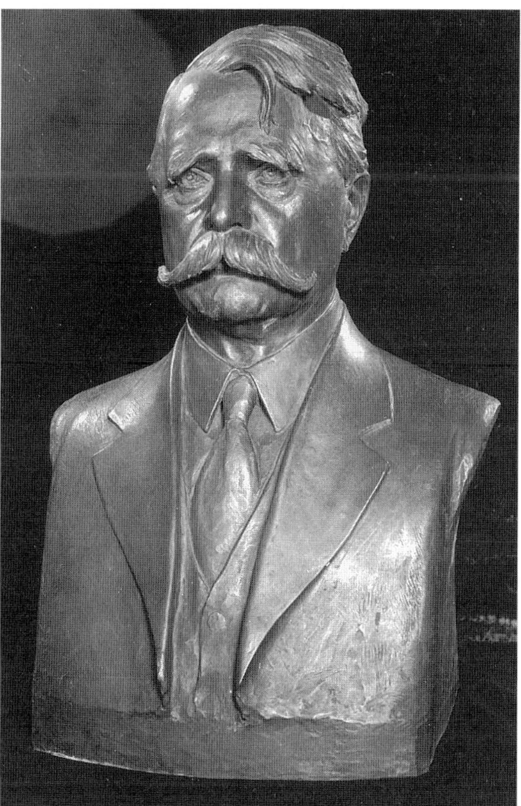

Figure 2.1 *Gov. George Clarke*, 1932.

Their situation was a common one for American artists in the early years of the Depression. Few could support themselves from the proceeds of their art, and prospects for improvement were slight. Within months of Franklin D. Roosevelt's inauguration after his victory over Herbert Hoover late in 1932, the emergency measures of the New Deal were instituted. Realizing that artists of every sort were in an especially hopeless plight, the new president set in motion plans to create special programs to address their needs. The first of several such programs during the Roosevelt years, the Public Works of Art Project (PWAP), began on December 8, 1933, with the goal of setting artists to work on approved, strictly supervised projects to produce art for the American public. Certainly one of the goals was to provide economic relief for artists who could barely, if at all, support themselves from their work, but equally important was the philosophical position that art and the people who produce it are fundamentally valuable in a civilization. In addition, New Dealers saw an opportunity to record the life of the nation in a systematic way that had never occurred in the United States. The head of the PWAP was Edward Bruce, who was able to articulate clearly (and persuasively) the aims of his program. "It is our belief that the Project will rescue many artists from their former position of isolation and will inspire them to create a record which will be of permanent value, of the American scene and of our American life today. ... The artistic record of every country remains ... the true measure of its civilization. We believe that the PWAP is not only a 'putting to work' plan affecting an important class of citizens in great distress but it is a Governmental step forward, toward bringing about a finer American civilization."[10]

One of the organizers of this government experiment in the arts was the director of the Little Gallery in Cedar Rapids, Edward Rowan, who was told when he was hired that he was to be involved with "the greatest artist relief work ever undertaken by any government and absolutely vital to the American artist."[11] The country was divided into twelve regions, with Missouri, Kansas, Nebraska, and Iowa making up Region 7. The director of the program for Iowa was the best known artist of the region and a friend of Rowan's, Grant Wood, who administered it from Iowa City. Wood quickly began to assemble a group of artists, several of whom had attended his summer art school and colony at Stone City. Petersen's friends in Des Moines were eager to bring him permanently to the state and began to lobby on his behalf to Wood. A rapid, but effective exchange of letters began less than a month after the Project started and resulted rather quickly in Petersen being brought from Illinois to join the Iowa Project.

The campaign may have been initiated when the *Des Moines Register* writer, Reece Stuart, Jr., mentioned to another *Register* writer, Harlan Miller, who knew Wood, that Petersen had enrolled in the Illinois Project with no results.[12] Miller wrote to Wood, who replied on January 10, 1934, "I only wish that I had known of him before the Iowa quota was filled," but added that he "hope[d] to be able to take care of him soon."[13] Wood wrote Petersen that same day, "I like your work and feel that you are just the kind who should receive every consideration. ... I do not wish to create false hopes, but something may happen in a week or two and I should like to be of service if possible."[14]

Within one week, Wood did indeed prove himself to be of service as he wrote to Petersen on January 16, 1934, offering a place on the Iowa PWAP at $26.50 per week, starting two days later, on January 18. His work was to be a set of bronze bas-reliefs for gate markers in state parks, and Wood encouraged him to be in Iowa City as soon as possible, although he recognized that even travel expenses were an obstacle in those days. "You may be broke and need car fare. Wish I could advance you some cash, but I am broke too."[15] Two days later, Petersen wrote Wood with elation: "Received your good news last night — Thanks heaps. Best letter I have had since I don't know when. You are right. I am broke — else I'd be there today — as it is I don't believe I can be there before Monday — have to raise a loan for traveling expenses. Wish I could make it sooner — but just now I don't see how I can make it before Monday — See you then. Make up for lost time. Rarin' to go."[16]

Soon after the Petersens joined the other artists in Iowa City, the idea for gate markers was dropped so that the sculptor could concentrate on a job more closely related to what the painters were doing. Although there were a number of requests for public works of art, the two major accomplishments of the PWAP in Iowa were both for Iowa State College in Ames. President R.M. Hughes of Iowa State College, whom Petersen had met the previous year and who wanted to create a higher cultural profile at the agricultural and mechanical school, proposed a fountain for the dairy industry building on campus. In their discussions during the fall of the previous year, the president had suggested a fountain that could be fabricated by the engineering department at the college and asked the sculptor to submit a design.[17] He admitted that there was no guarantee that he could "get [it] past a jury of two or three ... here on the staff," but offered to bring the Petersens to stay in his home as Petersen developed the design. The pay that he proposed for that month — $250.00 — was more than Petersen would later make on the Project (a little over $100.00 per month), and it is not clear whether Hughes planned to pay this amount himself or it would come from the college payroll.[18] His support of Petersen was such that he often provided a stipend for the sculptor from his own personal funds during the 1930s.[19] In addition to the Des Moines friends, Hughes may have been equally instrumental in Wood's decision to extend an invitation to Petersen. Considering that the PWAP was regarded as a temporary program whose goal was to place artists in permanent employment, the prospect of a possible job at Iowa State College for one of his artists would have been a persuasive factor for Wood. Considering further that the primary activity of the Iowa

Project was the murals that would go into the library there, it is not surprising that both Hughes and Wood would see the expanded opportunity for cooperation and accomplishment. As soon as Petersen had been transferred onto the Iowa Project, Hughes must have worked quickly to see that the request for state parks markers was shelved in favor of his own plan for a fountain that, as it happened, grew into an entire sculptural cycle. By the end of January, he wrote to Petersen expressing hope that this project might be only the beginning of the artist's work for Iowa State. "I wrote [Wood] ... that if you were successful in developing a design which we could all accept, I might later bring you here at our expense to work with us in casting it. ... I want you to do some work on our campus as soon as I can finance it."[20]

Petersen seems to have been the only professional sculptor on the Iowa Project — in fact, one of the very few in the Midwest who did not work in Chicago — and the only one who produced any sculpture that can still be identified.[21] In addition, he was older than most of the other artists (including Wood), had lived and worked in the East, and had already established his reputation. Finally, he appears to be the only participant who parlayed

his opportunities on the Iowa Project into a permanent job. In contrast to the primary task of the Iowa project — murals for the library at Iowa State (Figures 2.2–2.6) — Petersen's was not a group job, or as it might have been termed in Iowa at the time, a cooperative project. He alone was assigned to work on the dairy sculpture cycle, and the responsibility for its success was his alone, as Hughes must have understood. In his zeal to bring an artist to campus, the president presented both an opportunity and a challenge to Petersen, perhaps in hopes that he would demonstrate his competence to join the staff of the college as an independent, tested professional. Most artists on the Iowa project were employed primarily (several of them also produced easel paintings) in carrying out the designs that Wood had developed for the library murals. None were asked to contribute any major imagery to the mural cycle; they were expected only to paint exactly as Wood directed, which is what they did.[22] But Petersen developed his own designs for his separate assignment. Of course, they would have required the approval of Wood, but there would have been little reason to withhold that since the relief designs harmonized nearly seamlessly with Wood's two-dimensional ones for the mural paintings.

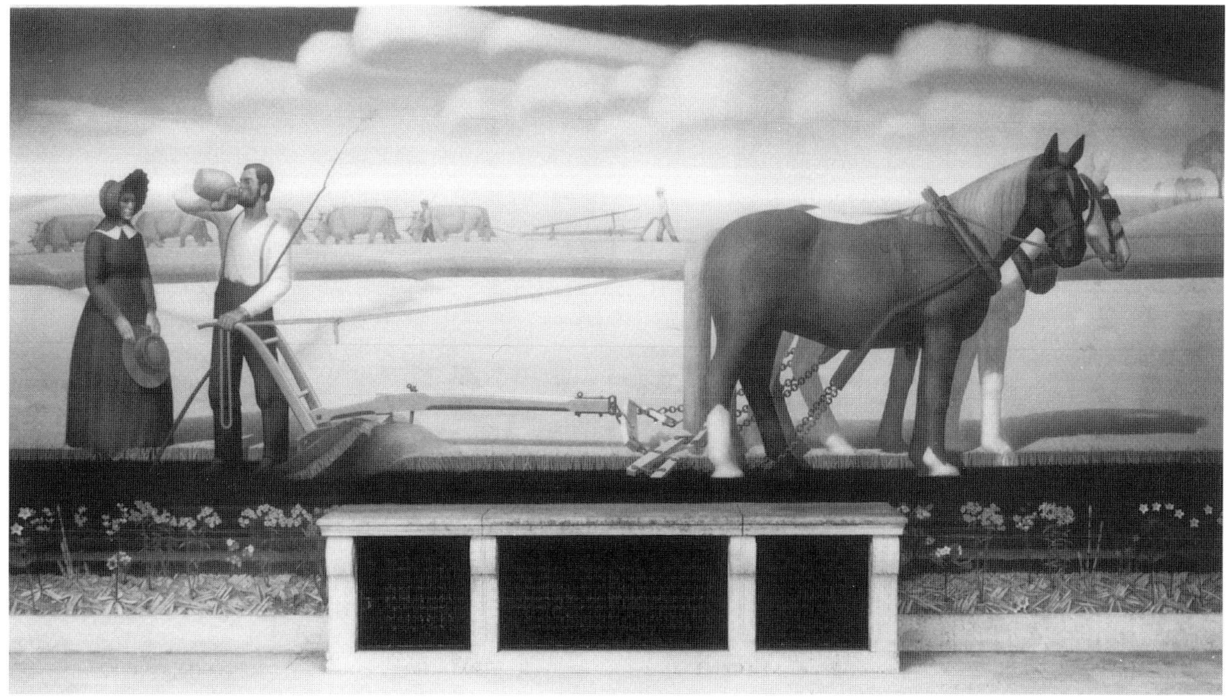

Figure 2.2 *Breaking the Prairie,* center panel, 1936–37.

Grant Wood

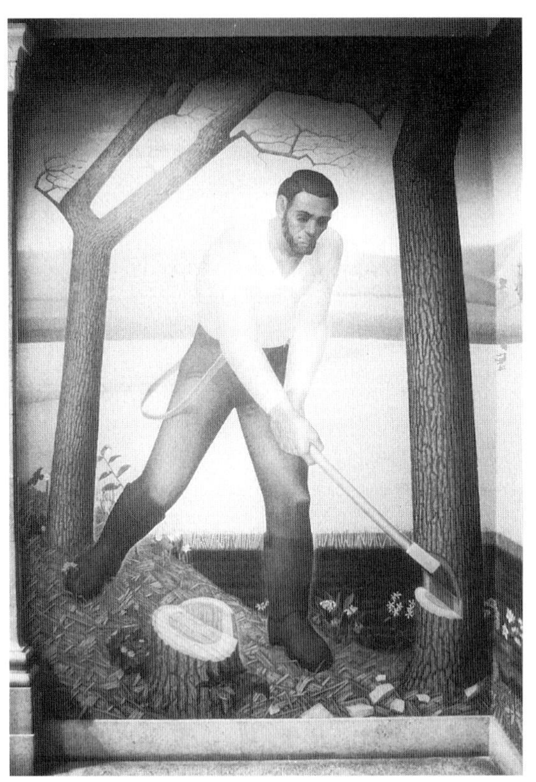

Figure 2.3 *Breaking the Prairie,* detail.

Grant Wood

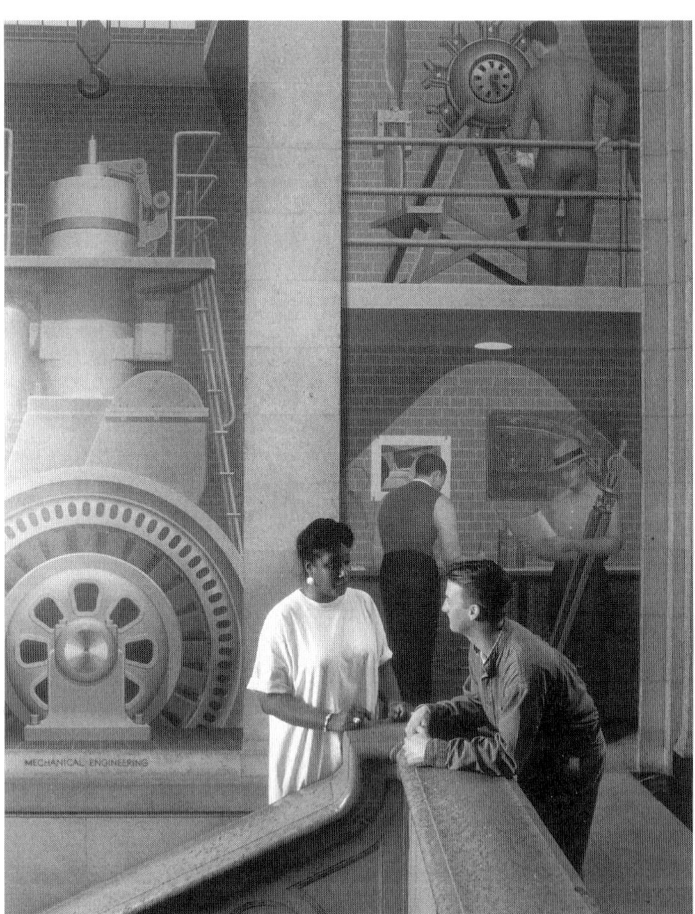

Figure 2.4 *When Tillage Begins, Other Arts Follow,* 1934.

Grant Wood

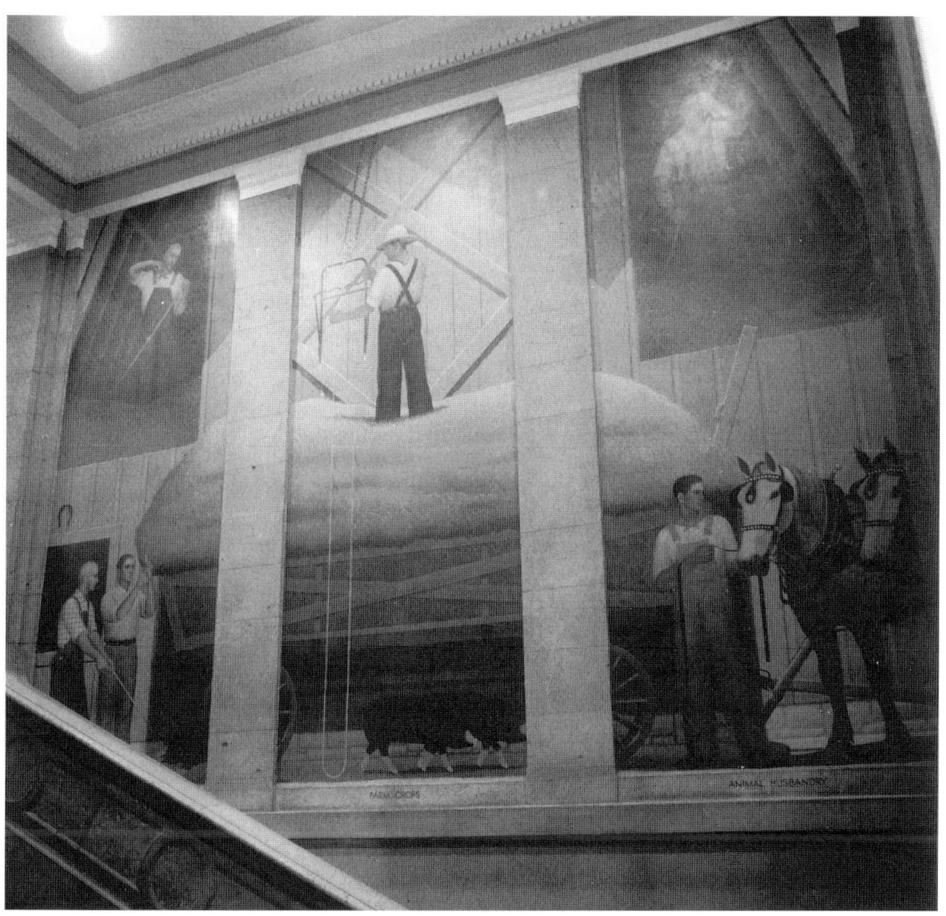

Figure 2.5 *When Tillage Begins*, detail.

Grant Wood

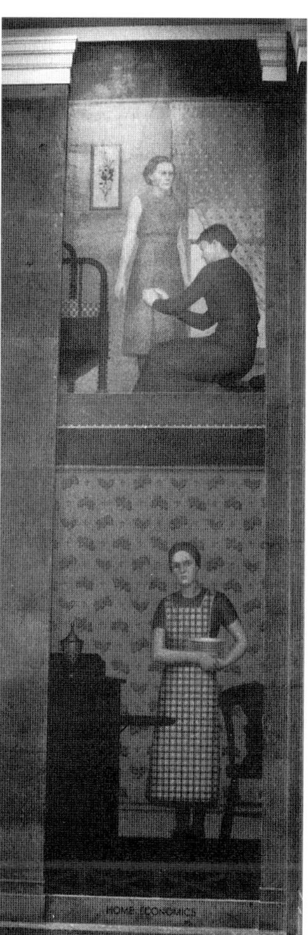

Figure 2.6 *When Tillage Begins*, detail.

Grant Wood

A 1934 photograph of the Iowa City studio (Figure 2.7), a converted swimming pool, shows the young men[23] at work on the canvases that would be installed on the library walls in Ames. In the lower right corner is Christian Petersen working on what appears to be a full-scale design for the first panel of his dairy relief, as another man looks on.[24] In another photograph, this one taken at the University of Iowa Armory, the sculptor has turned momentarily from modeling a full-scale plaster relief for the fourth panel of the cycle. The drawings and the models for the dairy industry cycle that are shown in these photographs reveal that Petersen made very few changes in the final sculptures that were installed in spring of 1935. Yet an elaborate sketch (Figures 2.8 and 2.9) on brown kraft paper shows that Petersen had initially developed a more complex plan for his dairy reliefs. The narrative of this sketch is similar to the final reliefs, but is more complicated and detailed: it also begins with cattle in the fields being brought in for milking and then follows the process of dairy production. The primary difference is that it is fluid and connected, without the episodic panels of the final installation.

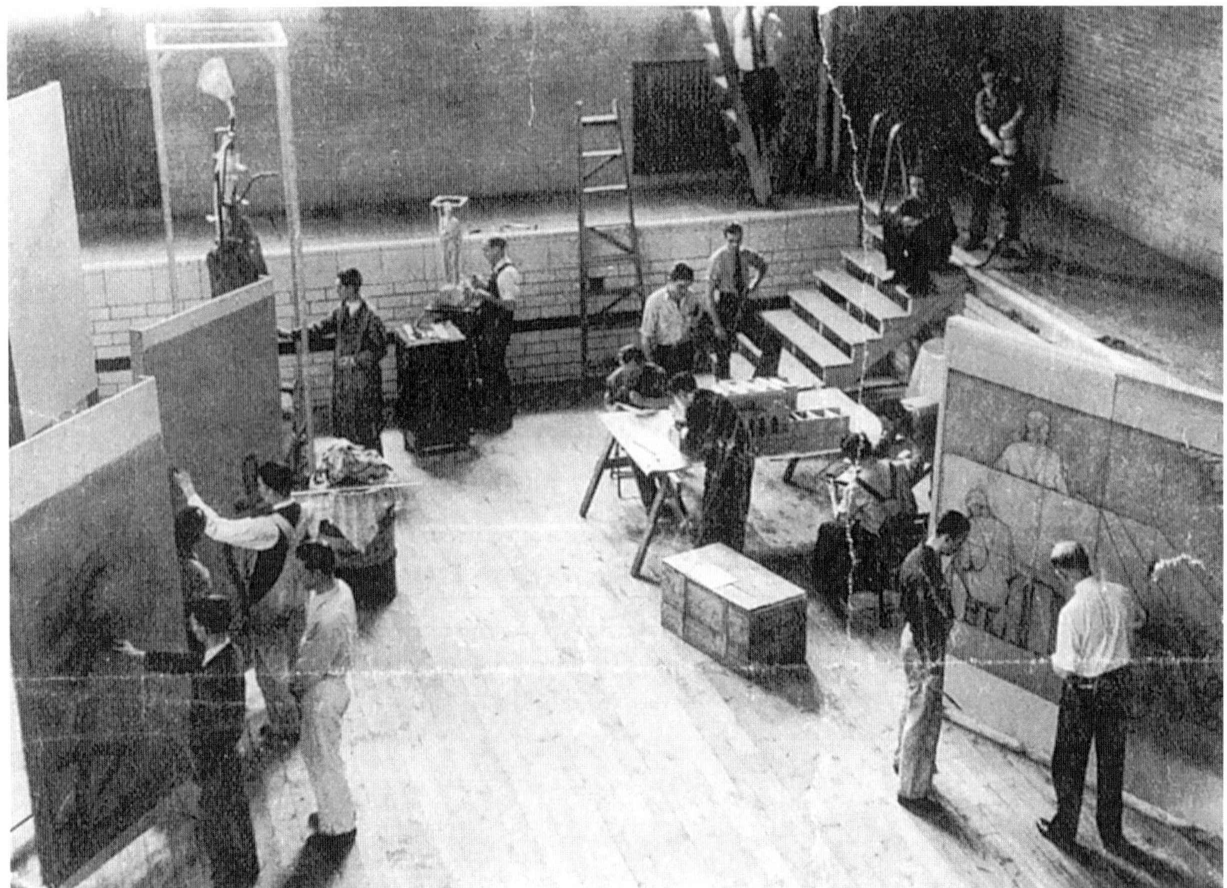

Figure 2.7 Public Works of Art Project studio, Iowa City.

Among the intriguing things about this sketch is that it already (assuming it was an earlier plan) shows Petersen's change of style. Considering that even his most unconventional sculptures of the past had been well within a Beaux Arts or a simple realist tradition, the dairy sculptures constituted a radical stylistic change — as radical a change for his sculpture as Wood had effected when he abandoned his loose impressionistic style for his precise, "regionalist" style in the late 1920s. There is little in Petersen's previous work to prepare us for the flattened, schematic simplicity,

the almost folk-like character of this new design. At no point in any of his public commentary or his papers (and there is not an abundance of either) did he indicate an interest in, admiration of, or even awareness of, folk art, which was one of the "discoveries" of the Depression era, as Wood's work partly demonstrates. It seems obvious that Petersen had adapted his sculptural style to Wood's painting style, and he had done it very quickly. None of the drawings from this period suggest a struggle to come to terms with new stylistic expectations. In fact, it is not known what

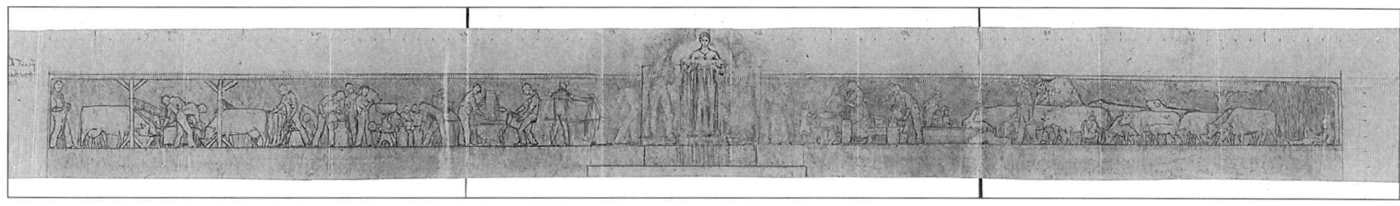

Figure 2.8 Sketch for Petersen's proposal for *History of Dairying Mural*.

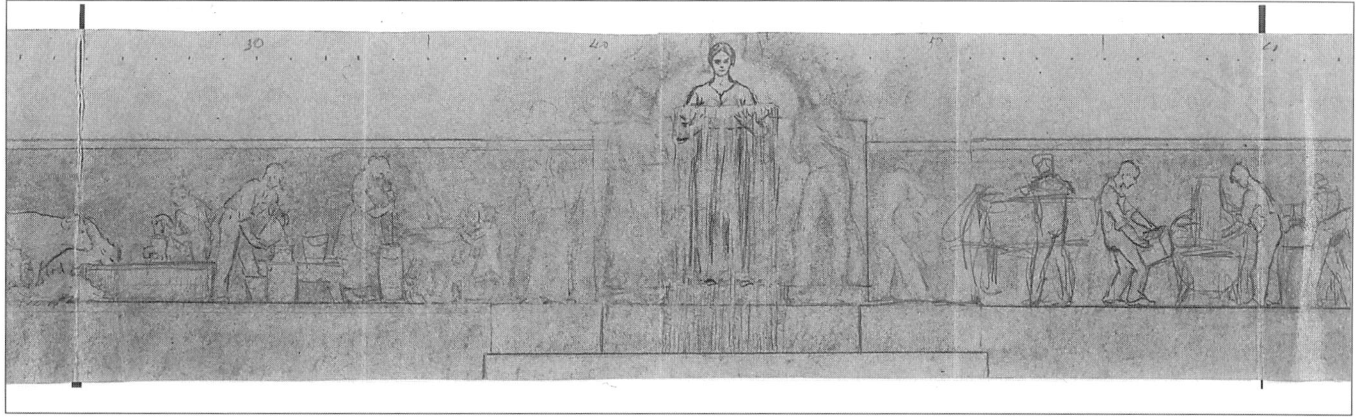

Figure 2.9 Sketch for Petersen's proposal for *History of Dairying Mural*, detail.

Wood's instructions to Petersen were in regard to either his sculpture project or what attempts he might have made to persuade the older artist to consider a new approach. Petersen certainly never suggested that he had been coerced into stylistic harmony with Wood's PWAP output. Like others who worked with Wood in Iowa, he emphasized Wood's certainty about his approach to painting, but never expressed any serious animosity toward him. "I don't believe Grant willfully imposed his methods on his students," he recalled. "It was just his intense desire to help."[25] Although it is true that the two artists do not seem to have been close friends and do not appear to have maintained a personal or professional relationship once the Project shut down, there may be a number of reasons for that, including Wood's preoccupation with his troubles at the University of Iowa. In an interview that probably occurred shortly after Wood's death in 1942, Petersen's comments refer mostly to the PWAP experience and do not indicate much familiarity with Wood's life after that. Wood himself made few comments about the artists with whom he worked at Iowa City. In one of them, he suggests that there were conflicts on the Project but poses himself more as the resolver than as the instigator of them. "He had twenty-four artists working with him on certain murals — and the twenty-four were fairly evenly divided between the modernist and the academic in their artistic leanings. At the outset they were at sword's points, but in the end he had them working harmoniously together."[26]

It is possible that the similarity between the styles of the dairy sculpture (Figure 2.10) and the library paintings was encouraged by President Hughes. It is likely as well that Petersen was reluctant to place himself in opposition to Wood who, although he had recently become quite well known, had not had the broad, though somewhat informal and piecemeal, artistic education or years of experience producing public art that Petersen had. In addition to his gratitude to Wood for his inclusion on the Project, Petersen

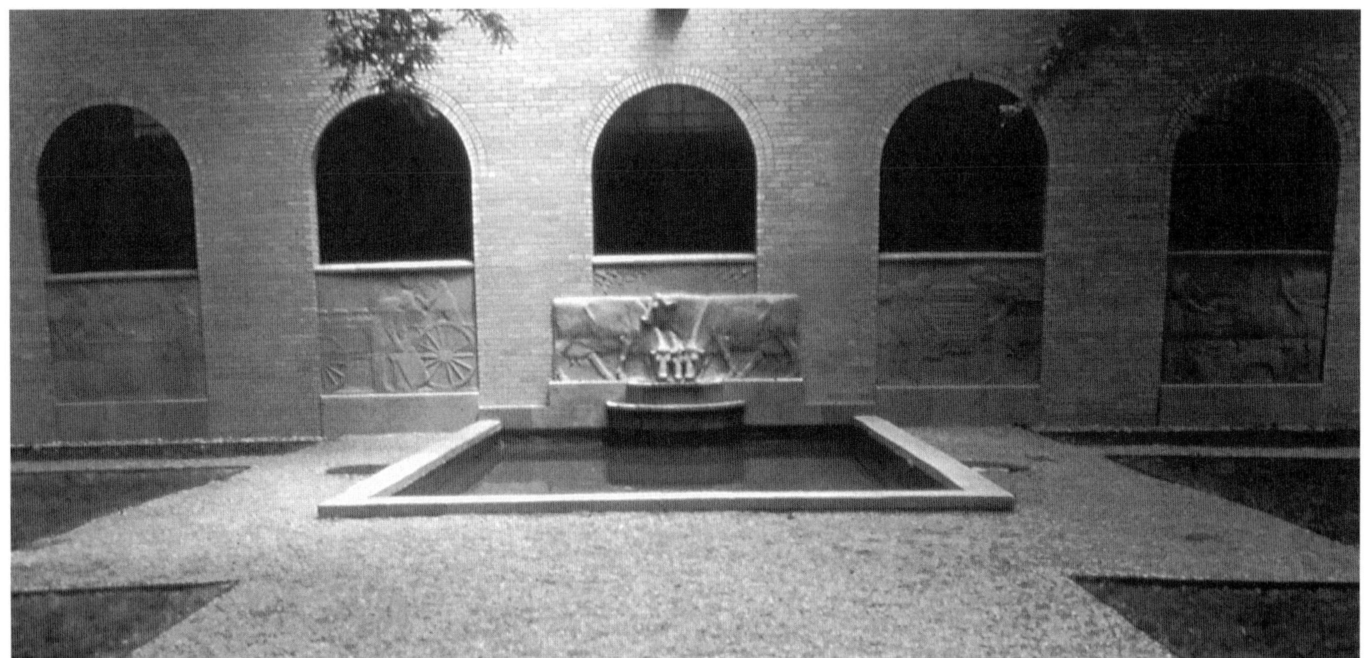
Figure 2.10 *History of Dairying Mural*, courtyard view.

had long been noted for his natural modesty and reticence. Whatever the reasons, he abruptly put aside the style he had used in his large sculpture for decades and never returned to it in works on that scale. For smaller scale work, especially the busts and plaques that he continued to produce for the rest of his life, he maintained a stylistic continuity that makes it nearly impossible to distinguish his early portraits from his late.

The dairy reliefs had a quiet, crisp simplicity in their design that suggests influences beyond the immediate one of Wood's regionalism. The finely tuned rhythms of the trio of cows in the first (Figure 2.11) and sixth (Figure 2.12) panels and the counterpoint between the two bending figures of the third panel (Figure 2.13) all imply an acquaintance with Egyptian painting and sculpture (which had been so admired in the years after the discovery of King Tut's tomb in 1922). The restrained and stately compositions recall the early neoclassicism of the nineteenth century, such as that seen in the engravings of John Flaxman and, perhaps more directly influential for Petersen, the marble carving of the Danish sculptor Thorwaldsen. Finally, Petersen shows a sharp awareness of Art Deco. The repeated forms, the overlapping geometric elements, and the radiating compositional devices are characteristics that he could have observed in Art Deco decoration from the East Coast to the Midwest. Certainly the closest example of the style was the elegant and modern Valley National Bank in Des Moines, built 1931–32, at just the time when Petersen was establishing himself in the city. He might also have noted the Northwestern Bell Telephone Company building of 1928, an example of the "Vertical style" of Art Deco.[27] If Petersen assimilated a number of sources for his designs, his dairy reliefs themselves generated influence on other artists in Iowa. John Bloom's post office murals from the late 1930s for the Iowa towns of DeWitt and Tipton (Figure 2.14) show a clear similarity in their handling of the animals to Peterson's compositions as does Thomas Savage's mural in Jefferson and Lee Allen's in Onawa (Figure 2.15).

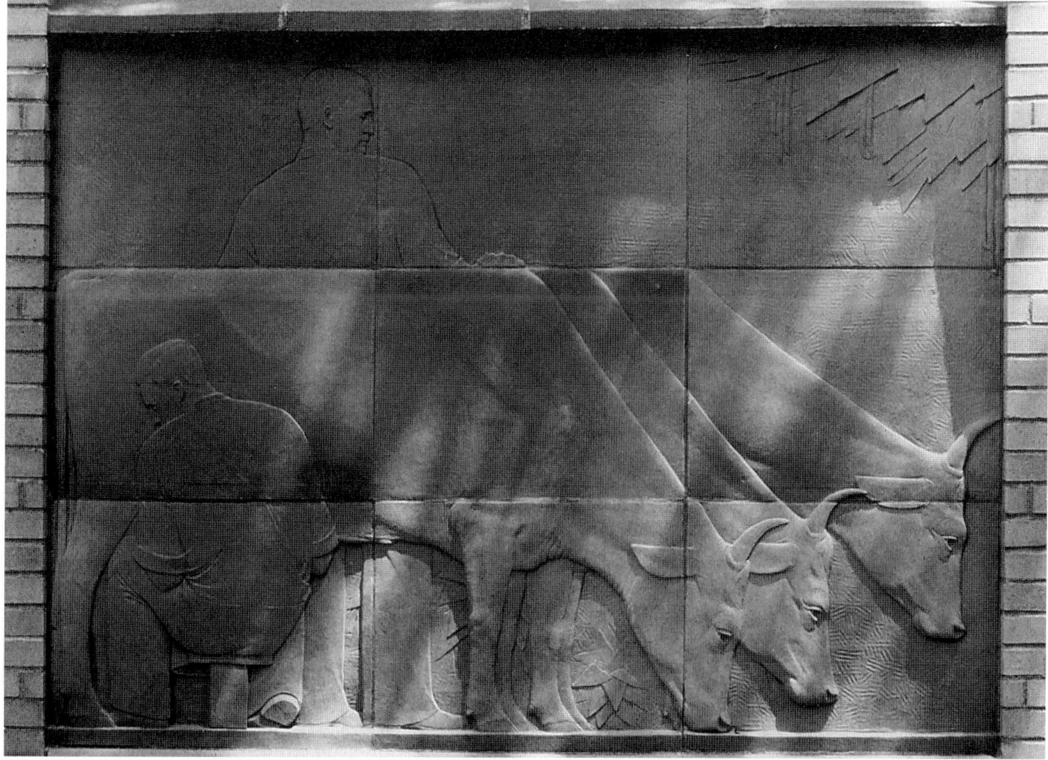

Figure 2.11 *History of Dairying Mural*, panel 1.

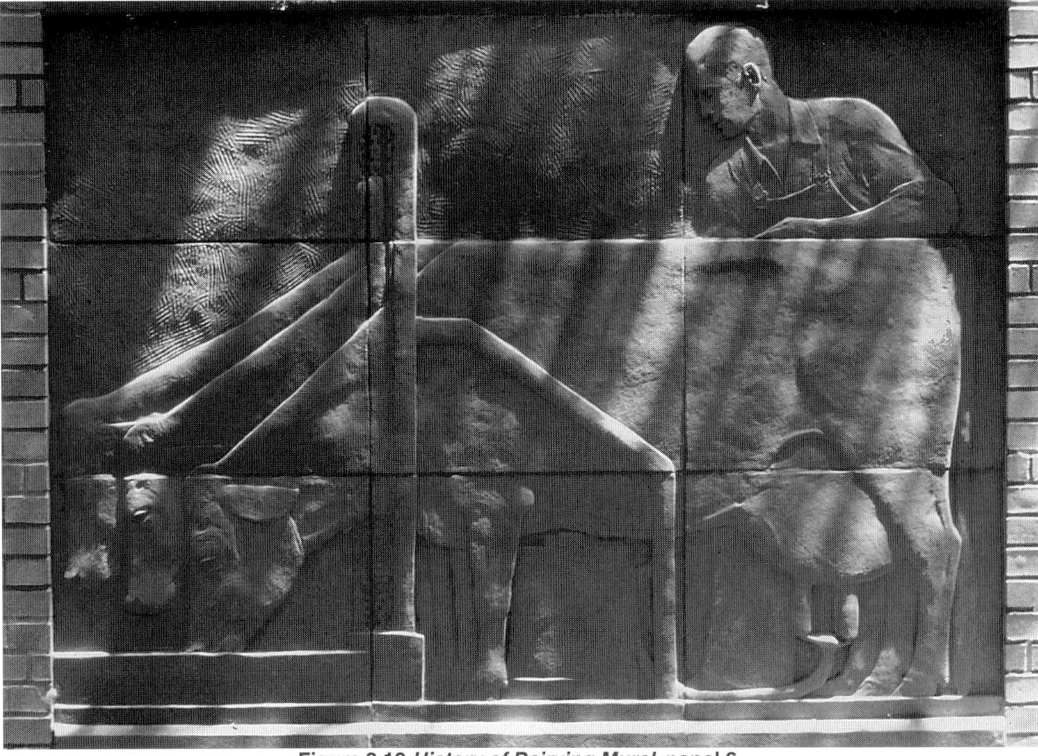

Figure 2.12 *History of Dairying Mural*, panel 6.

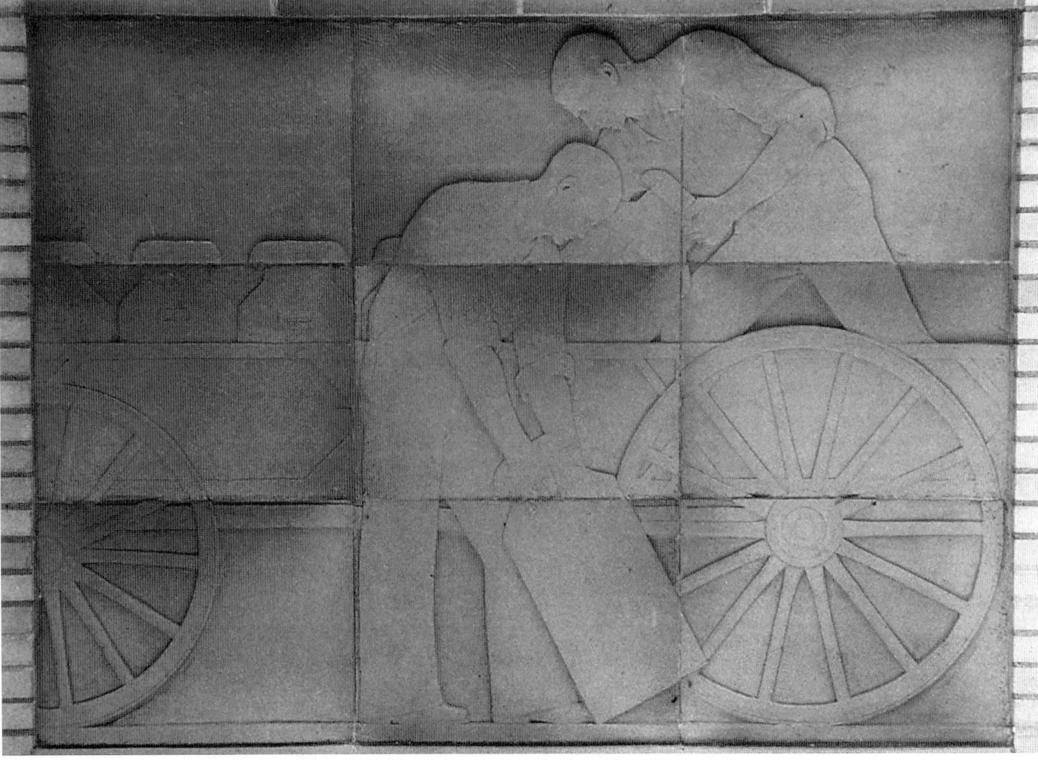

Figure 2.13 *History of Dairying Mural*, panel 3.

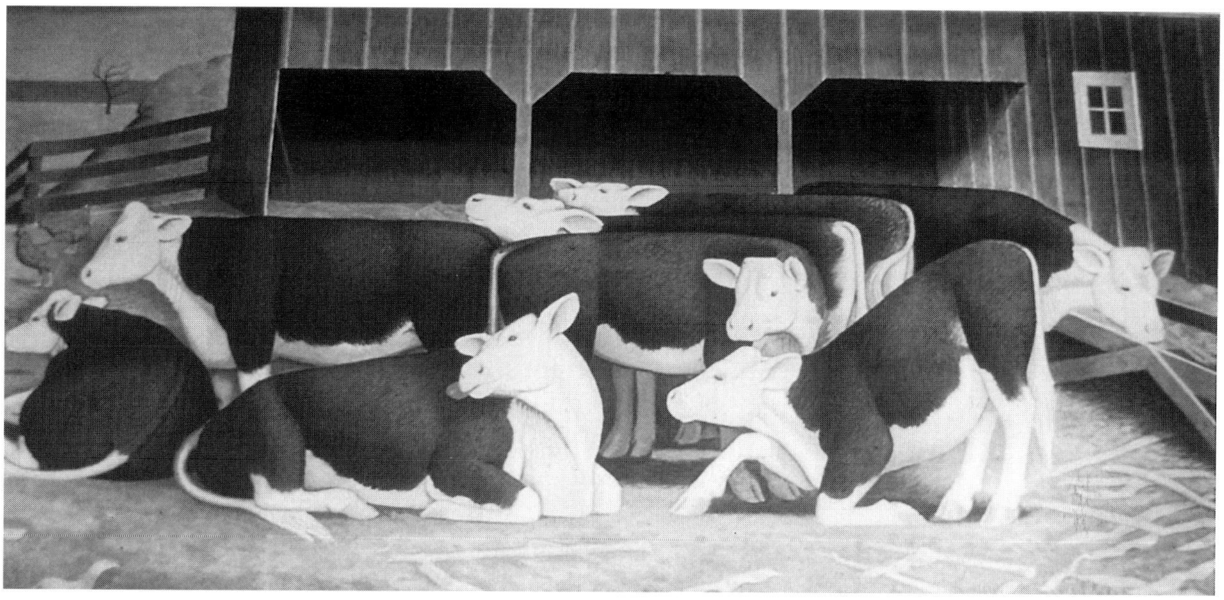

Figure 2.14 *Cattle*, Tipton Post Office, 1939–40.

John V. Bloom

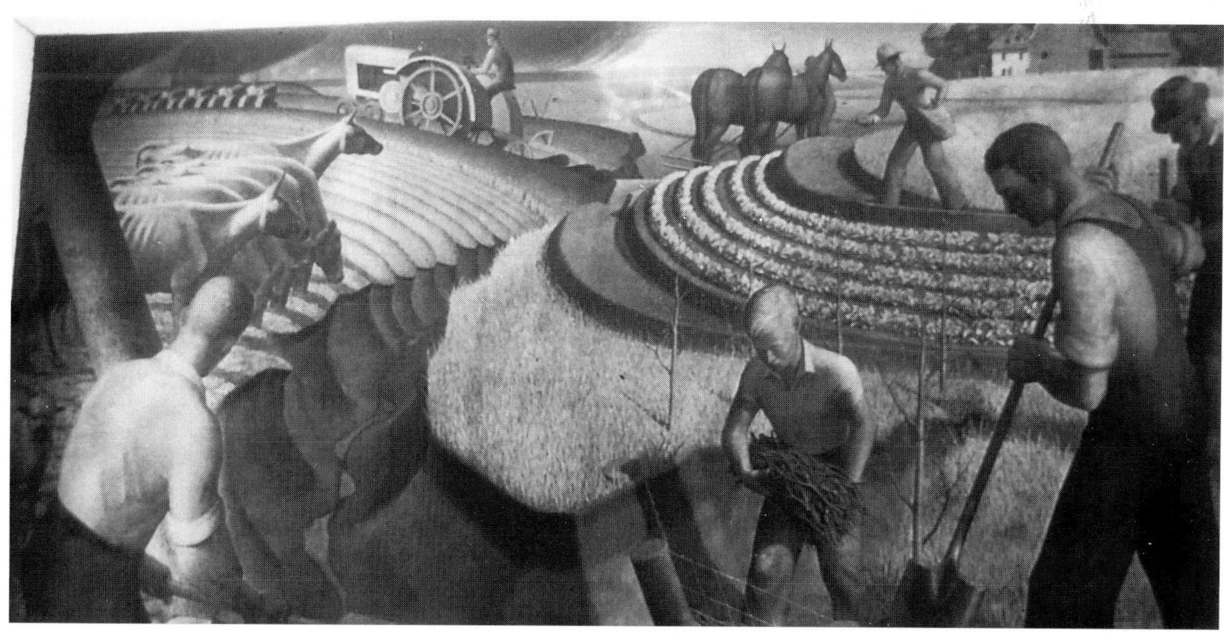

Figure 2.15 *Soil Erosion and Control*, Onawa Post Office, 1937–38.

Lee Allen

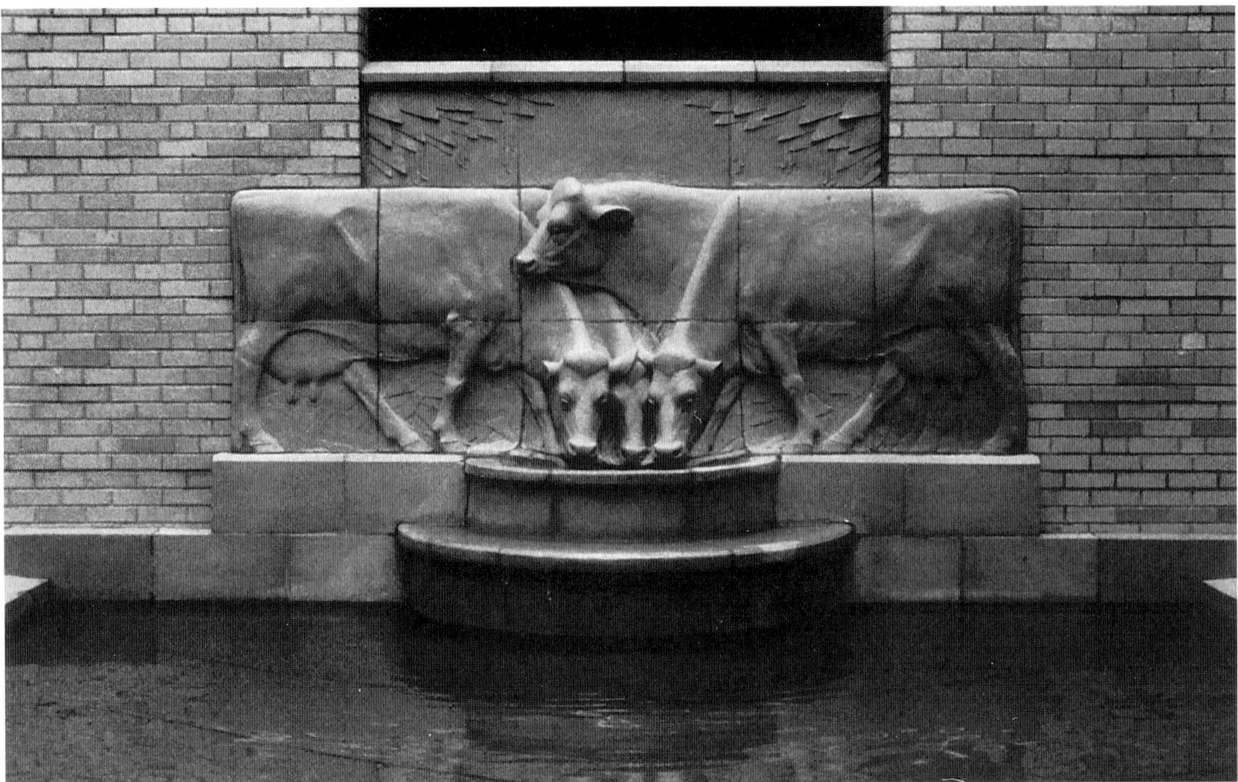

Figure 2.16 *History of Dairying Mural*, fountain.

The dairy industry reliefs were among the most extensive sculptural projects of the New Deal in the Midwest, and the only known sculptures that still exist in Iowa. The six panels were installed three on each side of a center panel whose depth extended out of the low relief into nearly freestanding in the heads of three Jersey cows who stretch out of the flattened panel toward an actual pool of water from which they seem to drink (Figure 2.16). The sophisticated trompe l'oeil effect that Petersen achieved here demonstrated not only his knowledge of art history but also his ability to adapt it to an Iowa subject. The series of sculptures is one side of an outdoor "room" bordered by terraces, plantings, and other buildings. Sensitivity to the site of his sculpture was an enduring characteristic of Petersen's as, over the years, he added a long series of outdoor sculptures to the campus. In every case, his designs took account of both the natural and the man-made aspects of the environment into which he would place his work. Some of his responsiveness to the landscape may have been heightened by his friendship with the landscape architect Jens Jensen (Figure 2.17), like himself a Danish-born American, whom he had met in Chicago and who had helped realize a plan for the Iowa State campus in 1916.[28] The inclusion of the pool in the dairy complex was the first of several instances in which Petersen would integrate water into his schemes for campus monuments.

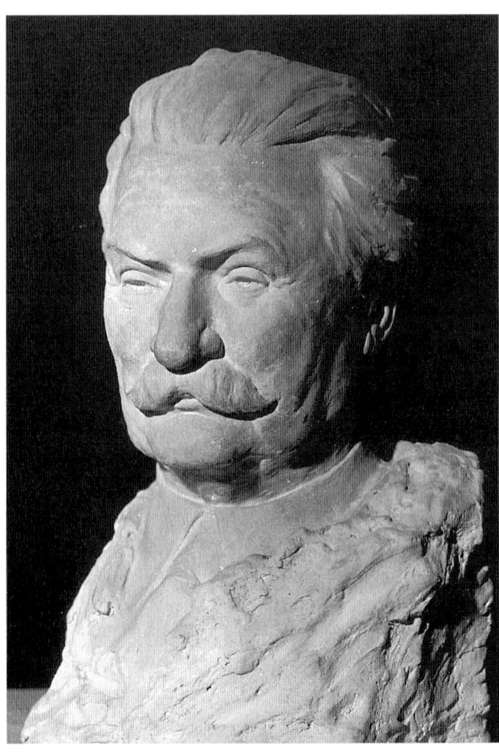

Figure 2.17 *Jens Jensen.*

Christian Petersen

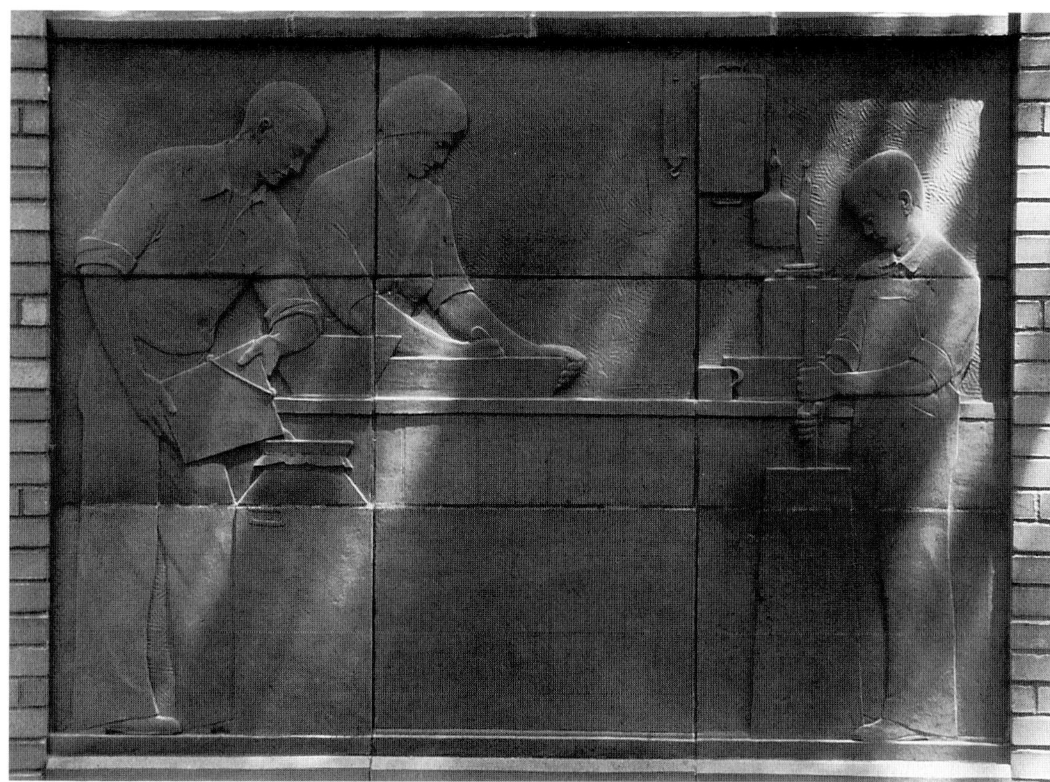

Figure 2.18 *History of Dairying Mural*, panel 2.

Like many artists working in the government's New Deal programs, Petersen was stringent in the accuracy of his portrayals of his subjects, in this case the history and current state of dairying. Just as Wood had been careful to show correct implements and practices in his depictions of agricultural and mechanical practice in his library murals, so Petersen kept in mind that his images would be seen and judged by people who were experts in the field and who were actually engaged daily with the industry. The first three panels dealt with the history of dairying, with its hand milking and laborious production and market procedures. With all of his actors dressed in 1930s styles, Petersen displayed activities that had gone on for decades if not centuries in the historical section.[29]

The first panel (Figure 2.11) depicts an age-old scene, with one man seated on a low stool and milking the first of three orderly, docile cows while a man standing between the second and third cows appears to position himself to also begin that task. There is no indication of a barn or any other setting except for a radiating design in an upper corner that may be an abstracted tree and a few precisely rendered plants along the ground. The second panel (Figure 2.18) brings the scene indoors to a very plain farmhouse where a family takes up the next stage. The raw milk is strained into a metal can by the father while the mother stirs a mixture in a bowl on the counter and a boy in overalls pensively operates a hand churn. Five pristine objects, each with simple but elegant contours, form a studied composition of the implements used in the farm kitchen. The approach that Petersen exhibits here, with a concentration on the restrained simplicity of the shapes of common objects, echoes that used by Wood in his domestic scenes in the library murals. In the last of the three historical panels (Figure 2.13), two men bend and lift in an almost musical rhythm as they load milk cans onto a large-wheeled wagon.

The contemporary section begins after the fountain panel with a scene in a milk processing plant that is a combination of laboratory and industry. This panel (Figure 2.19) demonstrates that Petersen was not immune to the fascination early modern artists had for the machine. Never before had his art portrayed the rapid transformation the machine was creating in the twentieth century. (Certainly his World War I work had implied that change, but the primary focus was on more humanistic themes.) Here, two men attend to an entire series of machines designed to mass produce dairy products. The fifth panel (Figure 2.20) continues that idea but presents the men in situations less subservient to the machines. One tests a sample of milk while the second pours milk into a separator. The sixth panel (Figure 2.12) depicts a single figure who oversees an efficient operation with three cows placed into their designated slots to be milked mechanically as they feed. The overall effect of the story Petersen tells is an evenhanded one, not trumpeting the superiority of modernism over the past, but also not dehumanizing workers in the grip of a machine.

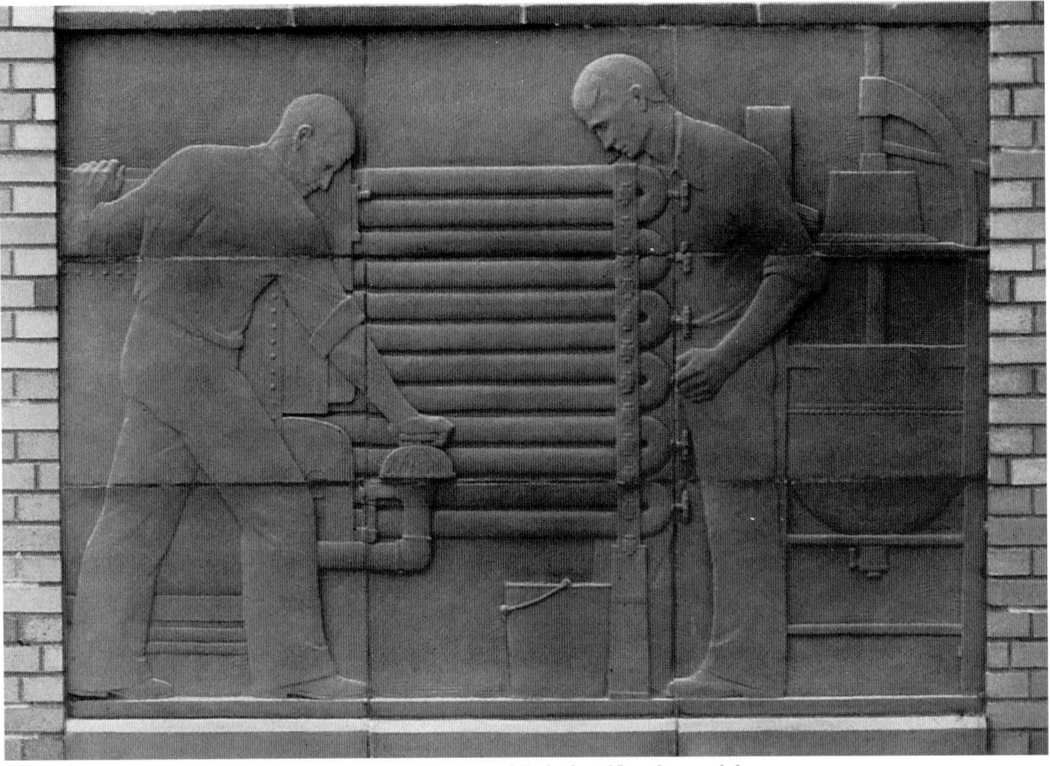

Figure 2.19 *History of Dairying Mural*, panel 4.

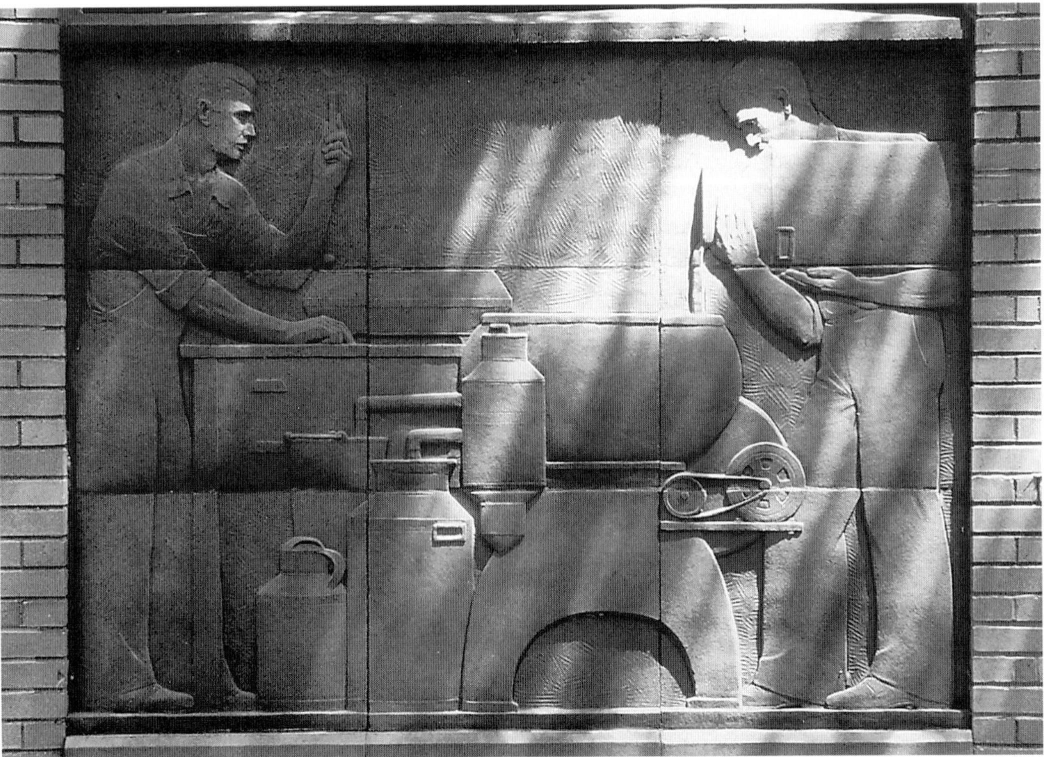

Figure 2.20 *History of Dairying Mural*, panel 5.

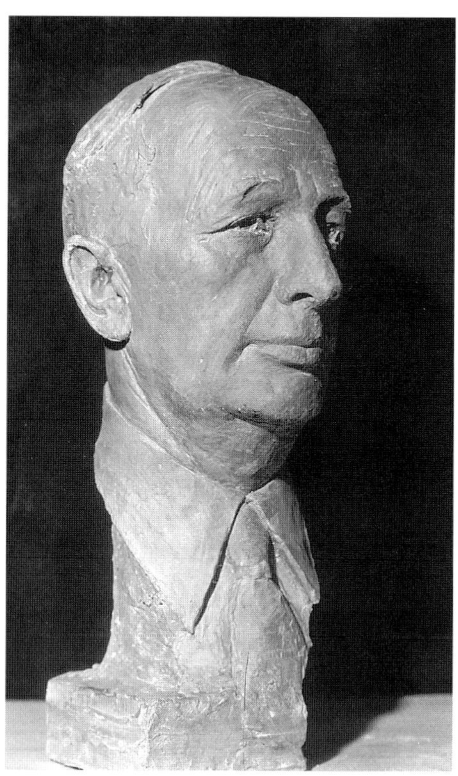

Figure 2.21 *Martin Mortensen.*

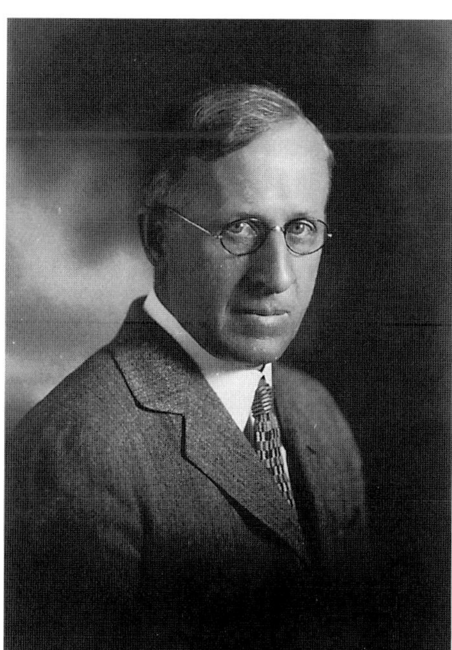

Figure 2.22 Paul Cox.

The installation of the sculpture cycle did not proceed with the calm certainty that characterizes the panels. The PWAP was the most short-lived of the New Deal programs for art, and by June of 1934, the funding had ended and the artist groups had disbanded. The Petersens stayed in Iowa City until August before moving to Ames, where Iowa State College had committed to the completion of his project. The finished panels were to be of terra cotta, which Petersen had planned to fire in a large commercial kiln in Chicago. But as financial responsibility for the sculpture cycle transferred to the college, Petersen was informed that it was beyond their ability to pay. President Hughes had managed to add the sculptor to the college payroll at a low salary (even by Depression standards), and the realization of the project also had to be achieved at minimal cost.[30] The head of the dairy industry department, Martin Mortensen (Figure 2.21) (also Danish-born), was eager to add the sculptural cycle to his building, and the president had enlisted the participation of the head of the college's ceramic engineering department, Paul E. Cox (Figure 2.22). By June of 1934, Petersen and Cox had worked together enough to understand what was required to accomplish their task in Ames, and Cox estimated that the whole project would cost around $552, assuming there were no serious problems and not counting "Sculptor Petersen's time here."[31] Throughout the fall of 1934 and spring of 1935, Cox and Petersen combined their expertise and long working hours to overcome the technical challenges of the panels.[32]

Professor Cox's kiln at the ceramic engineering department was simply not big enough to accommodate the full-scale panels, even if it had been possible to fire them without breakage and distortion. If the project was to be realized, Petersen had to adjust his designs to the dimensions of the college kiln, which meant they could not be fired as a single panel but would have to be divided into nine sections, each of which had to go into the kiln separately. It was Petersen's task to make sure these divisions did not disrupt the formal integrity of his designs. Determined to see the project through, Petersen cooperated fully with Cox until the two formed a highly effective team. Nearly a year later, in April of 1935, Cox wrote a letter to the dean of engineering detailing the problems they had met and overcome and heading off any criticism that might be made from elsewhere in a college which emphasized practice as well as theory. "Christian Petersen is not only a good sculptor but is a practical man," he wrote, and added that in the work they had done together, "We are entirely right and entirely correct in all the steps we took."[33] The effort had necessitated a new, deeper level of knowledge of ceramic practice for both Cox and Petersen. For the sculptor, it had also involved a willingness to help monitor the kiln and work alongside Cox and his students in the dirty, frustrating job of correcting and finishing the panels. Petersen's wife related how the couple would awaken in the middle of the night to bring coffee and sandwiches to the student who had the nighttime shift overseeing the round-the-clock operation of the kiln.[34]

In the end, the collaboration of Cox and Petersen produced a sculptural cycle unlike anything else produced by the New Deal art programs, not only in its scale but more especially in its regionalist theme and setting. The dairy complex has another, less well-known component in the interior of the building that continues the ideas and imagery of the dairy courtyard cycle. Petersen added two arched plaster panels, eleven by eight feet, on either side of the divided staircase in the foyer of the building, also contrasting old dairy methods with new. The first panel (Figure 2.23) depicts two women in classical garb, one churning cream in an animal skin hung from a tree limb as a second rests her arm on the back of a cow while balancing a Greek-like vessel on her left shoulder. A nude boy also carries that same kind of vessel as he steps toward the center of the composition. Although the cow has the same modern-looking geometric proportions of those in the Courtyard, the women resurrect the classicizing interpreta-

tion Petersen had used in his *Spanish-American War Memorial* and other works from early in his career. The Old English inscription below the scene was contributed by J.C. Cunningham, professor of corn genetics, who had befriended the Petersens and admired the artist's work: "For melke and chese and buttere for ther bred / The Abram wymmen slaved and laboured longe."

The second panel (Figure 2.24) dressed its two farm women in plain, long skirts that suggest pioneer days, while a young man dressed like a contemporary college student sits, one hand resting on his chin and the other clasping the handle of a milk pail. He stares thoughtfully at the wooden churn worked by the central female figure as the other woman approaches carrying a shallow, broad bowl. The background is a plain farmhouse with a few utilitarian objects of simple design. Arching over the scene are the branches of an Iowa oak tree. Cunningham's inscription does

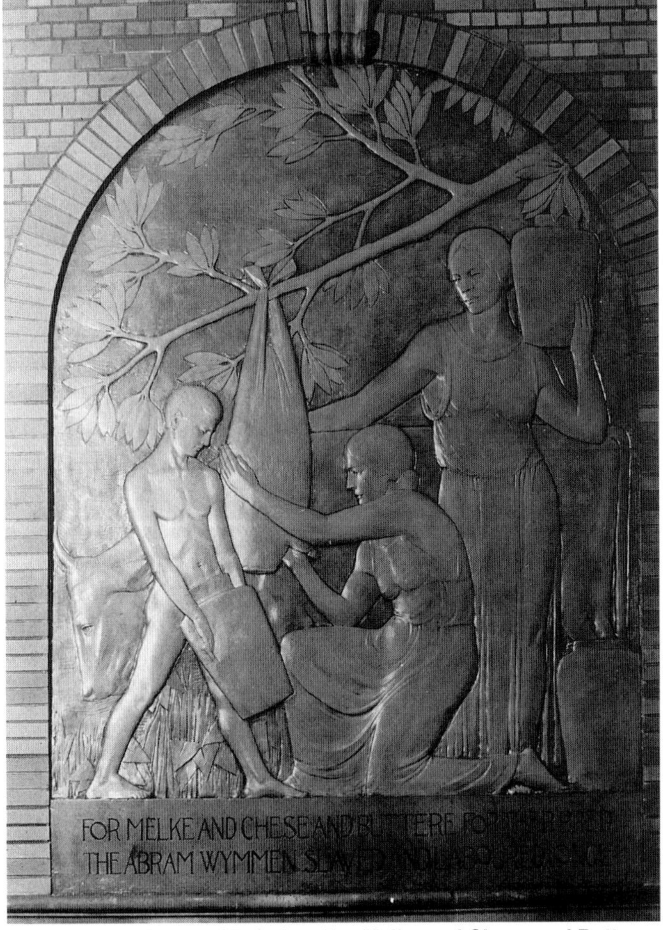

Figure 2.23 *History of Dairying: For Melke and Chese and Buttere.*

FOR MELKE AND CHESE AND BUTTERE FOR THER BRED
THE ABRAM WYMMEN SLAVED AND LABOURED LONGE.

Jules Cool Cunningham 1879–1948
American
(Writings used as inscriptions on bas-relief interior panels,
former Dairy Industry Building.)

not entirely reflect the serious, dignified tone of the image: "Four thousande yeers pass by before man thinkes / To chaunge these plodding houres to houres of songe."

President Raymond Hughes' desire to keep Petersen at Iowa State led him to add the sculptor to the college payroll in October of 1935 "at $100 a month for at least three months and such further time as our funds and your work make possible."[35] He was expected to teach a class in sculpture and to continue working on projects for the college. Hughes' push to add an artist to his faculty may reflect his awareness of similar movements at the University of Iowa and the University of Wisconsin. Grant Wood began his tumultuous tenure at the University of Iowa in April of 1934 with the assignment of finishing the mural project and teaching classes. In a joint announcement, President Walter A. Jessup of the University of Iowa and Hughes of Iowa State committed their institutions to the completion of both the library murals and the dairy reliefs begun under the government program.[36] Hughes may have seen this development as the opportunity he had been waiting for to create a more cultural atmosphere at his agriculture/engineering school and, at the same time, to give it more equal footing with the University of Iowa. Whereas Wood's appointment served to expand the fine arts curriculum in Iowa City, Petersen's created a foundation for a true fine arts program at Iowa State. After Wood joined the Iowa faculty in April, Hughes must have been eager to have a professional artist on his staff as well.

Hughes may also have known about plans at the University of Wisconsin, which resulted in the addition of John Steuart Curry as artist-in-residence in 1936. He would surely have been aware of "the Wisconsin idea" or the concept of the university as not just the teacher of college students but the populist teacher of

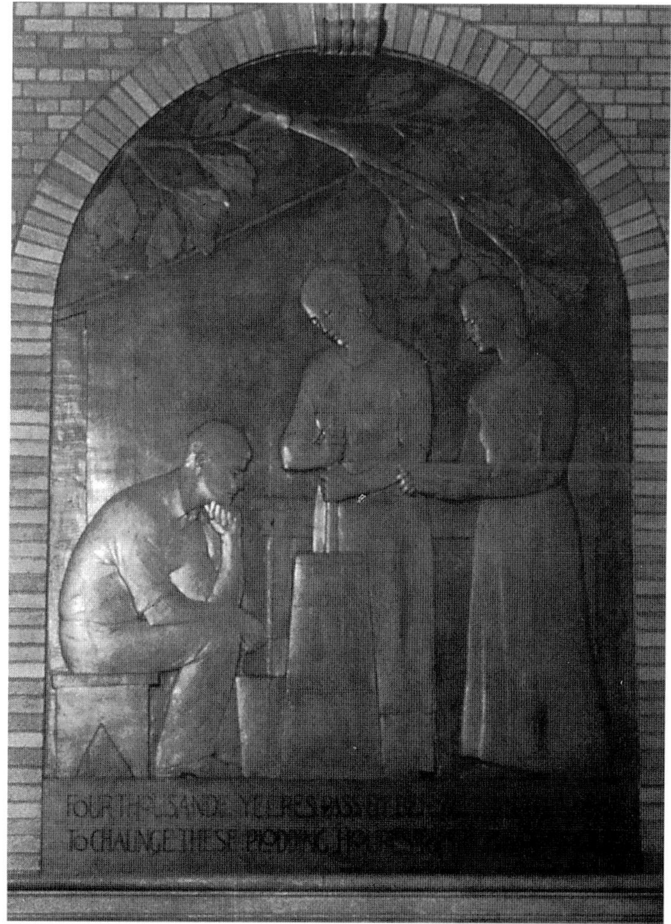

Figure 2.24 *History of Dairying: Four Thousande Yeeres.*

FOUR THOUSANDE YEERES PASS BY BEFORE MAN THINKES
TO CHAUNGE THESE PLODDING HOURES TO HOURES OF SONGE.

Jules Cool Cunningham 1879–1948
American
(Writings used as inscriptions on bas-relief interior panels,
former Dairy Industry Building.)

the state at large. The university's role as an educator of the state-wide population and a beacon for broad-based development in all aspects of both rural and urban life was the concept identified with the University of Wisconsin, and Hughes may have felt that his own upper Midwest, land-grant institution could share in that idea. Curry's position at Wisconsin, however, was far more generous than Petersen's. He was not required to teach classes, although he was expected to travel about the state and promote art, especially in rural districts. A studio was built especially for him and, in contrast to Petersen's low salary, Curry was paid $4,000 per year.[37]

Petersen began the winter quarter of 1934–35, meeting his all female class in a ceramics lab. Unlike the University of Iowa, which had an active (and very competitive) art department, Iowa State College offered only a few classes in what they called "applied art" through the home economics department. Since only women were allowed to enroll in home economics classes, only women made up Petersen's early classes in sculpture (Figure 2.25). But those classes were soon filled, and Petersen proved himself an effective, highly regarded teacher. For the next twenty years, until his retirement in 1955, he taught and produced, at every opportunity, sculpture for the campus.

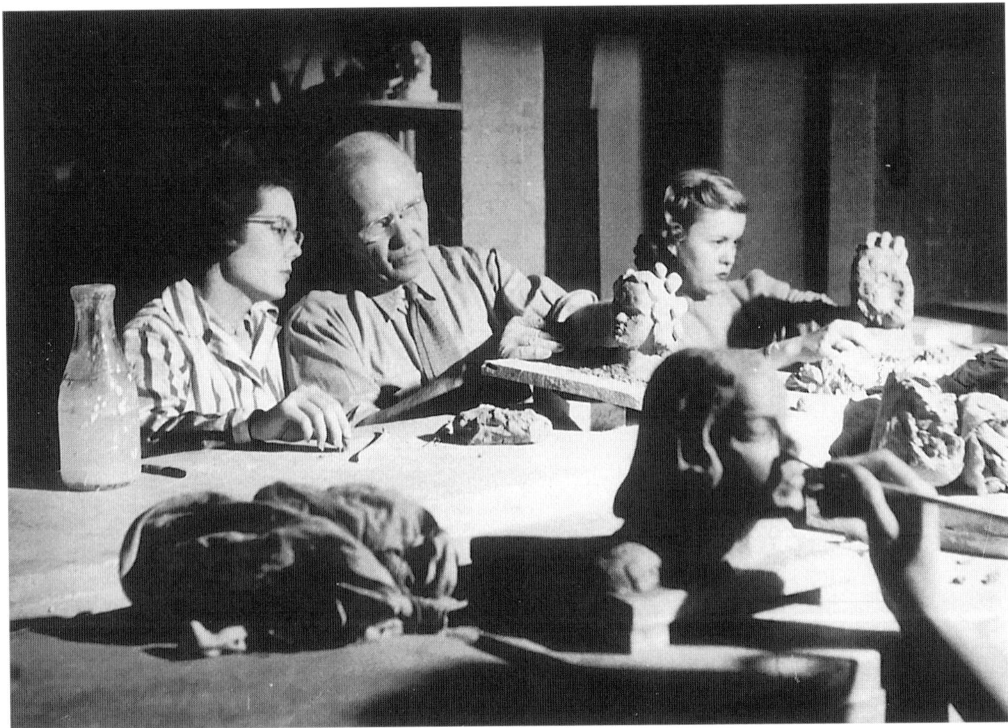

Figure 2.25 Petersen with students.

NOTES

1. Several sources indicate that Petersen was a member of the Chicago Galleries Association. The group was begun in 1926 to aid artists in obtaining exhibition opportunities, including the gallery space of the Association itself at 220 N. Michigan Avenue. Membership was $200.00 per year, by invitation only. A check by the Art Institute of Chicago provided information on this Association, but did not find Petersen's name among artist members up to 1930. Marcy Neth, Ryerson Library of the Art Institute of Chicago, to author, August 31, 1999. A search by Art and Architecture Archivist at the Art Institute revealed no information in *The Annual Exhibition Record of the Art Institute of Chicago, 1888–1950,* or any other exhibition records there. Reviews there of exhibition catalogues of the Association did not include Petersen. The author is indebted to the Archivist for a partial copy of *The Chicago Galleries Association; Prospectus for the Second 3-Year Period (1929–1931).* Letter from Mary K. Woolever, Art and Architecture Archivist, The Art Institute of Chicago, to author, September 22, 1999. Searches at the Chicago Historical Society and The Newberry Library also discovered no information about this phase of Petersen's career.

2. J.C. Cunningham, identified as "Research Professor, Iowa Corn Research Institute of the Iowa Agricultural Experiment Station, Ames, Iowa," handwritten notes for "An Appreciation," undated. Christian Petersen Papers.

3. Ibid. Another version of the story of Petersen's employment is given in Bliss, Patricia L., *Christian Petersen Remembered,* Ames: Iowa State University Press, 1986, 15–16. Taken from an interview with Charlotte Petersen, it is Mrs. Petersen's recollection not only of his employment, but of her first meeting with her future husband. Mrs. Petersen recalled his starting salary at $100.00 per week while Cunningham recorded it in his notes as $50.00.

4. The friend, Juliet G. Sager, and the Petersens drew up a handwritten contract in which they agreed to buy her house and three lots on Buchanan Street for $3,000.00 "as soon as they arrange to make a payment. ... Juliet Sager agrees that they may occupy the house rent-free until they buy it, provided they pay the taxes and insurance when due." Christian Petersen Papers.

5. On the Wood Brothers, see Renda Lutz, "3851 Delaware Ave," Des Moines *Register*, August 25, 1999. The plaque is in the collection of the State Historical Society of Iowa, I 11923.

6. Both of these works came into the collection of the State Historical Society, but that of Pushetonequa is currently unlocated. Petersen also sculpted a portrait bust of Edgar R. Harlan in 1930.

7. The bronze of this portrait is in the collection of the State Historical Museum of Iowa. Three plaques of the governor, also produced in 1932, are owned by descendants. His granddaughter, Louise Clarke Hobbs, remembered watching Petersen work on the bust while her grandfather sat for the modeling in Adel, the governor's hometown. Letter from Hobbs to author, February 9, 1999.

8. Bliss, 20–22. Eventually, Edgar R. Harlan, head of the State Historical, Memorial, and Art Department, had to alert friends and patrons in Des Moines that the Petersens desperately needed to be paid and that Petersen had actually fallen ill due to malnutrition.

9. An article in the Des Moines *Register*, "C. Petersons [*sic*] Return Home to Illinois," explains that Petersen had been occupied for "several months" on reliefs of "Iowa's distinguished citizens" and would return to Des Moines for the opening of the Younkers exhibition on July 17. Undated clipping, probably from 1933. Christian Petersen Papers.

10. Memorandum to the Advisory Committee on Fine Arts to the Treasury, December 20, 1933, Archives of American Art (AAA) Record Group 121, frame 487. This early memorandum also notes that one project was already approved and under way in Region 7 (Iowa, Missouri, Nebraska, Kansas), described as "Murals designed by Grant Wood for Library, Iowa State College, Ames, Iowa." frame 489.

11. Telegram to Rowan from Forbes Watson, Technical Director of the PWAP, December 12, 1933. Record Group 121, DC 3, frame 711.

12. Reece Stuart, Jr., to Petersen at Belvidere, Illinois, January 12, 1934. Christian Petersen Papers. Petersen had sculpted a plaque of Stuart's two young sons.

13. Letter from Grant Wood to Harlan Miller, January 10, 1934. Christian Petersen Papers.

14. Letter from Wood to Petersen, January 10, 1934. Christian Petersen Papers. It is not clear how Wood became acquainted with Petersen's work, but it is likely he knew him primarily through his portraiture and not through the monumental sculpture he had done in the East.

15. Letter from Wood to Petersen, January 16, 1934. Christian Petersen Papers.

16. Letter from Petersen to Wood, January 18, 1934. Christian Petersen Papers.

17. Letter from R.M. Hughes to Petersen, October 3, 1933. Christian Petersen Papers.

18. Letter from R.M. Hughes to Petersen, October 16, 1933, Christian Petersen Papers. Following this offer of support, Hughes added, "At this time I am not able to agree to finance the matter beyond that point, but later we might go further."

19. From this time until around 1937, Hughes personally provided a stipend, often monthly, to the Petersens, even after he had left his post as president. In a letter of December 12, 1936, as president emeritus, he made a formal record of this commitment. "I am very deeply interested in your success as a sculptor, and I believe you are

NOTES

approaching a point where you will receive more recognition than has hitherto been the case. It seems to me that without any doubt your tenure of appointment here at the College must remain very uncertain. This is not because you and your work are not appreciated by the administration, but because of the very nature of your work and the uncertainty of the College being able to finance it from quarter to quarter. In order to give you a greater sense of security and to enable you to go ahead with more confidence in the work in which you are engaged I am willing to agree ... to pay you $100 a month for any month that you are not employed by the College, up to a total of twelve." On November 5, 1937, he wrote to say he would no longer provide a regular stipend since Petersen was employed, but since Petersen's college contract was for nine months only, he would send money in the summers if he could.

20. Letter from Hughes to Petersen, January 29, 1934. Petersen must have already made a trip to Ames to discuss the proposed work with Hughes since he sent reimbursement for traveling expenses to Petersen at his Memorial Union address at the University of Iowa. Hughes to Petersen, January 31, 1934. Christian Petersen Papers.

21. According to the final tally for the entire Region 7, only ten sculptures were produced in comparison with 321 oils, fifteen murals, and forty-three murals in process. Forbes Watson, technical director to Louis LaBeaume (director for Region 7), May 22, 1934, AAA Record Group 121, DC 1, frame 755. Another listing of work completed in Region 7 includes Petersen's work with the mural, *When Tillage Begins, Other Arts Follow* at Iowa State College, Ames; the artists were "Grant Wood, Francis McCray, Christian Petersen and others" AAA Record Group 121, DC 1, frames 943–946.

22. There was opportunity to produce their own easel paintings under Wood's tutelage, which a number of them had already experienced at his Stone City art colony and school during the summers of 1932 and/or 1933. But the library murals were the primary products of the Project.

23. There were at least nine women on the Iowa Project, but it is not clear whether any of them were resident at Iowa City; no women are recorded as having contributed to the library murals. *Report of the Public Works of Art Project*, Washington, D.C., 1934, 58.

24. The photograph also shows two men each working on a sculpture with a wooden framework around it. The smaller is clearly a figurative piece while the larger one appears well over life-size and, in addition, looks rather abstract, although it may be simply an armature onto which the sculptor is adding clay from the pile to his left. The two men are unidentified, and no sculpture other than Petersen's is known to have survived from the Iowa PWAP or, indeed, from any of the New Deal art projects in Iowa.

25. Undated typescript with handwritten editions. Christian Petersen Papers.

26. "He Plans for a Native Art; Grant Wood Bases Faith on Regional Development," *The New York Sun*, October 10, 1934. Clipping in

Nan Wood Graham Scrapbook, Archives of American Art, Roll 1216, frame 405.

27. See Gebhard, David, and Mansheim, Gerald, *Buildings of Iowa* (Buildings of the United States), New York: Oxford University Press, 1993, 197, 199.

28. Bliss reports that Jensen was also from Dybbol, where he had been a boyhood friend of Petersen's father. 31.

29. The narrative sequence of the panels is somewhat unclear in that Petersen may have intended it to begin from the outermost panels (of cows being milked, as in the first panel) and move toward the center. For this essay, however, the panels are discussed and numbered by their physical sequence; thus the panel adjacent to the center fountain panel is designated as the fourth panel and so on.

30. Bliss records comparative salaries of other workers in Iowa and at the college, finding that Petersen's salary was considerably less than the lowest-paid Iowa State employee. Although his salary did gradually increase, he remained on the lowest rung of the financial ladder for the rest of his career at Iowa State College. 32–33.

31. Letter from Paul E. Cox to R.M. Hughes, June 12, 1934. Christian Petersen Papers.

32. Letter from Paul E. Cox to Dean T.R. Agg (dean of engineering), April 16, 1935.

33. The technical aspects of this job have been described in several places. Letter to Mrs. L. Worthington Smith from Petersen, February 6, 1935. Minton, Lewis G., "Ceramic Engineering Department Constructs Panels of Terra Cotta," *The Iowa Engineer*, March 1935, 84–85. "Students Turn Test Kiln to Aid of Unemployed Iowa Artists," *The Power Specialist*, September 1935, 2(9): 9–11. Bliss, 34–46.

34. Bliss, 42.

35. Handwritten letter from Hughes to Petersen, October 25, 1934. Christian Petersen Papers. In what would become a typical gesture of Hughes', he added, "If you need some money to pull along till (the first check of November 20) I will be glad to loan it to you or endorse your note at the bank."

36. "Name Grant Wood to Faculty," *The Daily Iowan*, April 26, 1934. Nan Wood Graham Scrapbook, Archives of American Art, Roll 1216, frame 385.

37. For a discussion of Curry's situation as artist-in-residence and a history of his career at the University of Wisconsin, see Mathiak, Lucy J., "A Stranger to the Ivory Tower: John Steuart Curry and the University of Wisconsin," in Junker, Patricia, *John Steuart Curry: Inventing the Middle West,* New York: Hudson Hills Press in association with the Elvehjem Museum of Art, University of Wisconsin-Madison, 1998, 183–194.

water from stone

The most beautiful spot
they say, in Ames,
in the fall or early summer
or mid-May is inside
the Dairy Industry Building.
Three gentle Jerseys
reach out from
the college hallway
stretching their necks
from the flat world
of their maker's hand
into yours, and
all of a sudden
you are no longer inside,
fresh water streams
from stone walls
and pours into
a pool at your feet
holding you
in its shimmering hands,
letting you
dance for a while
on its trembling surface,
you on the flagstone patio
talking with your friends and
smiling and eating ice cream.

Never have you been
so unsure of what
was real and what was not,
what was moving
and what was stone,
what inside, what out,
exactly whose luxuriant
imagination you lived in
and with anyway.

A huge Jersey bull coddles
and comforts his cows
as if you are the strangers here,
marvelous misshapen lumps
that have inexplicably found themselves
on this green and open plain
hardened by life
and sadness and curiosity.
Sixty-five years and no cracks
have yet ruined this firing,
these timeless moments in time,
this groggy Iowa clay
beaten into handmade ashlers
and burned sixty hours at a time
at 500 degrees Fahrenheit
the first day,
1800 the second
and 2000 the remaining 58.

It was hard work back then,
during the Depression, you
had better believe it, and hot.
It took stubbornness
and guts and pain
to make this quiet moment
in the Iowa shade,
this sweet air and sunshine,
this little bit of peace
deep inside your present,
modern, unfathomable work.
Oh what is beauty?
What is dust? I say.
What is dirt?
What is clay?
that the creator's hands
ever imagined to fashion it?

Michael Carey

Inspired by the History of Dairying Mural *by Christian Petersen.*
Commissioned by the University Museums, Iowa State University, 1999
as part of the Art on Campus Poetry Collection.

CHAPTER 3
FROM DAIRIES TO VETERINARIANS

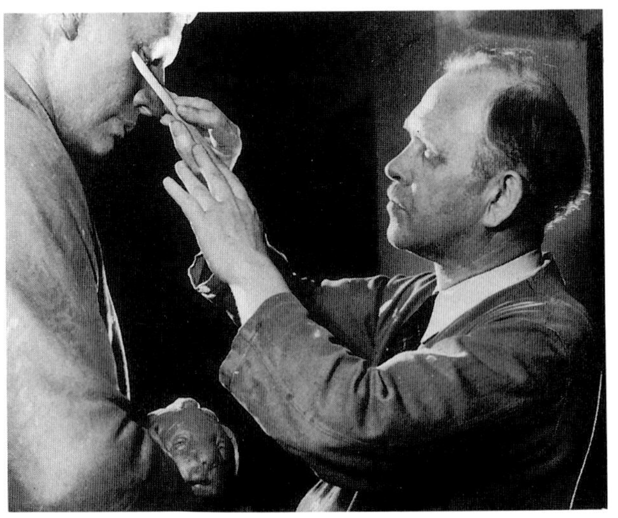

Petersen, 1937.

After the dairy building sculptures, inside and out, were unveiled in the spring of 1935, Petersen began developing ideas for his next major campus sculpture. The dean of veterinary medicine, Charles H. Stange, had requested a work of art for the veterinary complex, and during the summer of 1935, his discussions with Petersen helped the sculptor formulate the theme for a large sculptural panel (Figures 3.1 and 3.2). With help of his wife, Charlotte, Petersen acquainted himself with the history and recent developments in veterinary science, then composed an active scene of sturdy men and farm animals. Like the dairy sculptures, it was also to be a relief, but this time a single panel, not broken into seven separate scenes. Nothing of its size was produced in Iowa or perhaps in the entire Midwest during the 1930s. In proposing his new sculpture to the college administration, Petersen described the primary theme as "the protection of human health by guarding animal health through the development of vaccines."[1]

He continued with explanations of each portion of the composition. "Men with cow. Protection of the food animal by inspection for the recognition of contagious diseases, specifically foot-and-mouth disease. Since this is a transmissible disease to humans it also shows human protection." Working with a cow of clean, geometric character, similar to those in the dairy reliefs, one man pulls open the cow's jaws to peer into its mouth while a second clasps the cow's neck, pulling it upward and back. Like the determined soldier of the *Battery D Memorial* and two other major figures of the veterinary panel, he steps vigorously into his work.

The next incident drops the action to the ground plane where two men vaccinate a calf, according to Petersen: "Kneeling figures working with a calf. The protection of the human from smallpox by vaccine prepared from the calf." With the calf turned onto its back so that one veterinarian can extract fluid from its underside, a shirtless man grips the calf's front legs while its head is held fast between the man's arm and his side. His braced position as he keeps the animal still and the straining muscles of his upper body make it evident that all his strength and focus are required to carry out his part of the procedure.

In the next portion, the dominant panel, man must again overpower an animal. But this man's struggle is the greatest of the panel, as his exaggerated position shows. Petersen's clinical description of the scene contrasts markedly with the drama he infused into his representation of it: "The protection of the human through the production of diphtheria and tetanus antitoxin through the blood of the horse." The spirited horse, flexing his muscles and bending his head down sharply as if on the verge of rearing up, seems to be a twentieth-century incarnation of the horses and centaurs who paraded and fought across the pediments of the Parthenon.[2] The musculature of the shirtless man and the arch of his back as he strains to subdue the horse suggest that man and animal are equal contenders in this contest for dominance. Widespread legs planted on the ground, the man wraps his right arm over the shoulder of the horse as his left firmly tugs back on a bridle in the horse's mouth. The tone of struggle, of muscle against muscle, will against will, of these two massive and central forms is in contrast to the studious concentration of the vet who withdraws the horse's blood. This theme of struggle was one that hovered over a good deal of art in the 1930s, and in no other work does Petersen express so clearly that feature of his times. Perhaps the best known images of the period are the men and horses by Michael Lantz for the Federal Trade Commission on the Federal Triangle in Washington, D.C., but they were produced several years after Petersen's veterinary panel. For all of the vigor that courses across the panel, it is typical of much public, especially federal, sculpture of its time in that there is little aggressive emotion displayed, but rather a grim, determined, and concentrated focus on the task at hand. The emotional tone is expressed mainly through the action of the body. Much of Petersen's sculpture possesses a calm, steady, even introspective air, but this panel is lively and animated, full of quickened postures and tense contests.

The central figures of the tall, powerful, muscular horse and the man who battles to contain him dominate the entire panel. They are bracketed by two groups who kneel or bend to execute their procedures: the two men with the calf on the left and, to the right, two other men who vaccinate a hog. According to Petersen's description: "Figure[s] with hog — the protection of the food animal by vaccination against hog cholera." Their job appears less physically taxing for, while the hog does strain away from the men, the one holding the forelegs of the hog appears well able to manage his task. Both veterinarians are fully clothed, as if Petersen did not feel the need to emphasize their physical exertion.

The final scene depicts surgery on a dog, representing research on animal tissues leading to medicines for both humans and animals. "The protection of both humans and animals with rabies vaccine prepared from the spinal cord of rabbits and sheep which have been inoculated with the brain tissue of infected dogs. The figure at extreme right is that of a scientist making microscopic examination of the brain tissue for rabies." As they go about their research with a laboratory counter as a prop, two men hold a striding position very much like that of the men gripping the cow and the horse. These four figures, with their left legs forming a straight, strong line while the right leg takes a small angle, create an echoing rhythm across the panel.

As before, in the dairy reliefs, the veterinary panel had to be broken down into sections that could be fired in the twenty-by-thirty-inch Cox kiln. The long process of firing, correcting, and trimming forty-four terra cotta sections began in 1936 but was not finished until 1938. Petersen was worried about the height of the relief in this panel; his wife later recollected that Grant Wood (and perhaps others) had criticized the dairy reliefs as being too low.[3] When Petersen sent President Emeritus Hughes a photo-graph of his design for the veterinary panel in late 1935, his reply showed that he agreed with Wood. "I like the Veterinary Bas Relief very much indeed; the more I look at it, the better I like it. I hope you make this in much bolder relief than the dairy panels. I am sure that is the only valid criticism on the latter."[4] Petersen rarely commented extensively on his work and never defended it, except in this one instance, when he wrote back, "I am glad you like the design for the Vet panels. Please be at ease as to the relief — I hope it may be neither too bold nor too low — I agree with you that [the dairy reliefs] should have been bolder. This mistake will not occur on the Vet panel. May I say in my own defense that the others were kept so low under protest. That however does not constitute an excuse — but that "mistake" will not occur again."[5]

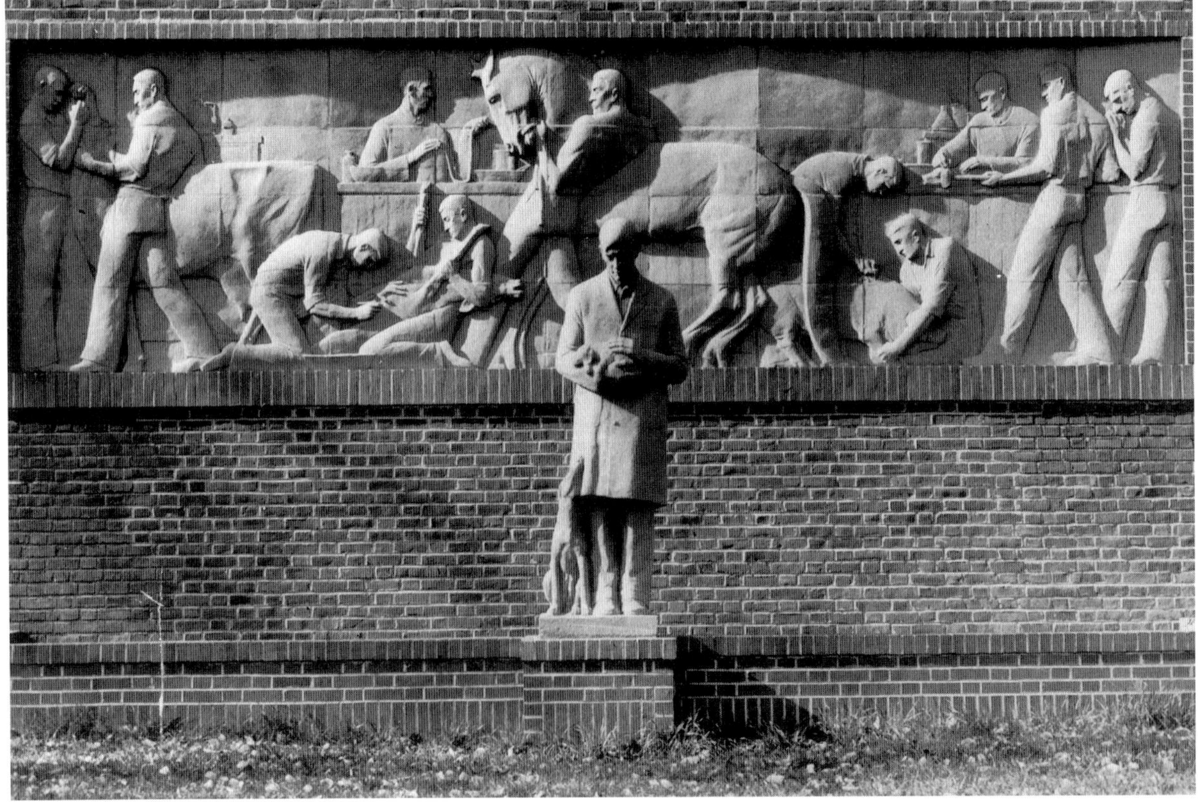

Figure 3.1 *Veterinary Medicine Mural,* 1937, original location.

His concerns about his relief were serious enough to cause him, in June of 1936, to solicit the opinion of the assistant director and dean at the Art Institute of Chicago. Why he wrote to this particular person and whether he even knew the dean personally is not clear. It is possible that they met when Petersen was in Chicago, although he left few traces of his activities and associations during those years. In any case, the dean replied that, based on the photograph he had been sent, "you certainly have gotten a very interesting composition for a most difficult problem and it has some very fine modeling in it." He passed on two main criticisms of the work. He felt that the relief was not "strong enough to stand out in outdoor light" and needed "more vigorous masses." Petersen may have been asked to work in a good deal of detail to fortify the scientific accuracy of the scenes depicted, detail that fragmented the impact of the artistic design, causing the dean to sympathize: "I know you have a lot of zealous veterinary surgeons to contend with and that your path has been beset with difficulties and too pointed suggestions, so I am hoping that any suggestions that I may make will not increase your difficulties." He then criticized a second element: he felt that "there was too much pain represented. Regardless of the beneficent purpose of the operation, I would see the stress and struggles of the animals. All this raises the question, can we suit the sculptor and the veterinary in the same piece of work?"[6]

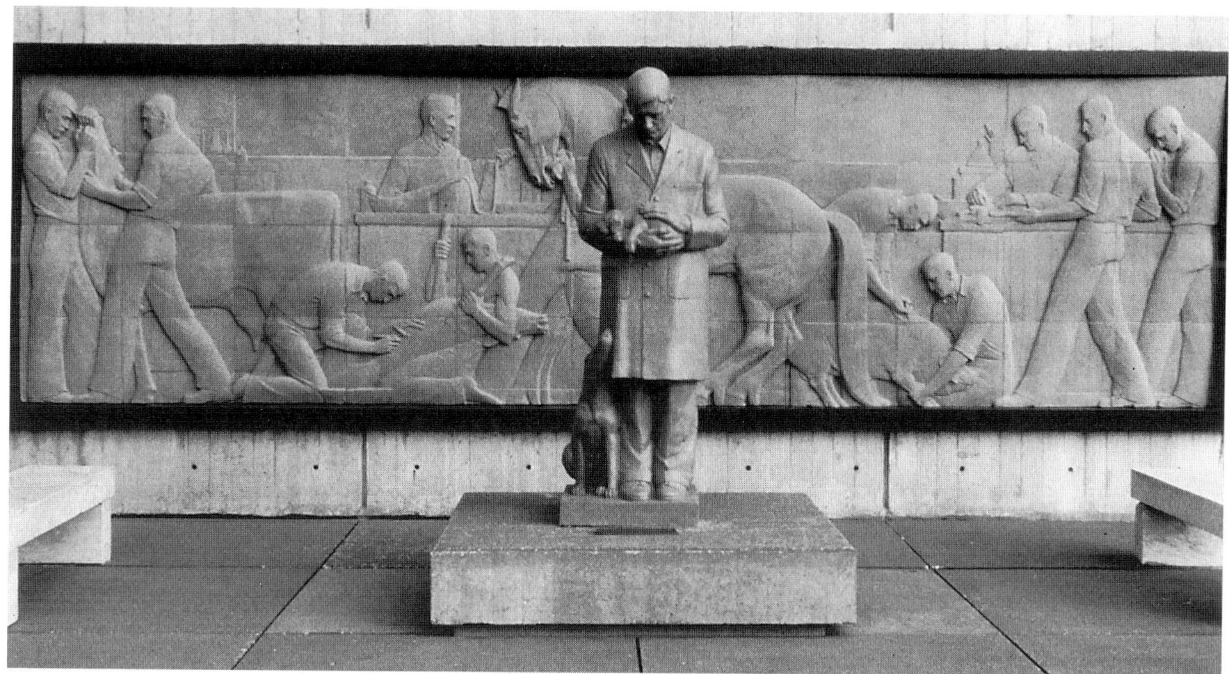

Figure 3.2 *Veterinary Medicine Mural,* 1937, current location.

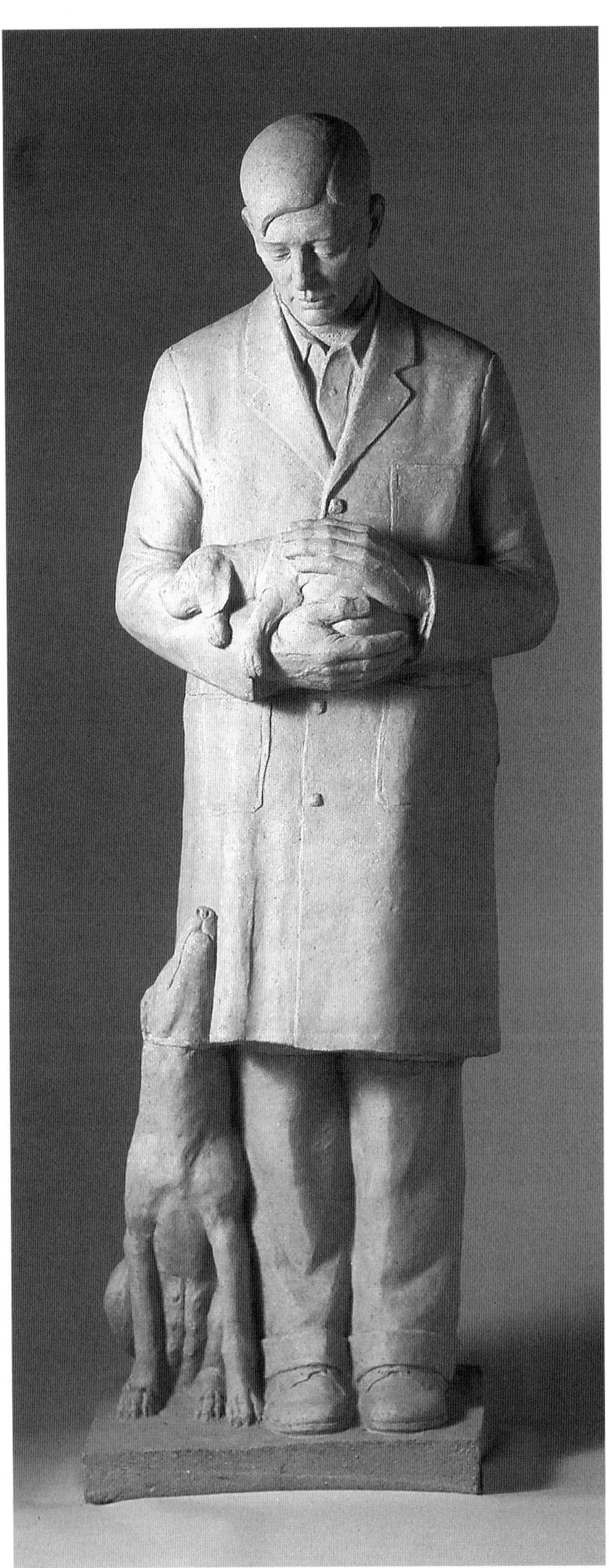

Figure 3.3 *The Gentle Doctor* (after conservation).

At an early point in the realization of this sculpture panel, Petersen conceived the idea of a figure to accompany the relief panel and expand the space to create an entire sculptural environment. Considering the scientific rigor of the themes on the panel and the tone of contention as the men submitted the animals to various procedures, Petersen may have wanted to "humanize" the profession somewhat. His solution was to present an individual, a figure who seemed to have an identity and was not just a participant in a scientific crusade for the health and betterment of men and animals. He worked through a number of designs that showed a veterinarian coming to the aid of an ailing family pet, sometimes accompanied by a concerned child. In the end, he settled upon a stalwart but sympathetic man dressed in plain clothes and a lab coat, holding a sick puppy while the mother dog worries at his feet (Figures 3.3 – 3.5). The doctor cradles the limp puppy in two oversize hands as he gazes down at it with both compassion and competence. The mother leans against his lower leg, her head lifted mournfully toward her pup.

The sculpture is the simplest composition Petersen had so far developed, and has been purged of any hint of his early Beaux Arts style. Compared with the animation and complexity of the relief, the figure is almost stark in the economy of its modeling.

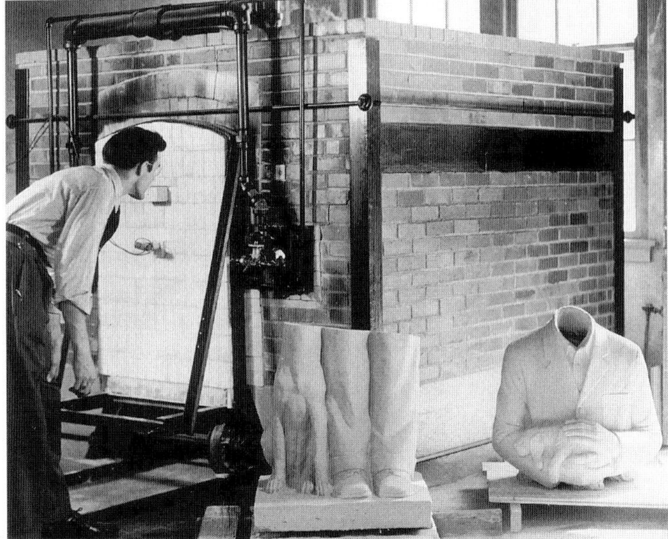

Figure 3.4 Firing of *The Gentle Doctor* **in the Cox kiln.**

In both, Petersen displays a certain geometric clarity, but the three-dimensional figure concentrates the form even more. He made the point at every opportunity that he had little regard for "modern" art, but starting with this work, *The Gentle Doctor,* much of his monumental sculpture would fit well under the broad term of modern. If one of the primary characteristics of modernism is its drive to reduce form to its essentials and strip away any element of decoration or elaboration, then certain of Petersen's work is a clear, if conservative, example of the style. His work was never what could be called abstract, yet an analysis of his form shows that he understood the fundamental idea behind abstraction. Just as Grant Wood's work is often thought of as quite traditional on the surface, a closer look at his actual principles of design and composition reveals a sophisticated eye for the underlying essence of a form. Petersen also was able to couch his artistic statements in a popular and accessible imagery that nevertheless employed the modernistic sensibility for honing a form down to its most elementary, basic, and abstract state.

In a work that appears so individual, the question of the model arises. Since the beginning of his career, portraiture had been a mainstay, and Petersen had a reliable faculty for producing a likeness. Even the profiled faces of some of the men in the veterinary relief are so distinct that they appear to have been based on specific individuals. In the case of *The Gentle Doctor*, three men may have had a part. The first model was chosen not just for his appearance but also because of his role in the commissioning of the veterinary sculptures. Dean Charles H. Stange had welcomed Petersen on campus and had solidified the rationale for having an artist on the staff of Iowa State College. The eagerness with which he took up the opportunity to have a sculptor give form to the ideals and accomplishments of his department gave Petersen an occupation during his early, most tenuous years at Iowa State. Stange had discussed his ideas with Petersen and had enthusiastically received his preliminary designs, but his unexpected death in April of 1936 left Petersen without his patron. The project was taken up without hesitation by Stange's successor as dean of veterinary medicine, Charles Murray, who soon became one of Petersen's most effective supporters. Within the year, Petersen produced a substantial portrait bust of Stange (Figure 3.6) whose broad, blunt features are clearly related to the face of *The Gentle Doctor*. The bust was cast in bronze and placed in the veterinary college, where it remains today. Although Petersen never specifically isolated Stange as the main model, it was popularly assumed that both the features and the demeanor of the figure were based on Stange's.[7]

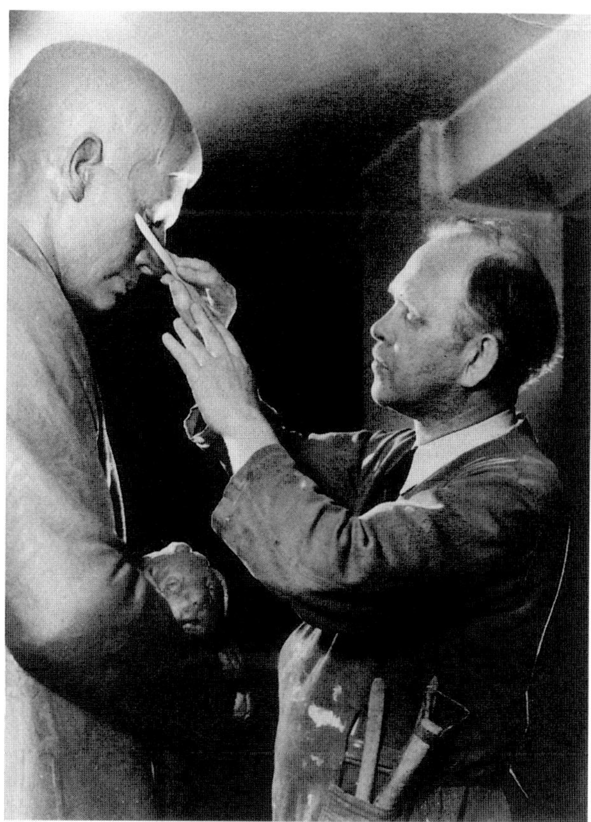

Figure 3.5 Petersen at work on *The Gentle Doctor*.

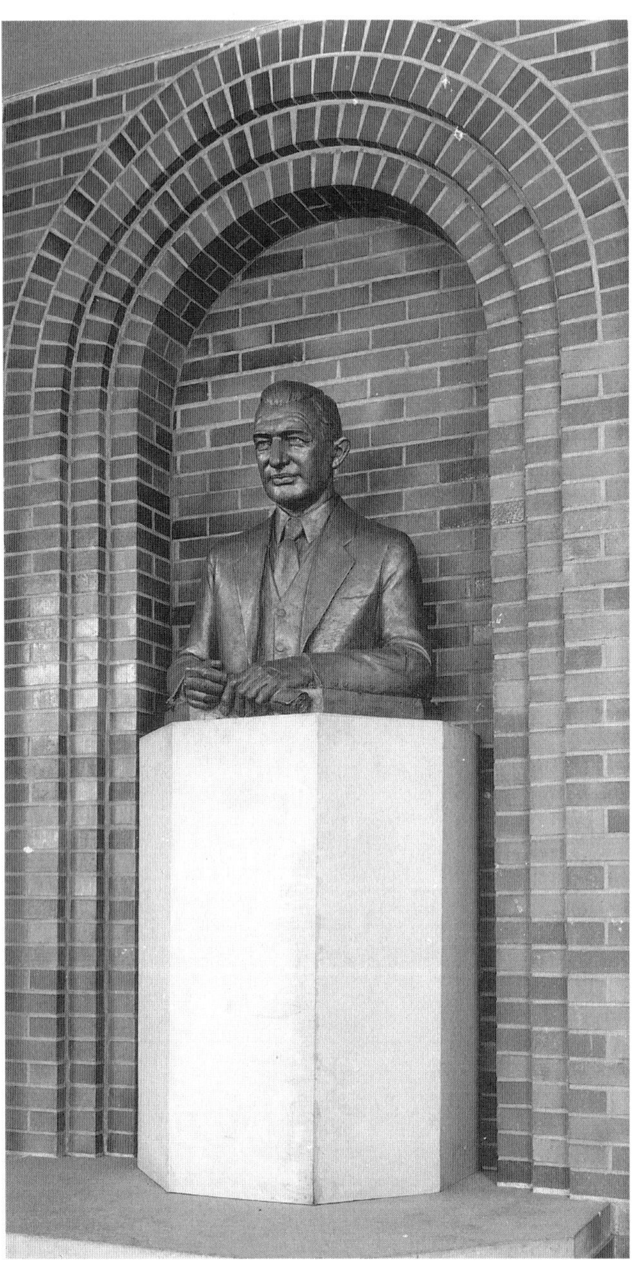

Figure 3.6 *Charles H. Stange.*

Not surprisingly, the two other models for *The Gentle Doctor* were students. L.M. Forland (Figure 3.7), who graduated from the veterinary school in 1941, was working his way through college as a janitor. One of his duties was to clean up the sculpture studio, and since Petersen often worked at night, the two struck up a friendship. In 1983, Dr. Forland recalled to Patricia Bliss the fall and winter quarter of 1936 and 1937 when he served as an impromptu model. "Mr. Petersen's studio was on the ground floor of the home economics building. I remember too well how heavy his garbage cans were! If we had a few minutes' time, he would ask me to stand for him while he carved away at a small pile of clay. He had me hold a small pillow between my forearms in a position similar to that of a little pup."[8] The hands of the figure were likely modeled after those of William R. Born, a 1940 graduate in veterinary science. Like Dr. Forland, Dr. Born was also working his way through school, and his schedule of 1937–1938 found him squeezing in a few early morning hours study near Petersen's studio, where he was enlisted as model from time to time. Noted for its welcoming and informal atmosphere, the studio was an inviting place for students, as the congenial sculptor often worked at all hours.[9]

Until the spring of 1938, Petersen worked and conducted classes in the basement of the exclusively female home economics building. Charlotte Petersen recalled the unpredictable messiness of a sculpture studio in the home economics atmosphere and how grateful her husband was when Dean Charles Murray offered a converted horse hospital in the veterinary building as a classroom and studio — space where he would work for the rest of his life (Figure 3.8).

The area was on the southwest corner of the vet quad, with a concrete floor and nice west sunlight ... plus its own entry. There was no phone, but there was running water and a bathroom nearby. The new Stange Memorial Clinic building had opened up the space, and Dean Murray gave Christian first chance at it. Of course, he said "yes" immediately.

Christian was absolutely delighted to move back into the company of men. He loved talking sports and swapping stories — and the vets became his closet friends on the campus. The students and faculty often dropped in to chat; it was the only classroom that had a coffeepot always going, and a radio, too. The students loved it; I can remember his sculpture classes always listened to Arthur Godfrey.[10]

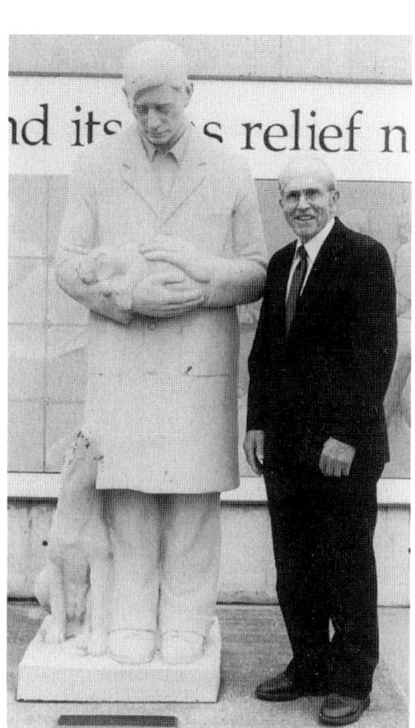

Figure 3.7 L.M. Forland next to *The Gentle Doctor* **for which he posed.**

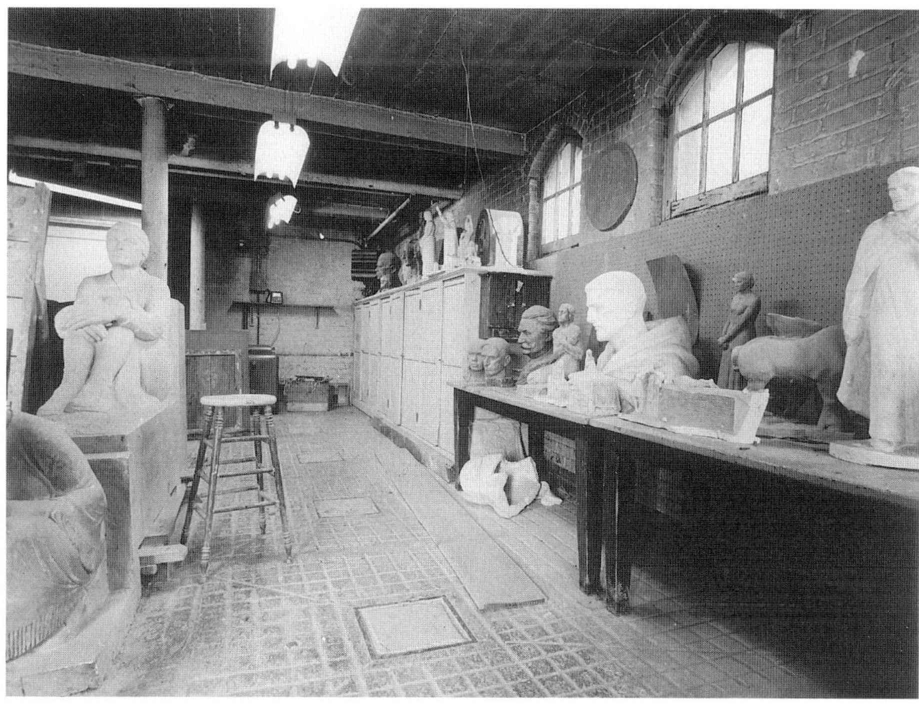

Figure 3.8 Petersen's studio, 1961.

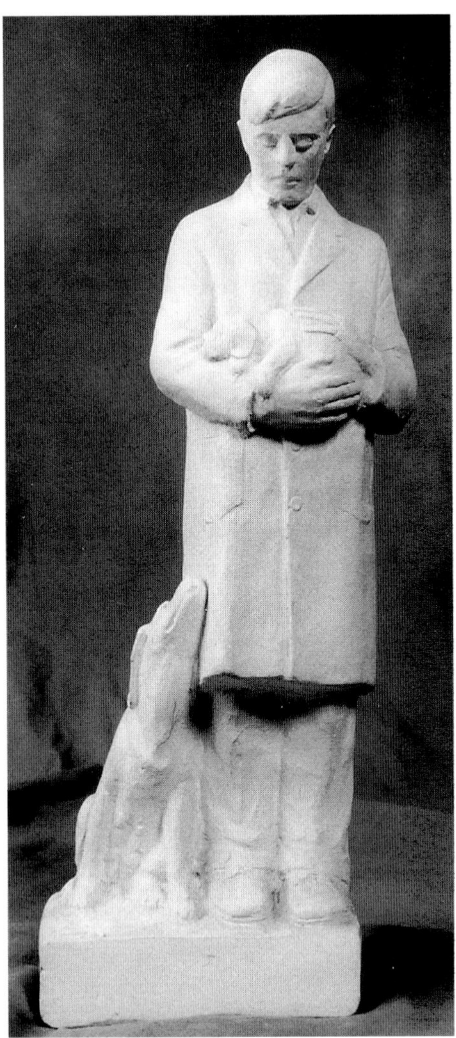

Figure 3.9 Plaster replica of
The Gentle Doctor.

The importance of Petersen's veterinary sculptures and his studio's proximity to the life of the school led to a special relationship between the artist and the doctors. *The Gentle Doctor* gradually became a symbol of the college and is often regarded as a symbol of the overall profession. If Petersen had been worried about the relief panel satisfying the veterinarians, there were no such worries about the vet figure: a 1941 article in *Veterinary Student* praised the sculpture as typifying "the fine type of men who make up our Veterinary profession today. Like the country doctor, he is motivated by the spirit to serve humbly and to save life. We believe that this excellent piece is a just symbol of our profession and the kindly, understanding spirit of the veterinarian has been caught by the artist."[11] During his lifetime, Petersen produced a mold for casting a long series of eighteen-inch plaster replicas that were sold or presented by the ISU veterinary college. (Figure 3.9)[12] When the mold for these was exhausted, a separate series of nine-and-a-half-inch figures was manufactured.[13]

When it was time to install the composition of both the relief panel and the freestanding figure, Petersen was, as always, quite specific as to the placement and environment of his work. In the dairy cycle, he had combined relief and in-the-round sculpture with a fountain and pool and shown sensitivity to the architecture and landscaping. Although the veterinary group was not as complex, he continued to be exacting as to its installation. Strangely enough, in light of his earlier request for the opinion of the Art Institute dean, Charles F. Kelley, it was Kelley who was invoked when the head of the landscape architecture department objected to Petersen's plan.[14] But the sculptor prevailed, and the panel was placed against a brick wall well above eye level. The figure was added immediately in front of the wall, though still low enough that the seven-foot tall form obscured the view of the panel only slightly, just enough to act as a transition from the scale and space of the viewer to that of the relief panel. When a new veterinary building was constructed in 1983, the relief panel and statue were moved to the new location. The original relationship of the panel to the figure was altered significantly when the panel was installed against a rough concrete wall and lowered to about two feet above the paved plaza. *The Gentle Doctor*, as the figure is known, stands on a broad concrete base about twelve inches high, with about six feet between it and the terra cotta panel. Both sculptures are now roughly on eye level with the viewer. The original terra cotta figure, however, was relocated to the Brunnier Art Museum building and replaced in the veterinary complex by a bronze cast.[15]

NOTES

1. The proposal which enunciates the theme and describes the five scenes of the panel is in the Christian Petersen Papers.

2. Although classicism is a hallmark of Petersen's style, he may have been inspired in a particular way to review the animals and the battles that coursed along the pedimental and relief sculptures of the Parthenon. In a May 10, 1935, letter from former president Raymond Hughes, he commented that the only fault with the dairy panels was that they were too low and encouraged Petersen to make these new reliefs "much bolder," then noted, "as I remember ... the reliefs on the Parthenon were very bold, were they not?" Possibly Petersen renewed his knowledge of that monument and, in the process, gleaned some ideas that could be applied to his own work.

3. Bliss, Patricia, L., *Christian Petersen Remembered,* Ames: Iowa State University Press, 1986, 54–55.

4. Hughes to Petersen, December 29, 1935.

5. Handwritten draft of letter from Petersen to Hughes, January 10, 1936.

6. Petersen to Charles Fabens Kelley, June 23, 1936. Christian Petersen Papers. The contact may have been made when staff from the Art Institute advised in the affixing of Wood's P.W.A.P. murals to the library walls.

7. Perhaps the most convincing evidence of the assumption of Stange as the main model is an undated clipping from *The Des Moines Tribune* of a photograph of Petersen with the nearly completed sculpture. According to the caption of the clipping entitled "I.S.C. Statue," Petersen is shown "applying finishing touches to memorial statue of the late Charles H. Stange, former dean of veterinary medicine."

8. Letter from L.M. Forland to Patricia L. Bliss, September 15, 1983. Quoted in Bliss, 64.

9. Letters to Bliss from Born's wife describe a post-graduation visit to Petersen in which he showed her the installed sculpture and confirmed her husband's role as model. See Bliss, 67–68, n.10. For a student-written account of the atmosphere in Petersen's studio, see "Murals, Figures, and Statues Hide Peterson [*sic*] While He Models," *Iowa State Student*, January 21, 1937.

10. Quoted in Bliss, 67.

11. Caption for cover photograph of sculpture, *Veterinary Student*, Winter 1941, 3(2).

12. According to Bliss, this series is dated 1960 to 1980, 70.

13. This smaller cast was produced by Herman Deaton of Newton, Iowa. Bliss, 70.

14. P.H. Elwood to B.H. Platt, May 10, 1938. Christian Petersen Papers.

15. The cost of the bronze cast, carried out by Prof. Paul Shao of the architecture faculty, was donated by Dr. and Mrs. J.E. Salsbury.

The Calling

*Up at midnight, shoe in hand,
a boy is stalking a cricket
in a corner of his bedroom
dappled by the street light.*

*Impossible to sleep
with such incessant chirring,
a noise like something rusty
turning in the wind.*

*Poised over silence, waiting
for another sound, he hears
his own breath rustling,
feels the shared air rushing in.*

*Such a stunning communion!
Spiders breathing, a moth
on the dark lamp shade,
even horseflies on the window screen,*

*everything needing the air
each life unrepeatable,
unique as any star
and brilliant,*

*the night itself shimmering,
bright with uncounted lives,
one cricket singing in the room,
one heart and whole fields answering!*

Neal Bowers

Inspired by The Gentle Doctor *by Christian Petersen.
Commissioned by the University Museums, Iowa State University, 1990
as part of the Art on Campus Poetry Collection.*

Faith

The mystery of suffering
She cannot understand,
Yet humbly at his feet she waits
To know his least command.

She cannot think her god is clay
Nor his neglect ill meant.
Waiting here she feels his touch
And is content.

Jules Cool Cunningham (1879–1948)
American

Published privately in 1943 by Jules Cool Cunningham
In From Dusk to Dawn *by Jules Cool Cunningham*
Written as a tribute to The Gentle Doctor, *shortly after its installation.*

Chapter 4
Campus Sculptor

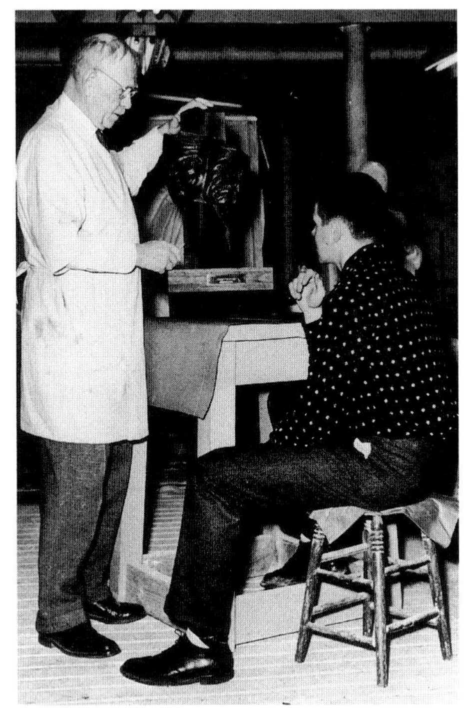

Figure 4.1 Petersen with student.

Over the next twenty years, Christian Petersen created six more public sculptures for the Iowa State campus, three of them major outdoor pieces: *The Fountain of the Four Seasons*, the *Marriage Ring*, and *Conversations*. The other three: the *Three Athletes*, the *Reclining Nudes*, and the *Library Boy and Girl*, were in less prominent spots, but were nevertheless an important part of the campus and of Petersen's career. In addition, he produced many other sculptures related to Iowa State or on other subjects at the same time that he maintained a constant stream of portrait busts and plaques. During these years, he was also a popular teacher whose classes each quarter were full to overflowing, making increasing demands on his time and energy. When he began, only women students were allowed into the sculpture course (because they were offered through the home economics curriculum), but by spring of 1939, men joined the classes.[1] Throughout this period, Petersen remained one of the lowest paid members of the faculty and staff at the college.[2]

While Petersen was still working on the dairy courtyard reliefs in 1935, the college was renovating its gymnasium, known as State Gym. When the dairy sculptures were finished and installed (and while he was developing the concepts for the veterinary complex), he inserted into the new staircase front of the building three reliefs of college athletes in action (Figure 4.2). The rectangular terra cotta panels with slightly arched tops are divided into five sections that could be fired in the Cox kiln. The man on the left is a football player running in one direction, ball tucked against his chest, while his upper torso and head turn in the opposite direction to ward off a tackle (Figure 4.3). It is a complex pose that is full of both rhythmic energy and stateliness, especially in its gestures. The middle figure (Figure 4.4) is as still as the other two figures are active. He stands, both feet planted firmly, as he brings a basketball up to the center of his chest and prepares to shoot a free throw. Petersen extended the feet out beyond the base of the panel so that they project out into space. It is only a slight projection, but enough to infuse this figure with an immediacy the others do not possess. On the right of the installation is a runner charging toward the center, leg muscles tense and precisely drawn (Figure 4.5). Yet, as in the football player, the design possesses an air of formality and stateliness. In all the figures, this quality comes from the sharp carving and bold outline of forms that do not just capture a moment in these athletic contests, but distill motions and poses so characteristic that they can typify an entire sport. Despite the action displayed, these reliefs are not expressionistic but formal, hierarchical, and universalized, an example of the innate classicism in Petersen's style.

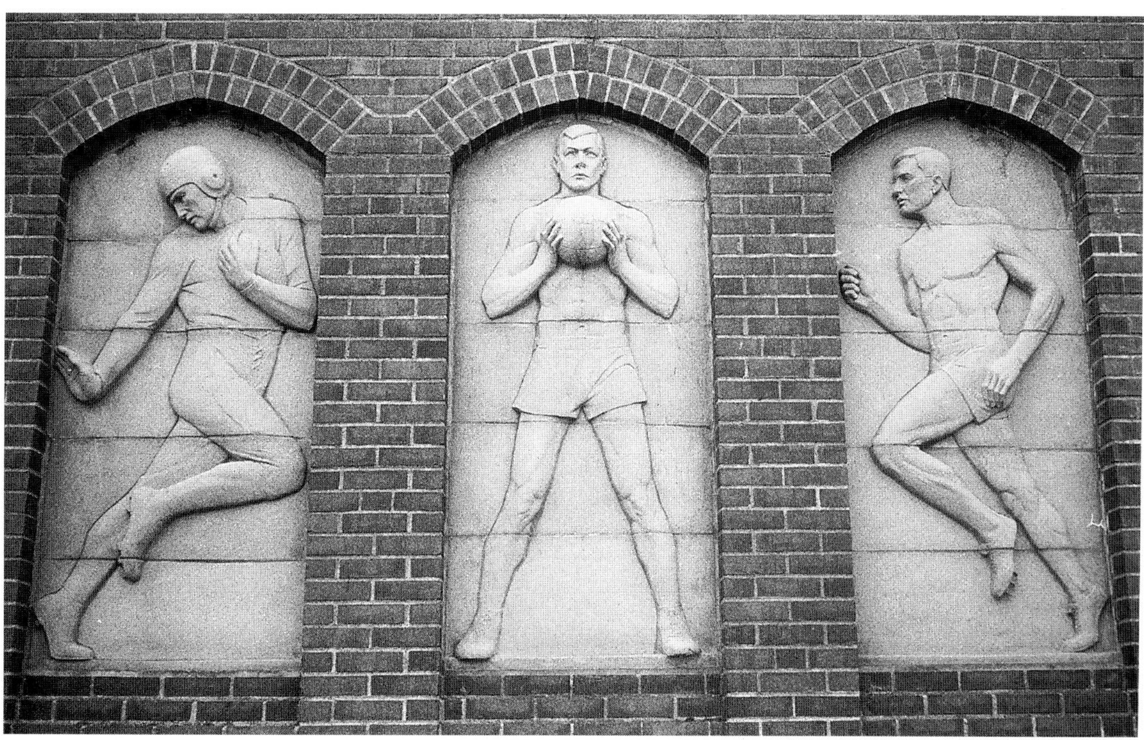

Figure 4.2 *Three Athletes*, 1935.

For this installation, Petersen seemed to be aware that there were challenges with the composition. The basketball player and the runner contribute to a conventionally balanced composition, but the football player, while sensible within himself, has a problematic relationship to the other two figures. His lower body, with one foot tucked into the outside corner of the relief, echoes almost exactly the runner's. The primary difference is that in the runner, Petersen was able to carve precise renditions of the musculature; the football player's uniform precluded the opportunity to explore those aspects of the anatomy. Both run toward the center of the overall composition, but the football player's head turns back in the opposite direction so that the focus moves to the outer edge of the composition. The figure is internally balanced in a knowledgeable, resourceful way, but the relationship beyond those confines remains somewhat unresolved.

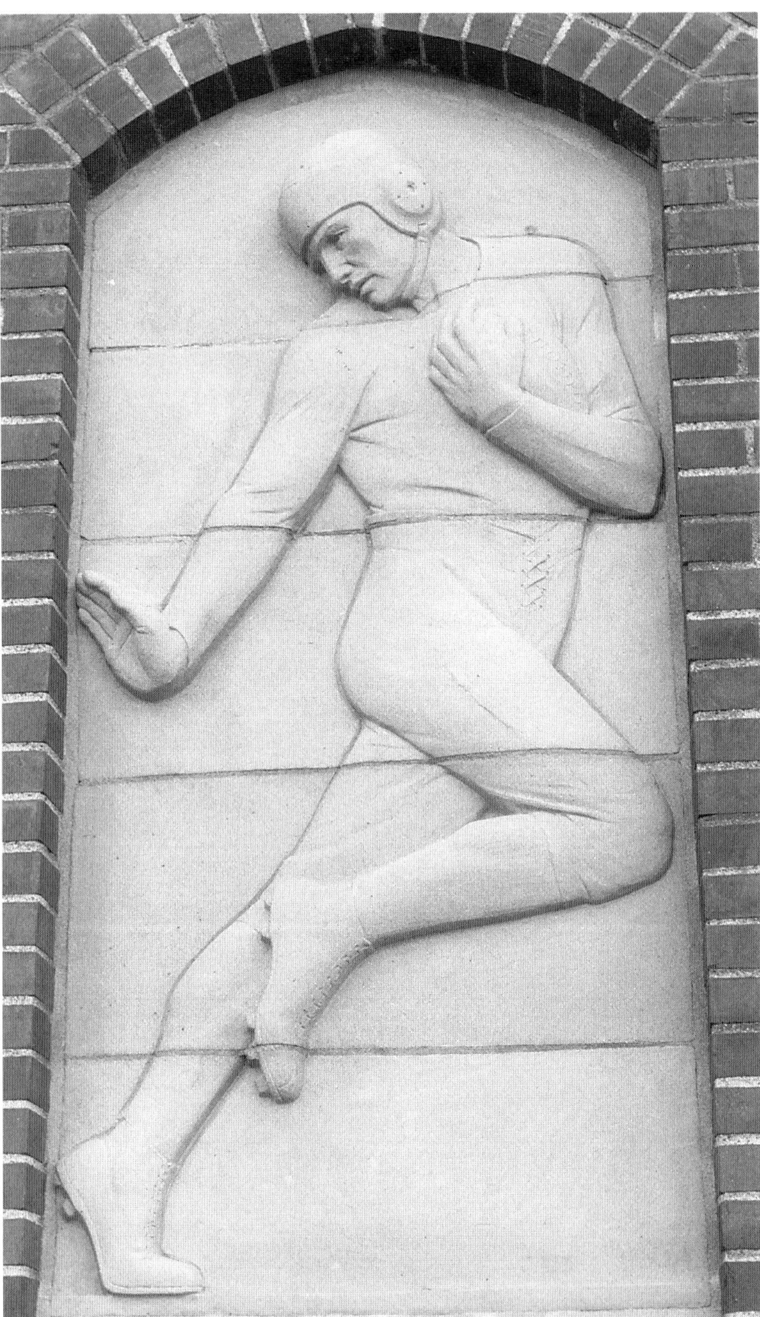

Figure 4.3 Football player from *Three Athletes*.

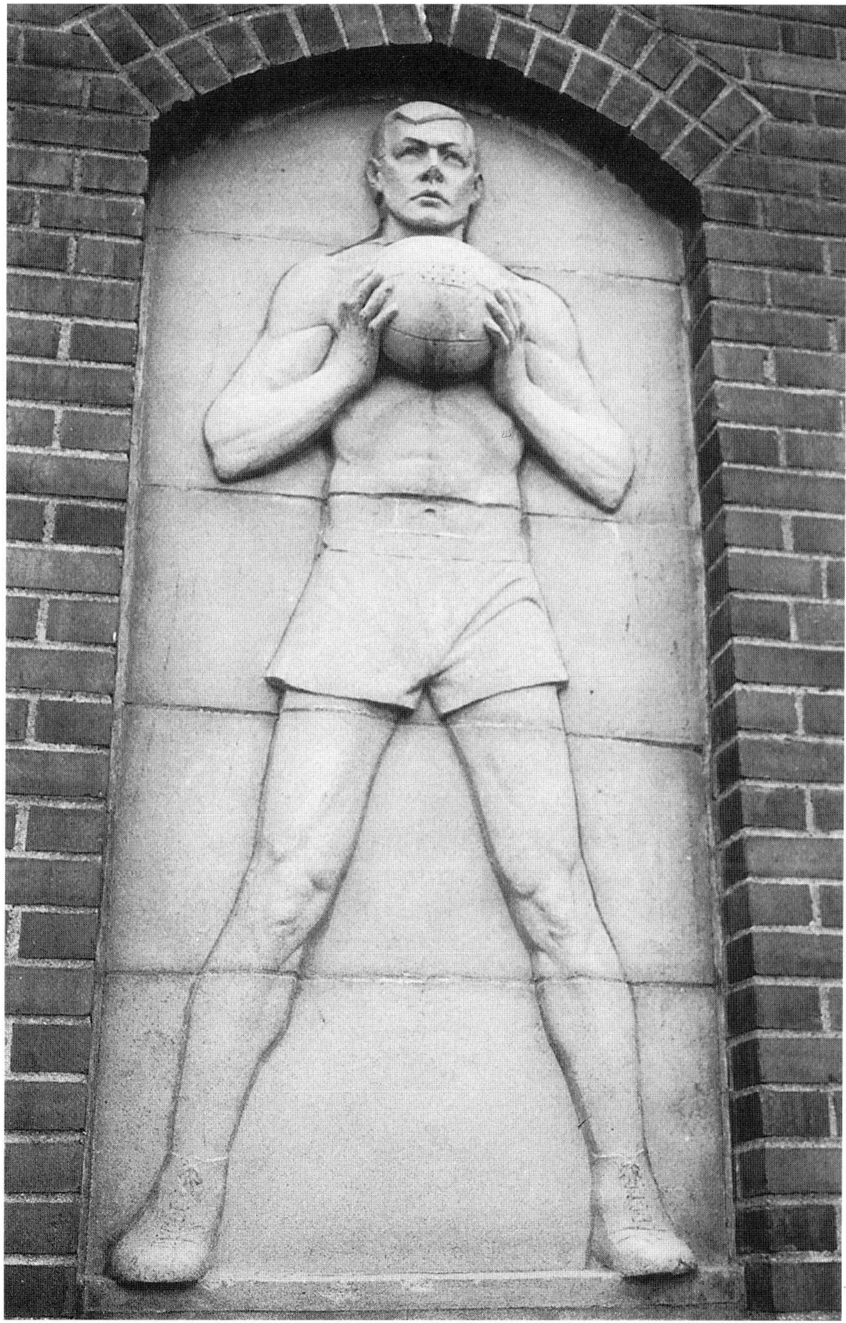

Figure 4.4 Basketball player from *Three Athletes*.

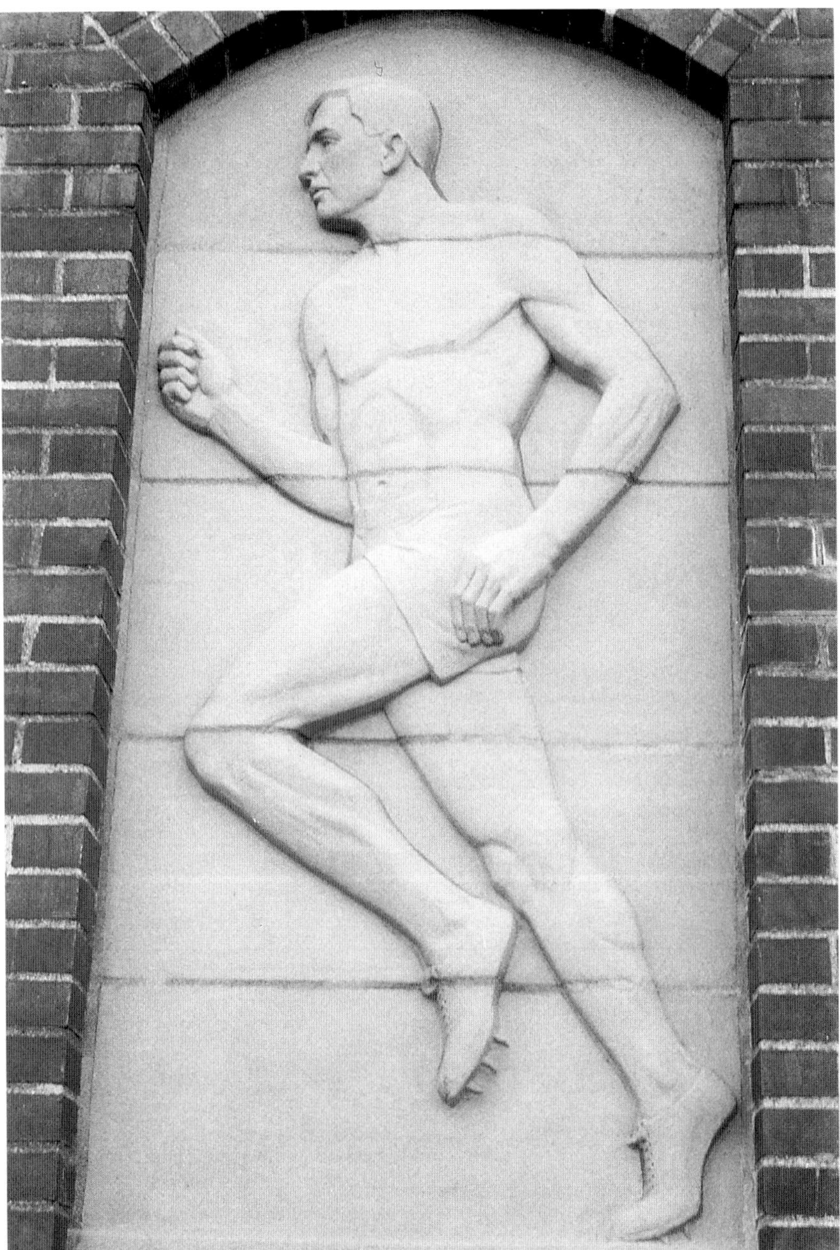

Figure 4.5 Runner from *Three Athletes*.

Petersen's next campus sculpture, *Reclining Nudes* (Figure 4.6), was far less public than the gymnasium athletes. For a new women's dormitory, Roberts Hall, Petersen designed another fountain-pool-sculpture complex. Again, he showed his interest not just in sculpture, but in a combination of elements, all responsive to each other and to the surrounding space. Compared to most of his other campus works, the Roberts Hall fountain is modest, unassuming and physically smaller. These characteristics may in part be because of the architecture itself, but they may partly relate to the subject matter. The two young women in the relief are nude, the first such instance in any of Petersen's public sculptures. The concern about nudity cannot be attributed to the provinciality of the Midwestern locale, for nudity was a problem almost anywhere during that period and, for that matter, would be even today. These attitudes were institutionalized in the New Deal art programs of the period, where nudity was generally discouraged and where its presence nearly always sent up a red flag for the administrators of the various programs. No official protest was made about the lack of clothing in the Roberts Hall work, but Petersen must have been aware that he was taking a risk because he noted in a financial memo to the college for this work, "No models used."[3]

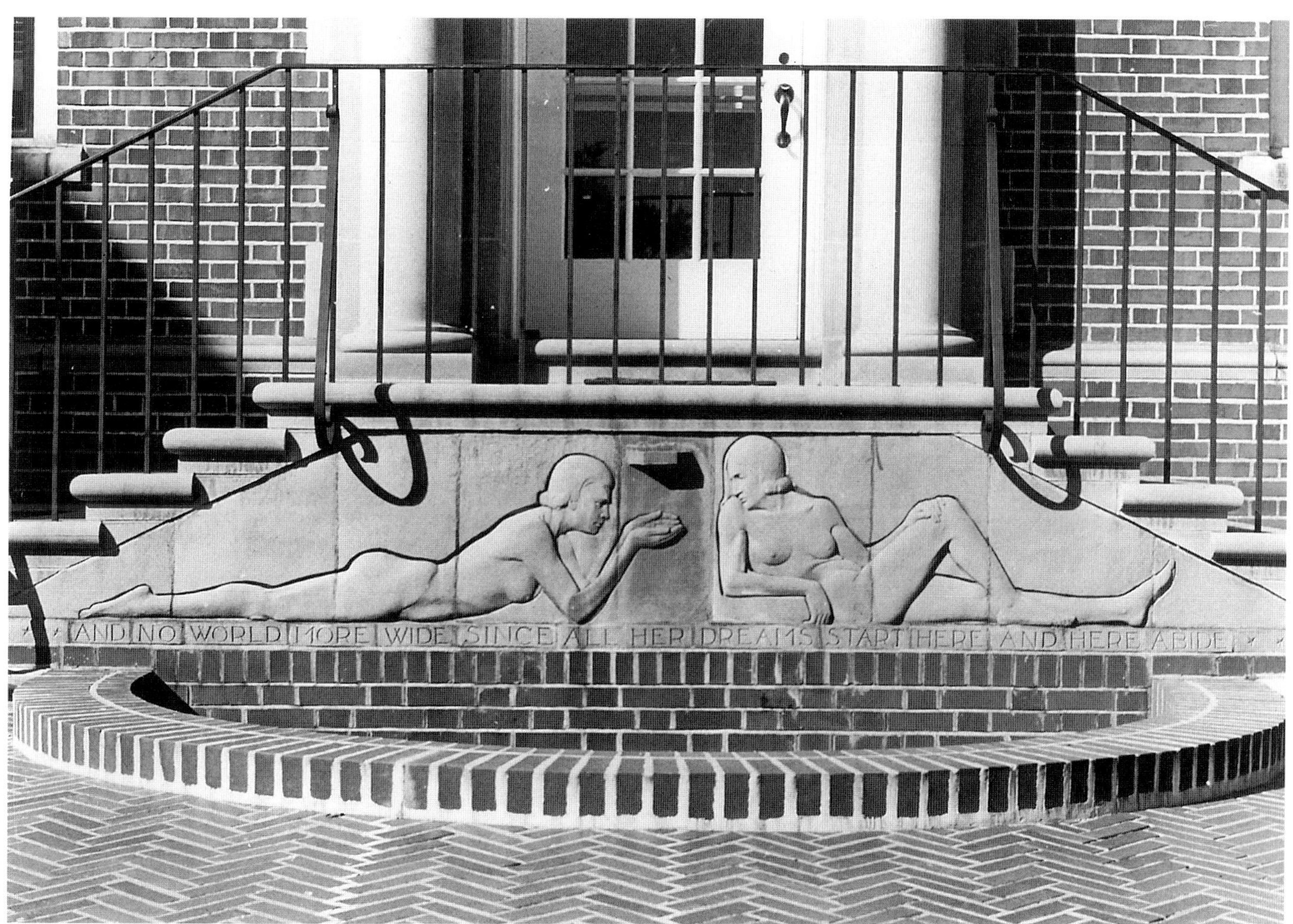

Figure 4.6 *Reclining Nudes* at Roberts Hall, 1936.

The reclining figures are fitted into a narrow, truncated pedimental shape on the facade of the two-sided staircase at the entrance to the dormitory. Originally, a semicircular, brick-lined pool caught the water from a small stream descending along the center of the relief. The young woman on the left lies on her stomach, but lifts her upper body to rest on her elbows as she cups her hands to catch water trickling over a small basin just above. As Petersen conceived the design, she would have been staring fixedly, as most observers would be, at the moving water. The second woman reclines in a pose related to that of the football player at State Gym. Her lower body rests with one leg extended and one bent while her torso twists, supported by her right elbow, and her head turns back against her shoulder to gaze at the stream of water. Both figures are stable and calm, conveying a state of quiet, centered contemplation.

An inscription accompanies the sculpture, as it does in many of Petersen's campus designs. Placed in a single line along the bottom of the narrow panel, it reads, "And no world more wide, Since all her dreams start here and here abide." Suggested by his wife, Charlotte, the inscription is taken from the last line and a half of a poem published in the July 1917 *Century* magazine. Long a favorite of his wife, the poem, "Sancta Ursula (After Carpaccio)," describes the small room of a female saint, Ursula, based on a painting of the early Renaissance by the Venetian painter, Carpaccio.[4]

In contrast to the quiet, rather secluded site for the Roberts Hall fountain, Petersen's next sculpture is the most prominent on campus, a work so frequently encountered that it has become one of the identifying images of the University. The *Fountain of the Four Seasons,* 1940–41, is placed at the entrance to the Memorial Union, the center of student life. According to Petersen's biographer, Patricia L. Bliss, it began with a call from President Charles Friley, who had grown exasperated with the situation of the fountain in front of Memorial Union. A gift of the 1936 VEISHEA[5] Central Committee, the fountain was the frequent target of jokesters, and the president wished the sculptor to transform it into something that would discourage such pranks.

Petersen took as his inspiration a subject he had explored thoroughly only a few years earlier. In 1936, he had illustrated *Cha-Ki-Shi* (Figure 4.7), a children's book on the Meskwaki Indians of Iowa, and had spent time at their Tama settlement. Deciding he would like to continue this theme of Native Americans, he consulted with his geneticist-poet friend J.C. Cunningham, who shared that interest. The professor soon supplied a four-line Osage chant:

Lo, I come
to the tender planting

Lo, a tender shoot
breaks forth

Lo, I collect
the golden harvest

Lo, there is joy
in my house

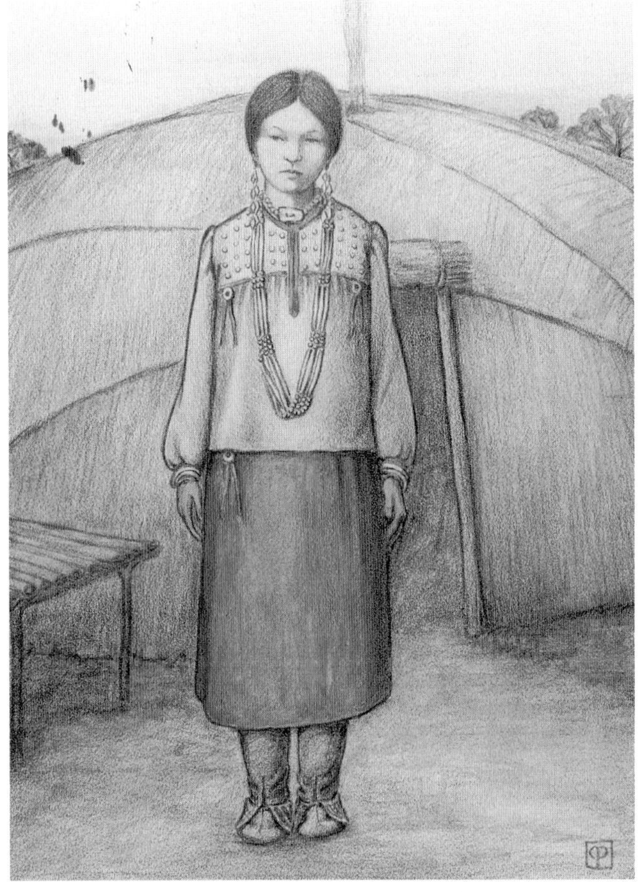

Figure 4.7 Book cover from *Cha-ki-shi, Cha-ki-shi Ready for Dance*, 1936.

Employing the original fountain as his centerpiece, Petersen designed a circular pool with an Indian woman placed at each of the four directions, picturing each of the lines of the chant. In his visualization of the first three lines, Petersen chose the grain most closely associated not only with Indians, but with Iowa and the agricultural curriculum of Iowa State as well: corn. The motif of corn is carried out in a decorative frieze along the bottom of the fountain (Figures 4.8 – 4.10). Stylized corn plants with two leaves bent back from an emerging ear of corn are similar to plants found in the dairy courtyard reliefs; both have a simple, rhythmic design that relates equally to Grant Wood and to Art Deco.

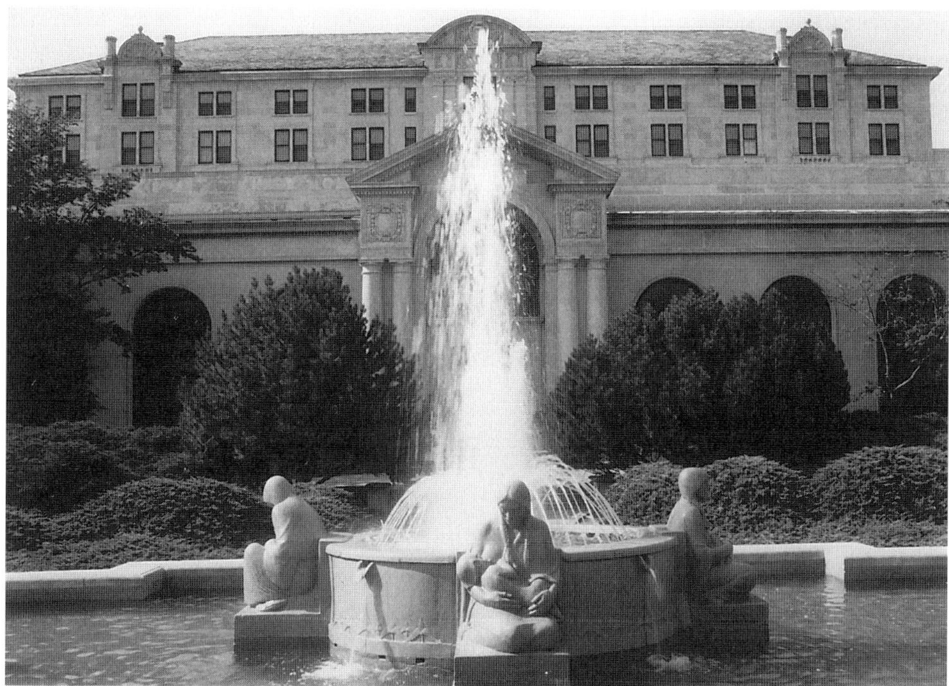

Figure 4.8 *Fountain of the Four Seasons* overview, facing Memorial Union, 1940–41.

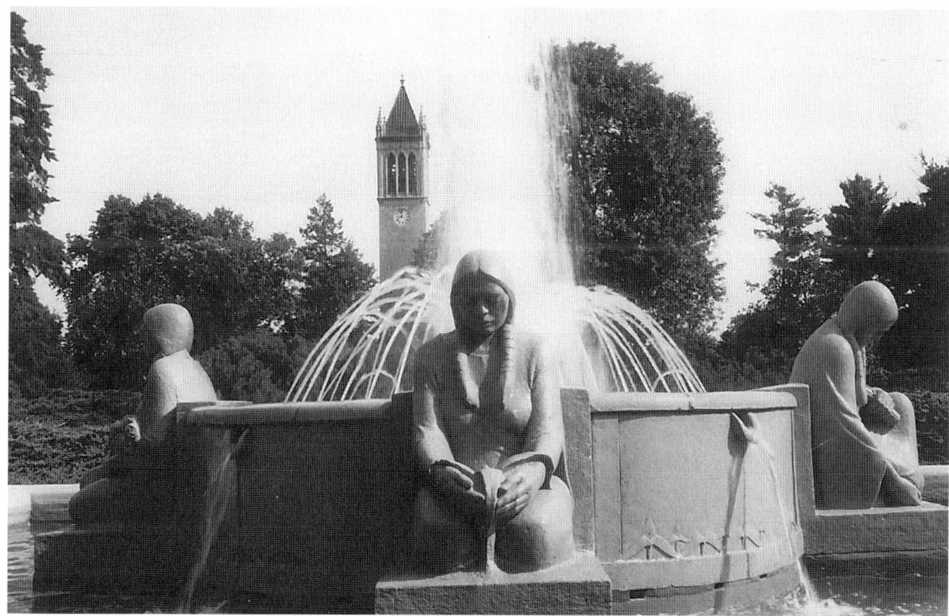

Figure 4.9 *Fountain of the Four Seasons* overview, facing Campanile.

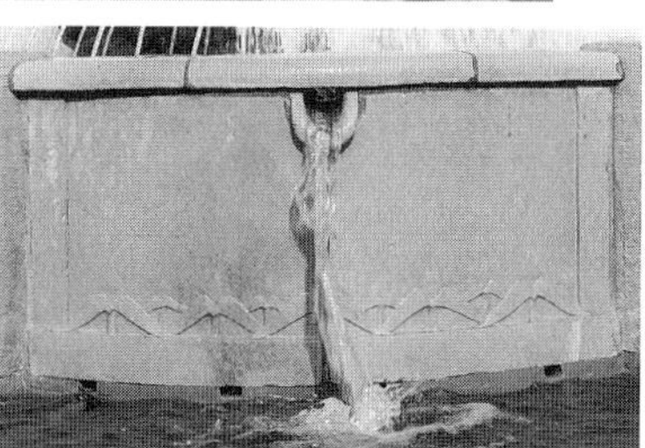

Figure 4.10 Stylized corn motif at bottom of fountain.

Each of the four figures is seated slightly differently, with different inclinations of the head. They are similar enough to provide continuity but distinct enough to illustrate the four separate narratives. Each is dressed identically, in clothing that Petersen had illustrated with such precision in his book illustrations. The figure who illustrates the first line of the chant: "Lo, I come to the tender planting," faces the east and kneels with one leg tucked under and the other bent at the knee (Figure 4.11). Holding in her left hand an ear of corn with several rows already gone, she reaches down to place a single kernel into the ground. The ends of her belt sweep across her lap to emphasize the rhythm of her pose. Her face is the least visible of the four figures, its angle directed downward toward the earth.

Facing south and representing the line "Lo, a tender shoot breaks forth," the second figure sits on a straight axis, both legs folded beneath her, as she gently supports two leaves from a small corn plant in front of her (Figure 4.12). A third corn leaf falls outward while the ear of corn is just emerging, creating a symmetrical design that is echoed in the pattern that rings the base of the fountain. Like all the other figures, her facial features are plain and her expression sober. The third woman, weight on her left hip, lifts her head and gazes out toward the west, six ears of corn gathered into her arms to illustrate "Lo, I collect the golden harvest." (Figure 4.13) All of the other figures attend to a task that preoccupies them, but the harvest figure looks out at the world as if surveying the rest of the earth's bounty or anticipating ac-

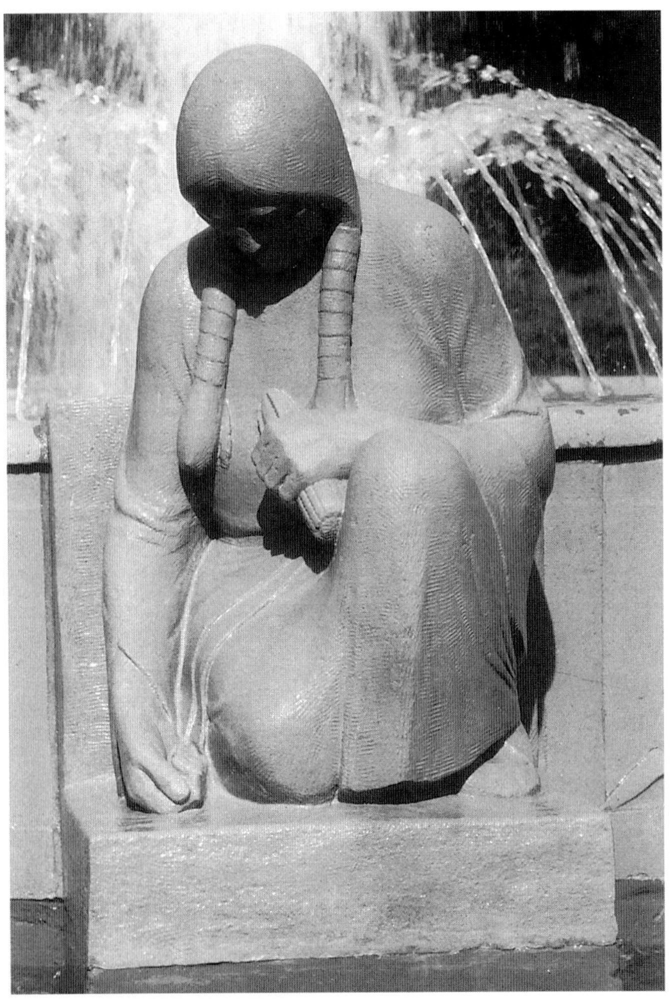

Figure 4.11 Detail of maiden.

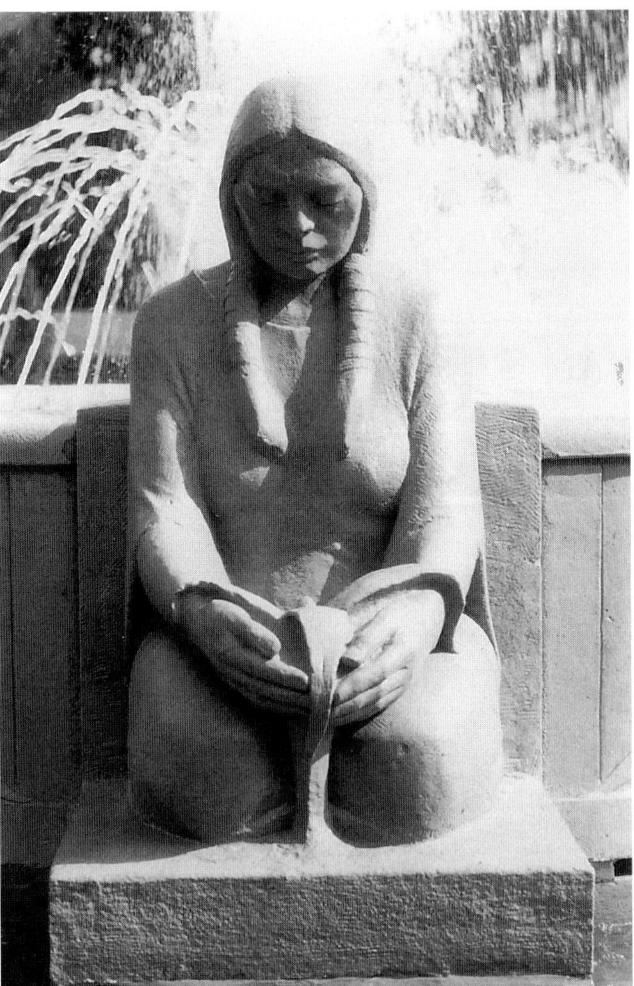

Figure 4.12 Detail of maiden.

knowledgment by the viewer. The final woman, facing north, symbolizes "the joy in my house" as she nurses an infant who plays with the end of one of her braids (Figure 4.14). Her position sways slightly as she supports the child, at which she looks fixedly.

All the figures are quiet, stately, and self-contained with composed and calm facial expressions. The narrative of the fountain is expressed in the positions of the bodies and the gestures of the hands, which are often cupped in a receiving or supporting form. The self-contained movements of the figures are in contrast to the animation and play of the water that arcs nearby. A large central column of water spouts directly upward while smaller jets of water arc toward it from the edge of an inner pool. Petersen rarely described his works, but in this case he explained how the curving jets that spout inward toward the center column of water reflect the shapes of nature, suggesting that the sculptures and water together with the poetry of the chant express balance and harmony with nature. Like other examples of his outdoor sculptures, the *Fountain of the Four Seasons* relates not only to nature but also to architecture. The Memorial Union is a Beaux Arts building with a row of large, arched windows along the facade and an arched entrance. It is at the southern end of a large, open, and grassy field that forms the "center" of the campus, with three other major Beaux Arts buildings marking the sides of a quadrangle.

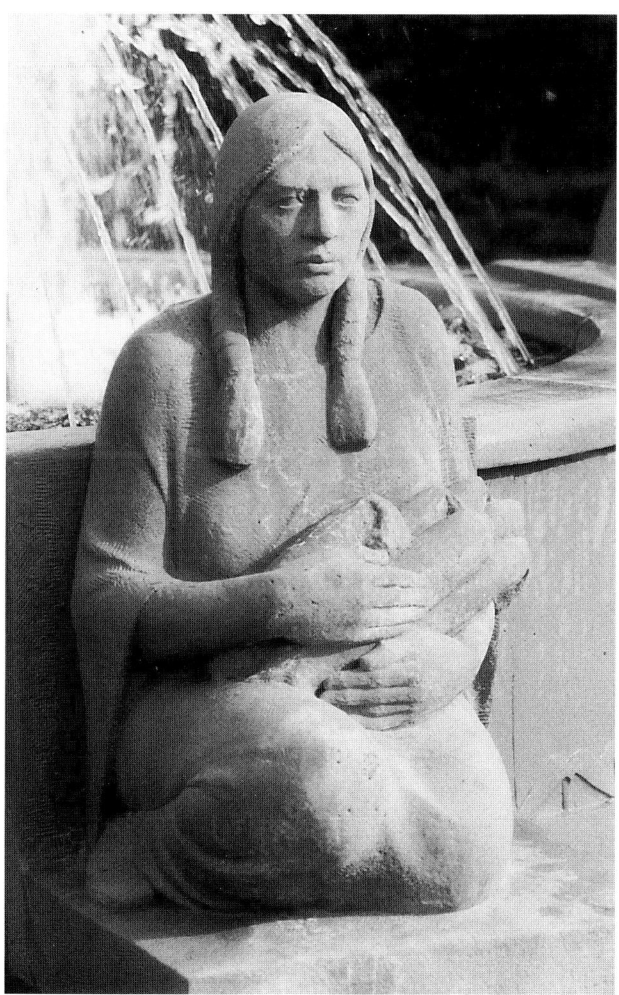

Figure 4.13 Detail of maiden.

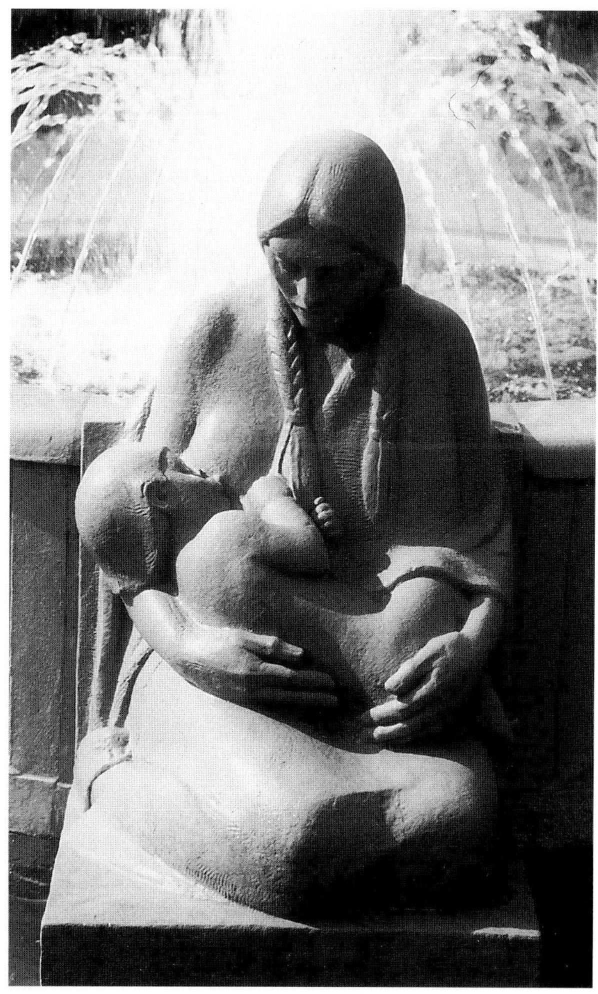

Figure 4.14 Detail of maiden.

Petersen's next project, on the grounds in front of the home economics building, would be the largest public space he had created since the Dairy Industry Courtyard in the mid-1930s. It was also his most metaphorical public work. Dealing again with water, he designed a large, round, shallow pool ringed by a low concrete band that rises less than a foot from ground level. Playing at water's edge along the south side of the circle are three small figures of children, all around three years of age. Entitled *The Marriage Ring* (Figure 4.15), the children symbolize the fruits, or the "jewels" of marriage, thus illustrating metaphorically the goal of the home economics program. This curriculum, restricted to women, taught them the skills of successful homemaking, often with an emphasis on the needs of children. Tellingly, the work is also known as *The Wedding Ring* and *The Ring of Life*.[6] The inscription incised along the top of the ring (Figure 4.16) celebrates children with a quotation from James Whitcomb Riley's poem "The Hired Man's Faith in Children": "I believe all children's good / if only they're understood / even bad ones, seems to me / 's jest as good as they can be." Petersen's wife, Charlotte, was familiar with a broad range of literature and here, as in nearly all of his major works, the influence of her tastes and her knowledge was likely significant.[7] A bronze plaque placed on the outside of the ring below the fountain explains that the sculpture was presented by the VEISHEA Committee of 1942.

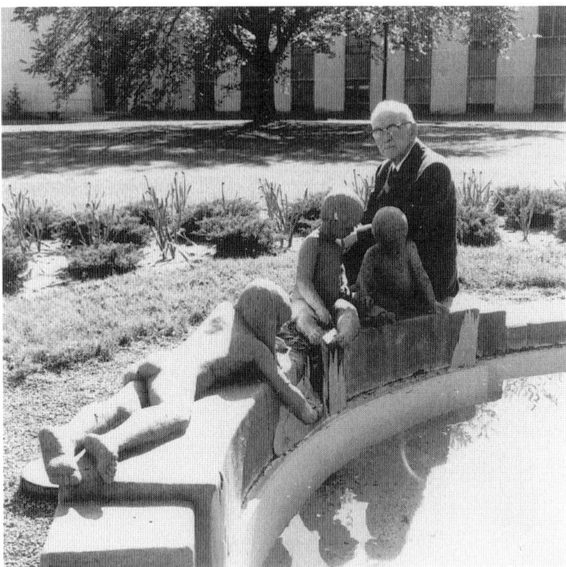

Figure 4.15 Petersen sitting at the *Marriage Ring* at original location.

The children are situated atop two low, stepped elevations in the center of which a small fountain burbles up from a shallow depression with two frogs along its edge. The water pools slightly before falling over into the basin. To the left is the figure of a girl who lies on her stomach (similar to one of the figures in the Roberts Hall fountain) as she reaches down to hold a sculpted water lily that seems to emerge from the pool. To the right of the fountain sit two toddler boys (like the girl, both are nude), who play with a turtle. One sits upright holding a spoon or toy sand shovel in his right hand as he turns his attention toward the turtle. The boy beside him leans sharply inward as he touches the turtle's shell with his right hand. The boys (like the girl) focus their attention downward and, as in a number of Petersen's public sculptures, present no awareness of the viewer. The composition is an asymmetric one that suggests the momentary nature of play, an effect that is heightened when the group is reflected on the surface of the water.

As in the Dairy Industry Courtyard and the *Fountain of the Four Seasons*, Petersen used a stylized plant motif to decorate his design. More than in the two earlier works, however, the plant forms link *The Marriage Ring* to natural surroundings. At the ends of the elevated portion containing the figures are blade-like bunches of foliage painted green. On both the outside and the inside of the ring, these and other painted grasses foster a heightened awareness of nature.

This work has been vandalized on a number of occasions and the figures nearly lost.[8] Today, the terra cotta originals have been taken into the lobby of the home economics building and placed within a circular pattern that resembles the outdoor installation (Figures 4.17 and 4.18). The sculptures that decorate the ring outside are concrete reproductions (Figure 4.19).

Most of Petersen's major campus works were intended for the outside, but the *Library Boy and Girl* of 1944 (Figures 4.20 and 4.21) are designed for an interior — ISU Library — in which they must deal not only with the architecture but with Grant Wood's painted murals. They are in the room containing Wood's *Breaking the Prairie*, and they are placed on pedestals framing both sides of the entrance to the staircase that leads up to his

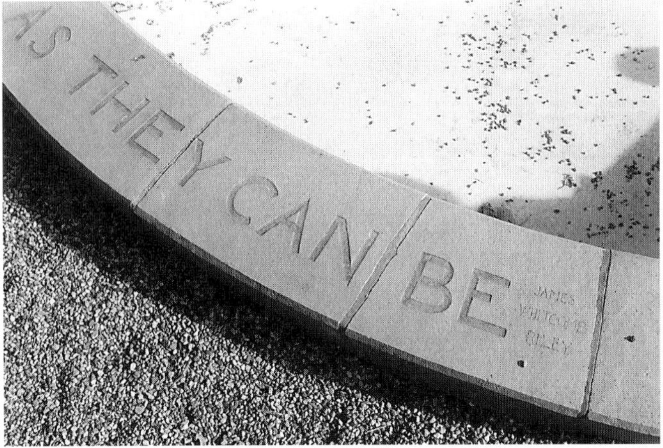

Figure 4.16 The *Marriage Ring* inscription, detail.

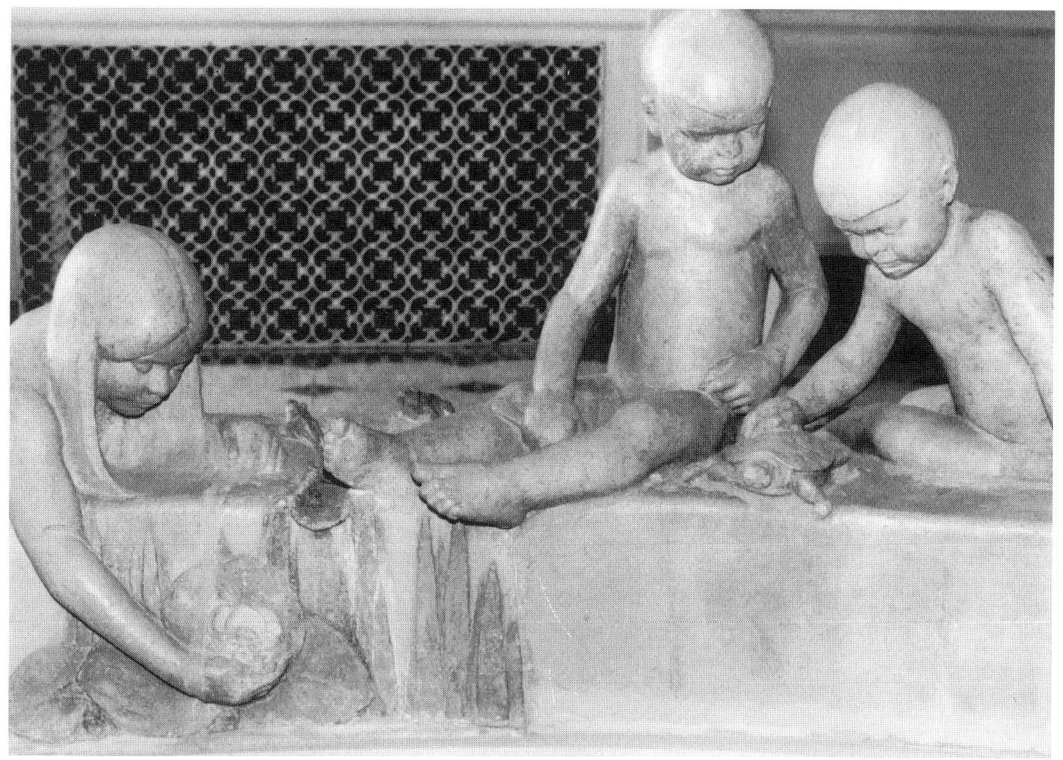

Figure 4.17 Close-up of the *Marriage Ring*.

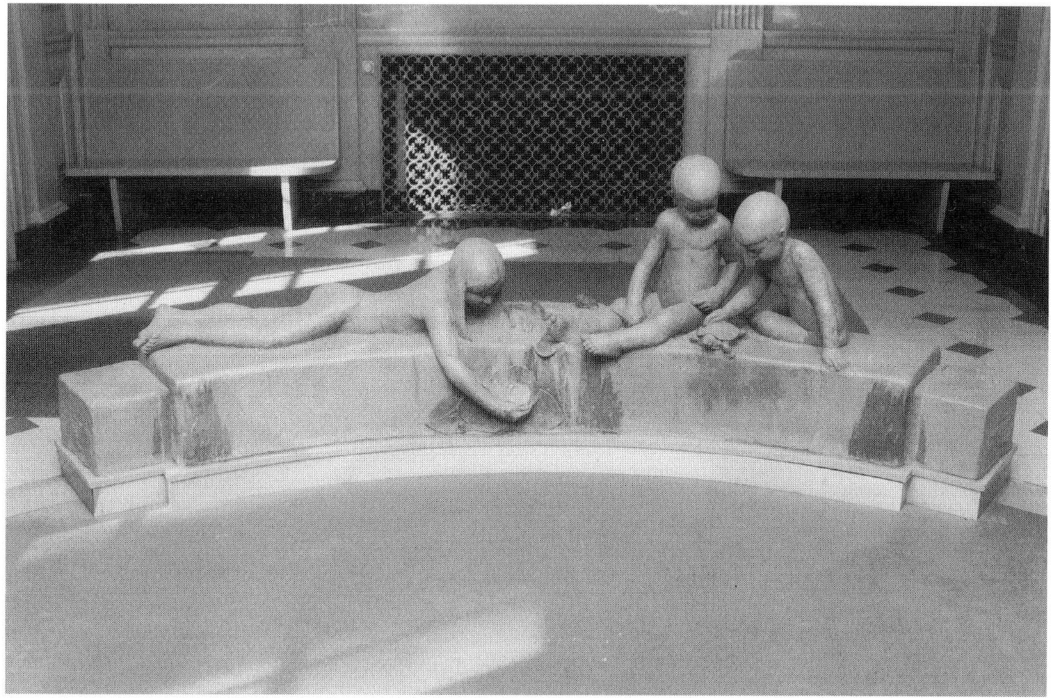

Figure 4.18 *Marriage Ring*, current view.

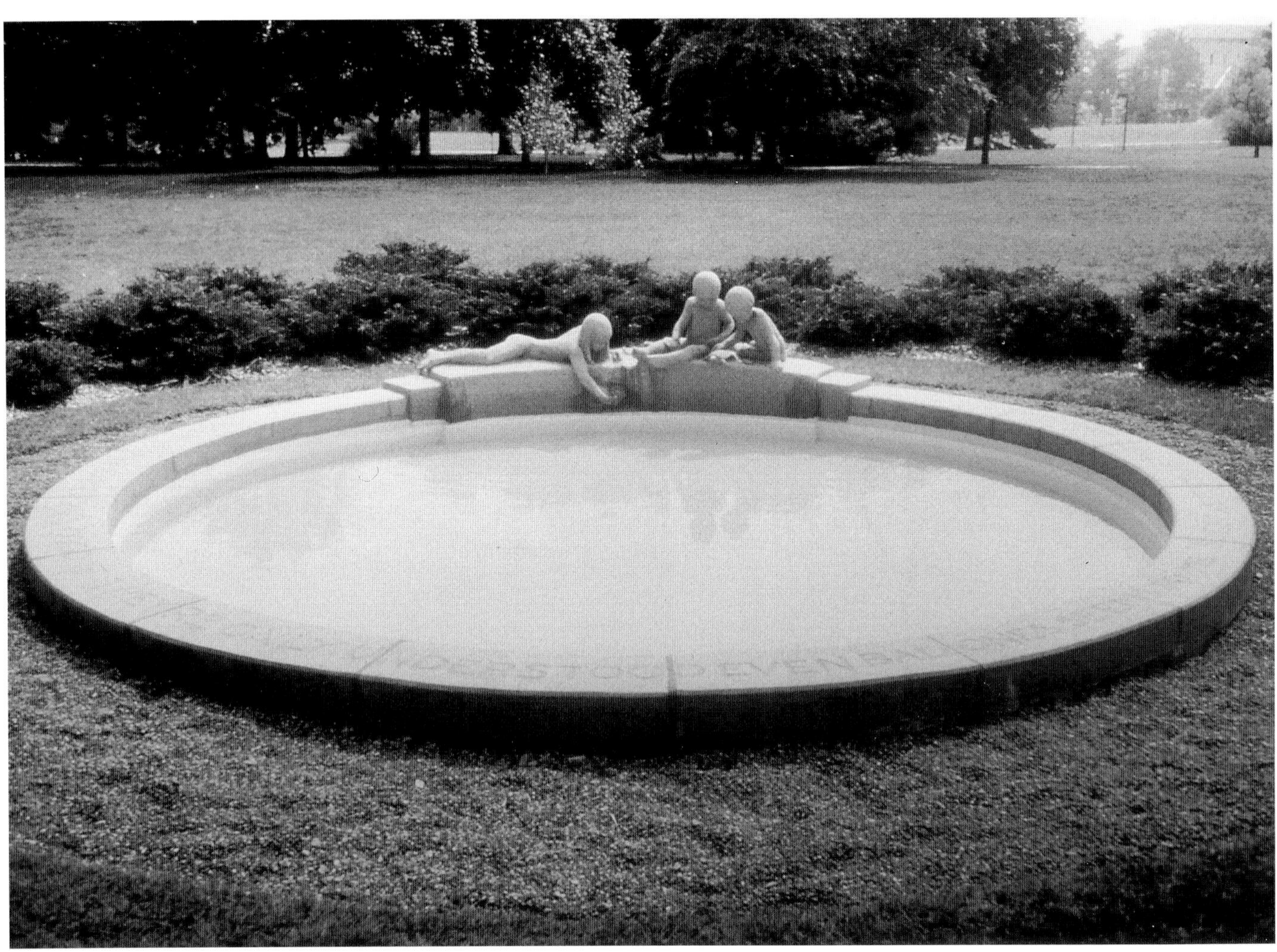

Figure 4.19 *Marriage Ring*, outside reproduction.

other PWAP murals. The carved limestone figures sit in quiet, perhaps even constrained, positions with open books poised on their knees. Their backs are bent slightly forward, their forearms rest on their laps, and the heads are angled downward, creating a self-contained sculptural character. Although both the *Boy* and the *Girl* incline their heads as if studying their books, it soon becomes apparent that they are also slightly angled in another direction: toward each other. It is clear that, although their body language is subtle, they are very much aware of one another.

Neither registers any marked emotion on the face, exhibiting the restrained, if not neutral, facial expressions that are typical of Petersen's public works. Absorbed less in their studies than in their modestly expressed but sharp awareness of each other, they seem not to notice the passersby who move up and down the staircase between them. Their quietly dramatic exchange activates the nearly seven feet of space between them, demonstrating again Petersen's ability to animate the space surrounding his sculptures. This charged space and the understated but engaging narrative of the sculpture group is accomplished primarily through his manipulation of posture and the relationship of the poses to the space around them. Sometimes the masses of the body are shifted to only a slight degree, but Petersen uses his understanding of human anatomy and its innate expressiveness to tell his story.

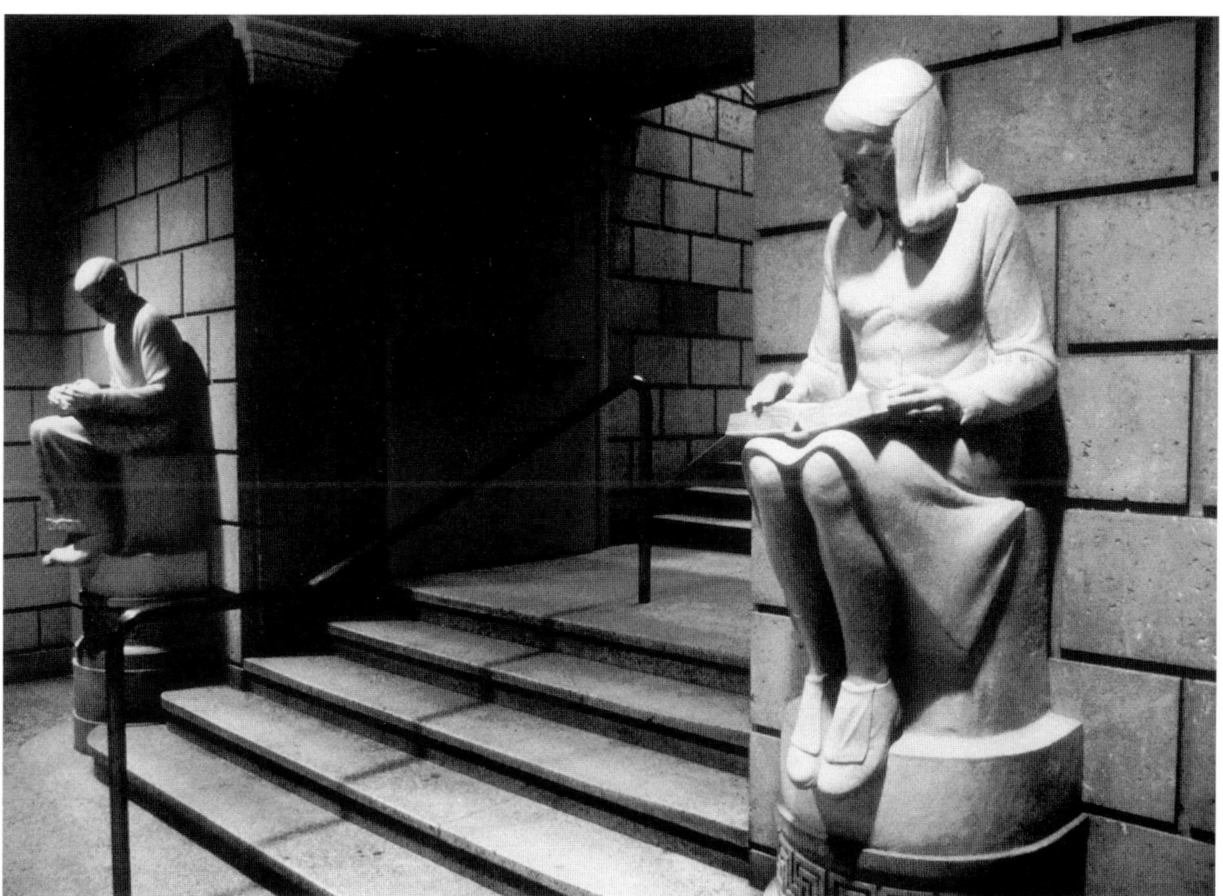

Figure 4.20 *Library Boy and Girl*, ISU Library, 1944.

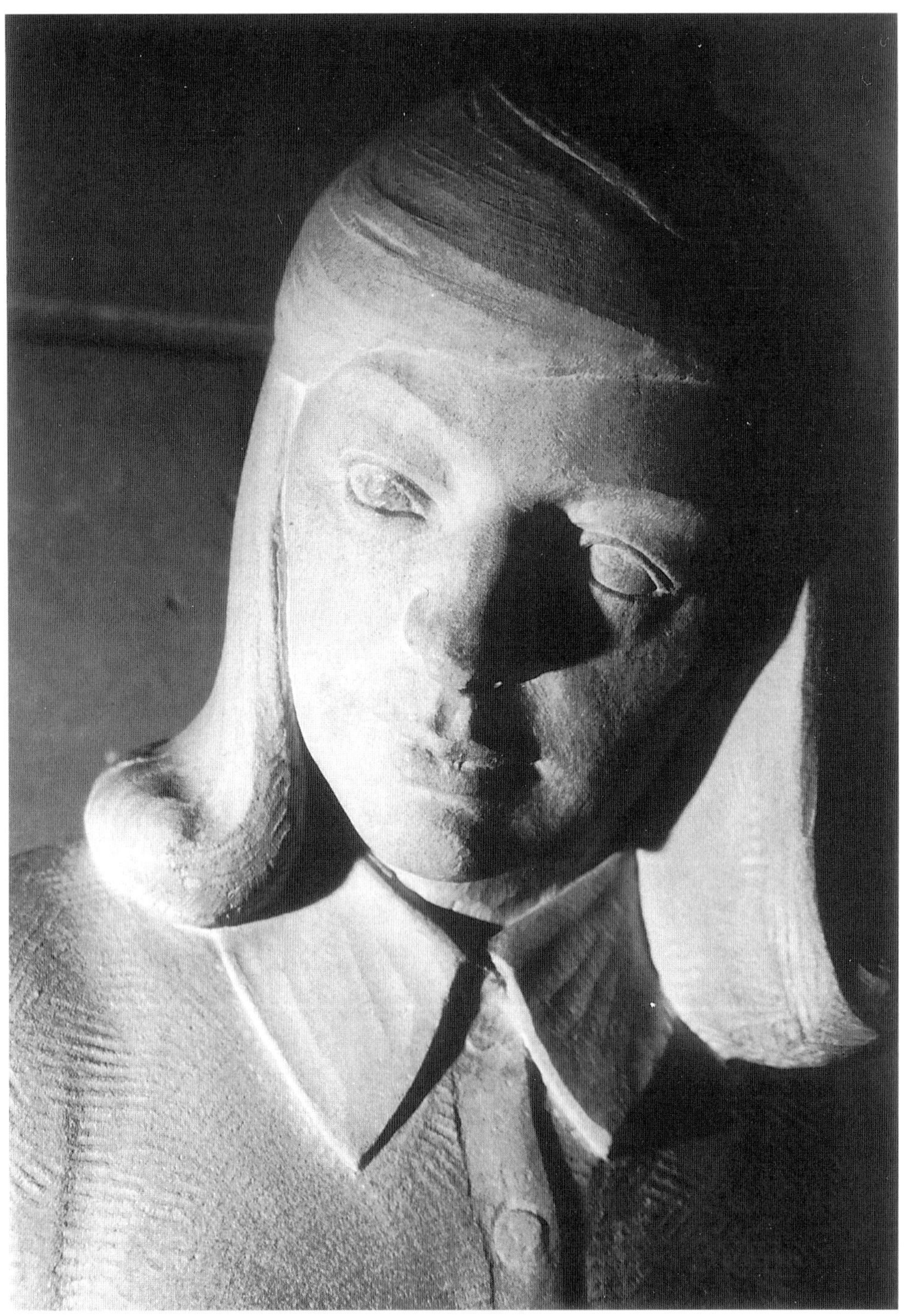

Figure 4.21 *Library Girl*'s head detail.

Petersen must have been acutely aware of the proximity of his sculptures to the Wood-designed paintings. Turning from the portrayal of these Iowa students' ancestors, the viewer encounters the three-dimensional student figures which remind us of the actual students who are at that moment in the library, doing what they have been doing since the college began. As we ascend the stairs, Wood's murals instruct us in the courses of study offered to students as they prepare not only for their own future but for the betterment of their society overall. Taken as a whole, Petersen has inserted his figures beneficially into the symbolic narrative of Wood's scheme. As he

had done for the veterinary complex, Petersen humanized a cycle that concentrated on historical and scientific issues. It also seems likely that the sweet earthiness of the *Library Boy and Girl* was especially poignant in 1944, as World War II moved into its third year for Americans. In two sculptures of soldiers, *Men of Two Wars* (Figure 4.22) and *Price of Victory* (Figure 4.23), Petersen had already shown his deep distress about war and the casualties that are felt so vividly on a college campus. Perhaps this sculpture dealing with the human cycle of life reminded him and others of the pleasures of peacetime and the hope for its restoration after the conflict.

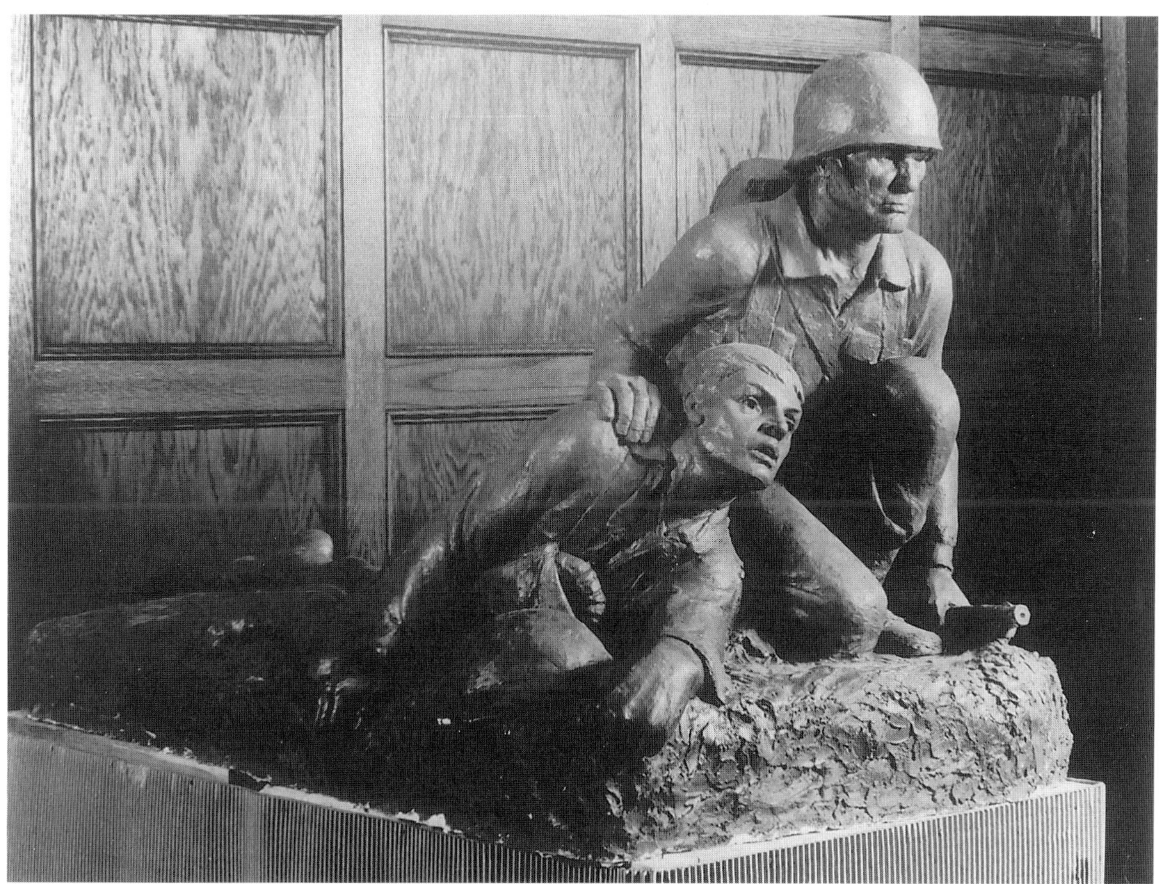

Figure 4.22 *Men of Two Wars*, 1942.

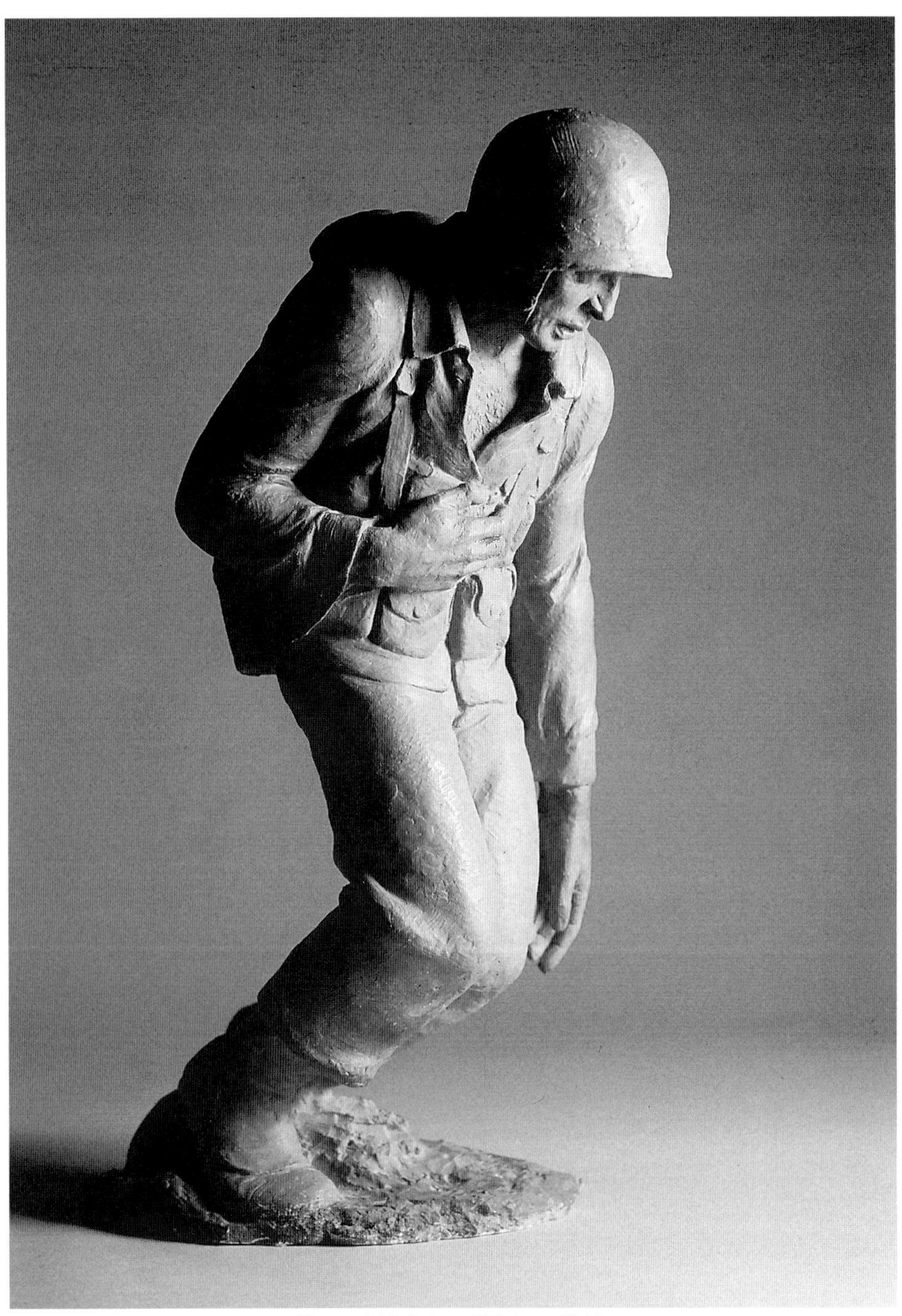

Figure 4.23 *Price of Victory*, 1944.

Petersen's major postwar campus sculpture is known as *Conversations*, or the *Oak-Elm Group* (Figure 4.24). It was begun in 1947 and completed in 1952, but not installed until after his death, in 1963 (Figure 4.25). Made up of three limestone groups arranged along a freestanding wall, it continues the theme found in the Iowa State University Library sculptures of the quiet moments of college life. Although there are a number of portraits of students, these two works and the State Gym *Three Athletes* are the only public sculptures that clearly portray the lives of students. The over life-size figures explore a range of personal experiences that typify the college years. The wall along which they are placed is brick with a light concrete cap that echoes the color of the limestone and links all of the sculptures. Except for one male, all the figures are young women, dressed in the cardigan sweaters and short skirts popular during and just after the war years. Except for the single end figure, all wear straight, medium-length, pageboy hairstyles that fit their heads like caps.

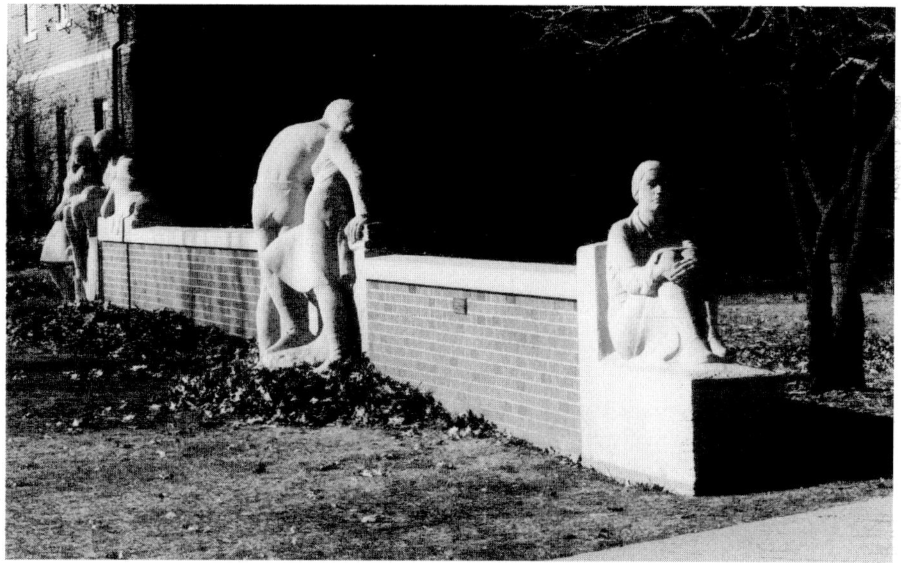

Figure 4.24 Overview of *Conversations*, 1999.

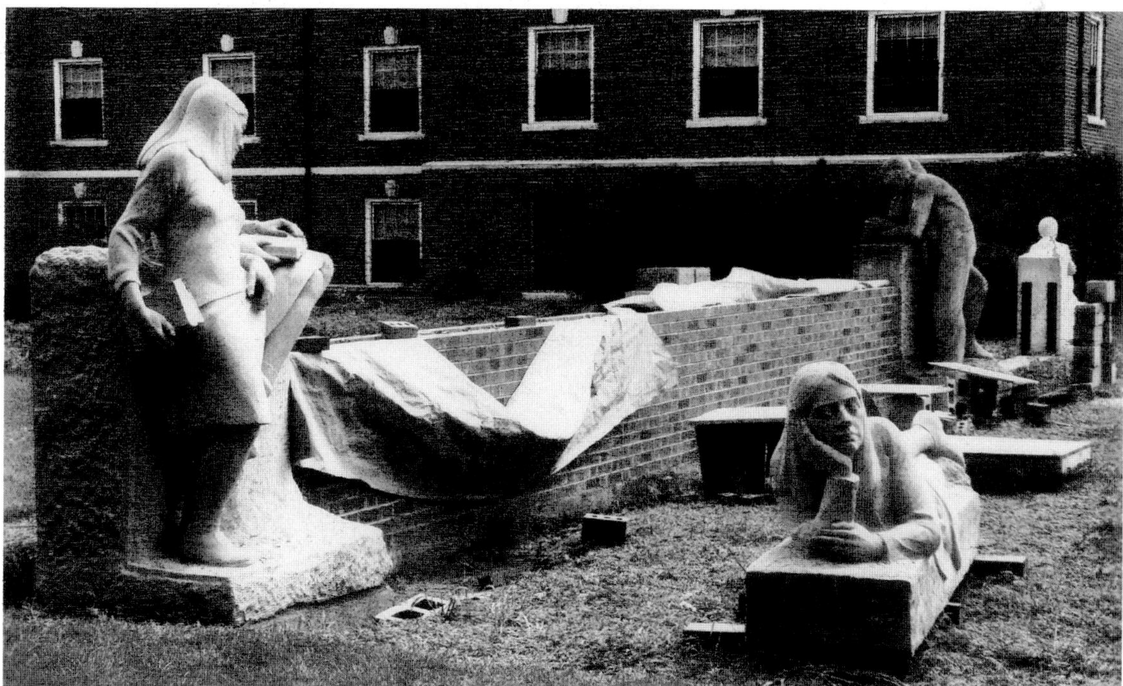

Figure 4.25 *Conversations* being installed, 1963.

The first group depicts three young women studying together (Figure 4.26). The central figure sits at the end of the wall, an open book on her lap. Her pose is similar to that of the *Library Girl*, but is more fluid and casual, with one ankle caught behind the other. A second figure leans in toward her in a languidly twisting posture, as if joining her in reading the book. She balances two books on her right hip as she distributes her weight on the left elbow and leg. The right leg bends at an angle only a little less sharp than that of the elbow, creating a somewhat exaggerated contrapposto posture. The third figure integrates the wall into the composition by stretching out along its top in a position related to that of the girl in *The Marriage Ring* and the *Reclining Nudes*. Her legs are crossed at the ankle and, like the second figure, she rests much of her weight on her elbow. She provides a contrast with the seated figure next to her, whose muscles must be tensed to maintain the position with the legs crossed at the ankles while the prone figure employs a similar ankles-crossed pose, but whose lower body seems completely relaxed.

The tone of the group is quiet and intimate. Despite the variety of postures, the group possesses a strong focus as the glance of each girl is drawn toward the open book. The standing figure is heavy and monumental,[9] and the pull of her leaning figure initiates the visual motion of the group, then leads the eye along the wall. Her head is very close to that of the central figure as they share the view of the open book. The seated central figure lightly holds the book with her right hand as the left seems to trace a passage on the page. The prone figure lifts her upper body and holds her head upright so that she looks, not down, but nearly straight across toward the book. This figure serves at least a dual purpose of intensifying the focus of this group while fostering the eye's movement out of this group and toward the second.

As in much of Petersen's sculpture, the style is a plain, unadorned one that gives an impression of simplicity. The treatment of the surfaces is indeed fairly simple and unelaborate, but the disposition of

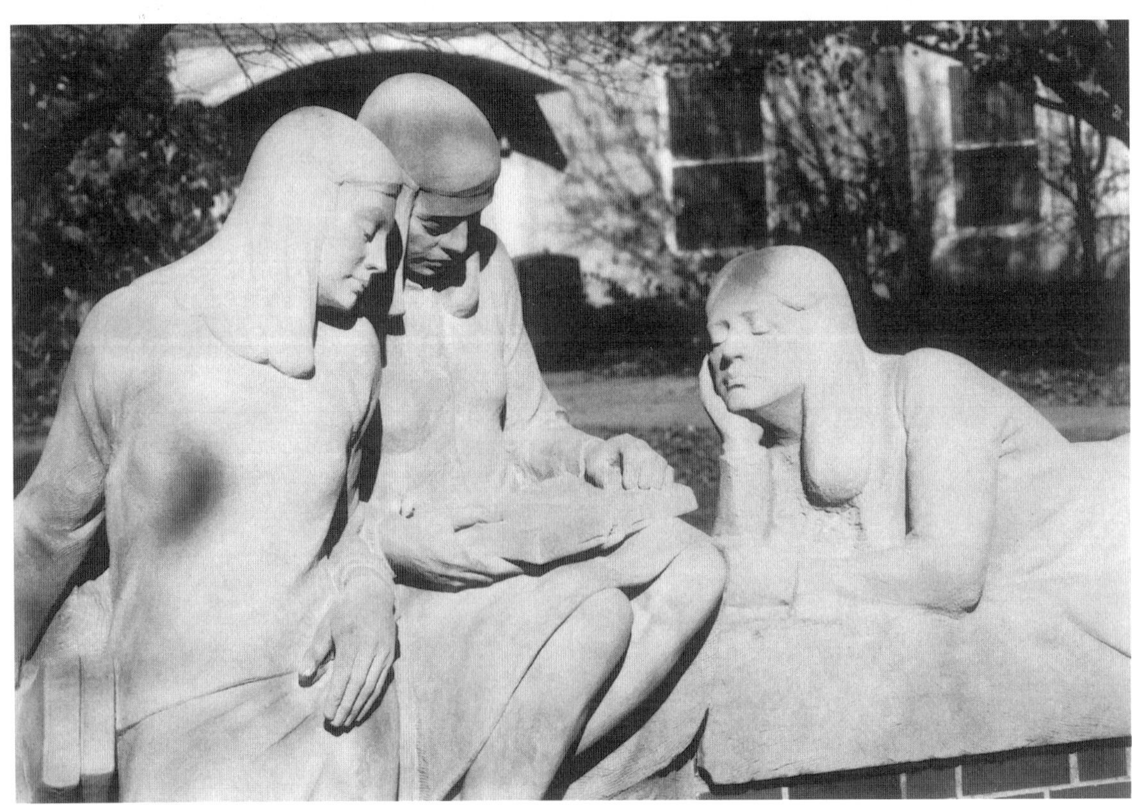

Figure 4.26 Detail of *Conversations*.

the internal masses of the figures and the compositions are often complex and sophisticated. Occasionally, some elements are unresolved, but it is clear that Petersen set himself challenges and avoided compositional cliches. That is the case here, with the combination of weighted and relaxed forms as well as the catalogue of poses: standing, sitting, and lying. Even the hands participate in a thoughtful, engaging design. Each figure holds something: the first two have books in their hands while the third "holds" her head. The hands of the first figure both are cupped inward toward her body, but one is tensed, holding her books, while the other hangs loosely in front of her. The two remaining figures have a similar configuration with one hand engaged, the other more relaxed.

The second group, placed about two-thirds of the way along the wall (not in the center), has only two figures, but it is an even more dynamic design (Figure 4.27). This is a couple, but a far more actively engaged couple than the reticent *Library Boy and Girl* of the ISU Library. The young man, who appears to be shirtless, drapes himself over the wall, his back to the viewer as he bends over an open book, which he seems to read with concentration. In a contrasting pose, the young woman beside him stands with her back to the wall. In order to look over his right shoulder at the book, she twists her body sharply and arches her torso as she leans back toward her partner. Her posture is related to that of the standing girl in the first group: she supports her inclined body on her elbow and the opposite arm swings out from the body, but it is much more pronounced and much more active. Her straight left leg is planted firmly on the limestone while the right steps vigorously toward the boy. The curving sway of the male body contrasts with the angles and energy of the female figure.

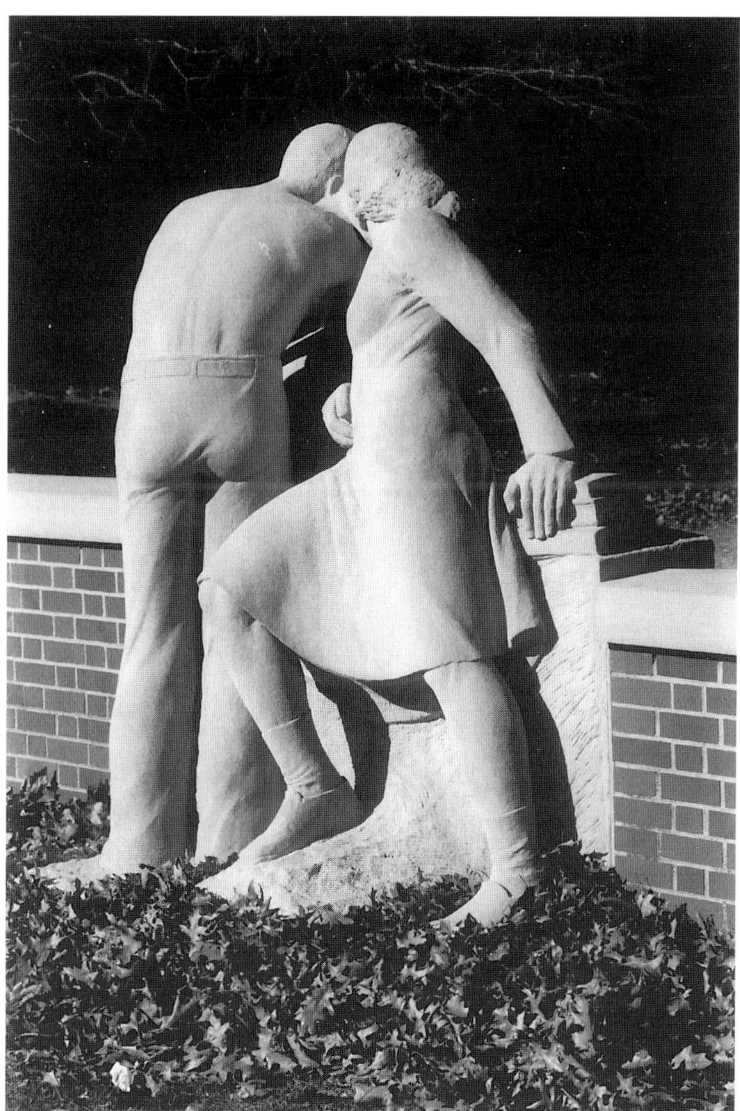

Figure 4.27 Detail of *Conversations*.

Petersen's campus installations had usually demonstrated his sensitivity to the space around the sculpture, but this work is the most compelling in its encouragement of the viewer to move about the space and experience the work from several viewpoints. Partly because of the narrative of a college couple together but partly also because of the arrangement of the forms themselves, the installation cannot be comprehended without the viewer actually walking along and around the wall. This level of participation in the spatial experience of the art is comparable to that required in site-specific works from the 1970s on. A full understanding of the installation demands not only that we become visually aware of the space around it, but that we experience that space directly. In setting up this quality in the piece, it is the second group — the couple — that is crucial to the success of *Conversations*.

From the back, which provides the only view of the faces (Figure 4.28) (they cannot be seen from the front at all), the complexity of the sculpture couple continues. The young man turns a little away from the young woman as he studies his book intently. He supports the book with his right arm, but it is a position that appears to pull away slightly from the woman. His upper right arm and her upper left are parallel, but his gesture almost seems to ward off the leaning woman while hers insinuates an intimacy. This confident postwar woman is very different from the modest, reserved 1944 *Library Girl*. Perhaps Petersen was responding in a subtle way to the changed atmosphere

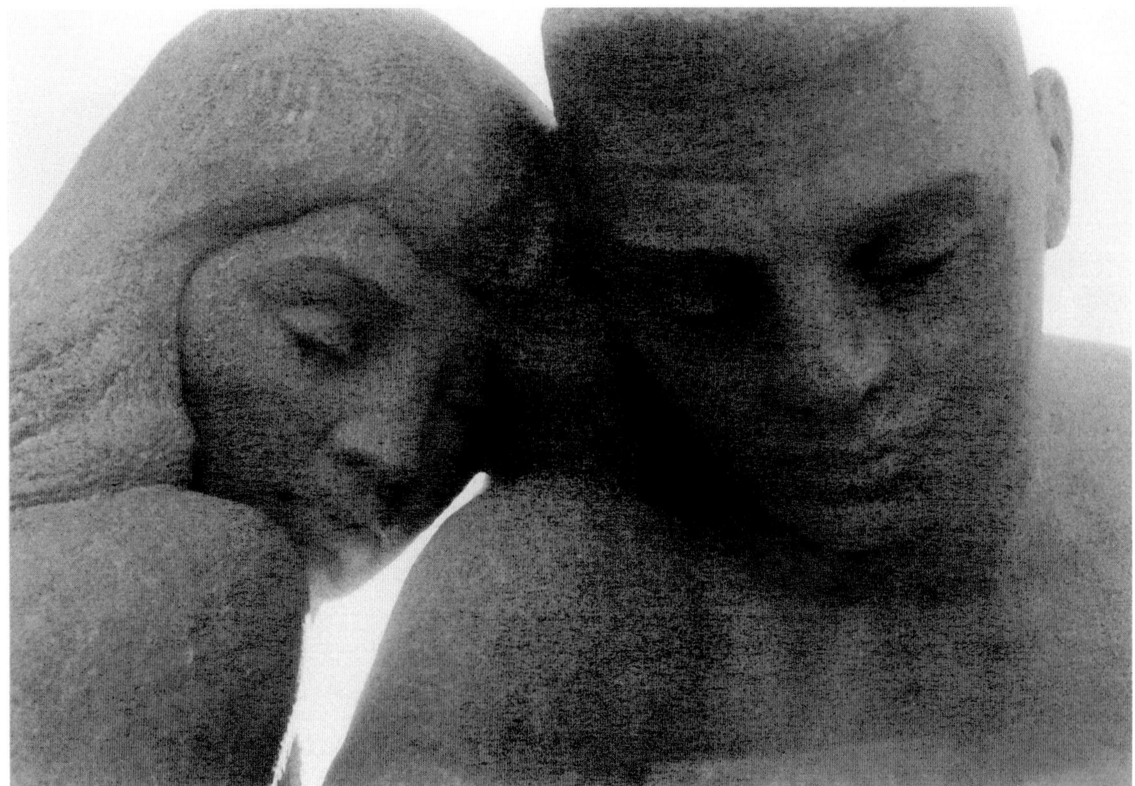

Figure 4.28 Detail of *Conversations*.

on American campuses when thousands of young men on the GI Bill took up their studies and their lives with focused intensity.

After the sculptural trio and then the couple, Petersen terminates his installation with a single figure (Figure 4.29). A young woman sits quietly and alone on a limestone pedestal, knees drawn toward her chest and hands folded calmly over her shins. A rose is sheltered in her lap. Back turned to the other depicted students, she gazes out toward the edge of campus. Her head is lifted and her facial expression is composed and thoughtful. This is perhaps the most simple, restful pose in the entire design. Without the complication of bodily gestures that relate one figure to another, Petersen's task here was to keep this one self-contained figure as visually and emotionally

compelling as the others. He accomplished it partly by the alert, attentive angle of the head and the slight tension in the neck muscles. In earlier sculptures of both humans and animals, Petersen had revealed his capacity to model subtle shifts in the planes of the bodies, shifts that intimate inner responses. While the lower body of the woman is relaxed, the upper possesses those minute adjustments that suggest something working beneath the surface. In a work entitled *Conversations*, this figure portrays the most important conversation of the college years: the conversation with oneself. This young woman does not seem inert, but rather highly engaged in some sort of mental activity, whether thinking or dreaming. As Petersen has positioned her in the design, she is part of the campus, but she looks out away from school toward the world beyond.

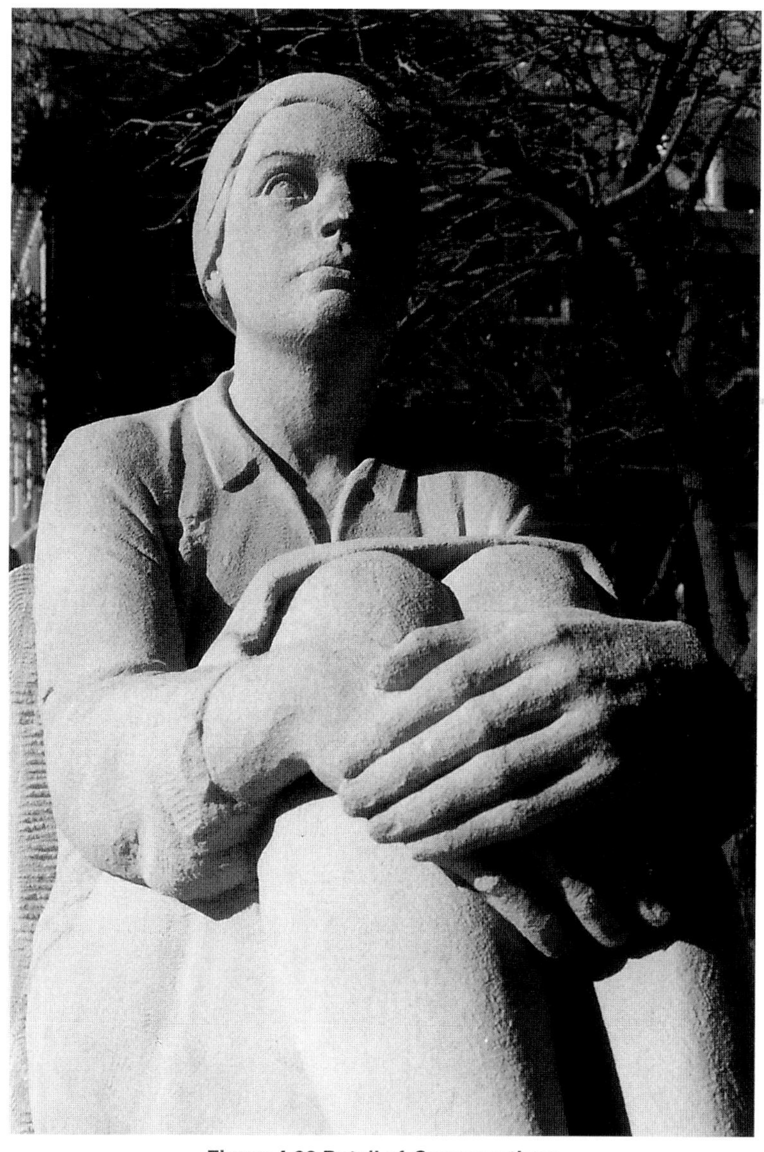

Figure 4.29 Detail of *Conversations*.

Conversations is Petersen's most complex sculpture, but it is only a portion of what would have been his most ambitious project. He proposed to create a large installation that would mark the eastern entrance to the campus along the old Lincoln Highway. He began his sculptural scheme in 1947 after "college officials gave him the nod to embark on his greatest venture to date."[10] Apparently, he carved the tons of limestone with such determination and energy that he exhausted himself. "Christian Petersen worked long hours into the night for years to complete the largest section of the job. He worked with such vigor and disregard for himself, that he became ill and was forced to remain home for many weeks to regain his strength."[11] The artist himself later confirmed the strenuousness of his efforts: "'I carved them directly without any assistance and my wife didn't like it when I used to come home at 2 or 3 in the morning', he said. Other than that Petersen refused to discuss his work. 'I never have spoken about my art — art should speak for itself.'"[12]

They were finished in 1952, but languished in his studio as the campus plan evolved to reflect the growth of the university. In addition, no funds were allotted for the completion of the project. Over the years, the unfinished status was noted by various publications. In 1954, *The Des Moines Register* featured on the cover of its Sunday picture magazine a color photograph of Petersen in front of the couple in *Conversations* with a model of the overall plan in his hands. The article explained that over the years Petersen spent creating the works, then waiting for their installation, the women's' fashions had changed. "The co-eds in the group will wear short skirts, about knee length, as that was the style seven years ago when the work was begun. Since fashion follows a cycle that takes hemlines up one year and down another year, it actually makes little difference in a permanent work what the skirt length is. Over a long period of years sometimes it will be in style and sometimes it won't. At any rate, this is a problem about which Christian Petersen is not worrying at all."[13] A magazine article of that same year commented about the delay: "Now, about two years after the sculptor completed his most monumental project, the work remains under the roof where it was created. Students at Iowa State College have been hopeful, each passing year, that they will be able to unveil the masterpiece at their annual VEISHEA celebration. Many have become impatient."[14] Their impatience was not relieved. When Petersen retired from teaching in 1959, another newspaper article acknowledged, "Probably the greatest artistic disappointment in Petersen's life has been the fact that his production of a four-section oversized 'campus entrance' group of student figures now gathers dust in his studio." The construction of new buildings and the widening of the highway eliminated the possibility of the installation ever being completed as Petersen initially planned. He recognized the changed circumstances but, in a rare public complaint, expressed some frustration with the situation. "'I don't think that corner entrance is a proper place for the figures now,' Petersen said. 'Still, there should be some place where they can be set up in a proper atmosphere.'"[15]

In 1960, a year before the sculptor's death, the art critic of *The Des Moines Register*, Nick Baldwin, wrote an article on the plight of the massive sculptures still waiting for placement. Questioning university officials about the delay, he learned that it would cost around $6,000 to install them and there was only $200 available from a fund established by the class of 1947. The university business manager agreed that it was "a worthwhile project," as did the college newspaper, which advised in an editorial: "Six thousand dollars has been estimated as the cost to erect the entrance project. Not a great deal, when you consider that it will identify the university as well as pay tribute to a great sculptor."[16] In Petersen's obituary in *The Des Moines Tribune* on April 5, 1961, it was reported that "a student movement, spearheaded by Phi Kappa Theta, a fraternity of which Mr. Petersen was an honorary member, raised funds to complete the project" and that Petersen had worked with the university to designate a site for his work.[17] Today, the sculpture is found on the lawn of a dormitory complex. It is only a short distance from the crossing of two main entrances to the campus, but it cannot be seen from either roadway.

Petersen had come to Iowa State in 1934 with the dairy project well underway and, at the time of his death, he was awaiting the installation of his last major campus sculpture. In between, his work had explored many aspects of college life, from the research of its professional faculty to the solitary moments of a young student. From athletics to home economics, from campus courtship to the history of corn, the themes in his sculpture addressed themselves to many audiences. The work was always representational and often narrative, carried out in a style which the head of the Department of Applied Art in 1941 called "fine simple work."[18] Most have been vandalized at some point, all have required some form of conservation, and a few are not where Petersen intended them to be, but none have been lost. For public, especially college, sculpture, this is an impressive record. The university has maintained each one and, since the founding of the Brunnier Art Museum, has encouraged and supported their sometimes costly and extensive conservation and restoration. It has been joined in this effort by alumni, some of whom have affectionate memories of their time spent in Petersen's sculpture class as well as many who recall these works of art as an integral part of their education at Iowa State.

NOTES

1. Bliss, Patricia, L., *Christian Petersen Remembered,* Ames: Iowa State University Press, 1986, 77.

2. Bliss reports that in 1938, he earned $150.00 a month, on a nine-month appointment.

3. Bliss, 76.

4. Bradley, William Aspenwall, "Sancta Ursula (After Carpaccio)," *Century*, 94(July 1917): 405. The entire poem is included in Bliss, 77.

5. VEISHEA is a spring celebration designed to showcase the colleges at ISU for the students, the community, and prospective students. The letters in VEISHEA stand for the original five colleges: Veterinary Medicine, Engineering, Industrial Sciences, Home Economics, and Agriculture.

6. *The Ring of Life* provides the title for the group who has made contributions to the program.

7. In the extensive interviews with Charlotte Petersen conducted 1983–84 by Bliss, it is evident that Petersen depended upon not only her knowledge, but also upon her research, for the subjects of several major works, including the Dairy Industry Courtyard and the veterinary reliefs. In the *Marrriage Ring* inscription, the Petersens slightly altered the poet's lines, probably for ease of reading.

8. Bliss gives an account of these cases, 85–87.

9. That monumentality was noted with some amusement in a student newspaper article: "Moo U's Beefy Babes," Iowa State University *Daily,* December 11, 1978.

10. Minser, Earl R. and Murray, Ray, "He Has Carved a Heritage," *The Iowan*, March 1954, 20.

11. Ibid.

12. Baldwin, Nick, "Sculptor's Work Stranded in Studio," *The Des Moines Tribune*, February 1, 1960.

13. "Seven-Year Sculpture Job Completed at Ames," *The Des Moines Register Picture Magazine*, January 10, 1954, 5-7.

14. Minser and Murray, 20.

15. Owens, Herb, "I.S.C. Sculptor: Freed of 'Duty,' He Enjoys Life," *The Des Moines Tribune*, January 12, 1959.

16. Baldwin, Nick, "At Iowa State University: Sculptor's Work Stranded in Studio," *The Des Moines Tribune*, February 1, 1960.

17. "Petersen, Sculptor, Is Dead; His Creations Adorn Iowa," *The Des Moines Tribune*, April 5, 1961.

18. Letter from Joanne M. Hansen, head of applied art, to *LIFE* magazine, October 28, 1941. Christian Petersen Papers. In this letter, Ms. Hansen suggested that the magazine consider publishing some photographs of Petersen's work, especially the Dairy Industry Courtyard and the veterinary installation. She noted that he gave sculpture demonstrations each year at the Iowa State Fair.

POETRY INSPIRATIONS

Sancta Ursula
(After Carpaccio)
1917

This is her room; this is her narrow bed
Whereon each night her golden hair is spread.
This is her glass, wherein she looks;
These are her pictures; these are all her books.
These are her trinkets, trophies girlish, gay;
These are the toys she touches every day.
This is her desk, whereat she sits to write
Letters that make the day that brings them bright.
These are her fish that swim in water clear;
This is her winged Love that she holds most dear.
This is her rug her eager feet have pressed,
This is her chair, wherein she sinks to rest
When wearied with some simple task or pleasure.
This is her clock, whose hands her young hours measure.
These are her walls that hold her heart at home.
These are her windows, tempting her to roam.
This is in fine her world; so world more wide,
Since all her dreams start here or here abide.

William Aspenwall Bradley (1878–1939)
American

Published in 1917 by The Century Company in Century
magazine
Inspiration for Reclining Nudes, *1936*

POETRY INSPIRATIONS

the seed:
chant of the indian maidens

After long suffering,
peace comes,
a kind of quiet
breaks over bent knees
and necks and falls softly
no matter how loud
the turbulence
in the distance.

Once in fertile ground,
the seed grows
come rain or snow,
or the brightest
of sunshine.
In sickness
and in health,
for better
or for worse
it blooms and blossoms.
When God wills,
it comes. Stop,
fellow nomad, and
gratefully gather in
whatever it is,
whatever it has become,
no matter how small or painful
or seemingly insignificant,
the gift, the joy, the life.
Oh hear, all,
north, east, south and west
now and forever,
our prayer sung in silence:
always and everywhere
give thanks, forever bend your
beautiful battle-weary bones
with tending

Michael Carey

Inspired by the Fountain of the Four Seasons, *by Christian Petersen, 1941.*
Commissioned by the University Museums, Iowa State University, 1999,
as part of the Art on Campus Poetry Collection.

POETRY INSPIRATIONS

Fountain of
the Four Seasons

No need to throw a coin
because this fountain itself is a wish,
a charm against everything
that can go wrong from seed to harvest,
from hand to soil and back again.

The water climbs, collapses, climbs
and falls upon itself
in that old paradigm of plenty,
while maidens guard the compass points,
invoke the seasons.

Look how they cradle the seeds,
the plant, the full-grown ears,
so much tender mothering
from corn to small child nursing.
Who could fail with such devotion?

If you walk around their circle
you can see the seasons turn,
feel the weather changing,
know that nothing stays the same,
that this is constancy.

Neal Bowers

Inspired by Fountain of the Four Seasons *by Christian Petersen.*
Commissioned by the University Museums, Iowa State University, 1990,
from the Art on Campus Poetry Collection.

Footprints I make: Smoke arises in their midst
Footprints I make: The soil lies mellowed
Footprints I make: The little hills stand in rows
Footprints I make: Lo, I come to the sacred planting

Footprints I make: Give me kernels, two, three, four
Footprints I make: Give me five, six, and final seven
Footprints I make: Lo, the tender stalk breaks the soil
Footprints I make: The stalk stands amidst the day
Footprints I make: The blades spread in the winds
Footprints I make: Lo! The plant has blossomed
Footprints I make: The blades sigh in the wind
Footprints I make: The ears branch from the stalk
Footprints I make: Lo! I gather the ripened grain
Footprints I make: There is joy in my house
Footprints I make: Lo! The day of fulfillment!

Osage Indian Chant and inspiration for the Fountain of the Four Seasons.

The Hired Man's Faith in Children
1900

I believe all children's good,
Ef they're only understood, -
Even bad ones, 'pears to me,
'S jes' as good as they kin be!

James Whitcomb Riley (1849–1916)
American

Published in 1900 by Braunworth, Munn, and Barber in Home — Folks
by James Whitcomb Riley
Inspiration for the Marriage Ring, 1942

POETRY INSPIRATIONS

the jewels

Water, they say,
we are mostly,
water and air
surrounded by
a few ounces
of minerals:
calcium, phosphorus,
potassium, salt,
the tiniest amount
of iron and zinc and copper.

Oh, but what
a fine mixture!
See these children
sitting and lying in the sun
by the low tangle of green bushes.
Such tender lumps of clay!
Such beautiful bags of water!
Bright jewels
on the wedding ring
of their parents!
staring at themselves
in the lily, in the turtle,
the frog and the surface
of the bubbling stream.
See the soft curves
on the gentle girl
and her two
plump brothers.
Nothing but skin and love
and a quiet curiosity
between their souls
and the heavens,
their hearts
and the sky and
the maze of students
walking by –
their busy brains
already reeling
about the tedious
contours of their
next day's assignment.

Michael Carey

Inspired by the Marriage Ring *by Christian Petersen.*
Commissioned by the University Museums, Iowa State University, 1999,
as part of the Art on Campus Poetry Collection.

POETRY INSPIRATIONS

his hands

How could something
so big and strong
make something
so fine and tender?
With a simple
twist of a wrist
the tip of his thumb
opened a young girl's eyes,
brought life to dead limbs,
put music in the air
around the hem
of a prancing dancer.

No one knew
how he did it
although they all
watched closely,
they all let him
touch calmly what their
young tentative hands were
slowly bringing into existence,
were trying to bring into existence,
or could not will to life.

Everyone began
with the same tools
the same wet
lump of soil,
the same arms
and heart and brain,
the same red dawn
calling to them
from the horizon,
but few felt loveliness
before it blossomed,
few could put their finger
on what could not be felt
until his warm sure hands
touched theirs
numb and shivering
in the untempered morning.

Michael Carey

In memory of the sculptor and teacher Christian Petersen, artist-in-residence,
Iowa State University, 1934 to 1955.
Commissioned by the University Museums, Iowa State University, 1999,
as part of the Art on Campus Poetry Collection.

CHAPTER 5
FARMS
AND WARS

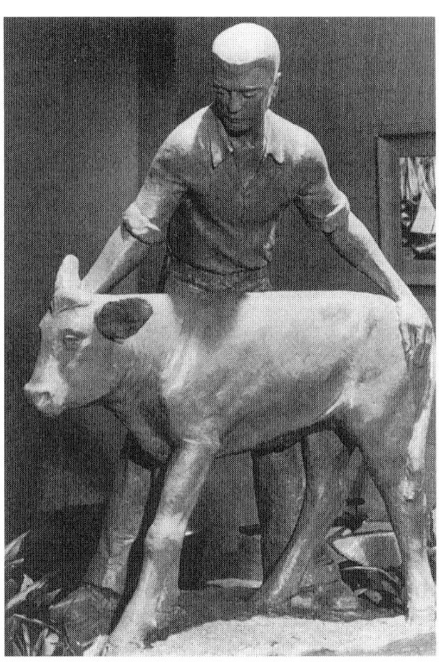

4-H Calf, 1941, a rural subject rarely portrayed in American sculpture.

Each time Iowa State presented Petersen with even the germ of an idea for a sculpture they might want, he amplified it as far as he could and created monumental works whenever he had the chance. But he also produced many smaller sculptures in which he expressed ideas that reflected his personal concerns and passions. Late in his life, many of these were religious sculptures, as will be seen, but earlier ones ranged over a number of subjects. And, of course, the demands for portraiture — everything from the president of the University of Kentucky to visitors at the Iowa State Fair — were ongoing. The small sculptures in particular reveal not only his sharp observations of human form and action, but also an acute interest in human beings. In 1937, when he was still something of a novelty on campus, a student reporter visited the studio and asked Petersen about his inspiration as a sculptor. "'I get most of my ideas from seeing groups of people together,' [he] explained. ... Petersen has a kindly, but penetrating gaze. While you talk to him, he is scrutinizing closely every change of expression on your face. 'Sometimes people think I'm staring at them,' Petersen said shyly: 'but all I'm doing is gaining material.'"[1]

With the material he gained, Petersen produced small sculptures that often crystallized larger, complex experiences. It was not until after he joined the faculty at Iowa State that he had much opportunity to explore such sculptures; most of his work before then had been either portraiture or memorial sculptures. His earliest years at the college were an intensely productive period when he accomplished six major pieces: the *History of Dairying* courtyard reliefs, the interior reliefs on the same subject, the State Gym *Three Athletes*, the *Reclining Nudes* of Roberts Hall, the *Veterinary Medicine* panel, and *The Gentle Doctor*. He also contributed the illustrations to a children's book on the Meskwaki Indians, *Cha-Ki-Shi,* in 1936. By 1938, with the work on all these mostly finished, Petersen and his wife traveled eastward, spending time in Kentucky, where Petersen worked on a plaque honoring Frank LeRonde McVey, president of the University of Kentucky. It seems certain that Petersen obtained this commission through his patron, Raymond Hughes, who was a friend of McVey's.[2] While there, Petersen was eager to see life away from an academic setting. His wife, Charlotte, wrote a lively letter back to a friend in Ames, exclaiming, "Oh, you should have come with us! A thrill in almost every mile. ... We are now in Augusta, Kentucky. ... Christian said this morning he'd like to get a real Kentucky hill-billy before he left. I hope he decides to do it."[3]

He did decide to visit the hill people of Kentucky, resulting in a number of small sculptures, all of which are of women and/or children, although a long series of sketches deal with a range of subjects. *Mountain Mother* (c. 1939) portrays a barefooted woman who may be in the early stages of a pregnancy, standing as firmly as a rooted tree (Figure 5.1). The three fearful, exhausted children who cling to her help create a sculptural composition that is

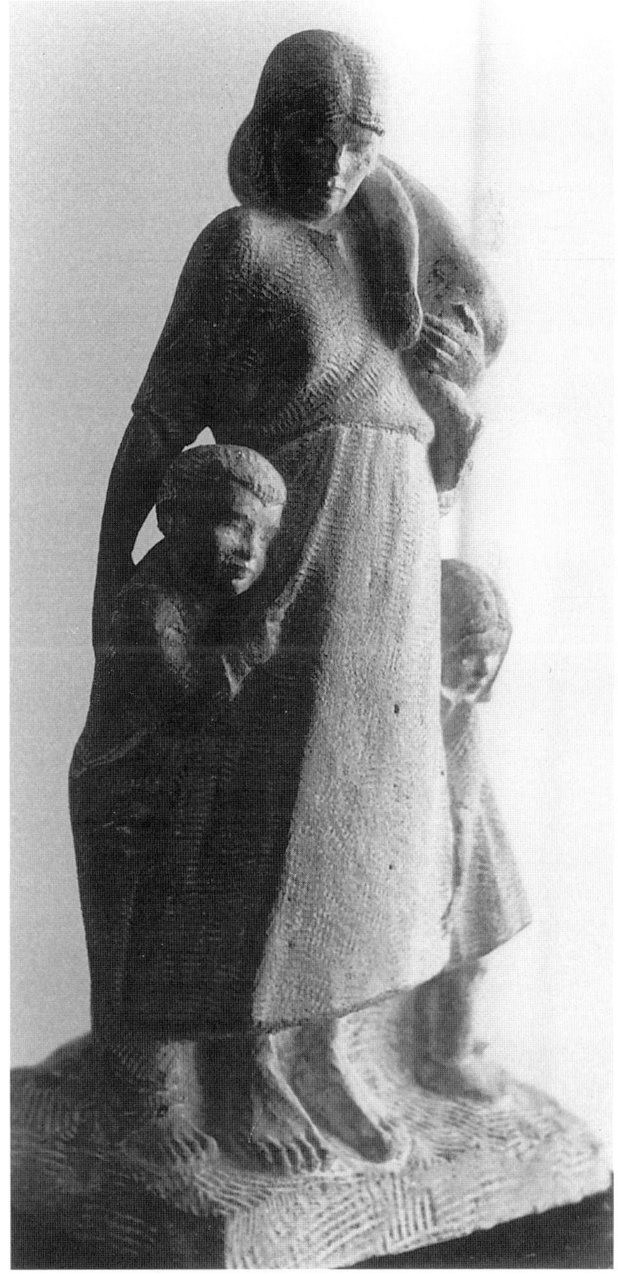

Figure 5.1 *Mountain Mother*, 1939.

concentrated and earthy.[4] At the time of the Petersen's visit, the area was recovering from floods, and the dogged endurance of these rural people in the face of both poverty and disaster seemed to inspire the sculptor. *Flood* (1938) (Figure 5.2) is as fluid an image as *Mountain Mother* is sturdy, with a woman climbing out of floodwaters that pull at her long skirts. Sheltering an infant in her arms, the figure looks down at the water behind her while her body moves away from the danger. In both of these sculptures, Petersen shows the essentializing quality that had come into his work after the move to Iowa in the early 1930s. *Soon after the Flood* (Figure 5.3) takes up a less dramatic moment as three children crowd onto the back of a mule to survey the damage left after the deluge. Two older children stare outward with sober expressions while a third — a toddler — slumps limply in sleep against the largest child.

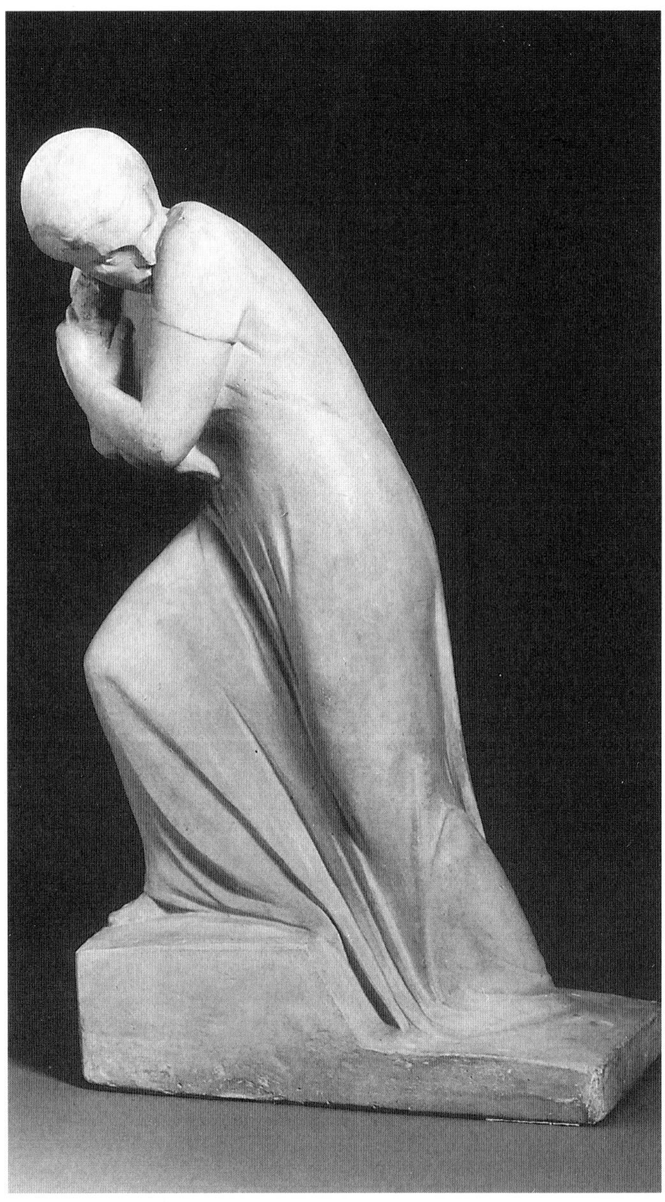

Figure 5.2 *Flood.*

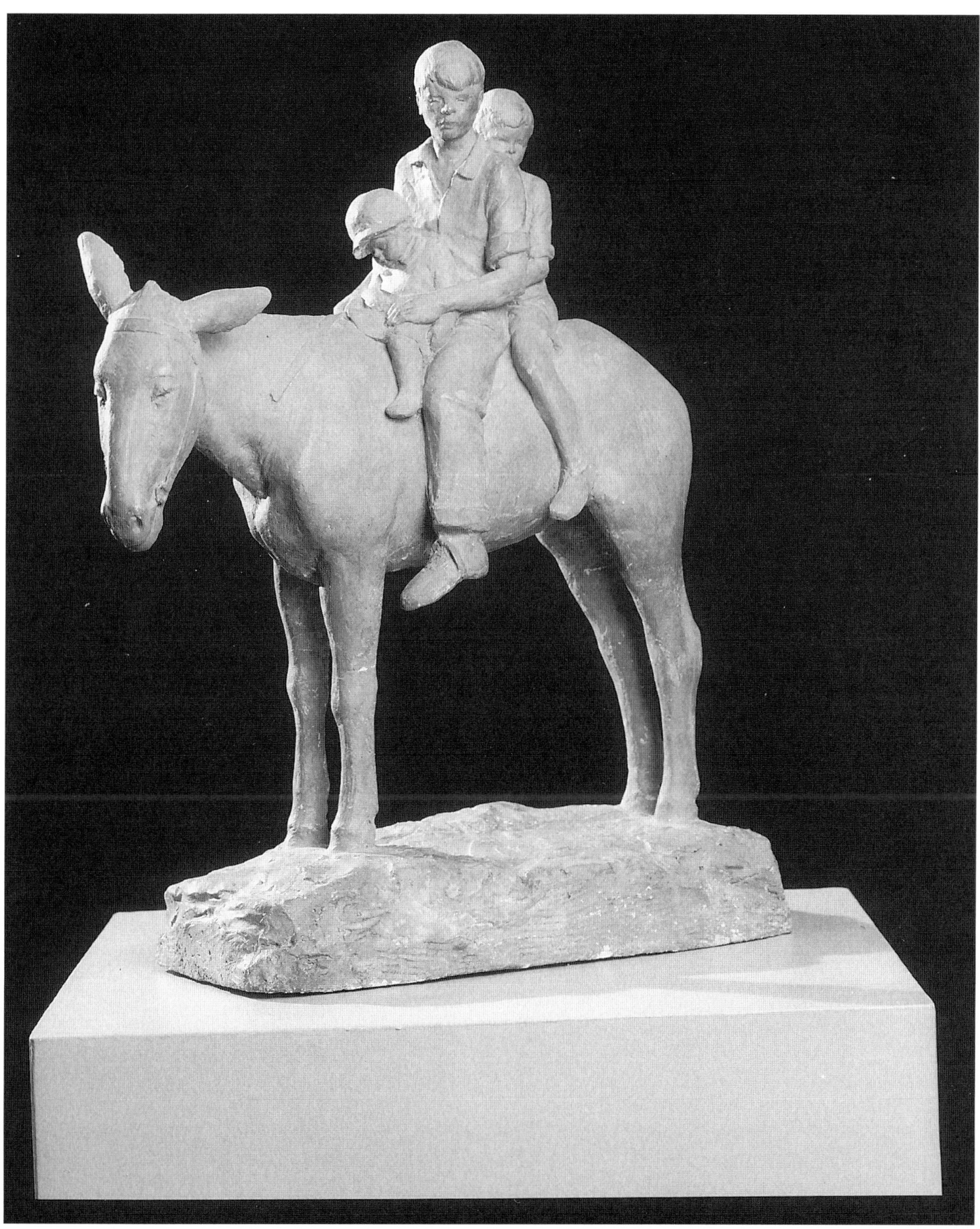

Figure 5.3 *Soon after the Flood*, 1939.

Two other sculptures may have been suggested by the Kentucky experience although they do not relate directly to it. *Pioneer Woman* (Figure 5.4), a plain, subdued woman whose clasped hands hang in a gesture of grief in front of her, may have been an interpretation of a funeral scene that Petersen sketched in Kentucky.[5] When he was working on *Flood* and, at the same time, hearing of the dust storms that stripped and parched the Great Plains in the late 1930s, it may have occurred to Petersen to produce a pendant figure entitled *Drought* (c. 1939) (Figure 5.5). In contrast to *Flood*, where the clinging garment is so important for the narrative, this sculpture is of a nude, almost desiccated looking woman. She too holds a child, but this one is not sheltered; rather, it is displayed as it lies on her lap, barely supported by the mother's slack arms. We cannot tell if the child is dead or alive, and the mother's expression is, like the figure in Saint-Gaudens' *Adams Memorial*, unreadable in specific terms. It may connote an entreating, despairingly prayerful state of mind or a stunned and speechless grief.

Such sculpture is as close as Petersen came during the Depression to referring to the disastrous situation in American agricul-

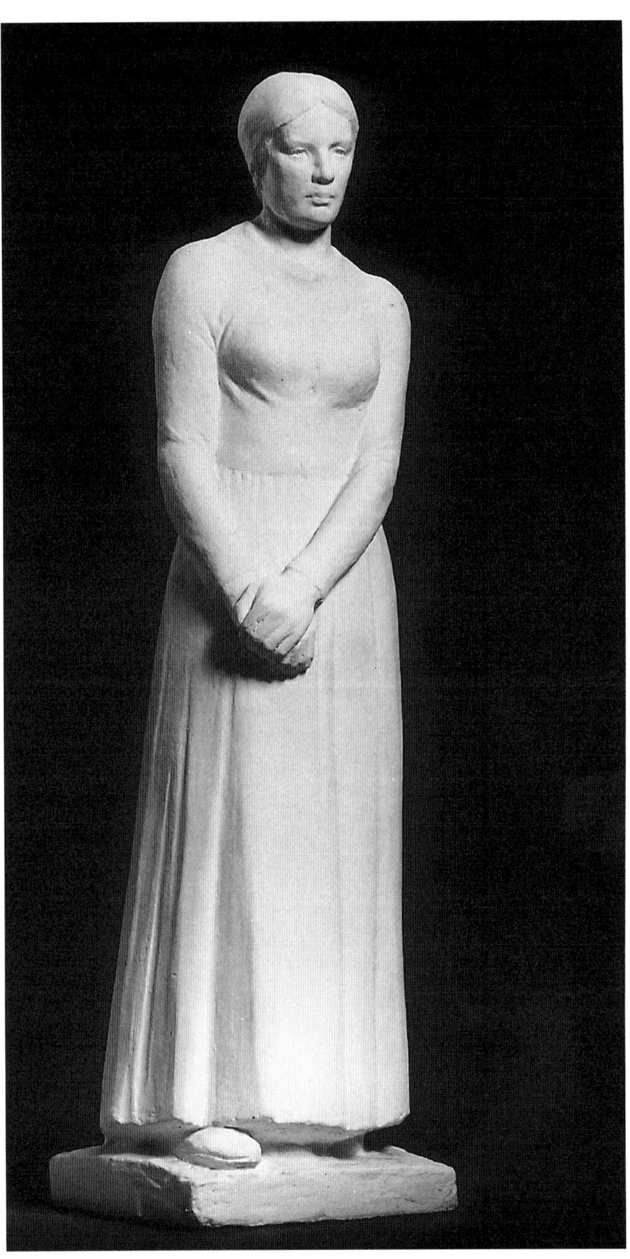

Figure 5.4 *Pioneer Woman*.

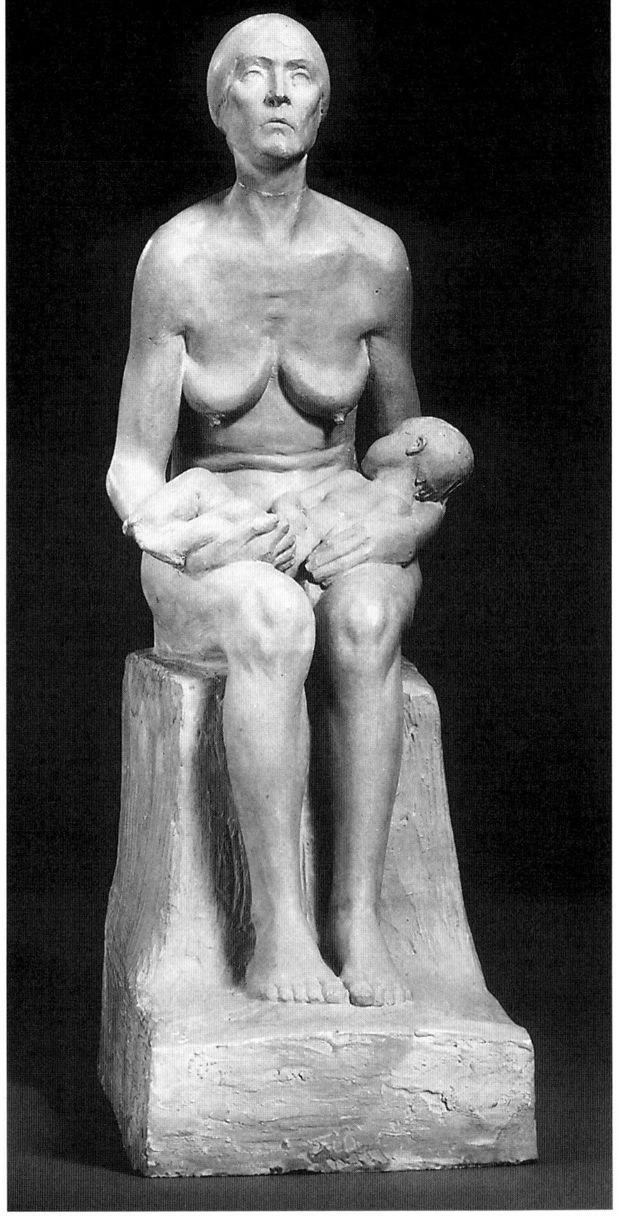

Figure 5.5 *Drought*.

ture. Like most artists of the period, he seldom dealt with it directly. Yet, rural life and what Grant Wood called "farmer material" was a part of his work, as one would expect it to be in an artist employed by Iowa State College. Not surprisingly, his versions of those subjects emphasized the productivity and enduring vigor of life on the land. With his colleagues in agriculture, genetics, and veterinary medicine, he must have been much more aware of research and new developments that were designed to enhance rural life than of its failures. While he might have been affected by bad social and natural conditions in Appalachia, he does not seem to have found correspondences in Iowa.

In 1941, as the country was pulling out of the Depression, Petersen produced two sculptures that address farm life, which are among the few instances at the time of a Midwestern artist taking up this theme in sculpture. *Cornhusker* (Figure 5.6) is based on a scene witnessed by Petersen and described by his friend in agricultural journalism, Charles Rogers.

One bright October afternoon on a farm near Nevada, Iowa, spectators at a corn husking contest watched the nimble, smoothly articulating form of a neighbor boy move rhythmically up and down the rows to win the first leg of a contest which was to carry him to the state championship and runner-up in the National.

Marion Link, Iowa husker champ, focused the spectators' attention that afternoon when he ran away with the county contest and started his climb to husker fame. ...

Perhaps some thought how fine a thing it would be to remember Marion just as he looked that afternoon, his shirt thrown off to free his supple muscles, striding down the corn rows, composing a corn dance as the yellow ears he flung caught the mellow afternoon sun, then struck the side board of the wagon in a symphony of percussion.

If an artist had been present this whole beautiful experience might be caught and held for others to enjoy forever.

That is exactly what did happen, for an artist was present. And Marion Link unwittingly inspired him to make an Iowa masterpiece. ...

The artist, Sculptor Christian Petersen, had seen what others saw, though no doubt, with his practiced sculptor's eyes, he saw a good deal more. He followed Marion through the contest, making careful mental notes. That evening, while the memory of Marion's fine athletic body was still fresh in his mind, he went to the studio and made the quick sketch in clay. Later Petersen persuaded Marion to pose in the studio, and then he completed this statue.[6]

The sculpture (originally entitled *Iowa Champ*) is about half life-size and depicts a muscular young farmer in overalls working his way, stride by stride, down the cornrow. Leaning into his work, he grasps an ear of corn to pull it from its stalk. According to Link's recollections after the war, he told Petersen, "'It'll be o.k. to make a statue of me as long as it doesn't look like me.' So the experienced hands of the sculptor patterned the arms and body after Link, but made the face entirely different."[7] Indeed, the face resembles the purposeful men of the veterinary panel more than it does that of the model. Like many young men whom Petersen knew, Marion Link soon went to war, in his case with the Seabees in the Pacific. But on a leave in 1942, he returned to

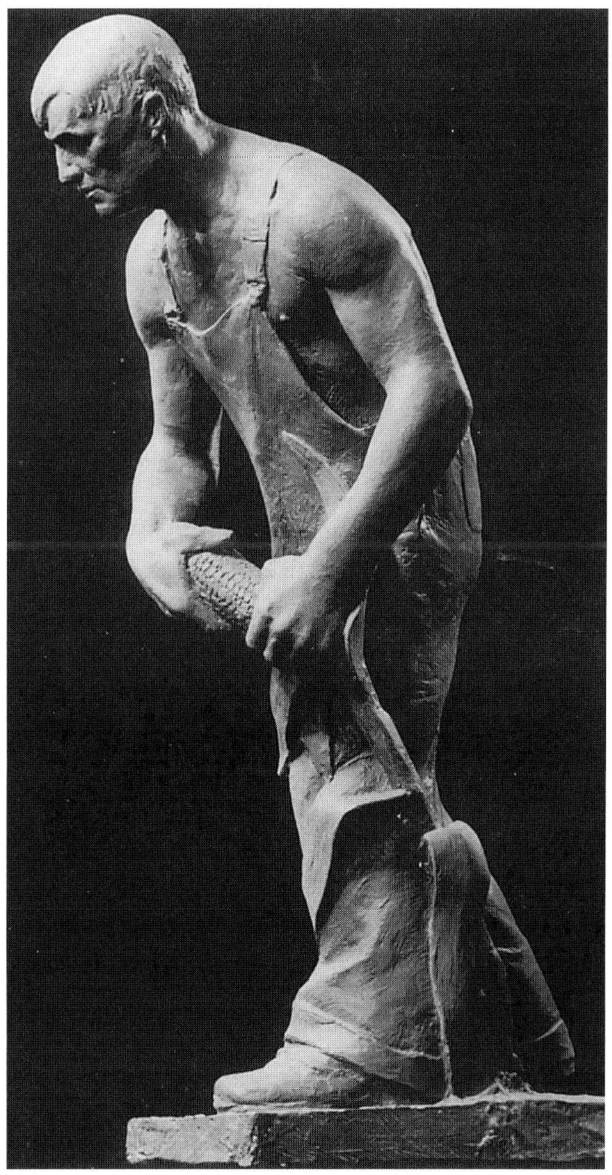

Figure 5.6 *Cornhusker,* 1941.

visit Petersen and see his statue, which was entitled, according to the caption for the newspaper photograph that showed the two men shaking hands, *Agricultural Labor.*[8]

That same year, Petersen made another sculpture that joined *Cornhusker* for many years on display in the Sheldon Munn Hotel in Ames and later the Kirkwood Hotel in Des Moines. *4-H Calf* (Figure 5.7) is a subject that Petersen must have observed many times as he did sculpture demonstrations at the Iowa State Fair. Here, an adolescent farm boy studiously positions his calf. The title suggests that this is not a farmyard scene but one in which the boy is showing his animal for judging at a fair. Though it does not have the abstracted simplification of the relief cattle in the dairy panels, it is still a very plain, unelaborated form, a description that could also apply in comparing the boy with the adult men who work to control their animals in the veterinary panel.

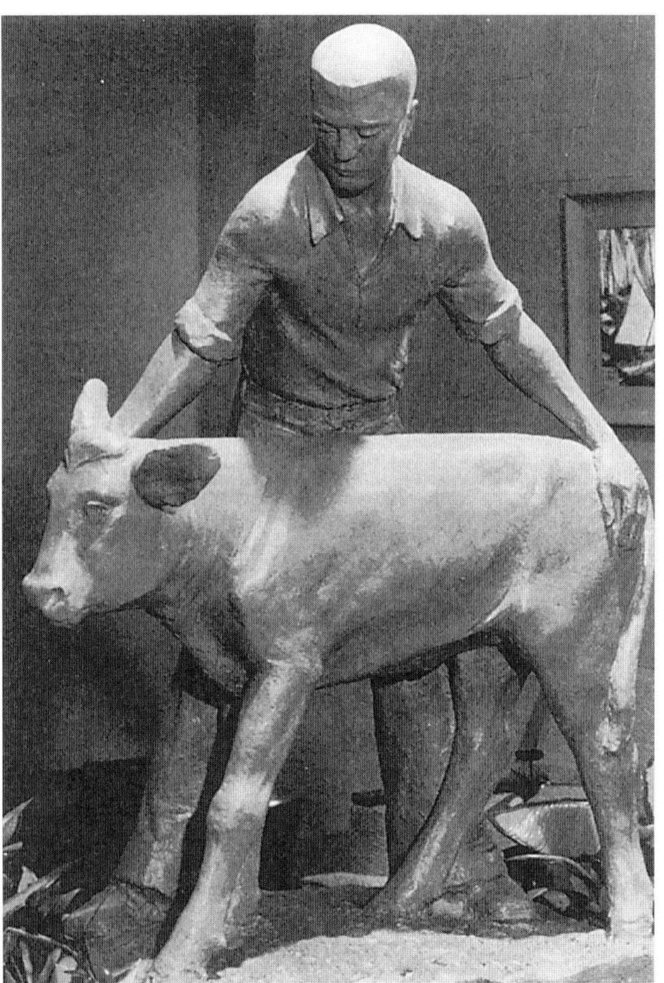

Figure 5.7 *4-H Calf*, 1941.

In producing sculptures on these themes, Petersen had little company among artists of the Depression era who were not working in federal programs. Even in those programs, however, relatively few freestanding sculptures (compared to the number of paintings) that depict the life of the farmer appear to have been created and preserved. Petersen's works are among the few that could be fitted into the regionalist program although, like most artists who found that term applied to them, he preferred not to be so narrowly labeled. "Regionalism is the bunk," he said when questioned about it in 1938. "That is putting it crudely, perhaps. Of course, my own work is regional in that it uses the material of the lives of Iowa and middlewestern people. It is natural that the artist uses the material around him. But I do not use a different style because of the regional subject matter," he explained.[9] He was right in that his style is not at all different from his other works, but regionalism can scarcely be said to be a "style" other than a general realism. But in terms of subject, he appears to be one of the few sculptors who was genuinely inspired by rural midwestern life and took it as a subject matter for art.

He was comfortable in the Midwest and, as has already been suggested, was an early proponent of that locale for the artist's life and work. In the same article where Petersen assailed any attempt to classify his work as regionalist, the writer proclaimed his association with the Midwest, then went on to describe him in a way that perhaps would make him, as an artist, a less suspicious figure here.

> *No one can doubt that this sculptor who came to the middlewest because he felt the region was more appreciative and more open minded to art, has his feet on the ground — planted firmly in fertile Iowa loam. He is no long haired effeminate artist. Sandy haired, with piercing blue eyes, stalwart, strong, nimble-fingered hands, he might be taken for a Viking following the trade of seafaring ancestors were it not for a tiny moustache.*
>
> *The only thing about him which remotely suggested the traditional conception of the artist were his dark colored smock and the fact that his trousers did not match his vest and coat. He wore a black felt hat with downturned brim similar to those affected by reporters in the movies.*[10]

Scenes of peaceful pursuits in the steady rhythm of rural American life were not on Petersen's mind during the years of World War II. He seems to have been especially saddened and appalled by the conflict, as he would later express in a different way in his religious sculptures of the 1950s. He addressed the war in both metaphorical and graphic ways, as he had in earlier sculptures on the subject. While the *Spanish-American War Memorial* in Newport and the *Janie Flynn Memorial* were honorific in a traditional way, the *Battery D Memorial* was not heroic and the *Albert E. Scott Memorial* was grimly realistic, at least for its time.

From early in the war — 1942 — *Carry On* or *Men of Two Wars* (Figure 4.22) expresses the idea of a continuing situation that links World War I and World War II. A fallen soldier, dressed in a World War I uniform with his doughboy hat on the ground, struggles with his last breath to lift his head and look outward. He is aided and comforted by a G.I., also dressed accurately, who kneels by his side and takes up the task of battle. The facial expression of the first figure is haggard, but that of the contemporary fighter is grim, as if steeling himself to confront his legacy and his duty. In late 1942, Petersen had been honored by the college with a dinner at which his old East Coast friend, George Nerney, had been asked to speak. While in Ames, he attended the opening of an exhibition of Petersen's work at the Memorial Union where *Men of Two Wars* was first displayed. "After studying it for several minutes, he remarked, 'Isn't it terrible?' Then, clarifying his statement, he continued to explain how masterfully Petersen had portrayed the terrible thought that a new soldier must carry on where an old soldier had failed."[11]

By 1944, Petersen must have been well enough acquainted with the losses caused by the war to produce a sculpture that is particularly moving in its immediacy. Although he gave it a metaphorical title — *Price of Victory* (Figure 4.23) — the image is disturbingly real. Petersen depicts an American soldier at the moment of death, as he is struck by a bullet. With his body already sagging toward the earth, one arm is drawn to his chest while the other hangs by his side, unable now to break the fall which will come in the next instant. The face is not agonized or contorted, but hovers between awareness and unconsciousness. Petersen must have sent a photograph of the piece to George Nerney and asked if he had any suggestions about it. Nerney replied, "I judge ... that it would stir the feeling of anyone so deeply that it ought to be of some great use to assist those boys who are giving up so much for us. It has so much that you have told so simply and so strongly."[12] According to Petersen's first biographer, the sculpture did affect those who saw it, for when it was shown in the Gold Star Hall of the Memorial Union after the war ended, college administrators were asked to take it off display. "The statue apparently had created too much grief for those who had seen it, particularly persons who had lost a loved one in combat." Upon learning of the reaction, Petersen reportedly commented, "It is the greatest compliment ever paid to my work."[13]

NOTES

1. Barlow, Walter, "Murals, Figures, and Statues Hide Petersen While He Models; Sculptor Smokes; Hangs Out in Ceramics Lab; Watches People for Ideas," *Iowa State Student*, January 21, 1937.

2. In a series of letters from 1937 through 1938, Petersen and Hughes discussed this sculpture. In one from May 1, 1938, Hughes wrote from Washington, D.C., encouraging Petersen: "Am tremendously keen on your relief of Dr. McVey. You must do your very best on that. ... I hope you catch the life in McVey's expression. Sometimes he has a rather dead poker face."

3. Charlotte Petersen to Joanna (Joanne M. Hansen?), undated. Christian Petersen Papers.

4. According to interviews conducted by Bliss with Charlotte Petersen, a sculpture entitled *Mother Earth* was produced in 1938, but stolen the following year from the studio. Bliss, Patricia L., *Christian Petersen Remembered,* Ames: Iowa State University Press, 107. No photographs exist, but it may have been related to *Mountain Mother* in theme.

5. In interviews with Bliss, Charlotte Petersen reported that this sculpture arose from Petersen's observation of a widow in the cemetery at Iowa State University containing the gravestones of Iowa settlers. Bliss, 107. A similar figure exists in the group of sketches from Kentucky.

6. "Corn Country Sculptor," undated typescript. The manuscript is attributed to Charles Rogers by a handwritten inscription "Probably by Chas. Rogers." Christian Petersen Papers.

7. "Iowa's Champion Husker," *Iowa Agriculturist*, October 1946, 45(3): 5.

8. "Model Sees Statue," *Iowa State Daily*, September 29, 1942.

9. Cook, Virginia, "Petersen in Discussion of Sculpture; Believe Midwest Is Open Minded to Art," Ames *Tribune*, January 1, 1938.

10. Ibid.

11. Dudgeon, Ellen, "Petersen Exhibit In Memorial Union Is Well Attended; 'Carry On' Is Newest Among Pieces On Exhibit," *Iowa State Daily*, December 5, 1942.

12. Nerney to Petersen, March 2, 1945. Christian Petersen Papers.

13. Bliss, 114.

Drought
1938

The brave child Hope
Lies starving on the mother's knees.
Her shrunken breasts have failed
When empty skies
Mocked back the cry for rain.

Both day and night
The cattle moan
For drink and parceled forks of hay.
High poised the ugly buzzards circle slow
To drop like plummets when some beast
Staggering falls to rise no more.
The dried up corn breaks from its roots
And burning winds suck added heat
From pastures dry as parchment from a desert tomb.

The Pueblo calls his clans
And hour by hour
And day on day
Repeats his chants
And thinks by agony and dance
To draw from gods displeased
The blessing of the rain.
The Pale-face knows no chant,
No dance.
He cannot think that God
Would change his laws for one small place,
He cannot pray for rain:
He can but dumbly stare
While Hope lies dying
On the mother's knees.

Outside the withering wind unwearied blows.
A sheltering tree, the grandsire's pride, is dead—
Others yet will die.

Another brazen sky
Stares at a new born day
But offers not one cloud to nourish Hope,
Starving – dying on the mother's knees.

Jules Cool Cunningham (1879–1948)
American

Published privately in 1943 by Jules Cool Cunningham
In From Dusk to Dawn *by Jules Cool Cunningham*
Inspiration by Drought, *created ca.1938.*

CHAPTER 6
RELIGIOUS SCULPTURE

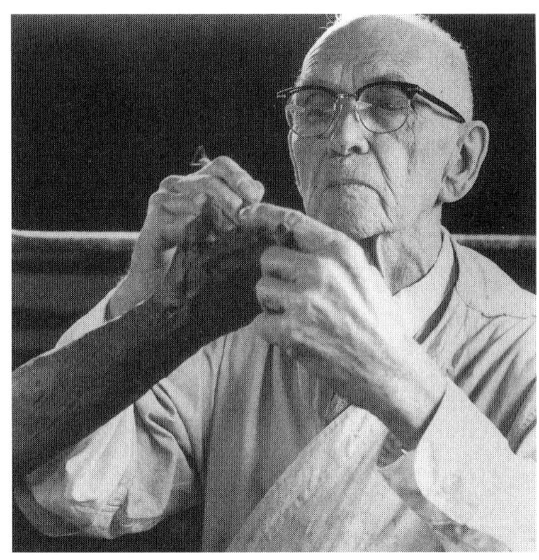

Petersen, 1961.

In the years after World War II until his death in 1961, Petersen completed only one major public sculpture for Iowa State: *Conversations*, begun in 1947 and completed in 1952. He continued to teach his classes, offering to students their only opportunity to study sculpture. Much of his activity in sculpture that was not portraiture of some variety was in religious sculpture. This genre — so unfashionable in the twentieth century — provided an important avenue of expression for Petersen in the last decade and a half of his life. In 1949 he converted to Catholicism in what was apparently a genuine and carefully deliberated conversion. His wife, Charlotte, was a life-long practicing Catholic, and he regularly attended Mass with her,[1] but it was not until his sixty-fourth year that he joined the Church.

His interest in religious sculpture seems to have begun around the end of World War II. It is possible that the carnage of the war and the explosive dawn of the Atomic Age prompted him to consider new topics dealing with spirituality. He had already demonstrated in his sculpture *Price of Victory* that he felt strongly about the cataclysm that was overtaking the world. Those feelings, in addition to his own advancing age, may have contributed to his turn toward religious imagery. As was typical of Petersen, he left little direct indication of his thinking about the changes in his art. In the past, he had produced sculpture that dealt with famous and distinctive individuals (Vitus Bering, Lincoln, George Washington Carver), attempting to give some idea of their strength of character. His task in his religious work was to translate that idea into the sense of divine mission that could animate the figures of Christ, the Madonna, and saints for the twentieth century.

One of Petersen's earliest and most affecting religious works was carved around the end of World War II: *St. Bernadette* (Figure 6.1). He depicts the nineteenth century French saint in a trance as she listens for the voice of "the Lady," or the Virgin Mary. She leans slightly forward, throws back her head, and holds her open-palmed hands out slightly from her body in a pose similar to that which has been indicative of prayer since Antiquity; it is commonly found in early Christian art. The rapt posture may also be related to an image well known to Americans at that time: the actress Jennifer Jones in her Academy Award-winning role as the saint of Lourdes in the 1943 film *The Song of Bernadette*. Petersen was able to capture the simple but intense tone of the uneducated, rural young woman transported into spiritual ecstasy. In 1945, he and his wife presented it as a gift to their parish church in Ames, St. Cecilia,[2] and in October of that year the sculpture served as a cover image for the small devotional magazine, *Women's Catholic Forester*.[3]

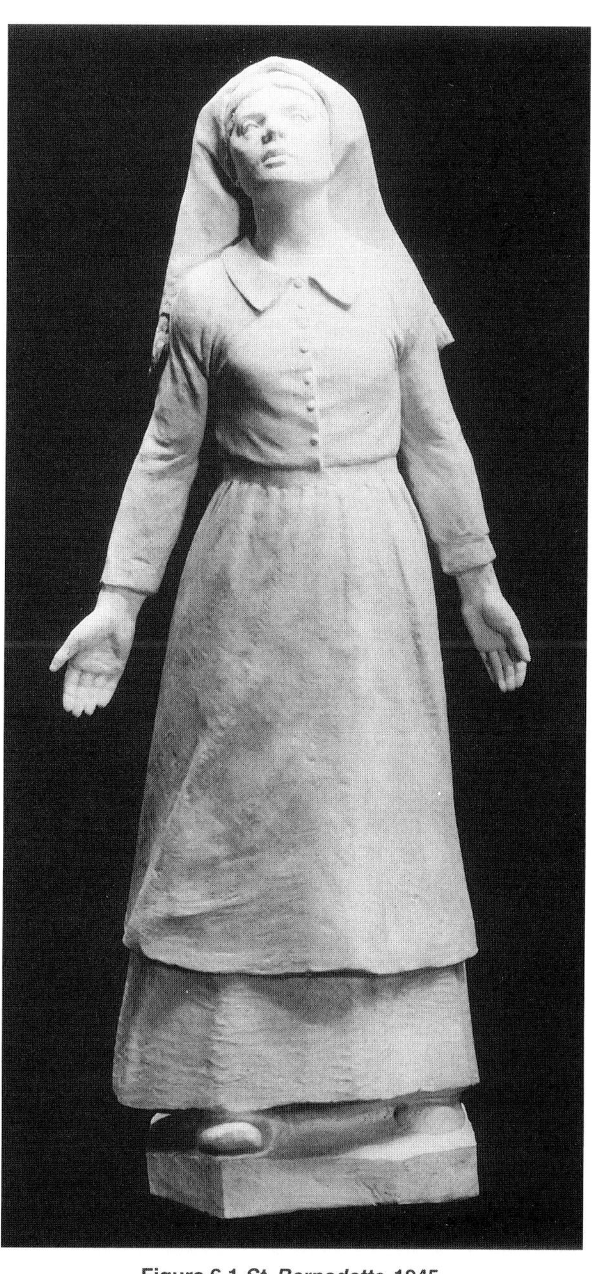

Figure 6.1 *St. Bernadette*, 1945.

His next work was his best-known religious sculpture and also marked the beginning of a short series of commissioned religious sculptures. After *Conversations* of 1947–52, Iowa State requested no further major work from Petersen, but his talents were taken up by several Catholic parishes and organizations. With the exception of some portrait commissions, most of his activity in the last decade of his life was devoted to what might be termed spiritual, if not outrightly religious, work. In fact, several of the portraits were also individuals from an ecumenical religious community (Presbyterian and Methodist churches in Ames; B'Nai Jeshurun congregation in Des Moines). It was his own St. Cecilia parish that asked Petersen to create a sculpture for their elementary school. The work that he produced was, like so many he had done for Iowa State, a sculptural complex. Within a multilevel brick architectural framework, Petersen placed a figure of the Madonna with her child and three other contemporary children (Figure 6.2). He pushed his work to its farthest point in the creation of a trompe l'oeil illusion. The dairy courtyard cows which bend their necks to drink from an actual fountain, the students who range themselves along the wall in *Conversations,* and especially, the children who play beside the pool in the *Marriage Ring* were all predecessors for Petersen's concept here. In fact, the two boys and one girl who interrupt their play to devote their attention to the Holy Mother and the Christ Child could be older versions of the same children who had earlier played alongside the pool of the *Marriage Ring.*

The Madonna (Figure 6.3) is the solid, solemn female figure who had populated so many earlier sculptures, and the child could have been drawn from the dozens he had sculpted for families in the Ames–Des Moines area over the previous ten to fifteen years. Petersen's practiced eye for the proportions and gestures of a child's body are nowhere displayed more clearly than in this sculpture. A substantial, realistic-looking child, the nude figure is both supported and presented by his Mother. The facial expressions of both are benign and pleasant; some observers have felt that they also reflected a pensive tone. Petersen's ability to capture a characteristic momentary pose is shown in the figures of the children, who retain a note of the spontaneity of play and its brief interruption. Two boys (Figure 6.4) put down their ball and bat to turn and look toward the Madonna and Child. One standing and one sitting on a step just below the pedestal holding the holy figures, both have their feet facing outward while their torsos twist to pay homage to her presence. On the right side of the complex, a girl (Figure 6.5) faces the Holy Mother with one knee resting on the first level and her arms placed along the top of a low wall. A sturdy child in braids, she resembles the Petersen's daughter, Mary, who was then ten years old and a student at St. Cecilia School.

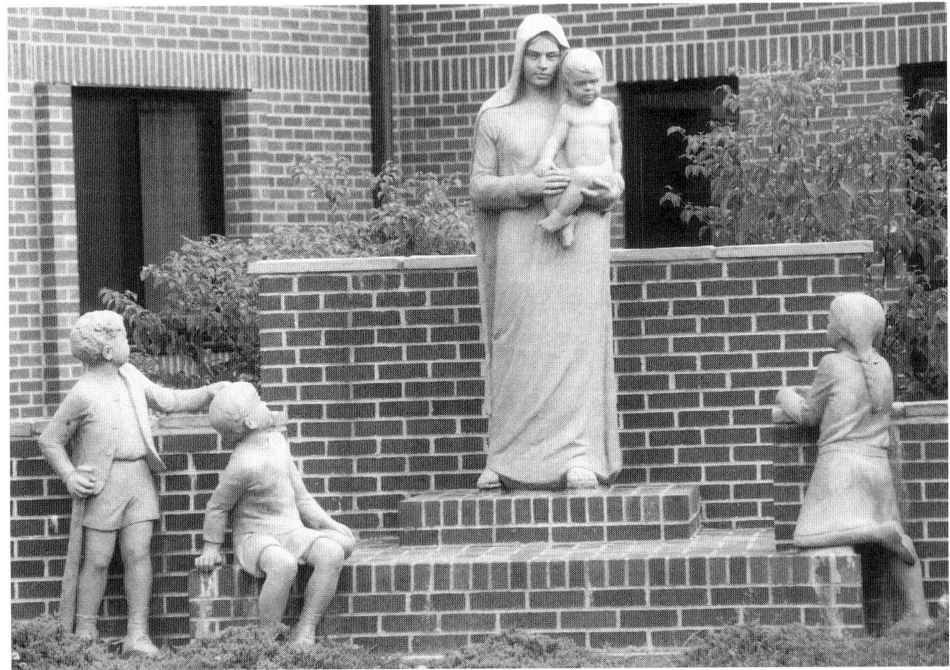

Figure 6.2 *Madonna of the Schools.*

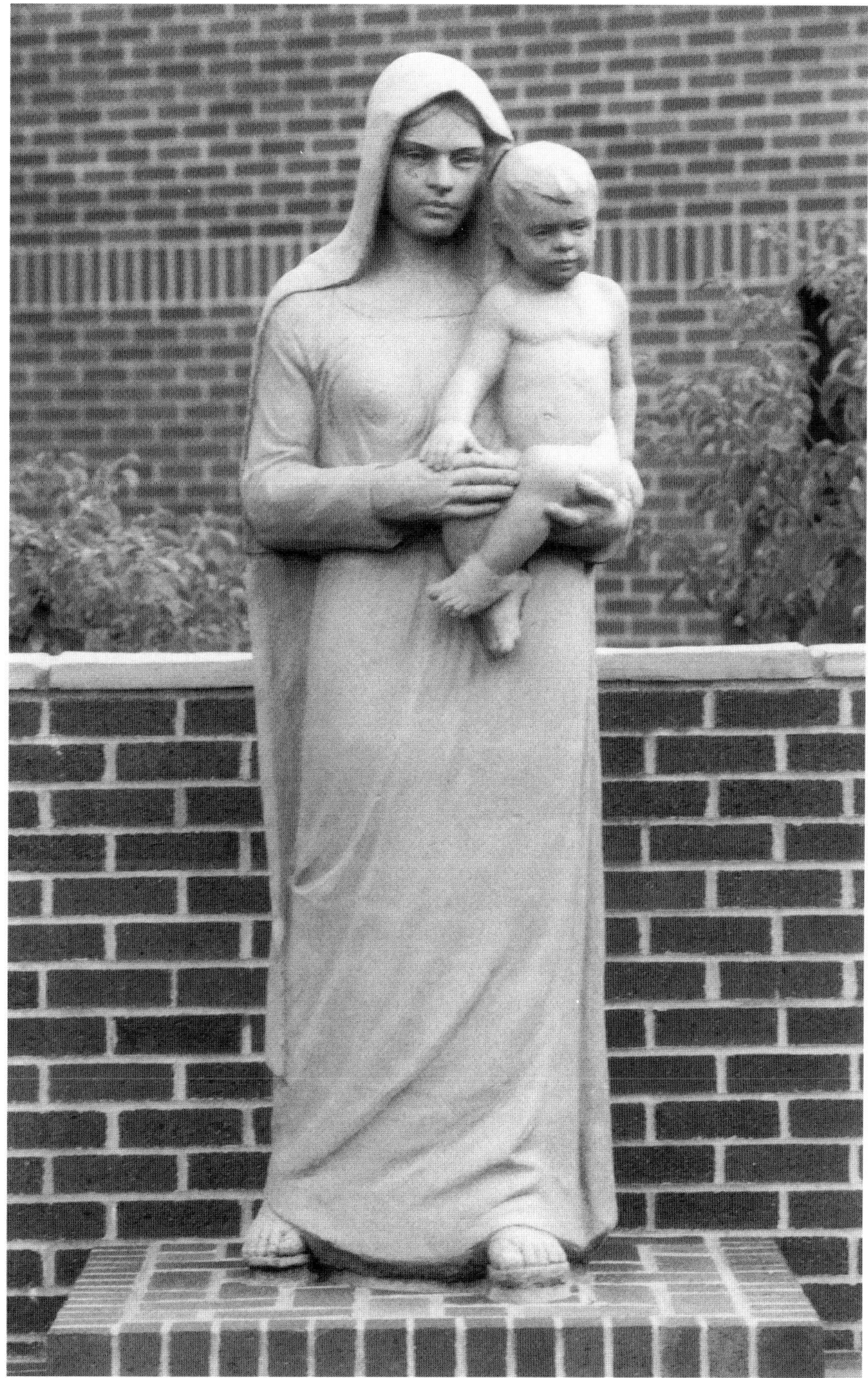

Figure 6.3 Madonna detail.

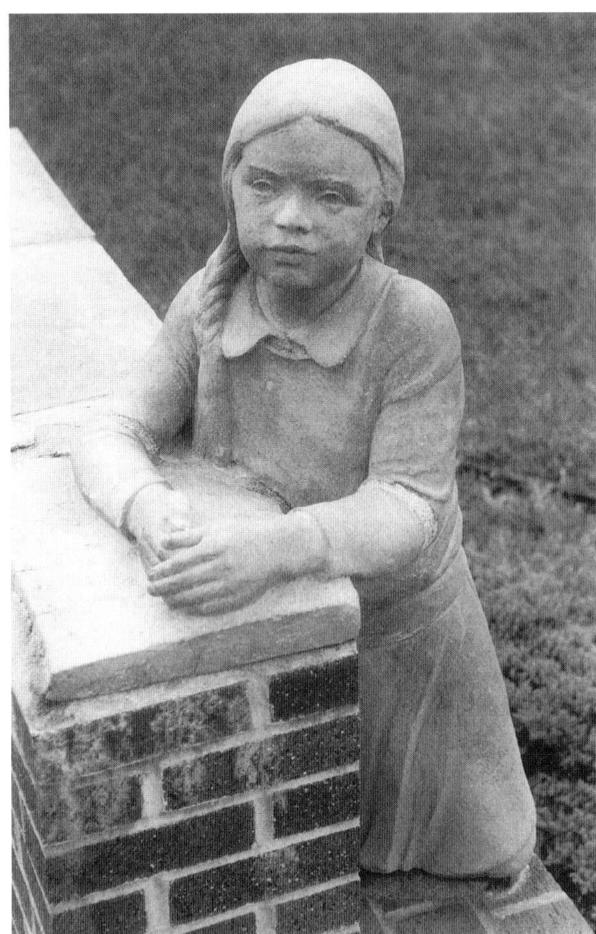

Figure 6.5 Girl detail.

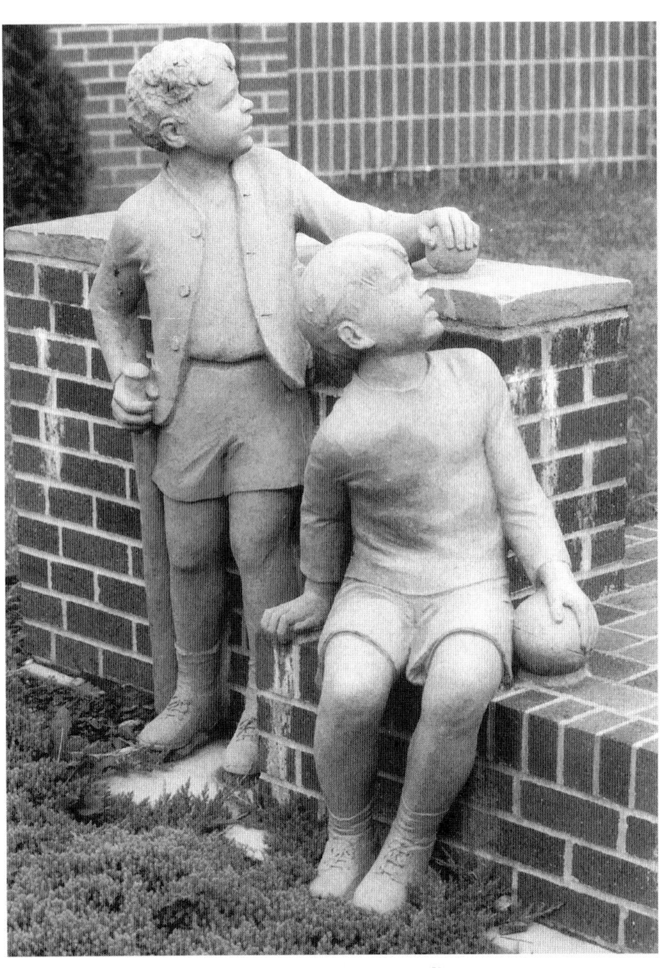

Figure 6.4 Boys detail.

Petersen's sculpture made a considerable stir in the Catholic press, especially since, not long after its installation in fall 1946, he was taken into the Church. It was pictured in or on the cover of a number of publications,[4] one of which described it in some detail, noting that it was "in easy view of the transcontinental Lincoln Highway at a point where more than 15,000 cars pass each day."

The statuary children are the artist's conception of the typical American boyhood and girlhood of the present generation, busy with studies and interested in sports, yet mindful of the indispensable influence of religion in their education and character formation. They have paused momentarily in their playing and studying to gaze up affectionately at the Virgin Mary and the Christ Child, who look down in approval upon them, but who yet seem to be gazing beyond the children with a suggestion of pensive sadness. Is it, perhaps, because they see the uncounted thousands upon thousands of other little children throughout the land who are receiving an "education" which concerns itself only with the mind and the body, but which neglects the soul? What profound symbolism and what a spiritual message for the fathers and mothers of America the artist has incorporated into his masterpiece![5]

Noting his conversion shortly after completion of *The Madonna of the Schools*, the magazine reported the observation of the priest at St. Cecilia, Father Nicholas Steffen: "I cannot but think that Our Lady secured the Grace of Faith for him as a reward for his beautiful and meaningful tribute to her and her Divine Son."[6] When Petersen was contacted a few years later by St. Ansgar's Scandinavian Catholic League for a photograph of *The Madonna of the Schools* and other information about himself and the recent changes in his life, he commented on his conversion. "I had long been in the position of a man looking into a window—seeing my family and my friends in the glow of a great love and wanting to join them, and yet not knowing how until the light of Grace dawned in my soul. Those who have been Catholics from infancy can scarcely realize the convert's peace and joy after his first confession and Holy Communion."[7] The sculpture was also featured in an edition of *Catholic Comics,* which characterized it as "a new original conception of the Blessed Virgin and the Christ Child which combines biblical and modern values in artistic unity." One frame of the comic strip showed a bishop and a parishioner saying, "Mr. Petersen, you are the foremost sculptor in Iowa. Here is our idea." A figure intended to be the artist replies, "Grand. It must be done in a new way, too."[8]

In 1949, the year of his conversion, and into 1950, Petersen produced at least five important religious sculptures, starting with a commission from Regis High School in Cedar Rapids for a figure of Christ the King (Figure 6.6). In the most conventional of his concepts, he depicts a robed figure wearing a crown and standing with arms extended forward slightly. The figure's welcoming or possibly entreating gesture is enhanced by the facial expression, which goes beyond the solemn mien usually found in Petersen's sculptures to suggest compassion or a similar active emotion.

In 1950, Petersen created another full-length figure of Christ, but this one presented a distinctive, highly personal interpretation.

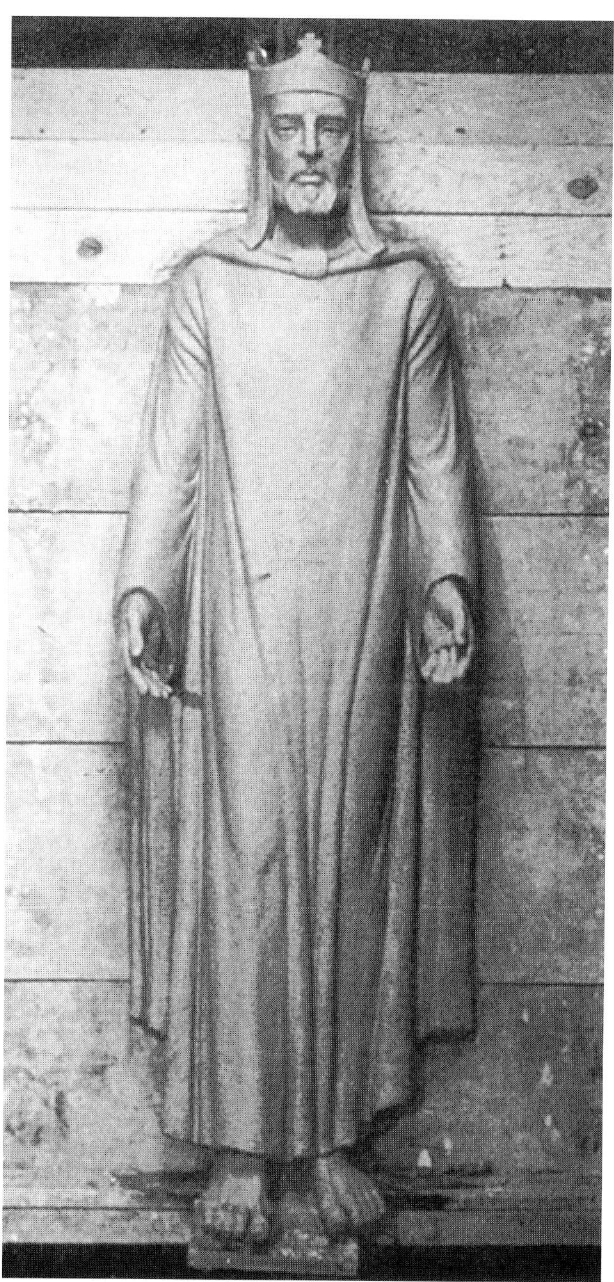

Figure 6.6 *Christ the King*.

Christ with Bound Hands (Figure 6.7) is a postwar image that reflects the sculptor's distress at the current state of humankind. The narrative of the statue arises from the trial and torment of Christ just before he was led to crucifixion. He stands firmly with weight distributed evenly and hands tied in front of him with a rope. He is clothed in the bottom half of a robe which covers his legs and feet almost entirely and creates a strong cylindrical base for the rest of the figure. His chest and arms are exposed, revealing a muscular, pointedly powerful body. The facial expression is one of the most acute of Petersen's career, suggesting a depth of emotion on several levels. A sketch for the piece carries the sculptor's handwritten caption: "all the evils which have kept Him prisoner."[9] On the back of a photograph of *Christ with Bound Hands* in the Christian Petersen Papers is an unattributed explanation: "This concept of Christ grew from Christian Petersen's feeling after World War II concerning the inhumanity of man toward man. The muscular Christ represents power, the power that was meant to be used in goodness by man. But conflict between nations and races, man's self-indulgence and greediness — 'All the evils which have kept him prisoner' — bind the hands, the power, of Christ."[10]

Petersen himself discussed some of the ideas behind his work in an unusually specific comment. An unidentified religious publication apparently ran a photograph of the sculpture and solicited remarks from the artist, whom it described as "a recent convert." The account declared that *Christ with Bound Hands* "embodies the sculptor's conception of Our Savior's appearance at the Court of Pilate," then Petersen explained further.

> *In Christian art, ... the Kingship of Christ has ordinarily been portrayed as the attribute of the Risen and Glorified Savior. It has always seemed significant to me that the exalted title had already been acknowledged during the Passion. In my attempt to crystallize the drama enacted in the presence of Pilate, I have acted upon the conviction that the royal bearing and divine power of the Son of Man must somehow have revealed themselves in His suffering countenance and manacled hands, and that His contempt for the insincerity and futility of the secular might arrayed against Him must have been softened by His infinite mercy. The Kingship of Christ is timeless; and the opposition to it seems timeless, too. In the statue I have tried to depict the timeless King judging His judges.[11]*

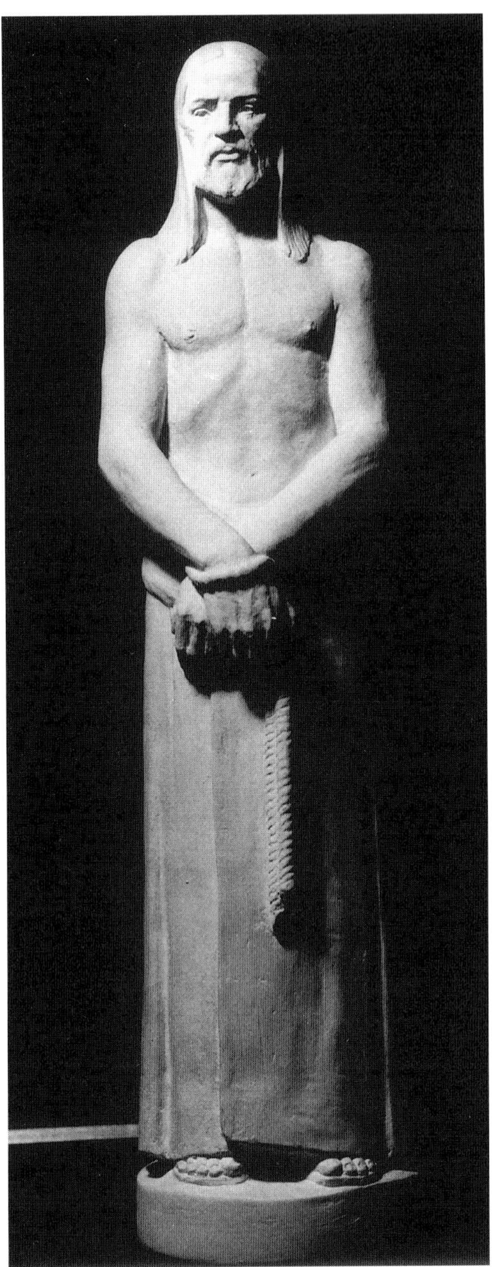

Figure 6.7 *Christ with Bound Hands.*

The original was given to Archbishop Rohlman of the Dubuque diocese,[12] who had presided over Petersen's confirmation in the Church. Soon after the ceremony, Petersen wrote to the Archbishop, "Words are inadequate as expression of my feelings upon being accepted into your family at the beautiful ceremony in your chapel last Friday evening at which you administered the Sacrament of Confirmation on me. ... The last weekend has been of such import that it takes time to assimilate the full significance thereof — I want you to know how much I appreciate all you have done and herewith express my most heartfelt thanks."[13] The sculpture had an impact on a young man who had apparently spent time at the Petersen's home in Gilbert. Bill Merrill, then at the Episcopal Theological Seminary in Cambridge, Massachusetts, wrote to them that he credited the statue with affecting his decision to enter the priesthood.[14]

With the winding down of his career at Iowa State College in the early 1950s, Petersen spent more time on his religious work. His sculpture classes continued to be full, he was occasionally called upon to produce portraits, and he was still waiting for the college to install *Conversations*. But his studio was fully occupied with the production of two monumental statues commissioned by the Catholic community in Iowa: *St. Francis Xavier* of 1950 and *St. Bernard of Clairvaux* of 1951. The earlier sculpture, *St. Francis Xavier*, was a monumental figure of the tireless Jesuit missionary known as the Apostle to the Indies. It was commissioned by the northeastern Iowa parish named for the saint and was to be placed in front of St. Francis Xavier School. The figure itself is twelve feet high, and when combined with its base, the entire piece is twenty-one feet. A newspaper photograph (Figure 6.8) shows the sculptor in his studio in 1950, standing on a giant stepladder as he worked on a full-scale model of the statue, which was cast in terra cotta sections and then mortared together.[15] The saint lifts his crucifix with both confidence and force while his other arm is kept close to the body and holds a gospel book. He wears the robe-like costume of the Jesuit order, with Rosary beads hanging from the belt, and a cloak from which emerges the arm holding the gospel book. The head looks out levelly with a fervent, focused expression at the world to which he displays his elevated crucifix. The figure does not move but stands firmly and evenly on both feet. Yet there is a sense of dynamism about it due largely to the angle at which Petersen places the body. The turn of the head and the presentation of the crucifix also add to the effect of the saint's engagement with the world outside. It is not a figure of contemplation but of action.

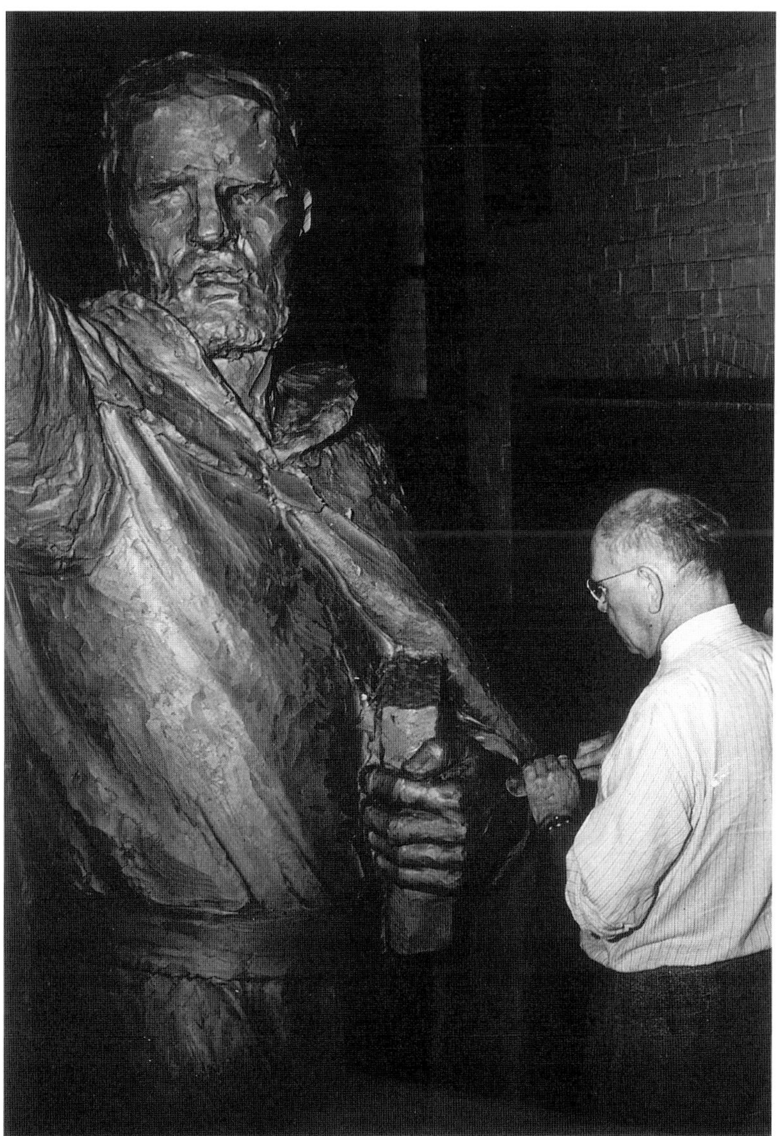

Figure 6.8 Petersen carving *St. Francis Xavier*.

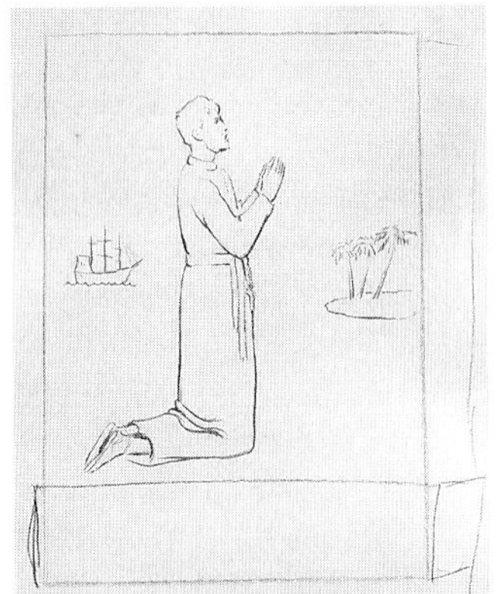

Figure 6.9 Sketch for the base of *St. Francis Xavier*.

The story of St. Francis Xavier (1506–1552) and the devotion he brought to the spread of his faith is further told by the reliefs of the base. Having helped to found the Society of Jesus, or the Jesuit order, with St. Ignatius of Loyola, he traveled in 1540 to southern India, where he gained thousands of converts. He disseminated the gospel throughout the region and into Japan (1549) and was even preparing to work in China when he died. A map of the part of the

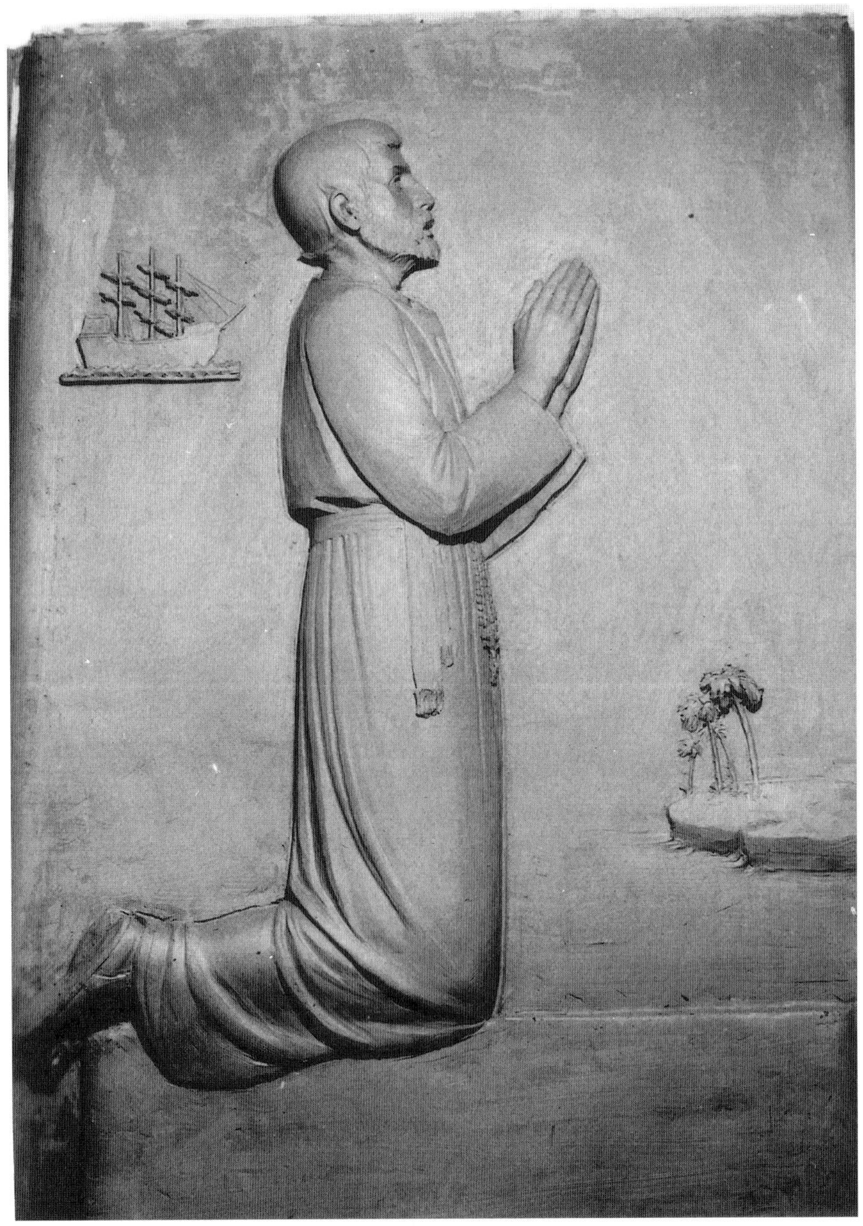

Figure 6.10 Bas-relief for base of *St. Francis Xavier*.

world to which he ministered is pictured on the front of the base. A second relief (Figures 6.9 and 6.10) shows St. Francis kneeling at prayer with small depictions of a sailing ship and an island of palm trees. The ship in the upper left appears to sail toward the saint while in the lower right relief, the palm trees arch toward him as well. The third relief (Figure 6.11) finds him seated on a small, square block teaching four Asian children, an open gospel book on his lap and his arm around one of the children. The large crucifix from his rosary dangles prominently against the block, and an even larger crucifix occupies the upper left corner of the relief. Everyone's attention is on the gospel book from which the saint reads, his pointing finger following along the sentences. The crisp, simple carving of the reliefs shares the calm classicism that characterized some of Petersen's work from the 1930s, such as the dairy building interior.

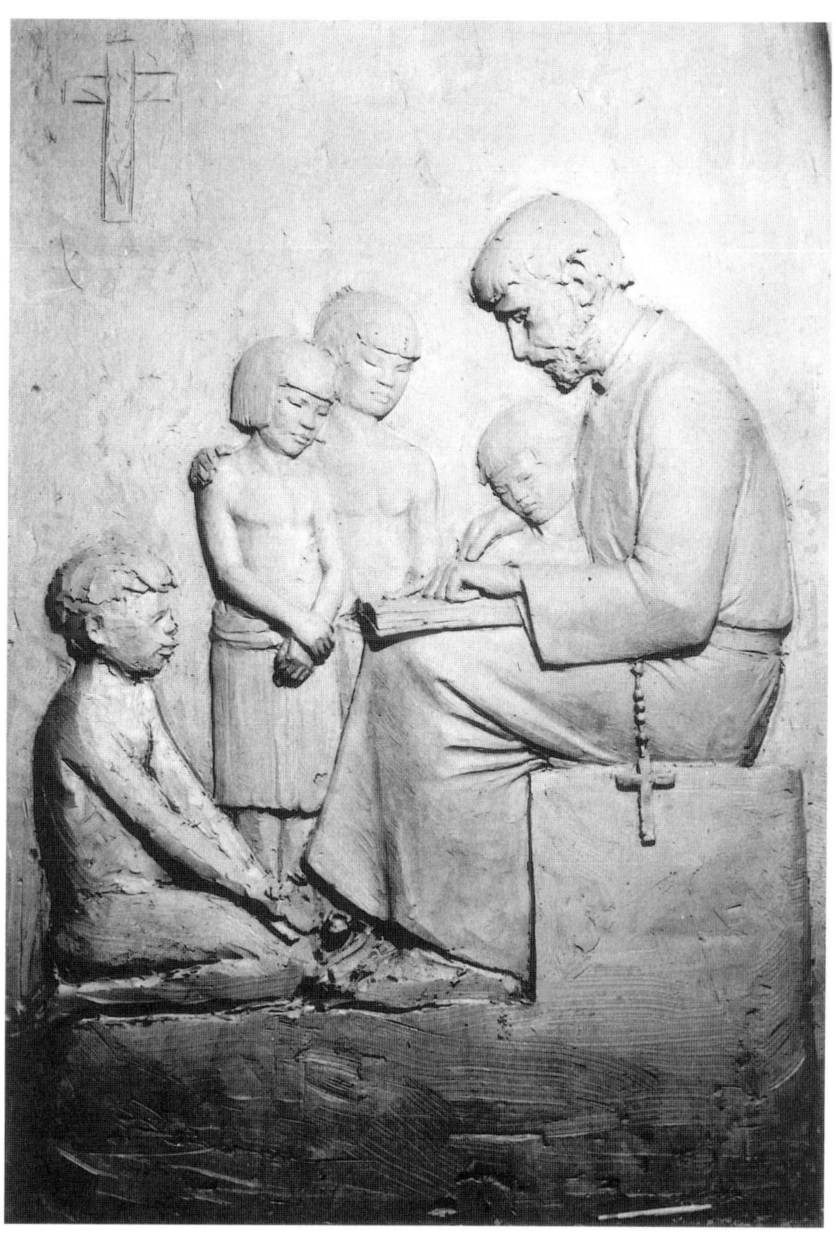

Figure 6.11 Bas-relief for base of *St. Francis Xavier*.

The second monumental sculpture of the early 1950s was the ten-and-a-half-foot-tall *St. Bernard of Clairvaux*, carved for a new theological seminary, Mount Saint Bernard, in Dubuque and now installed outside St. Bernard's parish church at Breda, Iowa. Petersen received the commission from the Board of Governors of the seminary on April 30, 1954, the cost of the statue having been donated by children in the Catholic schools throughout Iowa.[16] Petersen set to work looking at other depictions of the saint — one model came from a Cistercian monastery in northern California[17] — and carried out at least two highly finished clay models of the final conception. For the sculpture itself, Petersen used a twenty-ton block of Bedford limestone from Indiana that he began carving in his studio on St. Patrick's Day (March 17) of 1954 and completed on September 8 of that same year.[18]

The sculpture is a sturdy, straightforward one with no elaboration or excess in its carving. The pared-down simplicity and even plainness of the work is well suited to the depiction of the monk who was known for both his austerity and his energy, and who despised the twisting, dance-like stylings and "monstrous" inventions of the Romanesque (Cluniac) sculpture of his own day.[19] St. Bernard (1090/91–1153) was a wealthy young nobleman when he joined the Cistercian abbey of the Benedictine Order at Cîteaux in 1113. After founding a new abbey at Clairvaux three years later, he added hundreds of monasteries throughout Europe and the British Isles to the Cistercians. As a leader in the spiritual revival of the twelfth century, he used his eloquent speaking ability to preach the Second Crusade (1147–1149) and was a persuasive writer and an active participant in both ecclesiastical and secular life. He was known for his impulsiveness and zeal, both of which are suggested in Petersen's vigorous sculpture. Like St. Francis Xavier, St. Bernard is shown clutching his gospel book next to his body as he steps purposefully forward.

His left hand grips his crosier, a staff that is a symbol of the pastoral duties of a bishop or an abbot. Head looking straight forward, the saint is shown mid-stride with his cloak billowing out slightly behind him on both sides. The figure retains a clear evidence of the stone block from which it was carved, with only the right arm and its crosier breaking away from the mass of the body. The draperies are shallowly carved, but their lines often swing about the body enough to convey a steady, consistent pace as the saint journeys forward. Interestingly, the drapery along the lower leg resembles the whorls found in the sculpture of St. Bernard's time although, as earlier mentioned, it was not a style that the saint himself admired. The face is composed and unrevealing of any emotion other than a determined, focused resolution as the figure moves confidently out into space. The carving of the head is spare and angular, with the planes of the form set in clear juxtaposition to each other. This quality is especially effective as it highlights the cheekbones in the thin face of the ascetic monk who encouraged self-denial in religious practice. Petersen's pared-down sculptural style that presents only the essentials conveys the internal intensity and vitality of a saint who would have liked to retire to a life of religious contemplation but who found himself at the center of the events of his day.

As energetic as this figure is, a clay study for St. Bernard (Figure 6.12) shows that Petersen considered a design of even greater dynamism. The study also depicts the saint in the act of stepping forward, although it may be more of a bodily gesture than the suggestion of actual motion since he appears to be preaching. The body has an almost dramatic twist to it as it accommodates the vigorous gestures of both arms. The right moves up and out from the body as if exhorting his listeners while the left bends sharply across the body to point off to the side. The carving of the drapery follows the activity of the body, especially the loose-fitting sleeves, the left one of which flies out as if it has instantaneously been set in motion by the quick, pointing gesture of the arm. The mouth is open as if speaking, the expression is engaged and alert, and the entire figure is animated, even impassioned. In the end, however, Petersen rejected this spirited rendition for a more self-contained image. The final statue is a less personally interpreted sculpture, exchanging the narrative and emotional possibilities of the model for a less nuanced moment in the life of St. Bernard. Considering Petersen's personal reticence and the tendency throughout his career to downplay the overtly emotional in favor of a more generalized tone, the choice of a more circumspect saint is not surprising.

When Petersen finished his massive sculpture, he turned to the challenge of transporting it across the state and installing it in front of the seminary. According to an article in *The Witness*, the newspaper of the Dubuque diocese, its journey and placement were in themselves an event. For the trip of 246 miles, a support scaffolding was built around the statue,[20] and it was loaded onto a flatbed truck to ride upright. With a Highway Patrol escort, Petersen accompanied his sculpture on the nine-hour drive from Ames to Dubuque over two-lane roads.[21] At the seminary, it was unloaded from the trailer onto a block of ice whose gradual melting slowly settled the statue into place. What were described as "five heavy lines" were used to secure the work, even when uneven melting on one side called for the use of "carbon dioxide fire extinguishers to refreeze the ice and retard its melting." At last, reported the diocese newspaper, "With the final operation complete[,] the statue, which suffered only a few small specks of road tar, began its long vigil over Iowa's new Theological Seminary, Mount Saint Bernard."[22] At the installation ceremony, Joseph Mueller, the bishop of Sioux City, presented the homily during the solemn pontifical mass presided over by Bishop Daley of Des Moines, and the statue itself was blessed by the apostolic delegate to the United States.[23]

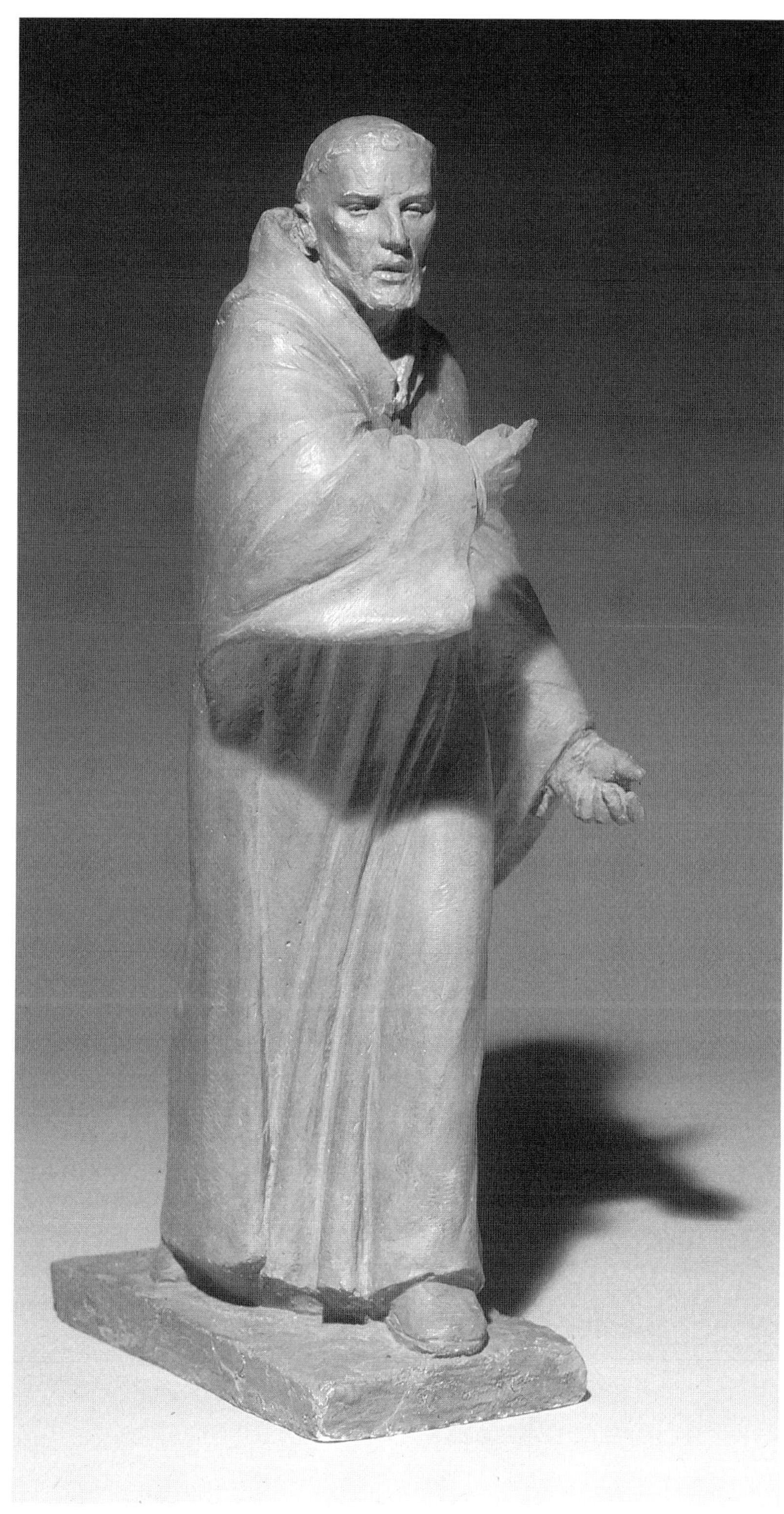

Figure 6.12 Petersen's clay model for *St. Bernard of Clairvaux*.

In fact, the sculpture's vigil was short-lived. Forty-three years later, the seminary having closed, the new owners of the property, the Sisters of the Presentation, offered it to St. Bernard's parish in the small west-central Iowa town of Breda, about eighty miles west of Ames.[24] When the parish council and Father James Hart agreed to accept the statue, their decision instigated a community effort, led by parish historian David Nieland, that once more put St. Bernard on a journey across the state (Figure 6.13). Nieland marshaled services and donations for the transfer to Breda beginning on June 9, 1997.[25] The sculpture again rode upright on a flatbed truck, but this time a crane was used on both ends of the trip to place the sculpture.

Five days later, on June 16, the site in Breda having been prepared and the sculpture sandblasted, the sculpture was settled into its new position in front of St Bernard's, between the church itself and the rectory. (Figure 6.14)[26] The following year, on July 26, 1998, the statue was officially rededicated by Bishop Daniel N. DiNardo of Sioux City, with Father Hart and the new priest at St. Bernard's, Father James R. Smith, participating in the special mass. The arrival of Petersen's monumental sculpture was followed by area publications that noted its welcome in the community, including that of Fr. Hart. "'It's a tremendous work of art and a tremendous gift for the people of the parish,' he declared."[27]

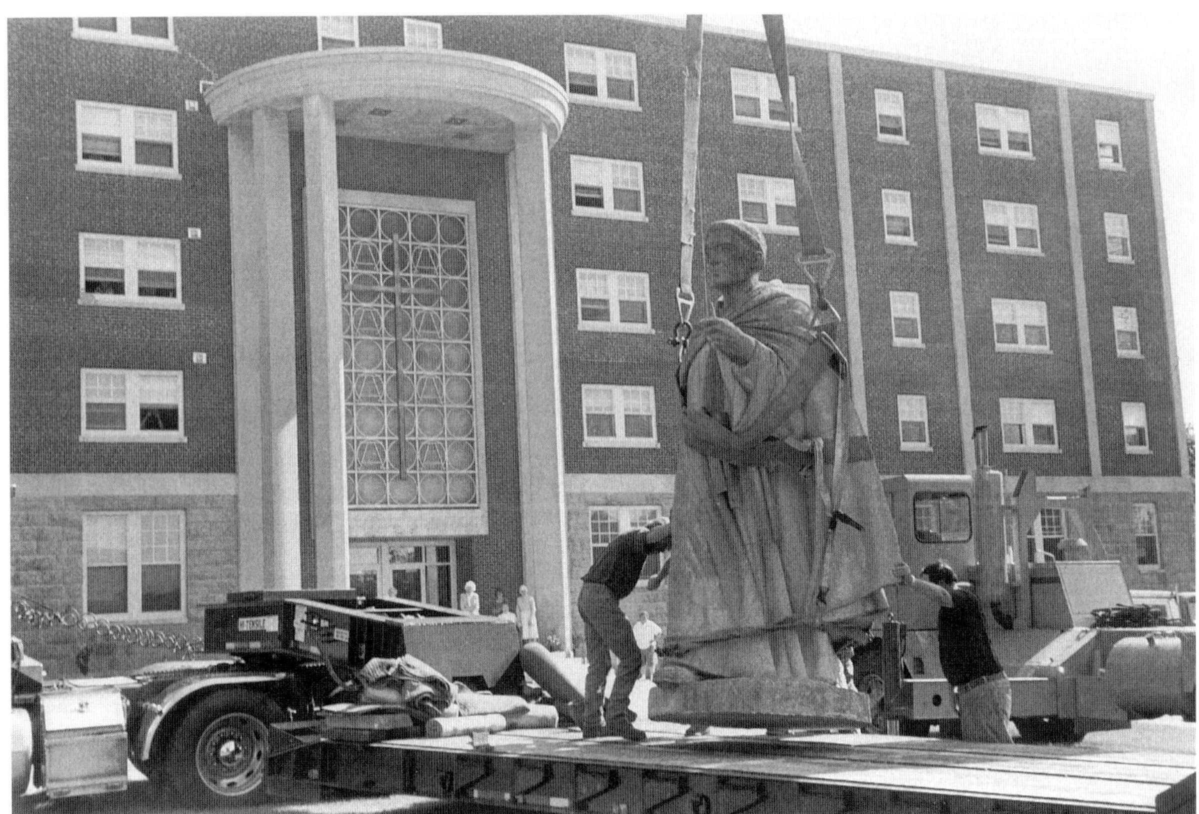

Figure 6.13 *St. Bernard of Clairvaux* being transported from St. Bernard Seminary in Dubuque to present location in Breda, 1998.

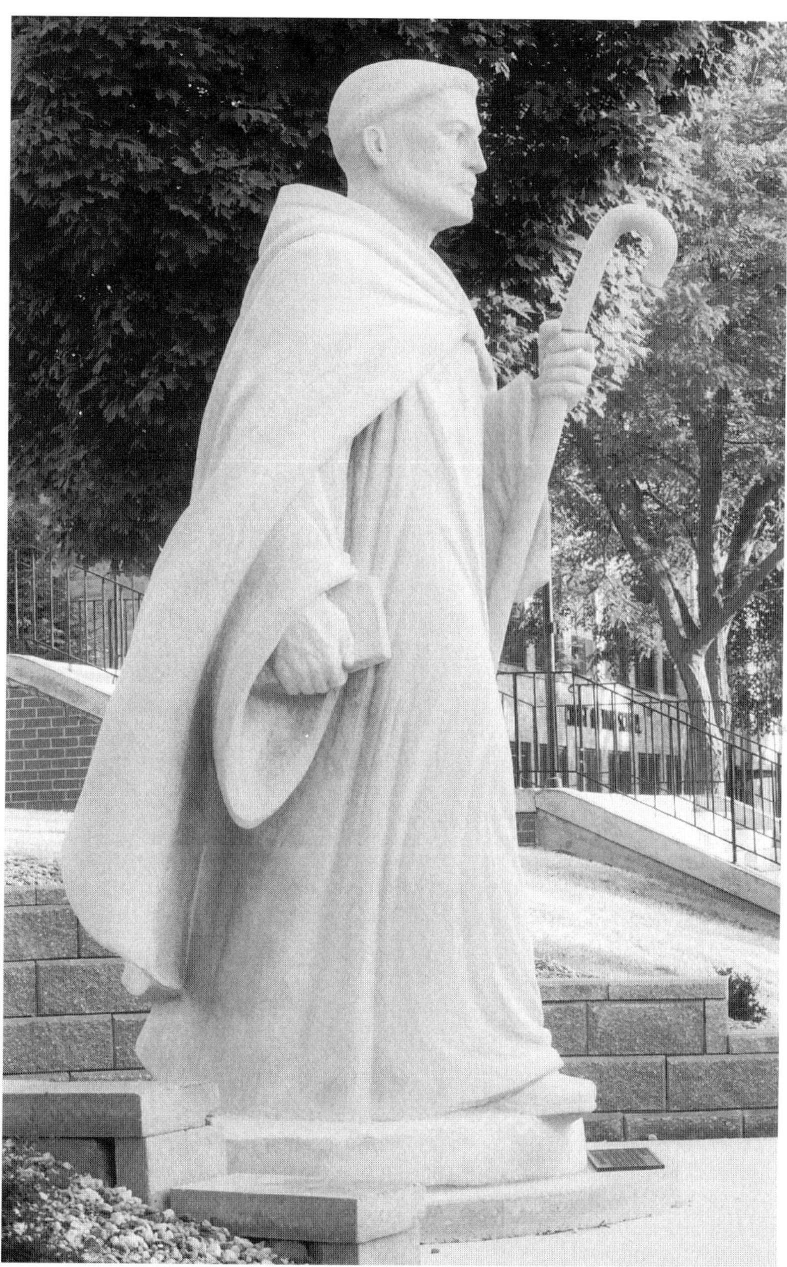

Figure 6.14 *St. Bernard of Clairvaux* at Breda, Iowa.

Near the end of his life, Petersen was given a commission that, while it was not strictly religious, can appropriately be discussed in the context of his late works that attend to matters of the spirit. In 1955, he retired from teaching at Iowa State, although he continued to work in his studio there. Interviewed for a 1959 newspaper article, Petersen reported that no one had replaced him and the courses he had taught for over twenty years. "'There are no classes in sculpture at I.S.C. now,' he said. 'It bothers me a bit — particularly since they set up the five-year architectural course. I don't think an architect can qualify completely unless he has some study of sculpture.'"[28] But he then began teaching a weekly class in sculpture at the Fisher Community Center at Marshalltown, about fifty miles east of Ames. When the founder of the Center and the head of the Fisher Governor Company of Marshalltown, J. William Fisher, modeled for a sculpture demonstration, he commissioned Petersen to continue his work and produce a finished portrait bust (Figure 6.15). As they talked while the work was going on, the idea of a major bronze sculpture for the Center began to be discussed, and in 1958 Fisher commissioned a major sculpture to be the centerpiece of a small lake at the community center. Sending Petersen some materials he would need to begin his work, Fisher wrote, "This will be, surely, a proper beginning for your dreaming and planning for an important sculpture for the grounds of our Community Center. Have fun."[29] He gave the sculptor no particular direction and no serious budget restraints so that he had an opportunity unequalled in his previous career. Unfortunately, this opportunity coincided with a serious decline of health so that Petersen struggled to complete this final work.

He begin designing the sculpture in fall of 1959 and presented his ideas to Fisher, who was pleased and wrote, "We thoroughly enjoyed the stimulating conversation ... and I really do believe we are on the right track for an important new piece of sculpture. I enclose your pencil sketches [which] look just as good to me this morning as they did Sunday evening."[30] But Petersen's plans had not gone far when he suffered a heart attack in November of 1959. This and other health problems delayed the development of his ideas, but by the fall of 1960 he was ready to begin the actual execution of the piece. His design consisted of a father lifting his small son over his head as his child opens wide his arms. (Figures 6.16 and 6.17) In a letter to his old friend from New Jersey, George Nerney, Petersen explained his concept.

I feel that this piece that I have just done is one of the most important pieces I have ever done. I have carried out an idea. ... I have an eight-foot figure there, holding aloft a child. I want to symbolize this generation helping the next generation to see beyond what it has been able to see ... so the child is looking into the future, having a little more light.[31]

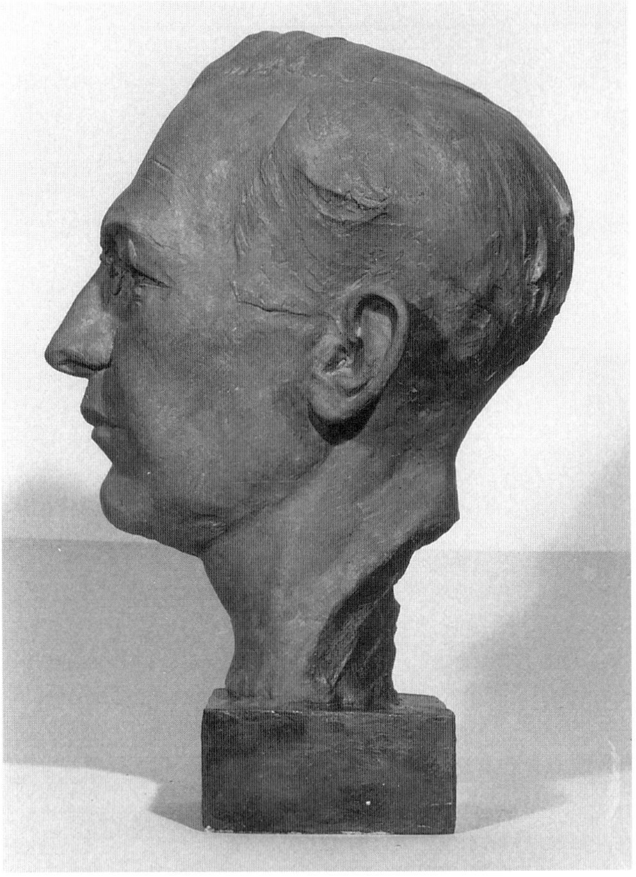

Figure 6.15 Portrait bust of J.W. Fisher by Petersen.

Mounted on a pedestal in the middle of a pool, the male figure steps forward, weight on the left leg and the right dragging slightly behind. The upper half of the body twists slightly to reorient it in a new direction, and the back arches as both hands lift the child. The father's head is tilted backward enough to observe his child's reaction. As the father grasps him at both hips, the boy's back is straight and his arms reach out in a gesture of embrace and also of awe, surprise, or joy. It is not a specifying gesture, since we cannot know the future, as Petersen must have been acutely aware as he designed it. Both father and son are nude figures, and the opportunity to display his capacity to model the anatomy and musculature of the human body must have been rewarding to Petersen after so many years of being careful not to offend by the use of nudity. Perhaps he recalled the classical rationale for the nude: that nudity represented idealism and was a symbol of the unadorned truth.

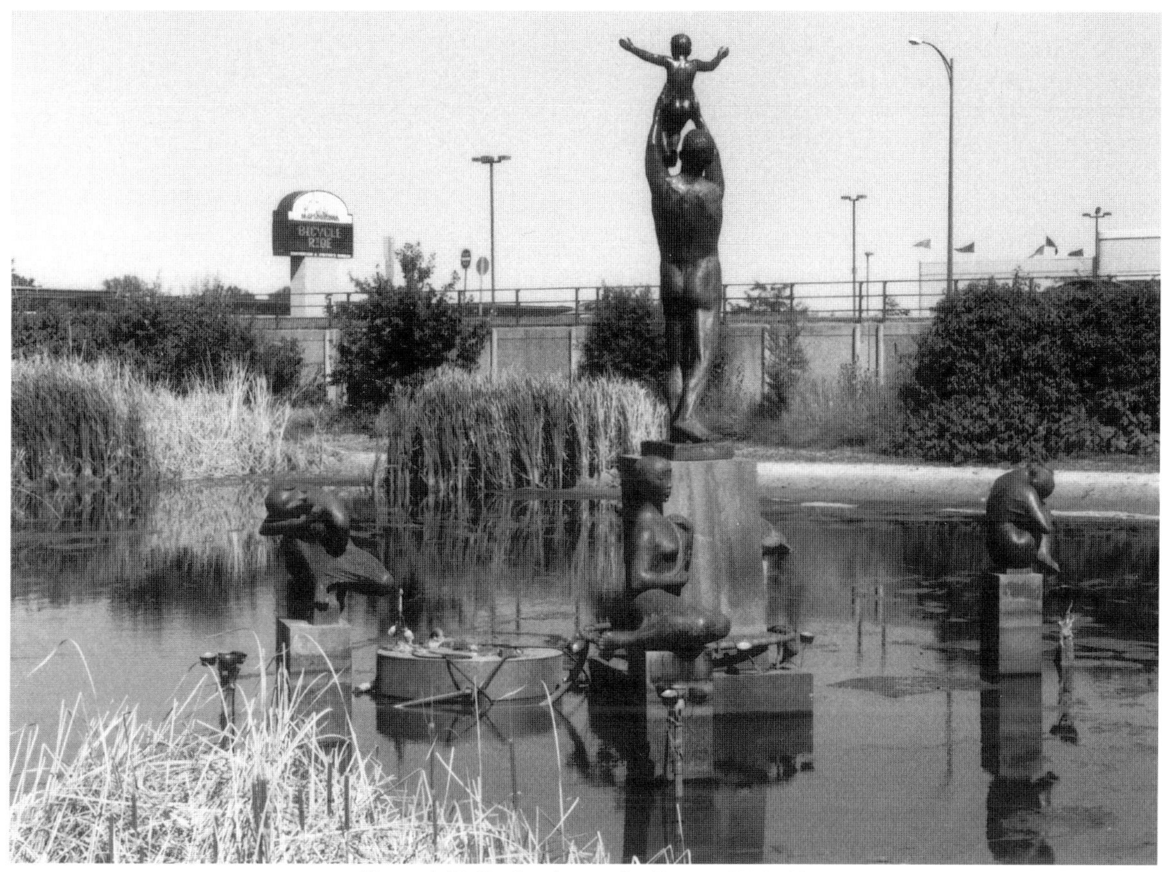

Figure 6.16 *Dedication to the Future*, 1959–61.

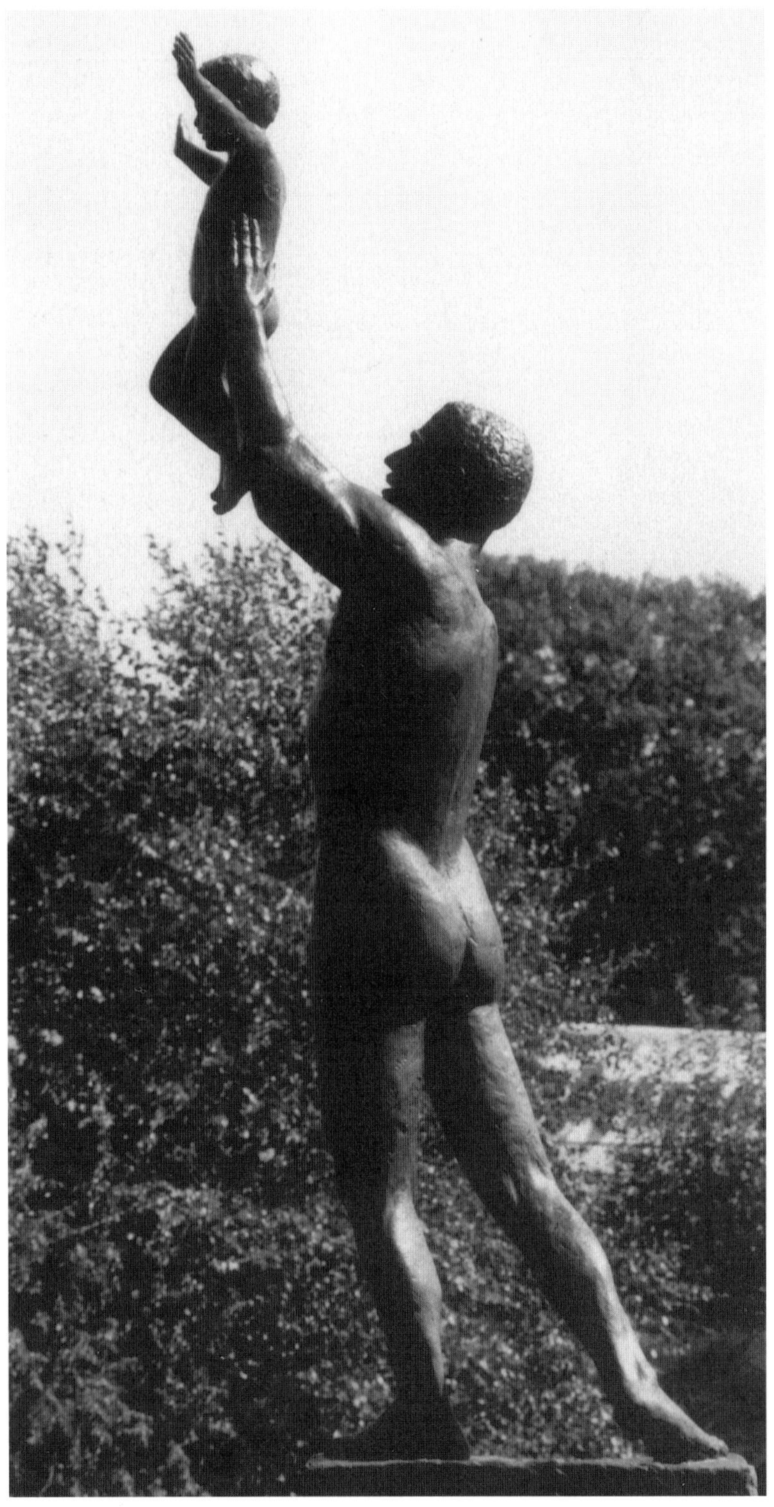

Figure 6.17 *Dedication to the Future*, detail.

The integration of architecture, landscape, and water had been an enduring concern throughout Petersen's career, and his last work involved all of them. The tall statue is centered in a large pool of water so that it must always be seen from afar and never close up enough to read details of expression or surface. The overall line and broad gestures, then, must succeed in conveying the idea of the heritage and hope of one generation passed to another. The considerable space between the viewer standing at the edge of the pool and the sculpture itself helps to isolate and focus the image, emphasizing its heroic quality. Jets of water spray along the pedestal, creating an almost cloudlike form from which the sculpture seems to emerge. The child is lifted so that he sees outward past the pool and the civility of the cultural center onto a world of increasing complexity and unpredictability.

Petersen battled pain, fatigue, and serious illness in this last year of his life as he struggled to complete this commission. After Fisher approved his model, Petersen planned to begin the actual sculpting in the fall of 1960. But ill health continued, and in December of 1960 he was diagnosed with cancer. Nevertheless, using three tons of clay brought in January, 1961, to a large room in the botany building, he modeled the full-scale figure from a special scaffolding arranged by Professor Bernard Slater of the architecture department, an old friend. (Figure 6.18) He also provided student assistants for the weakened artist, who could mount the scaffolding only by pulling himself with his arms.[32] In early February, he underwent surgery, but determined to finish his sculpture, he returned to the studio later that month. He finished working the clay in March and handed over the task of preparing it for bronze casting. Only days before his death, he approved the casting and signed the piece from his hospital bed. In a remarkable feat of perseverance, he saw the commission for *Dedication to the Future* through, just before his death on April 4, 1961. His wife, Charlotte, later attributed his determination to his concern over the "weakening of the idea of the dignity of man." Recalling his state of mind during those last days, she explained, "He wanted to leave this work to remind youth."[33]

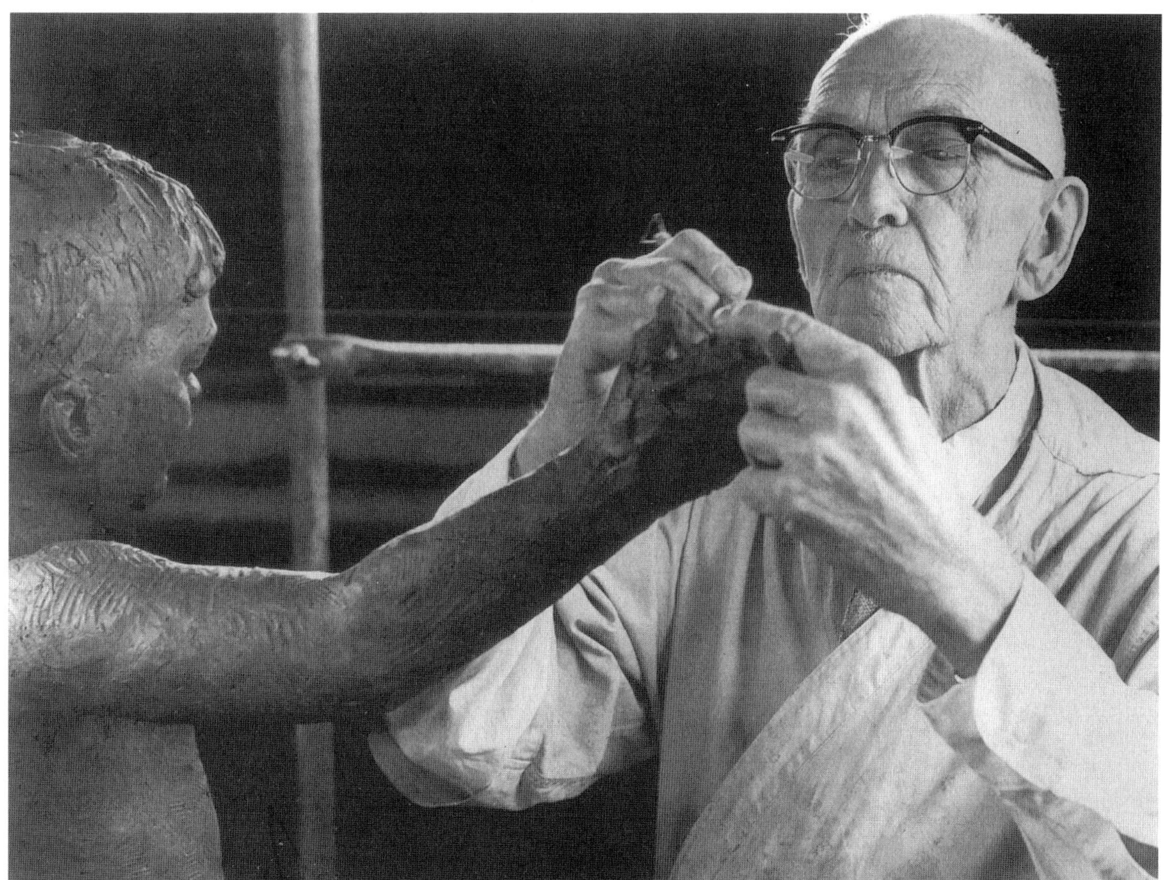

Figure 6.18 Petersen working on *Dedication to the Future*, 1961.

NOTES

1. Bliss, Patricia, L., *Christian Petersen Remembered,* Ames: Iowa State University Press, 1986, 147.

2. Bliss, 148.

3. "New Statue of St. Bernadette," *Women's Catholic Forester,* October 1945, 45(11): cover, 7.

4. Among the publications noting the sculpture were *Sorrowful Mother Novena Notes,* August 29, 1947, 11(34): cover illustration, 2; "Noted Sculptor Designs New Madonna," *The Catholic School Journal,* October 1947, 270; "Noted Iowa Sculptor Joins Church," *St. Ansgar's Bulletin*, undated clipping in Christian Petersen Papers; and an illustration included in an unidentified Danish publication, undated clipping in Christian Petersen Papers.

5. *The Apostle*, A Publication of the Mariannhill Fathers, September 1951, 34(9): cover and description inside.

6. Ibid., n.p.

7. Typescript attached to letter to Petersen from St. Ansgar's Scandinavian Catholic League, New York, April 12, 1950. Christian Petersen Papers.

8. "Shrines of America," *Catholic Comics*, December 1947, 2(3).

9. Reproduced in Wilson, Geraldine L., *Christian Petersen, Sculptor*, Ames: Iowa State University Press, 1962, 27.

10. Unattributed caption on back of photograph of *Christ with Bound Hands*, Christian Petersen Papers. This same caption reports that the original of the statue was given to Archbishop Rohlman and that three copies were made.

11. Unidentified, undated typescript on St. Cecilia's Rectory stationery, Christian Petersen Papers. The article was entitled "Convert Sculptor Completes Statue for Archbishop Rohlman" and was accompanied by a photograph. "News item" is written at the bottom of the sheet in what appears to be Petersen's handwriting.

12. According to the above-cited typescript, the sculpture was designed for the Archbishop "as an expression of long-standing admiration for His Excellency." The gift is also cited in a captioned photograph of the sculptor at work on *Christ with Bound Hands, The Des Moines Register*, March 6, 1966, clipping in Christian Petersen Papers.

13. Handwritten draft of letter from Petersen to Archbishop Rohlman, December 20, 1949. Christian Petersen Papers.

14. Undated letter to Petersen from Bill Merrill, Christian Petersen Papers.

15. "A Petersen Statue," undated, unidentified clipping, Christian Petersen Papers. The caption reads: "A 12-foot statue of St. Francis Xavier, which stands at entrance of St. Francis School at Dyersville, is work of Christian Petersen. Sculptor is shown at work on heroic-size figure in his studio in 1950."

16. "St. Bernard Statue Gift of Ia. Catholic School Children," *The Witness*, September 23, 1954. The brochure for the installation ceremonies at Breda adds the information that the money came from the children's Lenten savings. "Re-Dedication of the Statue of Saint Bernard at Breda, Iowa, July 26, 1998."

17. Ibid.

18. Owens, Herb, "I.S.C. Sculptor: Freed of 'Duty,' He Enjoys Life," *The Des Moines Tribune*, January 12, 1959. The reporter characterized this work as "one of Petersen's most strenuous productions." The sculptor was sixty-nine years old at the time.

NOTES

19. It was St. Bernard of Clairvaux who wrote the infamous criticism of the vividly carved, imaginative style of French Burgundian architecture and sculpture that issued from the abbey at Cluny. Considering Petersen's often-professed dislike of modern art, it is possible he had sympathy with the saint's displeasure with what he regarded as excess in art. Expressing his irritation with the elaborate architecture and decoration of churches and monasteries, St. Bernard wrote, "I say naught of the vast height of your churches, their immoderate length, their superfluous breadth, the costly polishings, the curious carvings and paintings which attract the worshipper's gaze and hinder his attention [to Christ]. ... What profit is there in those ridiculous monsters, in that marvelous and deformed comeliness, that comely deformity?" Quoted in Holt, Elizabeth Gilmore, *A Documentary History of Art*, Vol.I: *The Middle Ages and the Renaissance*, New York: Doubleday Anchor Books, 1957, 18–22.

20. Petersen apparently felt that the transporters took more trouble than they needed to. Handwritten on the back of a photograph of *St. Bernard of Clairvaux* crated up before the trip is his comment, probably to his daughter, Mary. "Hi Honey — here are some of the pictures Jon Morgan took for the A.P. — they show somewhat the crating job they did. Personally I think they went to an unnecessary lot of work but they went ahead on their own." Christian Petersen Papers.

21. Their route in 1954 started north from Ames on Highway 69, then east on Highway 175, north again on Highway 14 and then Highway 3 east to take Highway 52 into Dubuque. *The Witness*, September 23, 1954.

22. *The Witness*.

23. *The Witness* and brochure for reinstallation: "Re-Dedication of the Statue ..."

24. The statue was offered by the Congregational Leader of the Sisters of the Presentation, Sister Jacqueline Quillin, PBVM. Soon afterward, in the fall of 1996, Fr. Hart and David A. Nieland inspected the statue in Dubuque. "Re-Dedication of the Statue ..."

25. The cost of the transportation was underwritten by George Crouse, owner of Crouse Cartage Company in Carroll, Iowa. The truck tractor was driven by Todd and Teresa Crouse of Lake View and the semitrailer was the donation of Dale and Jean Tiefenthaler of Breda. The crane that lifted it off its base in front of the seminary was contributed by Conlon Construction Company of Dubuque. Burns, Douglas, "Statue finds home in name and spirit at St. Bernard," Carroll *Times Herald*, undated clipping in history files of St. Bernard parish.

26. The new base for the statue in Breda was supported in part by parishioners Herb and Marlys Schulte; Jerry Wessling sandblasted the limestone; and Dale Tiefenthaler contributed the crane. "Re-Dedication of the Statue ..."

27. Hauser, Tony, "St. Bernard graces parish," *Carroll Today*, June 13, 1997.

28. Owens.

29. J.W. Fisher to Petersen, October 3, 1958. Christian Petersen Papers.

30. J.W. Fisher to Petersen, September 15, 1959. Christian Petersen Papers.

31. Wilson, 83.

32. Bliss, 163. From an interview with Charlotte Petersen.

33. "Sculptor's message: Keep dignity of man," unidentified newspaper clipping, June 9, 1974. Christian Petersen Papers.

CHARLOTTE PETERSEN:
HER HUSBAND'S "MUSE"

PATRICIA LOUNSBURY BLISS

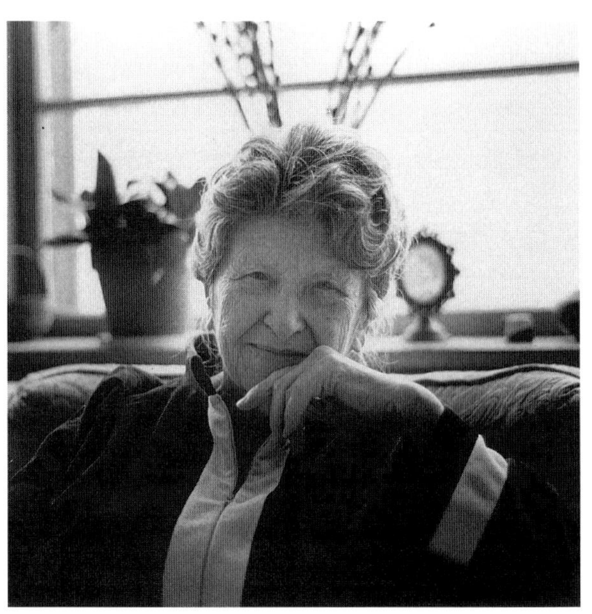

Charlotte Petersen.

Although friends and relatives were not enthusiastic about their wedding in 1931, both Christian Petersen and Charlotte Garvey were sure of themselves. For the next thirty years, the tall Danish-American sculptor and the small Irish woman were a contrasting but compatible pair. He was forty-five; she was thirty-one. "He needed my youth and enthusiasm, and I needed his maturity and strength. We were a good match and we knew it," Charlotte summed up in 1983.

All who knew her during their years together would agree that Charlotte was the perfect partner for Christian. She had a blithe spirit, was a born optimist, and possessed keen intellect. Combine those with her sturdy Irish character and leprechaun-style kind of humor, add a solid religious faith, and you have just a glimpse of the personality facets that made a delightful woman sparkle like a well-cut emerald.

During our many hours of interviews for the biography of her sculptor husband, Charlotte's often eloquent words and constant enthusiasm firmly established that she loved life, laughter, children, all the arts and artists, her friends, needy strangers, young people, and — above all — her husband Christian Petersen and their daughter, Mary.

A lifetime student of the Bible, Charlotte was totally dedicated to her Church. She would consult an appropriate patron saint on any stressful occasion. Once she asked one of her favorite saints to intercede for her in an "emergency." Charlotte had walked to St. Thomas Aquinas Church and was short on time. She prayed: "Please get me safely across this street, otherwise I'll either be dead or late for mass."

One of the parishioners who witnessed the scene later reported that Charlotte held her head high, both hands extended upward and outward, and immediately halted two-way, four-lane traffic on what then was U.S. Highway 30 through campustown Ames. She then jaywalked with dignity to St. Thomas Aquinas Church. Every car or truck had stopped, no one shouted epithets or insults, and no horns honked. Her friend noted: "The saint watching over transcontinental highway traffic drivers had heeded her plea. Charlotte was always in close touch with those saints."

She was also a woman with a firm sense of resolve. A close friend explained, "If Charlotte doesn't want to talk about something, she'll set her Irish jaw and simply 'clam up.'" During the research process for *Christian Petersen Remembered*, Charlotte politely evaded discussing her childhood and growing-up years, always saying firmly that her early life story wasn't important, so she would talk only about her "years with Christian." Not having met him until she was thirty-one years old, she also refrained from talking about Christian's forty-three years before they met, always insisting that "Because I wasn't there, and I won't even talk about that."

Despite Charlotte's reticence, it's important to emphasize that she did occasionally acknowledge that a few events in her early life had a later bearing on life with Christian — and these might be shared with readers. For example, she explained that her family had lived and farmed on the bleak plains of South Dakota, where country schools were sparse, underfunded, and operated only through the elementary grades.

When she was fourteen, her parents wanted Charlotte to have a high school education. They arranged to send her to Belvidere, Illinois, to live with and work for their friend Juliet Sager, a well-educated career woman who resided with her elderly mother in their large old family mansion. Charlotte worked her way through high school helping the Sagers with housework and kitchen chores and becoming part of their family.

In return, Miss Sager became Charlotte's benefactor, enrolling her in high school and encouraging her to learn all she could about literature, the arts, and secretarial skills. She often treated Charlotte with trips to Chicago for symphony concerts, libraries, art museums, educational lectures, ballet or dance programs, choral concerts, the opera — all the arts. Charlotte's mentor also financed a post–high school secretarial schooling for her bright seventeen-year-old friend, who ended up as the top student in the class and won an immediate job as an office secretary.

And that's how Charlotte Petersen became an earthly ambassador for all the "Muses" of the arts at an early age. She became another, special kind of "muse" in her later years with Christian, as we shall later see.

There's a difference in those two words "Muse" and "muse" that needs emphasis.

"Muses" with a capital "M" refers to the ancient classical Greek mythology of the nine "patron goddesses of the arts:" Calliope (Muse of epic poetry and eloquence), Euterpe (music or lyric poetry), Erato (love poetry), Polymnia (Muse of oratory or sacred poetry), Clio (history), Melpomene (tragedy), Thalia (comedy), Terpsichore (choral song and dance), and Urania (astronomy).

Charlotte loved all those arts and always encouraged and admired talented people who pursued them. She had wanted to be a ballet dancer when she was in her early teens, but explained "By the time I matured, I realized I wouldn't ever have a body built for professional dance. But I've always enjoyed dancing." (There's the influence of Terpsichore.)

She loved poetry and wrote it throughout her lifetime. But despite requests from her friends, she rarely shared it with others. And she wrote love poems for Christian that only he saw or heard. (There are Euterpe, Calliope, and Polymnia and Eros.)

The only published poems by Charlotte appeared in a Christmas greeting booklet, illustrated by Christian, of poems for their daughter Mary. This is one of them:

Charlotte could ferret out from memory a poem she loved fifty years previously and quote it verbatim. For example, when Christian was sketching his concept for the *Marriage Ring* fountain for the home economics school at Iowa State College, she suggested the legend and theme carved into the outer terra cotta tiles of the reflecting pool, quoting James Whitcomb Riley's "The Hired Man's Faith in Children."

When Christian was refining his sketches for a beautiful small sculpture and fountain for the outdoor entry façade of Roberts Hall in 1936, Charlotte remembered a poem by William Aspenwall Bradley, "Sancta Ursula." She had read it in 1917 in a *Century* magazine loaned by her friend and mentor Juliet Sager. "When I recited it to Christian," she recalled in 1984, "he loved it, too. It

*You wanted a penny
When there were so many
Lovely things to see.*

*Why, You did not even hear
The cheerful little note
From the Meadowlark's throat;
Nor see
The corn as it peeped through
And waved 'hello' to you,
Nor the turkey gobbler
Strut and spread his wings.
No,
You did not see these things.*

*You wanted a penny
When there were so many
Lovely things to see.*

*Oh, Mary!
Only grownups do that.*

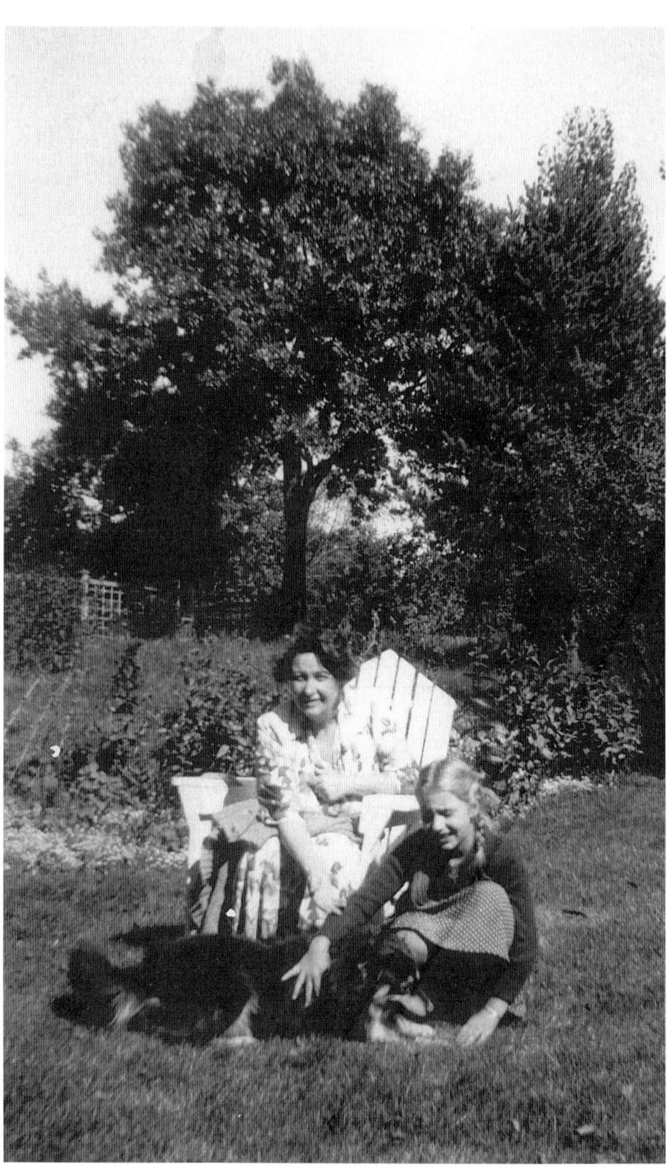

Charlotte and Mary Petersen with dog "Tink"
at their Gilbert home.

reminded both of us what life in a women's dormitory at a college might be like, and it tells of the hopes and dreams of a young woman — all young women, no matter what era they're in. I was young and full of dreams when I read it. I never forgot it."

Carved in the terra cotta tiles of the fountain is the last line of the poem, "... all her dreams start here or here abide."

As for the Muse of tragedy, Melpomene, Christian and Charlotte totally shared enjoyment of opera and always attended performances at the Chicago opera house "sitting up there in the cheap seats," she explained. She always brought extra handkerchiefs "in case it was an extra tragic opera." They also loved theater and drama, and often attended plays or movies. On Saturdays, through the decades, they listened to Metropolitan Opera performances on radio.

Thalia, the Muse of comedy, was a perennial influence on Christian and Charlotte's years together. In Ames, Iowa, Charlotte enjoyed participating in "Playmakers," a community theater performing group. Usually she was chosen to perform in comedies,

but once she won a major dramatic role that had earlier been played by famous actress Ethel Barrymore on Broadway. Studying her role in the script early one morning, she noticed Christian making a rapid sketch of her. He told her to stay just as she was because "You look just like you did when I fell in love with you."

He finished the sketch and handed it to her. "It was a marvelous cartoon," she said. "There I was, my hair in curlers, in my old housecoat ... looking just like I really did, not at all like Ethel Barrymore."

On another occasion, Charlotte dressed in her finest outfit for their first university president's reception honoring the faculty. She swept into the living room with her hat, gloves, and finery, and Christian complimented her elegant appearance. Charlotte remarked: "Tomorrow, all those people there tonight will remember me as one classy dame!"

The Muse in charge of history is Clio. Charlotte Petersen had an enduring sense of history: her friends accused her of being a "packrat" because she saved every scrap of paper, every sketch, every document regarding Christian's sculpture career. All those items comprise the Christian Petersen Papers, at the Department of Special Collections in the Iowa State University Library. They are a treasure trove of irreplaceable memorabilia. Charlotte gave the collection to the library a few years after Christian's death in 1961.

His wife's ability to research subjects and record historical data in her flawless shorthand and typed pages helped Christian in many ways. She wrote letters from his dictation, lecture notes for his speeches, and reports or inquiries regarding his work. In the formative stages of the magnificent *Dairy Industry Mural* and the dynamic *Veterinary Medicine Mural* with *The Gentle Doctor* figure, she researched and wrote concise proposal summaries of the dairy technology and veterinary technology depicted in the landmark sculptures Christian later created.

And what about Urania, the ninth Muse, of astronomy? One of Charlotte's favorite sayings was: "If you want to reach for the stars, first you have to plant your feet firmly on the ground and get to work." She loved the order of the heavenly universe and its Creator.

Thus the nine Muses (with a capital "M") influenced Charlotte's life. In her own special way, Charlotte became a contemporary "muse," spelled with a small "m." That word represents "the spirit regarded as inspiring a poet or other artist; source of genius or inspiration." (*New Heritage Dictionary*) From the day they met, she was Christian Petersen's one-woman muse, encouraging and enhancing his well-being and his long and productive career as a sculptor.

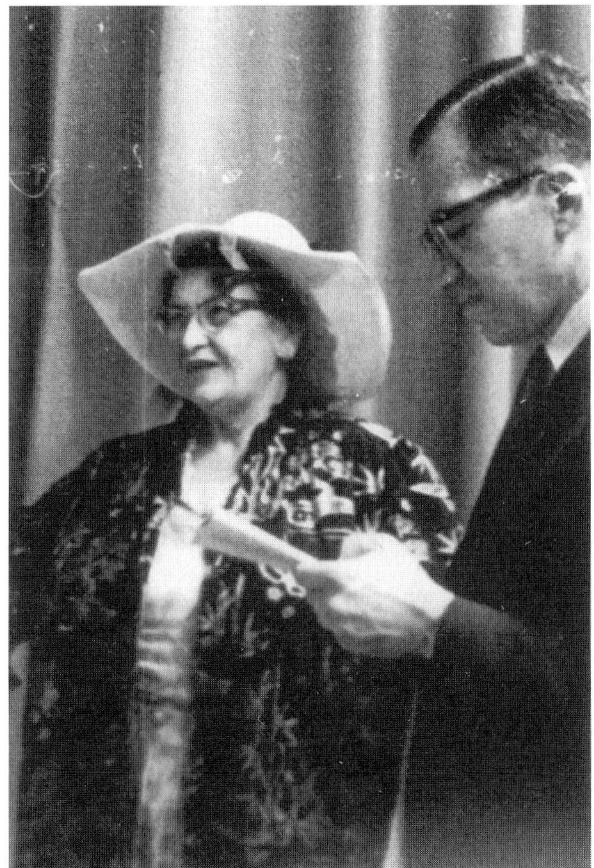

Charlotte dressed in costume for a
Playmakers' production.

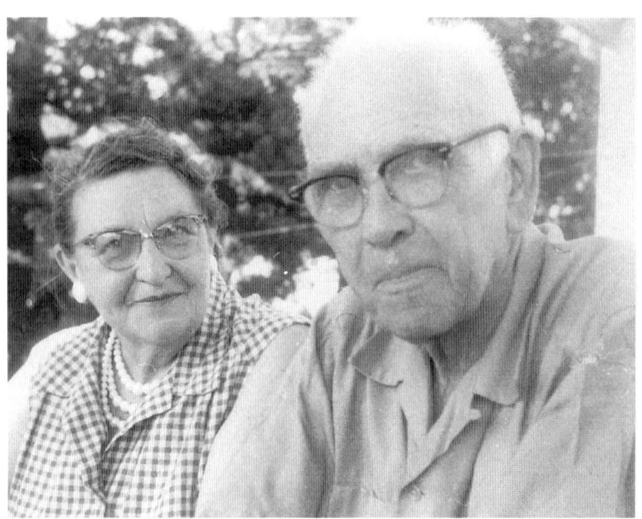

Charlotte and Christian near the end of the artist's life.

She never ceased being his artistic advocate.

In 1984, she wistfully expressed three special wishes:
1. That each of Christian's campus sculptures could be permanently marked with his name, the date, and title of the piece.
2. That his outdoor sculptures be preserved and protected from vandalism and weather deterioration.
3. That Christian would be honored and recognized as an American regional artist who left a lasting heritage of major landmark sculptures for future generations to enjoy.

Thanks to the combined efforts of Lynette Pohlman and her staff, Iowa State University, and the contributions of students, alumni, and friends of Iowa State, Charlotte's three wishes have been fulfilled.

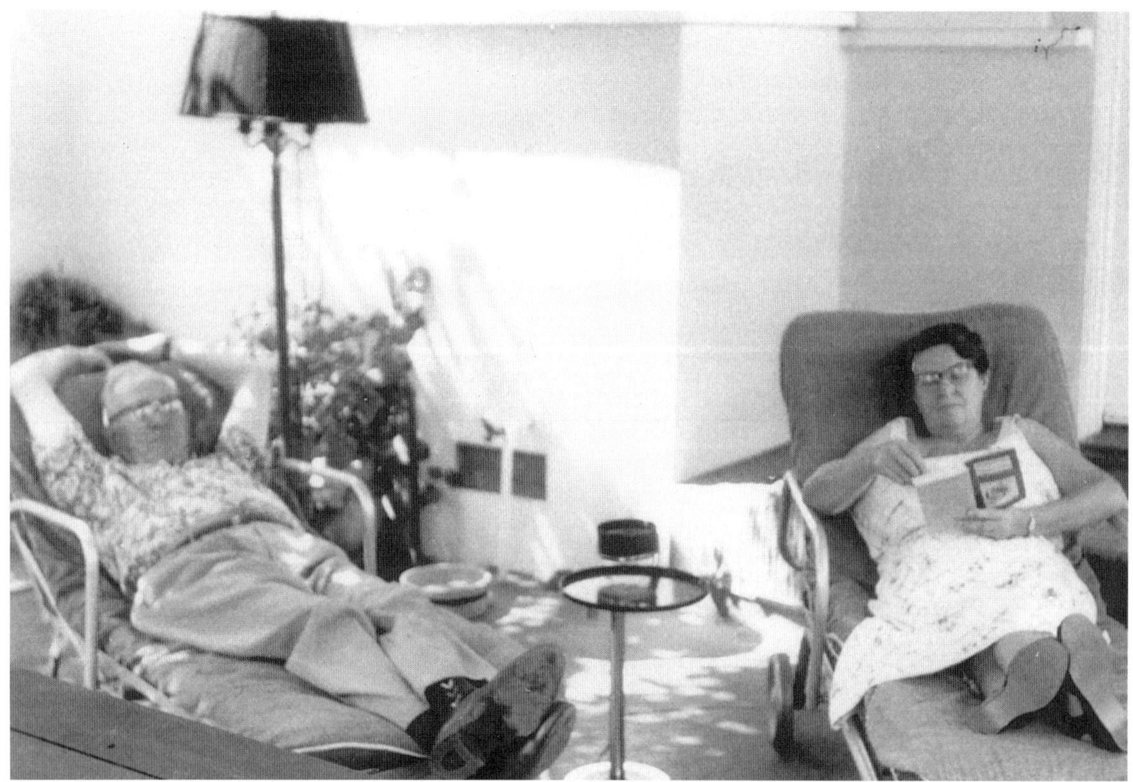

The couple relaxing at home.

INSIGHTS GAINED DURING CONSERVATION

LINDA MERK-GOULD

Inside Christian Petersen's Art:
Insights Gained during Conservation

During the creation of his artwork, Christian Petersen collaborated with Paul Cox, a ceramics engineer at Iowa State College, to produce plaster and terra cotta sculptures and murals of extremely fine quality. These works of art have endured for more than half a century, despite the fact that many of them were installed outdoors. The interrelationship between art and technology used to create these artworks also was used when conserving them. Through conservation technical studies prior to treatment and during the actual preservation work, reliance on technology became the foundation for decisions made regarding conservation.

Conservation is a profession that has evolved in the United States from an art-based guild tradition in the early twentieth century to one infusing more scientific research into materials to ensure that they preserve and do not damage the art. Since the 1930s, and at an accelerated rate since the 1970s, the challenge for conservators has been to utilize scientific technology while retaining what an Italian would express as "simpatico" for the art — thereby preserving the artist's intention.

In order to return the art to Christian Petersen's original intended appearance, it was necessary to analyze the materials used in the fabrication of the work, as well as subsequent changes in its condition. Treatment was often necessary due to manmade changes/relocations that had occurred in the art's original settings between the time they were first installed in the mid-twentieth century and the end of the twentieth century. Petersen's work was of such high quality that during only one instance was treatment necessary due to the fabrication method or materials used (and then it was only one aspect of that treatment).

PUBLIC ART IN PUBLIC SPACES
IN THE EARLY TWENTIETH CENTURY

Within the American artistic tradition of the first half of the twentieth century, sculpture and reliefs in terra cotta were predominantly created for outdoor use as tiles and glazed decorative elements on buildings. The majority of public sculptures and monuments were executed in bronze and in stone ssuch as granite, marble, or limestone.[1] Christian Petersen's profession as a sculptor started after the height of the city and park beautification period in the United States, which began with the end of the Civil War and ended with the advent of the Public Works Administration (1890–1930).[2]

During the height of the city beautification period, Petersen was working as a medal sculptor in New Jersey, but he found himself in search of work during the economically depressed years following the 1929 stock market crash. In 1934, mural painter Grant Wood extended an invitation for Petersen to come to Iowa. In Iowa, Petersen found support for his artistic endeavors from Iowa State College Presidents Raymond M. Hughes and Charles B. Friley.

Another pivotal relationship developed when Petersen began collaborating with Cox. With Cox, Petersen found support for pursuing his artwork and a team approach that enabled an artistic vision to be realized. Cox had an exceptional understanding of ceramic production. This understanding, coupled with Petersen's artistic abilities, helped create high quality works of art that have lasted outdoors for decades. This successful blending of art and technology also benefited the art preservation undertaken during the past decade.

ENJOYMENT AND CHALLENGES OF
TERRA COTTA AND PLASTER AS AN ARTISTIC MEDIA

During his years as a sculptor at Iowa State, Petersen worked in a variety of media, each requiring a markedly different approach in creating the art. His carving of Bedford stone sculptures, such as the Osage Indian figures in the *Fountain of Four Seasons* (1941) and the *Library Boy and Girl* (1944) required a subtractive carving process. The majority of his works produced on campus, however, were created through the additive process of modeling in clay.

The ease of adding and subtracting from the surfaces creates a fluid sculptural experience for an artist, and for Petersen working in clay complemented the broad, smooth curves used in his style of sculpting. His work in clay included murals and sculpture that were transformed into both terra cotta and plaster. For example, there are plaster murals in the lobby of the food sciences building and a terra cotta mural and fountain in that building's courtyard.

Modeling clay, an artist can explore different ideas and vary the sculptural form without destroying the sculpture. In contrast, a carved sculpture can be destroyed by chiseling into a fault line hidden within the block of stone. There may also be uneven (harder or softer) clusters of minerals within the stone that, when encountered, can cause the tool to skip. One cannot add back a form. The Bedford stone Petersen used was relatively soft, similar to Indiana limestone (commonly used at the turn of the century), and therefore was easier to carve than a dense granite.

For the terra cotta and plaster murals and sculptures, Petersen developed his sculptural concepts in drawings[3] or in a nondrying modeling clay. Often the clay sculptures were produced in smaller sizes known as maquettes and working models before they were transformed into a more permanent form. Once he was satisfied with the sculptural clay model, he created a plaster mold, the "negative" of the sculpture.

The terra cotta sculptural form was fabricated by pressing the clay mix into the plaster "negative," or mold. When doing this, great care was taken to avoid air pockets and unevenness in the thickness of the hollow sculpture. Both would cause the sculpture to crack while drying or firing, or even to burst in the firing cycle. It was technically challenging for Petersen to ensure success in this process because he worked in such a large scale. During the drying, and even more so in the firing of the large reliefs, Professor Cox's collaboration was critical to creating the artwork.

Terra cotta shrinks 8 to 15 percent during the drying-firing cycle; the stiffer the mix is, the lower the percentage. Having a consistent mix and build-up of the terra cotta is key to maintaining sculptural forms and avoiding large shrinkage cracks or bursting of the form during the firing cycle. The quality of Petersen's terra cotta mix and systematic, controlled handling during the drying-firing cycles resulted in works of the scale of *The Gentle Doctor* (1936) at ISU and *Madonna of the Schools* (1946) at St. Cecilia Church in Ames. Misalignment through uneven shrinkage would have been even more noticeable and distracting on a long mural, such as the 24-foot-long by 7-foot-tall *Veterinary Medicine Mural*. The collaboration of engineer and artist is evident in this large mural, designed as one continuous form, but cut into forty-four panels in order to fit the kiln and limit warpage.

Pressing the materials into molds is the usual fabrication method for large-scale terra cotta and many large plaster sculptures. The "clue" that this process was followed is that the sculpture is hollow. Smaller sculptures, such as a six-to-twelve-inch high standing figure, could be created by directly modeling in the terra cotta or plaster, using both additive and subtractive techniques. Such smaller sculptures are typically solid, or have only a small amount of the interior removed.

PETERSEN'S WORK WITH COX

Christian Petersen's collaboration with Professor Paul Cox[4] produced artwork seen throughout the Iowa State campus, including some pieces that have now come to symbolize the different colleges on campus, such as *The Gentle Doctor*. Others, such as the *Fountain of the Four Seasons,* have become campus icons. In addition to being important symbols to the thousands of Iowa State graduates, the collaboration produced extremely high quality art in a medium often fraught with technical problems that many artists are unable to overcome.

Several articles exist from the time period in which many of Christian Petersen's works of art were created. Both Professor Cox and engineering student Lewis Minton wrote these articles in the 1930s. They provide important details on the materials and processes used. From the article, *Ceramic Engineering Department Constructs Panels of Terra Cotta*, by Lewis Minton in *The Iowa Engineer* (March 1935), we learn:

> *Ten tons of plastic buff-burning clay, known as "Fort Dodge clay" was combined to control shrinkage of the clay in a proportion of 3 parts clay to 2 parts non-plastic grog by weight. The old furnace lining blocks from the college powerhouse were cleaned of slag and crushed to pass through a 60-mesh screen to use as the grog. An even, homogenous mix was critical to avoid uneven shrinkage and cracking during drying and firing. A small amount of barium carbonate was added to combine with soluble salts in the clays which otherwise could crystallize on the surface, thereby creating a delamination of any glaze or a "scumming" on the surface of the fired terra cotta.*

Petersen first sculptured an artistic design in clay, then followed with a plaster mold, hand-pressing the terra cotta mixture into the molds. The mold size was constructed to fit the Cox kiln's 30- x 24- x 48-inch chamber, resulting in terra cotta panels measuring approximately 20 x 28 inches. It was critical to evenly press the terra cotta into the mold to avoid air pockets that could burst apart the panel during firing. The three-inch thick panels were supported by a rectangular web on the reverse side to reduce shrinkage-cracking problems. The panels were dried under a cover to control evaporation for one week, with a specifically calculated drying angle of forty-five degrees.

Each firing in Cox's "Carboradiant car-type" kiln was completed over a period of five days. The first day, the panel was heated to 500°F to release any water that had not evaporated during drying. The second day, the temperature was raised to 1850°F to drive off the chemically combined water and organic material, and finally, on day three, the temperature was raised to 2050°F to enable fusion of the terra cotta. A controlled, slow cooling period of two days followed.[5]

1990s ANALYSIS FOR CONSERVATION TREATMENTS

As part of the treatment, conservators had x-ray diffraction and petrographic examinations conducted, and these concurred with most of what was written in *The Iowa Engineer* and *Ceramic Industry* articles of 1935. When removing three campus works of art for conservation treatment, small terra cotta samples were removed from the back and undersides. Sample 1 was obtained from the *Reclining Nudes* (1936) at Roberts Hall, sample 2 came from *The Gentle Doctor*, and sample 3 came from the *Veterinary Medicine Mural*. Analysis by James Murowchick of the University of Missouri geosciences department documented strong similarities in the terra cotta mix; however, there appear to be some differences in the firing temperatures attained in the kiln.

As described in Murowchick's reports:

> *The x-ray diffraction analysis [sic] of the three samples are quite similar with the dominant phases present being quartz (SiO_2), mullite ($Al_6Si_2O_{13}$), and cristobalite (SiO_2). Samples 1 and 2 have larger glass humps than sample 3.*

Petrographic examination by Murowchick identified the matrix in *The Gentle Doctor* and the *Veterinary Medicine Mural* to be virtually identical. The quartz is present as angular grains 5-125μm, mostly 12-60μm. No brown glass associated with iron-rich areas was found in these samples. For the *Reclining Nudes* sample, the quartz is present as angular grains 5-50μm across, and some areas have been enriched in iron where a brown glass is present and larger mullite crystals have formed with the glass.

Although absolute firing temperatures could not be determined due to small samples, it was possible to deduce relative firing temperatures of the artworks, assuming that the firing times were about the same for all three. The deduction regarding fire temperature was based on:

1. The quartz/cristobalite and quartz/mullite ratios decrease with an increased firing temperature, or with time at a sufficiently high firing temperature.
2. The amount of glass increases with an increased firing temperature.
3. The extent of iron diffusion into surrounding melt (forming an iron-rich glass) should increase with firing temperature.

The angularity or rounding of clasts was not used in this evaluation since all three samples were similar in this aspect. Based on the criteria listed above, sample 1, the *Reclining Nudes*, was probably fired at the highest temperature; sample 2, *The Gentle Doctor*, was fired at a slightly lower temperature; and sample 3, the *Veterinary Medicine Mural* was fired at the lowest temperature.[6]

It was not critical to determine precise firing temperatures of the terra cotta in order to perform the conservation treatments, but the removal of the artworks presented a unique opportunity to obtain discrete samplings and therefore to perform analysis that would help us to better understand the techniques Christian Petersen used.

An elemental analysis of the clay bodies was important in determining effective, yet preservation-safe, cleaning materials to be used in the conservation treatment. Samples from two different pieces on the ISU campus, the *History of Dairying Mural* (1934) and the *Fountain of the Four Seasons* (1941), illustrate remarkable consistency in the terra cotta, even though they were produced seven years apart.

Optical emission spectography was performed for a partial elemental analysis. The analysis identified the terra cotta mix as 20 percent aluminum, 20 percent silicon, 2 vs. 3 percent titanium, 2 percent iron, 2 vs. 0.5 percent calcium, 1 percent potassium, 0.7 vs. 0.5 percent magnesium, and the other elements each less than 0.5 percent.[7]

The most significant element in the analysis — with regard to determining the cleaning method — was the level of manganese in the terra cotta mix. Because all standard conservation cleaning methods were unsuccessful in cleaning the terra cotta, acidic cleaning solutions could not safely be field tested unless the manganese level was sufficiently low so colloidal silica staining, a potentially reoccurring purple-brown color, would not occur. Petersen's terra cotta mix contained a total manganese level of 0.01 or 0.008 percent, depending on the sample, and an acidic solubility of 0.0021 or 0.0013 percent, well below the level that would restrict a professional conservator's use of acidic cleaners.[8]

PETERSEN'S WORK ON THE ISU CAMPUS

The table below contains a list of the Christian Petersen sculptures in the ISU collection that Conservation Technical Associates has conserved through July 1999. Additional small-scale plaster sculptures are scheduled for conservation treatment in 2000. The artwork is located in public spaces on the ISU campus or was part of the collection treated at ISU unless otherwise noted.

Due to space limitations, only highlights of information learned about Petersen's techniques and materials are presented here. Some treatments spanned three years to include sufficient time to analyze the treatment issues, then develop and execute a well-planned conservation program. The detailed conservation reports with complete photographic documentation are filed in the Brunnier Art Museum at Iowa State University in Ames, Iowa.

Christian Petersen sculptures in the ISU collection conserved by Conservation Technical Associates (CTA) LLC, Westport, Connecticut

No.	Title	Date Sculpted	Material	Date Conserved by CTA
1	*History of Dairying Mural* and Fountain	1934–35	Terra Cotta	1994–95
2	*Four Thousande Yeeres*	1935	Plaster	1994
	For Melke and Chese and Buttere	1935	Plaster	1999
3	*The Gentle Doctor*	1936	Terra Cotta	1999
4	*Veterinary Medicine Mural*	1936–38	Terra Cotta	1997
5	*Three Athletes*	1936	Terra Cotta	1999
6	*Reclining Nudes*	1936	Terra Cotta	1999
7	*Flood*	1938	Plaster	1998
8	*Charlotte*	1938	Plaster	1998
9	*Drought*	1938	Plaster	1998
10	*Soon after the Flood*	1939	Plaster	1998
11	Full-scale Plaster Maidens (4)	1940	Plaster	1999
12	*Fountain of the Four Seasons*	1941	Terra Cotta/ Bedford Stone	1998
13	*Library Boy and Girl*	1944	Bedford Stone	1998
14	*Price of Victory*	1944	Plaster	1998
15	*Risen Christ* U89.25	1949	Plaster	1998
16	*The Gentle Doctor* Reproductions	1976	Bronze	1998
17	*Reverend W. Barlow* U89.33	1959	Plaster Mold	1998
18	*Country Doctor*	1936	Plaster	1999
19	*Charlotte and Mary* UM97.139	1946	Plaster Mold	1998
20	*Fallen Soldier*	ca. 1944	Plaster	1998
21	*Two Maidens* UM98.2,3	late 1930s	Plaster	1998
22	*Dean Helen Benitez* U89.34	ca. 1950s	Plaster	1998

CONSERVATION CHALLENGES IN THE 1990s

Since 1994, Conservation Technical Associates LLC of Westport, CT, has worked on more than twenty sculptures created by Christian Petersen. These have included large-scale outdoor terra cotta sculptures and murals as well as indoor murals and smaller sculptures. Many pieces are plaster painted and glazed to simulate terra cotta.

TERRA COTTA
History of Dairying Mural and Fountain

The first public artwork that Petersen undertook at ISU was the *History of Dairying Mural and Fountain* in 1934 for the Public Works of Art Project. Coincidentally, it also was the first of his outdoor artworks to undergo a technical study and conservation treatment by this author sixty years later. An analysis of the terra cotta and mortar was the key to developing the appropriate cleaning strategy and a historically accurate mortar mix for pointing the joints between the mural's terra cotta panels.

Upon first inspection, the creamy white surface was reminiscent of a thinly glazed terra cotta tile. The more thickly glazed tiles used on buildings in the early twentieth century often deteriorate over time, resulting in devitrification and detachment of the glaze from the clay substrate. With the majority of research and publications for terra cotta being on glazed architectural terra cotta, the conservation challenge was to develop a new body of research and knowledge for the treatment of Petersen's semivitreous (not glazed) terra cotta. The surface was covered at the start of the project with a visually disfiguring pattern of fine black lines from plants that once covered the surface. The mortar was a hard, granular reddish color, reportedly used in a pointing project in the mid-1970s.

Although certain cleaning chemicals may or may not generally be used on a material, in this case terra cotta, it is important to understand the scientific/chemical reaction reasons why so that an informed conservation treatment plan can be developed. Too often, surfaces are cleaned simply because "X" or "Y" was "always used." With the elemental analysis of the terra cotta, it was learned that Petersen's terra cotta mix did not include high levels of manganese, common to architectural terra cotta mixtures.

Because the actual composition of *this* terra cotta, the type of soiling, and the contents of manufacturers' cleaning solutions were known, the field tests of cleaning solutions demonstrated that the only effective *and preservation safe* method was to use a proprietary acidic cleaner[9] consisting of sulfamic and hydroxyacetic acids. This was the only cleaning solution that could actually clean the terra cotta without any deleterious effect to it. The surface was checked under a 30x field microscope followed by thorough rinsing and constant pH (acid-alkaline balance) verification to achieve on the terra cotta surface the same pH as the city water after the cleaning cycles were completed.

CTA was able to produce a historically accurate mortar mixture through x-ray diffraction analysis of the remaining mortar found behind the 1970s tuck-pointing. The mortar was used on this and other Petersen terra cotta sculptures, once analysis of each artwork's mortar confirmed that the mix was appropriate. Additional analysis of the mortar in the *Fountain of the Four Seasons*, *Madonna of the Schools* at St. Cecilia Church in Ames, and *The Gentle Doctor*, as well as samples removed from the reverse of the individual panels comprising the *Veterinary Medicine Mural*, confirmed that they were highly similar.

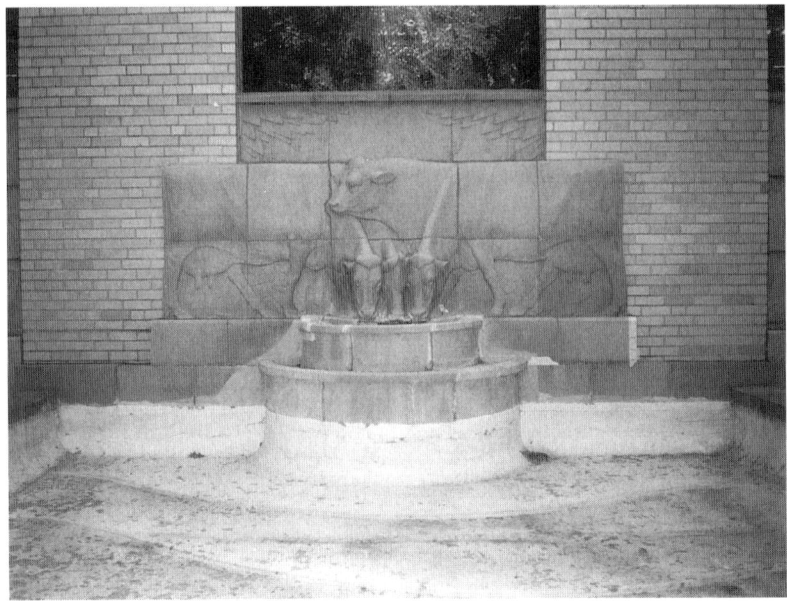

This view of the fountain panels shows rust stains and sandblasting damage on the sides.

The analysis of the mortar[10] determined that the sample contained major (>10 percent) quartz (SiO_2) and calcite ($CACO_3$), minor (1–10 percent) albite [$(NaAlSi_3)_8$], and traces (<1 percent) of microline [$(KAlSi_3)_8$] and dolomite [$CaMg(CO_3)_2$]. The average grain size is 0.7 mm in diameter, with some grains reaching 2 mm in diameter. A small amount of hematitic pigment is associated with the cement calcite. The mortar has a sandy pinkish brown color, with the sand grains well exposed on the weathered surface but not easily loosened from the cement.

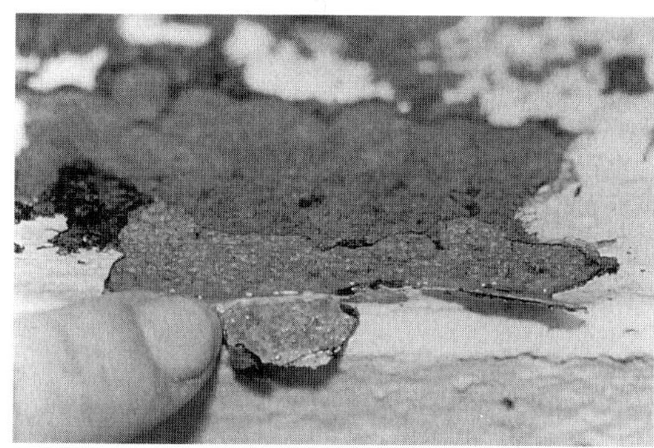

Conservators discovered dark blue specks, the original pool color, under the old paint.

sample revealed that the original paint color, as selected by Christian Petersen, was a deep blue (Munsell 5PB 2/8), not the 1995 light blue "swimming pool" color. The depth of this color and its relationship to the cleaned terra cotta increased visitors' appreciation of the mural and its courtyard setting.

Veterinary Medicine Mural

After the heavy rainfall and extensive flooding throughout the Midwest in 1993, white deposits formed on the surface of the *Veterinary Medicine Mural* (1936–38). The disfiguring appearance resulted in the mural being prioritized for conservation treatment. Salts were migrating through the tuck-pointing between many of the forty-four panels comprising the mural and even through some of the terra cotta itself. It was unknown what the source of the salts was — the heavy rainfall, the mortar, the building, the terra cotta itself, or something behind the mural. Given the comparative condition of other terra cotta murals and Petersen's ISU sculptures, which have no efflorescence on the surface, it seemed unlikely that terra cotta was the source.

With the anticipated arrival of President Clinton to the ISU campus in summer 1995, the opportunity to re-establish the use of the courtyard for ice cream socials as in the 1930–1960s became part of the university's plan. With the conservation treatment close to completion, attention turned to the fountain and pool.

CTA located some of the original paint through selective sampling of the pool, in spite of it having been sandblast cleaned in the 1970s. Under 160x magnification, a microscopic cross section of paint

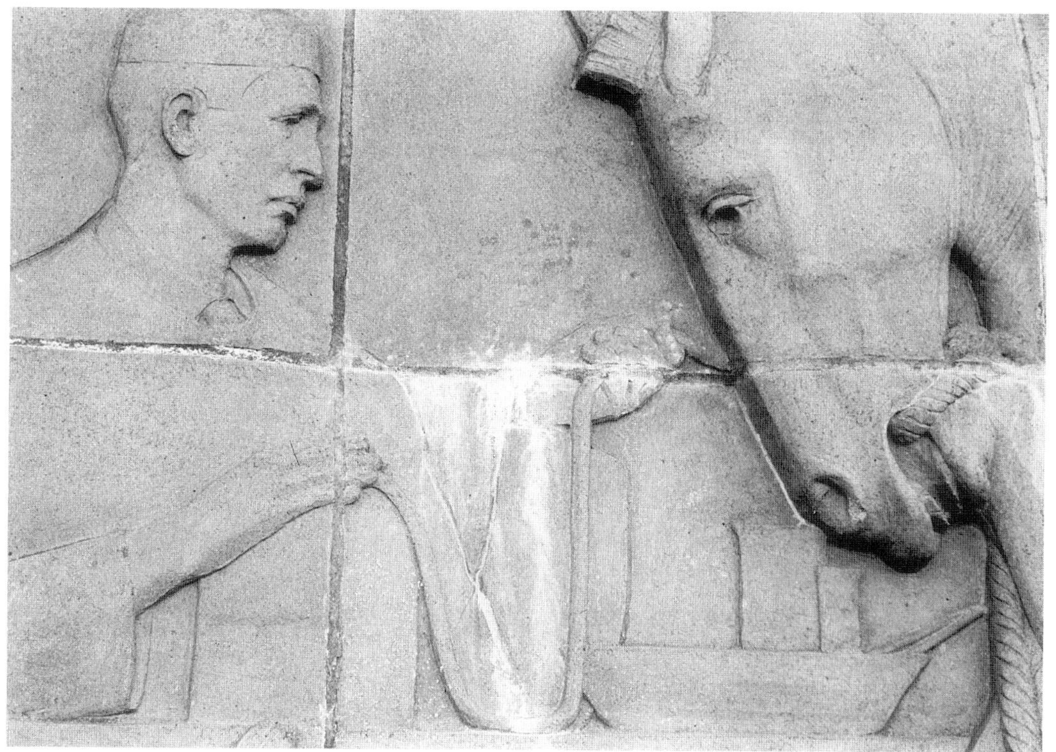

Salts had seeped from the mortar behind the mural to the surface.

To determine the source of the white deposit and then develop a conservation plan, CTA undertook an analysis of the white efflorescence on the terra cotta samples of the mortar and the building. X-ray diffraction at the Department of Geosciences at the University of Missouri–Kansas City indicated that the white deposits were solely calcite and that the mortar joints consisted of fine-grained reprecipitated calcite with trace amounts of quartz sand and white cement. The sample of the concrete building consisted of primarily Portlandite with some calcite present as well as fragments of dolomite, limestone and quartz sand.[11] The laboratory analysis in combination with the observed water migration tests led to the conclusion that the source of the white efflorescence was the setting mortar behind the terra cotta panels.

Further investigation with a structural engineer, Gary Strand PE, revealed that the mural had not been installed according to the mounting system specified by the architect when the mural was relocated to the new veterinary medicine building in 1976. The architectural drawing sheet A4-8 prepared by Henningson, Durham, and Richardson called for a one-inch air cavity between the building and mural. Soundings and discreet drilling through the tuck-pointing joints between the terra cotta panels demonstrated that the majority of the cavity was filled with a mortar-like material. This proved to be the source of the salts, requiring the removal of the mural in order to solve the efflorescence problem.

Back-filling with grout/mortar and unwashed sand in the mixture was not an uncommon construction practice for the 1970s; however, after twenty-five years and the extreme flood weather of the prior year, each day's humidity fluctuations brought more salt to the surface. The white streaks were visually disfiguring. The conservation challenges in the treatment were from earlier relocation, not Petersen's workmanship.

CTA had to remove the mural to correct the problem. For this, water-jet technology was used to cut the setting mortar behind the panels, thereby enabling the forty-four panels to be removed. Our familiarity with water-jet applications came from using the

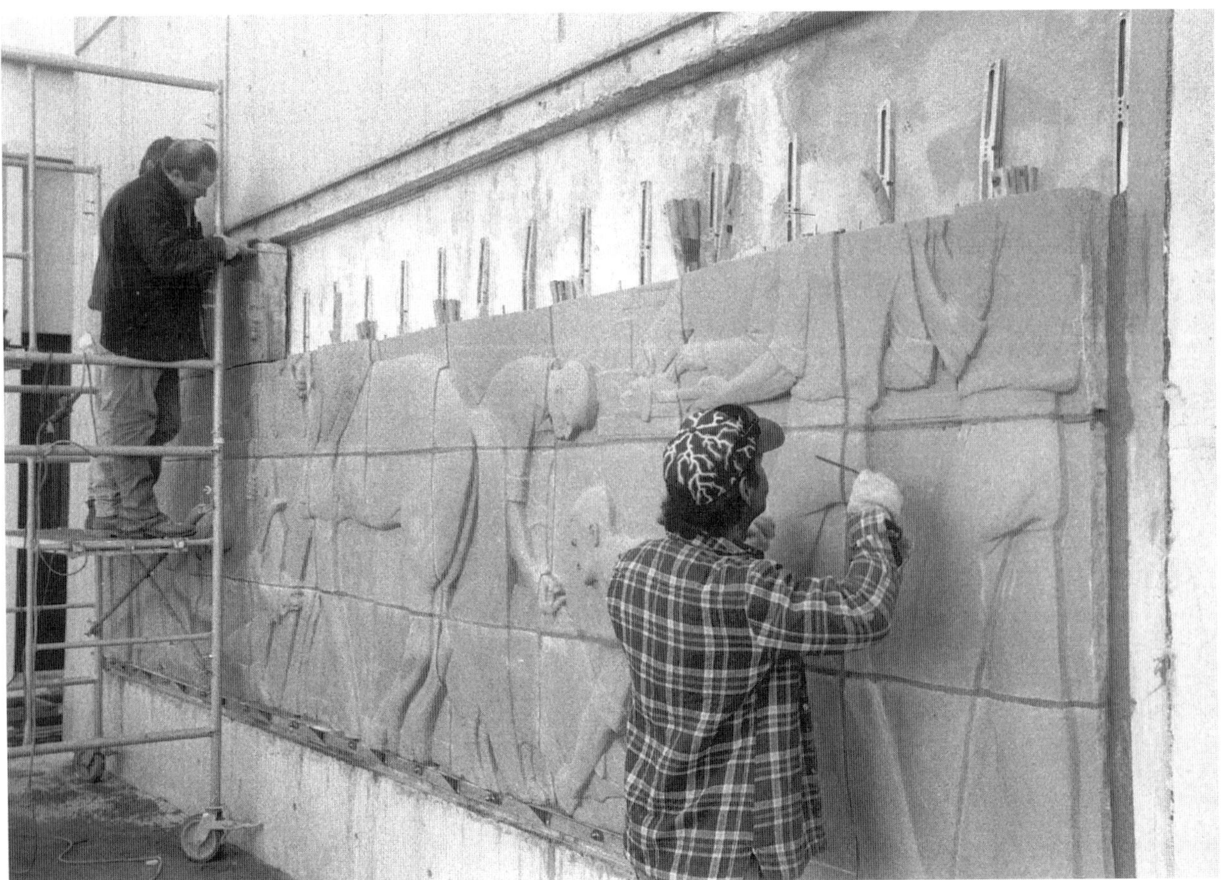

The mural is reinstalled after extensive conservation.

technology in other outdoor conservation treatments.[12] Although successful and used for removing those first few critical corner blocks, its cost proved prohibitive. The majority of the blocks were then removed using more traditional cutting wheels.

The bedding mortar in the terra cotta panels' reverse sides was initially chiseled out as each panel was removed. The waffle pattern construction revealed by this work illustrated the collaboration between engineer and artist to reduce the weight, increase the strength, and minimize shrinkage/deformation during firing of each panel.

With the terra cotta effectively "impregnated" with salt, the common conservation practices for salt removal (poultices, pulling the salt out as an aqueous clay material dries, or chemically chelating the salts) were not successful.

CTA made advances in the conservation field practices by adapting ultrasound cleaning technology to remove the salt. Ultrasonic technology is essentially molecular vibration that creates acoustic waves induced into an aqueous solution. The alternating high and low pressure develops cavitation in the solution. These alternating pressures enhance the likelihood that particles will be separated from the terra cotta substrate. Removal of the salts in this application was achieved using a frequency of 40 kHz and a piezoelectric transducer with deionized water and a proprietary mixture for six to eight hours followed by a cycle of soaking in distilled water for two to four hours and exposure to sunlight for two to four weeks. The salt extraction was monitored using an oxidation reduction potentiometer (ORP). Repetition of the procedures occurred as needed for some of the panels to eliminate salt recrystallization during wet-dry testing cycles.[13]

The use of ultrasound technology was adapted for the removal of hard water "scale" deposits and iron stains from the terra cotta panels in the *Fountain of the Four Seasons*. Although the basic approach remained the same, the temperature of the aqueous solution and the duration of immersion for the panels differed.[14]

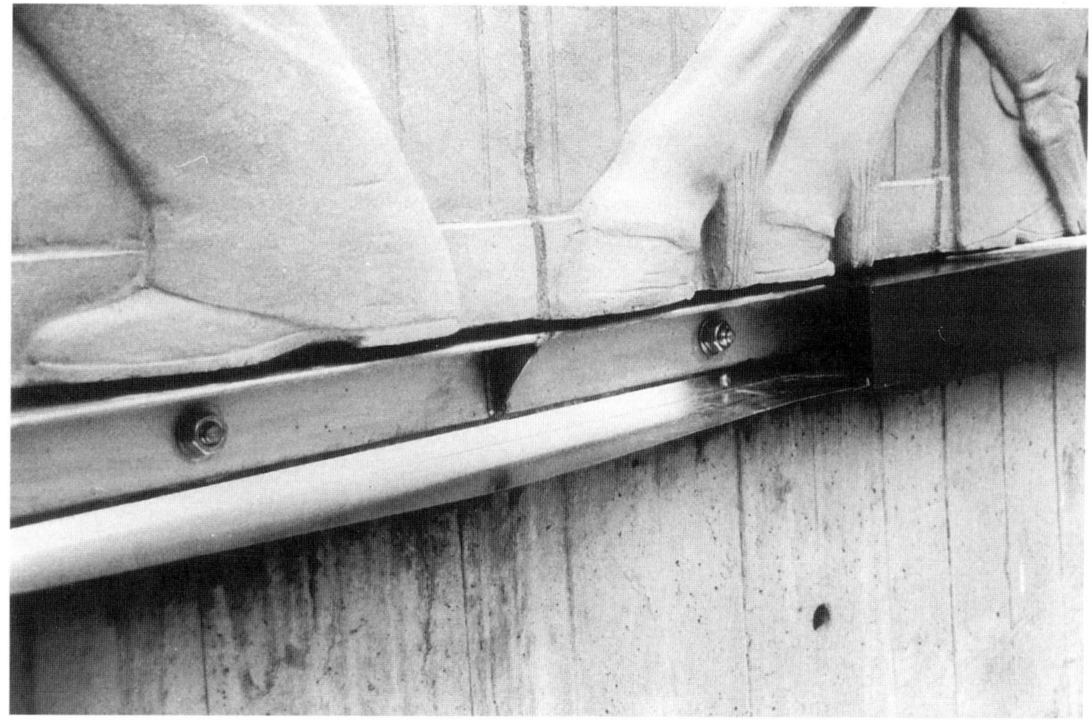

Close-up of new stainless steel support system.

The Gentle Doctor Sculpture

The terra cotta *The Gentle Doctor* sculpture had been moved indoors in the mid-1970s, and a bronze replica, painted to look like terra cotta, had been placed at the new veterinary medicine building. The concern at that time was that the terra cotta would not weather more harsh Iowa winters with repeated freeze-thaw cycles. During the 1999 conservation treatment, the surface overpaint was removed with solvent gels and a water-jet rinse. The gray body putty used in the 1970s to fill all the fissures and firing shrinkage cracks was revealed. Although ultrasound technology was tried to remove the fill material, it proved unsuccessful in this application. The more tedious approach of chemically softening the fills and manually removing the materials with dental tools was needed.

Numerous fissures in the surface and shrinkage cracks from the original firing, particularly in the doctor's hands by the small dog's head, resulted in our recommendation that the sculpture be exhibited indoors — unless a rigorous maintenance plan could be strictly followed. The gaps were filled with color-match mortar and tonal variations inpainted with Dutch Kiem silica-based paints. This is the only one of Petersen's fired ceramics in which the conservation problem resulted from the original firing fabrication.

The "man-induced" problem that needed correction during the conservation treatment was the concrete-filled interior of the sculpture. The imbalance in the sculpture caused by the slight forward lean of the sculptural form was accentuated with the increased weight from the concrete. The concrete was success-

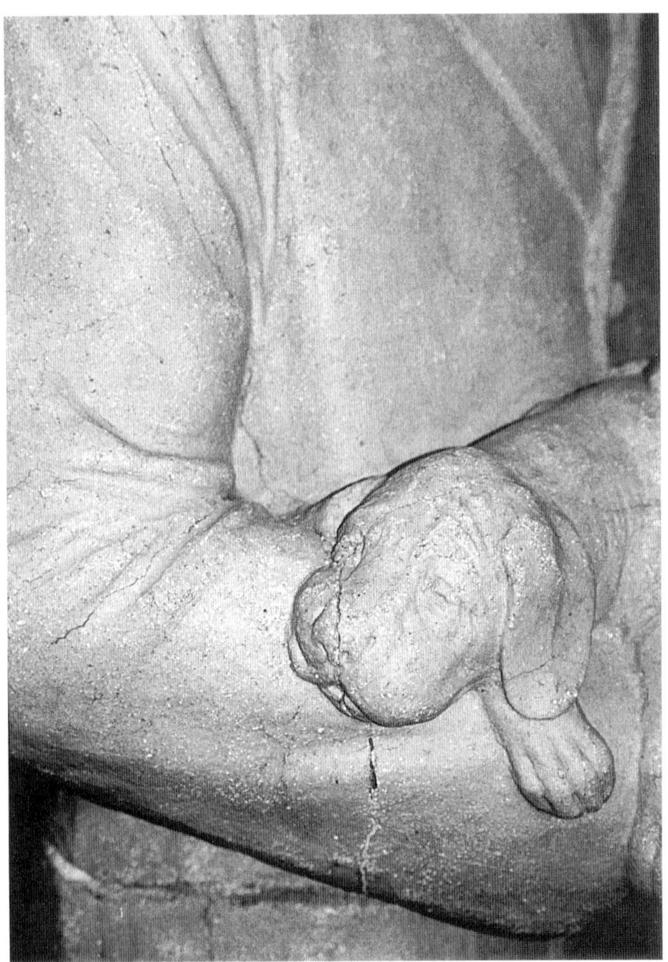

The face of the little dog in *The Gentle Doctor* reveals cracks under the paint.

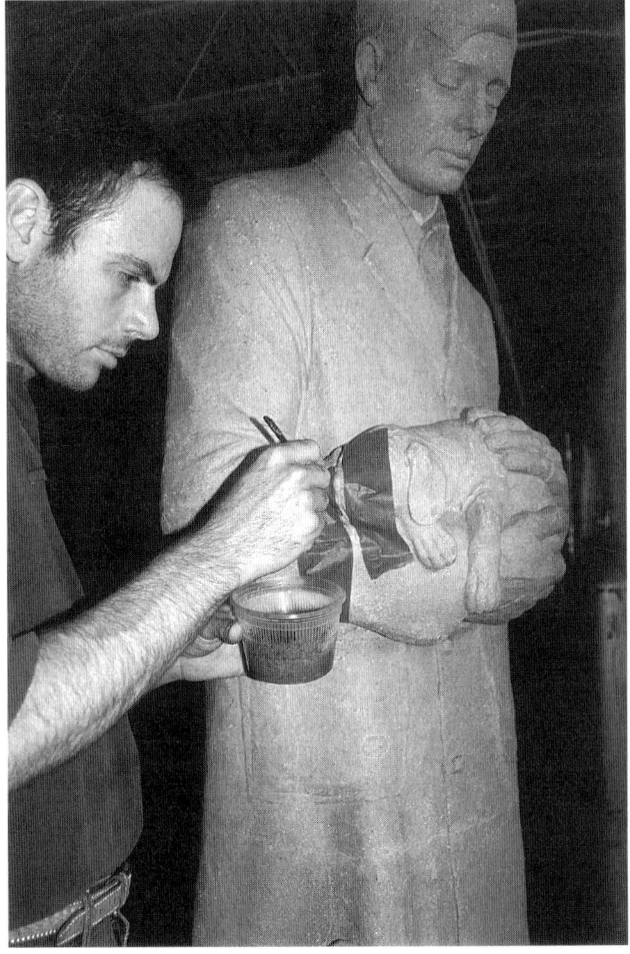

Francis Miller of Conservation Technical Associates fills the cracks in the dog's face with soft mortar.

fully removed from the self-base without damaging the terra cotta structural web on the bottom.

Unfortunately, the steel rods embedded in the concrete above the ankles could not be reached without likely damage to *The Gentle Doctor*. Even an attempt to remove the concrete by separating the mortar joint in the waist was not successful — the entire interior of *The Gentle Doctor* is filled solid with concrete and steel rods.

As a result, the concrete removed from the self-base was replaced with a lightweight synthetic aggregate mixed into the concrete. This helped counter the sculpture's forward lean without adding significant weight.[15]

PETERSEN'S PLASTER ARTWORK

A similar approach of starting with technical analysis to understand "how" Christian Petersen fabricated his artwork was undertaken for his painted plaster murals and large plaster sculptures. The information gathered was important in developing a treatment plan for the two projects described below as well as for numerous small plaster sculptures that have been conserved. Without knowledge of the methods of fabrication and, in this situation, the layers of paint on top of the plaster, it is possible to misinterpret what is visible. For example, is the color a glossy paint, a toned glaze, or clear glazes on top of paint? The answer will affect the materials used for cleaning. The wrong cleaning solutions or solvents could even dissolve the paint intended to be preserved!

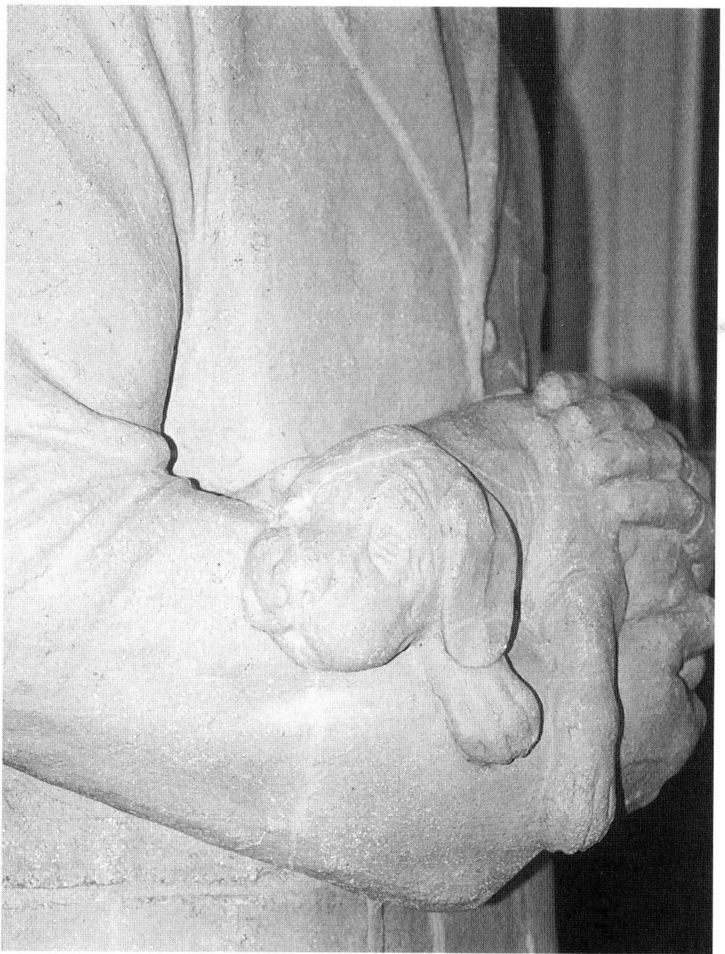

**The face of the little dog
after conservation treatment.**

Bas-Relief Murals in Food Sciences Building

The first of Petersen's plasters to be conserved was one of the two 11-foot-tall by 8-foot-wide plaster bas-relief murals in the historic entry to the dairy industry building, now known as Food Sciences. They were painted the color of terra cotta in 1934. Both the bas-reliefs, *Four Thousande Yeeres* and *For Melke and Chese and Buttere* were part of the 1994 technical study that included a conservation assessment by Linda Merk-Gould and an engineering assessment by Gary Strand, PE, of RGA Associates. The study focused on the cracks in bas-reliefs and the possible source for the dramatically different condition between the two reliefs.

While both bas-reliefs had paint losses and vertical-horizontal cracks through the midsections, one relief, *For Melke and Chese and Buttere*, had significantly more paint losses — so extensive that the stone wall ledge under the mural was covered by a layer of paint flakes. The cracks were inspected by the engineer and found to be old, inactive cracks associated with the shrinkage of plaster as it aged and released its residual moisture from the fabrication process.[16] In addition to the paint peeling off the surface, streaks in the viewer's upper left side indicated that either something had been spilled on the *For Melke and Chese and Buttere* mural or someone had tried to clean the dusty mural with the wrong product.

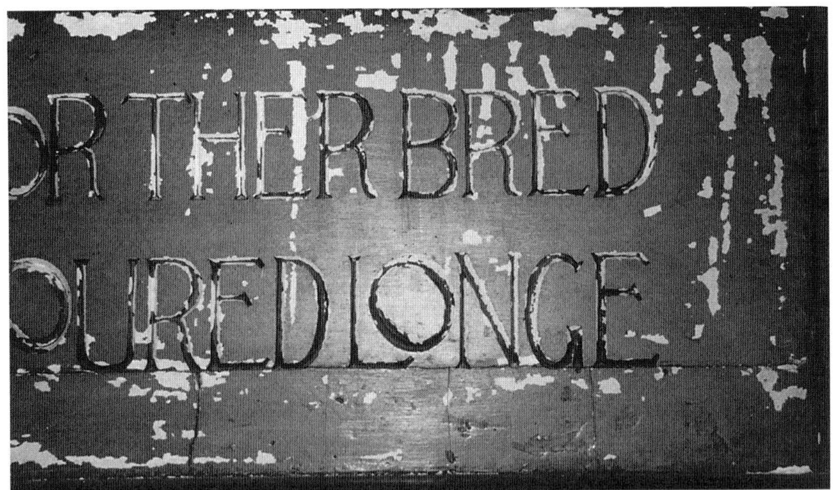

Close-up of paint losses on *For Melke and Chese and Buttere* before conservation.

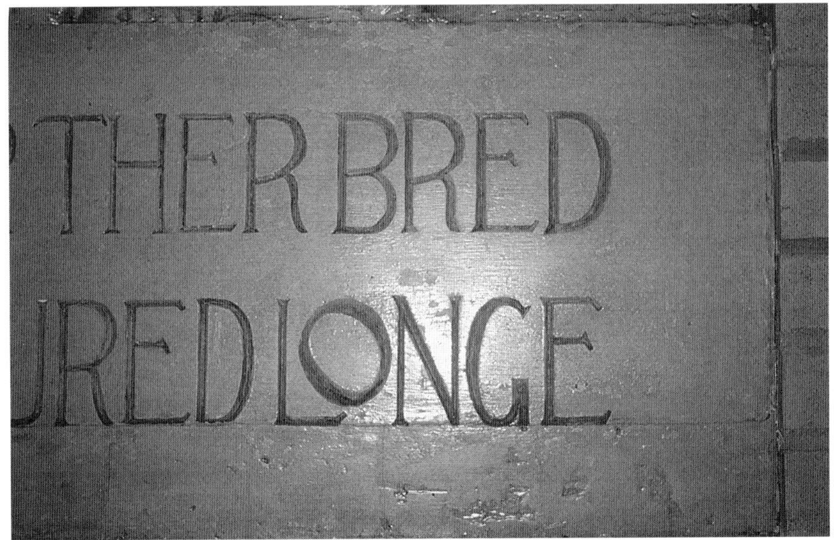

Close-up of *For Melke and Chese and Buttere* after conservation.

The engineer's inspection in 1994 brought into question the effects that the recently installed bathroom might have had on the paint; however, further study of the environment during the three weeks of conservation work on the *Four Thousande Yeeres* relief in January 1995 refocused the investigation to the entryway microclimate. The murals were undergoing thermal shock from rapid fluctuations in the temperature and humidity — opening and closing the front doors fifty or more times whenever classes changed. During work on the bas-reliefs in both May 1994 and January 1995, there were opportunities to document 30°F drops in temperature in less than five minutes. The additional deterioration found on the *For Melke and Chese and Buttere* relief can be attributed to the increased thermal changes from the raking angle of the sunlight through the west facing windows above the doors. Given the relative location of trees and buildings on campus, the *Four Thousande Yeeres* relief did not receive the same intensity of heat from the sunlight.

Faced with greatly different amounts of deterioration on the two reliefs, the time involved to conserve both murals using the same methods would have been prohibitively expensive. The philosophical approach for preservation was the same — stabilize the original surface, only paint in the areas of loss, that is, not the faster method of overpainting the entire relief as had been suggested by others. Additionally, all work should be reversible and identifiable as different from Petersen's original craftsmanship.

The scientific-based decision-making approach for the conservation treatments is illustrated in the work done on the bas-reliefs *Four Thousande Yeeres,* which was conserved in 1995, and *For Melke and Chese and Buttere*, conserved in 1999. This contrasts with the approach often taken by restorers trained prior to the 1960s and 1970s when the emphasis in the conservation field shifted from guild-like practices of "what has always been done" to understanding the materials used by the artist *and* conservator.

Prior to the start of "hands-on" work in the conservation treatment, paint samples were removed for analysis. Cross-sectional paint analysis differentiated the layers applied by the artist to achieve the terra cotta–like appearance. CIE and Munsell system computer identifications of the colors in those layers were prepared to facilitate color matching for inpainting losses on the surface.[17]

While the colors on the two murals tested numerically differently, the colors appear visually similar to viewers. This is consistent for an artwork in which the final appearance is achieved with multiple paint layers and not a single can of paint.

A microscopic view of the cross section on *For Melke and Chese and Buttere* showed many layers applied by Petersen: yellowish-white oil primer to seal the plaster, three similarly colored intermediate layers of yellowish-white oil paint, and the finish layers consisting of a yellowish-gray oil paint (Munsell 10 YR 8/2 or CIE L* = 81.27, a* = + 1.81, b* = +13.02) with a thin tinted toning glaze and a final clear but yellowed varnish. The layer of interest in this project was the top varnish layer that had drips and runs in the upper half. An infrared spectral analysis of the paint flakes revealed that the top layer is a phthalic-acid-modified resin. This is likely the original layer, given that in 1935, thirty-five million pounds of alkyd resin were produced in the United States. No dirt layer was seen in the cross section under the alkyd resin, so it appears that all the layers were applied in one sequence.[18]

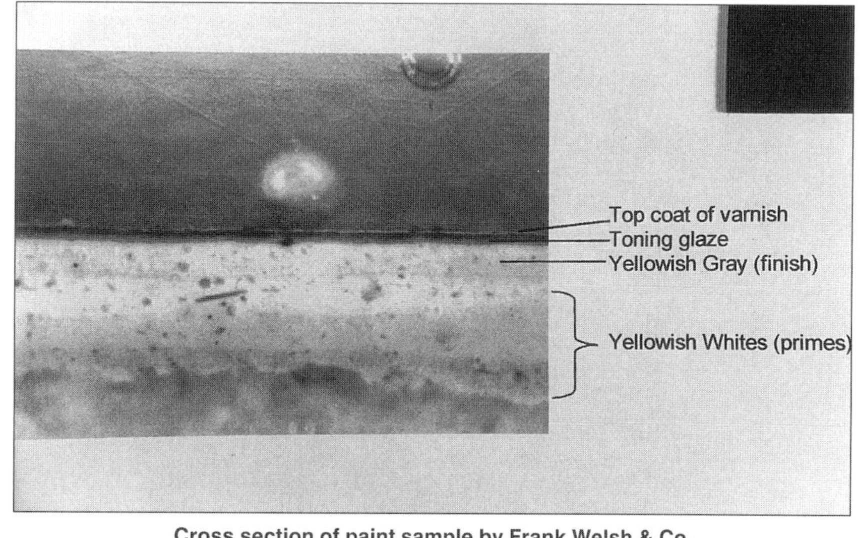

Cross section of paint sample by Frank Welsh & Co.

Knowing this information, the conservators meticulously inserted a thermosetting methacrylate resin behind the paper-thin paint layers, using syringes and 000 brushes. The solvent was allowed to evaporate from the resin for twenty-four hours, and then the paint was secured onto the plaster relief with silicon-coated, heated microspatulas imported from England.

Only after this work was done could the layers of dust and grime on the surface be cleaned off with a water-solvent mixture. The paint layer was too brittle and deteriorated to be cleaned prior to consolidation. Detergent was avoided due to the solubility of the paint and the desire to avoid a residue on the surface. The solvent increased the rate of evaporation of the distilled water, thereby reducing the likelihood of the aqueous solution softening the paint film.

An even more time-consuming process was filling losses where the paint had flaked off. Each spot had an acrylic-plaster putty laid into the 1-3 mm height difference between the plaster and the top layer of paint/varnish applied by Petersen. The fills were contoured to match the adjoining surface and then sanded to the level of the paint surface without going over the edge onto the original paint. This work was important to avoid shadows created by uneven surfaces that would produce, at certain sunlight angles, an appearance that the relief still had paint losses. The fill work was completed for the relief *Four Thousande Yeeres* but not on *For Melke and Chese and Buttere*, which had about 300 percent more paint loss that would have needed to be filled.

For the *For Melke and Chese and Buttere* relief, it was decided that the time and funds should be used to preserve all the original paint that could be saved (versus an earlier proposal by others to overpaint the mural). The preferred treatment with filling all losses was performed in 1995 but could not be done in 1999 due to the cost of such extensive work. Therefore, the areas of missing paint were inpainted on the level of the original plaster after a barrier layer of clear methacrylate resin had been applied to separate the conservator's work from the artist's 1934 work. As with any difficult decision, when the ideal approach cannot be taken, it is important to maintain a preservation-oriented philosophy as exemplified by the American Institute for Conservation's Guideline for Practice and Code of Ethics. For all the conservation treatments, the philosophy of giving highest priority to preserving the artist's original work was maintained — acknowledging that completing fills on this relief could always be undertaken in the future should funds become available — but any paint not saved *now* would be lost forever.

Although these bas-reliefs are indoors, they suffer from a somewhat uncontrolled environment, much like Petersen's art installed in outdoor settings. Until the temperature, humidity, and sunlight in the building's entryway can be controlled or at least moderated, the paint top layers and the plaster substrate will continue to differentially expand and contract, leading to cracking and flaking paint with its associated paint losses. Ironically, the dairy industry building was placed on the National Register of Historic Places as an act of preservation. Such a listing has restrictions that prevent any visible changes to its exterior. Unfortunately, this includes new doors and/or windows that could help preserve these important and equally historic reliefs located in the entryway.

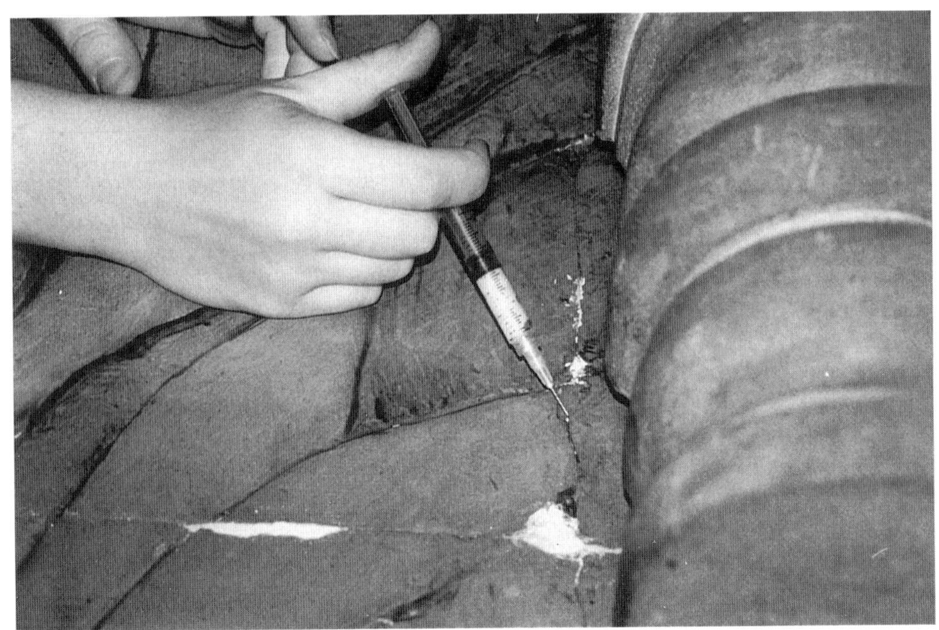

**Conservator fills losses with white plaster-acrylic mixture
with injection behind lifting paint.**

Fountain of the Four Seasons Plaster Sculptures

While plasterwork can be a finished sculptural expression for an artist, it can also serve as a sketch or a material in which to express and work out ideas before undertaking a sculpture in a more permanent medium such as a stone carving, bronze casting, or firing in terra cotta. The four plaster sculptures of kneeling American Indians are examples of Petersen working in plaster to formalize a concept for a sculpture prior to undertaking the carving of those sculptures.

The more familiar versions of these sculptures are in Bedford stone, a whitish-grayish stone similar to limestone, part of the *Fountain of the Four Seasons* in front of Memorial Union since 1941. During the conservation of the stone sculptures in 1998, the stone surface was uncovered after removing multiple layers of biological growth and calcium-based hard water deposits/scale. The scale was so thick that it was initially thought to be a waterproof coating erroneously smeared onto the sculpture. This one-half-inch layer covering most of the surface was solely scale from hard water buildup. With the fountain having iron pipes (a standard pipe material earlier in this century) to supply the water, extensive rust stains had been deposited on the terra cotta relief panels and the stone sculptures. The abraded condition of much of the surfaces indicated that sandblasting had been used in prior years to "clean off" the orange rust stains and scale.

The extent of surface detail loss that had occurred over the years was only known once the four original plasters of the sculptures by Christian Petersen were rediscovered and examined by the author. The tremendous amount of sculptural detail in the plaster's surface increased the importance of these full-scale working models.

These sculptural sketches presented an opportunity to study Petersen's creative process in more detail during the conservation treatment — to gain insights into his sculptural "building" techniques and aesthetic finishing or painting process. Two of the plaster sculptures were in good condition with small plaster chips missing and numerous small paint losses. However, two had extensive damage — cracked, broken in several pieces, and one missing the back vertical support near the sculpture's right shoulder.

With so many different paint colors visible on the back surface of the sculpture, questions arose about whether some of these paint splatters were the result of being left in an artist's atelier and/or storage *or* if these layers were intentionally applied by Petersen to achieve a specific effect. The visible colors on the surface included black, light blue-green, gold, and various shades of orange and beige — applied in a highly gestural manner, with the layers of paint broken and not continuous.

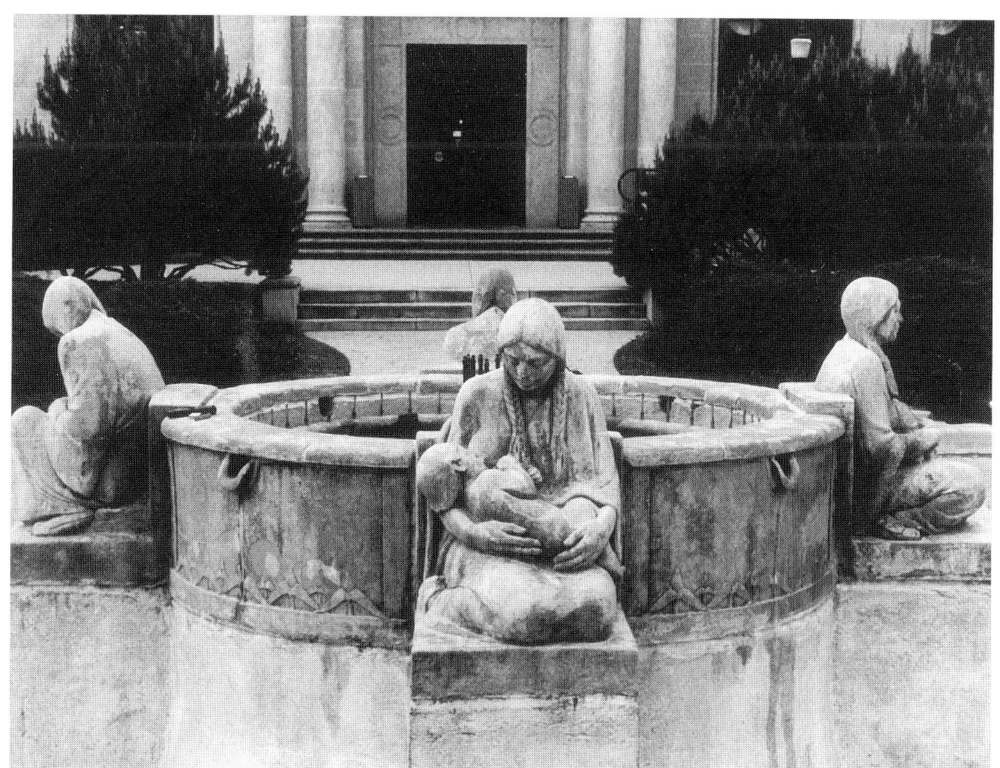

View of the condition of the *Fountain of the Four Seasons* before treatment began. The sculptures and terra cotta panels were covered with mineral and biological deposits.

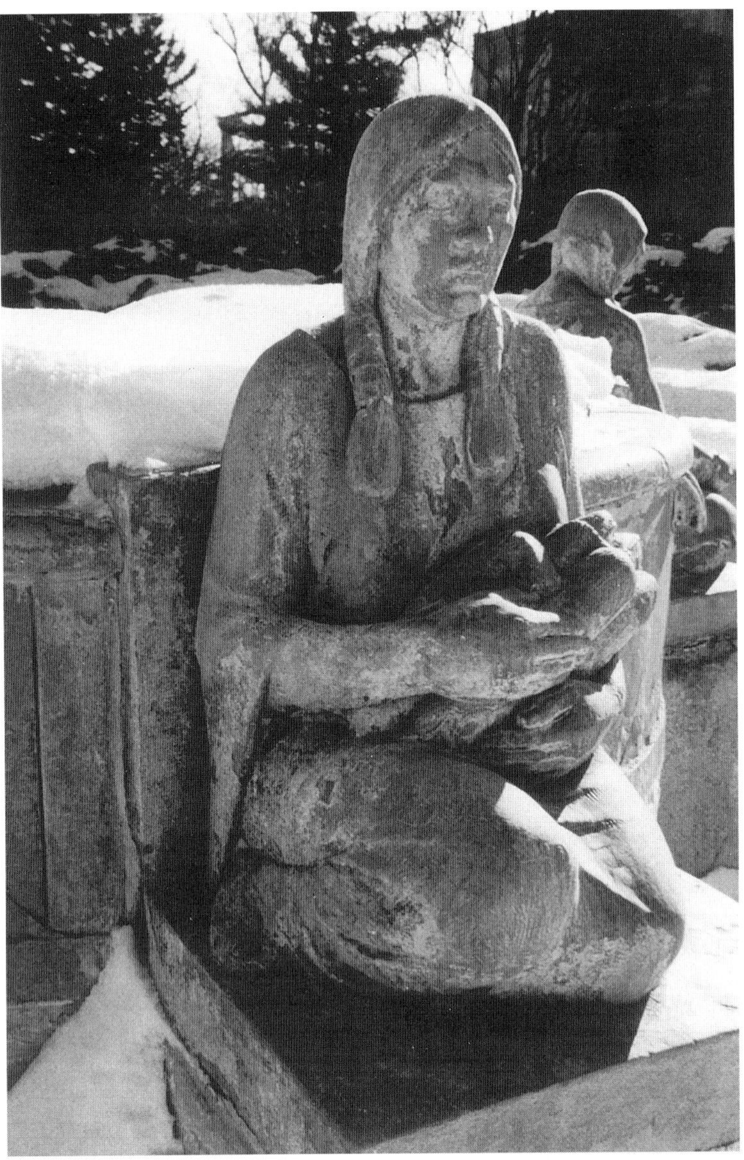

Close-up of the condition of a maiden of the *Fountain of the Four Seasons* before treatment began. The sculptures were covered with mineral and biological deposits.

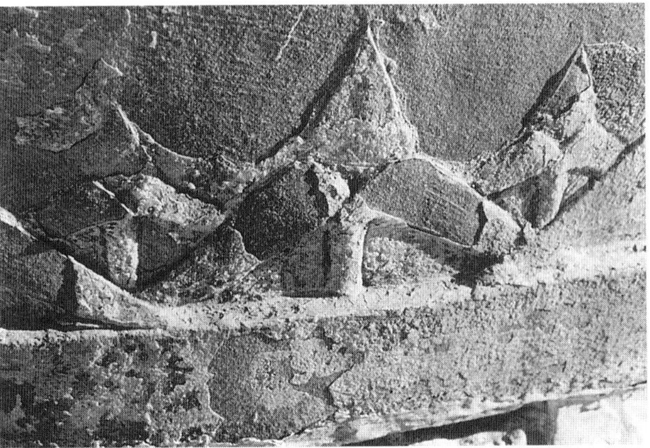

Close-up of the condition of the base of the *Fountain of the Four Seasons* before treatment began. The terra cotta panels were covered with mineral and biological deposits.

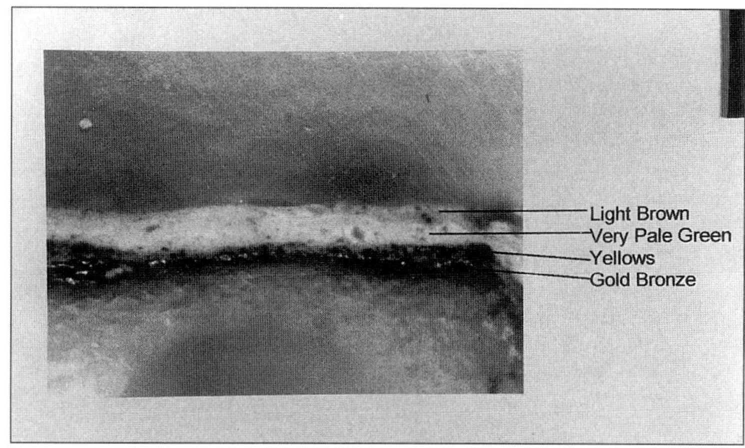

**The cross section of the paint layers in
one of the original maiden plaster sculptures
documents Petersen's paint application sequence.**

A paint cross section from the maiden representing fall prepared by Frank Welsh Company showed two distinct groupings of colors with a dirt layer between the groups. This typically indicates that the sculpture had been initially painted a medium yellow color, time had passed (that is, dirt had settled on the surface), and then the sculpture was painted with a thick pale green primer followed by an orange-brown terra cotta color.

The question is, what did the artist intend for their appearance? Did he repaint the sculpture at the later time or did someone else? Were the plaster sculptures made, painted a medium yellow to make a pure white plaster form easier to "read" and later adjusted to achieve the appearance he wanted? Perhaps after the carvings were completed? Or were they set aside in his studio for a while and then reconsidered and repainted by Christian Petersen himself? Or by someone else?

As a conservator, my first reaction was to undertake further analysis: If titanium white was part of the later color layers, then the paint would post-date the early 1940s when these plaster models were first created. However, Petersen remained artistically active until his death in 1961, when titanium white was commonly used. With a commitment to understanding and preserving the artist's original intent, it is a question worth investigating further. This is an example of when an instrumental analysis cannot conclusively provide an answer. However, in combination with historical sources or oral histories, one hopes the answer will be learned.

There are many indicators left in the plaster's structure regarding Christian Petersen's sculptural process. The hollow interior re-flects that his first versions for the maidens were carved in clay, a mold made of the clay, and then the plaster laid up by hand into the mold. The repeated, parallel grooved channels from Petersen's hand pressing the soft plaster into the mold are evidence of this. The broken pieces enabled us to see that two distinct plaster layers exist, sandwiching a reinforcing layer of burlap between them. In some areas, the burlap is readily visible on the back of the sculpture. The build up of the plaster varies from as little as three-sixteens inch to more than three inches thick, indicative that such a technically accomplished artist as Petersen was working out ideas and not constructing a finished sculpture.

The structural support work, which was part of the conservation treatment, was conceptualized to create the additional strength needed so the sculptures would not break apart again, but also to avoid obscuring the visual evidence of Petersen's working methods. The irregular bottom edge was filled with a fiberglass putty to differentiate the conservator's work from the artist's plaster work and to eliminate single loading-bearing points. These points created pressure points along which the plaster could crack apart. A fiberglass bottom panel was then attached to the bottom of the sculpture, effectively creating a single integral form and providing the necessary support. The bottom panel extends beyond the sculpture to facilitate handling of the piece.

The artist's original bracing varied from a steel pipe on *Summer* to a reused, broken piece of wood on *Fall*. These were kept by the conservators in the sculptures to preserve the artist's original working method, although they were no longer structurally required. The two other sculptures, *Winter* and *Spring,* did not have any braces in the back.

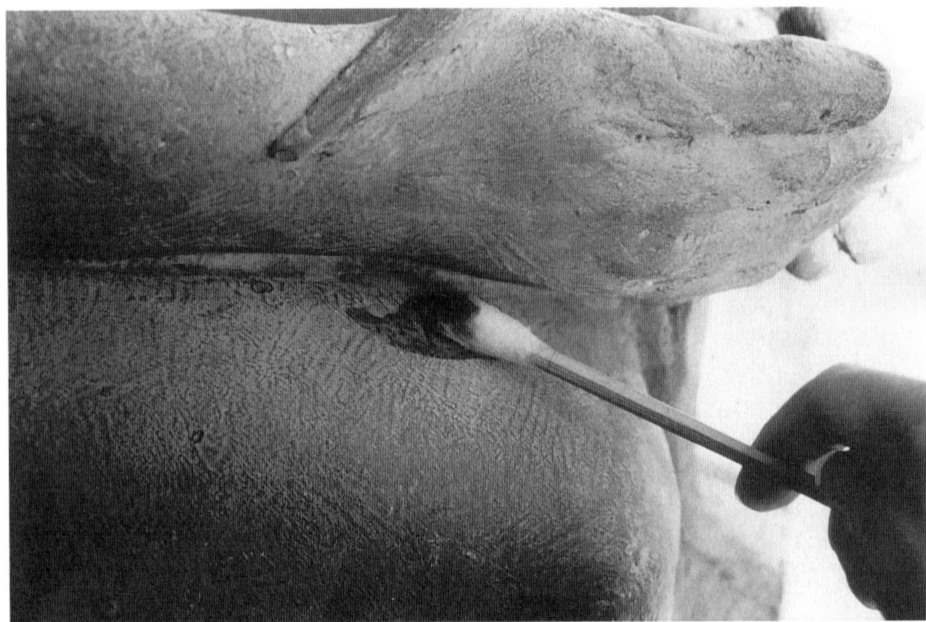

Dirt is removed from the surface of a plaster maiden.

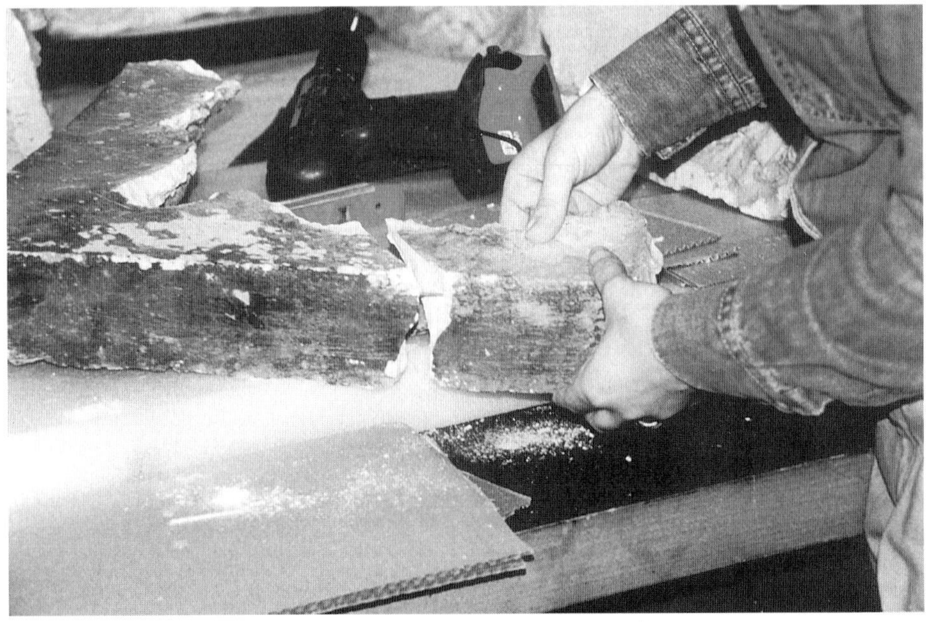

Broken sections are pinned back together.

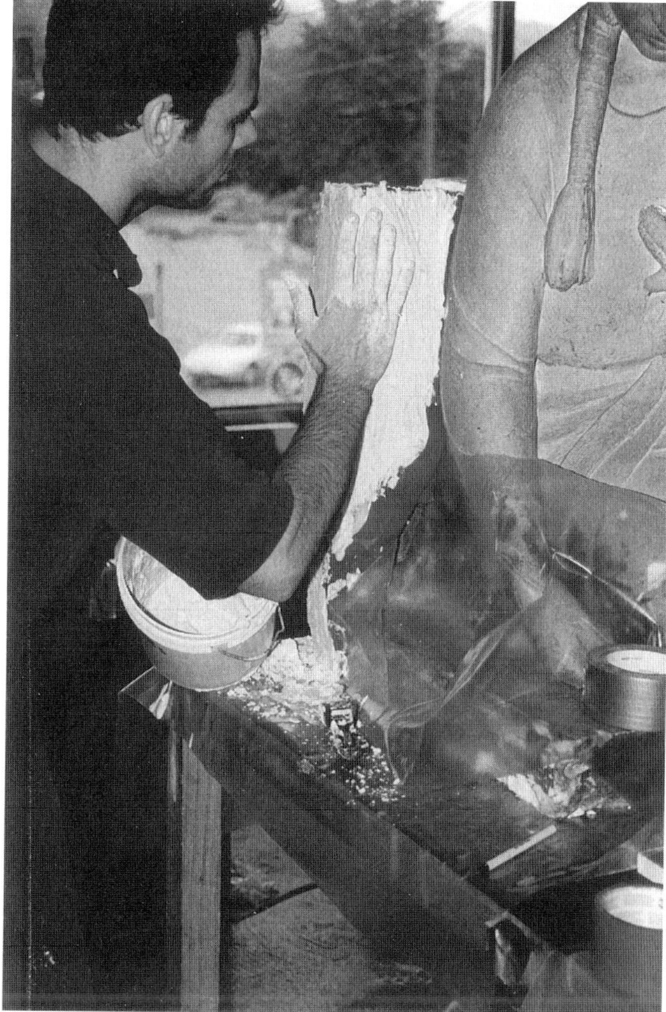

Conservator Francis Miller applies plaster on wire mesh.

CONCLUSION

The conservation treatment reports prepared by the author are part of the University Museums archives and contain numerous additional observations on Christian Petersen's craftsmanship and the materials that he used. Through the conservation work, we have helped preserve his artwork for future generations and have received the gift of being able to contribute to the understanding of this artist's oeuvre.

The collaboration between Christian Petersen, the artist, and Paul Cox, the engineer, produced works that are not only expressive but also must be of a very high caliber to have withstood an often aggressive outdoor environment. As the care for this art continues in an ever-growing academic environment, it will be everyone's collective challenge to preserve and not disturb the Christian Petersen sculptures that have come to symbolize Iowa State University. The sculptor's work is an exemplar of public art in public spaces by a regional artist in the United States.

NOTES

1. Inventory of American Sculpture Database. National Museum of American Art, Washington, D.C.

2. Bogart, Michele H., *Public Sculpture and the Civic Ideal in New York City 1890-1930,* Chicago: University of Chicago Press, 1989.

3. Bliss, Patricia L., *Christian Petersen Remembered,* Ames: Iowa State University Press, 1986.

4. Ibid., 41–42.

5. Burn Large Terra Cotta Panels in Small Special Kiln. *Ceramic Industry*, September 1935, 118, 148–150.

6. Complete analysis information available in April 16, 1999, correspondence from James B. Murowchick, Overland Park, Kansas.

7. Chicago Spectro Service Laboratory Report Number Four Season Fountain A1501-1 and Dairy Industries Mural A 1501-2. May 9,1995.

8. Weaver, Martin, *Conserving Buildings: A Guide to Techniques and Materials,* New York: John Wiley & Sons Inc., 1993, 122–124.

9. ProSoCo of Kansas City, Missouri. Labeled T-1804 Glass Cleaner by the manufacturer.

10. Petrographic and X-ray Diffraction Analyses. CGA Report # 9431. Dr. James Murowchick, July 1994.

11. Petrographic and XRD Analyses. CGA # 9431. James Murowchick, Overland Park, Kansas

12. Merk-Gould, Linda, et al., "Field Tests on Removing Corrosion From Outdoor Bronze Sculptures Using Waterjets," *ICOM Triennial Meeting Preprints,* 1993.

13. Conservation Technical Associates LLC: Conservation Treatment Report for the Terra Cotta Mural at ISU Veterinary Medicine Building. Submitted to University Museums, ISU, December 1997.

14. Sembrat, J., The Use of an Ultrasonic Cleaner for the Removal of Scale Deposits from a Terra Cotta Fountain, presented at ICOM Triennial Meeting, 1998.

15. Conservation Technical Associates LLC: Conservation Treatment Report for the Terra Cotta Gentle Doctor. Submitted to the University Museums, ISU, October 1999.

16. Merk-Gould, Linda, Conservation Treatment Report for Christian Petersen's Painted Plaster Mural Four Thousand Yeeres, CTALLC, May 17, 1995.

17. F. Welsh & Co. Report on C. Petersen Mural *Four Thousande Yeeres,* September 6, 1994.

18. F. Welsh & Co. Report on C. Petersen Mural *For Melke and Chese*, March 2, 1998.

HISTORICAL INFORMATION

ARTIST'S CHRONOLOGY[1]

DANA L. MICHELS

1 8 8 5 — Born on February 25 in Dybbol, Denmark, one of two sons and a daughter of Peter and Helene (Lorensen) Petersen.

1 8 9 4 — Immigrated to the United States with his parents and siblings, Peter (1891–unknown death date) and Anna (1888–1980s).

1 9 0 0 — Entered the Newark (New Jersey) Technical and Fine Arts School and began two years of studies as an apprentice in die-cutting.

1 9 0 2 — Worked as a beginning die-cutter while attending night classes at Fawcett School of Design in Newark for the next three years.

1 9 0 7 — Enrolled in the Art Students League in New York where he met George Nerney, who became his steadfast friend for the next fifty-four years. They worked for the Robbins Company, a firm that produced fine medallions and commemorative jewelry in Attleboro, Massachusetts. Petersen worked as design artist, intaglio engraver, and die-cutter. He studied life drawing at the Art Students League in New York under George Bridgeman and attended classes at the Beaux Arts Institute of Architecture and Design in New York.

1 9 0 8 — Married Emma L. Hoenicke (unknown birth date–1978).

1 9 0 9 — Daughter Helene born in Attleboro on July 24. Petersen worked as a freelance die-cutter for many of the fraternal jewelry manufacturers in the city, including the Robbins Company.

1 9 1 2 — Son Lawrence born on July 31 in Attleboro.

1 9 1 5 — Daughter Ruth born in Attleboro on April 4.

1 9 2 0 — Petersen was commissioned to create bronze portrait busts of former Rhode Island governors Emery J. Sans Souci and Aram Poithier. At an undetermined date, perhaps circa 1920, Petersen worked as assistant in the Quincy, Massachusetts, studio of sculptor Henry Hudson Kitson, an association which brought him sculpture commissions, including those from the state of Iowa.

1 9 2 3 — Petersen received what was probably his first sculpture-in-the-round commission, the *Spanish-American War Memorial* in Newport, Rhode Island. Received another commission from the State of Rhode Island for a portrait bust of former Rhode Island governor R.L. Beeckman.

1 9 2 0s — Throughout this period Petersen received many commissions for portraiture and medallion work. These included por-trait medallions of President Woodrow Wilson, General John Pershing, Rev. John Moore of Brooklyn College, Chief Justice Charles Evans Hughes of the United States Supreme Court, and Harvard President Charles W. Eliot; and bas reliefs or bust portraits of Prince and Princess Bibescu of Romania, Notre Dame football coach Knute Rockne, and John Cotton Dana, director of the Newark, New Jersey, Art Museum, among others.

MID-1 9 2 0s — Began receiving commissions in Des Moines for portraits of business and civic leaders.

LATE-1 9 2 0s — Invited to exhibit in a number of galleries, including the East Orange Art Center, New Jersey; a gallery in Providence, Rhode Island; and the Harcourt Studio in Boston. He decided to stop die-cutting work and turn his artistic efforts exclusively to fine art sculpture.

1 9 2 8 — Petersen and his wife Emma agreed to a divorce. He signed over their home and savings to her and left for Chicago in the late winter, determined to begin a new life and career in the Midwest. He took with him a contract to create the *Fountain of the Blue Herons* for the A.E. Staley Company in Decatur, Illinois.

1 9 2 9 — In late October, Petersen was living temporarily at the Chicago YMCA when the stock market collapsed and the financial disaster of the Great Depression began. In late November, Petersen was hired by Chicago jewelry manufacturers Dodge and Ascher.

1 9 3 1 — Married Charlotte Garvey (born February 23, 1899, died December 15, 1985), who was a secretary at Dodge and Ascher.

1 9 3 2 — Gave up his job at Dodge and Ascher to focus on sculpting. He and Charlotte moved to Belvidere, Illinois, and spent the summer in Des Moines where he did portrait commissions including one of Governor George Clarke arranged by Edgar Harlan, director of Iowa's State Historical, Memorial, and Art Department. Harlan introduced Petersen to Iowa State College President Raymond M. Hughes.

1 9 3 3 — Petersen completed the *Fountain of the Blue Herons* for A.E. Staley Company in Decatur, Illinois. His proposal for a monumental sculpture of Abraham Lincoln in Milwaukee won honorable mention from among forty-eight entries. He spent a second summer completing portrait commissions in Des Moines, where his sculptures were exhibited in the Younkers Department Store Gallery for eight weeks. Petersen was commissioned to produce his first portrait bust for Iowa State College, one of Louis Pammel, a pioneer scientist in botany and bacteriology. Patrons and friends such as Hughes and Harlan recommended Petersen to Grant Wood for the Public Works of Art Project (PWAP) in Iowa. On December 8, the federal PWAP program began.

1 9 3 4 — Invited on January 18 by Grant Wood to the PWAP in Iowa City, Petersen's assignment was a sculpted mural for what was then the Dairy Industry building. The federal Public Works of Art Project was disbanded in June. In August, Petersen moved to Ames, Iowa, where he became sculptor-in-residence at Iowa State College. His duties included creating sculptures for campus and teaching classes in sculpture to the all-female applied art program in the Home Economics Department. Petersen reported to Paul E. Cox, head of the Ceramic Engineering Department, who had been assigned to help him kiln fire panels for the dairy mural.

1 9 3 5 — At least a hundred firing periods of sixty hours each took place from September 1934 through April 1935 before Petersen's first large scale project for Iowa State College, the *History of Dairying Mural,* fountain sculpture, and reflecting pool were installed. Petersen and Dean of Veterinary Medicine Charles H. Stange planned the veterinary mural project.

1 9 3 6 — Petersen completed the *Three Athletes* for the State Gym and *Reclining Nudes* for Roberts Hall. *Cha-Ki-Shi,* a children's book on the Meskwaki Indians of Tama was published with illustrations by Petersen. His daughter, Mary Charlotte, was born on November 24.

1 9 3 8 — *Veterinary Medicine Mural* and *The Gentle Doctor* were completed. Petersen moved into a space offered by Dean Charles Murray in a converted horse hospital in the veterinary medicine building, a studio where Petersen would work for the rest of his life. As part of a commission for a portrait plaque of the University of Kentucky president, the Petersens took a summer trip to that state, where Petersen carried out a series of drawings of rural Kentucky scenes. These drawings were the basis of a series of small sculptures over the next several years.

1 9 3 9 — In the spring semester, men were allowed into Petersen's expanding sculpture class schedule for the first time.

1 9 4 1 — The *Fountain of the Four Seasons* unveiled at the Iowa State Memorial Union.

1 9 4 2 — The *Marriage Ring* installed in front of the home economics building. Iowa State College recognized Petersen with a dinner in his honor and an exhibition at the Memorial Union.

1 9 4 4 — *Library Boy* and *Girl* installed at the Iowa State College Library.

1 9 4 9 — Petersen converted to Catholicism at age 64.

LATE 1 9 4 0s and EARLY 1 9 5 0s — Petersen created a number of religious works of art, many of which were commissioned by churches and schools in Iowa.

1 9 5 3 — Petersen's daughter Mary entered Mount Carmel Convent in Dubuque, Iowa, where she remained for ten years.

1 9 5 5 — Completed *Conversations* before retiring at the age of 70.

LATE 1 9 5 0s — Continued to create portraits and reliefs for private and public commissions. He also taught clay modeling to handicapped children twice a week as a volunteer at Smouse Opportunity School in Des Moines.

1 9 5 9 — Began the design for *Dedication to the Future.* He suffered a heart attack later that year.

1 9 6 1 — Petersen died of cancer on April 4, four days after inspecting and signing the last casting mold for *Dedication to the Future* for the Fisher Community Center in Marshalltown, Iowa.

1 9 6 4 — Eighty of the remaining works in Petersen's studio were offered for sale to the public on behalf of Charlotte Petersen by close friends.

1 9 7 6 — The Brunnier Gallery, now the Brunnier Art Museum, presented the exhibition *Christian Petersen* from May 8 through 30. A new veterinary medicine building was constructed, and Petersen's relief mural was moved to its courtyard. The sculpture of *The Gentle Doctor* was placed on the main floor of the Scheman building in the Iowa State Center. A new bronze casting of the statue was made and placed in the courtyard of the new veterinary complex.

1 9 8 0 — The Iowa State University College of Design established the annual Christian Petersen Design Award to honor staff, faculty, alumni, and friends of the university.

1 9 8 1 — The artist's son Lawrence Christian Petersen died.

1 9 8 2 — The Iowa Veterinary Medical Association celebrated its centennial year by commissioning a commemorative bronze medallion featuring the image of *The Gentle Doctor,* international symbol of veterinary medicine.

1 9 8 5 — The Brunnier Museum and Gallery published a walking tour guide to the visual arts at Iowa State University including Petersen's works. In May, Charlotte moved into a retirement home. She and their daughter Mary sold many of Christian's studio sculptures. Mary also found more than four hundred of his sketches and early photographs that had been stored since 1945. They are now in the Christian Petersen Collection, Brunnier Art Museum, University Museums, Iowa State University. On December 15, Charlotte died.

1 9 8 6 — *Christian Petersen Remembered*, a biography by Patricia Lounsbury Bliss, was published by Iowa State University Press. The exhibition *Christian Petersen Remembered*, which included small sculptures and models from private collections, was held at the Octagon Center for the Arts in Ames, Iowa, from August 31 through October 15. The Brunnier Museum and Gallery announced a program to inspect and conserve Petersen's outdoor sculptures.

1 9 8 7 — Petersen's dairy courtyard sculptures, after a nomination submitted by Patricia L. Bliss, were accepted for the National Register of Historic Places on April 7. The artist's daughter Ruth Eleanor Sollenberger died on October 8.

1 9 8 8 — The exhibition *Christian Petersen: Images of Youth* was held at the Brunnier Gallery and Museum from January through March. Petersen's sculpture *Drought* was included in *New Deal Art of the Upper Midwest: An Anniversary Exhibition* at the Sioux City Art Center in Sioux City, Iowa.

1 9 9 1 — The *Marriage Ring* was moved inside MacKay Hall to prevent further damage. A reinforced concrete replica was made and placed outside.

1 9 9 3 — The replica of the *Marriage Ring* showed flaws and was redone. The molds used in making the replica were destroyed in a flood that summer; new molds were made and the sculpture was recast.

1 9 9 5 — Conservation of *For Melke and Chese and Buttere* and the fountain and *History of Dairying Mural* in the Food Sciences building, formerly Dairy Industry, completed.

1 9 9 6 – 1 9 9 7 — Petersen's *Two Children* were loaned to the Sioux City Art Center for the exhibition *A Decade of Motivation: Iowa and the Federal Arts Project, 1933–1943.*

1 9 9 7 — Bronze casting of *The Gentle Doctor* and the original *Veterinary Medicine Mural* conserved and rededicated at the College of Veterinary Medicine.

1 9 9 8 — Conservation completed on the *Fountain of the Four Seasons*, the *Boy* and *Girl* in Iowa State University Library, and on the following eleven small studio sculptures: *Flood, Charlotte, Drought, Soon after the Flood, Price of Victory, Risen Christ,* bronze casting of *The Gentle Doctor, Reverend W. Barlow, Mother and Child, Fallen Soldier, Two Maidens,* and *Dean Helen Benitez.*

1 9 9 9 — Completed conservation projects include *Three Athletes* at State Gym, *Four Thousande Yeeres* mural in the Food Sciences building, *Reclining Nudes* in Roberts Hall, *The Gentle Doctor* in terra cotta, four large plaster castings of the maidens of *Fountain of the Four Seasons*, the heads of the children's figures on *The Marriage Ring* at MacKay Hall, and *Converstaions* at Oak-Elm Residence Halls.

2 0 0 0 — Conservation completed by conservation Technical Associates on the following studio sculptures: *Saint Bernard of Clairvaux, Price of Victory, 4-H Calf, Cornhusker, Laura and Wallace, Francis McCray, Rose Shloss, Buffalo, Cowboy on a Cutting Horse, Library Boy* (model), *Library Girl* (model), *Bound Christ, George Washington Carver, Colonel Godson, Gentle Doctor* (model), *Charlotte and Mary* (mold), *Stephen Vincent Benet, Megan Norris,* and *Murray Children.* Retrospective exhibition, *Christian Petersen, Sculptor,* from August 22 through December 30, and publication with the same title of a series of essays and a catalog of Petersen's known lifetime works published in conjunction with the twenty-fifth Anniversary of the Brunnier Art Museum, University Museums, Iowa State University, Ames, Iowa.

NOTES

1. Information from 1885 through 1985 adapted from *Christian Petersen Remembered* by Patricia Lounsbury Bliss, Ames, Iowa: Iowa State University Press, 1986.

*Works of art by Christian Petersen are listed by date, and alphabetically
by title. Undated works of art appear alphabetically after those that are
dated. Measurements, unless otherwise noted, are in inches followed by
centimeters in parenthesis, with height preceding width and depth.*

DATED WORKS OF ART

Min Moder (My Mother), 1900
Silver, 2 (5.1) [diameter]
On loan from Mary Petersen, Beverly Hills, Florida.

Mother and Father, 1910
Bronze, 5 x 4 (12.7 x 10.2)
On loan from Scott Sollenberger, Clovis, California.

Nikh-Eiphnh, 1910
Plaster, 9 7/8 x 1 (25.1 x 2.5) [diameter x depth]
*On loan from Special Collections Department, Iowa State University
Library. Gift of Mrs. Helen Nerney Shaw. SC99.64.*

Theodore Roosevelt, ca. 1919
Bronze, 6 3/4 x 5 x 6 3/4 (17.1 x 12.7 x 17.1)
On loan from Lynn Sollenberger Lucido, Fresno, California.

Reverend George Endicott Osgood Medal, 1920
Bronze medal, 2 1/8 x 1/8 (5.4 x 0.3) [diameter x depth]
Steel positive mold, 2 1/2 x 2 (6.4 x 5.1) [diameter x depth]
Steel negative mold, 4 1/8 x 4 1/8 x 2 3/4 (10.5 x 10.5 x 7)
*On loan from Special Collections Department, Iowa State University
Library. Gift of Mrs. Helen Nerney Shaw. SC99.59abc.*

Medal, ca. 1920
Bronze, 1 1/2 x 1 x 1/8 (3.8 x 2.5 x 0.3)
On loan from Mary Petersen, Beverly Hills, Florida.

Medal, ca. 1920
Bronze, 1 1/2 x 1 x 1/8 (3.8 x 2.5 x 0.3)
On loan from Mary Petersen, Beverly Hills, Florida.

Winged Victory, ca. 1920
Bronze, 1 3/4 x 1 1/8 x 1/8 (4.4 x 2.8 x 0.3)
*On loan from Special Collections Department, Iowa State University
Library, Ames, Iowa. Purchased with Iowa State University Library
Funds. SC99.70.*

Prince Anton and Princess Elizabeth Bibescu of Romania, 1923
Bronze, 4 x 3 (10.2 x 7.6)
On loan from The Newark Museum, New Jersey. 29.2138.

Spoons, 1925
Sterling silver, 4 9/16 (11.6) [length]

Alma
*Christian Petersen Collection, Brunnier Art Museum, University
Museums, Iowa State University. Gift of Isabel Matterson. UM93.23c.*

California
*Christian Petersen Collection, Brunnier Art Museum, University
Museums, Iowa State University. Gift of Isabel Matterson. UM93.23a.*

Coal Miner
On loan from Mary Petersen, Beverly Hills, Florida.

General Jackson
*Christian Petersen Collection, Brunnier Art Museum, University
Museums, Iowa State University. Gift of Isabel Matterson. UM93.23b.*

Georgia Peaches
On loan from Mary Petersen, Beverly Hills, Florida.

Hibiscus
On loan from Mary Petersen, Beverly Hills, Florida.

Holly
On loan from Mary Petersen, Beverly Hills, Florida.

Lily
On loan from Mary Petersen, Beverly Hills, Florida.

Nantucket, Old Mill
On loan from Mary Petersen, Beverly Hills, Florida.

Nantucket, Stone Alley
On loan from Isabel Matterson, Ames, Iowa.

Palm Trees
On loan from Helene Petersen Male, Fresno, California.

Poppies
On loan from Mary Petersen, Beverly Hills, Florida.

Wood Brothers, 1925
Bronze, 48 x 33 x 3 (121.9 x 83.8 x 7.6)
*On loan from the State Historical Society of Iowa, Des Moines, Iowa.
I 11923.*

Henry Cantwell Wallace, Senior, 1926
Bronze, 28 x 21 x 10 (71.1 x 53.3 x 25.4)
On loan from the State Historical Society of Iowa, Des Moines, Iowa. I 525.

Cyrus Farnum, 1927
Bronze, 12 3/4 x 10 1/2 x 1/2 (32.4 x 26.7 x 1.3)
*Christian Petersen Collection, Brunnier Art Museum, University Museums,
Iowa State University. Gift of Joy Munn. UM99.296.*

Young Man in Profile, 1929
Plaster mold, 9 1/4 x 7 1/2 x 1 (23.5 x 19.1 x 2.5)
On loan from the State Historical Society of Iowa, Des Moines, Iowa. I 11919.

Edgar R. Harlan, ca. 1930
Painted plaster, 15 x 9 x 9 (38.1 x 22.7 x 22.7)
On loan from the State Historical Society of Iowa, Des Moines, Iowa. I 11917.

Young Bear, 1930
Painted plaster, 15 x 11 x 11 (38.1 x 27.9 x 27.9)
On loan from the State Historical Society of Iowa, Des Moines, Iowa. I 11916.

Jens Jensen, ca. 1930–1932
Painted plaster, 20 x 12 x 11 1/2 (50.8 x 30.5 x 29.2)
On loan from the Department of Landscape Architecture, Iowa State University. U94.2.

Vitus Bering, 1931
Painted plaster, 17 x 5 x 5 (43.2 x 12.7 x 12.7)
On loan from Margaret Hunziker, Ames, Iowa.

Stuart Boys, 1931
Plaster, 27 x 18 1/2 (68.6 x 47)
On loan from Reece Stuart III, Des Moines, Iowa.

Bear, ca. 1932
Charcoal on paper, 9 x 12 (22.9 x 30.5)
Christian Petersen Collection, Brunnier Art Museum, University Museums, Iowa State University. Purchased by the Christian Petersen Memorial Fund. UM92.177.

Governor George W. Clarke, 1932
Bronze, 26 x 22 x 11 (66 x 55.9 x 27.9)
On loan from the State Historical Society of Iowa, Des Moines, Iowa. I 528.

Rose Shloss, 1932
Painted plaster, 18 1/2 x 13 7/8 x 1 (47 x 35.1 x 2.5)
On loan from Marjorie Shloss Spevak and Frances M. Shloss.

Robert Mannheimer, 1933
Painted plaster, 19 x 11 1/2 (48.3 x 29.2)
On loan from Mr. and Mrs. Robert Mannheimer, Des Moines, Iowa.

Louis Herman Pammel, 1933
Bronze, 15 x 9 x 14 (38.1 x 22.9 x 35.6)
On loan from the Botany Department, Iowa State University. U99.295.

Colonel W.F. Godson, Fort Des Moines, ca. 1933
Painted plaster, 12 5/8 x 10 5/8 x 5/8 (32.1 x 27 x 1.6)
Christian Petersen Collection, Brunnier Art Museum, University Museums, Iowa State University. Gift of Helen J. Sebek. UM2000.3.

Bertrand R. Adams, 1934
Painted plaster, 18 1/2 x 8 x 8 1/2 (47 x 20.3 x 20.3)
On loan from Mary (Mrs. Bertrand) Adams, Ames, Iowa.

Buffalo, 1934
Painted plaster, 6 1/8 x 12 x 5 1/4 (20.3 x 35.6 x 15.2)
On loan from Special Collections Department, Iowa State University Library. Purchased with Iowa State University Library Funds. SC99.53.

Studies related to *History of Dairying Mural*, 1934–1935
  Courtyard
  Christian Petersen Collection, Brunnier Art Museum, University Museums, Iowa State University. Purchased by the Christian Petersen Memorial Fund. UM92.148.
  First Concept
  Colored pencil on paper, 6 3/4 x 50 1/2 (17.1 x 128.3);
  Image: 5 x 48 (12.7 x 121.9)
  On loan from Special Collections Department, Iowa State University Library. Gift of Charlotte Petersen. SC99.161.
  For Melke and Chese and Buttere: Preparatory Study
  Pencil or conté on paper, 8 1/2 x 11 (21.6 x 27.9)
  Christian Petersen Collection, Brunnier Art Museum, University Museums, Iowa State University. Purchased by the Christian Petersen Memorial Fund. UM92.128.

For Melke and Chese and Buttere: Final Model, 1934
Painted plaster, 24 x 18 3/8 x 2 (60.9 x 46.7 x 5.1)
On loan from Virginia Slater, Ames, Iowa.

History of Dairying Mural: Study of Cows, 1934
Painted plaster, 12 x 24 x 6 (30.5 x 60.9 x 15.2)
Christian Petersen Collection, Brunnier Art Museum, University Museums, Iowa State University. Gift of the Animal Science Department. U90.101.

Francis McCray, 1934
Plaster, 19 x 9 1/2 x 9 1/2 (48.3 x 24.1 x 24.1)
Christian Petersen Collection, Brunnier Art Museum, University Museums, Iowa State University. Gift of the Friends of the University Museums. U89.39.

Eli Lilly & Company Research Award: Study, ca. 1935
Colored pencil on paper, 8 1/2 x 11 (21.6 x 27.9)
Christian Petersen Collection, Brunnier Art Museum, University Museums, Iowa State University. Purchased by the Christian Petersen Memorial Fund. UM92.138.

Eli Lilly and Company Research Award, 1936
Bronze, 3 x 1/4 (7.6 x 0.6) [diameter x depth]
On loan from Special Collections Department, Iowa State University Library. Purchased with Iowa State University Library Funds. SC99.68.

Martin Mortensen, 1935
Painted plaster, 22 x 8 1/2 x 11 (55.9 x 21.6 x 27.9)
Christian Petersen Collection, Brunnier Art Museum, University Museums, Iowa State University. Gift of Mrs. Marie Beal. U90.27.

Studies related to *Veterinary Medicine Mural*, 1935–1936

Farm Animals and Final Concept

Orange pencil on paper, 8 1/2 x 11 (21.6 x 27.9)
Christian Petersen Collection, Brunnier Art Museum, University Museums. Purchased from Mary Petersen with funds from the Christian Petersen Memorial Fund. UM92.44b.

Final Design

Pencil or conté on paper, 11 x 7 3/4 (27.9 x 19.7)
Gift to Veterinary College by Charlotte and Mary Petersen. Gift of Veterinary College to Christian Petersen Collection, Brunnier Art Museum, University Museums. U89.41a.

Preliminary Study

Pencil or conté on paper, 8 1/2 x 11 (21.6 x 27.9)
Christian Petersen Collection, Brunnier Art Museum, University Museums. Purchased by the Christian Petersen Memorial Fund. UM92.45.

Veterinary Medicine Mural:
Studies related to *The Gentle Doctor,* 1935–1936

Preliminary Design

Black conté on paper, 12 x 9 (30.5 x 22.9)
Christian Petersen Collection, Brunnier Art Museum, University Museums. Gift of College of Veterinary Medicine, Iowa State University. U89.41d.

Preliminary Study

Pencil or conté on paper, 11 x 8 1/2 (27.9 x 21.6)
Christian Petersen Collection, Brunnier Art Museum, University Museums. Gift of College of Veterinary Medicine, Iowa State University. U89.41b.

Study of Dog

Pencil on paper, 11 3/4 x 8 3/4 (29.8 x 22.2)
On loan from Special Collections Department, Iowa State University Library. Gift of Charlotte Petersen. SC99.177.

Reclining Nudes: Preparatory Study, 1935–1936

Pencil or conté on paper, 8 1/2 x 11 (21.6 x 27.9)
Christian Petersen Collection, Brunnier Art Museum, University Museums. Purchased by the Christian Petersen Memorial Fund. UM92.123.

Studies related to *Three Athletes*, 1935–1936

Concept Study

Charcoal on paper, 9 x 12 (22.9 x 30.5)
Christian Petersen Collection, Brunnier Art Museum, University Museums. Purchased by the Christian Petersen Memorial Fund. UM92.176.

Figure Study

Charcoal on paper, 9 x 12 (22.9 x 30.5)
Christian Petersen Collection, Brunnier Art Museum, University Museums. Purchased by the Christian Petersen Memorial Fund. UM92.174.

Motion Studies

Brown pencil on paper, 8 1/2 x 11 (21.6 x 27.6)
Christian Petersen Collection, Brunnier Art Museum, University Museums. Purchased by the Christian Petersen Memorial Fund. UM92.135a.

Studies of Athletes

Pencil or conté on paper, 8 1/2 x 11 (21.6 x 27.9)
Christian Petersen Collection, Brunnier Art Museum, University Museums. Purchased by the Christian Petersen Memorial Fund. UM92.31.

Cha-Ki-Shi: Ba-wi-shi-ka Dressed for the Dance, ca. 1936

Pencil, conté, watercolor and colored pencil on paper, 12 x 9 (30.5 x 22.9);
Image: 10 1/4 x 7 3/8 (26 x 18.7)
On loan from Special Collections Department, Iowa State University Library. Gift of Charlotte Petersen. SC99.120.

Cha-Ki-Shi: The Baby and Her New Cradle, ca. 1936

Conté on paper, 13 1/2 x 10 3/4 (34.5 x 27.3);
Image: 3 1/2 x 4 (8.9 x 10.2)
On loan from Special Collections Department, Iowa State University Library. Gift of Charlotte Petersen. SC99.127.

Cha-Ki-Shi: Bearclaw Necklace, ca. 1936

Charcoal and pencil on paper, 12 x 9 1/4 (30.5 x 23.5);
Image: 12 x 5 (30.5 x 12.7)
On loan from Special Collections Department, Iowa State University Library. Gift of Charlotte Petersen. SC99.124.

Cha-Ki-Shi: The Brush Broom, ca. 1936

Pencil on paper, 12 x 9 1/8 (30.5 x 23.2)
On loan from Special Collections Department, Iowa State University Library. Gift of Charlotte Petersen. SC99.91.

Cha-Ki-Shi: The Buffalo Head Dance, ca. 1936

Conté on textured paper, 10 3/4 x 11 (23.2 x 27.9);
Image: 7 1/2 x 8 (19.1 x 20.3)
On loan from Special Collections Department, Iowa State University Library. Gift of Charlotte Petersen. SC99.130.

Cha-Ki-Shi: Cha-Ki-Shi Loses Her Doll, ca. 1936

Pencil, colored pencil and charcoal on paper, 12 x 9 (30.5 x 22.9)
On loan from Special Collections Department, Iowa State University Library. Gift of Charlotte Petersen. SC99.121.

Cha-Ki-Shi: Girl with Ko-Na-No, ca. 1936

Pencil and conté on textured paper, 13 1/2 x 10 5/8 (34.3 x 26);
Images 7 1/4 x 8 (18.4 x 20.3) and 2 x 3 1/2 (5.1 x 8.9)
On loan from Special Collections Department, Iowa State University Library. Gift of Charlotte Petersen. SC99.132.

Cha-Ki-Shi: Mesquakie Headdress, ca. 1936

Conté, pencil and pastel or crayon on paper, 12 x 9 (30.5 x 22.9)
On loan from Special Collections Department, Iowa State University Library. Gift of Charlotte Petersen. SC99.122.

Cha-Ki-Shi: The Runner, ca. 1936

Conté on paper, 9 1/4 x 12 (23.5 x 30.5)
On loan from Special Collections Department, Iowa State University Library. Gift of Charlotte Petersen. SC99.134.

**Cha-Ki-Shi: Stretching and Drying the Skins
for the Baby's New Dress,** ca. 1936
Conté on paper, 11 3/4 x 10 1/4 (29.8 x 26);
Image: 7 x 8 (17.8 x 20.3)
*On loan from Special Collections Department, Iowa State University
Library. Gift of Charlotte Petersen. SC99.111.*

Cha-Ki-Shi: Study for the Cover, ca. 1936
Watercolor on paper, 11 x 8 1/2 (27.9 x 21.6);
Image: 7 1/4 x 4 5/8 (18.4 x 11.7)
*On loan from Special Collections Department, Iowa State University
Library. Gift of Charlotte Petersen. SC99.133.*

Country Doctor, 1936
Painted plaster, 32 x 9 1/2 x 14 1/2 (81.3 x 24.1 x 36.8)
*Christian Petersen Collection, Brunnier Art Museum, University Museums,
Iowa State University. Gift of Helen J. Sebek. UM99.298.*

Farmer's Face, ca. 1936
Pencil and colored pencil on paper, 8 1/2 x 11 (21.6 x 27.9)
*Christian Petersen Collection, Brunnier Art Museum, University Museums,
Iowa State University. Purchased by the Christian Petersen Memorial
Fund. UM92.35.*

The Gentle Doctor: Model, 1936
Painted plaster, 16 x 5 1/4 x 4 (40.6 x 15.2 x 10.2)
*On loan from M. Burton Drexler. Promised gift to Christian Petersen Collec-
tion, Brunnier Art Museum, University Museums, Iowa State University.*

Mary Charlotte Petersen, 1936
Engraving on paper, 4 1/2 x 6 (11.4 x 15.2);
Image: 3 x 4 (7.6 x 10.2);
Copper plate, 3 x 4 x 1/16 (7.6 x 10.2 x 0.2)
*On loan from Special Collections Department, Iowa State University Library.
Gift of Charlotte Petersen. Engraving: SC99.286a. Plate: SC99.286b.*

Professors' Conference, ca. 1936
Pencil or conté on paper, 8 1/2 x 11 (21.6 x 27.9)
*Christian Petersen Collection, Brunnier Art Museum, University Museums,
Iowa State University Purchased from Mary Petersen with funds from
the Christian Petersen Memorial Fund. UM92.29.*

Reclining Nudes (Roberts Hall Fountain), 1936
Terra cotta cast in nine panels, 25" x 13'7" x 8" (63.5 x 414 x 20.3)
*Commissioned by Iowa State College, in the Art on Campus Collec-
tion, University Museums, Iowa State University. U88.74.*

Dean Charles Henry Stange, DVM, ca. 1936
Painted plaster, 38 x 33 x 21 (96.5 x 83.8 x 53.3)
On loan from the College of Veterinary Medicine, Iowa State University. U90.63.

Charles E. Friley, 1937
Bronze, 17 x 10 1/2 x 10 1/2 (43.2 x 26.7 x 26.7)
*Christian Petersen Collection, Brunnier Art Museum, University Museums.
Gift of Friley Hall, Department of Residence, Iowa State University. U94.36.*

Mary at Age One, 1937
Engraving on paper, 9 1/2 x 9 3/4 (24.1 x 24.8);
Copper plate: 6 1/4 x 5 1/8 x 1/32 (15.9 x 13 x 0.8)
*On loan from Special Collections Department, Iowa State University Li-
brary. Gifts of Charlotte Petersen. Engraving: SC99.276. Plate: SC99.230.*

Amphitheater: Sketch, ca. 1938
Pencil or conté on paper, 16 1/8 x 13 3/4 (41 x 34.9)
*Christian Petersen Collection, Brunnier Art Museum, University Museums,
Iowa State University. Purchased from Mary Petersen with funds from
the Christian Petersen Memorial Fund. UM92.217.*

Anson Marston Medal, 1938
Bronze medals, 1 5/8 x 1/8 (4.1 x 0.3) [diameter x depth]
Steel molds, 2 1/4 x 3/16 (5.7 x 0.5) [diameter x depth]
*On loan from Special Collections Department, Iowa State University
Library. Purchased with Iowa State University Library Funds.
SC99.60abc and SC99.61.*

Charlotte Sitting on a Rock at a Picnic, ca. 1938
Painted plaster, 11 3/16 x 9 3/8 x 7 3/4 (28.4 x 23.8 x 19.7)
*Christian Petersen Collection, Brunnier Art Museum, University Museums,
Iowa State University. Gift of Mary Petersen. UM92.610.*

Drought, ca. 1938
Painted plaster, 21 3/4 x 7 x 13 (55.2 x 17.8 x 33)
*Christian Petersen Collection, Brunnier Art Museum, University
Museums, Iowa State University. Gift of Class of 1919. UM85.49.*

Flood, 1938
Painted plaster cast, 16 1/2 x 9 (41.9 x 22.9)
*Christian Petersen Collection, Brunnier Art Museum, University
Museums, Iowa State University. Gift of Class of 1919. UM85.48.*

Laura and Wallace, 1938
Painted plaster, Laura: 11 1/2 x 9 x 12 (29.2 x 22.9 x 30.5);
 Wallace: 11 x 8 x 9 (27.9 x 20.3 x 22.9)
*Christian Petersen Collection, Brunnier Art Museum, University Museums,
Iowa State University. Gifts of Joy Munn. UM99.301 and UM99.300.*

Mother with Walking Child, ca. 1938
Fired clay, 16 x 6 (40.6 x 15.2)
*Christian Petersen Collection, Brunnier Art Museum, University Museums,
Iowa State University. Gift of James Borcherding. U92.402.*

Mother with Walking Child (unfinished), ca. 1938
Bedford limestone with charcoal, 26 1/2 x 6 (67.3 x 15.2)
*Christian Petersen Collection, Brunnier Art Museum, University Museums,
Iowa State University. Gift of James Borcherding. U92.401.*

Pioneer Woman (Alma Mater), 1938
Plaster, 23 x 7 x 6 (58.4 x 17.8 x 15.2)
*Christian Petersen Collection, Brunnier Art Museum, University Museums,
Iowa State University. Anonymous gift in memory of Charlotte Petersen.
UM89.19.*

**Studies related to Petersen's trip to Kentucky
in the summer of 1938**

  Kelly Caldwell
Pencil on paper, 7 1/2 x 10 3/8 (19 x 26.4)
On loan from Special Collections Department, Iowa State University Library. Gift of Charlotte Petersen. SC99.146.

  Man with Upraised Arms
Pencil on paper, 10 3/8 x 6 3/4 (26.4 x 17.1)
On loan from Special Collections Department, Iowa State University Library. Gift of Charlotte Petersen. SC99.148.

  Men on a Bench
Pencil on paper, 15 3/4 x 12 (40 x 30.5)
On loan from Special Collections Department, Iowa State University Library. Gift of Charlotte Petersen. SC99.149.

  Seated Woman
Pencil on paper, 10 1/2 x 7 1/4 (26.7 x 18.4)
On loan from Special Collections Department, Iowa State University Library. Gift of Charlotte Petersen. SC99.145.

  Storyteller
Pencil on paper, 10 3/8 x 7 3/8 (26.4 x 19)
On loan from Special Collections Department, Iowa State University Library. Gift of Charlotte Petersen. SC99.144.

  Uncle John
Pencil on paper, 10 3/8 x 7 1/4 (26.4 x 18.4)
On loan from Special Collections Department, Iowa State University Library. Gift of Charlotte Petersen. SC99.154.

  Uncle Miles Bach
Pencil on paper, 10 1/2 x 7 3/8 (26.7 x 18.6)
On loan from Special Collections Department, Iowa State University Library. Gift of Charlotte Petersen. SC99.155.

  Woman in Bonnet
Pencil on paper, 10 3/8 x 7 1/8 (26.2 x 18.1)
On loan from Special Collections Department, Iowa State University Library. Gift of Charlotte Petersen. SC99.157.

  Woman Hanging Laundry
Pencil on paper, 7 1/2 x 8 (19.1 x 20.3)
On loan from Special Collections Department, Iowa State University Library. Gift of Charlotte Petersen. SC99.151.

  Two Women in Prayer
Pencil on paper mounted on paper, 10 1/2 x 7 3/8 (26.7 x 19)
On loan from Special Collections Department, Iowa State University Library. Gift of Charlotte Petersen. SC99.158.

Charlotte and Mary, ca. 1939
Brown pencil on paper, 16 3/4 x 13 3/4 (42.5 x 34.9)
Christian Petersen Collection, Brunnier Art Museum, University Museums, Iowa State University. Purchased with funds from the Christian Petersen Memorial Fund. UM92.223.

Hello Beautiful, 1939
Booklet, 7 1/4 x 5 (23.8 x 16.4)
Christian Petersen Collection, Brunnier Art Museum, University Museums, Iowa State University. Gift of Charlotte Petersen.

Mountain Mother, ca. 1939
Bedford limestone, 18 (45.7) [height]
On loan from the Central Iowa Art Association, Marshalltown, Iowa.

Soon after Flood (Three Children on a Mule; After the Flood), 1939
Painted plaster, 26 x 22 x 8 (66 x 55.9 x 20.3)
Christian Petersen Collection, Brunnier Art Museum, University Museums, Iowa State University. Gift of Bernice Burns Donovan and Esther Burns. UM85.50.

Two Children, 1939
Fired clay, Boy: 12 1/2 x 5 1/4 x 4 (31.8 x 13.3. x 10.2);
Girl: 12 1/2 x 4 3/4 x 5 1/4 (31.8 x 12.1 x 13.3)
Christian Petersen Collection, Brunnier Art Museum, University Museums, Iowa State University. Gift of Patricia L. Bliss. UM89.20 and UM89.21.

Dancing Woman, late 1930s
Painted plaster, 13 1/2 x 9 x 3 1/2 (34.3 x 22.9 x 8.9)
Christian Petersen Collection, Brunnier Art Museum, University Museums, Iowa State University. Purchased in memory of Ruth Smith with funds from Friends of Ruth Smith. UM98.2.

Dancing Woman, late 1930s
Painted plaster, 13 1/8 x 9 x 3 1/2 (33.3 x 22.9 x 8.9)
Christian Petersen Collection, Brunnier Art Museum, University Museums, Iowa State University. Purchased in memory of Ruth Smith with funds from Friends of Ruth Smith. UM98.3.

Equitable of Iowa Companies Award, ca. late 1930s
Pencil or conté on paper, 8 1/2 x 11 (21.6 x 27.9)
Christian Petersen Collection, Brunnier Art Museum, University Museums, Iowa State University. Purchased by the Christian Petersen Memorial Fund. UM92.38a.

Mary Petersen and Her Friends, ca. late 1930s
Pencil or conté on paper, 13 3/4 x 16 3/4 (34.9 x 42.5)
Christian Petersen Collection, Brunnier Art Museum, University Museums, Iowa State University. Purchased by the Christian Petersen Memorial Fund. UM92.215.

Pin, ca. late 1930s
Silver, 2 x 1 1/2 (5.1 x 3.8)
On loan from Mary Petersen, Beverly Hills, Florida.

Bears, ca. 1930s
Pencil or conté on paper, 9 x 12 (22.9 x 30.5)
Christian Petersen Collection, Brunnier Art Museum, University Museums, Iowa State University. Purchased by the Christian Petersen Memorial Fund. UM92.166.

Fountain, ca. 1930s
Charcoal on paper, 9 x 12 (22.9 x 30.5)
Christian Petersen Collection, Brunnier Art Museum, University Museums, Iowa State University. Purchased by the Christian Petersen Memorial Fund. UM92.186.

Charlotte, ca. 1940
Pencil on paper, 9 x 12 (22.9 x 30.5)
Christian Petersen Collection, Brunnier Art Museum, University Museums, Iowa State University. Purchased by the Christian Petersen Memorial Fund. UM92.156.

Mary with a Doll, ca. 1940
Engraving on paper, 4 7/8 x 2 7/8;
Copper plate used in printing it: 4 1/2 x 2 1/4 x 1/32 (11.4 x 5.7 x .1)
On loan from Special Collections Department, Iowa State University Library. Gifts of Charlotte Petersen. Engraving: SC99.162. Plate: SC99.229.

Mary with a Doll, ca. 1940
Pencil and ink on paper, 5 1/2 x 3 3/4 (14 x 9.5)
On loan from Special Collections Department, Iowa State University Library. SC99.169.

War (After the Blitz War): Nude Woman, ca. 1940
Brown pencil on paper, 16 3/4 x 13 3/4 (42.5 x 34.9)
Christian Petersen Collection, Brunnier Art Museum, University Museums, Iowa State University. Purchased by the Christian Petersen Memorial Fund. UM92.224.

Dmitri Metroupolis [*sic*], 1940
Painted plaster, 10 3/4 x 12 3/4 (27.3 x 32.4)
On loan from Maridee Hegstrom, Ames, Iowa.

Madonna, 1940
Clay sketch, 7 3/4 x 1 5/8 x 3 1/2 (19.7 x 4.1 x 8.9)
Christian Petersen Collection, Brunnier Art Museum, University Museums, Iowa State University. Gift of Helen J. Sebek. UM2000.5.

Old Woman in Prayer (The Refugee), ca. 1940
Bedford limestone, 28 x 17 x 18 (71.1 x 43.2 x 45.7)
On loan from Iowa State University Library. Iowa Art in State Buildings Program Purchase by Iowa State University Library. Art on Campus Collection. U86.521.

Cornhusker, 1941
Painted plaster, 43 x 16 x 24 (109.2 x 40.6 x 60.9)
Christian Petersen Collection, Brunnier Art Musem, University Museums, Iowa State University. Gift in memory of Joseph M. Coppola, Sr., by the Coppola Family. UM99.329.

4-H Calf, 1941
Painted plaster, 40 1/2 x 31 1/2 x 18 (102.9 x 80 x 45.7)
Christian Petersen Collection, Brunnier Art Museum, University Museums, Iowa State University. Gift in memory of Joseph M. Coppola, Sr., by the Coppola Family. UM99.330.

Fountain of the Four Seasons: Maidens, 1941
Plaster models, A: 40 x 24 x 22 3/4 (101.6 x 60.9 x 57.8);
B: 40 x 24 x 24 (101.6 x 61 x 61);
C: 38 x 24 x 22 (96.5 x 60.9 x 55.9);
D: 40 x 24 x 24 (96.5 x 60.9 x 60.9)

Christian Petersen Collection, Brunnier Art Museum, University Museums, Iowa State University. Gift of the Friends of the University Museums. U89.26abcd.

Mary on a Swing, ca. 1942
Watercolor on linocut print on paper, 6 7/8 x 5 1/4 (17.5 x 13.3);
Image: 6 x 4 1/4 (15.2 x 10.8);
Incised linoleum on wood block: 5 1/2 x 4 3/8 x 1 1/8 (14 x 11.1 x 2.9)
On loan from Special Collections Department, Iowa State University Library, Ames, Iowa. Gifts of Charlotte Petersen. Print: SC99.163. Block: SC99.291.

Marriage Ring: Study of MacKay Hall, 1942
Pencil or conté on paper, 16 1/2 x 13 3/4 (41.9 x 34.9)
Christian Petersen Collection, Brunnier Art Museum, University Museums, Iowa State University. Purchased by the Christian Petersen Memorial Fund. UM92.222.

Marriage Ring: Model, 1942
Painted plaster, 5 1/2 x 20 1/2 x 4 /2 (14 x 52.1 x 11.4)
On loan from Eleanor and William Butler, White Bear Lake, Minnesota.

Men of Two Wars, 1942
Painted plaster, 33 x 55 x 29 (83.8 x 139.7 x 73.7)
On loan from the Memorial Union, Iowa State University.

Library Boy and Girl: Preliminary Studies, 1943
Pencil or conté on paper, 16 3/4 x 13 3/4 (42.5 x 34.9)
Christian Petersen Collection, Brunnier Art Museum, University Museums, Iowa State University. Purchased by the Christian Petersen Memorial Fund. UM92.252.

Library Boy and Girl: Models, 1944
Painted plaster, 24 x 12 x 12 (61 x 30.5 x 30.5) [each]
On loan from Wayne Moore, Ames, Iowa.

Library Boy: Model, 1944
Painted plaster, 20 1/2 x 7 1/4 x 6 1/2 (52.1 x 18.4 x 16.5)
On loan from Special Collections Department, Iowa State University Library. Gift of Charlotte Petersen. SC99.66.

Library Girl: Model, 1944
Painted plaster, 12 x 4 1/2 x 5 1/2 (30.5 x 11.4 x 14)
On loan from Special Collections Department, Iowa State University Library. Gift of Charlotte Petersen. SC99.65.

Price of Victory (Fallen Soldier), ca. 1944
Charcoal on paper, 8 3/4 x 11 7/8 (22.2 x 30.2)
Christian Petersen Collection, Brunnier Art Museum, University Museums, Iowa State University. Purchased by the Christian Petersen Memorial Fund. UM92.95.

Price of Victory (Fallen Soldier), 1944
Painted plaster, 36 x 18 x 16 (91.4 x 45.7 x 40.6)
Christian Petersen Collection, Brunnier Art Museum, University Museums, Iowa State University. Gift of Mary Petersen. UM99.297.

Soldiers, ca. 1944
Pencil or conté on paper, 13 3/4 x 16 3/4 (34.9 x 42.5)
Christian Petersen Collection, Brunnier Art Museum, University Museums, Iowa State University. Purchased by the Christian Petersen Memorial Fund. UM92.207.

Unknown Prisoner: Preparatory Study, ca. 1944
Pencil or conté on paper, 9 x 12 (22.9 x 30.5)
Christian Petersen Collection, Brunnier Art Museum, University Museums, Iowa State University. Purchased by the Christian Petersen Memorial Fund. UM92.359.

Unknown Prisoner, 1944
Plaster, 15 1/2 x 17 3/8 x 9 3/8 (39.4 x 44.1 x 23.8)
Christian Petersen Collection, Brunnier Art Museum, University Museums, Iowa State University. Gift of Helen J. Sebek. UM2000.6.

Father William Clark, ca. 1945
Pencil on paper, 10 1/2 x 9
On loan from Virginia Slater, Ames, Iowa.

Mary with Braids, ca. 1945
Brown pencil on paper, 13 x 11 (33 x 27.9)
On loan from Mary Petersen, Beverly Hills, Florida.

Landscape, ca. 1945–1955
Oil on masonite, 12 x 18 (30.5 x 45.7)
Christian Petersen Collection, Brunnier Art Museum, University Museums, Iowa State University. Gift of Mary Petersen. UM92.608.

Studies related to *Conversations*, 1946–1947
   Man and Woman
   Pencil or conté on paper, 8 x 10 (20.3 x 25.4)
   Christian Petersen Collection, Brunnier Art Museum, University Museums, Iowa State University. Purchased from Mary Petersen with funds from the Christian Petersen Memorial Fund. UM92.350.
   Preliminary Study
   Pencil or conté on paper, 13 3/4 x 16 3/4 (34.9 x 42.5)
   Christian Petersen Collection, Brunnier Art Museum, University Museums, Iowa State University. Purchased by the Christian Petersen Memorial Fund. UM92.210.
   Studies for Wall
   Pencil on paper, 9 1/2 x 12 (24.1 x 30.5)
   Christian Petersen Collection, Brunnier Art Museum, University Museums, Iowa State University. Gift of Charlotte Petersen. SC99.220.

Conversations: Students at Wall, 1946
Painted plaster and clay, approximately 10 x 18 x 4 (25.4 x 45.7 x 10.2)
On loan from Ms. Carol Mae Campbell, Menlo Park, California.

Madonna of the Schools: Figure Study, 1946
Pencil or conté on paper, 8 3/4 x 11 7/8 (22.2 x 30.2)
Christian Petersen Collection, Brunnier Art Museum, University Museums, Iowa State University. Purchased by the Christian Petersen Memorial Fund. UM92.86.

Madonna of the Schools, 1946
Clay, 16 x 15 1/2 x 1 3/8 (52.5 x 50.9 x 4.5)
On loan from Saint Cecilia's Catholic Church, Ames, Iowa. Gift of Florence Castonguay.

Saint Cecilia with Children, ca. 1946
Painted plaster, 8 5/8 x 16 x 7 1/2 (21.9 x 40.6 x 19.1)
On loan from Helen and Keith McRoberts, Woodward, Iowa.

Madonna and Child, ca. 1947
Pencil and conté on paper, 11 3/4 x 8 3/4 (29.8 x 22.2)
On loan from Special Collections Department, Iowa State University Library, Ames, Iowa. Gift of Charlotte Petersen. SC99.181.

Iowa State College Alumni Medallion, 1948
Bronze, 15 x 1/2 (38.1 x 1.3) [diameter x depth]
Art on Campus Collection, University Museums, Iowa State University. Funded by Alumni Association. U99.17.

Iowa State College Alumni Medal, 1948
Bronze, 2 7/8 x 1/2 (2.22 x .6) [diameter x depth]
On loan from Special Collections Department, Iowa State University Library, Ames, Iowa. Purchased with Iowa State University Library Funds. SC99.67.

George Washington Carver: Preparatory Sketch, ca. 1949
Pencil or conté on paper, 5 3/4 x 9 (14.6 x 22.7)
Christian Petersen Collection, Brunnier Art Museum, University Museums, Iowa State University. Purchased from Mary Petersen with funds from the Christian Petersen Memorial Fund. UM92.112.

George Washington Carver, 1949
Painted plaster, 43 x 12 x 11 (109.2 x 30.5 x 27.9)
Art on Campus Collection, University Museums, Iowa State University. Gift of the Class of 1968. U88.73.

Risen Jesus Christ, 1949
Plaster, 38 x 15 x 7 (96.5 x 38.1 x 17.8)
Christian Petersen Collection, Brunnier Art Museum, University Museums, Iowa State University. Gift of the Friends of the University Museums. U89.25.

Studies related to *Saint Francis Xavier,* 1949
   Figure Study
   Pencil or conté on paper, 8 3/4 x 11 7/8 (22.2 x 30.2)
   Christian Petersen Collection, Brunnier Art Museum, University Museums, Iowa State University. Purchased by the Christian Petersen Memorial Fund. UM92.85.
   Studies for Panels
   Pencil or conté on paper, 8 3/4 x 11 7/8 (22.2 x 30.2)
   Christian Petersen Collection, Brunnier Art Museum, University Museums, Iowa State University. Purchased by the Christian Petersen Memorial Fund. UM92.75.

Studies related to *Saint Francis Xavier,* continued

Study of a Priest
Pencil or conté on paper, 8 3/4 x 11 7/8 (22.2 x 30.2)
Christian Petersen Collection, Brunnier Art Museum, University Museums, Iowa State University. Purchased by the Christian Petersen Memorial Fund. UM92.73.

J.C. Cunningham Sleeping, ca. 1940s
Watercolor on paper, 9 3/4 x 9 7/8 (24.8 x 25.1)
Christian Petersen Collection, Brunnier Art Museum, University Museums, Iowa State University. Purchased by the Christian Petersen Memorial Fund. UM92.147.

Farm Scene, ca. 1940s
Colored pastels and pencil on paper, 13 3/4 x 16 1/2 (34.9 x 41.9)
Christian Petersen Collection, Brunnier Art Museum, University Museums, Iowa State University. Gift of Mary Petersen. UM92.612.

Farmer and His Wife Looking over Their Land, ca. 1940s
Colored pencil on paper, 10 x 13 3/4 (25.4 x 34.9)
Christian Petersen Collection, Brunnier Art Museum, University Museums, Iowa State University. Purchased by the Christian Petersen Memorial Fund. UM92.188a.

Girl with a Sick Pet, ca. 1940s
Pencil on paper, 12 x 9 3/4 (30.5 x 24.8)
On loan from Special Collections Department, Iowa State University Library. Gift of Charlotte Petersen. SC99.224.

Julegranen: Angel, ca. 1940s
Colored pencil on paper, 8 3/4 x 11 7/8 (22.2 x 30.2)
Christian Petersen Collection, Brunnier Art Museum, University Museums, Iowa State University. Purchased by the Christian Petersen Memorial Fund. UM92.94.

Abraham Lincoln, 1950
Bedford limestone, 28 x 11 1/2 x 13 (71.1 x 29.2 x 33)
Christian Petersen Collection, Brunnier Art Museum, University Museums, Iowa State University. Gift of WOI-TV. U82.133.

All the Evils Which Have Kept Him Prisoner, ca. 1950
Pencil on paper, 10 3/4 x 11 7/8 (27.3 x 30.2)
On loan from Special Collections Department, Iowa State University Library. Gift of Charlotte Petersen. SC99.223.

David, ca. 1950s
Plaster cast, 10 x 10 1/2 x 6 (25.4 x 26.7 x 15.2)
On loan from Joan Lange Kaas.

Saint Bernard of Clairvaux: Studies of Hands and Figure, 1950
Colored pencil on paper, 16 3/4 x 13 3/4 (42.5 x 34.9)
Christian Petersen Collection, Brunnier Art Museum, University Museums, Iowa State University. Purchased by the Christian Petersen Memorial Fund. UM92.255.

Saint Bernard of Clairvaux, ca. 1950
Painted plaster, 26 x 12 x 12 (66 x 30.5 x 30.5)
On loan from Robin Krueger, Charles City, Iowa.

Helen Benitez, ca. 1950s
Painted plaster, 21 x 22 x 10 (53.3 x 55.9 x 25.4)
Christian Petersen Collection, Brunnier Art Museum, University Museums, Iowa State University. Gift of Friends of the University Museums. U89.34.

Eugene Mannheimer, ca. 1950s
Painted plaster, 19 x 2 1/4 (48.3 x 5.7) [diameter x depth]
Christian Petersen Collection, Brunnier Art Museum, University Museums, Iowa State University. Gift of Joan and Robert E. Mannheimer. UM97.140.

Woman Washing Her Hair, ca. 1953
Terra cotta, 15 1/2 x 7 1/2 x 8 1/2 (39.4 x 19.1 x 21.6)
Nude woman, sitting on a rock, washing her hair.
On loan from Mary Lou and the late Jon Edwin Morgan, Chandler, Arizona.

Cowboy, Cutting Horse, and Two Polled Hereford Heifers, 1953–1954
Brown pencil on paper, 14 x 17 (35.6 x 43.2)
Christian Petersen Collection, Brunnier Art Museum, University Museums, Iowa State University. Purchased by the Christian Petersen Memorial Fund. UM92.288.

Cowboy, Cutting Horse, and Two Polled Hereford Heifers, 1953–1954
Painted plaster, 17 x 24 x 12 (43.2 x 61 x 30.5)
Model for cowboy is Dr. John J. Edenburn, DVM.
Christian Petersen Collection, Brunnier Art Museum, University Museums, Iowa State University. Gift of John J. Edenburn family. UM2000.2.

Woman and Child, ca. 1955
Unfired clay, 9 7/8 x 15 5/16 x 1 1/4 (25.1 x 38.9 x 3.2)
Christian Petersen Collection, Brunnier Art Museum, University Museums, Iowa State University. Gift of Neva Petersen. UM91.62.

Christ on the Cross, 1960–1961
Wood (walnut), 23 1/2 x 15 1/2 x 6 1/2 (59.7 x 39.4 x 16.5)
Christian Petersen Collection, Brunnier Art Museum, University Museums, Iowa State University. Gift of Leo Schmitz in memory of his brother Reverend John A. Schmitz. U92.404.

Dedication to the Future: Concept Study, ca. 1958
Pencil or conté on paper, 5 3/4 x 7 3/4 (16.6 x 19.7)
Christian Petersen Collection, Brunnier Art Museum, University Museums, Iowa State University. Purchased by the Christian Petersen Memorial Fund. UM92.105.

UNDATED WORKS OF ART

Charlotte
Pen on paper, 16 x 8 (40.6 x 20.3)
Christian Petersen Collection, Brunnier Art Museum, University Museums, Iowa State University. Purchased by the Christian Petersen Memorial Fund. UM92.271b.

Charlotte Petersen
Pencil on paper, 11 3/4 x 8 3/4 (29.8 x 22.2)
On loan from Special Collections Department, Iowa State University Library. Gift of Charlotte Petersen. SC99.173.

Charlotte Sitting in Her Garden
Oil on canvas, 10 x 14 (25.4 x 35.6)
Christian Petersen Collection, Brunnier Art Museum, University Museums, Iowa State University. Anonymous gift in memory of Charlotte Petersen. UM93.32.

Figure Studies
Pencil or conté on paper, 8 1/2 x 11 (21.6 x 27.9)
Christian Petersen Collection, Brunnier Art Museum, University Museums, Iowa State University. Purchased from Mary Petersen with funds from the Christian Petersen Memorial Fund. UM92.59.

Horse
Brown crayon on paper, 8 1/2 x 11 (21.6 x 27.9);
Image: 5 1/4 x 7 1/2 (13.3 x 19.1)
On loan from Special Collections Department, Iowa State University Library. Gift of Charlotte Petersen. SC99.197.

Jacob Kanengieser
Bronze, 6 7/8 x 5 x 1/4 (17.5 x 12.7 x 0.6)
On loan from the State Historical Society of Iowa, Des Moines, Iowa. I 4238.

Julegranen: Sketch of Religious Figures
Pencil or conté on paper, 8 3/4 x 11 7/8 (22.2 x 30.2)
Christian Petersen Collection, Brunnier Art Museum, University Museums, Iowa State University. Purchased by the Christian Petersen Memorial Fund. UM92.92.

Man
Charcoal or conté on paper, 8 1/2 x 11 (21.6 x 27.9)
Christian Petersen Collection, Brunnier Art Museum, University Museums, Iowa State University. Purchased by the Christian Petersen Memorial Fund. UM92.127.

Man Shooting Bow and Arrow II
Pencil or conté on paper, 8 1/2 x 11 (21.6 x 27.9)
Christian Petersen Collection, Brunnier Art Museum, University Museums, Iowa State University. Purchased by the Christian Petersen Memorial Fund. UM92.41.

Man with Violin
Plaster, 10 1/4 x 11 1/4 x 3/4 (26 x 28.6 x 1.9)
On loan from the State Historical Society of Iowa, Des Moines, Iowa. I 11921.

Running Horses
Brown crayon on paper, 8 1/2 x 11 (21.6 x 27.9)
On loan from Special Collections Department, Iowa State University Library. Gift of Charlotte Petersen. SC99.176.

Self-portrait
Watercolor and crayon on paper, 8 1/2 x 11 (21.6 x 27.9);
Image: 7 1/2 x 4 1/2 (19.1 x 11.4)
On loan from Special Collections Department, Iowa State University Library. Gift of Charlotte Petersen. SC99.175.

Theodore Roosevelt
Bronze, 6 3/4 x 5 x 6 3/4 (17.1 x 12.7 x 17.1)
On loan from Lynn Lucido, Fresno, California.

Two Men
Plaster mold with red latex liner, 19 x 18 3/4 x 5 1/2 (48.3 x 47.6 x 14)
Christian Petersen Collection, Brunnier Art Museum, University Museums, Iowa State University. Gift of Helen (Mrs. J. William) Uhrig. UM2000.7.

Virgin Mary Holding Jesus
Pencil on paper, 11 7/8 x 8 3/4 (30.2 x 22.2)
On loan from Special Collections Department, Iowa State University Library. Gift of Charlotte Petersen. SC99.201.

Virgin Mary Holding Jesus
Pencil or conté on paper, 5 3/4 x 9 (14.6 x 22.7)
Christian Petersen Collection, Brunnier Art Museum, University Museums, Iowa State University. Purchased by the Christian Petersen Memorial Fund. UM92.114.

EXHIBITION LIST OF OBJECTS
NOT CREATED BY PETERSEN

Works listed in date order.

Cha-Ki-Shi
Book written by Halla Rhode and Bessie Coon with drawings by Christen Petersen.
Printed by Charles Scribner's Sons, New York, 1936.
Christian Petersen Collection, Brunnier Art Museum, University Museums, Iowa State University.

Christian Petersen, ca. 1940
Oil on canvas, 16 x 20 (40.6 x 50.8)
Painted by Frank Johnson.
Christian Petersen Collection, Brunnier Art Museum, University Museums, Iowa State University, Ames, Iowa. Gift of Mary Petersen. UM92.609.

Christian Petersen, 1943
Black pencil on paper
Drawn by Frank Johnson.
Christian Petersen Collection, Brunnier Art Museum, University Museums, Iowa State University, Ames, Iowa. Anonymous gift in memory of Charlotte Petersen. UM94.1.

Tools Used by Christian Petersen
On loan from Special Collections Department, Iowa State University Library. Gifts of Charlotte Petersen. SC99.71 through SC99.85.

Tools Used by Christian Petersen
Christian Petersen Collection, Brunnier Art Museum, University Museums, Iowa State University. Gift of Francis L. Pisney, M.D. UM99.303abcd.

Catalogue Raisonné

DANA L. MICHELS
LEA ROSSON DELONG
LYNETTE L. POHLMAN

Available object information is
listed in the following format:

Title, Date
Material, Dimensions
Description
Markings
Provenance

Works of art by Christian Petersen are listed by date, and alphabetically by title. Undated works of art appear alphabetically after those that are dated. Three-dimensional works of art appear before those that are two-dimensional. Measurements, unless otherwise noted, are in inches followed by centimeters in parentheses, with height preceding width and depth.

If no collection, media, dimensions, date, or location is given, that information is unknown. If works of art are known only from a published source, that source is given. Works of art known to have existed based on documents and/or photographs, with no evidence to suggest they have been destroyed, are included in the catalogue. Works of art that are known to have been destroyed are listed in Appendix A at the end of the catalogue.

Unauthorized castings, where noted, means castings for which the artist is not known to have given permission.

Petersen titled and dated very few of his works of art. Most titles listed for his untitled works of art are common usage titles or have been assigned either by Patricia L. Bliss, author of *Christian Petersen Remembered* or by staff of the Brunnier Art Museum, University Museums, Iowa State University, Ames, Iowa. Where the artist dated the object, that information is given as part of the object's inscription. Other dates are assigned through documentation in the Christian Petersen Papers or the Brunnier files or by Bliss based on interviews with the artist's wife, Charlotte Petersen. Dates designated "circa" are assigned by the staff of the Brunnier Art Museum.

In 1959, Iowa State College changed its name to Iowa State University.

In 1964, works of art remaining in the artist's studio were made available for public purchase. Works of art sold at that time are noted.

In 1992, 393 sketches, studies, and drawings were purchased by the Brunnier Art Museum, University Museums, Iowa State University, from Mary Petersen with funds donated by the following people to the Christian Petersen Memorial Fund: Beverly J. and Robert G. Bole; Patricia L. Bliss; Mary A. and William H. Reinhardt, Jr.; and Rita Kay and Norman Riis. The sketches and drawings are listed below with the credit line, "Purchased by the Christian Petersen Memorial Fund."

The following abbreviations appear in the provenance listings:
"CPC" denotes works of art in The Christian Petersen Collection at the Brunnier Art Museum, University Museums, Iowa State University, Ames, Iowa.
"CPC/AOC" denotes sculptures in The Christian Petersen Collection in the Art on Campus Program, University Museums, Iowa State University.
"SC" denotes Special Collections Department, Iowa State University Library.
"CPP" denotes the Christian Petersen Papers in the Special Collections Department, Iowa State University Library.

Numbers listed at the end of some entries refer to accessioned objects at museums and libraries.

DATED THREE-DIMENSIONAL WORKS OF ART

1. Min Moder (My Mother), 1900
Silver, 2 (5.1) [diameter]
Medal of Petersen's mother, Helene, in profile sitting in a chair.
Charlotte Petersen; Mary Petersen, Beverly Hills, Florida.

2. Mother and Father, 1910
Bronze, 5 x 4 (12.7 x 10.2)
Bas-relief of Petersen's parents, Helene and Peter Petersen.
Charlotte Petersen; Mary Petersen; Ruth Petersen Sollenberger;
Scott Sollenberger, Clovis, California.

3. Nikh-Eiphnh, 1910
Plaster, 9 7/8 x 1 (25.1 x 2.5) [diameter x depth]
Plaque of Greek goddess of victory in profile wearing a
crown of leaves. This is one of Petersen's earliest works of art and
possibly his earliest bas-relief.
George Nerney; Mrs. Helen Nerney Shaw; SC, Gift of Mrs. Helen
Nerney Shaw. SC99.64.

4. Athena, ca. 1915
Bronze, 1 5/8 x 1/8 (3.5 x .3) [diameter x depth]
Medal of Greek goddess Athena holding branch, with owl on a
pile of books and a lamp on a pedestal.
Charlotte Petersen; SC, Purchased with Iowa State University
Library Funds. SC99.62.

5. Lawrence (Private Jack), ca. 1916
Fired clay, approximately 18 (45.7) [height]
Standing figure of the artist's son Lawrence playing soldier.
The boy is wearing a toy pail helmet and holding a wooden sword.
Known from photograph in Littman, Minna, "From a Die Cutter
to a Sculptor…", undated clipping in CPP and from Macdonald,
William A., "The Rise of a New Paul Revere." *Boston Transcript,*
January 23, 1918.

6. Caleb Arnold Slade, 1916
Painted plaster, 10 1/2 x 7 3/4 (26.7 x 19.7)
Bas-relief. Three-quarters view of painter facing right, palette and
brushes in hand.
Inscription top right: C. Arnold Slade
Signed lower right: Christian Petersen Sc May 1916
The Old Dartmouth Historical Society – New Bedford
Whaling Museum, New Bedford, Massachusetts.

7. War, 1917
Early medal design by Petersen.

8. Liberty, Justice, Peace, Honor, ca. 1919
Bronze, 1 3/8 x 1/8 (3.5 x 0.3)[diameter x depth]
Medal. Recto: Winged female with battleground behind.
Verso: Surround of leaves.
Recto inscription: LIBERTY / JUSTICE / PEACE / HONOR /
1917–1919
Verso inscription: FOR SERVICE IN THE WORLD WAR /
PRESENTED TO (a blank box) BY GRATEFUL CITIZENS /
TOWN OF NORTH ATTLEBORO, INCORPORATED (date rubbed
off from wear)

Charlotte Petersen; SC, Purchased with Iowa State University
Library Funds. SC99.69.

9. Theodore Roosevelt, ca. 1919
Bronze, 6 3/4 x 5 x 6 3/4 (17.1 x 12.7 x 17.1)
Bookend.
Charlotte Petersen; Mary Petersen; Helene Petersen Male;
Lynn Sollenberger Lucido, Fresno, California.

10. Bear, 1920
Bronze, 3 x 5 1/2 x 2 1/2 (7.6 x 14 x 6.4)
Bear at ledge. May have been intended for Yellowstone National Park.
Signed on base in square: CP
George Nerney; Mrs. Helen Nerney Shaw; SC, Gift of Mrs. Helen
Nerney Shaw. SC99.56.

11. Carry On, ca. 1920
Proposal for World War I memorial. Fallen soldier lifting a torch.

12. Joe Mitchell Chappel, 1920
Portrait bust or bas-relief.

13. Christopher Columbus, ca. 1920
Standing figure of Columbus with a cross in his upraised right
hand. Known from a photograph in Littman.

14. Daniel C. Crandon, 1920
Sculpture of the first president of the Boston Ethical Society,
founded in 1920.

15. John Cotton Dana, 1920
Bronze
Bust portrait of Petersen's friend who was Director of the Newark
Museum in Newark, New Jersey.

16. General Focht, 1920
Bronze
Bas-relief medallion honoring World War I general.

17. Helene, 1920
Portrait bust or bas-relief, possibly of Petersen's eldest daughter.

18. Helene, ca. 1920
Free-standing figure of Petersen's daughter standing in a fur-trimmed
hooded coat while wind blows her skirts. Described in Littman.

19. Medal, ca. 1920
Bronze, 1 1/2 x 1 x 1/8 (3.8 x 2.5 x .03)
Medal featuring a woman with her hands and arms extended with
two young children next to her.
Charlotte Petersen; Mary Petersen, Beverly Hills, Florida.

20. Medal, ca. 1920
Bronze, 1 1/2 x 1 x 1/8 (3.8 x 2.5 x .03)
Medal featuring a woman holding a torch in one hand, a laurel leaf
in the other. A bird with spread wings is in the lower left corner.
Charlotte Petersen; Mary Petersen, Beverly Hills, Florida.

21. Reverend John Moore, Brooklyn College, ca. 1920
Portrait medallion.

22. Reverend John W. Moore, 1920
Bronze
Bust portrait.

23. Samuel F. B. Morse, ca. 1920
Painted plaster, 6 1/2 x 7/8 (16.5 x 2.2) [diameter x depth]
Bas-relief of the inventor of the telegraph, wearing medals.
George Nerney; Mrs. Helen Nerney Shaw; SC, Gift of Mrs. Helen Nerney Shaw. SC99.52.

24. Albert Edward Scott Memorial (Newsboys Memorial), ca. 1920
Bronze
Bas-relief cast by T.F. McGann & Son.
Inscription: NEWSBOYS MEMORIAL TO ALBERT EDWARD SCOTT / COMPANY H 101 UNITED STATES INFANTRY A.E.F. / KILLED IN ACTION AT EPIEDS, FRANCE, JULY 23, 1918

25. Reverend George Endicott Osgood Medal, 1920
Bronze medal, 2 1/8 x 1/8 (5.4 x 0.3) [diameter x depth]
Steel positive mold, 2 1/2 x 2 (6.4 x 5.1) [diameter x depth]
Steel negative mold, 4 1/8 x 4 1/8 x 2 3/4 (10.5 x 10.5 x 7)
Medal with a profile view of the father of Helen Nerney Shaw and father-in-law of Petersen's friend, George Nerney. Commissioned by a personal friend.
Signed right center in square: CP
Medal and molds: George Nerney; Mrs. Helen Nerney Shaw; SC, Gift of Mrs. Helen Nerney Shaw. SC99.59abc.

26. Aram Poithier, 1920
Bronze
Portrait bust of a governor of Rhode Island.

27. Paul Revere, 1920
Plaster casting
Figure of Paul Revere. Known from photograph in William A. Macdonald, "The Rise of a New Paul Revere," *Boston Transcript*, January 23, 1918.

28. Serenity, 1920
Bronze
Memorial bas-relief plaque for World War I soldiers.

29. Emery J. Sans Souci, 1920
Bronze, 22 (55.9) [height]
Portrait bust of governor of Rhode Island.
Rhode Island Historical Society.

30. Tigers, 1920
Bronze, approximately 24 x 18 x 40 (61 x 45.7 x 101.6)
A pair of tigers commissioned for the entrance gate to the Charles J. Davol East Greenwich Estate in Providence, Rhode Island.

31. Woodrow Wilson, ca. 1921
Bronze, 2 (5) [diameter]
Uniface medal with bust of Wilson facing left.
Inscription: WOODROW WILSON PRESIDENT OF THE U.S.A.
Signed: C. Petersen

32. R.L. Beeckman, 1923
Bronze
Bust of Beeckman (1866–1935), Governor of Rhode Island from 1915 to 1921.
Known from photograph in Littman.

33. Prince Anton and Princess Elizabeth Bibescu of Romania, 1926
Bronze, 4 x 3 (10.2 x 7.6)
Bas-relief portrait plaque of Prince Anton Bibescu (1878–1951)

and Princess Elizabeth Asquith Bibescu (1897–1945). Bibescu was Minister of the Romanian Legation in Washington, D.C. 1920–1926. Cast by Whitehead and Hoag Company, Newark, New Jersey.
Inscription: "MCMXXVI, Elizabeth-Anton / Bibesco." The spelling of the family name "Bibesco" is current Romanian usage.
The Newark Museum, New Jersey. 29.2138. Gift of Whitehead and Hoag, Co., 1929.

34. Frank Ormand Draper, 1923
Bronze
Memorial plaque of superintendent of Pawtucket, Rhode Island, School System, 1906–1920s.
Pawtucket School System, Pawtucket, Rhode Island.

35. Janie Flynn Memorial, ca. 1923
Bronze, 33 x 18 (83.8 x 45.7)
Memorial plaque of World War I nurse in her uniform.
Inscription: IN MEMORIAM / JANIE FLYNN. T.S.H. NURSE / 1893–1918 / STRICKEN WHILE / SERVING THE / CITY OF TAUNTON / AS VOLUNTEER / NURSE DURING / THE INFLUENZA / EPIDEMIC.
Taunton State Hospital, Taunton, Massachusetts.

36. The Frontiersman, 1923
Believed to have been cast in bronze.
Figure of a young Abraham Lincoln.

37. Charles Evans Hughes, 1923
Bronze, 9 3/4 x 6 1/2 (24.8 x 16.5)
Bas-relief portrait medallion of United States Supreme Court Justice, made for Balfour Company.
Inscription: Made for Balfour Company. The Gorham Company, Founders
Signed: CP, Sc

38. George Kuhn, 1923
Portrait bust or bas-relief.

39. Spanish-American War Memorial, 1923
Bronze, 94 x 34 3/4 x 10 3/4 (238.8 x 88.3 x 27.3)
Pedestal: 26 x 8 1/2 x 4 1/2 (66 x 21.6 x 11.4)
Stone monolith: 92 1/4 x 49 x 27 (234.3 x 124.5 x 68.6)
Overall: 120 x 102 x 54 (3.05 m x 2.59 m x 1.37 m)
Female figure with torch and sword. Cast by Tilden-Thurber Company, Providence, Rhode Island. Known locally as the Liberty Monument.
Inscription on north elevation: DEDICATED TO THE MEMORY OF CITIZENS OF / NEWPORT WHO SERVED IN THE WAR WITH SPAIN / A BRIEF WAR BUT ONE WHERE RESULTS WERE / MANY STARTLING AND OF WORLD WIDE MEANING / 1898–1925
Inscription on south elevation: CUBA, / USA, / PORTO RICO [*sic*], / PHILIPPINE ISLANDS, / SPANISH WAR VICTIMS, / 1898–1902
Equality Park, City of Newport, Rhode Island.

40. Battery D Memorial, ca. 1924
Bronze, approximately 7' (2.13 m) [height]
Soldier in field uniform carrying an artillery shell ready to be loaded. Mounted on stone boulder at the corner of Kempton and Watson Streets.
City of New Bedford, Massachusetts.

41. The Seabury Memorial, 1924
Bronze, 27 3/4 x 19 3/4 (70.5 x 50.2)
Bas-relief of a whaleship under full sail.
Inscription: IN MEMORY OF / WILLIAM SEABURY, HIS
SONS, OTIS, EDWARD, WILLIAM, / HUMPHREY,
CHARLES AND JASON AND HIS SON-IN-LAW, /
BENJAMIN CUSHMAN. A RACE OF SEAFARING MEN — /
THIS TABLET PLACED 1924 BY / ANNIE SEABURY WOOD
Signed in upper right: Christian Petersen Sculptor
The Old Dartmouth Historical Society – New Bedford Whaling
Museum, New Bedford, Massachusetts, Gift of Annie Seabury
Wood, 1924.

42. John Burroughs, 1925
Fired clay or plaster
Figure study of Danish explorer and naturalist. Known from
photograph in Littman.

43. Charles W. Eliot, 1925
Bronze
Portrait medallion of Harvard University president.
Harvard University.

44. Prudential Insurance Company Medal, 1925
Bronze, 3 (7.6) [diameter]
One of 30,000 medals struck by Whitehead and Hoag for the
company's fiftieth anniversary. Recto: Rock of Gibraltar.
Verso: Headquarters at top, inscription at center, oak leaves at bottom.
Recto inscription: PRUDENTIAL / HAS THE / STRENGTH OF /
GIBRALTAR
Verso inscription: COMMEMORATING / THE / FIFTIETH
ANNIVERSARY / OF / THE PRUDENTIAL / INSURANCE
COMPANY / OF AMERICA / 1875 1925
The Newark Museum, New Jersey. 29.2128.

45. Arthur Henry Rostrom, 1925
Painted plaster, 6 x 4 3/8 x 1/2 (15.2 x 11.1 x 1.3)
Portrait medallion. Rostrom was the Captain of the Titanic, which
sunk April 14, 1912. Petersen probably created this medallion for
the Robbins Company of Attleboro, Massachusetts.
George Nerney; Mrs. Helen Nerney Shaw; SC, Gift of Mrs. Helen
Nerney Shaw. SC99.54.

Spoons, 1925
Twelve spoons designed by George Nerney and die-cut by Petersen for
the Robbins Company, Attleboro, Massachusetts. The backs of all of the
images are depicted on the reverse side of the spoons.

46. Alma
Sterling silver, 4 9/16 (11.6) [length]
A donkey and the name "Alma."
1) Helene Petersen Male, Fresno, California.
2) CPC, Gift of Isabel Matterson. UM93.23c.

47. California
Sterling silver, 4 9/16 (11.6) [length]
A bear standing on its hind legs and the word "California."
1) Mary Petersen, Beverly Hills, Florida.
2) CPC, Gift of Isabel Matterson. UM93.23a.

48. Coal Miner
Sterling silver, 4 9/16 (11.6) [length]
A man swinging a pick. Other tools below him.
Mary Petersen, Beverly Hills, Florida.

49. General Jackson
Sterling silver, 4 9/16 (11.6) [length]
Man on a rearing horse and the words "General Jackson."
1) Mary Petersen, Beverly Hills, Florida.
2) CPC, Gift of Isabel Matterson. UM93.23b.

50. Georgia Peaches
Sterling silver, 4 9/16 (11.6) [length]
Peaches on a tree branch.
Mary Petersen, Beverly Hills, Florida.

51. Hibiscus
Sterling silver, 4 9/16 (11.6) [length]
Two clusters of flowers.
Mary Petersen, Beverly Hills, Florida.

52. Holly
Sterling silver, 4 9/16 (11.6) [length]
A branch of holly and ivy.
Mary Petersen, Beverly Hills, Florida.

53. Lily
Sterling silver, 4 9/16 (11.6) [length]
A stem of an Easter lily.
Mary Petersen, Beverly Hills, Florida.

54. Nantucket, Old Mill
Sterling silver, 4 9/16 (11.6) [length]
A windmill and the words "Old Mill" and "Nantucket."
Mary Petersen, Beverly Hills, Florida.

55. Nantucket, Stone Alley
Sterling silver, 4 9/16 (11.6) [length]
A clock tower and the words "Stone Alley" and "Nantucket."
1) Mary Petersen, Beverly Hills, Florida.
2) Isabel Matterson, Ames, Iowa.

56. Palm Trees
Sterling silver, 4 9/16 (11.6) [length]
Two palm trees.
Helene Petersen Male, Fresno, California.

57. Poppies
Sterling silver, 4 9/16 (11.6) [length]
Three poppies.
Mary Petersen, Beverly Hills, Florida.

58. Wood Brothers, 1925
Bronze, 48 x 33 x 3 (121.9 x 83.8 x 7.6)
Plaque with two men, bust length, in profile facing left.
Honoring founders of Wood Brothers Thresher Company.
Inscription at top: THEY FOLLOWED THEIR VISION THRU [sic]
Inscription below: FOUNDERS - WOOD BROTHERS
THRESHER CO.; FRANZ J. WOOD - BORN - MARCH - 7 -1864;
ROBERT L. WOOD - BORN - AUGUST - 31 - 1862.
State Historical Society of Iowa, Des Moines, Iowa. I 11923.

59. Reverend Father Silvester Escalante, 1926
Bronze
Memorial tablet honoring missionary.
City of Cedar City, Utah.

60. Warren G. Harding, 1926
Bronze, 1 1/4 (3.2) [diameter]
Memorial medallion struck by Whitehead and Hoag. Recto: President Harding facing left. Verso: cornerstone of monument dedicated at Marion, Ohio on May 30, 1926.

61. Visit of Queen Marie of Romania to Hotel Sinton, 1926
Bronze, 4 x 2 3/4 (10.1 x 7)
Half portrait bas-relief of the Queen facing left and wearing crown and jewels. Cast by Whitehead and Hoag.
Inscription top: HOTEL SINTON / CINCINNATI / OHIO / NOVEMBER 19TH 1926
Inscription bottom: MARIE / QUEEN OF ROUMANIA
Signed: C. Petersen, Sc. (W & H)

62. Henry Cantwell Wallace, Senior, 1926
Bronze, 28 x 21 x 10 (71.1 x 53.3 x 25.4)
Portrait bust of pioneer agricultural researcher at Iowa State College, and father of United States Vice President Henry A. Wallace. Cantwell Wallace was secretary of agriculture under President Warren G. Harding and publisher of *Wallace's Farmer* magazine.
Inscription: WALLACE.
State Historical Society of Iowa, Des Moines, Iowa. I 525.

63. Cyrus Farnum, 1927
Bronze, 12 3/4 x 10 1/2 x 1/2 (32.4 x 26.7 x 1.3)
Bas-relief portrait of New York and Paris painter, seated with painter's brushes and palette.
Charlotte Petersen; Joy Munn, Ames, Iowa; CPC, Gift of Joy Munn. UM99.296.

64. Dr. Albert Goldspohn, 1929
Bronze, 21 1/2 x 14 1/2 x 1 1/2 (54.6 x 36.8 x 3.8)
Bas-relief portrait.
North Central College, Naperville, Illinois.

65. Young Man in Profile, 1929
Plaster mold, 9 1/4 x 7 1/2 x 1 (23.5 x 19.1 x 2.5)
Man with hair brushed back.
Upper left: Christian Petersen, 1929.
State Historical Society of Iowa, Des Moines, Iowa. I 11919.

66. Doughboy of World War I, ca. 1920s
Bronze medal, 2 1/4 x 1/8 (5.7 x 0.3) [diameter x depth]
Steel mold, 2 1/2 x 1 1/2 (6.4 x 3.8) [diameter x depth]
Medal shows a soldier bayoneting a grotesque beast attacking a woman. God-like figure stands behind the soldier.
Medal and mold: Charlotte Petersen; SC, Purchased with Iowa State University Library Funds. SC99.57ab.

67. Female Nude, ca. 1920s
Clay, approximately 18 (45.7) [height]

Standing woman with head tilted back and arms reaching behind her. Created in a class taught by Petersen.

68. General John Pershing, ca. 1920s
Medallion design.

69. Edgar Allen Poe, ca. 1920s
Bronze
Photograph in Littman. Bust of Poe wearing a jacket, vest, and tie.
Jordan Hall, New England Conservatory of Music, Boston, Massachusetts.

70. Winged Victory, ca. 1920s
Bronze, 1 3/4 x 1 1/8 x 1/8 (4.4 x 2.8 x .3)
Medal with sculpture of the Winged Victory of Samothrace at the center, and a scroll and leaves at the top.
Charlotte Petersen; SC, Purchased with Iowa State University Library Funds. SC99.70.

71. Baby Allan, 1930
Figure or bas-relief.

72. Consul-General Baumann of Denmark, 1930
Bas-relief portrait.

73. Alfred Caldwell, 1930
Terra cotta, approximately 30 [height] (76.2)
Portrait bust of Chicago architect.

74. Carol Caldwell, 1930
Plaster, 12 1/4 x 10 1/4 x 3/4 (31.1 x 26 x 1.9)
Bas-relief portrait of the daughter of Alfred Caldwell of Chicago, Illinois, shown sitting in a high chair.
Gretchen Greenwood Weber, Ames, Iowa.

75. George C. Duffield, 1930
Plaster
Bas-relief portrait of president of Duffield Motor Company.

76. James D. Edmundson, 1930
Bronze, 22 1/2 x 14 1/4 x 10 (57.2 x 37.5 x 25.4)
Portrait bust done at the request of Edgar R. Harlan.
Des Moines Art Center, Des Moines, Iowa.

77. El and Bill, 1930
Portrait busts or bas-relief.

78. Benjamin F. Hadley, 1930
Hadley was second vice-president of Equitable of Iowa Companies, Des Moines, Iowa.

79. Kenneth Haines, 1930
Portrait bust.

80. Edgar R. Harlan, ca. 1930
Portrait bust of Harlan (1869–1941), Curator (1908–1937), Iowa's State Historical, Memorial, and Art Department in the 1920s and 1930s, who arranged some of Petersen's early Iowa commissions and introduced him to Iowa State College President Hughes.
Painted plaster, 15 x 9 x 9 (38.1 x 22.7 x 22.7)
State Historical Society of Iowa, Des Moines, Iowa. I 11917.

81. Robert S. Laird Trophy, 1930
Probably silver, approximately 26 x 20 (66 x 50.8)
Industrial safety award medallion. Figure in Trojan dress with a shield and arm out protecting a male figure in modern dress holding a hammer. The figures are in the center of a structure with columns to each side with reliefs of oats and places to add the winner's names. It was awarded in March and October of each year from 1930 through 1935.
Inscription: ROBERT S. LAIRD TROPHY / FOR OUTSTANDING ACHIEVEMENT / IN THE PREVENTION OF ACCIDENTS / IN PLANTS OF THE QUAKER OATS COMPANY
Signed, lower left: Christian Petersen, Sc
Quaker Oats Company, Cedar Rapids, Iowa.

82. Little Girl, ca. 1930
Painted plaster, 11 1/2 x 7 1/2 x 7 (29.2 x 19.1 x 17.8)
Profile of a little girl with curly hair. Daughter of Chicago friend of Petersen's.
Charlotte Petersen; Frank E. Brandt, Deming, New Mexico.

83. Pilgrim Man and Wife, ca.1930
Male and female free-standing figures.

84. Pushetonequa, 1930
Painted plaster, 15 1/2 x 11 1/2 x 1 1/4 (39.4 x 29.2 x 3.2)
Portrait plaque of Meskwaki Native American.
State Historical Society of Iowa, Des Moines, Iowa. I 11392.

85. Dr. Nelson Voldeng, 1930
Portrait bust or bas-relief.

86. Young Bear, 1930
Painted plaster, 15 x 11 x 11 (38.1 x 27.9 x 27.9)
Meskwaki Native American, son of Pushetonequa.
State Historical Society of Iowa, Des Moines, Iowa. I 11916.

87. Baby Boy, 1931
Painted plaster, 12 1/2 x 9 1/2 x 1/2 (31.8 x 24.1 x 1.3)
Bas-relief of unknown boy.
Inscription: April 26, 1931 Christian Petersen
Private collection.

88. Vitus Bering, 1931
Painted plaster, 17 x 5 x 5 (43.2 x 12.7 x 12.7)
Figure of Vitus Bering (1681–1741), Danish explorer and discoverer of the Bering Strait.
Signed: Christian Petersen
Charlotte Petersen; Margaret Hunziker, Ames, Iowa.

89. Johnson Brigham, 1931
Bas-relief medallion of director of State of Iowa Library.

90. Leslie Young Correthiers, 1931
Approximately 30 (76.2) [height]
Portrait bust done in lieu of hotel rent in Belvidere, Illinois.

91. Dean Peter Christian Lutkin, ca. 1931
Bronze, 24 x 17 x 9 1/2 (61 x 43.2 x 24.1)
Bust portrait of dean of the School of Music at Northwestern University in Evanston, Illinois.
Deering Library, Northwestern University, Evanston, Illinois.

92. Annie Merner Pfeiffer, 1931
Portrait bust or bas-relief.

93. Bishop George Craig Stewart, 1931
Portrait bust or bas-relief of bishop.
Northwestern University, Evanston, Illinois.

94. Stuart Boys, 1931
Plaster, 27 x 18 1/2 (68.6 x 47)
Reece Stuart III and Hamilton B. Stuart; children of Reece Stuart, Jr., writer at *Des Moines Register.*
Reece Stuart, Jr.; Reece Stuart III, Des Moines, Iowa.

95. Jens Jensen, ca. 1930–1932
Painted plaster, 20 x 12 x 11 1/2 (50.8 x 30.5 x 29.2)
Bust of landscape architect Jens Jensen created to honor his work with the Chicago parks system.
Signed in square: CP
Two castings: Casting 1: Garfield Conservatory, Chicago, Illinois. Casting 2: Charlotte Petersen; Purchased at 1964 sale by students of the Department of Landscape Architecture, Iowa State University; CPC/AOC. U94.2.

96. Governor George W. Clarke, 1932
Bronze, 26 x 22 x 11 (66 x 55.9 x 27.9)
Portrait bust of Governor of Iowa from 1913 to 1917.
Inscription: G. W. CLARKE / JUNE 8, 1932
Signed lower left: Christian Petersen
State Historical Society of Iowa, Des Moines, Iowa. I 528.

97. Governor George W. Clarke, 1932
Bronze plaque, 11 x 8 1/4 x 5/8 (27.9 x 21 x 1.6)
George W. and Arletta G. Clarke; Fred G. Clarke, Sr.; Fred G. and Lee Vinal Clarke.

98. Governor George W. Clarke, 1932
Plaster plaque, 11 x 8 1/4 x 5/8 (27.9 x 21 x 1.6)
Casting 1: George W. and Arletta G. Clarke; Charles F. and Kate Macomber Clarke; Louise Clarke Hobbs. Casting 2: George W. and Arletta G. Clarke; Charles F. and Kate Macomber Clarke; Theodora Clarke Bell; Allyson Armstrong.

99. Robert Cook, 1932
Bronze, 36 x 48 (91.4 x 121.9)
Bas-relief portrait of first principal of Theodore Roosevelt High School, Des Moines, Iowa.
Inscription: ROBERT ROY COOK / 1923 - FIRST PRINCIPAL - 1932 / LEADER COUNSELLOR FRIEND.
Signed: Christian Petersen
Des Moines Public Schools, Roosevelt High School, Des Moines, Iowa.

100. Couple (Man and Woman), ca. 1932
Plaster mold, 10 1/4 x 1 1/8 (26 x 2.9) [diameter x depth]
Signed lower right in cursive: Christian Petersen
State Historical Society of Iowa, Des Moines, Iowa. I 11920.

101. Diana D., 1932
Portrait bust or bas-relief.

102. De Jong Girls, 1932
Portrait busts or bas-relief.
Mr. & Mrs. Richard De Jong.

103. Richard De Jong, 1932
Bas-relief portrait; commissioned by vice presidents of Iowa Des Moines National Bank.
Johannes De Jong.

104. George Dumphy, Jr., 1932
Portrait bust or bas-relief.

105. Mr. and Mrs. Amos Emery, 1932
Portraits of Amos and Alice Emery. Mr. Emery provided Petersen with studio space in his architectural office.
Amos Emery, Des Moines, Iowa.

106. Farmer, 1932
Portrait bust of a young man.

107. William and Ella Garvey (Salt of the Earth), 1932
Painted plaster, 24 3/4 x 17 (62.9 x 43.2)
Bas-relief portrait mounted on wood, of Charlotte Petersen's parents.
Charlotte Petersen; Private Collection.

108. Glen Duffield Harlan, 1932
Painted plaster, 10 x 8 x 1 1/2 (25.4 x 20.3 x 4)
Bas-relief portrait of the nephew of Margaret Wilhelm.
Inscription bottom left: G.D.H.
Signed: Christian Petersen Sc May 29, 1932
Margaret Wilhelm, Urbandale, Iowa.

109. Lorentzen Boys, 1932
Portrait busts or bas-relief.
Mr. and Mrs. Joe Lorentzen.

110. Ellis Newsome, 1932
Portrait, done in lieu of rent due, of owner of the Elliott Hotel, Des Moines, Iowa.

111. Dr. William Ryan, 1932
Portrait bust of a Des Moines physician.

112. Rose Shloss, 1932
Painted plaster, 18 1/2 x 13 7/8 x 1 (47 x 35.1 x 2.5)
Portrait plaque.
Marjorie Shloss Spevak and Frances M. Shloss.

113. Lewis Worthington Smith, 1932
Bas-relief portrait of Chairman, English Department, Drake University, Des Moines, Iowa.

114. Mrs. Forrest Spaulding, 1932
Portrait bust or bas-relief. Wife of director of Des Moines Public Library.

115. Eastman Weaver, 1932
Portrait bust or bas-relief.

116. James B. Weaver, 1932
Portrait bust or bas-relief of Des Moines attorney.

117. Zuni, 1932
From exhibition checklist at Younkers Department Store, 1933.

118. Cemetery Christ, Model for Campus Cemetery, ca. 1930–1935
Painted plaster, approximately 24 (61) [height]

119. Children of Mr. And Mrs. Harlan Miller, early 1930s
Portraits.

120. Old Character from Cherry Valley, Illinois, early 1930s
Clay
Bust of a man wearing a train engineer's hat.

121. Margaret A., 1933
Portrait bust or bas-relief.

Equitable of Iowa Portraits, 1933
A series of portrait plaques of company presidents and city founders of Des Moines commissioned by Equitable of Iowa Companies. (The chronology of the castings and addenda to this series of portraits has not been established.)

122. Benjamin F. Allen
Bronze, 16 3/4 x 10 7/8 x 1 (42.5 x 27.6 x 2.5)
Inscription: BENJAMIN FRANKLIN ALLEN 1829–1914
Signed at lower left: Christian Petersen
Equitable of Iowa Companies, Des Moines, Iowa.

123. Phineas McCray Casady
Bronze, 16 3/4 x 10 7/8 x 1 (42.5 x 27.5 x 2.5)
Inscription: PHINEAS McCRAY CASADY 1818–1908
Signed lower left: Christian Petersen
Equitable of Iowa Companies, Des Moines, Iowa.

124. James Calvin Cummins
Bronze, 16 7/8 x 10 7/8 x 1 (42.7 x 27.5 x 2.5)
Inscription: JAMES CALVIN CUMMINS 1852–1933
Signed lower left: Christian Petersen
Equitable of Iowa Companies, Des Moines, Iowa.

125. Frederick Cooper Hubbell
Bronze, 17 x 11 x 1 (43.2 x 27.9 x 2.5)
Inscription: FREDERICK COOPER HUBBELL
Signed lower right: Christian Petersen Sc
Equitable of Iowa Companies, Des Moines, Iowa.

126. Frederick Marion Hubbell
Bronze, 16 7/8 x 11 x 1 (42.7 x 27.9 x 2.5)
Inscription: FREDERICK MARION HUBBELL 1839–1930
Signed right: Christian Petersen Sc
Equitable of Iowa Companies, Des Moines, Iowa.

127. Frederick Marion Hubbell
Bronze, 9 1/8 x 12 3/4 x 3/4 (23.2 x 32.4 x 1.9)
Hubbell founded the company on January 21, 1867.
Signed lower left: CP
Equitable of Iowa Companies, Des Moines, Iowa.

128. Frederick Windsor Hubbell
Bronze, 16 3/4 x 10 3/4 x 1 1/2 (42.5 x 27.3 x 3.8)
Inscription: FREDERICK WINDSOR HUBBELL 1891–1959
Signed center right: Christian Petersen Sc
Equitable of Iowa Companies, Des Moines, Iowa.

129. Cyrus Kirk
Bronze, 16 7/8 x 10 7/8 x 1 (42.7 x 27.5 x 2.5)
Inscription: CYRUS KIRK 1844–1912
Signed at lower left: Christian Petersen
Equitable of Iowa Companies, Des Moines, Iowa.

130. Henry Scholte Nollen
Bronze, 17 x 11 1/8 x 1 1/4 (43.2 x 28.3 x 3.2)
Inscription: HENRY SCHOLTE NOLLEN
Signed lower right: Christian Petersen Sc
Equitable of Iowa Companies, Des Moines, Iowa.

131. Hoyt Sherman
Bronze, 16 7/8 x 10 3/4 x 1 (42.9 x 27.3 x 2.5)
Inscription: HOYT SHERMAN 1827–1904
Signed lower left: Christian Petersen
Equitable of Iowa Companies, Des Moines, Iowa.

132. Simon Casady, 1933
Bronze
Portrait plaque.

133. Florence Cassidy Reclining in a Chair, 1933
Plaster, 7 1/2 x 9 (19.1 x 22.9)
Bas-relief.
Signed upper left: Christian Petersen 1933
Signed upper left in square: CP
Florence Cassidy; Mary Petersen, Beverly Hills, Florida.

134. Gardner Cowles, 1933
Bronze, 13 x 10 1/2 x 1/2 (33 x 26.7 x 1.3)
Portrait plaque of *Des Moines Register and Tribune* publisher.
Signed top right: Christian Petersen
Des Moines Register and Tribune Company, Des Moines, Iowa.

135. Billie George, 1933
Portrait bust or bas-relief.

136. Colonel W.F. Godson, Fort Des Moines, ca. 1933
Painted plaster, 12 5/8 x 10 5/8 x 5/8 (32.1 x 27 x 1.6)
Bas-relief of man in profile, sitting in a chair.
Inscription at upper left: TO COL. GODSON / AN
APPRECIATION FROM
Signature below inscription: Christian Petersen
Charlotte Petersen; Purchased at 1964 sale by Helen J. Sebek,
Fort Dodge, Iowa; CPC, Gift of Helen J. Sebek. UM 2000.3.

137. Clyde Herring, 1933
Bronze
Iowa senator, and governor from 1933 to 1937.

138. George Jewett, 1933
Clay portrait bust or bas-relief.

139. Governor Nelson Kraschel, 1933
Bronze
Portrait bust of Iowa governor from 1937 to 1939.

140. Abraham Lincoln, 1933
Painted plaster, 25 x 13 x 18 (63.5 x 33 x 45.7)
Model done for a competition in Chicago among forty-eight artists from
across the United States; received honorable mention.
Charlotte Petersen; Gilbert Community Schools, Gilbert, Iowa.

141. Richard Mannheimer, 1933
Painted plaster, 19 x 11 1/2 (48.3 x 29.2)
Bas-relief of son of Rabbi and Mrs. Eugene Mannheimer.
Signed center right: Christian Petersen
Rabbi and Mrs. Eugene Mannheimer; Richard Mannheimer,
Los Angeles, California.

142. Robert Mannheimer, 1933
Painted plaster, 19 x 11 1/2 (48.3 x 29.2)
Bas-relief of son of Rabbi and Mrs. Eugene Mannheimer.
Signed: Christian Petersen
Rabbi and Mrs. Eugene Mannheimer; Mr. and Mrs. Robert
Mannheimer, Des Moines, Iowa.

143. Julia Bloom Mayer, 1933
Bronze, 30 x 20 x 3 (76.2 x 50.8 x 7.6)
Portrait plaque of director of the Jewish Federation of Greater Des
Moines.

Top inscription: JULIA BLOOM MAYER / SEPTEMBER 28 1872 /
APRIL 14 1945
Bottom inscription: BORN IN IOWA CITY A TIRELESS
WORKER IN THE / CAUSES OF PEACE, EDUCATION,
CITIZENSHIP AND COMMUNITY / LOYALTY WHO GAVE
A LIFETIME OF FINEST SOCIAL SERVICE / AND CIVIC
LEADERSHIP TO THE PEOPLE OF IOWA, THE JEWISH /
COMMUNITY CENTER WHICH SHE LOVED AND
BRILLIANTLY DIRECTED / FOR 20 YEARS STANDS AS A
LIVING TRIBUTE TO HER / GREATNESS OF HEART /
WHICH KNEW NO DISTINCTION OF RACE, COLOR OR CREED
Jewish Federation of Greater Des Moines, Des Moines, Iowa.

144. E. T. Meredith, 1933
Portrait bust of the United States Secretary of Agriculture under
President Woodrow Wilson and later editor and publisher of
Successful Farming magazine.

145. Princess Mishawaka, 1933
Fired clay, 8 x 13 (20.3 x 33)
Low relief plaque for consideration for commission for
Mishawaka, Indiana, Centennial.

146. Princess Mishawaka, 1933
Fired clay, 18 (45.7) [height]
Model for commission for Mishawaka, Indiana, Centennial.

147. Princess Mishawaka, 1933
Fired clay, 18 (45.7) [height]
One of two small-scale figure sketches which were models for
commission for Mishawaka, Indiana, Centennial.

148. David. N., 1933
Portrait bust or bas-relief.

149. Louis Herman Pammel, 1933
Bronze, 15 x 9 x 14 (38.1 x 22.9 x 35.6)
Portrait bust of academic head of Department of Botany,
Iowa State College.
Botany Department, CPC/AOC. U99.295.

150. Knute Rockne, ca. 1933
Bust and medallion of Notre Dame football coach. Commission
awarded by competition.
Notre Dame University, South Bend, Indiana.

151. Jessica Wellbourn Smith, ca. 1933
Painted plaster, 17 3/4 x 13 3/4 x 1/2 (45.1 x 34.9 x 1.3)
One of three bas-reliefs for his friends Jessica Wellbourn Smith,
Professor Lewis Worthington Smith of Drake University,
Des Moines, Iowa, and their daughter Marjorie E.B.W. Smith.
Private collection.

152. Lewis Worthington Smith, ca. 1933
Painted plaster, 6 x 6 (15.2 x 15.2)
One of three bas-reliefs of the Smith family.
Private collection.

153. Marjorie E.B.W. Smith, ca. 1933
Painted plaster, 11 x 7 1/2 x 1/2 (27.9 x 19.1 x 1.3)
One of three bas-reliefs of the Smith family.
Private collection.

154. Forrest Spaulding, 1933
Bronze, approximately 14 (35.6) [height]
Portrait bust of Director of Public Library of Des Moines,
1918–1920 and 1928–1951. Spaulding wrote the Des Moines
Library Bill of Rights in 1938, adopted by the American Library
Association in 1939.

155. Billie Wadelton, 1933
Portrait of son of Major Willard Wadelton, Fort Des Moines Army Post.

156. Wilcke Children (Carol and Janet), 1933
Daughters of Mr. and Mrs. A. L. Wilcke. Mr. Wilcke was a
poultry husbandry professor at Iowa State College.
Mr. and Mrs. A. L. Wilcke.

157. Bertrand R. Adams, 1934
Painted plaster, 18 1/2 x 8 x 8 1/2 (47 x 20.3 x 21.6)
Portrait bust. Adams was Petersen's colleague on Public Works of
Art Project at Iowa City.
Signed back of neck: Christian Petersen 1934
Bertrand Adams; Mary (Mrs. Bertrand) Adams, Ames, Iowa.

158. E.B. Bieghler, 1934
Bronze
Portrait bust commissioned by the Des Moines City Railway Company.
Des Moines City Railway Company.

159. Buffalo, 1934
Painted plaster, 6 1/8 x 12 x 5 1/4 (20.3 x 35.6 x 15.2)
Created on Public Works of Art Project in Iowa City, a
preliminary model for a proposed bridgehead sculpture that was
never commissioned. It depicts four buffalo running.
*Charlotte Petersen; SC, Purchased with Iowa State University
Library Funds. SC99.53.*

160. History of Dairying Mural: For Melke and Chese and Buttere, 1934
Painted plaster, 24 x 18 3/8 x 2 (60.9 x 46.7 x 5.1)
Final model for mural inside Dairy Industry Building. Two women
in Grecian clothing and a boy with jugs. Bull in background. This
also shows the brickwork and ledge which frame the final piece,
which is one of a pair of murals inside the entrance to the Dairy
Industry Building. It is assumed there is a similar model for *Four
Thousande Yeere*s, the companion mural, but that model has not
been located.
Gift of Charlotte Petersen to Virginia Slater, Ames, Iowa.

161. History of Dairying Mural: Study of Cows, 1934
Painted plaster, 12 x 24 x 6 (30.5 x 60.9 x 15.2)
Cast, study for central fountain sculpture in Dairy Industry Building
Courtyard. Three Jersey cows are bending their heads low to drink
water while a bull stands and looks over their heads.
*Charlotte Petersen; Animal Science Department; ISU; CPC,
Gift of Animal Science Department. U90.101.*

162. History of Dairying Mural, 1934
Terra cotta. Fountain: 82 x 132 x 40 (208.3 x 335.3 x 101.6).
Panels: 62 x 86 x 8 each (157.5 x 218.4 x 20.3)
Seven panels depicting the history of dairying with fountain at center
panel. Designed and modeled at the Iowa City studio of the Public
Works of Art Project, administered by Grant Wood. Terra cotta panels
fired at the Department of Ceramic Engineering at Iowa State College.
This mural is the primary sculpture produced by the Iowa PWAP

and one of the largest remaining
sculptural works of art produced
under the federal art programs
in the Midwest. The mural was
named to National Register of
Historic Places, 1987.
Signed:
CHRISTIAN PETERSEN,
SCULPTOR
*Commissioned by Iowa State
College and partially carried out
under the Iowa Public Works of
Art Project. Permanent installation
at the Dairy Industry Courtyard.
CPC/AOC. U88.64a-g.*

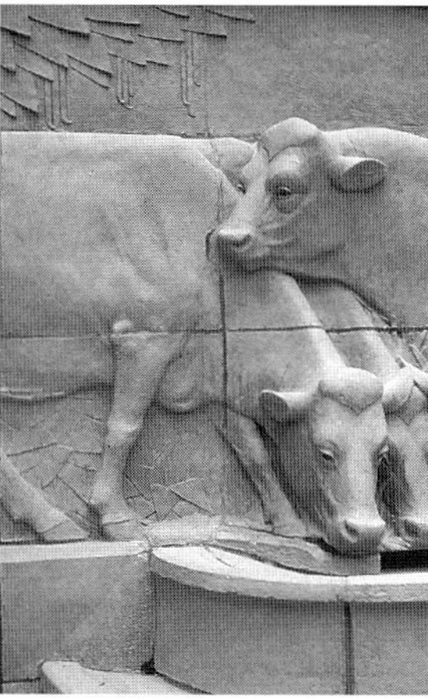
Detail.

163. The Immigrants, 1934
Clay, approximately 16 x 8 x 4 (40.6 x 20.3 x 10.2)
Family group with father, mother holding toddler, and young son.

164. Francis McCray, 1934
Painted plaster, 19 x 9 1/2 x 9 1/2 (48.3 x 24.1 x 24.1)
Portrait bust of Petersen's friend, head of the University of Iowa
art department, Iowa City, Iowa, and one of the artists for the Iowa
State College Library murals in 1934.
*Charlotte Petersen; Mary Petersen; CPC, Gift of the Friends of the
University Museums. U89.39.*

165. John Pusey, 1934
Portrait bust of Petersen's Iowa City friend who worked on Grant Wood's
Public Works of Art murals for the Iowa State College Library.

166. Sons of Dr. and Mrs. William Ryan, 1934
Terra cotta
Bas-relief portraits of the sons of close friends of Petersens in
Des Moines, Iowa.
Dr. & Mrs. William Ryan, Des Moines, Iowa.

167. Mark Thornburg, 1934
Bronze
Portrait bust of Gardner Cowles' grandson.

168. Niels Bukh, 1935
Bukh was a gymnastics professor from Denmark.

169. History of Dairying Mural: For Melke and Chese and Buttere, 1935
Painted plaster, 11' x 7'(3.35 m x 2.13 m)
Inscription: FOR MELKE AND CHESE AND BUTTERE FOR
THER BRED / THE ABRAM WYMMEN SLAVED AND
LABOURED LONGE
*Commissioned by Iowa State College. Permanent installation in
the Dairy Industry Building, ISU. CPC/AOC. U88.65a.*

170. History of Dairying Mural: Four Thousande Yeeres, 1935
Painted plaster, 11' x 7' (3.35 m x 2.13 m)
Inscription: FOUR THOUSANDE YEERES PASS BY BEFORE
MAN THINKES / TO CHAUNGE THESE PLODDING
HOURES TO HOURES OF SONGE
*Commissioned by Iowa State College. Permanent installation at
the Dairy Industry Building, ISU. CPC/AOC. U88.65b.*

171. Neale Knowles, 1935
Portrait bust.

172. Francis McCray, ca. 1935
Fired clay, 10 x 7 x 9 1/2 (25.4 x 17.8 x 24.1)
McCray was head of the University of Iowa art department and a
friend of Petersen. This sculpture depicts his head only.
*Charlotte Petersen; Mary Petersen; CPC, Gift of the Friends of the
University Museums. U89.35.*

173. Martin Mortensen, 1935
Painted plaster, 22 x 8 1/2 x 11 (55.9 x 21.6 x 27.9)
Portrait bust of academic chairman of Department of Dairy Industry.
*Martin Mortensen; Mrs. Marie Mortensen Beal; CPC, Gift of
Mrs. Marie Beal. U90.27.*

174. Mother and Child, 1935
Wood (black walnut), 7 1/2 x 5 1/2 x 3/4 (19.1 x 14 x 1.9)
The outline of figures carved into a flat piece of wood for use as a trivet.
Charlotte Petersen; Mary Petersen, Beverly Hills, Florida.

175. Marjorie and Frances M. Shloss, ca.1935
Bronze, 17 1/2 x 22 1/2 x 3 (44.5 x 57.2 x 7.6)
Portrait of two sisters.
Marjorie Shloss Spevak and Frances M. Shloss.

176. James Stevens, 1935
Terra cotta, 4 1/2 (11.4) [diameter]
This plaque commemorates the visit to Iowa State College of
Ireland's poet laureate, working under the auspices of the Authors
and Poets Club.
Charlotte Petersen; Mr. and Mrs. Clair Watson.

177. Carrie Chapman Catt, 1936
Iowa State College graduate and president of the Women's
Suffrage Alliance from 1904 to 1923.

178. Country Doctor, 1936
Painted plaster,
32 x 9 1/2 x 14 1/2
(81.3 x 24.1 x 36.8)
Medical doctor in a winter coat
and hat carrying medical bag.
*Charlotte Petersen; Purchased
at 1964 sale by Helen J. Sebek;
CPC, Gift of Helen J. Sebek.
UM99.298.*

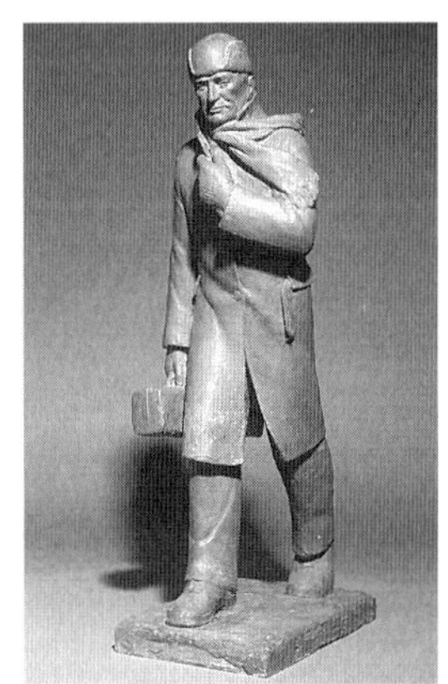

179. J. C. (Jules Cool) Cunningham, 1936
Painted plaster, approximately 16 (40.6) [height]
Portrait bust of Petersen's friend, Cunningham (1879–1948),
a research professor at the Iowa Corn Institute, and amateur poet
who inspired several of Petersen's campus sculptures.

180. Eli Lilly and Company Research Award, 1936
Bronze, 3 x 1/4 (7.6 x 0.6) [diameter x depth]
Recto: Chemist in a lab coat looking into a microscope.
Verso: Man seated under a tree.
Inscription: THE ELI LILLY AND COMPANY RESEARCH

AWARD / for FUNDAMENTAL RESEARCH IN BIOLOGICAL
CHEMISTRY / ADMINISTERED BY THE AMERICAN
CHEMICAL SOCIETY
*Charlotte Petersen; SC, Purchased with Iowa State University
Library Funds. SC99.68.*

181. The Gentle Doctor: Model, 1936
Painted plaster, 10 1/2 x 2 1/2 x 3 (26.7 x 6.4 x 7.6)
*Charles Murray; Madelyn (Murray) and Jerome Miller; Barbara
Haskins, Des Moines, Iowa.*

182. The Gentle Doctor: Model, 1936
Painted plaster, 16 x 5 1/4 x 4 (40.6 x 15.2 x 10.2)
*Charlotte Petersen; Purchased in 1964 sale by M. Burton Drexler.
Promised gift of M. Burton Drexler to CPC.*

183. The Gentle Doctor: Model, 1936
Plaster cast, 16 x 5 1/4 x 4 (40.6 x 13.3 x 10.2)
Charlotte Petersen; Dr. and Mrs. Fred Davison, Augusta, Georgia.

184. Haugen Children, 1936
Terra cotta
Busts of six children in one bas-relief. A gift from Christian Petersen.
Dr. and Mrs. A. I. Haugen.

185. Holl Children (Bruce, Bill, and Beth), 1936
Bas-relief portrait plaque of the children of Mr. and Mrs. D.L. Holl.

186. Phillip Lyendecker, 1936
Portrait bust.
Veracruz University, Jalapa, Mexico.

187. Mask of Lincoln, 1936
Plaster, 8 1/2 (21.6) [height]
Mask of a young, beardless Lincoln. Reproductions were cast by
Pegasus Productions in 1986.
*Charlotte Petersen; Patricia L. Bliss; CPC, Gift of
Patricia L. Bliss. UM89.18.*

188. Frank Luther Mott, 1936
Bronze
Portrait bust of director of University of Missouri school of journalism.

189. Reclining Nudes (Roberts Hall Fountain), 1936
Terra cotta cast in nine panels, 25"x 13'7" x 8"
(63.5 cm x 4.14 m x 20.3 cm)
Two reclining nude figures on either side of a small fountain. Fountain
and pool were removed for conservation from Roberts Hall in 1998.
Inscription: AND NO WORLD MORE WIDE, SINCE ALL HER
DREAMS START HERE AND HERE ABIDE
Commissioned by Iowa State College. CPC/AOC. U88.74.

190. The Surgeon, 1936
Bronze, 23 1/2 x 6 x 4 1/2 (59.7 x 15.2 x 11.4)
Sculpture created for Dr. and Mrs. Charles Ryan, friends of the Petersens,
after Dr. Ryan operated on the artist's wife, Charlotte, for a toxic goiter.
Dr. Ryan practiced surgery in Des Moines until his death in 1942.
Signed: Christian Petersen
Dr. and Mrs. Charles Ryan; Charles J. Ryan, M.D., Naples, Florida.

191. Three Athletes, 1936
Terra cotta, Overall: 73 x 136.5 x 10 (185.4 x 346.7 x 25.4)
Each panel: 73 x 34 x 10 (185.4 x 86.4 x 25.4)
Three bas-reliefs of athletes: football player carrying ball; male
basketball player poised shooting free throw, and a man sprinting.

Each panel is composed of five horizontal panel sections.
Commissioned by Iowa State College. Permanent installation at State Gymnasium. CPC/AOC. U88.75abc.

192. Madonna and Child, ca. 1936
Wood (black walnut), 17 1/2 x 6 1/2 x 4 1/2 (44.5 x 16.5 x 11.4)
Petersen used Charlotte and newborn daughter Mary as models for the sculpture.
Charlotte Petersen; Gift to Fr. Bill Clark; Monsignor Dan Tarrant; Brother Joshua Turley, Saint Benedict, Oregon; Turley Family, Kansas City, Missouri.

193. Pioneer Mother (Portrait Bust of Mary Coon Howell), ca. 1936
Painted plaster, 15 3/4 x 7 1/2 x 10 (40 x 19.1 x 25.4)
The model (great-aunt of Neva Hamann) was cousin to Bessie Coon, author of *Cha-Ki-Shi.* Shows an elderly woman with hair in bun at back of neck.
Signed lower right of pedestal: Christian Petersen
Mary Coon Howell; Neva Hamann; State Historical Society of Iowa, Des Moines, Iowa.1997.74.

194. Dean Charles Henry Stange, DVM, ca. 1936
Painted plaster, 38 x 33 x 21 (96.5 x 83.8 x 53.3)
Waist view of Dean Stange, Veterinary College, Iowa State College. He holds his hand in front of him with a scroll in his left hand.
Commissioned by Iowa State College, College of Veterinary Medicine. CPC/AOC. U90.63.

195. Charles E. Friley, 1937
Bronze, 17 x 10 1/2 x 10 1/2 (43.2 x 26.7 x 26.7)
Portrait bust of Dr. Friley, president of Iowa State College, 1936 to 1953.
Signed lower left of base: Christian Petersen, ISC
Commissioned by Iowa State College; Friley Hall; Department of Residence Life; CPC, Gift of Friley Hall, Department of Residence Life. U94.36.

196. The Gentle Doctor, 1937
Terra cotta, 80 x 24 1/2 x 23 (203.2 x 62.2 x 58.4)
Doctor holding an injured or ill puppy, with mother dog sitting at the veterinarian's feet and leaning against his knee. The sculpture is widely accepted as the international symbol of veterinary medicine.
Commissioned by Iowa State College, College of Veterinary Medicine; CPC/AOC. U84.179.

197. Frances Reis Quinn, ca. 1937
Plaster
Bas relief of Petersen's student at Iowa State College.
Frances Reis Quinn; Barbara Reis Sandblom, Paradise Valley, Arizona.

198. Dancing Woman, late 1930s
Painted plaster, 13 1/2 x 9 x 3 1/2 (34.3 x 22.9 x 8.9)
Woman in a dance pose, dressed in an off-the-shoulder Grecian gown.
Getrude Cox; Jean C. Davis; CPC, Purchased in memory of Ruth Smith with funds from Friends of Ruth Smith. UM98.2.

199. Dancing Woman, late 1930s
Painted plaster, 13 1/8 x 9 x 3 1/2 (33.3 x 22.9 x 8.9)
Woman in a dance pose, dressed in an off-the-shoulder Grecian gown.
Getrude Cox; Jean C. Davis; CPC, Purchased in memory of Ruth Smith with funds from Friends of Ruth Smith. UM98.3.

200. Equitable of Iowa Companies Award, ca. late 1930s
Medallion.
Equitable of Iowa Companies, Des Moines, Iowa.

201. Abraham Lincoln, late 1930s
Plaster, 9 1/2 x 6 1/4 x 1 (24.1 x 15.9 x 2.5)
Arched plaque with a frontal portrait.
Inscription: ABRAHAM LINCOLN
George Nerney; Mrs. Helen Nerney Shaw; SC, Gift of Mrs. Helen Nerney Shaw. SC99.262.

202. Madonna of the Prairie, late 1930s
Clay sketch, 12 x 10 3/4 x 15 1/4 (30.5 x 27.3 x 38.7)
Charlotte Petersen; Purchased at 1964 sale by Helen J. Sebek; CPC, Gift of Helen J. Sebek. UM2000.4.

203. William Holmes McGuffey, late 1930s
Small model for a proposed memorial to McGuffey, whose *McGuffey Readers* were written for school children in the late nineteenth century.

204. Pin, late 1930s
Silver, 2 x 1 1/2 (5.1 x 3.8)
Nude male and female holding hands across a flower. Made to wear with a particular dress of Charlotte Petersen.
Charlotte Petersen; Mary Petersen, Beverly Hills, Florida.

205. Thomas R. Agg, 1938
Portrait of dean, College of Engineering, Iowa State College from 1932 to 1946.

206. Myron Boozer, 1938
Painted plaster, 29 1/2 x 21 1/4 x 2 1/8 (74.9 x 54 x 5.4)
Bas-relief portrait of pastor of Collegiate Presbyterian Church.
Collegiate Presbyterian Church, Ames, Iowa.

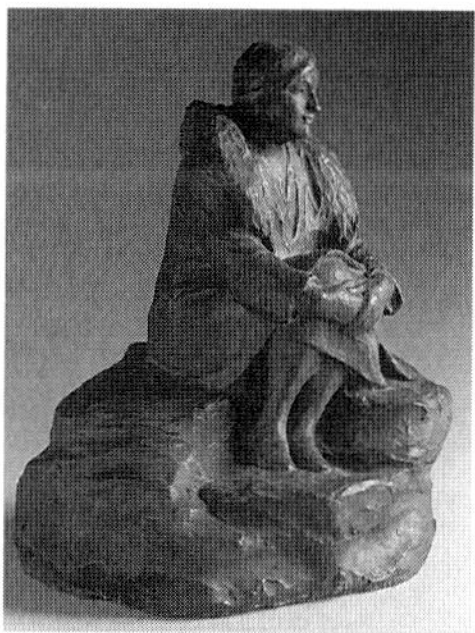

207. Charlotte Sitting on a Rock at a Picnic, ca. 1938
Painted plaster,
11 3/16 x 9 3/8 x 7 3/4
(28.4 x 23.8 x 19.7)
Woman seated on a rock formation with hands around knees. She wears a hat and coat with fur collar.
Charlotte Petersen; Mary Petersen; CPC, Gift of Mary Petersen.UM92.610.

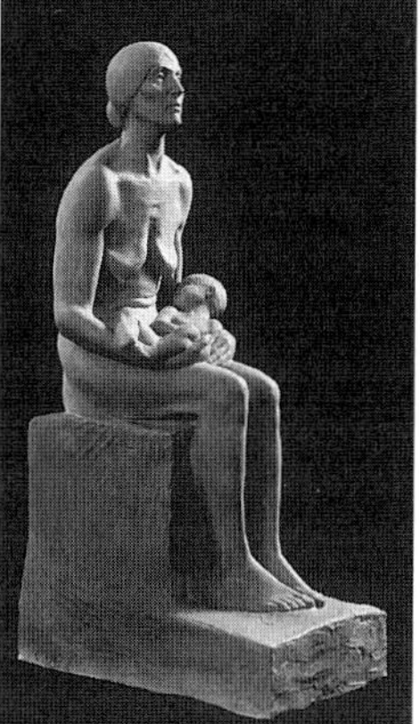

208. Drought, ca. 1938
Painted plaster, 21 3/4 x 7 x 13
(55.2 x 17.8 x 33)
Seated nude woman holding child.
Mary Petersen; CPC, Gift of Class of 1919. UM85.49.

209. Sara Porter Ellis, 1938

Portrait bust of director of home economics extension, Iowa State College.

210. Genevieve Fisher, 1938

Bronze

Portrait bust of dean, Home Economics College, Iowa State College.

211. Flood, 1938

Painted plaster cast, 16 1/2 x 9 (41.9 x 22.9)

Woman standing holding a small child in her arms while looking back over her shoulder.

1) *Mary Petersen; CPC, Gift of Class of 1919. UM85.48.*
2) *Dr. and Mrs. Charles Ryan; Charles J. Ryan, M.D. Naples, Florida.*

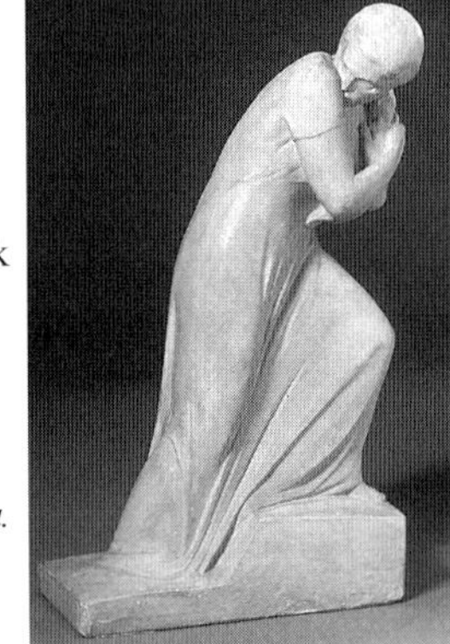

212. Cynthia Kendall, 1938

Plaster, 20 (50.8) [diameter]

Bas-relief medallion. Woman in profile facing right.

Charlotte Petersen; Purchased at 1964 sale by Harriet Adams, Ames, Iowa.

213. Laura and Wallace, 1938

Painted plaster, Laura: 11 1/2 x 9 x 12 (29.2 x 22.9 x 30.5). Wallace: 11 x 8 x 9 (27.9 x 20.3 x 22.9)

Two bust sketches of a man and woman Petersen met in Kentucky, both of whom were sharecroppers, and one of whom was a former slave.

Charlotte Petersen; Purchased at the 1964 sale by Joy Munn; CPC, Gifts of Joy Munn. UM99.301 and UM99.300.

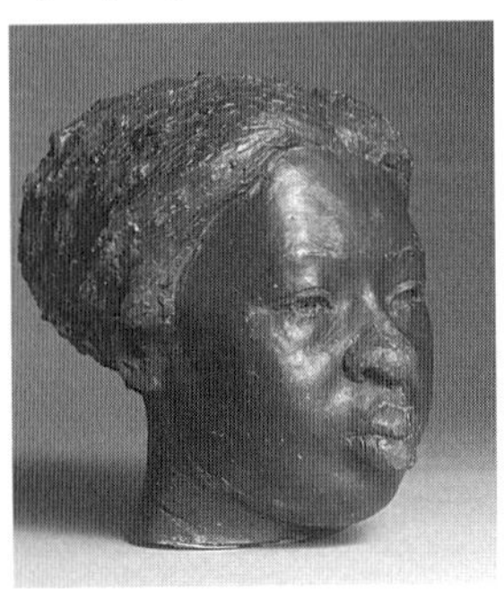
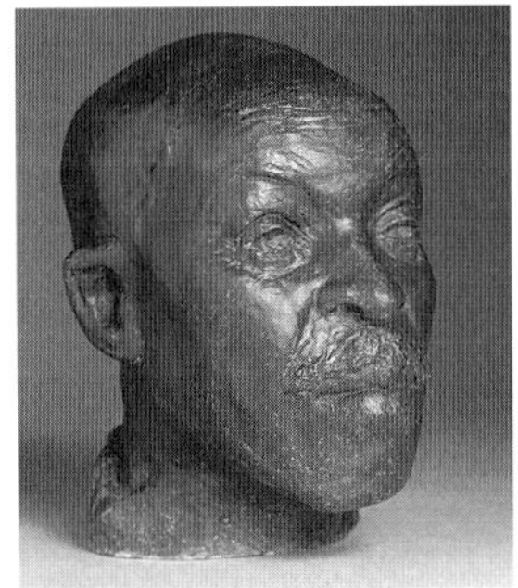

214. Anson Marston Medal, 1938

Bronze medals, 1 5/8 x 1/8 (4.1 x 0.3) [diameter x depth]

Steel molds, 2 1/4 x 3/16 (5.7 x 0.5) [diameter x depth]

Medals awarded for achievement in engineering.

Recto: Anson Marston in profile with a mustache, wearing a suit and tie.

Verso: A scene with bridges, a river, a dam, a tower, and buildings.

Recto inscription: THE ANSON MARSTON AWARD - IOWA STATE COLLEGE

Verso inscription: AWARDED FOR ACHIEVEMENT IN ENGINEERING

Two medals and two molds: Charlotte Petersen; SC, Purchased with Iowa State University Library Funds. SC99.60abc and SC99.61.

215. Anson Marston, 1938

Bust portrait or bas-relief.

216. Frank LeRonde McVey, 1938

Bronze, approximately 48 x 36 x 3 (121.9 x 91.4 x 7.6)

Signed: Christian Petersen Sc '38 Bronze Incorporated.

Inscription at top: FRANK LERONDE MCVEY / FIFTH PRESIDENT / UNIVERSITY / OF / KENTUCKY

Inscription at bottom: BELIEVE IN TRUTH / PROTEST AGAINST ERROR/LEAD MEN BY REASON RATHER THAN FORCE

University of Kentucky.

217. Mother Earth, 1938

Terra cotta, approximately 66 (1.7 m) [height]

Life size figure of a pregnant pioneer woman. Stolen from Petersen's studio, ca. 1939.

218. Mother with Walking Child, ca. 1938

Fired clay, 16 x 6 (40.6 x 15.2)

Small maquette of preparatory work to be carved in Bedford limestone.

Charlotte Petersen; Purchased at 1964 sale by James Borcherding; CPC, Gift of James Borcherding. U92.402.

219. Mother with Walking Child (unfinished), ca. 1938

Bedford limestone with charcoal, 26 1/2 x 6 (67.3 x 15.2)

Image of mother and child are drawn on limestone in anticipation of being sculpted.

Charlotte Petersen; Purchased at 1964 sale by James Borcherding; CPC, Gift of James Borcherding. U92.401.

220. Mrs. Christian Petersen Washing Her Hair, 1938

Glazed and fired clay, 6 x 5 x 6 (15.2 x 12.7 x 15.2)

Spoof on sculpture by Hugo Robus.

Charlotte Petersen; Mary Petersen, Beverly Hills, Florida.

221. A. H. Munn, 1938

Terra cotta, 15 x 9 x 10 (38.1 x 22.9 x 25.4)

Portrait bust of the patriarch of the Munn family of Ames, Iowa.

A.H. Munn; Hiram Munn; Fritz Munn; Joy Munn, Ames, Iowa.

222. George Nerney, 1938

Fired clay

Portrait bust of Petersen's lifelong friend from Attleboro, Massachusetts.

223. Old Lady (Old Woman), 1938

Clay

Charlotte Petersen; Purchased at 1964 sale by Mr. G. A. Englesson, Ames, Iowa.

224. Pegasus in Iowa, 1938

Painted plaster, 15 x 12 x 7 (38.1 x 30.5 x 17.8)

A spoof of a draft horse getting a pair of wings. Three limited edition bronzes of this sculpture were created and offered in 1984 on behalf of Charlotte Petersen by Pegasus Productions, the first of which was purchased by the College of Veterinary Medicine, ISU.

225. Pioneer Woman (Alma Mater), 1938

Plaster, 23 x 7 x 6 (58.4 x 17.8 x 15.2)

Proposal for the Iowa State College Cemetery, this depicts a female figure in long skirts. The pioneer theme was used to suggest the rural background of the State of Iowa and Iowa State College.

Charlotte Petersen; Private collection; CPC, Anonymous gift in memory of Charlotte Petersen. UM89.19.

226. Edward and David Rall, 1938
Bas-relief portrait of sons of the president of North Central College, Naperville, Illinois.
Edward E. Rall.

227. George Shull, 1938
Plaster
Casting from bust portrait. Shull was on the Iowa State Board of Regents.

228. Thomas J. Sloss, 1938
Painted plaster, 29 1/2 x 21 x 3 (74.9 x 53.3 x 7.6)
Bas-relief portrait of Sunday school superintendent of Collegiate Presbyterian Church.
Collegiate Presbyterian Church, Ames, Iowa.

229. Orland Russell Sweeney, 1938
Bronze, 28 1/4 x 34 1/2 x 3/4 (71.8 x 87.6 x 1.9)
Portrait bas-relief of academic chairman, Chemical Engineering, Iowa State College.
Inscription: ORLAND RUSSELL SWEENEY/ 1882–1958/ FIRST HEAD OF DEPARTMENT OF CHEMICAL ENGINEERING 1920–1947. AN INSPIRING EDUCATOR, ADMINISTRATOR AND RESEARCH WORKER. KNOWN FOR HIS WARM PERSONALITY, REMARKABLE FORESIGHT AND INVENTIVE MIND. A DEVOTED FRIEND TO STUDENTS AND COLLEAGUES ALIKE. PRESENTED WITH AFFECTION BY SWEENEY'S BOYS OF THE CLASS OF 1927.
Commissioned by Iowa State College, Department of Chemical Engineering; CPC/AOC. U99.294.

230. Veterinary Medicine Mural, 1935–1938
Unglazed terra cotta, 76" x 22'9" x 8" (193 cm x 6.93 m x 20.3 cm)
The mural consists of forty-four blocks. It depicts the services the veterinary profession performs in conserving the life and health of domestic animals, thereby safeguarding the health of humans.
Commissioned by Iowa State College. Permanent installation at the College of Veterinary Medicine Courtyard. CPC/AOC. U88.71.

231. Children's Fountain Base, ca. 1938
Plaster, 30 x 30 (76.2 x 76.2) [height x diameter]
Model of a children's fountain which depicts children in bas-relief playing and dancing around the periphery of the fountain. The drinking fountain was proposed for Brookside Park in Ames, Iowa.
Charlotte Petersen; Mary Petersen; CPC, Purchased by Home Economics Development Fund. 88.39.

232. Edward R., 1939
The subject is the son of Florence Walls, Iowa State College faculty member.
Florence Walls.

233. Mary Jean Stoddard Fowler, 1939
A portrait mentioned in correspondence.

234. Gerber Baby, 1939
Award or medal commissioned by the Gerber Company.

235. Grateful Farmer, 1939
Clay or plaster
Charlotte Petersen; Purchased in 1964 as gift to the Mason City School System.

236. Charles F. Murray, 1939
Clay or bronze
Portrait bust of dean, Veterinary Medicine College, Iowa State College.

237. Princess and the Pea, 1939
Clay study, 10 x 7 x 5 (25.4 x 17.8 x 12.7)
Whimsical study, based on Hans Christian Andersen fairy tale.
Charlotte Petersen; Purchased at 1964 sale by Maridee Hegstrom, Ames, Iowa.

238. Michael Schroeder, 1939
Plaster
Son of Iowa State College music professor and wife, Mr. and Mrs. Ira Schroeder.
Michael Schroeder, Perry, Iowa.

239. Albert Edward Scott, 1939
Plaster
Bas-relief portrait created for close friends of Petersens.
Mr. & Mrs. Ira Schroder.

240. Soon after Flood (Three Children on a Mule; After the Flood), 1939
Painted plaster, 26 x 22 x 8 (66 x 55.9 x 20.3)
Petersen saw children on a mule after the 1938 flood in Kentucky. An unauthorized bronze casting of this piece was created after Petersen's death.
Bernice Burns Donovan and Esther Burns; CPC, Gift of Bernice Burns Donovan and Esther Burns. UM85.50.

241. Two Children, 1939
Fired clay, Boy: 12 1/2 x 5 1/4 x 4 (31.8 x 13.3. x 10.2); Girl: 12 1/2 x 4 3/4 x 5 1/4 (31.8 x 12.1 x 13.3)
One sculpture depicts Mary Petersen, the artist's daughter, holding her rag doll in dejection and the other depicts her playmate — a neighborhood boy — holding his new puppy after bragging about it and telling her, "You can't play with it." Five plaster castings were sold at the 1964 sale, and others were sold around that time. Thirty-six pairs of Permastone castings of the originals were done by Pegasus Productions in 1986 by royalty arrangement with Charlotte and Mary Petersen.
Charlotte Petersen; Patricia L. Bliss; CPC, Gift of Patricia L. Bliss. UM89.20 and UM89.21.

242. Mountain Mother, ca. 1939
Bedford limestone, 18 (45.7) [height]
Figures of mother and two small children, believed to be from Appalachia.
Purchased from the sculptor's studio in 1961 by his students at Central Iowa Art Association as a memorial to their friend and teacher. Located at the Community Center, Marshalltown, Iowa.

243. Helen Gilkey, ca. 1930s
Clay

244. John Pusey, ca. 1930s
Bust portrait of Petersen's Iowa City friend, painter John Pusey, a painter on Public Works of Art Project in Iowa.

245. B.G., 1940
Bronze
Portrait bust of a daughter of a *Des Moines Register and Tribune* columnist.
Harlan Miller, Des Moines, Iowa.

246. Basketball Player, 1940
Cast concrete, approximately 73 x 34 x 10 (185.4 x 86.4 x 25.4)
Bas-relief sculpture of an athlete.
Ventura Public Schools, Ventura, Iowa.

247. Frederick William Beckman, 1940
Bronze, 18 x 17 1/2 x 10 3/4 (45.7 x 44.5 x 27.3)
Portrait bust of Fredrick W. Beckman, founder of Iowa State
College Press in 1934 and head of the Department of Technical
Journalism, 1911–1927.
Signed: Christian Petersen SC
Commissioned by Iowa State College, CPC. U94.4.

248. Dorothy Beemer, 1940
Portrait bust.

249. Mrs. Blanding, 1940
Painted plaster, 12 x 8 1/2 x 1/2 (30.5 x 21.6)
President of Vassar College in the 1940s. Mrs. Blanding,
originally from Kentucky, was the mother of Sara Gibson Blanding
and met Petersen during his trip there in the summer of 1938.
Bas-relief: Sally Peterson, Ames, Iowa.
Plaster mold: Charlotte Petersen; Purchased at 1964 sale by Mrs.
Percy A. Johnson, Saint Paul, Minnesota.

250. Boy with Dog, 1940
Fired clay
Demonstration sketch, probably done at the Iowa State Fair.

251. Charles F. Curtiss, 1940
Portrait of dean, College of Agriculture, Iowa State College.

252. The Drama, 1940
Created for the artist's wife, Charlotte, and the Playmakers
community theater group.

253. Clyde Beals Fletcher, 1940
Bronze
Bas-relief portrait of founder, Home Federal Savings and Loan,
Des Moines, Iowa.

254. Kirk Fox, 1940
Portrait bust of *Successful Farming* editor.

255. A. Maurice Hanson, 1940
Portrait bust of professor of landscape architecture at Iowa State College.

256. Indian Mother, 1940
Clay

257. Frank Johnson, 1940
Plaster, 19 (48.3) [height]
Portrait bust of an artist and friend of Petersen.
Charlotte Petersen; Mary Petersen; CPC, Gift of the Friends of
the University Museums. U89.40.

258. H. H. Kildee, 1940
Portrait bust of dean, College of Agriculture, Iowa State College.
ISU, Ames, Iowa.

259. Kuhn Children, 1940
Bas-relief.
George Kuhn.

260. Anna B. Lawther, 1940
Portrait bust.

261. Ernest N. Lindstrom, 1940
Bronze, 23 x 16 x 2 1/4 (58.4 x 40.6 x 7)
Memorial plaque with bust of genetics professor at Iowa State College.
Inscription: LINDSTROM MEMORIAL GENETICS LIBRARY /
ESTABLISHED BY HIS FAMILY STUDENTS AND FRIENDS
TO COMMEMORATE HIS LASTING INTEREST IN GENETICS

Plaque: Charlotte Petersen; SC, Purchased with Iowa State
University Library Funds. SC99.58.
Mold: Charlotte Petersen; Listed in 1964 sale records.

262. Madonna, 1940
Clay sketch, 7 3/4 x 1 5/8 x 3 1/2 (19.7 x 4.1 x 8.9)
Charlotte Petersen; Purchased at 1964 sale by Helen J. Sebek; CPC,
Gift of Helen J. Sebek. UM2000.5.

263. Dmitri Metroupolis [*sic*], 1940
Bronze, 10 3/4 x 12 3/4 (27.3 x 32.4)
Portrait bas-relief of conductor Mitroupolis presented to him when
he left as Music Director of the Minneapolis Symphony,
participant in the Iowa State Concert Series, for the New York
Philharmonic. Commissioned by Tolbert MacRae, head of the Iowa
State College Music Department from 1920 to the 1960s.

264. Dmitri Metroupolis [*sic*], 1940
Painted plaster, 10 3/4 x 12 3/4 (27.3 x 32.4)
Two castings given to Tolbert MacRae, head of the Iowa State
College Music Department from 1920 to the 1960s. Both given
to MacRae's children: Casting 1: John MacRae, Los Gatos,
California. Casting 2: Estate of Rebecca Josephine (MacRae)
Boswell, Roswell, New Mexico.

265. Dmitri Metroupolis [*sic*], 1940
Plaster, 10 3/4 x 12 3/4 (27.3 x 32.4)
Portrait bas-relief of conductor; copy of bronze one given to him
when he left his position as Music Director for the Minneapolis
Symphony, participant in the Iowa State Concert Series, for the
New York Philharmonic.
Charlotte Petersen; Purchased from 1964 sale by Maridee
Hegstrom, Ames, Iowa.

266. Mood, 1940
Created for the artist's wife, Charlotte, and the Playmakers
community theater group.

267. Moyer Children, 1940
Plaster
Bas-relief of two children.

268. Ole Nelson, 1940
Portrait bust of national commander of the Grand Army of the Republic.
Listed as "Not for Sale" in 1964 sale records.

269. G. Samuel Nichols, 1940
Terra cotta
Bas-relief portrait of the pastor of Collegiate Methodist Church in
Ames, Iowa, from 1935 to 1960.
Collegiate United Methodist Church — Wesley Foundation,
Ames, Iowa.

270. Don Reynolds, 1940
Clay
Portrait bust of Ames attorney, sculpted as demonstration for
Kiwanis Club.

271. Viking, 1940
Cast concrete, approximately 32 x 8 (81.3 x 20.3) [diameter x depth]
High relief of head of a Viking.
Ventura Public Schools.

272. War (After the Blitz War), 1940
Bedford limestone, approximately 36 x 18 x 12 (91 x 49 x 30)
Half-figure sculpture of nude mother figure holding nude child close
to her chest, both wearing expressions of horror. Inspired by World
War II bombings in Europe.
*Gift from Martha Ellen Fisher Tye to the Central Iowa Art
Association. Dedicated in 1961 at the Fisher Community Center,
Marshalltown, Iowa.*

273. Gary and Sandra Weiss, 1940
Plaster, 12 1/2 x 13 1/4 x 1 1/2 (31.8 x 33.7 x 3.8)
Bas-relief portrait plaque of children of Mr. and Mrs. Martin Weiss.
*Plaque: Mary Meixner; Beth Harvey, Minneapolis, Minnesota.
Mold: Charlotte Petersen; Purchased at 1964 sale by Mary
Meixner; CPC, Gift of Mary Meixner. UM97.138.*

274. George Wilson, 1940
Painted plaster, 18 x 9 x 11 (45.7 x 22.9 x 27.9)
Wilson (1884–1953) was Governor of Iowa 1939–1943.
State Historical Society of Iowa, Des Moines, Iowa. I 523.

275. Gutzon Borglum, ca. 1940
Probably plaster
Portrait bust of sculptor of Mount Rushmore; Borglum possibly
known from Petersen's early career in New York.

276. Head of a Girl, ca. 1940
Painted cast concrete, 12 x 10 x 9 (30.1 x 25.4 x 22.9)
Hair is pulled back into two buns worn in the middle/back of her head.
*Charlotte Petersen; Mary Petersen; CPC, Gift of the Friends of
the University Museums. U89.36.*

277. Madonna of the Prairie, ca. 1940
Bedford limestone, Overall: 69 1/2 x 28 x 24 (176.5 x 71.1 x 61);
Image: 54 1/2 (138.4) [height]
Figure portraying a young pioneer mother carrying a small child in
her arms.
*Charlotte Petersen; Iowa Art in State Buildings Program
Purchase by College of Education. Permanent installation at
Lagomarcino Hall Courtyard. CPC/AOC. U86.590.*

278. Old Woman in Prayer (The Refugee), ca. 1940
Bedford limestone, 28 x 17 x 18 (71.1 x 43.2 x 45.7)
Aged female with her hands placed together in prayer and eyes
looking upward.
*Charlotte Petersen; Iowa Art in State Buildings Program
Purchase by Iowa State University Library. CPC/AOC. U86.521.*

279. Oscar Woody, ca. 1940
Fired clay, 5 1/4 x 4 x 4 (13.3 x 10.2 x 10.2)
Linda Craven, Laramie, Wyoming.

280. Pickle Spear, ca. 1940–1941
Wood (black walnut), 6 inches (15.2) long
A sculpture of a woman fades into a two-pronged spear.
Charlotte Petersen; Mary Petersen, Beverly Hills, Florida.

281. Salad Spoon, ca. 1940–1941
Wood (black walnut), 10 x 2 (25.4 x 5.1) [height x width]
Sculpture of a woman who fades into the bowl of the spoon. Tree
rings are centered in the bowl of the spoon.
Charlotte Petersen; Mary Petersen, Beverly Hills, Florida.

282. Blair Converse, 1941
Bronze, 20 x 16 x 8 (50.8 x 40.6 x 20.3)
Portrait of Converse, Department of Journalism, 1919–1939.
Dedicated October 1941 in the Department of Technical Journalism,
Iowa State College, Ames, Iowa.
Signed on back of left arm: Christian Petersen SC
*Commissioned by Iowa State College, Department of Technical
Journalism; CPC. U94.5.*

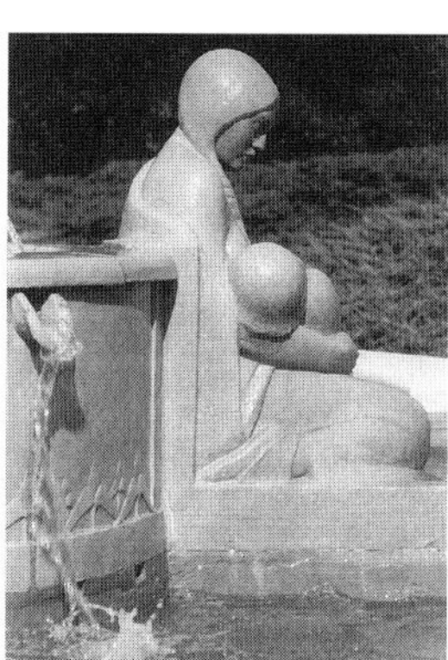

Detail.

283. Cornhusker (Iowa Champ, Agricultural Labor), 1941
Painted plaster, 43 x 16 x 24
(109.2 x 40.6 x 60.9)
The model, Marion Link of
Nevada, won second in the
National Cornhusking Champ-
ionship in 1940 and first place in
the Iowa championship in 1941.
*Hotel Sheldon Munn, Ames,
Iowa; Kirkwood Civic Center
Hotel, Des Moines, Iowa;
CPC, Gift in memory of Joseph
M. Coppola, Sr., by the Coppola
Family. UM99.329.*

284. Fountain of the Four Seasons, 1941
Bedford limestone sculptures,
installation: 40 x 144
(1.02 m x 3.66 m) [height x
 diameter]
Terra cotta fountain ring, 30 x 96
(76.2 x 243.8)[height x diameter]
Four kneeling figures of Native
American women equally
spaced around a fountain ring.
The ring design is sprouting corn.
*Commissioned by Iowa State
College. Permanent installation
at the Memorial Union Courtyard. CPC/AOC. U88.69.*

285. 4-H Calf, 1941
Painted plaster,
40 1/2 x 31 1/2 x 18
(102.9 x 80 x 45.7)
Figure of boy with calf.
Commissioned by Hotel
Sheldon Munn, Ames, Iowa,
along with *Cornhusker* in 1941.
*Hotel Sheldon Munn, Ames,
Iowa; Kirkwood Civic Center
Hotel, Des Moines, Iowa; CPC,
Gift in memory of Joseph M.
Coppola, Sr., by the Coppola
Family. UM99.330.*

286. Fountain of the Four Seasons: Maidens, 1941
Plaster models, A: 40 x 24 x 22 3/4 (101.6 x 60.9 x 57.8);
B: approximately 40 x 24 x 24 (101.6 x 61 x 61);
C: 38 x 24 x 22 (96.5 x 60.9 x 55.9);
D: 40 x 24 x 24 (96.5 x 60.9 x 60.9)
Original plaster casts for *Fountain of the Four Seasons* figures.
*Charlotte Petersen; Mary Petersen; CPC, Gift of the Friends of
the University Museums. U89.26abcd.*

287. William Wheelock Peet, 1941 or 1942
Plaster, 10 1/2 x 14 1/2 x 3/4 (26.7 x 36.8 x 1.9)
Relief portrait of business and diplomatic head of a Congregational
missionary society in Istanbul, Turkey, who spent the last two years
of his life in Ames and became friends with the Petersen family.
Signed: CP
Louise J. Peet and William Hartwell Peet; William H. Peet, Jr.

288. August Bang, 1942
Painted plaster, 15 1/2 x 8 x 10 1/2 (39.4 x 20.3 x 26.7)
Portrait bust of the Danish editor of *Julegranen* magazine.
*Charlotte Petersen; Purchased at 1964 sale by Marion
Gunderson; Clara G. Hoover, Omaha, Nebraska.*

289. Mildred Finegan, 1942
Painted plaster, 11 x 9 x 9 (27.9 x 22.9 x 22.9)
Portrait bust of Mildred Catherine Meader Finegan, sculpted at a
Faculty Women's Club meeting at Iowa State. Her husband, Jack,
was head of the department and professor of Religious Education.
The model was a close friend of the artist's wife Charlotte.
Jack Finegan, Oakland, California.

290. Mildred Finegan, ca. 1942
Terra cotta, 9 1/2 x 4 1/2 x 4 1/2 (24.1 x 11.4 x 11.4)
Charlotte Petersen; Mary Petersen, Beverly Hills, Florida.

291. Marriage Ring: Model, 1942
Painted plaster, 5 1/2 x 20 1/2 x 4 1/2 (14 x 52.1 x 11.4)
Model for sculpture and fountain.
*Gift of the artist to Frances Clarke Kinnick; Nile Kinnick, Sr.;
Eleanor White Kinnick Butler and William Butler, White Bear
Lake, Minnesota.*

292. Marriage Ring (Wedding Ring, Ring of Life), 1942
Terra cotta, sculpture group: 37 x 117 x 16 1/2
(94 x 297.2 x 41.9) with pool 17' (5.18m) [diameter]
Three toddlers, approximately life-size, sitting at the edge of a pool.
Designed for grounds of College of Home Economics, MacKay
Hall. Figures moved indoors inside MacKay Hall after being con-
served in 1991. 1994 outdoor reproduction of reinforced concrete
by Mayda Jensen, Omaha, permanently installed outside of MacKay Hall.
Signed: CHRISTIAN PETERSEN
*Commissioned by Iowa State College. Permanent installation
inside MacKay Hall entrance. CPC/AOC, Gift of the 1941
VEISHEA Central Committee. U88.66.*

293. Men of Two Wars, 1942
Painted plaster, 33 x 55 x 29 (83.8 x 139.7 x 73.7)
Crouching World War II soldier beside fallen World War I
doughboy. Proposed war memorial honoring service men from
World Wars I and II. Originally intended to be sponsored by the
American Legion of Iowa, this project was never commissioned.
Charlotte Petersen; Memorial Union, ISU, Ames, Iowa.

294. Murray Children, 1942
Painted plaster, 17 3/4 x 25 x 1 1/4 (45.1 x 63.5 x 3.2)
Bas-relief plaque. Side view of three children (Dave, John, Jean),
all facing to the left.
*Plaque: Mr. and Mrs. William Murray; CPC, Gift of Alice Murray.
U93.25a*
*Mold: Mr. and Mrs. William Murray; CPC, Gift of Alice Murray.
UM93.25b*

295. Stephen Vincent Benet, 1943
Painted plaster, 16 1/2 x 5 1/2 x 9 1/2 (41.9 x 14 x 24.1)
Portrait bust of Benet (1898–1943), a writer best known for
the Civil War narrative poem *John Brown's Body* (1928). Benet
had visited Iowa State College in 1939, and Petersen created two
busts after his death.
*Charlotte Petersen; Mary Petersen; CPC, Gift of the Friends of
the University Museums. U89.37.*

296. Charles Rogers, 1943
Plaster
Portrait bust of Department of Journalism faculty member who
did publicity for Petersen.

297. Clifford V. Gregory, 1934–1944
Terra cotta, 14 1/4 x 6 1/2 x 8 1/2 (39.2 x 16.5 x 21.6)
Portrait of the academic head of Agriculture Journalism from 1908
to 1911, for the Department of Technical Journalism.
Signed left side of neck: CP
Commissioned by Iowa State College; CPC. U94.3.

298. Library Boy and Girl, 1944
Bedford limestone, Boy: 84 x 26 x 26 (213.3 x 66 x 66);
Girl: 84 x 23 1/2 x 24 (213.3 x 59.7 x 60.9)
Seated boy and girl mounted on low pedestals on each side of the
stairway leading to the second floor, the figures represent two
college students admiring each other.
*Commissioned by Iowa State College. Permanent installation
inside Iowa State University Library. CPC/AOC. U88.67ab.*

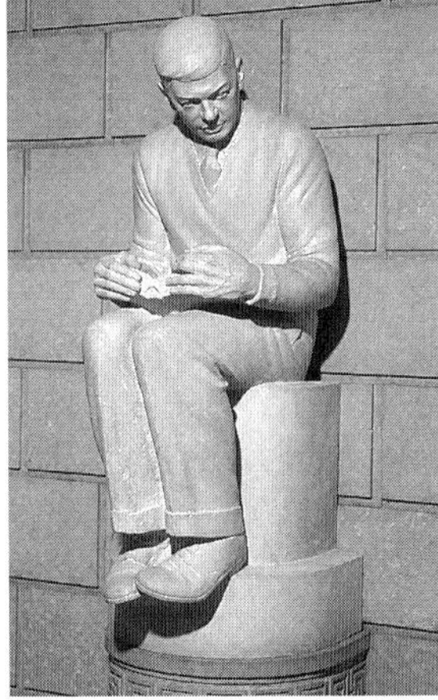 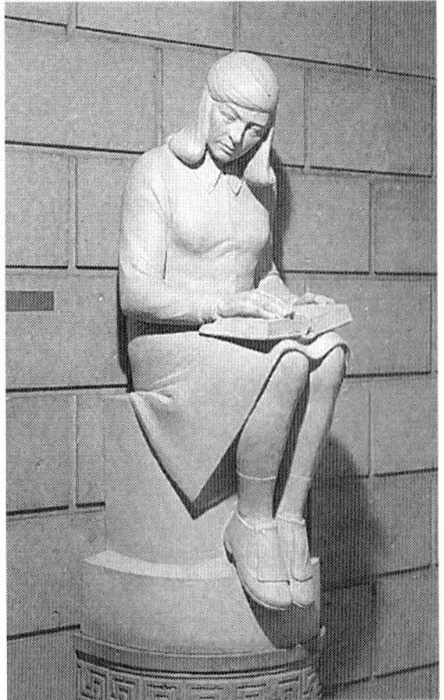

299. Library Boy and Girl: Models, 1944
Painted plaster, 24 x 12 x 12 (61 x 30.5 x 30.5) [each]
*Charlotte Petersen; Purchased at 1964 sale by Wayne and Mary
Moore, Ames, Iowa.*

300. Library Boy: Model, 1944
Painted plaster, 20 1/2 x 7 1/4 x 6 1/2 (52.1 x 18.4 x 16.5)
A concept for *Library Boy*. Figure sits on an anvil, with a wheel to his left and tools to the right. The boy and objects are on a two-tiered, curved pedestal.
Charlotte Petersen; SC, Gift of Charlotte Petersen. SC99.66.

301. Library Girl: Model, 1944
Painted plaster, 12 x 4 1/2 x 5 1/2 (30.5 x 11.4 x 14)
A concept for *Library Girl*. Seated female student glancing to her right with a book on her lap.
Charlotte Petersen; SC, Gift of Charlotte Petersen. SC99.65.

302. Fallen Soldier, ca. 1944
Clay, 17 1/2 x 6 x 5 1/2 (44.5 x 15.2 x 14)
Study of fallen soldier. A man grasping a wounded soldier under the arms and holding him upright.
Charlotte Petersen; Mary Petersen; CPC, Gift of Friends of the University Museums. U89.38ab.

**303. Price of Victory
(Fallen Soldier),** 1944
Painted plaster, 36 x 18 x 16
(91.4 x 45.7 x 40.6)
World War II soldier slumps toward ground as he is hit by a bullet.
Charlotte Petersen; Mary Petersen; CPC, Gift of Mary Petersen. UM99.297.

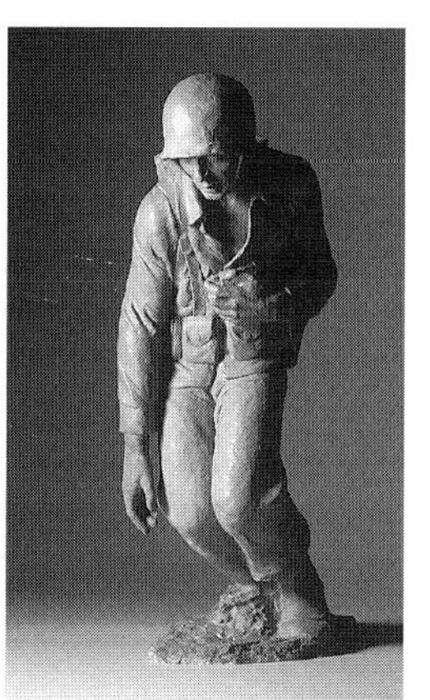

304. Unknown Prisoner, 1944
Plaster, 15 1/2 x 17 3/8 x 9 3/8
(39.4 x 44.1 x 23.8)
Scourged figure of Christ tied to the Cross, with his back to the viewer.
Charlotte Petersen; Purchased at 1964 sale by Helen J. Sebek; CPC, Gift of Helen J. Sebek. UM2000.6.

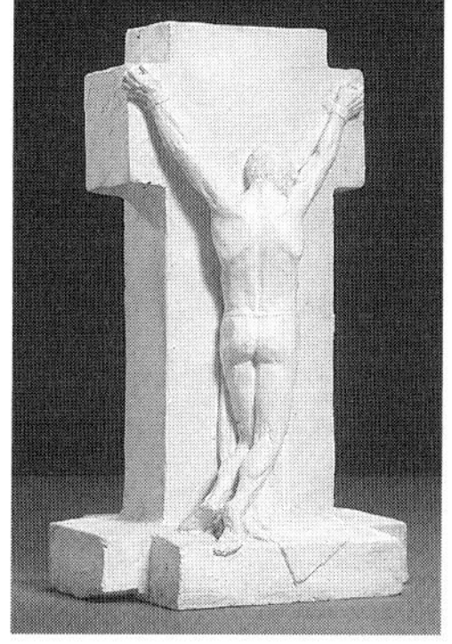

305. Baby John, 1945
Bronze, approximately 12 x 9 x 1 (30.5 x 22.9 x 2.5)
Plaster plaques are 13 1/2 x 9 1/2 x 1 3/4 (34.3 x 24.1 x 4.4)
Two plaster plaques commissioned by Alice M. and Jack D. Rector of their son John at five months. A bronze was cast by the owner from one of the two molds given them by Petersen.
Bronze: Alice M. and Jack D. Rector, Cedar Rapids, Iowa; Collection of John Rector, Iowa City, Iowa.
Two plaster plaques: Alice M. and Jack D. Rector, Cedar Rapids, Iowa.

306. Romantic Thoughts, ca. 1940
Exhibited at the Memorial Union, 1942.

307. Saint Bernadette, 1945
Painted plaster, 23 1/2 x 10 1/2 x 7 1/4 (59.7 x 26.7 x 18.4)
Figure of Saint Bernadette of Lourdes.
Gift from Petersens to Saint Cecilia Church, Ames, Iowa.

308. Charlotte and Mary, 1946
Relief: Painted plaster, 18 1/2 x 14 (47 x 35.6)
Mold: Plaster, 16 1/2 x 20 1/2 x 1 1/4 (41.9 x 52.1 x 3.2) [in two pieces]
Bas-relief, mounted on wood, of the artist's wife and daughter. Charlotte is portrayed with short cropped hair in a side view with her daughter Mary in front of her also with short hair. The mold is of the head and shoulders.
Bas-relief: Charlotte Petersen, Ames, Iowa; private collection. Mold: Charlotte Petersen; Purchased at 1964 sale by Mary Meixner, Hartland, WI; CPC, Gift of Mary Meixner. UM97.139ab.

309. Conversations: Students at Wall, 1946
Painted plaster and clay, approximately 10 x 18 x 4 (25.4 x 45.7 x 10.2)
This model shows the central sculpture grouping depicting a male and a female student.
Charlotte Petersen; Purchased at 1964 sale by Ms. Carol Mae Campbell, Menlo Park, California.

310. Dr. Martin Fritz, 1946
Fired clay, 4 3/4 x 2 1/2 x 4 (12.1 x 6.4 x 10.2)
Portrait bust of Dr. Martin Fritz, head of Department of Psychology at Iowa State from 1927 to 1972.
Gift of the artist to Dr. Martin Fritz; Dr. Kentner and Linda Fritz; CPC, Gift of Dr. Kentner and Linda Fritz. UM97.144.

311. Jo Ann and Betty, 1944–1946
Plaster, 19 x 22 x 3 (48.3 x 55.9 x 7.6)
Bas-relief of two young girls in profile. Daughters of William H. Schrampfer, who helped establish the College of Business, and Frances N. Schrampfer, a teacher and counselor in the Ames Public School System.
Two castings: Casting 1: Betty (Schrampfer) Azar-Harris, Freeland, Washington. Casting 2: Jo Ann (Schrampfer) Ruckman, Pocatello, Idaho.

312. Madonna of the Schools: Saint Cecilia with Children, ca. 1946
Painted plaster, 8 5/8 x 16 x 7 1/2 (21.9 x 40.6 x 19.1)
Preliminary sketch of Saint Cecilia seated with children at the end of a pool. Pool was later removed by owner. Saint Cecilia was replaced with the Virgin Mary in the final version.
Charlotte Petersen; Purchased at 1964 sale by Joy Munn, Ames, Iowa; Helen and Keith McRoberts, Woodward, Iowa.

313. Madonna of the Schools, 1946
Clay, 16 x 15 1/2 x 1 3/8 (52.5 x 50.9 x 4.5)
Model for terra cotta *Madonna of the Schools* at Saint Cecilia School in Ames, Iowa.
Florence (Barr) Castonguay; Saint Cecilia Church, Ames, Iowa, Gift of Florence Castonguay.

314. Madonna of the Schools, 1946

Terra cotta, Overall: 67" x 14' x 100" (1.7 m x 4.3 m x 2.6 m);
Mary: 68 1/2 x 27 1/2 x 16 (174 x 70 x 40.6);
Kneeling girl: 46 1/2 x 13 3/4 x 16 (118.1 x 34.9 x 40.6);
Seated boy; 38 x 23 x 16 (96.5 x 58.4 x 40.6);
Boy with bat: 46 1/2 x 30 x 10 (118.1 x 76.2 x 25.4)
Full-length figure of Madonna holding the infant Christ. She stands on a tiered base with a wall. Two boys wearing contemporary clothing are on the left, and a girl kneels on the right. The children are looking at Mary.
Saint Cecilia's Catholic School, Ames, Iowa.

315. Steerhead, 1946

Medal done for Josten's of Owatonna, Minnesota.

316. A.H. and Anna Blank, 1947

Bronze, 40 x 25 x 1 1/2 (101.6 x 63.5 x 3.8)
Bas-relief portraits of owners of Tri-States Theaters and donors of Blank Children's Hospital in Des Moines, Iowa.
Inscription upper left: A.H. AND ANNA BLANK / CHILDREN RISE UP AND CALL THEM BLESSED
Inscription bottom: A TRIBUTE BY THE PEOPLE OF DES MOINES TO MR. AND MRS. BLANK WHOSE WISE AND GREAT-HEARTED GENEROSITY FINDS MAGNIFICENT EXPRESSION IN THIS RAYMOND BLANK MEMORIAL HOSPITAL FOR CHILDREN. JULY 27, 1947
Signed center right: Christian Petersen
Blank Children's Hospital, Des Moines, Iowa.

317. Don Ricardo Jiminez, 1947

Clay study
University of Costa Rica; San Jose, Costa Rica.

318. Andrea Johnson, 1947

Approximately 18 (45.7) [height]
Portrait bust.
Andy and Virginia Johnson.

319. W. David Frevert, 1946–1947

Plaster, 13 x 7 x 15 (33 x 17.8 x 38.1)
Portrait bust. The model was a student in art appreciation at an Iowa State College class during a Petersen sculpture demonstration, and later he was an architect for the Agronomy Building at Iowa State who invited Petersen to create the relief sculpture for the main entrance in 1951.
W. David Frevert, Fairfield Bay, Arizona.

320. Campanile, 1948

Clay, 4 1/2 x 4 1/2 (11.4 x 11.4)
Green glazed tile designed by Petersen, produced by the Department of Ceramic Engineering and Iowa State College and given as 1948 VEISHEA souvenirs.
Dr. Henry Black, Ames, Iowa; CPC, Gift of Dr. Henry Black. UM86.128.

321. Goeppinger Children, 1948

Painted plaster, 20 x 23 x 10 (50.8 x 58.4 x 25.4)
Combined busts of two sons, Hans Hall and Neil Woods Goeppinger, at ages eight and three. They were created in thirteen sittings arranged by Joanne M. Hansen, former academic head of the Iowa State College Art Department.
Walter and Marnie Goeppinger, Ames, Iowa.

322. Hans Hall Goeppinger, 1948

Painted plaster, 11 15/16 x 7 1/4 x 8 (30.2 x 18.4 x 20.3)
Bust study done in preparation for *Goeppinger Children.*
Signed on base: Christian Petersen
Gift of the artist to Walter and Marnie Goeppinger; Hans and Wanda Goeppinger, Boone, Iowa.

323. Neil Woods Goeppinger, 1948

Painted plaster, 10 x 5 1/2 x 7 (25.4 x 14 x 17.8)
Bust study done in preparation for *Goeppinger Children.*
Signed on base: Christian Petersen
Gift of the artist to Walter and Marnie Goeppinger; Neil Goeppinger, Boone, Iowa.

324. Iowa State College Alumni Medallion, 1948

Bronze, 15 x 1/2 (38.1 x 1.3) [diameter x depth]
The round plaque is designed with a center image of a woman who wears a long dress. Both arms are extended out and appear to rest on a ledge. There are smaller images along the edge and across the middle of the plaque.
Signed in square: CP
Commissioned by Alumni Association, Iowa State College; CPC. UM99.17.

325. Iowa State College Alumni Medal, 1948

Bronze, 2 7/8 x 1/4 (7.3 x 0.6) [diameter x depth]
Medal with the same image as the Iowa State College Alumni Medallion.
Signed in square: CP
Charlotte Petersen; Charlotte Petersen; SC, Purchased with Iowa State University Library Funds. SC99.67.

326. Pope Pius X, ca. 1948

Painted plaster, 24 x 12 1/2 x 8 (61 x 31.8 x 20.3)
Sculpture of Pope who was canonized and known as the Children's Pope. Created as gift for Saint Cecilia Church, Ames, Iowa.
Gift from Petersens to Saint Cecilia Church, Ames, Iowa.

327. George Washington Carver, 1949

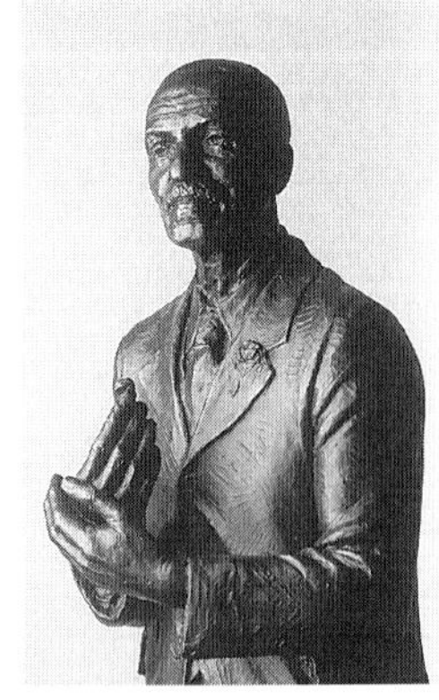

Painted plaster, 43 x 12 x 11 (109.2 x 30.5 x 27.9)
Figure study of Dr. Carver holding peanut, for which he discovered over one hundred industrial processing projects. Carver received a bachelor of science degree from Iowa State College in 1894 and a master's degree in 1896.
Charlotte Petersen; Purchased by Class of 1968 at 1964 sale; CPC, Gift of Class of 1968. UM88.73.

Detail.

328. Christ the King, 1949

48 (121.9) [height]
Figure of Christ in crown and robes. The commission was arranged by the architect who designed the Saint Regis High School building project and was a former student of Petersen.
Saint Regis High School, Cedar Rapids, Iowa; Saint Regis Middle School, Cedar Rapids, Iowa.

329. Risen Jesus Christ, 1949
Plaster, 38 x 15 x 7 (96.5 x 38.1 x 17.8)
Figure sculpture of the Risen Christ with extended hands.
Mary Petersen; CPC, Gift of the Friends of the University Museums. U89.25.

330. Head of a Young Woman, ca. 1940s
Unfired clay, 10 1/2 x 9 x 9 1/2 (26.7 x 22.9 x 24.1)
Young female with short hair; slate base.
Charlotte Petersen; Purchased at 1964 sale by Esther Whetstone; CPC, Gift of the Estate of Esther Whetstone. UM96.51ab.

331. Nude Male Working on Ceramic Pot, ca. 1940s
Clay, 4 5/8 x 4 5/8 x 3/8 (11.4 x 11.4 x 1)
Square unglazed ceramic tile, natural beige color. Top has design inscribed of nude male, squatting, working on a tall ceramic pot. Inscription: Ceramic Engineers VEISHEA ISC
Charlotte Petersen; Mary Petersen; CPC, Gift of Mary Petersen. UM92.619.

332. Horse, ca. 1948–1951
Terra cotta, 6 x 4 x 3 (15.2 x 10.2 x 7.6)
A bookend made as a Christmas gift for Mary Petersen, who wrote that the other bookend was destroyed in the firing process. Inscription on back: Merry Xmas Mary
Mary Petersen, Beverly Hills, Florida.

333. Bertrand R. Adams, ca. 1950
Painted plaster, 11 x 8 x 1 1/8 (27.9 x 20.3 x 2.9)
Bas-relief plaque. Adams was Petersen's colleague on Public Works of Art Project at Iowa City, and they became reacquainted when they both lived in Ames. Signed to right: CHRISTIAN PETERSEN
Two castings in the collection of Mary (Mrs. Bertrand) Adams, Ames, Iowa.

334. After the Bath, 1950
Wood

335. Jack Beckemeyer, 1950
Plaster, 17 x 15 x 11 (43.2 x 38.1 x 27.9)
Portrait bust of the son of Louise and Harry Beckemeyer at eighteen months.
Gift of the artist to Dr. and Mrs. Harry Beckemeyer, Shaker Heights, Ohio.

336. Jack Beckemeyer, 1950
Terra cotta, 11 x 8 x 9 1/2 (27.9 x 20.3 x 24.1)
Portrait bust of the son of Louise and Harry Beckemeyer.
Gift of the artist to Dr. and Mrs. Harry Beckemeyer, Shaker Heights, Ohio.

337. Ralph K. Bliss, 1950
Painted plaster, 24 x 17 1/2 x 1 1/2 (60.9 x 44.5 x 3.8)
A side profile of Ralph K. Bliss, Director of Agricultural Extension at Iowa State. He wears a coat and tie and glasses.
Charlotte Petersen; Mary Petersen; CPC, Gift of the Friends of the University Museums. U89.27.

338. Boy with Cattle, 1950
4-H boy with Jersey cows which was commissioned by an Iowa State College professor.

339. Christ with Bound Hands, 1950
Plaster, 25 x 6 1/4 x 6 1/2 (63.5 x 15.9 x 16.5)
Three casts of this figure were originally made. Additional reproductions of the cast were produced and sold at Saint Thomas Aquinas Church and Catholic Student Center in Ames, Iowa, in 1960.
1) Charlotte Petersen's gift to Fr. Bill Clark; Monsignor Dan Tarrant; Brother Joshua Turley, Saint Benedict, Oregon; Turley Family, Kansas City, Missouri. 2) Unknown.

340. Christ with Bound Hands, 1950
Painted plaster, 39 x 8 1/2 x 10 (99.1 x 21.6 x 25.4)
Archbishop Rohlman officiated at Petersen's confirmation ceremonies in Dubuque, Iowa, in 1949. A gift to Archbishop Rohlman for his personal chapel.
Gift of the artist to Archbishop Rohlman; Reverend William Robert Merrill; CPC, Gift of Reverend William Robert Merrill. UM99.299.

341. Christ on the Cross, ca. 1950
Plaster, 25 x 29 x 2 1/2 (63.5 x 73.7 x 6.4)
Plaster mold of *Christ on the Cross.* It is a front view to the waist and shows his arms only to the elbows.
Charlotte Petersen; Mary Petersen; CPC, Gift of the Friends of the University Museums. U89.29.

342. Gardner Cowles, Jr., 1950
Bronze, 13 x 9 1/2 x 11 1/2 (33 x 24.1 x 29.2)
Portrait bust.
Cowles Library, Drake University, Des Moines, Iowa.

343. Crucifix, 1950
Wood, 28 x 20 (78.1 x 50.8)
Christ on the Cross. A gift from Petersen to the Iowa State University's Xi Chapter of Phi Kappa Theta Fraternity. Charlotte was housemother in mid-1960s and Petersen was an honorary member.
Gift of the artist to Iowa Xi Chapter of Phi Kappa Theta Fraternity, Ames, Iowa.

344. Head of a Young Girl, 1950
Clay, 11 3/4 x 8 1/4 x 9 (29.8 x 21 x 22.9)
Young girl with long hair.
Marjorie Garfield; Department of Home Economics, Gift of Marjorie Garfield, Head of Applied Art; CPC. UM83.216.

345. Head of Christ, 1950
Bedford limestone, 33 x 16 x 15 (83.8 x 40.3 x 38.1)
Study of Christ
Saint Thomas Aquinas Church and Catholic Student Center, Ames, Iowa.

346. Lloyd Hedrick, 1950
Clay
Portrait bust done as demonstration for Rotary Club or Kiwanis.

347. Mrs. Hiram Houghton, 1950
Member of the Iowa State Board of Regents.

348. Koss Baby, 1950
Portrait relief of the son of one of Petersen's students.

349. Katy Jo, 1950
Portrait relief.

350. Abraham Lincoln, 1950
Bedford limestone, 28 x 11 1/2 x 13 (71.1 x 29.2 x 33)
Portrait bust of Abraham Lincoln, roughly chiseled.
Charlotte Petersen; Purchased by WOI-TV, ISU; CPC/AOC. U82.133.

351. Mary, Joseph, Boy Jesus, 1950
Terra cotta, Mary and Jesus: 35 x 7 1/4 x 6(88.9 x 18.4 x 15.2);
Joseph: 34 x 9 3/4 x 4 3/4 (86.3 x 24.8 x 12.1)
Collection of Saint Cecilia Church, Ames, Iowa.

352. Mutual of Omaha Logo, 1950
Corporate symbol designed by Petersen.

353. Saint Bernard of Clairvaux, 1950
Painted plaster, 26 x 12 x 12 (66 x 30.5 x 30.5)
Standing, robed saint, striding forward with right hand pointing to left.
Charlotte Petersen; Purchased at 1964 sale by Jon Morgan;
Robin Krueger, Charles City, Iowa.

354. Saint Bernard of Clairvaux, 1950
Plaster
Preliminary model depicting St. Bernard standing in a hooded robe
and holding a crosier.
Charlotte Petersen; Purchased at 1964 sale by Dr. Malcolm David
Tobey; Estate of Dr. Malcolm Tobey, Marshall, Minnesota.

355. Saint Bernard of Clairvaux, 1950–1951
Plaster, 36 (91.4) [height]
Figure holding a staff. Preliminary model for monumental sculpture.
Charlotte Petersen; Purchased at 1964 sale by Frankie Schwenk;
Lee and Frankie Schwenk, Columbia, Maryland.

356. Saint Cecilia, 1950
Mankato limestone, 28 x 22 1/2 x 2 1/2 (71.1 x 57.2 x 6.4)
Figures of the patron saint of music and a cherub in a lunette.
Saint Cecilia Church, Ames, Iowa.

357. Saint Francis Xavier, 1950
Clay, 17 x 7 3/4 x 5 1/4 (43.2 x 19.7 x 13.3)
Unfinished figure.
Charlotte Petersen; Mary Petersen; CPC, Gift of the Friends of
the University Museums. UM98.32

358. Saint Francis Xavier, 1950
A model for the sculpture for the Parish of Saint Francis Xavier in
Dyersville, Iowa.
Charlotte Petersen; Purchased at 1964 sale by Dr. William
Fennessey; Patrick and Betty Anne Scherrman, Dyersville, Iowa.

359. Saint Francis Xavier, 1950
Painted terra cotta, Overall: approximately 21' x 56" x 48"
(6.4 m x 1.43 m x 1.23 m);
Figure: 14' (4.27 m) [height]
Monumental figure of Saint Francis Xavier. The base includes three
terra cotta bas-reliefs. Dedicated in 1951 at the Saint Francis Xavier
Elementary School in Dyersville, Iowa.
Inscription: GO & ENKINDLE AND INFLAME ALL HEARTS /
XAVIER'S TRAVELS / 1542–1552
Inscription on base, right: WHO WILL DO MY BIDDING / TO
THE LAST? I WILL GIVE HIM / AUTHORITY OVER THE
NATIONS / APOCALYPSE 2:26
Inscription on base, left: SUFFER THE LITTLE ONES TO / COME
UNTO ME FOR OF THEM / IS THE KINGDOM OF HEAVEN
Signed: Christian Petersen
Saint Francis Xavier Parish, Dyersville, Iowa.

360. Agronomy Mural, 1951
Bedford limestone, 12' x 12'8" (3.7 m x 3.9 m)

Bas-relief on the west façade of the Agronomy Building. An Iowa
farmland theme depicting sky, seed, and soil, the fundamental
agronomy study areas.
Commissioned by Iowa State College. Permanent installation on
the Agronomy Building. CPC/AOC. U99.302.

361. Cookie Time, 1951
Painted plaster, 6 x 5 x 8 (15.2 x 12.7 x 20.3)
The artist's daughter Helene's dogs, Micky and Laddy.
Helene Petersen Male; Lynn Sollenberger Lucido; Jane
Sollenberger Crivello, Fresno, California.

362. Saint Bernard of Clairvaux, 1951
Plaster, 38 1/2 x 18 x 18 (97.8 x 45.7 x 45.7)
Figure study for *Saint Bernard of Clairvaux* in Breda, Iowa.
Charlotte Petersen; Mary Petersen; CPC, Gift of Friends of
University Museums. U89.23.

363. Saint Bernard of Clairvaux, 1951
Plaster, 25 x 27 x 21 (63.5 x 68.6 x 53.3)
Bust portrait. His head is shaved with a fringe of hair around his head.
Charlotte Petersen; Mary Petersen; CPC, Gift of Friends of
University Museums. U89.24.

364. Christ, 1951
Painted plaster, 15 x 9 x 10 (38.1 x 22.9 x 25.4)
Portrait bust.
Signed: Christian Petersen
Ruth E. Petersen Sollenberger; Lynn Sollenberger Lucido, Fresno,
California.

365. Helene and Burt Hemmingway, ca. 1951
Painted plaster, 9 x 4 x 5 (22.9 x 10.2 x 12.7) [each]
Busts.
Both signed: Christian Petersen
Helene Petersen Male; Lynn Sollenberger Lucido, Fresno, California.

366. Madonna and Jesus, 1951
Plaster, 35 1/2 x 7 1/2 x 6 1/2 (90.2 x 19.1 x 16.5)
Copy of Saint Cecilia's terra cotta *Mary and Jesus.*
Saint Cecilia Church, Ames, Iowa.

367. Philip Conrad Peet, 1951
Plaster, 12 x 1 3/4 (30.5 x 4.4)
Bas-relief portrait. Christian and Charlotte Petersen were godparents
at Philip's baptism.
Gift of the Petersens to the Peet family; Philip C. and Susan Peet,
Manassa, Virginia.

368. Arthur E. Thomas, 1951
Bas-relief: Bronze, 23 1/2 x 16 (59.7 x 40.6)
Mold: Plaster, 26 x 18 x 1 (66 x 45.7 x 2.54)
Bas-relief profile portrait of manager of the Des Moines
Municipal Airport.
Inscription: ARTHUR E. THOMAS / BORN DES MOINES MAY 13,
1900 / MANAGER DES MOINES MUNICIPAL AIRPORT / SINCE
AUGUST 5, 1925/ PRESENTED SEPTEMBER 1951 BY A GROUP
OF CITIZENS IN RECOGNITION OF HIS MORE THAN TWENTY-
FIVE YEARS DEVOTED TO THE CONSTRUCTION AND
OPERATION OF THE DES MOINES AIRPORT AND HIS
CONTRIBUTION TO LOCAL, STATE AND NATIONAL AVIATION
Signed lower left in square: CP

*Bas-relief: Des Moines Municipal
Airport, Des Moines, Iowa.
Mold: CPC, Gift of the Friends of the
University Museums. U89.32.*

369. **Conversations,** 1947–1952
Bedford limestone, Overall: 80 x 62 x 41
(203.3 x 157.5 x 104.1);
Three women: 75 x 129 x 40
(190.5 x 327.7 x 101.6);
Couple: 80 x 81 x 40
(203.3 x 205.7 x 101.6);
Woman: 60 x 66 x 19 1/4
(152.4 x 167.6 x 48.9)
Three groups of students along brick wall: three females; male
and female; female.
*Commissioned by Iowa State College.
Permanent installation outside of the Oak-Elm
Residence Hall complex.CPC/AOC. U88.63.*

370. **Henry J. Miles, Jr.** 1953
Plaster, 14 x 9 x 9 (35.6 x 22.9 x 22.9)
An unfired clay bust of a student made as a demonstration at a meeting of
the American Institute of Architects, and given to him by Petersen. An
unauthorized plaster casting was made at a later date.
Gift of the artist to Henry J. Miles, Jr., New London, Wisconsin.

371. **Woman Washing Her Hair,** ca. 1953
Terra cotta, 15 1/2 x 7 1/2 x 8 1/2 (39.4 x 19.1 x 21.6)
Nude woman, sitting on a rock, washing her hair.
Signed: Christian Petersen
*Gift of the artist to Mary Lou and Jon Edwin Morgan, Chandler,
Arizona.*

372. **Cowboy, Cutting Horse, and Two Polled Hereford Heifers,**
1953–1954
Painted plaster, 17 x 24 x 12 (43.2 x 61 x 30.5)
Model for cowboy was Dr. John J. Edenburn, DVM.
*Gift of the artist to Dr. John J. Edenburn, Hollister, Missouri;
CPC, Gift of John J. Edenburn Family. UM2000.2.*

373. **Saint Bernard of Clairvaux,** 1954
Bedford limestone, 126 (3.2 m) [height]
Figure purchased for the seminary with funds from Catholic school-
children of Dubuque Diocese. Commissioned and dedicated in
original location in 1954. When the seminary closed, the sculpture
was restored and relocated in 1997 to Saint Bernard's Catholic
Church in Breda, Iowa.
*Mount Saint Bernard Seminary, Dubuque, Iowa; Saint Bernard's
Catholic Church, Breda, Iowa.*

374. **Emmett J. Hasty,** 1955
Bronze, 15 x 22 (38.1 x 55.9)
Bas-relief portrait plaque.
Inscription: EMMETT J. HASTY/ 1941 - PRINCIPAL - 1954/
HE WAS HERE TO HELP
Signed: Christian Petersen
*Des Moines Public Schools, Roosevelt High School, Des Moines,
Iowa.*

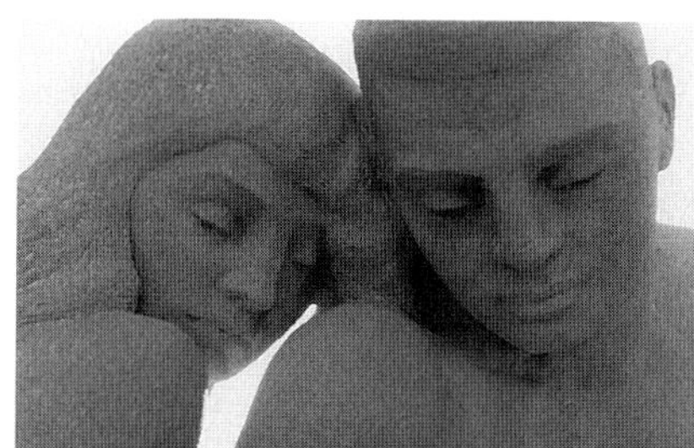

Detail of *Conversations*.

375. **Richard B. Hull,** 1955
Portrait bust.
Ohio State University.

376. **Eugene Mannheimer,** 1955
Painted plaster, 19 x 5 (48.3 x 12.7)
[diameter x depth]
Frontal view of Rabbi Eugene Mannheimer.
Signed center right: CHRISTIAN
PETERSEN SC
*Plaque: Casting 1: Eugene Mannheimer; Joan
and Robert E.
Mannheimer; CPC, Ames, Iowa. Gift of Joan
and Robert E. Mannheimer. UM97.140.*
*Casting 2: Richard Mannheimer, Los Angeles, California.
Mold: Charlotte Petersen; Mary Petersen; CPC, Gift of the
Friends of the University Museums. U89.31.*

377. **Eugene Mannheimer,** 1955
Bronze, 31 x 10 (78.7 x 25.4)
Portrait plaque.
Inscription: 1880–1952; EUGENE MANNHEIMER / RABBI
TEMPLE B'NAI/ JESHURUN 1905–1943 / RABBI
EMERITUS / 1943–1952
Signed center right: CHRISTIAN PETERSEN SC
Temple B'nai Jeshurun, Des Moines, Iowa.

378. **Woman and Child,** ca. 1955
Unfired clay, 9 7/8 x 15 5/16 x 1 1/4 (25.1 x 38.9 x 3.2)
Seated woman in profile with legs bent upward at knees. On her
knees she holds a small child.
*Charlotte Petersen; Purchased at 1964 sale by Neva Petersen;
CPC, Gift of Neva Petersen. UM91.62.*

379. **Crucifix,** ca. 1956
Wood (black walnut), 6 1/2 x 4 (16.5 x 10.2)
Carved as a Christmas present for the artist's daughter Mary when
she was in college.
Mary Petersen, Beverly Hills, Florida.

380. **Amos Emery,** 1956
Portrait bust of Petersen's friend, whom he knew beginning in 1933.
Amos Emery, Des Moines, Iowa.

381. **Megan Norris,** ca. 1956
Painted plaster, 13 1/4 x 10 1/2 x 7 3/4 (33.7 x 26.7 x 19.7)
Portrait bust of Marshalltown, Iowa, child.
Signed back lower band: Christian Petersen SC
*Irene W. Johnson; Robert W. Johnson; Mark W. Johnson; CPC,
Purchased with funds from Mary Alice and William Reinhardt.
UM98.35.*

382. **Steven Lofgren Memorial,** 1956
Plaster
Memorial bas-relief for ten-year-old at Roosevelt School, Ames, Iowa.
Inscription: MORE TO BE DESIRED ARE THEY THAN GOLD;
PSALM 19 / IN MEMORY OF STEVEN LOFGREN
Collection of Ames Community Schools, Ames, Iowa.

383. VEISHEA Varieties Trophy, 1956
Wood, 28 x 13 x 10 (71.1 x 33 x 25.4)
Travelling trophy given annually to the winners of the Iowa State VEISHEA Varieties show. Now a different supplementary trophy is presented in its place.
Memorial Union, ISU, Ames, Iowa.

384. Christine Fisher, 1957
Terra cotta, approximately 18 (45.7) [height]
Portrait bust of daughter of J.W. and Dorothy Fisher.
Signed: Christian Petersen
J.W. Fisher; Central Iowa Art Association, Marshalltown, Iowa.

385. Russell Fisher, 1957
Terra cotta, approximately 18 (45.7) [height]
Portrait bust of son of J.W. and Dorothy Fisher at age fifteen.
Signed: Christian Petersen
J.W. Fisher; Central Iowa Art Association, Marshalltown, Iowa.

386. The Awakening, 1958
Marble, 8 x 13 3/4 x 6 (20.3 x 34.9 x 15.2)
Reclining female nude figure, also possibly known as *Siesta.*
J.W. Fisher; Dorothy Fisher; Estate of Dorothy Fisher.

387. J.W. ("Bill") Fisher, 1958
Bronze
Medallion commissioned by the Fisher family.
Central Iowa Art Association, Marshalltown, Iowa.

388. Ann Munn, ca. 1958
Terra cotta, 19 x 16 x 11 (48.3 x 40.6 x 27.9)
Portrait bust.
Ann Munn McCormack, Naples, Florida.

389. J.W. ("Bill") Fisher, 1959
Bronze
Portrait bust commissioned by Fisher family.
Central Iowa Art Association, Gift of Mrs. F. Edna Fisher, J.W. Fisher's mother, to the Fisher Community Center, Marshalltown, Iowa.

390. James D. Edmundson, 1959
Bronze, 19 x 1 3/4 (48.3 x 4.4) [diameter x depth]
Memorial medallion honoring original donor of Des Moines Art Center.
Des Moines Art Center, Des Moines, Iowa.

391. Walter Barlow, 1959
Plaque: Terra cotta, 29 1/8 x 18 3/4 x 2 (74 x 47.6 x 5.1)
Mold: Plaster, 30 x 19 x 2 (76.2 x 48.3 x 5.1)
Bas-relief portrait of pastor of Collegiate Presbyterian Church from 1934–1961.
Signed at right: Christian Petersen
Plaque: Collegiate Presbyterian Church, Ames, Iowa.
Mold: Charlotte Petersen; Mary Petersen; CPC, Gift of the Friends of the University Museums. U89.33.

392. Helen Benitez, ca. 1950s
Painted plaster, 21 x 22 x 10 (53.3 x 55.9 x 25.4)
Portrait bust of Dean Helen Benitez, Women's University, The Philippines.
Charlotte Petersen; Mary Petersen; CPC, Gift of Friends of the University Museums. U89.34.

393. David, ca. 1950s
Plaster cast, 10 x 10 1/2 x 6 (25.4 x 26.7 x 15.2)
Son of Joan Lange Kaas.
Joan Lange Kaas, Los Angeles, California.

394. Head of Christ, ca. 1949–1961
Clay study, 12 x 10 x 8 (30.5 x 25.4 x 20.3)
Made as a demonstration at the Newman Catholic Student Center in Saint Thomas Aquinas Church and Catholic Student Center in Ames, Iowa.
Gift of the artist to Saint Thomas Aquinas Church and Catholic Student Center, Newman Club, Ames, Iowa.

395. Frederick J. Weertz, ca. 1956–1961
Painted plaster
Profile bas-relief.
Inscription: FREDERICK J. WEERTZ / SENIOR PASTOR / 1925–1956 / A BUILDER WITH GOD WHO SOUGHT / TO BRING THE CITY TO CHRIST / DEDICATED WITH LOVING MEMORIES BY THE SONS OF DR. J. CHARLES AND ESTHER RYAN
Bas-relief: Saint John's Lutheran Church, Des Moines, Iowa. Commissioned in honor of Dr. J. Charles and Esther Ryan by their sons.
Mold listed in 1964 sale records.

396. Christ on the Cross, 1960–1961
Wood (walnut), 23 1/2 x 15 1/2 x 6 1/2 (59.7 x 39.4 x 16.5)
Gift of the artist to Reverend Joseph Kleiner; Reverend John A. Schmitz; CPC, Gift of Leo Schmitz in memory of his brother Reverend John A. Schmitz. U92.404.

397. Dedication to the Future: Model, 1961
Painted plaster, 16 1/2 x 6 x 6 (41.9 x 15.2)
Charlotte Petersen; Mary Petersen, Beverly Hills, Florida.

398. Dedication to the Future, 1961
Bronze, 10' x 4' x 3' (304.8 x 121.9 x 91.4)
Nude man holds nude male child in his upraised hands. Sculpture sits on a rectangular base in a pond. Petersen's final sculpture, modeled and signed by the artist, but cast after his death.
Inscription on plaque: A DEDICATION / TO THE FUTURE / WE LIFT UP OUR YOUNG / TO SEE BEYOND / THAT WHICH WE CAN'T SEE / BY / CHRISTIAN PETERSEN / 1961
Signed at base: CHRISTIAN PETERSEN
Commissioned by J.W. Fisher for the Fisher Community Center, Marshalltown, Iowa.

UNDATED THREE-DIMENSIONAL WORKS OF ART

399. Baby plaque

Clay

Charlotte Petersen; Purchased at 1964 sale by Mrs. Joseph C. Picken, Ames, Iowa.

400. Barlow

Plaster mold

Listed in 1964 sale records.

401. Ralph K. Bliss

Plaster

Mold of sculpture of director of extension at Iowa State College. *Listed as not for sale in 1964 sale records.*

402. Elijah Buell

Bronze

Plaque shows a bust view of a man wearing a tie, in a circle. The signature "Elijah Buell" is reproduced below the image. Inscription: BORN APRIL 1, 1801 AT UTICA N.Y. / SETTLED AT LYONS, IOWA JULY 25 / 1835 — DIED MARCH 1, 1889 / A TRIBUTE TO HIS MEMORY BY W. ELIJAH BUELL AND DOROTHY BUELL HUGHES

Signed at right: Christian Petersen, Sc

Elijah Buell Elementary School, Clinton Community School District, Clinton, Iowa.

Three plaster copies of the plaque listed in 1964 sale records. Charlotte Petersen gave one to Petersen House, a floor in Friley Residence Hall, ISU, Ames, Iowa.

403. Johnson Brigham

Bust or plaque.

404. Campus Chest Sweepstakes

Wood (black walnut), 10 3/4 x 17 1/2 x 3 3/4 (27.3 x 44.5 x 9.5) Kneeling robed, male figure supporting a reclining figure of Christ. Inscription on base: CAMPUS CHEST SWEEPSTAKES

Charlotte Petersen; Charlotte Petersen; SC, Gift of Charlotte Petersen. SC99.55.

405. Carol

Sculpture of the daughter of a family from Marshalltown.

406. Cat

Glazed and fired clay, 6 x 4 x 3 (15.2 x 10.2 x 7.6)

Mary Petersen, Beverly Hills, Florida.

407. Christ

Plaster mold, 18 (45.7) [height]

Charlotte Petersen; Mary Petersen; CPC, Gift of the Friends of the University Museums. U89.30a-f.

408. Crucifix

Wood (black walnut), 6 1/4 x 4 3/4 x 1 1/2 (15.9 x 12 x 3.8) This was a gift to John Slater from Charlotte Petersen, who was his godmother.

Charlotte Petersen; John Slater, Chicago, Illinois.

409. Jay N. "Ding" Darling

Painted plaster

Portrait bust of *Des Moines Register* editorial cartoonist.

410. Double Plaque

Plaster

Charlotte Petersen; Purchased at 1964 sale by Dr. and Mrs. Arnold K. Webster, Des Moines, Iowa.

411. Elderly Woman in Glasses

Plaster mold, 12 1/4 x 9 1/2 x 1 1/8 (31.1 x 24.1 x 2.9)

State Historical Society of Iowa, Des Moines, Iowa. I 11928.

412. Girl

Plaster plaque

Charlotte Petersen; Purchased at 1964 sale by Mr. and Mrs. John T. Mason, Ames, Iowa.

413. Kenneth Haines

Bust or plaque.

414. Head of a Girl

Bedford limestone, 15 x 6 1/2 x 6 (38.1 x 16.5 x 15.2)

Charlotte Petersen; Purchased at 1964 sale by Marie Baird, Ames, Iowa.

415. Head of a Man

Clay

Charlotte Petersen; Purchased at 1964 sale by Leonard Degen, Independence, Iowa.

416. Hubbell

Plaster mold

Charlotte Petersen; Purchased at 1964 sale by Dr. Louis David Ducommun, Cleghorn, Iowa.

417. Jacob Kanengieser

Bronze, 6 7/8 x 5 x 1/4 (17.5 x 12.7 x 0.6)

Bas-relief portrait of man with moustache facing viewer and writing in a book.

Inscription: IN MEMORY OF / OUR ESTEEMED FRIEND / EX-PRESIDENT JACOB KANENGIESER / GOMBINER LODGE 174 — I.O.B.S.

Signed upper left: Christian Petersen, Sc.

State Historical Society of Iowa, Des Moines, Iowa. I 4238.

418. Kneeling Woman

Charlotte Petersen; Purchased at 1964 sale by Dr. Robert Kent Gillette, Kokomo, Indiana.

419. Lady in Gown

Plaster

Young woman in a long gown holding an object in her hand.

Hilda Been.

420. Man Facing Viewer

Plaster mold, 13 1/2 x 9 1/2 x 13/16 (34.3 x 24.1 x 2.1)

State Historical Society of Iowa, Des Moines, Iowa. I 11927.

421. Man with Van Dyke Beard

Bronze, 10 x 6 3/4 x 3/16 (25.4 x 17.1 x 0.5)

Signed: Christian Petersen, SC

State Historical Society of Iowa, Des Moines, Iowa. I 4239.

422. Man with Violin
Plaster, 10 1/4 x 11 1/4 x 3/4 (26 x 28.6 x 1.9)
Figure depicted down to knees, holding violin to right of plaque.
Inscription: ALL ONE'S LIFE IS MUSIC IF ONE TOUCHES
THE NOTES RIGHTLY AND IN TIME - RUSKIN.
State Historical Society of Iowa, Des Moines, Iowa. I 11921.

423. Alice Marston
Bas-relief. Anson Marston commissioned bas-reliefs of daughters
Alice and Lucy.
Alice Marston Barney, Springfield, Virginia.

424. Lucy Marston
Bas-relief. Anson Marston commissioned bas-reliefs of daughters
Alice and Lucy.
Lucy Marston Carruthers, Tucson, Arizona.

425. Mary Holding Baby Jesus
Engraving: 7 1/2 x 4 1/2 (19.1 x 11.4);
Image: 7 1/2 x 4 1/2 (19.1 x 11.4)
Madonna and child.
*Charlotte Petersen; Private Collection; CPC. Anonymous gift in
memory of Charlotte Petersen. UM93.33.*

426. Mother with Children
Plasticene
*Charlotte Petersen; Purchased at 1964 sale by Harriet Adams,
Ames, Iowa.*

427. Mother and Two Children
Clay study
*Charlotte Petersen; Purchased at 1964 sale by Emelda Kunaui;
private collection.*

428. Plaque
Plaster
*Charlotte Petersen; Purchased at 1964 sale by Mrs. George R.
West, Ames, Iowa.*

429. Elsie Robertson
Painted plaster, 18 1/2 x 13 x 11 (47 x 33 x 27.9)
Portrait bust. Robertson was active in the arts in Ames.
Elsie Robertson; Mr. and Mrs. Gary Coenen, Creston, Iowa.

430. Sedes Sapeintiae (Seat of Wisdom)
Painted plaster, 12 1/2 x 7 1/4 x 10 1/2 (31.2 x 18.4 x 26.7)
Seated Madonna with young Jesus standing near her, both reading a book.
*Charlotte Petersen's gift to Father Bill Clark; Monsignor Dan
Tarrant; Brother Joshua Turley, Saint Benedict, Oregon; Turley
Family, Kansas City, Missouri.*

431. Sketch
Plasticene
*Charlotte Petersen; Purchased at 1964 sale by Marie Baird,
Ames, Iowa.*

432. Standing Man with Book
Plaster, 16 1/2 x 8 1/2 x 1/2 (41.9 x 21.6 x 1.3)
State Historical Society of Iowa, Des Moines, Iowa. I 11925.

433. Three Children
Clay
*Charlotte Petersen; Purchased at 1964 sale by Mrs. Harry Cook
and Mrs. Glen Kenney, both of Nevada, Iowa.*

434. Two Men
Plaster mold with red latex liner, 19 x 18 3/4 x 5 1/2 (48.3 x 47.6 x 14)
The artist's wife, Charlotte, told Mrs. Uhrig that the two men shown
in profile are Charlotte's nephews.
*Charlotte Petersen; Purchased at 1964 sale by Mrs. J.W. Uhrig;
CPC, Gift of Helen (Mrs. J. William) Uhrig. UM2000.7.*

435. Wall Study
Clay
*Charlotte Petersen; Purchased at 1964 sale by Dr. Robert Kent
Gillette, Kokomo, Indiana.*

436. Dr. Wilhaus
Plaster, 17 (43.2) [height]
Charlotte Petersen; listed in 1964 sale records; location unknown.

437. Woman's Head
Plaster

438. Woman's Head
Terra cotta
*Charlotte Petersen; Purchased at 1964 sale by Helen (Mrs. J. William)
Uhrig, West Lafayette, Indiana.*

439. R. L. Wood
Plaster, 13 x 9 x 1 (33 x 22.9 x 2.5)
Man in profile facing left.
Inscription: R.L. Wood, April 23, 1929.
State Historical Society of Iowa, Des Moines, Iowa: I 11924.

440. Young Boy
Painted plaster, 13 1/2 x 9 1/2 x 1 (34.3 x 24.1 x 2.5)
Sculpture of Michael Schroeder, son of Mr. and Mrs. Ira Schroeder.
Charlotte Petersen; purchased at 1964 sale by Marie Baird, Ames, Iowa.

441. Young Girl with Puppy
Plaster mold, 16 1/8 x 10 x 7/8 (20.3 x 25.4 x 2.2)
Girl wears 1920s style short dress with bows at shoulders; holds
puppy with both arms, head bent down slightly.
State Historical Society of Iowa, Des Moines, Iowa. I 11922.

442. Young Woman
Painted plaster, 23 1/2 x 18 x 10 (59.7 x 45.7 x 25.4)
Portrait bust.
State Historical Society of Iowa, Des Moines, Iowa. I 11740.

443. Young Woman in Profile
Painted plaster, 10 x 8 3/4 x 5/8 (25.4 x 22.2 x 1.6)
Woman with bobbed hair.
Signed right in square: CP
State Historical Society of Iowa, Des Moines, Iowa. I 11918.

DATED TWO-DIMENSIONAL WORKS OF ART

444. Death of First Born, 1887
Oil on canvas, 18 x 24
Painted after a print depicting two adult lions standing over a lion cub.
Lee Sollenberger, Abbotsville, British Columbia.

445. Medallion, ca. 1920s
Pencil and colored pencil on paper, 8 1/2 x 11 (21.6 x 27.9)
Bottom is a man stabbing dog or wolf, with a woman and a child
crouched behind him; middle sketch is of man shooting bow and
arrow with woman crouched behind him holding a child; top right
is a sketch of a man with a shield and sword.
*Charlotte Petersen; Mary Petersen; CPC, Purchased by the
Christian Petersen Memorial Fund. UM92.39.*

446. Fountain of the Blue Herons: Preparatory Studies, ca. 1930
Black graphite or conté on paper, 9 1/4 x 11 1/2 (23.5 x 29.2)
Studies for fountain for A. E. Staley Manufacturing Company in
Decatur, Illinois. Fountain and reflecting pool were completed in
1930 and destroyed in 1950.
*Charlotte Petersen; Mary Petersen; CPC, Purchased by the
Christian Petersen Memorial Fund. UM92.160.*

447. Bear, ca. 1932
Charcoal on paper, 9 x 12 (22.9 x 30.5)
Drawing of a bear, probably for the Yellowstone National Park project.
*Charlotte Petersen; Mary Petersen; CPC, Purchased by the
Christian Petersen Memorial Fund. UM92.177.*

448. Bear, ca. 1932
Charcoal on paper, 8 1/2 x 11 (21.6 x 27.9)
Probably for a bronze bear figure Petersen designed for Balfour
Jewelry for Yellowstone National Park.
*Charlotte Petersen; Mary Petersen; CPC, Purchased by the
Christian Petersen Memorial Fund. UM92.115.*

449. David and Bob, 1932
Charcoal on paper
Two sons of an Iowa State College professor.
Mr. and Mrs. Walter E. Loomis, Ames, Iowa.

450. Steerhead, ca. 1932
Pencil or conté on paper, 8 x 10 (20.3 x 25.4)
Two pencil studies of an animal skull, possibly for a medal or award
called *Steerhead* for Balfour Jewelry.
*Charlotte Petersen; Mary Petersen; CPC, Purchased by the
Christian Petersen Memorial Fund. UM92.356.*

451. Artist and Model, ca. 1930–1935
Pencil on paper, 6 7/8 x 4 7/8 (17.5 x 12.4)
Recto: Quick sketches of a male artist in profile with a goatee and
moustache, hand held to forehead in contemplation of stylized
seated nude. Verso: Small medallion shape with a male kneeling in
profile, with his arms outstretched working on a bas-relief with a
sculpting tool.
Charlotte Petersen; SC, Gift of Charlotte Petersen. SC99.231ab.

452. Cemetery Christ, ca. 1930–1935
Pencil on paper, 6 7/8 x 4 7/8 (17.5 x 12.4)
Possible study for Campus *Cemetery Christ* with outstretched

upraised arms, and three other figures nearby in kneeling positions.
Charlotte Petersen; SC, Gift of Charlotte Petersen. SC99.236.

453. Cemetery Christ, ca. 1930–1935
Pencil on paper, 11 x 8 1/2 (27.9 x 21.6);
Images: 5 1/2 x 1 1/2 (14 x 3.8) and 6 x 2 1/4 (15.2 x 5.7)
Quick studies (one frontal, one profile) of a model of Christ
standing in front of a cross. He is wrapped in a garment from the
waist down, with his head down and arms out to front.
Charlotte Petersen; SC, Gift of Charlotte Petersen. SC99.166.

454. Cemetery Christ, ca. 1930–1935
Pencil on paper, 11 x 8 1/2 (27.9 x 21.6)
Quick studies (one frontal, one profile) of Christ rising up off the ground.
Charlotte Petersen; SC, Gift of Charlotte Petersen. SC99.167.

455. Cemetery Christ: Preliminary Sketch, ca. 1930–1935
Pencil or conté on paper, 16 3/4 x 13 3/4 (42.5 x 34.9)
Risen Christ, suspended over a crevice in the earth, with a cross at
the crevice's end.
*Charlotte Petersen; Mary Petersen; CPC, Purchased by the
Christian Petersen Memorial Fund. UM92.258.*

456. Cemetery Christ: Sketch, ca. 1930–1935
Black graphite and ink on paper, 11 x 8 1/2 (27.9 x 21.6)
Study of a standing figure, possibly Christ, robed from the waist
down, with his right arm in the air and rough rocks behind him on
the ground.
Charlotte Petersen; SC, Gift of Charlotte Petersen. SC99.188.

457. Cemetery Christ: Sketch, ca. 1930–1935
Ink on paper, 11 x 8 1/2 (27.9 x 21.6)
Study of a standing figure, possibly Christ, robed from the waist
down, with his hands at his sides and palms facing upward.
Charlotte Petersen; SC, Gift of Charlotte Petersen. SC99.189.

458. Cemetery Christ: Sketch, ca. 1930–1935
Black graphite and ink on paper, 11 x 8 1/2 (27.9 x 21.6)
Study of a standing robed figure, possibly Christ, surrounded by
rocks. His right arm is upraised.
Charlotte Petersen; SC, Gift of Charlotte Petersen. SC99.190.

459. Cemetery Christ: Sketch, ca. 1930 –1935
Black graphite on paper, 11 x 8 1/2 (27.9 x 21.6)
Study of a figure, possibly Christ, looking to the sky with arms
down and back. He is robed from the waist down. His feet are off
the ground, but his robes reach the ground.
Charlotte Petersen; SC, Gift of Charlotte Petersen. SC99.192.

460. Christ and the Cross, ca. 1930–1935
Colored pencil on paper, 4 x 6 (10.2 x 15.2)
Sketch of Christ trying to lift the cross on his back.
Charlotte Petersen; SC, Gift of Charlotte Petersen. SC99.263.

461. Christ and the Cross, ca. 1930–1935
Pencil on paper, 4 x 6 (10.2 x 15.2)
Sketch of Christ trying to lift cross, with another figure behind
him helping.
Charlotte Petersen; SC, Gift of Charlotte Petersen. SC99.267.

462. Christ Carrying the Cross, ca. 1930–1935
Colored pencil on paper, 4 x 6 (10.2 x 15.2)
Sketch of Christ, wearing crown of thorns and carrying cross on his back.
Charlotte Petersen; SC, Gift of Charlotte Petersen. SC99.264.

463. Christ Carrying the Cross, ca. 1930–1935
Pencil on paper, 4 x 6 (10.2 x 15.2)
Sketch of standing Christ, carrying cross on his back, with his right
hand raised toward three women who are watching him and crying
in the lower left corner.
Charlotte Petersen; SC, Gift of Charlotte Petersen. SC99.268.

464. Christ Carrying the Cross, ca. 1930–1935
Pencil on paper, 4 x 6 (10.2 x 15.2)
Sketch of Christ carrying a cross and three women weeping in the
lower left corner.
Charlotte Petersen; SC, Gift of Charlotte Petersen. SC99.269.

465. Christ Wearing Blindfold, ca. 1930–1935
Pencil on paper, 4 x 6 (10.2 x 15.2)
Sketch of Christ, wearing a blindfold, and a male figure looking at him.
Charlotte Petersen; SC, Gift of Charlotte Petersen. SC99.265.

466. Couple, ca. 1930–1935
Pencil on paper, 6 7/8 x 4 7/8 (17.5 x 12.4)
Sketch of striding man with one arm extended and the other arm
around a woman. Both are on single pedestal in a landscape.
Charlotte Petersen; SC, Gift of Charlotte Petersen. SC99.253.

467. Courtyard, ca. 1930–1935
Pencil on paper, 4 x 6 (10.2 x 15.2)
Aerial view of a courtyard, with measurements of sidewalks, lawn
areas and circular pool, marked "12 ½ feet."
Charlotte Petersen; SC, Gift of Charlotte Petersen. SC99.274.

468. Figures in a Landscape with Trees, ca. 1930–1935
Pencil on paper, 6 7/8 x 4 7/8 (17.5 x 12.4)
Sketches of three figures in a landscape.
Charlotte Petersen; SC, Gift of Charlotte Petersen. SC99.234.

469. Figures by a Pool, ca. 1930–1935
Pencil on paper, 6 7/8 x 4 7/8 (17.5 x 12.4)
Sketch of a male and a female figure by a small pool.
Charlotte Petersen; SC, Gift of Charlotte Petersen. SC99.251.

470. Four Figure Sketches, ca. 1930–1935
Pencil on paper, 6 7/8 x 4 7/8 (17.5 x 12.4)
1) Standing nude with arms outstretched, draped in cloth. 2) Draped
man with arms extending toward ground. 3 and 4) Figure sketches of
a child and two parents with the word "Confidence" in pencil under one.
Charlotte Petersen; SC, Gift of Charlotte Petersen. SC99.247.

471. Horse and Rider, ca. 1930–1935
Pencil on paper, 6 7/8 x 4 7/8 (17.5 x 12.4)
Charlotte Petersen; SC, Gift of Charlotte Petersen. SC99.257.

472. Nude, ca. 1930–1935
Pencil on paper, 6 7/8 x 4 7/8 (17.5 x 12.4)
Sketch of a leaning nude figure.
Charlotte Petersen; SC, Gift of Charlotte Petersen. SC99.261.

473. Robed Figure, ca. 1930–1935
Pencil on paper, 4 x 6 (10.2 x 15.2)
Sketch of a robed figure. Detail of washing hands in a bowl at lower right.
Charlotte Petersen; SC, Gift of Charlotte Petersen. SC99.266.

474. Three Arches, ca. 1930–1935
Pencil on paper, 6 7/8 x 4 7/8 (17.5 x 12.4)
Sketch of three arches for *The History of Dairying Mural* or *Three
Athletes* of State Gym.
Charlotte Petersen; SC, Gift of Charlotte Petersen. SC99.237.

475. Two Robed Figures, ca. 1930–1935
Colored pencil on paper, 4 x 6 (10.2 x 15.2)
Sketch within a circle of two robed figures facing each other and
standing in a street.
Charlotte Petersen; SC, Gift of Charlotte Petersen. SC99.272.

476. Two Sketches, ca. 1930–1935
Colored pencil on paper, 4 x 6 (10.2 x 15.2)
Two sketches, each within a circle. The top one appears to be a
base and a broken off column which seems to be blowing away.
The bottom sketch shows a figure seated on a pyramid of large blocks.
Charlotte Petersen; SC, Gift of Charlotte Petersen. SC99.271.

477. Two Sketches, ca. 1930–1935
Pencil on paper, 6 7/8 x 4 7/8 (17.5 x 12.4)
Two sketches of an adult and child on a pedestal.
Charlotte Petersen; SC, Gift of Charlotte Petersen. SC99.252.

478. Two Sketches of Two Figures, ca. 1930–1935
Colored pencil on paper, 4 x 6 (10.2 x 15.2)
Two sketches, each within a circle. Both show two seated or
kneeling figures facing each other.
Charlotte Petersen; SC, Gift of Charlotte Petersen. SC99.270.

479. Wall Installation, ca. 1930–1935
Pencil on paper, 6 7/8 x 4 7/8 (17.5 x 12.4)
Sketch of an unknown wall installation.
Inscription: 10 x 30 feet
Charlotte Petersen; SC, Gift of Charlotte Petersen. SC99.232.

480. Winged Horse and Rider, ca. 1930–1935
Colored pencil on paper, 4 x 6 (10.2 x 15.2)
Winged horse and rider, leaping at the edge of a cliff.
Charlotte Petersen; SC, Gift of Charlotte Petersen. SC99.275.

481. Woman Wearing Veil, ca. 1930–1935
Ink on paper, 4 x 6 (10.2 x 15.2)
Profile of the head of a religious woman, facing left and wearing a veil.
Charlotte Petersen; SC, Gift of Charlotte Petersen. SC99.273.

482. Mantelpiece, ca. 1933–1934
Orange pencil on paper, 8 x 10 (20.3 x 25.4)
Sketch of a fireplace with mantel sculptures of cattle, figures, and trees.
*Charlotte Petersen; Mary Petersen; CPC, Purchased by the
Christian Petersen Memorial Fund. UM92.346.*

483. Julegranen: Boboli Gardens, 1934
Pencil or conté on paper, 13 3/4 x 16 3/4 (34.9 x 42.5)
A sketch which may have been done for *Julegranen* magazine.
Inscription at bottom: Boboli Gardens
*Charlotte Petersen; Mary Petersen; CPC, Purchased by the
Christian Petersen Memorial Fund. UM92.278.*

484. Francis McCray, ca. 1934
Pencil or conté on paper, 8 3/4 x 11 7/8 (22.2 x 30.2)
Possibly a study of Francis McCray.
*Charlotte Petersen; Mary Petersen; CPC, Purchased by the
Christian Petersen Memorial Fund. UM92.98.*

485. Concept for Fountain of Five Colleges, ca. 1934
Black graphite or conté on paper, 8 1/2 x 11 (21.6 x 27.9)
Sketch of a three-tiered fountain surrounded by three figures.
Charlotte Petersen; Mary Petersen; CPC, Purchased by the Christian Petersen Memorial Fund. UM92.18.

Studies related to *History of Dairying Mural,* 1934–1935

486. Concept Study
Pencil on page, 6 7/8 x 4 7/8 (17.5 x 12.4)
Early concept study for the fountain with a square pool and two figures, one standing and one seated, holding a container out of which water pours.
Charlotte Petersen; SC, Gift of Charlotte Petersen. SC99.233.

487. Courtyard
Pencil or conté on paper, 8 1/2 x 11 (21.6 x 27.9)
Circular fountain with sculpture in center front; central area with sculpted panel; arched openings to either side.
Charlotte Petersen; Mary Petersen; CPC, Purchased by the Christian Petersen Memorial Fund. UM92.17.

488. Courtyard
Colored pencil on paper, 14 x 10 (35.6 x 25.4)
Perspective study of courtyard and fountain concept with cattle. Mathematical figuring done in center of paper.
Charlotte Petersen; Mary Petersen; CPC, Purchased by the Christian Petersen Memorial Fund. UM92.148.

489. Courtyard
Charcoal on paper, 8 1/2 x 11 (21.6 x 27.9)
Study for a courtyard, with series of panels as a wall decoration.
Charlotte Petersen; Mary Petersen; CPC, Purchased by the Christian Petersen Memorial Fund. UM92.116.

490. Cow
Colored pencil on paper, 8 3/4 x 9 7/8 (22.2 x 25.1)
Studies of a cow.
Charlotte Petersen; Mary Petersen; CPC, Purchased by the Christian Petersen Memorial Fund. UM92.146.

491. Cow
Colored pencil on paper, 10 x 11 1/2 (25.4 x 29.2)
Two studies of a cow's head, a preliminary study for fountain figures.
Charlotte Petersen; Mary Petersen; CPC, Purchased by the Christian Petersen Memorial Fund. UM92.151b.

492. Cows
Pencil or conté on paper, 16 3/4 x 13 3/4 (42.5 x 34.9)
Study of cows being milked by man and woman.
Charlotte Petersen; Mary Petersen; CPC, Purchased by the Christian Petersen Memorial Fund. UM92.238.

493. Cows
Pencil or conté on paper, 16 3/4 x 13 3/4 (42.5 x 34.9)
Studies of sculptures with cows for a mantelpiece sculpture.
Charlotte Petersen; Mary Petersen; CPC, Purchased by the Christian Petersen Memorial Fund. UM92.241.

494. First Concept
Colored pencil on paper, 6 3/4 x 50 1/2 (17.1 x 128.3);
Image: 5 x 48 (12.7 x 121.9)
Men, women, and cattle involved in dairying activities in

a mural behind a central sculpture of a standing female holding a container out of which water pours. Marked and numbered "10, 20 ... 80" in pencil across top. The words, "first thot [sic] for dairy panels" in pencil at top right.
Charlotte Petersen; SC, Gift of Charlotte Petersen. SC99.161.

495. For Melke and Chese and Buttere: Figure Study
Pencil or conté on paper, 8 1/2 x 11 (21.6 x 27.9)
Sketch of a nude woman holding an urn.
Charlotte Petersen; Mary Petersen; CPC, Purchased by the Christian Petersen Memorial Fund. UM92.129.

496. For Melke and Chese and Buttere: Preparatory Study
Pencil or conté on paper, 8 1/2 x 11 (21.6 x 27.9)
Study of a man sitting in the pose of Rodin's *The Thinker* and two women, one of whom is churning butter.
Charlotte Petersen; Mary Petersen; CPC, Purchased by the Christian Petersen Memorial Fund. UM92.128.

497. Four Thousande Yeeres: Figure Study
Pencil and colored pencil on paper, 8 1/2 x 11 (21.6 x 27.9)
Three studies of a woman with hands extended, as if holding the dasher for a dairy churn.
Charlotte Petersen; Mary Petersen; CPC, Purchased by the Christian Petersen Memorial Fund. UM92.125.

498. Four Thousande Yeeres: Figure Studies
Pencil or conté on paper, 8 1/2 x 11 (21.6 x 27.9)
Three sizes of studies of a woman holding a bowl.
Charlotte Petersen; Mary Petersen; CPC, Purchased by the Christian Petersen Memorial Fund. UM92.32.

499. For Melke and Chese and Buttere and
Four Thousande Yeeres: Concept Studies
Pencil on paper, 7 1/4 x 13 3/8 (8.4 x 34);
Image sheets: 6 1/8 x 4 7/8 (15.6 x 12.3) [each]
Early concepts for interior panels of Dairy Industry Building. Two studies on separate pages attached to a larger sheet. Left sketch shows a kneeling female figure in profile, and the words "1000 BC" in pencil. Right study shows a standing male figure using a churn and the words "1900 AD" in pencil. Both in arched shapes as are final reliefs.
Charlotte Petersen; SC, Gift of Charlotte Petersen. SC99.226ab.

500. Pedestals
Pencil or conté on paper, 9 x 12 (22.9 x 30.5)
Studies of pedestal and footing installations.
Charlotte Petersen; Mary Petersen; CPC, Purchased by the Christian Petersen Memorial Fund. UM92.165.

501. Preliminary Study
Pencil or conté on paper, 8 1/2 x 11 (21.6 x 27.9)
Study of central panel, depicting three cows and a bull.
Charlotte Petersen; Mary Petersen; CPC, Purchased by the Christian Petersen Memorial Fund. UM92.144.

502. Preparatory Study
Pencil or conté on paper, 9 3/4 x 14 (24.8 x 35.6)
Study of a cow laying down in a center panel with three panels to each side.
Charlotte Petersen; Mary Petersen; CPC, Purchased by the Christian Petersen Memorial Fund. UM92.265.

Studies related to *History of Dairying Mural*, continued.

503. Study

Pencil or conté on paper, 9 x 12 (22.9 x 30.5)
Study of a cow with veterinarians, animal scientists, or herdsmen.
Charlotte Petersen; Mary Petersen; CPC, Purchased by the Christian Petersen Memorial Fund. UM92.185a.

504. Study

Pencil or conté on paper, 9 x 12 (22.9 x 30.5)
Study of a cow and people milking cows.
Inscription: Out in back
Charlotte Petersen; Mary Petersen; CPC, Purchased by the Christian Petersen Memorial Fund. UM92.185b.

505. Studies of Fountains

Charcoal on paper, 9 3/4 x 14 (24.8 x 35.6)
Sketches of three fountains: cows, three figures, two figures.
Charlotte Petersen; Mary Petersen; CPC, Purchased by the Christian Petersen Memorial Fund. UM92.268.

506. Studies of Nudes

Pencil on page of a sketchbook, 6 7/8 x 4 7/8 (17.5 x 12.4)
Full-length figure studies of nudes.
Charlotte Petersen; SC, Gift of Charlotte Petersen. SC99.248.

507. Figure Studies

Pencil on page of a sketchbook, 6 7/8 x 4 7/8 (17.5 x 12.4)
Four figure studies. One man and child, the others of one kneeling and one standing man. Possibly for *History of Dairying Mural.*
Charlotte Petersen; SC, Gift of Charlotte Petersen. SC99.250.

508. Figure Studies for Central Figure

Pencil on page of a sketchbook, 6 7/8 x 4 7/8 (17.5 x 12.4)
Four small figure studies, possibly early concepts for central figure of Dairy Industry fountain.
Charlotte Petersen; SC, Gift of Charlotte Petersen. SC99.249.

509. Circular Fountain, ca. 1935

Pencil or conté on paper, 9 x 12 (22.9 x 30.5)
Sketch of a fountain or pool with a nude female figure in front of a building.
Charlotte Petersen; Mary Petersen; CPC, Purchased by the Christian Petersen Memorial Fund. UM92.155b.

510. Circular Fountain, ca. 1935

Pencil or conté on paper, 9 x 12 (22.9 x 30.5)
Sketch of a nude female figure standing in the middle of a pool.
Charlotte Petersen; Mary Petersen; CPC, Purchased by the Christian Petersen Memorial Fund. UM92.155a.

511. Eli Lilly & Company Research Award: Study, ca. 1935

Pencil or conté on paper, 8 1/2 x 11 (21.6 x 27.9)
Study of a man looking into a microscope, in a circle frame and with two hexagonal projected shapes.
Charlotte Petersen; Mary Petersen; CPC, Purchased by the Christian Petersen Memorial Fund. UM92.132.

512. Eli Lilly & Company Research Award: Study, ca. 1935

Pencil or conté on paper, 8 1/2 x 11 (21.6 x 27.9)
Two studies of a man looking into a microscope. Probably done in preparation for the Eli Lilly medal.

Charlotte Petersen; Mary Petersen; CPC, Purchased by the Christian Petersen Memorial Fund. UM92.140.

513. Eli Lilly & Company Research Award: Study, ca. 1935

Brown pencil on paper, 8 1/2 x 11 (21.6 x 27.9)
Study of figure in motion within a rectangle including a seated figure with hunched head, arms, and legs.
Charlotte Petersen; Mary Petersen; CPC, Purchased by the Christian Petersen Memorial Fund. UM92.15.

514. Eli Lilly & Company Research Award: Study, ca. 1935

Pencil or conté on paper, 8 1/2 x 11 (21.6 x 27.9)
Study of a man in a circular frame looking into a microscope.
Charlotte Petersen; Mary Petersen; CPC, Purchased by the Christian Petersen Memorial Fund. UM92.141.

515. Eli Lilly & Company Research Award: Study, ca. 1935

Colored pencil on paper, 8 1/2 x 11 (21.6 x 27.9)
Study of a man in a circular frame sitting at a table looking into a microscope.
Charlotte Petersen; Mary Petersen; CPC, Purchased by the Christian Petersen Memorial Fund. UM92.138.

516. Eli Lilly & Company Research Award: Study, ca. 1935

Pencil or conté on paper, 8 1/2 x 11 (21.6 x 27.9)
Study of a man looking into a microscope. May have been done in preparation for the Eli Lilly medal or veterinary medicine panels.
Charlotte Petersen; Mary Petersen; CPC, Purchased by the Christian Petersen Memorial Fund. UM92.139.

517. Eli Lilly & Company Research Award: Study, ca. 1935

Pencil or conté on paper, 8 1/2 x 11 (21.6 x 27.9)
The Eli Lilly and Company Research Award for fundamental research in Biological Chemistry, administered by the American Chemical Society. Recto: A man underneath a tree. Verso: Study of a woman and two children.
Charlotte Petersen; Mary Petersen; CPC, Purchased by the Christian Petersen Memorial Fund. UM92.145ab.

518. Man, ca. 1935

Pencil or conté on paper, 9 x 12 (22.9 x 30.5)
Sketches of a man carrying a heavy load on his back as he leans into the wind.
Charlotte Petersen; Mary Petersen; CPC, Purchased by the Christian Petersen Memorial Fund. UM92.157b.

519. Seated Man, ca. 1935

Conté on paper, 8 1/2 x 11 (21.6 x 27.9)
Detailed sketch of a full-length, nude male model in a seated position.
Charlotte Petersen; Mary Petersen; CPC, Purchased by the Christian Petersen Memorial Fund. UM92.136a.

Studies related to *Three Athletes*, 1935–1936

520. Concept Study

Colored pencil on paper, 8 1/2 x 11 (21.6 x 27.9)
Panel concepts with details and a fountain.
Charlotte Petersen; Mary Petersen; CPC, Purchased by the Christian Petersen Memorial Fund. UM92.142ab.

521. Concept Study

Charcoal on paper, 9 x 12 (22.9 x 30.5)

Study of a sculpture and a fountain.

CPC, Purchased from Mary Petersen with funds from the Christian Petersen Memorial Fund. UM92.171.

522. Concept Study

Charcoal on paper, 9 x 12 (22.9 x 30.5)

Study of an athlete leaning on a vaulting pole.

Charlotte Petersen; Mary Petersen; CPC, Purchased by the Christian Petersen Memorial Fund. UM92.176.

523. Concept Studies

Conté on paper, 9 x 12 (22.9 x 30.5)

Studies of sculptures of athletes for the State Gym, Iowa State. Two tennis, two baseball players, one runner and a swimmer.

Charlotte Petersen; Mary Petersen; CPC, Purchased by the Christian Petersen Memorial Fund. UM92.23.

524. Figure Study

Charcoal on paper, 9 x 12 (22.9 x 30.5)

Study of a seated athlete.

Charlotte Petersen; Mary Petersen; CPC, Purchased by the Christian Petersen Memorial Fund. UM92.172.

525. Figure Study

Charcoal on paper, 9 x 12 (22.9 x 30.5)

Drawing of a pole vaulter.

Charlotte Petersen; Mary Petersen; CPC, Purchased by the Christian Petersen Memorial Fund. UM92.169.

526. Figure Study

Charcoal on paper, 9 x 12 (22.9 x 30.5)

Study of an athlete holding a discus. Concept for State Gym panels.

Charlotte Petersen; Mary Petersen; CPC, Purchased by the Christian Petersen Memorial Fund. UM92.174.

527. Figure Study of an Athlete

Charcoal on paper, 9 x 12 (22.9 x 30.5)

Charlotte Petersen; Mary Petersen; CPC, Purchased by the Christian Petersen Memorial Fund. UM92.180.

528. Figure Study of a Discus Thrower

Charcoal on paper, 9 x 12 (22.9 x 30.5)

Charlotte Petersen; Mary Petersen; CPC, Purchased by the Christian Petersen Memorial Fund. UM92.179.

529. Figure Study of a Pole Vaulter

Pencil or conté on paper, 9 x 12 (22.9 x 30.5)

Charlotte Petersen; Mary Petersen; CPC, Purchased by the Christian Petersen Memorial Fund. UM92.181.

530. Figures in Various Athletic Positions

Brown pencil on paper, 6 3/4 x 10 1/4 (17.1 x 26)

Four panels with figures in various athletic positions.

Charlotte Petersen; Mary Petersen; CPC, Purchased by the Christian Petersen Memorial Fund. UM92.126a.

531. Football Player

Pencil or conté on paper, 8 1/2 x 11 (21.6 x 27.9)

Study of football player wearing a helmet and carrying a football in his right hand.

Charlotte Petersen; Mary Petersen; CPC, Purchased by the Christian Petersen Memorial Fund. UM92.20.

532. Motion Studies

Brown pencil on paper, 8 1/2 x 11 (21.6 x 27.6)

Six panels of athletes in various stages of motion involved in the sports of football and track.

Charlotte Petersen; Mary Petersen; CPC, Purchased by the Christian Petersen Memorial Fund. UM92.135a.

533. Pole Vaulter

Charcoal on paper, 9 x 12 (22.9 x 30.5)

Study of a pole vaulter. Concept for State Gym athletes.

Charlotte Petersen; Mary Petersen; CPC, Purchased by the Christian Petersen Memorial Fund. UM92.170.

534. Pole Vaulter

Charcoal on paper, 9 x 12 (22.9 x 30.5)

Study of an athlete leaning on a vaulting pole.

Charlotte Petersen; Mary Petersen; CPC, Purchased by the Christian Petersen Memorial Fund. UM92.173.

535. Pole Vaulter

Charcoal on paper, 9 x 12 (22.9 x 30.5)

Charlotte Petersen; Mary Petersen; CPC, Purchased by the Christian Petersen Memorial Fund. UM92.178.

536. Studies of Athletes

Pencil or conté on paper, 8 1/2 x 11 (21.6 x 27.9)

Five studies of athletes, one baseball player, two tennis players.

Charlotte Petersen; Mary Petersen; CPC, Purchased by the Christian Petersen Memorial Fund. UM92.22.

537. Studies of Athletes

Pencil or conté on paper, 8 1/2 x 11 (21.6 x 27.9)

Seven studies of athletes in football, basketball, and track: the three sports chosen for the State Gym panels.

Charlotte Petersen; Mary Petersen; CPC, Purchased by the Christian Petersen Memorial Fund. UM92.31.

538. Studies of a Runner

Pencil or conté on paper, 8 1/2 x 11 (21.6 x 27.9)

Charlotte Petersen; Mary Petersen; CPC, Purchased by the Christian Petersen Memorial Fund. UM92.34.

539. Studies of Athletes in Motion

Colored pencil on paper, 8 1/2 x 11 (21.6 x 27.9)

Nine figures in various stages of motion.

Charlotte Petersen; Mary Petersen; CPC, Purchased by the Christian Petersen Memorial Fund. UM92.134.

540. Study of an Athlete

Pencil or conté on paper, 8 1/2 x 11 (21.6 x 27.9)

Three studies of an athletic figure.

Charlotte Petersen; Mary Petersen; CPC, Purchased by the Christian Petersen Memorial Fund. UM92.21.

Studies related to *Veterinary Medicine Mural*, 1935–1936

541. Farm Animals and Final Concept

Orange pencil on paper, 8 1/2 x 11 (21.6 x 27.9)
Recto: Top study is a horse, a cow, and a pig being restrained; bottom study is final concept. Verso: Panel concepts of animals being treated by veterinarians.
CPC, Purchased from Mary Petersen with funds from the Christian Petersen Memorial Fund. UM92.44ab.

542. Man and Calf

Pencil or conté on paper, 8 1/2 x 11 (21.6 x 27.9)
Preparatory study of a man and a calf.
CPC, Purchased from Mary Petersen with funds from the Christian Petersen Memorial Fund. UM92.135b.

543. Man and Calf

Pencil or conté on paper, 8 1/2 x 11 (21.6 x 27.9)
Veterinary Medicine Mural and siting of mural in Veterinary Quadrangle.
Charlotte Petersen; Mary Petersen; CPC, Purchased by the Christian Petersen Memorial Fund. UM92.136b.

544. Preliminary Study

Pencil or conté on paper, 8 1/2 x 11 (21.6 x 27.9)
Three studies of animals being treated and examined.
Charlotte Petersen; Mary Petersen; CPC, Purchased by the Christian Petersen Memorial Fund. UM92.45.

545. Preliminary Study

Pencil or conté on paper, 8 1/2 x 11 (21.6 x 27.9)
Three studies of animals being treated by veterinarians.
Charlotte Petersen; Mary Petersen; CPC, Purchased by the Christian Petersen Memorial Fund. UM92.46.

546. Preliminary Study

Pencil or conté on paper, 8 1/2 x 11 (21.6 x 27.9)
A veterinarian restraining a calf.
Charlotte Petersen; Mary Petersen; CPC, Purchased by the Christian Petersen Memorial Fund. UM92.47a.

547. Preparatory Studies

Pencil or conté on paper, 9 x 12 (22.9 x 30.5)
Five pencil studies of men and animals.
Charlotte Petersen; Mary Petersen; CPC, Purchased by the Christian Petersen Memorial Fund. UM92.367.

548. Quadrangle

Pencil or conté on paper, 8 1/2 x 11 (21.6 x 27.9)
Entrance into a structure, possibly the former veterinary quadrangle.
Charlotte Petersen; Mary Petersen; CPC, Purchased by the Christian Petersen Memorial Fund. UM92.47b.

549. Two Men Working

Colored pencil on paper, 6 3/4 x 10 1/4 (17.1 x 26)
Multiple studies of two men working on an animal.
Charlotte Petersen; Mary Petersen; CPC, Purchased by the Christian Petersen Memorial Fund. UM92.126b.

550. Preparatory Sketch

Pencil or conté on paper, 8 1/2 x 11 (21.6 x 27.9)
Sketch of a buffalo in a circle and of a sow and piglets, probably for *Veterinary Medicine Mural*.
Charlotte Petersen; Mary Petersen; CPC, Purchased by the Christian Petersen Memorial Fund. UM92.143.

551. Sketch

Brown pencil and conté on paper, 9 x 12 (22.9 x 30.5
Very faint sketch of a building which could be the veterinary quadrangle.
Charlotte Petersen; Mary Petersen; CPC, Purchased by the Christian Petersen Memorial Fund. UM92.184.

***Veterinary Medicine Mural*:**
Studies related to *The Gentle Doctor*, 1935–1936

552. Final Design

Pencil or conté on paper, 11 x 7 3/4 (27.9 x 19.7)
Final design for the figure of *The Gentle Doctor*.
Gift to Veterinary College by Charlotte and Mary Petersen; CPC. U89.41a.

553. Preliminary Study

Pencil or conté on paper, 11 x 8 1/2 (27.9 x 21.6)
Study for the figure, *The Gentle Doctor*. Doctor in profile holding puppy.
Gift to Veterinary College by Charlotte and Mary Petersen; CPC. U89.41b.

554. Preliminary Study

Pencil on paper, 11 x 7 7/8 (27.9 x 20)
Five studies for *The Gentle Doctor*.
Gift to Veterinary College by Charlotte and Mary Petersen; CPC. U89.41c.

555. Preliminary Design

Black conté on paper, 12 x 9 (30.5 x 22.9)
Three-quarter view of the final design of *The Gentle Doctor*.
Gift to Veterinary College by Charlotte and Mary Petersen; CPC. U89.41d.

556. Study of Dog

Pencil on paper, 11 3/4 x 8 3/4 (29.8 x 22.2)
Profile of mother dog.
Charlotte Petersen; SC, Gift of Charlotte Petersen. SC99.177.

557. Working Man, ca. 1935

Colored pencil on paper, 8 1/2 x 11 (21.6 x 27.9)
Sketches of a man prying or leveling rocks from the ground.
Charlotte Petersen; Mary Petersen; CPC, Purchased by the Christian Petersen Memorial Fund. UM92.137.

558. Equitable of Iowa Life Insurance Company: Sketch, ca. 1933–1938

Pencil or conté on paper, 8 1/2 x 11 (21.6 x 27.9)
Sketch of an octagonal fountain with two figures and one head of a pig. May have been a concept for Equitable of Iowa Life Insurance Company in Des Moines, Iowa.
Charlotte Petersen; Mary Petersen; CPC, Purchased by the Christian Petersen Memorial Fund. UM92.38b.

559. Boy, ca. 1936

Pencil or conté on paper, 13 3/4 x 16 3/4 (34.9 x 42.5)
Sketch of a boy.
Charlotte Petersen; Mary Petersen; CPC, Purchased by the Christian Petersen Memorial Fund. UM92.285.

560. Child's Face, ca. 1936
Pencil or conté on paper, 8 1/2 x 11 (21.6 x 27.9)
Charlotte Petersen; Mary Petersen; CPC, Purchased by the Christian Petersen Memorial Fund. UM92.122.

561. J.C. Cunningham, ca. 1936
Pencil or conté on paper, 14 x 10 (35.6 x 25.4)
Sketch of the profile of a man's head. Cunningham was a friend of Petersen.
Charlotte Petersen; Mary Petersen; CPC, Purchased by the Christian Petersen Memorial Fund. UM92.153.

562. Mary Charlotte Petersen, 1936
Engraving on paper, 4 1/2 x 6 (11.4 x 15.2);
Image: 3 x 4 (7.6 x 10.2);
Copper plate, 3 x 4 x 1/16 (7.6 x 10.2 x 0.2)
Birth announcement. The back of a baby, wearing a diaper and standing with a tool in her right hand, carving the words, "Mary Charlotte Petersen, November 24, 1936."
SC. Engraving: SC99.286a. Plate: SC99.286b.

Studies related to *Reclining Nudes*, 1935–1936

563. Archways of a Building
Colored pencil on paper, 14 x 17 (35.6 x 43.2)
Study of archways of a building with two figures in the foreground.
Charlotte Petersen; Mary Petersen; CPC, Purchased by the Christian Petersen Memorial Fund. UM92.293.

564. Figure Studies
Pencil or conté on paper, 16 3/4 x 13 3/4 (42.5 x 34.9)
Study of three nude women and a nude young girl.
Charlotte Petersen; Mary Petersen; CPC, Purchased by the Christian Petersen Memorial Fund. UM92.245.

565. Fountain Study
Pencil or conté on paper, 8 1/2 x 11 (21.6 x 27.9)
Two roughly sketched figures, railing, circular shaped fountain below.
Inscription: "8" and "9"
Charlotte Petersen; Mary Petersen; CPC, Purchased by the Christian Petersen Memorial Fund. UM92.6.

566. Preparatory Study
Pencil or conté on paper, 8 1/2 x 11 (21.6 x 27.9)
A preparatory study for the *Reclining Nudes* fountain, with two people lying down.
Charlotte Petersen; Mary Petersen; CPC, Purchased by the Christian Petersen Memorial Fund. UM92.123.

567. Three Studies
Pencil on paper, 14 x 17 (35.6 x 43.2)
Three studies of a sculpture with a woman on her knees by a reflecting pool, possibly for *Reclining Nudes*.
Charlotte Petersen; Mary Petersen; CPC, Purchased by the Christian Petersen Memorial Fund. UM92.299a.

568. Anson Marston Medal: Concept Study, ca. 1936
Brown pencil on paper, 7 3/4 x 11 (19.7 x 27.9)
Two circles with the words "annual award to the outstanding senior engineer."
Charlotte Petersen; Mary Petersen; CPC, Purchased by the Christian Petersen Memorial Fund. UM92.64ab.

569. Anson Marston Medal: Design Studies, ca. 1936
Pencil or conté on paper, 8 1/2 x 11 (21.6 x 27.9)
Three large circles, with two smaller circles at the bottom. Awarded annually to the outstanding senior engineer from Iowa State.
CPC, Purchased from Mary Petersen with funds from the Christian Petersen Memorial Fund. UM92.1a.

570. Anson Marston Medal: Study of Engineers, ca. 1936
Pencil or conté on paper, 8 1/2 x 11 (21.6 x 27.9)
Two studies of engineers at a desk in a circle, with the words "annual award for achievement in engineering."
Charlotte Petersen; Mary Petersen; CPC, Purchased by the Christian Petersen Memorial Fund. UM92.64a.

571. Anson Marston Medal: Preliminary Study, ca. 1936
Brown pencil on paper, 5 x 5 3/4 (12.7 x 14.6)
Study of engineers. One is using a transit instrument.
Charlotte Petersen; Mary Petersen; CPC, Purchased by the Christian Petersen Memorial Fund. UM92.53.

572. Cha-Ki-Shi: Armlet, ca. 1936
Pencil on paper, 12 x 9 1/4 (30.5 x 23.5)
For schoolbook *Cha-Ki-Shi* by Bessie Coon and Halla Rhode, published by Charles Scribner's Sons, New York, in 1936 for elementary school children, with illustrations by Petersen. Study of a Meskwaki armlet with diamond patterns.
Signed lower right: CP
Charlotte Petersen; SC, Gift of Charlotte Petersen. SC99.104.

573. Cha-Ki-Shi: Ba-wi-shi-ka Dressed for the Dance, ca. 1936
Pencil, conté, watercolor, and colored pencil on paper, 12 x 9 (30.5 x 22.9);
Image: 10 1/4 x 7 3/8 (26 x 18.7)
Study of a man wearing a headdress, necklaces, armlets, a loincloth, leglets, and moccasins standing in front of a hut. Printer's marks in pencil in margins of front and on back.
Signed lower right: Christian Petersen
Charlotte Petersen; SC, Gift of Charlotte Petersen. SC99.120.

574. Cha-Ki-Shi: Ba-wi-shi-ka Dressed for the Dance, ca. 1936
Watercolor and charcoal on paper, 11 x 8 3/8 (27.9 x 12.3)
Preparatory study of a man wearing a headdress, necklaces, armlets, a loincloth, leglets, and moccasins standing on a path between two huts.
Signed lower right: CP
Charlotte Petersen; SC, Gift of Charlotte Petersen. SC99.135.

575. Cha-Ki-Shi: Ba-wi-shi-ka Rode at the Head of His Party, ca. 1936
Ink and pencil on paper, 8 1/2 x 11 (21.6 x 27.9)
Study of a Meskwaki family setting off on a hunting expedition. One horse is pulling a travois.
Signed lower left: CP
Charlotte Petersen; SC, Gift of Charlotte Petersen. SC99.88.

576. Cha-Ki-Shi: The Baby and Her New Cradle, ca. 1936
Conté on paper, 13 1/2 x 10 3/4 (34.5 x 27.3);
Image: 3 1/2 x 4 (8.9 x 10.2)
Study of a Meskwaki baby wrapped tightly in skins in a beaded cradle. Printer's marks in pencil to left of image and on back of paper.
Signed lower left: CP
Charlotte Petersen; SC, Gift of Charlotte Petersen. SC99.127.

577. Cha-Ki-Shi: The Baby and Her New Cradle, ca. 1936
Pencil and charcoal on paper, 12 x 9 (30.5 x 22.9);
Image: 10 x 7 (25.4 x 17.8)
Study of a Meskwaki baby wrapped tightly in skins in a beaded cradle.
Signed lower right: CP
Charlotte Petersen; SC, Gift of Charlotte Petersen. SC99.98.

578. Cha-Ki-Shi: The Bark House or Permanent Home, ca. 1936
Pencil on paper, 14 x 9 (35.6 x 22.9)
Study of two bark homes with smoke coming from holes in the center of each roof.
Signed lower left: CP
Charlotte Petersen; SC, Gift of Charlotte Petersen. SC99.90.

579. Cha-Ki-Shi: Bearclaw Necklace, ca. 1936
Charcoal and pencil on paper, 12 x 9 1/4 (30.5 x 23.5);
Image: 12 x 5 (30.5 x 12.7)
Study of a circular necklace made of beads between bearclaws for the book *Cha-Ki-Shi.*
Signed lower right: CP
Charlotte Petersen; SC, Gift of Charlotte Petersen. SC99.124.

580. Cha-Ki-Shi: Bison, ca. 1936
Pencil on paper, 9 x 12 (22.9 x 30.5)
Study of a row of bison walking in a landscape.
Charlotte Petersen; SC, Gift of Charlotte Petersen. SC99.97.

581. Cha-Ki-Shi: The Brush Broom, ca. 1936
Pencil on paper, 12 x 9 1/8 (30.5 x 23.2)
Study of a broom made of a long stick with twigs tied together at one end.
Signed bottom: CP
Charlotte Petersen; SC, Gift of Charlotte Petersen. SC99.91.

582. Cha-Ki-Shi: The Buffalo Head Dance, ca. 1936
Conté on textured paper, 10 3/4 x 11 (23.2 x 27.9);
Image: 7 1/2 x 8 (19.1 x 20.3)
Study of a male facing left, wearing a wig or buffalo headdress withhorns, a loincloth, and moccasins with fur at the ankles. He carries a shield and spear, both decorated with fringes.
Signed lower right: CP
Charlotte Petersen; SC, Gift of Charlotte Petersen. SC99.130.

583. Cha-Ki-Shi: Buffalo in the Snow, ca. 1936
Pencil on paper, 9 1/4 x 12 (23.5 x 30.5)
Study of a row of buffaloes walking in knee-deep snow. Two large ones at front, others in the distance.
Signed lower right: CP
Charlotte Petersen; SC, Gift of Charlotte Petersen. SC99.94.

584. Cha-Ki-Shi: Cha-Ki-Shi Dressed for the Dance, ca. 1936
Pencil, conté and colored pencil on paper, 12 x 9 (30.5 x 22.9)
Study of the central character dressed in a skin dress with shell jewelry at her neck and buckles and bracelets. Printer's notes in pencil in margins.

Signed lower right: CP
Charlotte Petersen; SC, Gift of Charlotte Petersen. SC99.115.

585. Cha-Ki-Shi: Cha-Ki-Shi Loses Her Doll, ca. 1936
Colored pencil on paper, 10 3/8 x 12 5/16 (26.4 x 31.3);
Image: 8 7/16 x 10 (21.4 x 25.4)
Study of a woman and girl on a rearing horse. The girl is looking back at her dropped doll which is on the ground behind the horse.
Signed lower left: Christian Petersen
Charlotte Petersen; SC, Gift of Charlotte Petersen. SC99.107.

586. Cha-Ki-Shi: Cha-Ki-Shi Loses Her Doll, ca. 1936
Pencil, colored pencil and charcoal on paper, 12 x 9 (30.5 x 22.9)
Study for the illustration of a woman and girl on a rearing horse. The girl is looking back at her dropped doll which is on the ground behind the horse.
Signed lower left: Christian Petersen
Charlotte Petersen; SC, Gift of Charlotte Petersen. SC99.121.

587. Cha-Ki-Shi: Cha-Ki-Shi with Her Doll, ca. 1936
Pencil, charcoal, and watercolor on paper, 12 x 9 (30.5 x 22.9);
Image: 5 x 3 5/8 (12.7 x 9.2)
Study for an illustration of a bust view of a girl facing front holding a doll in her right hand.
Charlotte Petersen; SC, Gift of Charlotte Petersen. SC99.129.

588. Cha-Ki-Shi: Drying Meat, ca. 1936
Pencil on paper, 14 x 10 1/2 (35.6 x 26.7);
Image: 10 1/2 x 8 (26.7 x 20.3)
Study of a Meskwaki woman carving strips of meat while her daughter hangs them near a fire to dry. Printer's marks in pencil at bottom.
Signed lower right: CP
Charlotte Petersen; SC, Gift of Charlotte Petersen. SC99.116.

589. Cha-Ki-Shi: Drying Meat, ca. 1936
Pencil on paper, 12 x 9 3/4 (30.5 x 24.8)
Study of a Meskwaki woman carving strips of meat while her daughter hangs them near a fire to dry.
Signed lower right: Christian Petersen
Charlotte Petersen; SC, Gift of Charlotte Petersen. SC99.93.

590. Cha-Ki-Shi: Earrings, ca. 1936
Pencil on paper, 12 x 9 1/4 (30.5 x 23.5)
Study depicting a pair of long beaded earrings with hoops at the tops.
Signed lower right: CP
Charlotte Petersen; SC, Gift of Charlotte Petersen. SC99.128.

591. Cha-Ki-Shi: Food, Clothing, Shelter, Culture, ca. 1936
Ink and colored pencil on paper, 11 x 8 1/2 (27.9 x 21.6)
Study of a Meskwaki girl with a doll in a square at the center, with boxes at each corner with the words, "Food," "Clothing," "Shelter" and "Culture" and corresponding images.
Signed right: CP
Charlotte Petersen; SC, Gift of Charlotte Petersen. SC99.86.

592. Cha-Ki-Shi: Garden Time, ca. 1936
Colored pencil, conté and pencil on paper, 12 x 9 (30.5 x 22.9);
Image: 8 1/4 x 6 1/4 (21 x 15.9)
Study showing a Meskwaki woman digging in the dirt with a girl holding a bowl of seeds standing to her right. Printer's marks in pencil in margin.
Signed lower right: Christian Petersen
Charlotte Petersen; SC, Gift of Charlotte Petersen. SC99.113.

593. Cha-Ki-Shi: Garden Time, ca. 1936
Pencil on paper, 12 x 9 (30.5 x 22.9)
Study for an illustration of a Meskwaki woman digging in the dirt with a girl holding a bowl of seeds standing to her right.
Signed lower right: Christian Petersen
Charlotte Petersen; SC, Gift of Charlotte Petersen. SC99.89.

594. Cha-Ki-Shi: Gathering the Nettles, ca. 1936
Pencil, charcoal and watercolor on paper, 9 1/4 x 12 (23.5 x 30.5);
Image: 7 3/4 x 11 (19.7 x 27.9)
Study showing women, one large in the foreground, gathering nettles.
Signed lower right: Christian Petersen
Charlotte Petersen; SC, Gift of Charlotte Petersen. SC99.136.

595. Cha-Ki-Shi: Gathering the Nettles, ca. 1936
Pencil on paper, 9 x 12 (22.9 x 30.5)
Preparatory study for an illustration showing two men near a lake or pond. One is cutting nettles while the other carries them.
Charlotte Petersen; SC, Gift of Charlotte Petersen. SC99.108.

596. Cha-Ki-Shi: Girl with Ko-Na-No, ca. 1936
Pencil and conté on textured paper, 13 1/2 x 10 5/8 (34.3 x 26);
Images: 7 1/4 x 8 (18.4 x 20.3) and 2 x 3 1/2 (5.1 x 8.9)
Preparatory studies of a girl playing a game with a pole and leather bag filled with ashes; and a smaller study of the front of a hut.
Signed lower right: CP
Charlotte Petersen; SC, Gift of Charlotte Petersen. SC99.132.

597. Cha-Ki-Shi: The Hair Roll, ca. 1936
Conté on paper, 14 x 10 1/2 (35.6 x 26.7);
Image: 11 1/2 x 10 1/8 (29.2 x 25.7)
Study depicting a profile view of a standing girl with her hair in a wrapped ponytail at her back. The ponytail wrappings are four long, beaded strips which reach down to her ankles. She is holding a doll.
Signed lower right: Christian Petersen
Charlotte Petersen; SC, Gift of Charlotte Petersen. SC99.138.

598. Cha-Ki-Shi: The Hair Roll, ca. 1936
Watercolor and pencil on paper, 12 x 9 1/4 (30.5 x 23.5)
Study for an illustration depicting a profile view of a standing girl with her hair in a wrapped ponytail at her back. The ponytail wrappings are four long beaded strips which reach down to her ankles. She is holding a doll.
Signed lower left: CP
Charlotte Petersen; SC, Gift of Charlotte Petersen. SC99.126.

599. Cha-Ki-Shi: Inside the Wickiup, ca. 1936
Pencil on paper, 12 x 9 (30.5 x 22.9)
Study of a Meskwaki family involved in various daily activities inside their home.
Signed lower right: Christian Petersen
Charlotte Petersen; SC, Gift of Charlotte Petersen. SC99.92.

600. Cha-Ki-Shi: Inside the Wickiup, ca. 1936
Pencil, charcoal, colored pencil and watercolor on paper, 9 1/4 x 12 (23.5 x 30.5);
Image: 8 1/8 x 11 (20.6 x 27.9)
Preliminary study for illustration of a Meskwaki family involved in various daily activities inside their home.
Signed lower left: Christian Petersen
Charlotte Petersen; SC, Gift of Charlotte Petersen. SC99.137.

601. Cha-Ki-Shi: Ko-Na-No, ca. 1936
Charcoal and pencil on paper, 12 x 9 1/4 (30.5 x 23.5)
Study of a Ko-Na-No (a pole and leather bag used for playing a Meskwaki game), and smaller studies of a person playing the game and a figure at the entrance to a hut.
Signed bottom: CP
Charlotte Petersen; SC, Gift of Charlotte Petersen. SC99.125.

602. Cha-Ki-Shi: Making Nettle String, ca. 1936
Pencil on paper, 13 1/4 x 10 1/4 (33.7 x 26);
Image: 7 x 8 (17.8 x 20.3)
Study of a young woman wearing braids, seated on the ground rolling a string along the inside of her left calf.
Signed lower right: CP
Charlotte Petersen; SC, Gift of Charlotte Petersen. SC99.112.

603. Cha-Ki-Shi: Maple Sugar Making, ca. 1936
Paper and charcoal on paper, 12 3/4 x 10 (32.8 x 25.4);
Image: 10 1/2 x 8 (26.7 x 20.3)
Study depicting a seated woman wrapped in a robe cooking over a fire, with a girl holding a bowl standing in the background.
Signed lower right: Christian Petersen
Charlotte Petersen; SC, Gift of Charlotte Petersen. SC99.96.

604. Cha-Ki-Shi: Maple Sugar Making, ca. 1936
Paper and charcoal on paper, 12 3/4 x 10 (32.8 x 25.4);
Image: 10 1/2 x 8 (26.7 x 20.3)
Preparatory study for illustration depicting a seated woman cooking over a fire, with a girl bringing her a bowl in the background.
Signed lower left: Christian Petersen
Charlotte Petersen; SC, Gift of Charlotte Petersen. SC99.119.

605. Cha-Ki-Shi: Meskwaki Family in Their Wickiup, ca. 1936
Watercolor and pencil on paper, 8 1/4 x 11 (21 x 27.9);
Image: 6 1/2 x 8 (16.5 x 20.3)
Study depicting a family involved in various activities in their home.
Signed lower right: CP
Charlotte Petersen; SC, Gift of Charlotte Petersen. SC99.101.

606. Cha-Ki-Shi: Meskwaki Headdress, ca. 1936
Conté on paper, 13 3/4 x 10 5/8 (34.9 x 27)
Study of a feathered and beaded headdress with printer's notes in pencil at left and bottom of image.
Signed lower left: CP
Charlotte Petersen; SC, Gift of Charlotte Petersen. SC99.117.

607. Cha-Ki-Shi: Meskwaki Headdress, ca. 1936
Conté, pencil and pastel, or crayon on paper, 12 x 9 (30.5 x 22.9)
Study for an illustration of a feathered and beaded headdress. Unlike the final printed image in the book, this one is in color with red, purple, yellow, and black elements.
Signed lower left: CP
Charlotte Petersen; SC, Gift of Charlotte Petersen. SC99.122.

608. Cha-Ki-Shi: The New Doll, ca. 1936
Pencil on paper, 12 x 9 (30.5 x 22.9)
Study of a girl in profile facing left, holding a doll. Printer's marks in pencil at bottom and on back.
Signed lower right: CP
Charlotte Petersen; SC, Gift of Charlotte Petersen. SC99.114.

609. Cha-Ki-Shi: The New Pair of Moccasins, ca. 1936
Pencil and charcoal on paper, 12 x 9 1/4 (30.5 x 23.5)
Study of a pair of moccasins.
Signed right: CP
Charlotte Petersen; SC, Gift of Charlotte Petersen. SC99.95.

610. Cha-Ki-Shi: The People Begin to Arrive for the Feast, ca. 1936
Colored pencil on paper, 12 x 9 (30.5 x 22.9)
Study of a Meskwaki family walking along a trail through the
hills toward a village where people are waiting and waving.
Signed lower right: Christian Petersen
Charlotte Petersen; SC, Gift of Charlotte Petersen. SC99.87.

611. Cha-Ki-Shi: Preparatory Studies, ca. 1936
Pencil on paper, 16 x 5 1/4 (40.6 x 13.3);
Images: 5 1/4 x 4 (13.3 x 10.2) [each]
Studies for the book *Cha-Ki-Shi*. Top study shows a Meskwaki
family involved in daily activities in their home. Bottom study shows
a woman stirring a pot which is hanging over a fire and a girl
standing in the background holding a bowl.
Top study signed lower left: Christian Petersen
Bottom study signed lower right: Christian Petersen
Charlotte Petersen; SC, Gift of Charlotte Petersen. SC99.103.

612. Cha-Ki-Shi: Rearing Horse, ca. 1936
Pencil on paper, 9 x 12 (22.9 x 30.5)
Preparatory study of a rearing horse with two riders.
Charlotte Petersen; SC, Gift of Charlotte Petersen. SC99.102.

613. Cha-Ki-Shi: The Runner, ca. 1936
Conté on paper, 9 1/4 x 12 (23.5 x 30.5)
Study of a male figure facing left, wearing a headdress, loincloth,
leglets and moccasins. He holds a bundle of "inviting" sticks.
Signed lower right: CP
Charlotte Petersen; SC, Gift of Charlotte Petersen. SC99.134.

614. Cha-Ki-Shi: Studies of Cha-Ki-Shi, ca. 1936
Pencil on paper, 12 x 10 1/2 (30.5 x 26.7);
Images: 2 1/2 x 2 (6.4 x 5.1) [each]
Studies of the central character of the book *Cha-Ki-Shi*. The top
study shows a profile of a Meskwaki girl with a braid facing to the
right. The bottom one shows the same girl facing forward with
long earrings and a necklace.
Signed right: CP
Charlotte Petersen; SC, Gift of Charlotte Petersen. SC99.105.

**615. Cha-Ki-Shi: Stretching and Drying the Skins for
the Baby's New Dress,** ca. 1936
Conté on paper, 7 x 8 (17.8 x 20.3)
A concept study for an illustration of a young woman outdoors on
a small piece of hide stretched on the ground. Two larger stretched
hides are hung on wooden frames behind her.
Charlotte Petersen; SC, Gift of Charlotte Petersen. SC99.123.

**616. Cha-Ki-Shi: Stretching and Drying the Skins
for the Baby's New Dress,** ca. 1936
Conté on paper, 11 3/4 x 10 1/4 (29.8 x 26);
Image: 7 x 8 (17.8 x 20.3)
Study of a young woman working on a small piece of hide stretched
on the ground. A larger stretched hide is hung on a frame behind her.

Signed lower right: CP
Charlotte Petersen; SC, Gift of Charlotte Petersen. SC99.111.

617. Cha-Ki-Shi: Studies of Meskwaki Accessories, ca. 1936
Pencil and colored pencil on paper, 12 x 9 (30.5 x 22.9)
Preparatory studies of headdresses and a necklace for the book
Cha-Ki-Shi. Back of paper has rough geometrical patterns in bands.
Charlotte Petersen; SC, Gift of Charlotte Petersen. SC99.109ab.

618. Cha-Ki-Shi: Studies of Meskwaki Accessories, ca. 1936
Pencil and pastels on paper, 12 x 9 (30.5 x 22.9)
Preparatory studies of moccasins and headwear for the book *Cha-Ki-Shi*.
Charlotte Petersen; SC, Gift of Charlotte Petersen. SC99.100.

619. Cha-Ki-Shi: Study for the Cover, ca. 1936
Watercolor on paper, 11 x 8 1/2 (27.9 x 21.6);
Image: 7 1/4 x 4 5/8 (18.4 x 11.7)
Concept study for the cover of the book *Cha-Ki-Shi*, with a girl
wearing jewelry and a dress made of skins standing between two huts.
Signed lower right: CP
Charlotte Petersen; SC, Gift of Charlotte Petersen. SC99.133.

620. Cha-Ki-Shi: Study of Meskwaki Housing, ca. 1936
Watercolor on paper, 11 x 8 1/2 (27.9 x 21.6);
Image: 8 x 5 1/8 (20.3 x 13)
Study of stick hut for the book *Cha-Ki-Shi*.
Signed lower right: CP
Charlotte Petersen; SC, Gift of Charlotte Petersen. SC99.99.

621. Cha-Ki-Shi: Two Figures, ca. 1936
Pencil or conté on paper, 8 1/2 x 11 (21.6 x 27.9)
Study of two kneeling figures.
*Charlotte Petersen; Mary Petersen; CPC, Purchased by the
Christian Petersen Memorial Fund. UM92.19*

622. Cha-Ki-Shi: The Women Gather the Cattails, ca. 1936
Watercolor and pencil on paper, 9 3/4 x 9 (24.8 x 22.9)
Preparatory study for an illustration shows three figures: a young
man carrying nettles, a young man cutting them, and a woman laying
them out in neat rows. Although two of the figures are male, the
words "The women gather the cattails" is written in pencil on the back.
Signed lower right: CP
Charlotte Petersen; SC, Gift of Charlotte Petersen. SC99.110.

623. Cha-Ki-Shi: The Woman Sitting, ca. 1936
Pencil on paper, 11 x 8 1/2 (27.9 x 21.6)
Studies for illustration. Recto: A woman cooking over a fire near a
tree, with a girl holding a bowl out to her. Verso: "The woman
sitting," in pencil with various watercolor marks and words.
Signed lower right: CP
Charlotte Petersen; SC, Gift of Charlotte Petersen. SC99.118ab.

624. Farmer's Face, ca. 1936
Pencil and colored pencil on paper, 8 1/2 x 11 (21.6 x 27.9)
Two sketches of a farmer's face, chin resting on one hand; one
drawn in black pencil, the other in colored pencil.
*Charlotte Petersen; Mary Petersen; CPC, Purchased by the
Christian Petersen Memorial Fund. UM92.35.*

625. Professors' Conference, ca. 1936
Pencil or conté on paper, 8 1/2 x 11 (21.6 x 27.9)
Character sketches on the back of an American Association of University Professors conference sheet. Three rows: frontal, side, and back views of male heads.
CPC, Purchased from Mary Petersen with funds from the Christian Petersen Memorial Fund. UM92.29.

626. Workers, ca. 1936
Pencil or conté on paper, 8 1/2 x 11 (21.6 x 27.9)
Sketches of workers wielding picks and surveyors. Six characters.
Charlotte Petersen; Mary Petersen; CPC, Purchased by the Christian Petersen Memorial Fund. UM92.42.

627. Mary at Age One, 1937
Two engravings, one on paper, 9 1/2 x 9 3/4 (24.1 x 24.8), one on a paper folded into a card, 18 7/8 x 8 (47.9 x 20.3);
Image: 6 1/4 x 5 1/8 (15.9 x 13);
Copper plate: 6 1/4 x 5 1/8 x 1/32 (15.9 x 13 x 0.8)
Head view in profile of the artist's daughter.
Inscription at bottom of SC99.219: Mary, 1 yr. An engraving.
In ink at the top of SC99.276, "Greetings from Charlotte Christian and Mary Petersen."
Charlotte Petersen; SC, Gift of Charlotte Petersen. Engravings: SC99.219 and SC99.276. Plate: SC99.230.

628. Equitable of Iowa Companies Award, ca. late 1930s
Pencil or conté on paper, 8 1/2 x 11 (21.6 x 27.9)
Medallion circle with a man stabbing a dog, defending a woman crouched, holding a child. Concept for medallion.
Charlotte Petersen; Mary Petersen; CPC, Purchased by the Christian Petersen Memorial Fund. UM92.38a.

629. Amphitheater, ca. 1938
Pencil or conté on paper, 8 1/2 x 11 (21.6 x 27.9)
A sculpture centered on a semi-circular fountain.
Charlotte Petersen; Mary Petersen; CPC, Purchased by the Christian Petersen Memorial Fund. UM92.4a.

630. Amphitheater, ca. 1938
Pencil or conté on paper, 8 1/2 x 11 (21.6 x 27.9)
Courtyard with figures leading to a major sculpture.
Charlotte Petersen; Mary Petersen; CPC, Purchased by the Christian Petersen Memorial Fund. UM92.11.

631. Amphitheater: Concept Study, ca. 1938
Charcoal on paper, 8 1/2 x 11 (21.6 x 27.9)
Charcoal sketches of stepped panels, with center panel at the apex.
Charlotte Petersen; Mary Petersen; CPC, Purchased by the Christian Petersen Memorial Fund. UM92.13.

632. Amphitheater: Flame of Learning, ca. 1938
Brown pencil on paper, 14 x 17 (35.6 x 43.2)
Sketch of a sculpture for "flame of learning" central campus amphitheater.
Charlotte Petersen; Mary Petersen; CPC, Purchased by the Christian Petersen Memorial Fund. UM92.301.

633. Amphitheater: Iowa State Campanile, ca. 1948
Brown pencil on paper, 14 x 17 (35.6 x 43.2)
Amphitheater proposal with five panels for a proposed site south of the Campanile.

Charlotte Petersen; Mary Petersen; CPC, Purchased by the Christian Petersen Memorial Fund. UM92.299b.

634. Amphitheater: Light of Learning, 1938
Colored pencil on paper, 14 x 17 (35.6 x 43.2)
Sketch of a sculpture depicting a "light of learning" theme, possibly for his amphitheater idea.
Charlotte Petersen; Mary Petersen; CPC, Purchased by the Christian Petersen Memorial Fund. UM92.298.

635. Amphitheater: Sketch, ca. 1938
Pencil or conté on paper, 16 1/8 x 13 3/4 (41 x 34.9)
Sketch of a group of women. Depicts figures for campus entry or major amphitheater work on central campus.
CPC, Purchased from Mary Petersen with funds from the Christian Petersen Memorial Fund. UM92.217.

636. Amphitheater Dream, ca. 1938
Colored pencil on paper, 14 x 17 (35.6 x 43.2)
Sketch of Iowa State's campanile with a vision of an amphitheater in background.
Charlotte Petersen; Mary Petersen; CPC, Purchased by the Christian Petersen Memorial Fund. UM92.297.

Studies related to Petersen's trip to Kentucky in the summer of 1938.

637. Miles Bach
Pencil on paper, 10 1/2 x 7 1/2 (26.8 x 19.1)
Three-quarter frontal bust view of a man wearing a collared shirt, suspenders and a rimmed hat.
Inscription lower right: Miles Bach, Quicksands, Ky
Charlotte Petersen; SC, Gift of Charlotte Petersen. SC99.142.

638. Blackberry Picker
Pencil on paper, 7 3/8 x 10 3/8 (18.7 x 26.4)
Man wearing hat, shirt and suspenders, standing surrounded by large containers full of blackberries.
Inscription lower left: Jackson Co blackberry picker bet. Chrisbonow and Big Hill
Charlotte Petersen; SC, Gift of Charlotte Petersen. SC99.143.

639. Blackberry Picker
Pencil on paper, 10 3/8 x 7 3/8 (26.4 x 8.7)
Three-quarters bust view of a man wearing overalls, shirt unbuttoned at the neck, and a hat with the rim turned down.
Inscription in pencil at lower right: Blackberry picker
Charlotte Petersen; SC, Gift of Charlotte Petersen. SC99.160.

640. Boy
Brown pencil on paper, 12 3/4 x 13 3/4 (32.4 x 34.9)
Profile sketch of a small boy.
Charlotte Petersen; Mary Petersen; CPC, Purchased by the Christian Petersen Memorial Fund. UM92.259.

641. Kelly Caldwell
Pencil on paper, 7 1/2 x 10 3/8 (19 x 26.4)
Sketch of a man wearing an engineer's hat, shirt, and pants with suspenders, walking away with a bag slung over his left shoulder.
Inscription lower right: Kelly Caldwell
Charlotte Petersen; SC, Gift of Charlotte Petersen. SC99.146.

Studies related to Petersen's trip to Kentucky, continued

642. Charlotte Sitting on a Rock at a Picnic
Colored pencil on paper, 4 x 6 (10.2 x 15.2)
Sketch of Charlotte seated, with her head resting on one hand, by a stream with her feet in the water.
Charlotte Petersen; Mary Petersen; CPC, Purchased by the Christian Petersen Memorial Fund. UM92.57.

643. Kentucky Building
Pencil on paper, 7 3/8 x 10 3/8 (19 x 26.4)
A small building with one window behind a group of trees.
Charlotte Petersen; SC, Gift of Charlotte Petersen. SC99.152.

644. Kentucky Church
Pencil on paper, 10 3/8 x 7 1/4 (26.4 x 18.4)
A small wooden church with a steeple and cross on top, in hills surrounded by trees.
Charlotte Petersen; SC, Gift of Charlotte Petersen. SC99.159.

645. Man
Charcoal on paper, 13 3/4 x 16 (34.9 x 40.6)
Drawing of a male, frontal view.
CPC, Purchased from Mary Petersen with funds from the Christian Petersen Memorial Fund. UM92.260.

646. Man
Pencil or conté on paper, 7 3/4 x 11 (19.7 x 27.9)
Profile sketch.
Charlotte Petersen; Mary Petersen; CPC, Purchased by the Christian Petersen Memorial Fund. UM92.65.

647. Man with Upraised Arms
Pencil on paper, 10 3/8 x 6 3/4 (26.4 x 17.1)
Full front view of a standing man with upraised arms (hands are unfinished) and his mouth open. He seems to be telling a story or preaching.
Charlotte Petersen; SC, Gift of Charlotte Petersen. SC99.148.

648. Frank LeRonde McVey
Pencil or conté on paper, 8 1/2 x 11 (21.6 x 27.9)
Study of Frank LeRonde McVey, President of the University of Kentucky.
Inscription: BELIEVE IN TRUTH, PROTEST AGAINST ERROR, LEAD MEN BY REASON RATHER THAN FORCE
Charlotte Petersen; Mary Petersen; CPC, Purchased by the Christian Petersen Memorial Fund. UM92.28.

649. Frank LeRonde McVey
Pencil or conté on paper, 8 1/2 x 11 (21.6 x 27.9)
Male figure seated in profile chair, leaning forward and turning to viewer. Three quick studies.
Charlotte Petersen; Mary Petersen; CPC, Purchased by the Christian Petersen Memorial Fund. UM92.1b.

650. Frank LeRonde McVey
Purple pencil on paper, 9 3/4 x 14 (24.8 x 35.6)
Study of Frank LeRonde McVey and text in a rectangle.
Charlotte Petersen; Mary Petersen; CPC, Purchased by the Christian Petersen Memorial Fund. UM92.264.

651. Frank LeRonde McVey
Pencil or conté on paper, 8 1/2 x 11 (21.6 x 27.9)
Study of a seated Frank LeRonde McVey, fifth president of The University of Kentucky.
Charlotte Petersen; Mary Petersen; CPC, Purchased by the Christian Petersen Memorial Fund. UM92.27.

652. Frank LeRonde McVey
Pencil or conté on paper, 8 1/2 x 11 (21.6 x 27.9)
Study of a seated Frank LeRonde McVey, fifth president of The University of Kentucky.
Charlotte Petersen; Mary Petersen; CPC, Purchased by the Christian Petersen Memorial Fund. UM92.26.

653. Frank LeRonde McVey
Pink pencil on paper, 9 3/4 x 14 (24.8 x 35.6)
Study of a seated Frank LeRonde McVey.
Charlotte Petersen; Mary Petersen; CPC, Purchased by the Christian Petersen Memorial Fund. UM92.263.

654. Frank LeRonde McVey Seated
Pencil or conté on paper, 9 3/4 x 14 (24.8 x 35.6)
Charlotte Petersen; Mary Petersen; CPC, Purchased by the Christian Petersen Memorial Fund. UM92.267.

655. Men on a Bench
Pencil on paper, 15 3/4 x 12 (40 x 30.5)
Three men in hats sitting on a bench along a wall of a building. Two are listening to the third man talking.
Charlotte Petersen; SC, Gift of Charlotte Petersen. SC99.149.

656. Mother Earth
Pencil or conté on paper, 8 1/2 x 11 (21.6 x 27.9)
Sketch of a very pregnant, nude woman, possibly for *Mother Earth*.
Charlotte Petersen; Mary Petersen; CPC, Purchased by the Christian Petersen Memorial Fund. UM92.33.

657. Mountain Mother
Pencil or conté on paper, 13 3/4 x 16 3/4 (34.9 x 42.5)
Sketch of a woman with three children.
Charlotte Petersen; Mary Petersen; CPC, Purchased by the Christian Petersen Memorial Fund. UM92.277.

658. Mountain Mother and Child
Pencil or conté on paper, 8 1/2 x 11 (21.6 x 27.9)
Small sketch of a woman with a child at her feet.
Charlotte Petersen; Mary Petersen; CPC, Purchased by the Christian Petersen Memorial Fund. UM92.37b.

659. Preparing Food
Pencil on paper, 7 1/2 x 10 1/2 (19.1 x 26.7)
Three women and one man are around a table in front of a house. They are gathering bowls and food on the table.
Charlotte Petersen; SC, Gift of Charlotte Petersen. SC99.147.

660. Seated Woman
Pencil on paper, 10 1/2 x 7 1/4 (26.7 x 18.4)
Seated woman wearing a hat and dress and facing left.
Charlotte Petersen; SC, Gift of Charlotte Petersen. SC99.145.

661. Arthur Sewell
Pencil on paper, 10 3/8 x 7 1/4 (26.4 x 18.7)
Bust view of a young man in a collared shirt looking at the viewer.
Inscription at bottom: Arthur Sewell
Charlotte Petersen; SC, Gift of Charlotte Petersen. SC99.150.

662. Storyteller

Pencil on paper, 10 3/8 x 7 3/8 (26.4 x 19)

Three figures in foreground walking toward a group of seated figures in the shade of a tree. One man stands with arms upraised in front of them with his back to the viewer.

Charlotte Petersen; SC, Gift of Charlotte Petersen. SC99.144.

663. Two Drawings

Pencil on paper mounted on paper, 13 3/4 x 11 1/8 (34.9 x 28.3); Images: 5 1/2 x 3 1/4 (14 x 8.3) and 5 3/4 x 3 3/4 (14.6 x 9.5)

Two sketches, both cut out of a sketch book and attached to a sheet of paper. Woman seated on chair with a child on her lap at upper right. Speaking or singing man in overalls standing with his mouth open.

Charlotte Petersen; SC, Gift of Charlotte Petersen. SC99.153.

664. Two Women in Prayer

Pencil on paper mounted on paper, 10 1/2 x 7 3/8 (26.7 x 19)

Two standing women, surrounded by hills, wearing long dresses. One wears a bonnet. Both have hands together in prayer. Inscription at bottom: "I've prayed all over these hills!"

Charlotte Petersen; SC, Gift of Charlotte Petersen. SC99.158.

665. Uncle Bill

Pencil on paper, 11 x 7 3/4 (27.9 x 19.7)

Man outside a doorway, seated in a chair which he's tilting back. Inscription lower right: Uncle Bill, W.H. Reams, Orlando, Ky

Charlotte Petersen; SC, Gift of Charlotte Petersen. SC99.156.

666. Uncle John

Pencil on paper, 10 3/8 x 7 1/4 (26.4 x 18.4)

Three-quarter bust view of an older man with whiskers, wearing a rimmed hat, shirt and overalls. Inscription at bottom: Uncle John, Quicksands, Ky

Charlotte Petersen; SC, Gift of Charlotte Petersen. SC99.154.

667. Uncle Miles Bach

Pencil on paper, 10 1/2 x 7 1/8 (26.7 x 18.6)

Bust view of a man in profile facing left and wearing a rimmed hat. Inscription lower right: Uncle Miles Bach, Quicksands, Ky

Charlotte Petersen; SC, Gift of Charlotte Petersen. SC99.141.

668. Uncle Miles Bach

Pencil on paper, 10 1/2 x 7 3/8 (26.7 x 18.6)

Full view of a man seated in a chair with his legs crossed, wearing glasses and reading a paper. Inscription lower right: Uncle Miles Bach, Quicksands, Ky

Charlotte Petersen; SC, Gift of Charlotte Petersen. SC99.155.

669. Woman Hanging Laundry

Pencil on paper, 7 1/2 x 8 (19.1 x 20.3)

A scantily clad woman in profile, standing and hanging laundry on a clothesline hung between trees. A young boy watches her from the bottom right corner.

Charlotte Petersen; SC, Gift of Charlotte Petersen. SC99.151.

670. Woman in Bonnet

Pencil on paper, 10 3/8 x 7 1/8 (26.2 x 18.1)

Profile view of a woman facing left, wearing a collared dress and her hair in a bun at the back of her neck.

Charlotte Petersen; SC, Gift of Charlotte Petersen. SC99.157.

671. Young Boy Sitting on a Step

Charcoal on paper, 16 x 14 (40.6 x 35.6)

Charlotte Petersen; Mary Petersen, Beverly Hills, Florida.

672. Boy Scout Fountain, ca. 1938

Pencil or conté on paper, 8 1/2 x 11 (21.6 x 27.9)

Rapid sketch of what could have been Petersen's idea for an Ames Brookside Park Fountain, including an image of a Boy Scout.

Charlotte Petersen; Mary Petersen; CPC, Purchased by the Christian Petersen Memorial Fund. UM92.133.

673. Children's Fountain: Concept, 1938

Pencil or conté on paper, 14 x 17 (35.6 x 43.2)

Study of a sculpture. An idea for Brookside Park fountain.

Charlotte Petersen; Mary Petersen; CPC, Purchased by the Christian Petersen Memorial Fund. UM92.303.

674. Children's Fountain Base: Proposal for Brookside Park, ca. 1938

Charcoal on paper, 8 1/2 x 11 (21.6 x 27.9)

Side and top views of an octagonal shaped fountain with bas-relief panels.

Charlotte Petersen; Mary Petersen; CPC, Purchased by the Christian Petersen Memorial Fund. UM92.12.

675. Liberty Dime, 1938

Pencil or conté on paper, 8 1/2 x 11 (21.6 x 27.9)

Circle with the bust of a man and the writing; "Liberty & 1938."

CPC, Purchased from Mary Petersen with funds from the Christian Petersen Memorial Fund. UM92.2.

676. Mother and a Child, ca. 1938

Pencil or conté on paper, 12 x 18 (30.5 x 45.7)

Charlotte Petersen; Mary Petersen; CPC, Purchased by the Christian Petersen Memorial Fund. UM92.308.

677. Mother Feeding a Baby, ca. 1938

Colored pencil on paper, 12 x 18 (30.5 x 45.7)

CPC, Purchased from Mary Petersen with funds from the Christian Petersen Memorial Fund. UM92.310.

678. Mother and Two Children, ca. 1938

Pencil on paper, 12 x 18 (30.5 x 45.7)

Charlotte Petersen; Mary Petersen; CPC, Purchased by the Christian Petersen Memorial Fund. UM92.309.

679. Pegasus, ca. 1938

Pencil or conté on paper, 8 1/2 x 11 (21.6 x 27.9)

Circle with a horse jumping out of a hexagon design in the center.

Charlotte Petersen; Mary Petersen; CPC, Purchased by the Christian Petersen Memorial Fund. UM92.3.

680. Pioneer Woman, ca. 1938

Charcoal on paper, 14 x 17 (35.6 x 43.2)

Studies for *Pioneer Woman.* The model may have been Hazel Allen Lipa, professor of English at Iowa State College.

Charlotte Petersen; Mary Petersen; CPC, Purchased by the Christian Petersen Memorial Fund. UM92.290.

681. Pioneer Woman: Study, 1938

Pencil or conté on paper, 12 x 18 (30.5 x 45.7)

Charlotte Petersen; Mary Petersen; CPC, Purchased by the Christian Petersen Memorial Fund. UM92.311.

682. Pioneer Woman: Study, ca. 1938
Pencil or conté on paper, 8 x 10 (20.3 x 25.4)
Inscription: For Pioneer Woman
CPC, Purchased from Mary Petersen with funds from the Christian Petersen Memorial Fund. UM92.354.

683. Pioneer Woman: Study, ca. 1938
Pencil or conté on paper, 8 x 10 (20.3 x 25.4)
Charlotte Petersen; Mary Petersen; CPC, Purchased by the Christian Petersen Memorial Fund. UM92.355.

684. Lenore Sullivan, ca. 1938
Pencil and colored pencil on paper, 4 x 6 (10.2 x 15.2)
Lenore Sullivan, friend of the Petersens, with her feet in a stream.
Charlotte Petersen; Mary Petersen; CPC, Purchased by the Christian Petersen Memorial Fund. UM92.56.

685. Two Sketches of a Person Working with a Microscope, ca. 1938
Pencil or conté on paper, 8 1/2 x 11 (21.6 x 27.9)
Two sketches in a circular frame of a person working with a microscope at a lab table or bench.
Charlotte Petersen; Mary Petersen; CPC, Purchased by the Christian Petersen Memorial Fund. UM92.120.

686. Charlotte and Mary, ca. 1939
Brown pencil on paper, 16 3/4 x 13 3/4 (42.5 x 34.9)
CPC, Purchased from Mary Petersen with funds from the Christian Petersen Memorial Fund. UM92.223.

687. Hello Beautiful, 1939
Booklet, 7 1/4 x 5 (23.8 x 16.4)
A twenty-page booklet with "Motives by Mary, Words by Mommie, Drawings by Daddy." Includes fifteen illustrations of Mary at age three. Self-published in unknown quantity by the Petersen family for Christmas 1939.
Charlotte Petersen; CPC, Gift of Charlotte Petersen.

688. Mary and Charlotte, ca. 1939
Pencil on paper, 11 3/4 x 8 3/4 (29.8 x 22.2)
The back of the artist's wife seated with arm around their daughter who is turned playing with a cat. All are on a blanket.
Charlotte Petersen; SC, Gift of Charlotte Petersen. SC99.174.

689. Petersen Christmas Card, ca. 1939
Pencil or conté on paper, 8 1/2 x 11 (21.6 x 27.9)
Three studies, all are of Mary Petersen as a small child, after a bath, playing a toy piano, and with their dog Tink. Two of them are in borders.
Charlotte Petersen; Mary Petersen; CPC, Purchased by the Christian Petersen Memorial Fund. UM92.131.

690. Mary Petersen and Her Friends, ca. late 1930s
Pencil or conté on paper, 13 3/4 x 16 3/4 (34.9 x 42.5)
Seven sketches of Mary Petersen and her friends.
Charlotte Petersen; Mary Petersen; CPC, Purchased by the Christian Petersen Memorial Fund. UM92.215.

691. Bears, ca. 1930s
Pencil or conté on paper, 9 x 12 (22.9 x 30.5)
Sketches of two bears standing up. One sketch of bear on all four legs. Probably in preparation for Yellowstone National Park bronze sculpture.
Charlotte Petersen; Mary Petersen; CPC, Purchased by the Christian Petersen Memorial Fund. UM92.166.

692. Fountain, ca. 1930s
Charcoal on paper, 9 x 12 (22.9 x 30.5)
Sketch of a sculpture and fountain with figures, of which two have upraised arms.
Charlotte Petersen; Mary Petersen; CPC, Purchased by the Christian Petersen Memorial Fund. UM92.186.

693. Fountain, ca. 1930s
Pencil or conté on paper, 8 1/2 x 11 (21.6 x 27.9)
A rapid sketch concept for a fountain.
Charlotte Petersen; Mary Petersen; CPC, Purchased by the Christian Petersen Memorial Fund. UM92.25.

694. Fountain, ca. 1930s
Charcoal on paper, 9 x 12 (22.9 x 30.5)
Sketch of an adult and child by a three-stepped fountain pool.
Charlotte Petersen; Mary Petersen; CPC, Purchased by the Christian Petersen Memorial Fund. UM92.154.

695. Fountain Studies, ca. 1930s
Pencil or conté on paper, 8 1/2 x 11 (21.6 x 27.9)
Various assortment of figure motion studies for a fountain.
Charlotte Petersen; Mary Petersen; CPC, Purchased by the Christian Petersen Memorial Fund. UM92.4b.

696. Marston Hall: Concept Study, ca. 1930s
Pencil or conté on paper, 16 3/4 x 13 3/4 (42.5 x 34.9)
Sketch of Marston Hall, with figure sculptures placed in entry alcoves.
Charlotte Petersen; Mary Petersen; CPC, Purchased by the Christian Petersen Memorial Fund. UM92.243a.

697. Men Doing Farm Work, ca. 1930s
Pencil or conté on paper, 8 1/2 x 11 (21.6 x 27.9)
Four sketches including one of a man pouring from a long handled pan, others of men cutting grain and doing other farmwork, and one of a bull with a farmhand.
Charlotte Petersen; Mary Petersen; CPC, Purchased by the Christian Petersen Memorial Fund. UM92.43.

698. Portrait Sketch, ca. 1930s
Pencil on paper, 11 7/8 x 8 3/4 (30.2 x 22.2)
Sketch of a bas-relief with a bust view of a man wearing a tie and glasses in the upper section, and a blank box in the bottom third for an inscription.
Charlotte Petersen; SC, Gift of Charlotte Petersen. SC99.207.

699. Seated Woman, ca. 1930s
Pencil and purple colored pencil on paper, 11 3/4 x 8 3/4 (29.8 x 22.2)
Sketch of the back of a woman seated on the floor.
Charlotte Petersen; SC, Gift of Charlotte Petersen. SC99.172.

700. Woman Holding Child, ca. 1930s
Pencil or conté on paper, 8 1/2 x 11 (21.6 x 27.9)
Three sketches of sculptures, the largest is of a woman holding a child.
Charlotte Petersen; Mary Petersen; CPC, Purchased by the Christian Petersen Memorial Fund. UM92.24.

701. Charlotte, ca. 1940
Pencil on paper, 9 x 12 (22.9 x 30.5)
Sketch of Petersen's wife, Charlotte, frontal view, reading a book on her lap.
Charlotte Petersen; Mary Petersen; CPC, Purchased by the Christian Petersen Memorial Fund. UM92.156.

702. Charlotte, ca. 1940

Pencil or conté on paper, 9 x 12 (22.9 x 30.5)

Sketch of Charlotte Petersen, the artist's wife, full length, side profile, wearing a coat and hat.

Charlotte Petersen; Mary Petersen; CPC, Purchased by the Christian Petersen Memorial Fund. UM92.161.

703. Charlotte and Mary, ca. 1940

Pencil on paper, 8 1/4 x 9 (21 x 22.9)

Sketch depicting the artist's wife Charlotte with daughter Mary on her lap. Both are asleep in a chair.

Joanne M. Hansen; Neva Petersen, Rochester, Minnesota.

704. Children, ca. 1939–1941

Pencil or conté on paper, 13 3/4 x 16 3/4 (34.9 x 42.5)

Sketches of a sculpture with children.

Charlotte Petersen; Mary Petersen; CPC, Purchased by the Christian Petersen Memorial Fund. UM92.212.

Studies related to *Fountain of the Four Seasons*, 1940

705. Farmer and Pigs

Red pencil on paper, 9 x 12 (22.9 x 30.5)

Study of a farmer with two pigs in a circular frame. Concept for *Fountain of the Four Seasons.*

Charlotte Petersen; Mary Petersen; CPC, Purchased by the Christian Petersen Memorial Fund. UM92.162b.

706. Preliminary Study

Red pencil and conté on paper, 9 x 12 (22.9 x 30.5)

Four studies of an ear of corn in stylistic motifs and different stages of development.

Charlotte Petersen; Mary Petersen; CPC, Purchased by the Christian Petersen Memorial Fund. UM92.159a.

707. Preliminary Study

Pencil or conté on paper, 9 x 12 (22.9 x 30.5)

A farmer and a hog.

CPC, Purchased from Mary Petersen with funds from the Christian Petersen Memorial Fund. UM92.159b.

708. Preliminary Study

Red pencil on paper, 9 x 12 (22.9 x 30.5)

Study of a farmer, pigs, outline of the State of Iowa with two pigs and an ear of corn within.

Charlotte Petersen; Mary Petersen; CPC, Purchased by the Christian Petersen Memorial Fund. UM92.162a.

709. Studies

Pencil or conté on paper, 9 x 12 (22.9 x 30.5)

Studies of a cat, Native American, an ear of corn, and three arrows.

Charlotte Petersen; Mary Petersen; CPC, Purchased by the Christian Petersen Memorial Fund. UM92.168.

710. Woman

Pencil or conté on paper, 11 3/4 x 18 (29.8 X 45.7)

Sketches of a nude woman in motion. Appears to be a preliminary drawing.

CPC, Purchased from Mary Petersen with funds from the Christian Petersen Memorial Fund. UM92.281a.

711. Woman

Pencil or conté on paper, 11 3/4 x 18 (29.8 x 45.7)

Sketches of a nude woman in motion, likely in preparation for the *Fountain of the Four Seasons.*

Charlotte Petersen; Mary Petersen; CPC, Purchased by the Christian Petersen Memorial Fund. UM92.281b.

712. Site Sketch

Pencil or conté on paper, 9 x 12 (22.9 x 30.5)

Sketch of a building comparable to the north elevation of the Iowa State Memorial Union. Probably a siting sketch.

Charlotte Petersen; Mary Petersen; CPC, Purchased by the Christian Petersen Memorial Fund. UM92.158.

713. Ernest N. Lindstrom Memorial Plaque, 1940

Pencil or conté on paper, 14 x 17 (35.6 x 43.2)

Study for memorial plaque of professor in Iowa State's Genetics Department.

Charlotte Petersen; Mary Petersen; CPC, Purchased by the Christian Petersen Memorial Fund. UM92.292.

714. G. Samuel Nichols, ca. 1940

Pencil or conté on paper, 12 x 18 (30.5 x 45.7)

Pastor of Collegiate Methodist Church in Ames, Iowa, from 1935 to 1960. Preliminary study for bas-relief.

Charlotte Petersen; Mary Petersen; CPC, Purchased by the Christian Petersen Memorial Fund. UM92.324.

715. G. Samuel Nichols, ca. 1940

Pencil or conté on paper, 12 x 18 (30.5 x 45.7)

Pastor of Collegiate Methodist Church in Ames, Iowa, from 1935 to 1960. Preliminary study for bas-relief.

Charlotte Petersen; Mary Petersen; CPC, Purchased by the Christian Petersen Memorial Fund. UM92.323.

716. Two Dancers, ca. 1940

Pencil or conté on paper, 8 1/2 x 11 (21.6 x 27.9)

Charlotte Petersen; Mary Petersen; CPC, Purchased by the Christian Petersen Memorial Fund. UM92.36.

717. House and Street, ca. 1940

Pencil or conté on paper, 18 x 11 3/4 (45.7 x 29.8)

Sketch of a house and street.

Inscription on verso: 2 elms, Wisteria Vine, Japanese Lilac, 4 Japanese yews, 1 lilac kitchen door, 2 highbush cranberry.

Charlotte Petersen; Mary Petersen; CPC, Purchased by the Christian Petersen Memorial Fund. UM92.191a.

718. Mary with a Doll, ca. 1940

Engraving on paper, 4 7/8 x 2 7/8;

Copper plate used in printing it: 4 1/2 x 2 1/4¼ x 1/32 (11.4 x 5.7 x 0.1)

The artist's daughter wearing a dress and holding and gazing at a doll.

Charlotte Petersen; SC, Gift of Charlotte Petersen. Engraving: SC99.162. Plate: SC99.229.

719. Mary with a Doll, ca. 1940

Pencil and ink on paper, 5 1/2 x 3 3/4 (14 x 9.5)

Preliminary study for engraving of artist's daughter wearing a dress and holding and gazing at a doll.

Charlotte Petersen; SC, Gift of Charlotte Petersen. SC99.169.

720. Margaret Morgan, ca. 1940
Pencil on paper, 8 1/2 x 11 (21.6 x 27.9)
Sketch of daughter of the Petersens' neighbors.
Margaret Morgan Hauptman, Harrisburg, Illinois.

721. War (After the Blitz War): Nude Woman, ca. 1940
Brown pencil on paper, 16 3/4 x 13 3/4 (42.5 x 34.9)
CPC, Purchased from Mary Petersen with funds from the Christian Petersen Memorial Fund. UM92.224.

722. Cornhusker: Preparatory Study, ca. 1941
Pencil or conté on paper, 11 x 14 (27.9 x 35.6)
Preparatory study of two men taking a step grasping a stalk, and a sketch of a man leaning on another man standing next to a box, with a detail of a head.
Charlotte Petersen; Mary Petersen; CPC, Purchased by the Christian Petersen Memorial Fund. UM92.262.

723. Charlotte and Mary, ca. 1941
Ink and pencil on paper, 3 3/4 x 6 3/4 (9.5 x 17.1);
Image: 3 1/2 x 3 1/8 (8.9 x 7.9)
Sketch of Charlotte seated on a chair with a cigarette in her right hand, held up away from her daughter Mary, who is reading a book on her lap.
Charlotte Petersen; SC, Gift of Charlotte Petersen. SC99.277.

724. Children, ca. 1941
Brown pencil on paper, 16 3/4 x 13 3/4 (42.5 x 34.9)
Profile sketch of two children for portrait bas-relief.
Charlotte Petersen; Mary Petersen; CPC, Purchased by the Christian Petersen Memorial Fund. UM92.248.

725. 4-H Calf: Preparatory Study, ca. 1941
Colored pencil on paper, 9 3/4 x 14 (24.8 x 35.6)
Study of a newborn calf.
Charlotte Petersen; Mary Petersen; CPC, Purchased by the Christian Petersen Memorial Fund. UM92.269.

726. Mary, ca. 1941
Pencil on paper, 11 3/4 x 11 7/8 (29.8 x 30.2);
Image: 6 3/4 x 3 (17.1 x 7.6)
Sketch of the artist's daughter Mary standing and looking down.
Charlotte Petersen; SC, Gift of Charlotte Petersen. SC99.178.

727. Mary Petersen, ca. 1941
Pencil or conté on paper, 8 1/2 x 11 (21.6 x 27.9)
Two sketches of Mary Petersen reading and writing.
Charlotte Petersen; Mary Petersen; CPC, Purchased by the Christian Petersen Memorial Fund. UM92.130.

728. Merry Christmas, Happy New Year, ca. 1941
Two linocut prints on colored paper, 6 1/2 x 4 3/4 (16.5 x 12.1) [each];
Images: 5 3/8 x 4 1/8 (13.7 x 10.5) [each];
Incised linoleum used to make linocut: 5 1/2 x 4 3/8 x 1/4 (14 x 11.1 x 0.6)
Reverse image of Charlotte, Christian, and Mary Petersen standing and looking in shock at a globe on a pedestal as explosions come out of two sides. "Merry Christmas, Happy New Year" at top and "The Petersens" in linocut at bottom.
Charlotte Petersen; SC, Gift of Charlotte Petersen. Prints: SC99.164 and SC99.165. Block: SC99.290.

729. Boy and a Girl and Flowers, ca. 1942
Colored pencil on paper, 10 x 13 3/4 (25.4 x 34.9)
Charlotte Petersen; Mary Petersen; CPC, Purchased by the Christian Petersen Memorial Fund. UM92.188b.

Studies related to *Marriage Ring*, 1942

730. Children
Pencil or conté on paper, 14 x 17 (40.6 x 43.2)
Studies of children playing at Iowa State's Child Development lab.
CPC, Purchased from Mary Petersen with funds from the Christian Petersen Memorial Fund. UM92.287.

731. Concept Study
Pencil or conté on paper, 16 3/4 x 13 3/4 (42.5 x 34.9)
This series shows the progression of ideas for shapes of the reflecting pool, themes for figures, and orientation with the south facade of MacKay Hall.
Charlotte Petersen; Mary Petersen; CPC, Purchased by the Christian Petersen Memorial Fund. UM92.228b.

732. Concept Study
Pencil or conté on paper, 16 3/4 x 13 3/4 (42.5 x 34.9)
Study of a fountain.
Charlotte Petersen; Mary Petersen; CPC, Purchased by the Christian Petersen Memorial Fund. UM92.229.

733. Concept Study
Pencil or conté on paper, 16 3/4 x 13 3/4 (42.5 x 34.9)
Study of three nude figures standing at the edge of a rectangular reflecting pool.
Charlotte Petersen; Mary Petersen; CPC, Purchased by the Christian Petersen Memorial Fund. UM92.230.

734. Figure Studies
Pencil or conté on paper, 16 3/4 x 13 3/4 (42.5 x 34.9)
Study depicting woman and children seated and standing around a pool basin.
Charlotte Petersen; Mary Petersen; CPC, Purchased by the Christian Petersen Memorial Fund. UM92.219.

735. Figure Studies
Pencil or conté on paper, 8 1/2 x 11 (21.6 x 27.9)
Studies of three figures, one kneeling and holding a plant, another one lying down, and the third sitting and holding a plant.
Charlotte Petersen; Mary Petersen; CPC, Purchased by the Christian Petersen Memorial Fund. UM92.121

736. Figure Studies
Pencil or conté on paper, 16 3/4 x 13 3/4 (42.5 x 34.9)
Seven studies of children playing. When Petersen was mulling over ideas for the Home Economics fountain sculpture, his wife, Charlotte, suggested he observe children playing at the child development lab nursery school. He later used those ideas for the fountain proposal.
CPC, Purchased from Mary Petersen with funds from the Christian Petersen Memorial Fund. UM92.234.

737. Figures

Pencil or conté on paper, 16 3/4 x 13 3/4 (42.5 x 34.9)
Study of three figures.
CPC, Purchased from Mary Petersen with funds from the
Christian Petersen Memorial Fund. UM92.231.

738. Preliminary Concept

Pencil or conté on paper, 13 3/4 x 16 3/4 (34.9 x 42.5)
Study of a fountain and MacKay Hall.
Charlotte Petersen; Mary Petersen; CPC, Purchased by the
Christian Petersen Memorial Fund. UM92.209.

739. Preliminary Concept Study

Charcoal on paper, 16 3/4 x 13 3/4 (42.5 x 34.9)
Study of a fountain.
Charlotte Petersen; Mary Petersen; CPC, Purchased by the
Christian Petersen Memorial Fund. UM92.218.

740. Preliminary Concept Study

Pencil or conté on paper, 16 1/2 x 13 3/4 (41.9 x 34.9)
Detailed study of one of many preliminary concepts. Depicts
round and rectangular pools.
Charlotte Petersen; Mary Petersen; CPC, Purchased by the
Christian Petersen Memorial Fund. UM92.249.

741. Preliminary Study

Pencil and blue pencil on paper, 16 3/4 x 13 3/4 (42.5 x 34.9)
Depicts two female students sitting atop a wall around a
circular pool.
Charlotte Petersen; Mary Petersen; CPC, Purchased by the
Christian Petersen Memorial Fund. UM92.227a.

742. Preliminary Study

Pencil or conté on paper, 16 3/4 x 13 3/4 (42.5 x 34.9)
Study of fountain.
CPC, Purchased from Mary Petersen with funds from the
Christian Petersen Memorial Fund. UM92.227b.

743. Preliminary Study

Pencil or conté on paper, 16 3/4 x 13 3/4 (42.5 x 34.9)
Charlotte Petersen; Mary Petersen; CPC, Purchased by the
Christian Petersen Memorial Fund. UM92.235.

744. Preliminary Study

Pencil or conté on paper, 16 3/4 x 13 3/4 (42.5 x 34.9)
Study depicting rectangular and circular pools with small children.
Charlotte Petersen; Mary Petersen; CPC, Purchased by the
Christian Petersen Memorial Fund. UM92.236.

745. Preliminary Study

Pencil or conté on paper, 13 3/4 x 16 3/4 (34.9 x 42.5)
Study of two children at play on the edge of a circular pool.
Charlotte Petersen; Mary Petersen; CPC, Purchased by the
Christian Petersen Memorial Fund. UM92.279.

746. Study

Pencil or conté on paper, 16 3/4 x 13 3/4 (42.5 x 34.9)
Preliminary study of MacKay Hall and fountain.
Charlotte Petersen; Mary Petersen; CPC, Purchased by the
Christian Petersen Memorial Fund. UM92.228a.

747. Study

Pencil or conté on paper, 14 x 7 (35.6 x 17.8)
Concept study for siting of fountain and sculptures at MacKay Hall.
CPC, Purchased from Mary Petersen with funds from the
Christian Petersen Memorial Fund. UM92.386.

748. Study

Pencil or conté on paper, 14 x 7 (35.6 x 17.8)
Concept study siting of fountain and sculptures at MacKay Hall.
Charlotte Petersen; Mary Petersen; CPC, Purchased by the
Christian Petersen Memorial Fund. UM92.387.

749. Study of MacKay Hall

Pencil or conté on paper, 16 1/2 x 13 3/4 (41.9 x 34.9)
Study of proposed fountain.
Charlotte Petersen; Mary Petersen; CPC, Purchased by the
Christian Petersen Memorial Fund. UM92.222.

750. Men of Two Wars: Soldier, 1942

Pencil or conté on paper, 9 x 12 (22.9 x 30.5)
Seated profile, front view and various other sketches of a soldier.
Probably a preliminary sketch for *Men of Two Wars.*
Charlotte Petersen; Mary Petersen; CPC, Purchased by the
Christian Petersen Memorial Fund. UM92.175.

751. Mary on a Swing, ca. 1942

Watercolor on linocut print on paper, 6 7/8 x 5 1/4 (17.5 x 13.3);
Image: 6 x 4 1/4 (15.2 x 10.8);
Incised linoleum nailed to wooden block used to make linocut:
5 1/2 x 4 3/8 x 1 1/8 (14 x 11.1 x 2.9)
The artist's daughter wearing winter clothes with a hood and scarf.
She is on a swing.
Inscription at top: Merry Christmas
Inscription at bottom: The Petersens
Charlotte Petersen; SC, Gift of Charlotte Petersen.
Print: SC99.163 . Block SC99.291.

752. Murray Children: Preparatory Sketch, ca. 1942

Pencil or conté on paper, 15 3/4 x 13 3/4 (40 x 34.9)
Three children in profile.
Charlotte Petersen; Mary Petersen; CPC, Purchased by the
Christian Petersen Memorial Fund. UM92.247.

753. Five Divisions of the College, early 1940s

Pencil or conté on paper, 8 3/4 x 11 7/8 (22.2 x 30.2)
Sketches of two semicircles with figures and a sculpture and
lectern on the center.
Charlotte Petersen; Mary Petersen; CPC, Purchased by the
Christian Petersen Memorial Fund. UM92.71.

754. Mary Petersen, early 1940s

Two engravings on paper, 4 3/8 x 3 3/8 (11.1 x 8.6);
Image: 4 x 3 (10.2 x 7.6);
Copper plate, 4 x 3 x 1/8 (10.2 x 7.6 x 0.3)
The artist's daughter in profile in a short-sleeved dress, with
braids tied at the back of her head with ribbon.
Charlotte Petersen; SC, Gift of Charlotte Petersen.
Engravings: SC99.287a and SC99.288. Plate: SC99.287b.

Studies related to *Library Boy and Girl,* 1943

755. Figure Study
Pencil or conté on paper, 8 3/4 x 11 7/8 (22.2 x 30.2)
Study of seated boy reading a book.
Charlotte Petersen; Mary Petersen; CPC, Purchased by the Christian Petersen Memorial Fund. UM92.68.

756. Preliminary Studies
Pencil on paper, 6 7/8 x 4 7/8 (17.5 x 12.4)
Frontal and profile studies for *Library Boy.*
Charlotte Petersen; SC, Gift of Charlotte Petersen. SC99.235.

757. Preliminary Studies
Pencil or conté on paper, 16 3/4 x 13 3/4 (42.5 x 34.9)
Studies of a religious sculpture, and a preliminary study of *Library Girl.*
Charlotte Petersen; Mary Petersen; CPC, Purchased by the Christian Petersen Memorial Fund. UM92.243b.

758. Preliminary Studies
Pencil or conté on paper, 16 3/4 x 13 3/4 (42.5 x 34.9)
Studies of a seated girl with a book on her lap.
Charlotte Petersen; Mary Petersen; CPC, Purchased by the Christian Petersen Memorial Fund. UM92.253.

759. Preliminary Studies
Pencil or conté on paper, 16 3/4 x 13 3/4 (42.5 x 34.9)
Studies of *Library Boy and Girl,* and sketches of *War* sculpture.
Charlotte Petersen; Mary Petersen; CPC, Purchased by the Christian Petersen Memorial Fund. UM92.252.

760. Armory, ca. 1944
Pencil or conté on paper, 14 x 17 (35.6 x 43.2)
Sketch of the Armory for a war memorial concept.
Charlotte Petersen; Mary Petersen; CPC, Purchased by the Christian Petersen Memorial Fund. UM92.30.2

761. Let the Voice of Silence Speak for Those Who Made the Sacrifice for God and Country, ca. 1944
Pencil or conté on paper, 12 x 18 (30.5 x 45.7)
Image of children, a World War II memorial concept.
Inscription: LET THE VOICE OF SILENCE SPEAK FOR THOSE LOVED ONES WHO MADE THE SACRIFICE FOR GOD AND COUNTRY
Charlotte Petersen; Mary Petersen; CPC, Purchased by the Christian Petersen Memorial Fund. UM92.318.

762. Mary Petersen, ca. 1944
Pencil or conté on paper, 8 1/2 x 11 (21.6 x 27.9)
Two sketches of Mary Petersen in braids in rectangular frames, one in profile facing right.
CPC, Purchased from Mary Petersen with funds from the Christian Petersen Memorial Fund. UM92.124.

763. Price of Victory (Fallen Soldier), ca. 1944
Charcoal on paper, 8 3/4 x 11 7/8 (22.2 x 30.2)
Five sketches of a fallen soldier; possibly a war memorial.
Charlotte Petersen; Mary Petersen; CPC, Purchased by the Christian Petersen Memorial Fund. UM92.95.

764. Returning Wounded World War II Veteran, ca. 1944
Pencil or conté on paper, 16 3/4 x 13 3/4 (42.5 x 34.9)
Sketch of returning a wounded World War II veteran to his mother.
Charlotte Petersen; Mary Petersen; CPC, Purchased by the Christian Petersen Memorial Fund. UM92.239.

765. Soldiers, ca. 1944
Pencil or conté on paper, 13 3/4 x 16 3/4 (34.9 x 42.5)
Sketch of soldiers for a World War II Memorial.
Charlotte Petersen; Mary Petersen; CPC, Purchased by the Christian Petersen Memorial Fund. UM92.207.

766. Unknown Prisoner: Concept Sketch, ca. 1944
Pencil on paper, 9 x 12 (22.9 x 30.5)
Study of a T-shaped monument.
Charlotte Petersen; Mary Petersen; CPC, Purchased by the Christian Petersen Memorial Fund. UM92.96.

767. Unknown Prisoner: Preparatory Study, ca. 1944
Pencil or conté on paper, 9 x 12 (22.9 x 30.5)
Study of a man tied to a cross — unknown prisoner of war. Notation by Charlotte Petersen on cover of the sketch book states that it was for a competition for sculptors.
Charlotte Petersen; Mary Petersen; CPC, Purchased by the Christian Petersen Memorial Fund. UM92.359.

768. War Memorial Monument, ca. 1944
Pencil or conté on paper, 12 x 18 (30.5 x 45.7)
Sketch of a war memorial monument, with a woman.
Charlotte Petersen; Mary Petersen; CPC, Purchased by the Christian Petersen Memorial Fund. UM92.317.

769. Wounded Veteran, ca. 1944
Pencil or conté on paper, 16 3/4 x 13 3/4 (42.5 x 34.9)
Sketch of a wounded veteran returning and being greeted by his mother.
Charlotte Petersen; Mary Petersen; CPC, Purchased by the Christian Petersen Memorial Fund. UM92.232.

770. Wounded Veteran, ca. 1944
Pencil or conté on paper, 13 3/4 x 16 3/4 (34.9 x 42.5)
Sketches of a wounded World War II veteran returning home to his family.
CPC, Purchased from Mary Petersen with funds from the Christian Petersen Memorial Fund. UM92.211.

771. Father William Clark, ca. 1945
Pencil on paper, 10 1/2 x 9 (26.7 x 22.9)
Drawing of a priest who instructed Petersen when he was in the process of converting to Catholicism. Shows a priest reading from a breviary.
Signed: Christian Petersen
Virginia Slater, Ames, Iowa.

772. Crouching Figure, ca. 1945
Pencil or conté on paper, 8 x 10 (20.3 x 25.4)
Charlotte Petersen; Mary Petersen; CPC, Purchased by the Christian Petersen Memorial Fund. UM92.340.

773. Mary with Braids, ca. 1945
Brown pencil on paper,
13 x 11 (33 x 27.9)
The artist's daughter Mary
with braids in her hair.
Signed: Christian Petersen
*Charlotte Petersen; Mary
Petersen, Beverly Hills,
Florida.*

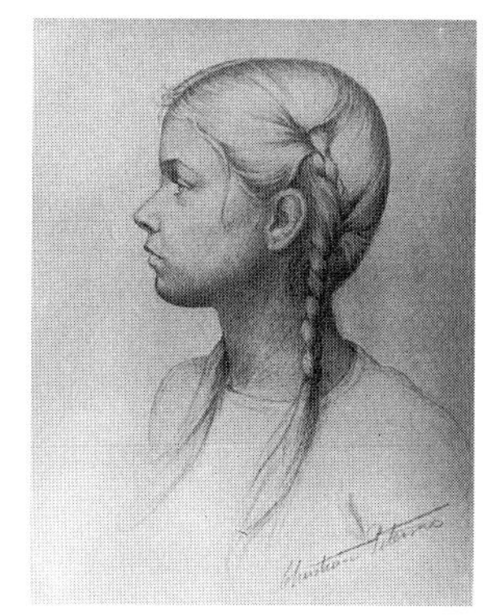

774. Mother and Baby, ca. 1945
Pencil or conté on paper, 12 x 18 (30.5 x 45.7)
Profile view of a mother with a baby on her lap.
*Charlotte Petersen; Mary Petersen; CPC, Purchased by the
Christian Petersen Memorial Fund. UM92.306.*

Religious Figures, ca. 1945
Colored pencil on connected pages from a sketchbook, 5 x 3 (12.7 x 7.6)

775. Rough sketch of Saint Cecilia standing on a pedestal,
holding a lyre.
*Charlotte Petersen; SC, Gift of Charlotte Petersen.
SC99.279.*

776. Sculpture of a woman with a boy standing in front of
her on a pedestal.
*Charlotte Petersen; SC, Gift of Charlotte Petersen.
SC99.280.*

777. Sketch of standing robed figure with her hands on the
shoulders of a child.
*Charlotte Petersen; SC, Gift of Charlotte Petersen.
SC99.281.*

778. Recto: Robed male standing on a pedestal.
Verso: Two heads in profile facing left in a round medallion.
*Charlotte Petersen; SC, Gift of Charlotte Petersen.
SC99.282ab.*

779. Saint Cecilia Church Figures, 1945
Pencil or conté on paper, 8 1/2 x 11 (21.6 x 27.9)
Study of a plaque depicting a person kneeling and holding a flower;
plaque is mounted on a brick column.
*Charlotte Petersen; Mary Petersen; CPC, Purchased by the
Christian Petersen Memorial Fund. UM92.60.*

780. Woman Looking at Helmet and Sword, mid 1940s
Pencil and colored pencil on paper, 12 x 9 (30.5 x 22.9)
A woman in a dress with her hands together in front of her, and a
large cross behind her. She is looking down at a helmet and sword,
all on a base.
Charlotte Petersen; SC, Gift of Charlotte Petersen. SC99.225.

781. Campus Entrance, ca. 1946
Pencil or conté on paper, 16 3/4 x 13 3/4 (42.5 x 34.9)
Sketch of some sculptures along a road. A concept for a campus entry.
*Charlotte Petersen; Mary Petersen; CPC, Purchased by the
Christian Petersen Memorial Fund. UM92.250.*

782. Campus Entrance, ca. 1946
Pencil or conté on paper, 14 x 17 (35.6 x 43.2)
Several sketches of standing students with graduation caps and gowns,
and a farmer holding a calf. Concept for campus entrance.
*Charlotte Petersen; Mary Petersen; CPC, Purchased by the
Christian Petersen Memorial Fund. UM92.304.*

783. Campus Entrance, ca. 1946
Charcoal on paper, 14 x 17 (35.6 x 43.2)
Sketches of standing graduating students.
*Charlotte Petersen; Mary Petersen; CPC, Purchased by the
Christian Petersen Memorial Fund. UM92.305.*

784. Campus Entrance, ca. 1946
Charcoal on paper, 13 3/4 x 16 3/4 (34.9 x 42.5)
Five sketches depicting students in graduation attire.
*Charlotte Petersen; Mary Petersen; CPC, Purchased by the
Christian Petersen Memorial Fund. UM92.395.*

785. Campus Entrance, 1946
Pencil or conté on paper, 8 1/2 x 11 (21.6 x 27.9)
Female in long gown with arms on two profile figures in gowns,
mortarboards, and diplomas, both facing to center. Against geo-
metric background.
*Charlotte Petersen; Mary Petersen; CPC, Purchased by the
Christian Petersen Memorial Fund. UM92.5.*

Studies related to *Madonna of the Schools*, 1946

786. Concept Studies
Pencil or conté on paper, 8 3/4 x 11 7/8 (22.2 x 30.2)
Studies of children and nun holding hands circling a three-
tiered fountain, with five studies of side elevation, three from
the top view, and two other details.
*Charlotte Petersen; Mary Petersen; CPC, Purchased by the
Christian Petersen Memorial Fund. UM92.77a.*

787. Concept Studies
Pencil or conté on paper, 16 3/4 x 13 3/4 (42.5 x 34.9)
Studies of a religious sculpture.
*Charlotte Petersen; Mary Petersen; CPC, Purchased by the
Christian Petersen Memorial Fund. UM92.233.*

788. Concept Study
Pencil or conté on paper, 12 x 18 (30.5 x 45.7)
Study of a fountain sculpture with children and nuns.
*Charlotte Petersen; Mary Petersen; CPC, Purchased by the
Christian Petersen Memorial Fund. UM92.374.*

789. Figure Study
Pencil or conté on paper, 8 3/4 x 11 7/8 (22.2 x 30.2)
Study of figures around a fountain: two women, two
children, and a nun.
*Charlotte Petersen; Mary Petersen; CPC, Purchased by the
Christian Petersen Memorial Fund. UM92.76a.*

Studies related to *Madonna of the Schools*, continued

790. Figure study
Pencil or conté on paper, 8 3/4 x 11 7/8 (22.2 x 30.2)
Study of the artist's daughter Mary. A preliminary study for children of *Madonna of the Schools.*
Charlotte Petersen; Mary Petersen; CPC, Purchased by the Christian Petersen Memorial Fund. UM92.86.

791. Figure Studies
Brown pencil on paper, 8 1/2 x 10 1/2 (21.6 x 26.7)
Two studies of a woman kneeling, framed by a brick column.
Charlotte Petersen; Mary Petersen; CPC, Purchased by the Christian Petersen Memorial Fund. UM92.62.

792. Figure Studies
Pencil or conté on paper, 8 1/2 x 11 (21.6 x 27.9)
Studies of four figures, three kneeling.
Charlotte Petersen; Mary Petersen; CPC, Purchased by the Christian Petersen Memorial Fund. UM92.58.

793. Figure Studies
Pencil or conté on paper, 13 3/4 x 16 3/4 (34.9 x 42.5)
Studies of religious figures around a circular pool.
Charlotte Petersen; Mary Petersen; CPC, Purchased by the Christian Petersen Memorial Fund. UM92.76.

794. Figure Studies
Colored pencil on paper, 8 x 10 (20.3 x 25.4)
Seated Virgin Mary holding Christ on her lap, with children standing near.
Charlotte Petersen; Mary Petersen; CPC, Purchased by the Christian Petersen Memorial Fund. UM92.33.1

795. Figure Studies
Colored pencil on paper, 8 x 10 (20.3 x 25.4)
Virgin Mary, Jesus, and several children.
Charlotte Petersen; Mary Petersen; CPC, Purchased by the Christian Petersen Memorial Fund. UM92.332.

796. Figure Studies
Colored pencil on paper, 8 x 10 (20.3 x 25.4)
Standing Virgin Mary holding Christ, with children standing by her.
Charlotte Petersen; Mary Petersen; CPC, Purchased by the Christian Petersen Memorial Fund. UM92.334.

797. Five Studies
Pencil or conté on paper, 8 3/4 x 11 7/8 (22.2 x 30.2)
Five small studies of children, nuns, and a priest surrounding a pool.
Charlotte Petersen; Mary Petersen; CPC, Purchased by the Christian Petersen Memorial Fund. UM92.76b.

798. Fountain Study
Pencil or conté on paper, 5 3/4 x 7 3/4 (14.6 x 19.7)
Study of fountain concept and landscape.
Charlotte Petersen; Mary Petersen; CPC, Purchased by the Christian Petersen Memorial Fund. UM92.113.

799. Mary Petersen
Pencil or conté on paper, 8 3/4 x 11 7/8 (22.2 x 30.2)
Study of the artist's daughter Mary. A preliminary study for children of *Madonna of the Schools.*

Charlotte Petersen; Mary Petersen; CPC, Purchased by the Christian Petersen Memorial Fund. UM92.88.

800. Mary Petersen
Pencil or conté on paper, 8 3/4 x 11 7/8 (22.2 x 30.2)
Study of the artist's daughter Mary. A preliminary study for children of *Madonna of the Schools.*
Charlotte Petersen; Mary Petersen; CPC, Purchased by the Christian Petersen Memorial Fund. UM92.89.

801. Mary Petersen
Pencil or conté on paper, 8 3/4 x 11 7/8 (22.2 x 30.2)
Study of the artist's daughter, Mary Petersen. A preliminary study for children of *Madonna of the Schools.*
Charlotte Petersen; Mary Petersen; CPC, Purchased by the Christian Petersen Memorial Fund. UM92.87.

802. Preliminary Study
Brown pencil on paper, 8 1/2 x 10 1/2 (21.6 x 26.7)
Study of person kneeling and holding a flower.
Charlotte Petersen; Mary Petersen; CPC, Purchased by the Christian Petersen Memorial Fund. UM92.61.

803. Studies of Children
Pencil or conté on paper, 8 1/2 x 10 1/2 (21.6 x 26.7)
Two studies of children and a study of a rock post.
Charlotte Petersen; Mary Petersen; CPC, Purchased by the Christian Petersen Memorial Fund. UM92.63.

804. Dmitri Metroupolis [*sic*]: Preliminary Studies, ca. 1946
Pencil or charcoal on paper, 16 x 8 (40.6 x 20.3)
Three studies of a conductor.
Charlotte Petersen; Mary Petersen; CPC, Purchased by the Christian Petersen Memorial Fund. UM92.272.

805. Dmitri Metroupolis [*sic*]: Study, ca. 1946
Pencil or conté on paper, 16 x 8 (40.6 x 20.3)
Study of a man in front of a sheet of music, believed to be Dimitri Mitropoulos, conductor of the Minneapolis Symphony.
Charlotte Petersen; Mary Petersen; CPC, Purchased by the Christian Petersen Memorial Fund. UM92.273.

Studies related to *Conversations*, 1946–1947

806. Aerial Studies
Pencil on paper, 12 1/4 x 15 1/4 (31.1 x 38.7)
Study of an aerial view of the locations of trees, stop signs, and the ISC sign with distances between them. Measurements and elevations are marked.
Inscription at bottom: Scale 1" = 20'
Charlotte Petersen; SC, Gift of Charlotte Petersen. SC99.213.

807. Campus Entry
Pencil or conté on paper, 16 3/4 x 13 3/4 (42.5 x 34.9)
Five studies for monumental sculptural markers. One is a woman and the others are groups. Concepts for campus entry and *Conversations.*
Charlotte Petersen; Mary Petersen; CPC, Purchased by the Christian Petersen Memorial Fund. UM92.251a.

808. Figure Study
Pencil or conté on paper, 8 x 10 (20.3 x 25.4)
Seated figure of a girl.
Charlotte Petersen; Mary Petersen; CPC, Purchased by the Christian Petersen Memorial Fund. UM92.341.

809. Figure Study
Pencil or conté on paper, 8 x 10 (20.3 x 25.4)
Figures leaning against a wall.
Charlotte Petersen; Mary Petersen; CPC, Purchased by the Christian Petersen Memorial Fund. UM92.347.

810. Figure Studies
Pencil or conté on paper, 8 x 10 (20.3 x 25.4)
Five studies of a seated, nude woman.
CPC, Purchased from Mary Petersen with funds from the Christian Petersen Memorial Fund. UM92.343.

811. Figure Study
Pencil or conté on paper, 8 x 10 (20.3 x 25.4)
Woman seated looking at a book.
Charlotte Petersen; Mary Petersen; CPC, Purchased by the Christian Petersen Memorial Fund. UM92.344.

812. Figure Study
Pencil or conté on paper, 8 x 10 (20.3 x 25.4)
Man and woman leaning on a wall.
Charlotte Petersen; Mary Petersen; CPC, Purchased by the Christian Petersen Memorial Fund. UM92.345.

813. Figure Study
Pencil or conté on paper, 8 x 10 (20.3 x 25.4)
Study of a man, and a woman who is holding a child on her hip.
Charlotte Petersen; Mary Petersen; CPC, Purchased by the Christian Petersen Memorial Fund. UM92.348.

814. Figure Study
Pencil or conté on paper, 8 x 10 (20.3 x 25.4)
Study of a man, and a woman who is holding a child on her hip.
Charlotte Petersen; Mary Petersen; CPC, Purchased by the Christian Petersen Memorial Fund. UM92.349.

815. Figure Study
Pencil or conté on paper, 9 x 12 (22.9 x 30.5)
Woman seated with hands clasped around knees.
Charlotte Petersen; Mary Petersen; CPC, Purchased by the Christian Petersen Memorial Fund. UM92.360.

816. Figure Study
Colored pencil on paper, 12 x 18 (30.5 x 45.7)
Woman seated with arms around legs.
Charlotte Petersen; Mary Petersen; CPC, Purchased by the Christian Petersen Memorial Fund. UM92.376.

817. Figures
Pencil or conté on paper, 5 3/4 x 7 3/4 (14.6 x 19.7)
Study of three figures.
Charlotte Petersen; Mary Petersen; CPC, Purchased by the Christian Petersen Memorial Fund. UM92.108.

818. Intersection
Pencil or conté on paper, 16 3/4 x 13 3/4 (42.5 x 34.9)
Study of an intersection. Concept for campus entry.

Charlotte Petersen; Mary Petersen; CPC, Purchased by the Christian Petersen Memorial Fund. UM92.225.

819. Man with Glasses
Pencil or conté on paper, 16 3/4 x 13 3/4 (42.5 x 34.9)
Study of a man with glasses.
Charlotte Petersen; Mary Petersen; CPC, Purchased by the Christian Petersen Memorial Fund. UM92.244.

820. Man and Woman
Brown pencil on paper, 4 x 6 (10.2 x 15.2)
Study of a man and woman.
Charlotte Petersen; Mary Petersen; CPC, Purchased by the Christian Petersen Memorial Fund. UM92.48.

821. Man and Woman
Brown pencil on paper, 4 x 6 (10.2 x 15.2)
Study of a couple leaning on a wall, studying a book.
Charlotte Petersen; Mary Petersen; CPC, Purchased by the Christian Petersen Memorial Fund. UM92.55.

822. Man and Woman
Pencil or conté on paper, 8 x 10 (20.3 x 25.4)
Man, and a woman holding a child on her lap.
CPC, Purchased from Mary Petersen with funds from the Christian Petersen Memorial Fund. UM92.350.

823. Preliminary Figure Studies
Pencil or conté on paper, 8 3/4 x 11 7/8 (22.2 x 30.2)
Study of three people grouped together looking at a book and of a single person sitting and looking at a book.
Charlotte Petersen; Mary Petersen; CPC, Purchased by the Christian Petersen Memorial Fund. UM92.70.

824. Preliminary Study
Pencil or conté on paper, 13 3/4 x 16 3/4 (34.9 x 42.5)
Study of clustered sculptures and corner detail of Lincoln Way and Beach where Petersen proposed a major sculpture grouping for the entrance to Iowa State College campus.
Charlotte Petersen; Mary Petersen; CPC, Purchased by the Christian Petersen Memorial Fund. UM92.210.

825. Preliminary Studies
Pencil or conté on paper, 14 x 17 (35.6 x 43.2)
Three studies for *Conversations* and/or campus entry wall at Lincoln Way and Beach intersection.
Charlotte Petersen; Mary Petersen; CPC, Purchased by the Christian Petersen Memorial Fund. UM92.300.

826. Preliminary Studies
Pencil or conté on paper, 8 x 10 (20.3 x 25.4)
Two pencil studies with two figures in each.
Charlotte Petersen; Mary Petersen; CPC, Purchased by the Christian Petersen Memorial Fund. UM92.351.

827. Preliminary Studies
Pencil or conté on paper, 8 x 10 (20.3 x 25.4)
Two studies of seated woman.
Charlotte Petersen; Mary Petersen; CPC, Purchased by the Christian Petersen Memorial Fund. UM92.342.

Studies related to *Conversations*, continued

828. Preliminary Studies

Pencil or conté on paper, 14 x 7 (35.6 x 17.8)

Study of three people.

Charlotte Petersen; Mary Petersen; CPC, Purchased by the Christian Petersen Memorial Fund. UM92.378.

829. Preliminary Study

Charcoal on paper, 14 x 17 (35.6 x 43.2)

Woman sitting on the ground with knees pulled toward her and her hands clasped around her knees.

Charlotte Petersen; Mary Petersen; CPC, Purchased by the Christian Petersen Memorial Fund. UM92.291.

830. Studies of People

Pencil or conté on paper, 16 3/4 x 13 3/4 (42.5 x 34.9)

Studies of people. Concepts for campus entry, with the notation: "food — clothing — ed — arts — ag — animal husbandry — engineering."

Charlotte Petersen; Mary Petersen; CPC, Purchased by the Christian Petersen Memorial Fund. UM92.226.

831. Studies for Wall

Pencil on paper, 12 x 9 1/2 (30.5 x 24.1)

Distance study with measurements and calculations for brick wall between groupings.

Charlotte Petersen; SC, Gift of Charlotte Petersen. SC99.218.

832. Studies for Wall

Pencil on paper, 12 x 9 1/2 (30.5 x 24.1)

Instructions and measurements for building the brick wall.

Charlotte Petersen; SC, Gift of Charlotte Petersen. SC99.216.

833. Studies for Wall

Pencil on graph paper, 12 x 9 1/2 (30.5 x 24.1)

Lines with measurements of distances for the wall construction. Inscriptions: "Boy & Girl," "stone," "foundation walls," "footings," and "stone coping"

Charlotte Petersen; SC, Gift of Charlotte Petersen. SC99.214.

834. Studies for Wall

Pencil on paper, 11 7/8 x 9 1/2 (30.2 x 24.1)

Study of proposed dimensions for a bench, wall, stone, foundation and footing. Includes measurements, instructions, and the words, "Two Girls" and "Prone Figure" in pencil.

Charlotte Petersen; SC, Gift of Charlotte Petersen. SC99.222.

835. Studies for Wall

Pencil on paper, 12 x 9 1/2 (30.5 x 24.1)

Studies and measurements for bases for the three groupings of figures.

Charlotte Petersen; SC, Gift of Charlotte Petersen. SC99.215.

836. Studies for wall

Pencil on paper, 9 1/2 x 12 (24.1 x 30.5)

Studies for proposed wall, with measurements and instructions for its construction including weights of the sculpture groupings in tons.

Inscription: Center of gravity of statues should be in line with center of gravity of footing.

Charlotte Petersen; SC, Gift of Charlotte Petersen. SC99.220.

837. Two Men

Pencil or conté on paper, 8 3/4 x 11 7/8 (22.2 x 30.2)

Study of two young men, one is sitting and the other is standing with objects in his hands. Stairsteps indicate an entry of foyer.

Charlotte Petersen; Mary Petersen; CPC, Purchased by the Christian Petersen Memorial Fund. UM92.69.

838. Christ, ca. 1947

Pencil on paper, 11 x 8 1/2 (27.9 x 21.6)

Three-quarter length standing Christ with outstretched arms. His garment has an inverted triangular shaped front. The robe and pose are similar to *Christ the King* at Regis High School in Cedar Rapids, Iowa, and may be an early concept.

Charlotte Petersen; SC, Gift of Charlotte Petersen. SC99.194.

839. Home, ca. 1947

Pencil or conté on paper, 18 x 11 3/4 (45.7 x 29.8)

Smaller sketch of a home in Gilbert, Iowa.

Charlotte Petersen; Mary Petersen; CPC, Purchased by the Christian Petersen Memorial Fund. UM92.191b.

840. Madonna and Child, ca. 1947

Conté on paper, 11 3/4 x 8 3/4 (29.8 x 22.2)

Standing Madonna with child Jesus.

Charlotte Petersen; SC, Gift of Charlotte Petersen. SC99.170.

841. Madonna and Child, ca. 1947

Pencil and conté on paper, 11 3/4 x 8 3/4 (29.8 x 22.2)

Robed, standing Madonna in profile with her arm and garment around a smaller figure. Both are on a pedestal.

Charlotte Petersen; SC, Gift of Charlotte Petersen. SC99.181.

842. Iowa State College Alumni Medal: Group of People, ca. 1948

Brown pencil on paper, 13 3/4 x 16 3/4 (34.9 x 42.5)

Study of a group of people in three circles with a rectangular frame.

Charlotte Petersen; Mary Petersen; CPC, Purchased by the Christian Petersen Memorial Fund. UM92.204.

843. George Washington Carver: Preparatory Sketch, ca. 1949

Pencil or conté on paper, 5 3/4 x 9 (14.6 x 22.7)

Preparatory study for George Washington Carver sculpture.

CPC, Purchased from Mary Petersen with funds from the Christian Petersen Memorial Fund. UM92.112.

844. Christ, ca. 1949

Pencil or conté on paper, 5 3/4 x 9 (14.6 x 22.7)

Two sketches of Christ with a sash tied around his waist, and an image of Christ.

Charlotte Petersen; Mary Petersen; CPC, Purchased by the Christian Petersen Memorial Fund. UM92.111.

845. Christ, ca. 1949

Pencil or conté on paper, 12 x 18 (30.5 x 45.7)

Sketch of Christ with outstretched hands.

CPC, Purchased from Mary Petersen with funds from the Christian Petersen Memorial Fund. UM92.328a.

846. Christ, ca. 1949
Pencil or conté on paper, 14 x 17 (35.6 x 43.2)
Charlotte Petersen; Mary Petersen; CPC, Purchased by the Christian Petersen Memorial Fund. UM92.391.

847. Saint Francis of Assisi, ca. 1949
Pencil on yellow paper, 11 x 8 1/2 (27.9 x 21.6)
Sketch of Saint Francis with an arm out and birds landing on him. The head of the robed figure is in profile and has a halo.
Charlotte Petersen; SC, Gift of Charlotte Petersen. SC99.184.

848. Saint Francis of Assisi, ca. 1949
Pencil on paper, 11 x 8 1/2 (27.9 x 21.6)
Sketch of Saint Francis standing with outstretched arms. Birds are landing on his hands. His robe is tied at the waist and he has a halo. Inscription at bottom: 1250 No Central Park Ave
Charlotte Petersen; SC, Gift of Charlotte Petersen. SC99.186.

849. Saint Francis of Assisi, ca. 1949
Pencil on paper, 11 x 8 1/2 (27.9 x 21.6)
Sketch of Saint Francis with a tie around his waist. His arms are upstretched and a bird is about to land in his right hand.
Charlotte Petersen; SC, Gift of Charlotte Petersen. SC99.191.

850. Saint Francis of Assisi, ca. 1949
Pencil or conté on paper, 8 3/4 x 11 7/8 (22.2 x 30.2)
Charlotte Petersen; Mary Petersen; CPC, Purchased by the Christian Petersen Memorial Fund. UM92.77b.

851. Saint Francis of Assisi, ca. 1949
Pencil on paper, 11 7/8 x 8 3/4 (30.2 x 22.2)
Two sketches (one small and one large) of a side of two figures, one standing and holding a bird and one seated and looking toward a bird. Both are on pedestals.
Charlotte Petersen; SC, Gift of Charlotte Petersen. SC99.200.

852. Saint Francis of Assisi: Preliminary Sketch, ca. 1949
Pencil on paper, 11 x 8 1/2 (27.9 x 21.6)
Sketch of a bas-relief with a profile of Saint Francis holding one bird in his left hand as another lands in his right hand. Lines representing text are marked on bottom half of sketch of relief.
Charlotte Petersen; SC, Gift of Charlotte Petersen. SC99.195.

Studies related to *Saint Francis Xavier,* 1949

853. Base Panel Study
Violet pencil on paper, 9 x 12 (22.9 x 30.5)
Study of a man seated on a long bench wall with his arms around three children.
Charlotte Petersen; Mary Petersen; CPC, Purchased by the Christian Petersen Memorial Fund. UM92.167.

854. Concept Study
Pencil or conté on paper, 8 3/4 x 11 7/8 (22.2 x 30.2)
Study of a priest kneeling and praying; an island and a ship are in the background.
Charlotte Petersen; Mary Petersen; CPC, Purchased by the Christian Petersen Memorial Fund. UM92.74.

855. Concept Study
Pencil or conté on paper, 8 3/4 x 11 7/8 (22.2 x 30.2)
Highly detailed study of a sculpture of Saint Francis Xavier, with the base being a map of his travels.
Charlotte Petersen; Mary Petersen; CPC, Purchased by the Christian Petersen Memorial Fund. UM92.84.

856. Figure Studies
Pencil or conté on paper, 8 3/4 x 11 7/8 (22.2 x 30.2)
Close-up study of head and of figure sculpture.
Charlotte Petersen; Mary Petersen; CPC, Purchased by the Christian Petersen Memorial Fund. UM92.90.

857. Figure Studies
Pencil or conté on paper, 8 3/4 x 11 7/8 (22.2 x 30.2)
Three versions of Saint Francis Xavier, one seated and two standing with one arm in raised position.
CPC, Purchased from Mary Petersen with funds from the Christian Petersen Memorial Fund. UM92.93.

858. Figure Studies
Pencil or conté on paper, 8 x 10 (20.3 x 25.4)
Studies, one of a man standing and one of a man kneeling.
Charlotte Petersen; Mary Petersen; CPC, Purchased by the Christian Petersen Memorial Fund. UM92.358.

859. Figure Studies
Pencil or conté on paper, 14 x 17 (35.6 x 43.2)
Five studies of a monk, possibly Saint Francis Xavier.
Charlotte Petersen; Mary Petersen; CPC, Purchased by the Christian Petersen Memorial Fund. UM92.392.

860. Figure Study
Pencil or conté on paper, 8 3/4 x 11 7/8 (22.2 x 30.2)
Saint Francis Xavier holding a cross in the air.
Charlotte Petersen; Mary Petersen; CPC, Purchased by the Christian Petersen Memorial Fund. UM92.83.

861. Figure Study
Pencil or conté on paper, 8 3/4 x 11 7/8 (22.2 x 30.2)
Saint Francis Xavier with children.
Charlotte Petersen; Mary Petersen; CPC, Purchased by the Christian Petersen Memorial Fund. UM92.85.

862. Preliminary Study
Pencil or conté on paper, 8 3/4 x 11 7/8 (22.2 x 30.2)
His right hand holds a cross with his arm extended in the air. Left hand holds a book.
Charlotte Petersen; Mary Petersen; CPC, Purchased by the Christian Petersen Memorial Fund. UM92.78.

863. Preliminary Studies
Blue pencil on paper, 8 3/4 x 11 7/8 (22.2 x 30.2)
Studies of a sculpture of Saint Francis Xavier. One is standing on pedestal, the other is kneeling with hands in praying position.
Charlotte Petersen; Mary Petersen; CPC, Purchased by the Christian Petersen Memorial Fund. UM92.91.

864. Study of a Priest
Pencil or conté on paper, 8 3/4 x 11 7/8 (22.2 x 30.2)
Study of a priest holding a cross in the air.
Charlotte Petersen; Mary Petersen; CPC, Purchased by the Christian Petersen Memorial Fund. UM92.73.

865. Study of Saint Holding a Book
Pencil or conté on paper, 8 3/4 x 11 7/8 (22.2 x 30.2)
Charlotte Petersen; Mary Petersen; CPC, Purchased by the Christian Petersen Memorial Fund. UM92.82.

Studies related to *Saint Francis Xavier,* continued

866. Study of Saint Holding a Cross
Pencil or conté on paper, 8 3/4 x 11 7/8 (22.2 x 30.2)
Charlotte Petersen; Mary Petersen; CPC, Purchased by the Christian Petersen Memorial Fund. UM92.80.

867. Study of a Ship
Pencil or conté on paper, 8 1/2 x 11 (21.6 x 27.9)
Ship in a rectangular frame for base panels of *Saint Francis Xavier.*
Charlotte Petersen; Mary Petersen; CPC, Purchased by the Christian Petersen Memorial Fund. UM92.117.

868. Studies for Bas-Reliefs
Pencil or conté on paper, 12 x 18 (30.5 x 45.7)
Three studies of Christ for bas-reliefs at the base of *Saint Francis Xavier.*
Charlotte Petersen; Mary Petersen; CPC, Purchased by the Christian Petersen Memorial Fund. UM92.373.

869. Studies for Panels
Pencil or conté on paper, 8 3/4 x 11 7/8 (22.2 x 30.2)
Study of a priest blessing a boy while another boy waits behind him. Several boys in the background.
Charlotte Petersen; Mary Petersen; CPC, Purchased by the Christian Petersen Memorial Fund. UM92.75.

870. Two Studies
Pencil or conté on paper, 8 3/4 x 11 7/8 (22.2 x 30.2)
Charlotte Petersen; Mary Petersen; CPC, Purchased by the Christian Petersen Memorial Fund. UM92.79.

871. Two Studies
Pencil or conté on paper, 8 3/4 x 11 7/8 (22.2 x 30.2)
Charlotte Petersen; Mary Petersen; CPC, Purchased by the Christian Petersen Memorial Fund. UM92.81.

872. Boy, ca. 1940s
Charcoal on paper, 8 1/2 x 11 (21.6 x 27.9)
Detailed sketch of a boy in profile.
Charlotte Petersen; Mary Petersen; CPC, Purchased by the Christian Petersen Memorial Fund. UM92.119.

873. Charlotte, ca. 1940s
Pencil or conté on paper, 9 1/4 x 11 1/2 (23.5 x 29.2)
Sketch of Charlotte resting in bed, head in profile on pillow, with covers pulled over her arm.
Charlotte Petersen; Mary Petersen; CPC, Purchased by the Christian Petersen Memorial Fund. UM92.274b.

874. J.C. Cunningham Sleeping, ca. 1940s
Watercolor on paper, 9 3/4 x 9 7/8 (24.8 x 25.1)
A man lying underneath of a tree. The image is of Petersen's friend, J. C. Cunningham, taking a nap while they were on a canoe trip. A rare medium for Petersen.
Charlotte Petersen; Mary Petersen; CPC, Purchased by the Christian Petersen Memorial Fund. UM92.147.

875. Farm Scene, ca. 1940s
Colored pastels and pencil on paper, 13 3/4 x 16 1/2 (34.9 x 41.9)
Two men working at unloading grain or hay into farm machinery from wagons which have horses hitched to them. Barn and windmill center right, corn in background left center, and fence across lower right and center section.
Charlotte Petersen; Mary Petersen; CPC, Gift of Mary Petersen. UM92.612.

876. Farmer and His Wife Looking over Their Land, ca. 1940s
Colored pencil on paper, 10 x 13 3/4 (25.4 x 34.9)
Long range perspective sketch of a farmer and his wife looking over their land. Cattle in fields and fence along road. Barn and windmill in background.
Charlotte Petersen; Mary Petersen; CPC, Purchased by the Christian Petersen Memorial Fund. UM92.188a.

877. Future Dormitory, ca. 1940s
Pencil on paper, 13 3/8 x 16 3/8 (34 x 41.6)
Elevation sketches of an area on the Iowa State College campus, with trees and distances marked.
Inscription: Scale 1" = 20'0" / Future Dormitory
Charlotte Petersen; SC, Gift of Charlotte Petersen. SC99.226ab.

878. Girl Playing with a Dog, ca. 1940s
Colored pencil on paper, 14 x 17 (35.6 x 43.2)
Sketch of a sculpture of a girl playing with a dog.
Charlotte Petersen; Mary Petersen; CPC, Purchased by the Christian Petersen Memorial Fund. UM92.294.

879. Girl with a Sick Pet, ca. 1940s
Pencil on paper, 12 x 9 3/4 (30.5 x 24.8)
Three sketches of two figures on bases. In all of them, a man is helping a young girl with a sick pet. There is also a small sketch of a plant at the center of the three groupings.
Charlotte Petersen; SC, Gift of Charlotte Petersen. SC99.224.

880. Julegranen: Angel, ca. 1940s
Colored pencil on paper, 8 3/4 x 11 7/8 (22.2 x 30.2)
Three figures looking at an angel with a bright light coming down from the sky.
Charlotte Petersen; Mary Petersen; CPC, Purchased by the Christian Petersen Memorial Fund. UM92.94.

881. Julengranen: Christmas Scenes, ca. 1940s
Colored pencil on tracing paper, 8 3/4 x 11 3/4 (22.2 x 29.8)
Four sketches of Christmas scenes.
Charlotte Petersen; Mary Petersen; CPC, Purchased by the Christian Petersen Memorial Fund. UM92.196.

882. Julegranen: Sketch of Two Shepherds, ca. 1940s
Chalk on red paper, 9 x 12 (22.9 x 30.5)
Charlotte Petersen; Mary Petersen; CPC, Purchased by the Christian Petersen Memorial Fund. UM92.197.

883. Julegranen: Sketch of Two Shepherds, ca. 1940s
Chalk on green paper, 9 x 12 (22.9 x 30.5)
Charlotte Petersen; Mary Petersen; CPC, Purchased by the Christian Petersen Memorial Fund. UM92.198.

884. Julegranen: Sketch of Two Shepherds, ca. 1940s
Chalk on blue paper, 9 x 12 (22.9 x 30.5)
Charlotte Petersen; Mary Petersen; CPC, Purchased by the Christian Petersen Memorial Fund. UM92.199.

885. Julegranen: Sketch of Two Shepherds, ca. 1940s
Chalk on black paper, 9 x 12 (22.9 x 30.5)
Charlotte Petersen; Mary Petersen; CPC, Purchased by the Christian Petersen Memorial Fund. UM92.200.

886. Julegranen: Sketch of Two Shepherds, ca. 1940s
Chalk on purple paper, 9 x 12 (22.9 x 30.5)
Charlotte Petersen; Mary Petersen; CPC, Purchased by the Christian Petersen Memorial Fund. UM92.201.

887. Julegranen: Small Sketches of Christmas Scenes, ca. 1940s
Colored pencil on paper, 8 3/4 x 11 3/4 (22.2 x 30.2)
Charlotte Petersen; Mary Petersen; CPC, Purchased by the Christian Petersen Memorial Fund. UM92.202a.

888. Julegranen: Virgin Mary and Jesus, ca. 1940s
Colored pencil on paper, 8 x 10 (20.3 x 25.4)
Two sketches of Mary and Christ with a cross glowing behind them.
Inscription: For Julegranen
Charlotte Petersen; Mary Petersen; CPC, Purchased by the Christian Petersen Memorial Fund. UM92.336.

889. Landscape with Pigs, Buildings, and a Smokestack, ca. 1940s
Colored pencil on paper, 13 3/4 x 10 1/2 (34.9 x 26.7)
Charlotte Petersen; Mary Petersen; CPC, Purchased by the Christian Petersen Memorial Fund. UM92.190a.

890. Mary, Jesus, and Three Wise Men, ca. 1940s
Copper plate for engraving, 4 1/2 x 3 1/4 x 1/8 (11.4 x 8.3 x 0.3)
Virgin Mary holding a nude infant Jesus with a halo around them. Three bearded men in front are kneeling and looking at them.
Charlotte Petersen; SC, Gift of Charlotte Petersen. SC99.174.

891. Mary Petersen, ca. 1940s
Pencil or conté on paper, 5 3/4 x 6 3/4 (14.6 x 17.1)
Pocket notebook sketches of the artist's daughter Mary.
Charlotte Petersen; Mary Petersen; CPC, Purchased by the Christian Petersen Memorial Fund. UM92.50.

892. Nun Comforting a Child, ca. 1940s
Pencil or conté on paper, 5 3/4 x 9 (14.6 X 22.7)
Charlotte Petersen; Mary Petersen; CPC, Purchased by the Christian Petersen Memorial Fund. UM92.110.

893. Cowboy, Cutting Horse, and Two Polled Hereford Heifers, 1953–1954
Brown pencil on paper, 14 x 17 (35.6 x 43.2)
Study of cowboy and cattle. Model was John Edenburn, DVM.
Charlotte Petersen; Mary Petersen; CPC, Purchased by the Christian Petersen Memorial Fund. UM92.288.

894. Julegranen: Sketch of Two Shepherds, 1950
Pencil or conté on tracing paper, 8 3/4 x 11 3/4 (22.2 x 29.8)
Inscription: Julegranen 1950
Charlotte Petersen; Mary Petersen; CPC, Purchased by the Christian Petersen Memorial Fund. UM92.195.

895. All the Evils which Have Kept Him Prisoner, ca. 1950
Pencil on paper, 10 3/4 x 11 7/8 (27.3 x 30.2)
Three sketches. Left to right: 1) large one of a Bound Christ standing on a globe, with sketched figures around it and the above title below in pencil. 2) detail of Christ's head. 3) similar to 1, but from a distance and with a base.
Charlotte Petersen; SC, Gift of Charlotte Petersen. SC99.223.

896. Angels, ca. 1950
Pencil or conté on paper, 8 x 10 (20.3 x 25.4)
Sketches of two angels.

Charlotte Petersen; Mary Petersen; CPC, Purchased by the Christian Petersen Memorial Fund. UM92.353.

897. Madonna and Child, ca. 1950
Colored pencil on paper, 9 x 12 (22.9 x 30.5)
Charlotte Petersen; Mary Petersen; CPC, Purchased by the Christian Petersen Memorial Fund. UM92.365.

898. Priest, ca. 1950
Colored pencil on paper, 14 x 17 (35.6 x 43.2)
Figure sketch of a priest on a raised pedestal.
Charlotte Petersen; Mary Petersen; CPC, Purchased by the Christian Petersen Memorial Fund. UM92.389.

899. Priest, ca. 1950
Pencil or conté on paper, 14 x 17 (35.6 x 43.2)
Figure sketch of a priest with clasped hands, on a pedestal.
Charlotte Petersen; Mary Petersen; CPC, Purchased by the Christian Petersen Memorial Fund. UM92.390.

Studies related to *Saint Bernard of Clairvaux,* 1950

900. Concept Study
Charcoal on paper, 14 x 7 (35.6 x 17.8)
Charlotte Petersen; Mary Petersen; CPC, Purchased by the Christian Petersen Memorial Fund. UM92.380.

901. Concept Study
Charcoal on paper, 14 x 7 (35.6 x 17.8)
Charlotte Petersen; Mary Petersen; CPC, Purchased by the Christian Petersen Memorial Fund. UM92.381.

902. Figure Studies
Orange crayon on paper, 16 3/4 x 13 3/4 (42.5 x 34.9)
Studies of Saint Bernard, a kneeling novitiate nun, and one of Petersen's sculpture students.
Charlotte Petersen; Mary Petersen; CPC, Purchased by the Christian Petersen Memorial Fund. UM92.257.

903. Figure Studies
Colored pencil on paper, 14 x 7 (35.6 x 17.8)
Five studies of Saint Bernard.
Charlotte Petersen; Mary Petersen; CPC, Purchased by the Christian Petersen Memorial Fund. UM92.388.

904. Figure Study
Charcoal on paper, 14 x 7 (35.6 x 17.8)
Saint with a book at his side.
Charlotte Petersen; Mary Petersen; CPC, Purchased by the Christian Petersen Memorial Fund. UM92.382.

905. Figure Study
Charcoal on paper, 14 x 7 (35.6 x 17.8)
Saint with a book in front.
Charlotte Petersen; Mary Petersen; CPC, Purchased by the Christian Petersen Memorial Fund. UM92.383.

906. Figure Study
Charcoal on paper, 14 x 7 (35.6 x 17.8)
Saint Bernard with crozier.
CPC, Purchased from Mary Petersen with funds from the Christian Petersen Memorial Fund. UM92.384.

Studies related to *Saint Bernard of Clairvaux,* continued

907. Studies of Hands and Figure
Colored pencil on paper, 16 3/4 x 13 3/4 (42.5 x 34.9)
Studies of two hands holding a staff. Gestural study of *Saint Bernard of Clairvaux.*
Charlotte Petersen; Mary Petersen; CPC, Purchased by the Christian Petersen Memorial Fund. UM92.255.

908. Agronomy Mural: Man with a Seed Bag, ca. 1951
Ink and pencil on paper, 9 x 12 (22.9 x 30.5)
Study of a man with a seed bag for sowing alfalfa.
Charlotte Petersen; Mary Petersen; CPC, Purchased by the Christian Petersen Memorial Fund. UM92.182.

909. Fancy, 1951
Charcoal on paper, 12 x 9 (30.5 x 22.9)
This drawing is of Mary Petersen's cat, which was given the name "Fancy" because of a little V-shaped mark on its right ear.
Inscription: to Mary from Daddy, Xmas '51
Signed in square: CP
Mary Petersen, Beverly Hills, Florida.

910. My Grandchildren, 1951
Pencil on paper, 16 x 20 (40.6 x 50.8)
Drawing made on a trip to California. Grandchildren Jane, Lee, Scott, and Lynn.
Signed lower right: Christian Petersen
Jane Crivello, Fresno, California.

911. Cecil B. DeMille, 1952
Colored pencil on paper, 9 x 12 (22.9 x 30.5)
Study of DeMille, the movie director.
Charlotte Petersen; Mary Petersen; CPC, Purchased by the Christian Petersen Memorial Fund. UM92.361a.

912. Cecil B. DeMille, 1952
Pencil or conté on paper, 9 x 12 (22.9 x 30.5)
Four studies for a sculpture of Cecil B. DeMille.
Charlotte Petersen; Mary Petersen; CPC, Purchased by the Christian Petersen Memorial Fund. UM92.362.

913. Cecil B. DeMille, 1952
Paper and brown pencil, 9 x 12 (22.9 x 30.5)
Charlotte Petersen; Mary Petersen; CPC, Purchased by the Christian Petersen Memorial Fund. UM92.361b.

914. Cecil B. DeMille, 1952
Paper and brown pencil, 9 x 12 (22.9 x 30.5)
Study of the outline of a man's face.
Inscription: Cecil B. DeMille — VEISHEA 1952
Charlotte Petersen; Mary Petersen; CPC, Purchased by the Christian Petersen Memorial Fund. UM92.363.

915. Tink, December 1952
Charcoal, pencils, 13 x 9 3/4 (33 x 24.8)
Head and shoulders of a dog, maybe a German Shepherd.
Inscription: TO MARY CHRISTMAS 1952 FROM DADDY
Mary Petersen; CPC, Gift of Mary Petersen. UM92.613.

916. Prayer of Saint Francis, 1954
Watercolor, 7 x 5 (17.8 x 12.7)
Painting given to Mary Petersen as a Christmas gift.

Inscription: Christmas 1954. With all my love, Dad.
Mary Petersen, Beverly Hills, Florida.

917. Emmett J. Hasty: Study, 1955
Pencil or conté on paper, 12 x 18 (30.5 x 45.7)
Study of bas-relief portrait of principal of Roosevelt Junior High School, Des Moines, Iowa.
Charlotte Petersen; Mary Petersen; CPC, Purchased by the Christian Petersen Memorial Fund. UM92.328b.

918. Landscape, ca. 1945–1955
Oil on masonite, 12 x 18 (30.5 x 45.7)
County line on Gilbert Road, Johnson's farm. Impressionist style, trees on rolling hills. Signed on back in black, "Petersen." A rare medium for Petersen.
Charlotte Petersen; Mary Petersen; CPC, Gift of Mary Petersen. UM92.608.

919. Happy, 1956
Charcoal and pencil on paper, 16 3/4 x 13 3/4 (42.5 x 34.9)
Bent head and shoulders of a man.
Inscription: Happy
Signed: CP
Charlotte Petersen; Mary Petersen; CPC, Gift of Mary Petersen. UM92.614.

920. An Infant in the Hands of Her Mother, 1958
Pencil on paper, 3 3/4 x 5 1/2 (9.5 x 14)
Virginia Slater's infant daughter, Regina, in her hands.
Gift of Charlotte Petersen to Virginia Slater, Ames, Iowa.

921. Dedication to the Future: Concept Study, ca. 1958
Pencil or conté on paper, 5 3/4 x 7 3/4 (16.6 x 19.7)
Study of man, woman, two children standing, and one being lifted up.
Charlotte Petersen; Mary Petersen; CPC, Purchased by the Christian Petersen Memorial Fund. UM92.105.

922. Cat, ca. 1950s
Pencil or conté on paper, 3 3/4 x 6 3/4 (9.5 x 17.1)
Four sketches of a cat.
Charlotte Petersen; Mary Petersen; CPC, Purchased by the Christian Petersen Memorial Fund. UM92.51.

923. Christ, ca. 1950s
Colored pencil on paper, 14 x 16 3/4 (35.6 x 42.5)
Religious figures, three of Christ and two of two people.
Charlotte Petersen; Mary Petersen; CPC, Purchased by the Christian Petersen Memorial Fund. UM92.397.

924. Christ with Arms Outstretched, ca. 1950s
Pencil or conté on paper, 8 x 10 (20.3 x 25.4)
Christ with child followers.
Charlotte Petersen; Mary Petersen; CPC, Purchased by the Christian Petersen Memorial Fund. UM92.339.

925. Christ with Followers, ca. 1950s
Pencil or conté on paper, 12 x 18 (30.5 x 45.7)
Four sketches of Christ with followers.
Charlotte Petersen; Mary Petersen; CPC, Purchased by the Christian Petersen Memorial Fund. UM92.372.

926. Crucifixion, ca. 1950s
Pencil or conté on paper, 8 3/4 x 11 7/8 (22.2 x 30.2)
Charlotte Petersen; Mary Petersen; CPC, Purchased by the Christian Petersen Memorial Fund. UM92.97.

927. Figure Sketches, ca. 1950s
Pencil or conté on paper, 12 x 18 (30.5 x 45.7)
Sixteen sketches of swimmers and people kneeling.
Charlotte Petersen; Mary Petersen; CPC, Purchased by the Christian Petersen Memorial Fund. UM92.315.

928. Home, ca. 1950s
Pencil or conté on paper, 16 3/4 x 13 3/4 (42.5 x 34.9)
Sketch of a house plan. May be the Petersen home in Gilbert, which they remodeled over a long period of time.
Charlotte Petersen; Mary Petersen; CPC, Purchased by the Christian Petersen Memorial Fund. UM92.251b.

929. Jesus Carrying a Cross, ca. 1950s
Colored pencil on paper, 8 x 10 (20.3 x 25.4)
Charlotte Petersen; Mary Petersen; CPC, Purchased by the Christian Petersen Memorial Fund. UM92.329.

930. Jesus Carrying a Cross, ca. 1950s
Colored pencil on paper, 8 x 10 (20.3 x 25.4)
Charlotte Petersen; Mary Petersen; CPC, Purchased by the Christian Petersen Memorial Fund. UM92.330.

931. Abraham Lincoln: Sketch, ca. 1950s
Pencil or conté on paper, 12 x 18 (30.5 x 45.7)
Charlotte Petersen; Mary Petersen; CPC, Purchased by the Christian Petersen Memorial Fund. UM92.370.

932. Abraham Lincoln: Sketch, ca. 1950s
Pencil or conté on paper, 12 x 18 (30.5 x 45.7)
Charlotte Petersen; Mary Petersen; CPC, Purchased by the Christian Petersen Memorial Fund. UM92.371.

933. Madonna and Child, ca. 1950s
Purple pencil on paper, 9 x 12 (22.9 x 30.5)
Seated Madonna and Child atop plinth.
Charlotte Petersen; Mary Petersen; CPC, Purchased by the Christian Petersen Memorial Fund. UM92.364.

934. Man with Arms Raised, ca. 1950s
Pencil or conté on paper, 8 x 10 (20.3 x 25.4)
Man with extended belly and arms raised.
Charlotte Petersen; Mary Petersen; CPC, Purchased by the Christian Petersen Memorial Fund. UM92.338.

935. Man in Profile, ca. 1950s
Colored pencil on paper, 12 x 18 (30.5 x 45.7)
Charlotte Petersen; Mary Petersen; CPC, Purchased by the Christian Petersen Memorial Fund. UM92.313.

936. Man's Face, ca. 1950s
Brown pencil on paper, 12 x 18 (30.5 x 45.7)
Two sketches of a man in profile.
Charlotte Petersen; Mary Petersen; CPC, Purchased by the Christian Petersen Memorial Fund. UM92.312.

937. Mary and Jesus, ca. 1950s
Colored pencil on paper, 8 x 10 (20.3 x 25.4)
Mary and Jesus with a cross glowing behind them.
Charlotte Petersen; Mary Petersen; CPC, Purchased by the Christian Petersen Memorial Fund. UM92.337.

938. Mary and Jesus, ca. 1950s
Colored pencil on paper, 8 x 10 (20.3 x 25.4)
Full figure sketch of Virgin Mary holding baby Jesus, both with halos.
Charlotte Petersen; Mary Petersen; CPC, Purchased by the Christian Petersen Memorial Fund. UM92.333.

939. Men, ca. 1950s
Pencil or conté on paper, 12 x 18 (30.5 x 45.7)
Five whimsical sketches, two men with a bug on one man's nose, in profile and a front view with a man in a corner. One sketch of the Holy Family with Mary and Jesus on a donkey.
Charlotte Petersen; Mary Petersen; CPC, Purchased by the Christian Petersen Memorial Fund. UM92.319b.

940. Charlotte Petersen, ca. 1950s
Charcoal and pencil on paper, 10 1/4 x 14 (26 x 35.6)
The artist's wife sitting in a chair reading a book, with a small lamp, plant, and bowl on the table in the background.
Charlotte Petersen; Mary Petersen; CPC, Gift of Mary Petersen. UM92.615.

941. Religious Figures, ca. 1950s
Brown pencil on paper, 11 3/4 x 18 (29.8 x 45.7)
Studies of *Christ with Bound Hands* with various gestures.
Charlotte Petersen; Mary Petersen; CPC, Purchased by the Christian Petersen Memorial Fund. UM92.261.

942. Religious Figures, ca. 1950s
Colored pencil on paper, 12 x 9 (30.5 x 22.9)
Eight sketches of varying sizes of religious figures, most on pedestals and some with crosses behind them.
Charlotte Petersen; SC, Gift of Charlotte Petersen. SC99.203.

943. Religious Figures, ca. 1950s
Colored pencil on paper, 12 x 18 (30.5 x 45.7)
Charlotte Petersen; Mary Petersen; CPC, Purchased by the Christian Petersen Memorial Fund. UM92.314.

944. Religious Figures, ca. 1950s
Pencil and ink on paper, 11 3/4 x 11 3/4 (29.8 x 29.8)
Sketch of six religious figures.
Charlotte Petersen; Mary Petersen; CPC, Purchased by the Christian Petersen Memorial Fund. UM92.396

945. Religious Panels, ca. 1950s
Colored pencil on paper, 8 3/4 x 11 7/8 (22.2 x 30.2)
Five panels with sketches in them, all religious concepts.
Charlotte Petersen; Mary Petersen; CPC, Purchased by the Christian Petersen Memorial Fund. UM92.100.

946. Robed Figures, ca. 1950s
Pencil on paper, 11 3/4 x 8 3/4 (29.8 x 22.2)
Five rough sketches of groups of figures in robes. Many seem to be in prayer and some appear as sculptures on pedestals.
Charlotte Petersen; SC, Gift of Charlotte Petersen. SC99.168.

947. Woman, ca. 1950s
Pencil or conté on paper, 9 x 12 (22.9 x 30.5)
Seated woman with her right hand raised, seated on a plinth.
Charlotte Petersen; Mary Petersen; CPC, Purchased by the Christian Petersen Memorial Fund. UM92.366.

948. Woman, ca. 1950s
Colored pencil on paper, 12 x 18 (30.5 x 45.7)
A stylishly dressed woman in fur trimmed coat and feather hat, walking away from the viewer.
Charlotte Petersen; Mary Petersen; CPC, Purchased by the Christian Petersen Memorial Fund. UM92.375.

UNDATED TWO-DIMENSIONAL WORKS OF ART

949. Hans Christian Andersen
Pencil or conté on paper, 12 x 18 (30.5 x 45.7)
Sketch of Hans Christian Andersen study; as well as one of a tennis player.
Charlotte Petersen; Mary Petersen; CPC, Purchased by the Christian Petersen Memorial Fund. UM92.326.

950. Animals
Pencil or conté on paper, 13 3/4 x 16 3/4 (34.9 x 42.5)
Sketch.
Charlotte Petersen; Mary Petersen; CPC, Purchased by the Christian Petersen Memorial Fund. UM92.283b.

951. Arm
Pencil or conté on paper, 9 x 12 (22.9 x 30.5)
Charlotte Petersen; Mary Petersen; CPC, Purchased by the Christian Petersen Memorial Fund. UM92.357.

952. Bowls
Pencil or conté on paper, 9 x 12 (22.9 x 30.5)
Drawing of two bowls.
Charlotte Petersen; Mary Petersen; CPC, Purchased by the Christian Petersen Memorial Fund. UM92.157a.

953. Boys: Preparatory Study for Bas-Relief
Pencil or conté on paper, 14 x 16 1/2 (35.6 x 41.9)
Sketch of two young boys.
Charlotte Petersen; Mary Petersen; CPC, Purchased by the Christian Petersen Memorial Fund. UM92.242.

954. Building
Green pencil on paper, 11 3/4 x 18 (29.8 x 45.7)
Charlotte Petersen; Mary Petersen; CPC, Purchased by the Christian Petersen Memorial Fund. UM92.282.

955. Building
Pencil or conté on paper, 14 x 17 (35.6 x 43.2)
Sketch of a building entrance.
Charlotte Petersen; Mary Petersen; CPC, Purchased by the Christian Petersen Memorial Fund. UM92.295.

956. Building Interior
Pencil or conté on paper, 10 x 11 1/2 (25.4 x 29.2)
Sketches of the interior of a building.
Charlotte Petersen; Mary Petersen; CPC, Purchased by the Christian Petersen Memorial Fund. UM92.151a.

957. Calvin Church and School, Des Moines, Iowa
Pencil or conté on paper, 8 3/4 x 11 7/8 (22.2 x 30.2)
Study of a street intersection and a sculpture. Concept for Calvin Church and School, Des Moines, Iowa.
Charlotte Petersen; Mary Petersen; CPC, Purchased by the Christian Petersen Memorial Fund. UM92.67.

958. Campus Entrance: Figures and Fountain
Pencil or conté on paper, 14 x 7 (35.6 x 17.8)
Sketch of five figures and a fountain.
Charlotte Petersen; Mary Petersen; CPC, Purchased by the Christian Petersen Memorial Fund. UM92.379

959. Cartoon for Charlotte
Pencil or conté on paper, 7 x 9 7/8 (17.8 x 25.1)
Sketch of a svelte woman dancing with three men and another plump woman watching.
Inscription: Where did you learn that Sis?
Charlotte Petersen; Mary Petersen; CPC, Purchased by the Christian Petersen Memorial Fund. UM92.66.

960. Chalice
Colored pencil on paper, 8 3/4 x 11 7/8 (22.2 x 30.2)
Sketch of a chalice with a seated satyr or devil.
Charlotte Petersen; Mary Petersen; CPC, Purchased by the Christian Petersen Memorial Fund. UM92.103.

961. Charlotte
Colored pencil on paper, 3 3/4 x 6 3/4 (9.5 x 17.1)
Sketch of Charlotte seated with her legs crossed and head down. She may be sleeping.
Charlotte Petersen; SC, Gift of Charlotte Petersen. SC99.278.

962. Charlotte
Pen on paper, 16 x 8 (40.6 x 20.3)
Cartoon sketches of Charlotte seated in a chair watching a cat lick milk from a dish.
Charlotte Petersen; Mary Petersen; CPC, Purchased by the Christian Petersen Memorial Fund. UM92.271b.

963. Charlotte
Pen on paper, 16 x 8 (40.6 x 20.3)
Cartoon sketch of Charlotte lying on a couch while the dog watches her.
Charlotte Petersen; Mary Petersen; CPC, Purchased by the Christian Petersen Memorial Fund. UM92.271a.

964. Charlotte Petersen
Pencil on paper, 11 3/4 x 8 3/4 (29.8 x 22.2)
Sketch of a standing woman with hands on her hips. She is wearing a dress and high heels.
Charlotte Petersen; SC, Gift of Charlotte Petersen. SC99.173.

965. Charlotte Sitting in Her Garden
Oil on canvas, 10 x 14 (25.4 x 35.6)
Portrait of the artist's wife sitting in her garden.
Charlotte Petersen; Private collection; CPC, Anonymous gift in memory of Charlotte Petersen. UM93.32.

966. Child
Pencil on paper, 6 3/4 x 3 3/4 (17.1 x 9.5);
Image: 5 x 2 1/4 (12.7 x 5.7)
A sketch of the back of a child, probably the artist's daughter Mary, wearing a skirt and shawl.
Charlotte Petersen; SC, Gift of Charlotte Petersen. SC99.212.

967. Child
Pencil or conté on paper, 8 1/2 x 11 (21.6 x 27.9)
Drawing of a child's face.
Charlotte Petersen; Mary Petersen; CPC, Purchased by the Christian Petersen Memorial Fund. UM92.7.

968. Children
Pencil or conté on paper, 12 x 18 (30.5 x 45.7)
Sketch of two children in profile for bas-relief plaque.
Charlotte Petersen; Mary Petersen; CPC, Purchased by the Christian Petersen Memorial Fund. UM92.325b.

969. Children
Pencil or conté on paper, 12 x 18 (30.5 x 45.7)
Sketch of two children in profile for bas-relief plaque.
Charlotte Petersen; Mary Petersen; CPC, Purchased by the Christian Petersen Memorial Fund. UM92.325a.

970. Christ
Pencil on paper, 11 x 8 1/2 (27.9 x 21.6)
Three sketches. Two are small and rough with figure with arms out on bases (one cloudlike, one hemispherical); large sketch of Christ with a robe draped across his chest and over one arm.
Charlotte Petersen; SC, Gift of Charlotte Petersen. SC99.193.

971. Christ
Charcoal on paper, 12 x 9 1/4 (30.5 x 23.5)
Two sketches of Christ, one standing in a robe with a heart in his hands, the other a head study with a crown of thorns.
Charlotte Petersen; SC, Gift of Charlotte Petersen. SC99.180.

972. Christ
Pencil or conté on paper, 12 x 18 (30.5 x 45.7)
Two sketches of Christ with arms stretched horizontally.
Charlotte Petersen; Mary Petersen; CPC, Purchased by the Christian Petersen Memorial Fund. UM92.369.

973. Christ with Child and Three Wise Men
Colored pencil on paper, 8 1/2 x 11 (21.6 x 27.9)
Christ with child and three wise men, used for the *Julegranen* magazine cover.
Charlotte Petersen; Mary Petersen; CPC, Purchased by the Christian Petersen Memorial Fund. UM92.194.

974. Civil War Soldiers
Purple pencil on paper, 10 x 13 3/4 (25.4 x 34.9)
Sketches of Civil War soldiers for war memorial.
Charlotte Petersen; Mary Petersen; CPC, Purchased by the Christian Petersen Memorial Fund. UM92.189.

975. Cloaked Woman
Charcoal on paper, 12 x 18 (30.5 x 45.7)
Figure sketch of a woman draped in a long cloth and seven smaller sketches including a fountain pool.
Charlotte Petersen; Mary Petersen; CPC, Purchased by the Christian Petersen Memorial Fund. UM92.316.

976. Kattke and Harry Collins
Pencil or conté on paper, 8 1/2 x 11 (21.6 x 27.9)
Half circle sketch.
Inscription: "Kattke" and "Harry Collins, Luginbuhl"
Charlotte Petersen; Mary Petersen; CPC, Purchased by the Christian Petersen Memorial Fund. UM92.37a.

977. Courtyard
Pencil on paper, 11 3/4 x 8 3/4 (29.8 x 22.2)
Recto: Two sketches, an aerial view of a circular courtyard or structure and one front view of a wall. Verso: A standing figure holding a stick with a marshmallow into a fire.
Charlotte Petersen; SC, Gift of Charlotte Petersen. SC99.182ab.

978. Crucifixion
Pencil or conté on paper, 8 3/4 x11 7/8 (22.2 x 30.2)
Sketch.
Charlotte Petersen; Mary Petersen; CPC, Purchased by the Christian Petersen Memorial Fund. UM92.99.

979. Figure
Pencil or conté on paper, 11 3/4 x 18 (29.8 x 45.7)
Sketch of a figure.
Charlotte Petersen; Mary Petersen; CPC, Purchased by the Christian Petersen Memorial Fund. UM92.281c.

980. Figure Studies
Pencil or conté on paper, 8 1/2 x 11 (21.6 x 27.9)
Eleven detailed sketches of a primitive man, buffalo, wolf, study of hands, and mother nursing child.
CPC, Purchased from Mary Petersen with funds from the Christian Petersen Memorial Fund. UM92.59.

981. Figure Studies
Charcoal on paper, 14 x 7 (35.6 x 17.8)
Charlotte Petersen; Mary Petersen; CPC, Purchased by the Christian Petersen Memorial Fund. UM92.385.

982. Figure Study
Charcoal and pencil on paper, 5 3/4 x 7 3/4 (14.6 x 19.7)
Sketch of two standing figures.
Charlotte Petersen; Mary Petersen; CPC, Purchased by the Christian Petersen Memorial Fund. UM92.109.

983. Figures
Pencil or conté on paper, 8 x 10 (20.3 x 25.4)
Sketch of couple dancing and a standing woman in profile.
Charlotte Petersen; Mary Petersen; CPC, Purchased by the Christian Petersen Memorial Fund. UM92.352.

984. Figures and Animals
Pencil or conté on paper, 9 x 12 (22.9 x 30.5)
Charlotte Petersen; Mary Petersen; CPC, Purchased by the Christian Petersen Memorial Fund. UM92.368.

985. Foundry Workers Pouring Metal into a Form
Brown pencil on paper, 5 1/2 x 8 1/2 (14 x 21.6)
Sketch of three workers pouring molten metal into a form, following procedures in a casting foundry for sculpting bronzes.
Charlotte Petersen; Mary Petersen; CPC, Purchased by the Christian Petersen Memorial Fund. UM92.104.

986. Grove of Trees
Conté on paper, 8 1/2 x 11 (21.6 x 27.9)
Charlotte Petersen; Mary Petersen; CPC, Purchased by the Christian Petersen Memorial Fund. UM92.8.

987. Horse
Brown crayon on paper, 8 1/2 x 11 (21.6 x 27.9);
Image: 5 1/4 x 7 1/2 (13.3 x 19.1)
Horse in profile. It seems to have come to a sudden stop or be backing away from something.
Charlotte Petersen; SC, Gift of Charlotte Petersen. SC99.197.

988. Jesus, Joseph, and Mary
Pencil or conté on paper, 16 3/4 x 13 3/4 (42.5 x 34.9)
Multiple sketches of the Holy Family.
Charlotte Petersen; Mary Petersen; CPC, Purchased by the Christian Petersen Memorial Fund. UM92.221.

989. Jesus, Joseph, and Mary
Pencil or conté on paper, 16 3/4 x 13 3/4 (42.5 x 34.9)
Sketches of the Holy Family.
Charlotte Petersen; Mary Petersen; CPC, Purchased by the Christian Petersen Memorial Fund. UM92.220.

990. Julegranen: Christmas Magazine Cover
Pencil or conté on paper, 13 3/4 x 16 3/4 (34.9 x 42.5)
Suggestions for Christmas issue cover for *Julegranen* magazine.
Charlotte Petersen; Mary Petersen; CPC, Purchased by the Christian Petersen Memorial Fund. UM92.286.

991. Julegranen: Christmas Sketch of a Girl
Pencil on paper, 13 7/8 x 9 1/2 (35.2 x 24.1);
Image: 12 x 7 1/2 (30.5 x 19.1)
Bust view of a young girl with a scarf tied around her head, looking up. There is a candle to her right and two windows above her, each with three candles and three faces behind them. Concept for cover for *Julegranen* magazine.
Charlotte Petersen; SC, Gift of Charlotte Petersen. SC99.209.

992. Julegranen: Christmas Sketches of Three Children Singing
Colored pencil on paper, 13 3/4 x 16 3/4 (34.9 x 42.5)
Charlotte Petersen; Mary Petersen; CPC, Purchased by the Christian Petersen Memorial Fund. UM92.208.

993. Julegranen: Sketch of Religious Figures
Pencil or conté on paper, 8 3/4 x 11 7/8 (22.2 x 30.2)
Sketch of three shepherds in a landscape with an angel coming down from the sky.
Charlotte Petersen; Mary Petersen; CPC, Purchased by the Christian Petersen Memorial Fund. UM92.92.

994. Julegranen: Villa Aldobrandini
Pencil or conté on paper, 13 3/4 x 16 3/4 (34.9 x 42.5)
Sketch of a building, possibly for an illustration for *Julegranen* magazine.
Inscription at bottom: Villa Aldobrandini
Charlotte Petersen; Mary Petersen; CPC, Purchased by the Christian Petersen Memorial Fund. UM92.203.

995. Kneeling Female and Child
Conté on paper, 11 x 8 1/2 (27.9 x 21.6)
Sketch of a kneeling female figure with hands on the shoulders of a child standing in front of her.
Charlotte Petersen; SC, Gift of Charlotte Petersen. SC99.185.

996. Kneeling Figure
Colored pencil on paper, 8 x 10 (20.3 x 25.4)
Sketch of a kneeling figure with arms extended to back.
Charlotte Petersen; Mary Petersen; CPC, Purchased by the Christian Petersen Memorial Fund. UM92.335.

997. Man
Pencil or conté on paper, 8 3/4 x 11 7/8 (22.2 x 30.2)
Sketch of a man's profile.
Charlotte Petersen; Mary Petersen; CPC, Purchased by the Christian Petersen Memorial Fund. UM92.101.

998. Man
Pencil or conté on paper, 8 3/4 x 11 7/8 (22.2 x 30.2)
Profile sketch of a man.
Charlotte Petersen; Mary Petersen; CPC, Purchased by the Christian Petersen Memorial Fund. UM92.102.

999. Man
Charcoal or conté on paper, 8 1/2 x 11 (21.6 x 27.9)
Sketch of a man in motion.
Charlotte Petersen; Mary Petersen; CPC, Purchased by the Christian Petersen Memorial Fund. UM92.127.

1000. Man
Pencil or conté on paper, 9 x 12 (22.9 x 30.5)
Sketch of a man in profile.
Charlotte Petersen; Mary Petersen; CPC, Purchased by the Christian Petersen Memorial Fund. UM92.164.

1001. Man and Children
Colored pencil on paper, 8 1/2 x 11 (21.6 x 27.9)
Man with two children seated on a long stone bench.
Charlotte Petersen; Mary Petersen; CPC, Purchased by the Christian Petersen Memorial Fund. UM92.14.

1002. Man Bending Over
Brown pencil on paper, 14 x 16 3/4 (35.6 x 42.5)
CPC, Purchased from Mary Petersen with funds from the Christian Petersen Memorial Fund. UM92.398.

1003. Man Shooting Bow and Arrow I
Pencil or conté on paper, 8 1/2 x 11 (21.6 x 27.9)
Sketch of man shooting a bow and arrow with woman crouched behind him holding a child; drawn in a circle.
Charlotte Petersen; Mary Petersen; CPC, Purchased by the Christian Petersen Memorial Fund. UM92.40.

1004. Man Shooting Bow and Arrow II
Pencil or conté on paper, 8 1/2 x 11 (21.6 x 27.9)
Man shooting a bow and arrow with woman crouched behind him holding a child; drawn in a rectangle.
Charlotte Petersen; Mary Petersen; CPC, Purchased by the Christian Petersen Memorial Fund. UM92.41.

1005. Man with Sideburns
Pencil or conté on paper, 8 1/2 x 11 (21.6 x 27.9)
Finely sketched and detailed profile of a man with long sideburns.
Charlotte Petersen; Mary Petersen; CPC, Purchased by the Christian Petersen Memorial Fund. UM92.30.

1006. Man Walking
Conté on paper, 11 7/8 x 8 3/4 (30.2 x 22.2);
Central image: 8 1/4 x 3 1/2 (21 x 8.9)
Four sketches. The three smaller ones are crossed out. The large sketch is of a nude male walking with fabric draped from his back, under his right arm to his left hand.
Charlotte Petersen; SC, Gift of Charlotte Petersen. SC99.208.

1007. Man Wearing Glasses
Purple colored pencil on paper, 11 7/8 x 8 3/4 (30.2 x 22.2)
Very faint sketch of a man in profile wearing glasses.
Charlotte Petersen; SC, Gift of Charlotte Petersen. SC99.183.

1008. Man's Face

Pencil or conté on paper, 9 3/4 x 14 (24.8 x 35.6)
Charlotte Petersen; Mary Petersen; CPC, Purchased by the Christian Petersen Memorial Fund. UM92.266.

1009. Mary and Friend

Pencil or conté on paper, 14 x 10 (35.6 x 25.4)
Sketches of two children, one of whom is the artist's daughter, Mary Petersen.
Charlotte Petersen; Mary Petersen; CPC, Purchased by the Christian Petersen Memorial Fund. UM92.150.

1010. "Merry Christmas, Happy New Year, The Petersens"

Linocut on paper, 4 1/4 x 5 7/8 (10.8 x 14.9)
Inscription: Merry Christmas, Happy New Year, The Petersens
Charlotte Petersen; Mary Petersen; CPC, Purchased by the Christian Petersen Memorial Fund. UM92.193.

1011. Mind's Eye Sketch

Pencil or conté on paper, 3 3/4 x 6 3/4 (9.5 x 17.1)
Pocket notebook with sketch of a building.
Inscription: 4 times 39 equals 166 [*sic*]
Charlotte Petersen; Mary Petersen; CPC, Purchased by the Christian Petersen Memorial Fund. UM92.52.

1012. Monument

Pencil on paper, 11 7/8 x 8 3/4 (30.2 x 22.2);
Images: 7 x 4 5/8 (17.8 x 11.7) and 6 1/2 x 2 1/2 (16.5 x 6.4)
Two views (frontal and profile) of a monument with three adult figures standing in front of a cross and behind a branch. The central figure holds a book or *Bible*.
Charlotte Petersen; SC, Gift of Charlotte Petersen. SC99.199.

1013. Mother and Child

Colored pencil on paper, 16 3/4 x 13 3/4 (42.5 x 34.9)
Charlotte Petersen; Mary Petersen; CPC, Purchased by the Christian Petersen Memorial Fund. UM92.254.

1014. Nude Figure

Pencil on paper, 11 x 8 1/2 (27.9 x 21.6)
Sketch on the left of a nude, leaning figure. Sketch on the right is crosslike and leaning in the opposite direction.
Charlotte Petersen; SC, Gift of Charlotte Petersen. SC99.210.

1015. Nude Sketches

Pencil or conté on paper, 14 x 10 (35.6 x 25.4)
Sketches of two nude figures at fountain, one with arms above head holding a tray.
Charlotte Petersen; Mary Petersen; CPC, Purchased by the Christian Petersen Memorial Fund. UM92.152.

1016. Old Man in Shorts

Ink on paper, 11 x 8 1/2 (27.9 x 21.6)
Sketch of an old man in shorts, on a beach, trying to catch a nude woman. Petersen would often leave very early in the morning for his studio after leaving a small sketch at Charlotte's place on the breakfast table as a "good morning" greeting.
Charlotte Petersen; Mary Petersen; CPC, Purchased by the Christian Petersen Memorial Fund. UM92.275.

1017. Oval Sculpture

Pencil or conté on paper, 14 x 17 (35.6 x 43.2)
Sketch.
Charlotte Petersen; Mary Petersen; CPC, Purchased by the Christian Petersen Memorial Fund. UM92.296.

1018. Person

Charcoal on paper, 9 x 12 (22.9 x 30.5)
Sketch of a person in a reaching pose.
Charlotte Petersen; Mary Petersen; CPC, Purchased by the Christian Petersen Memorial Fund. UM92.187.

1019. Plant

Brown pencil and conté on paper, 9 x 12 (22.9 x 30.5)
Sketch of a plant.
Charlotte Petersen; Mary Petersen; CPC, Purchased by the Christian Petersen Memorial Fund. UM92.183.

1020. Pool Studies

Pencil or conté on paper, 5 3/4 x 7 3/4 (14.6 x 19.7)
Two gestural sketches of circular and rectangular pools.
Charlotte Petersen; Mary Petersen; CPC, Purchased by the Christian Petersen Memorial Fund. UM92.107.

1021. Preparatory Sketch

Pencil or conté on paper, 9 1/4 x 11 1/2 (23.5 x 29.2)
Sketch of a sculpture.
Charlotte Petersen; Mary Petersen; CPC, Purchased by the Christian Petersen Memorial Fund. UM92.274a.

1022. Rectangular Sketches with Figures

Pencil or conté on paper, 8 3/4 x 11 7/8 (22.2 x 30.2)
Three sketches.
Charlotte Petersen; Mary Petersen; CPC, Purchased by the Christian Petersen Memorial Fund. UM92.72.

1023. Religious Event

Pencil or conté on paper, 13 3/4 x 16 3/4 (34.9 x 42.5)
Charlotte Petersen; Mary Petersen; CPC, Purchased by the Christian Petersen Memorial Fund. UM92.280.

1024. Religious Figures

Pencil on paper, 11 7/8 x 8 3/4 (30.2 x 22.2);
Image: 3 3/4 x 6 1/2 (9.5 x 16.5)
Two small sketches of figures on bases. One on the left is a robed female with an infant in her left arm. The one on the right is a standing figure with a bird, and a kneeling figure to his left is looking at the bird.
Charlotte Petersen; SC, Gift of Charlotte Petersen. SC99.205.

1025. Religious Figures

Pencil or conté on paper, 12 x 18 (30.5 x 45.7)
Three sketches with two figures in each sketch. Two sketches of a person supporting a fallen Christ, and one sketch of two robed figures walking.
Charlotte Petersen; Mary Petersen; CPC, Purchased by the Christian Petersen Memorial Fund. UM92.320.

1026. Running Horses

Brown crayon on paper, 8 1/2 x 11 (21.6 x 27.9)
Sketches (small at top, large at bottom) of a horse running.
Charlotte Petersen; SC, Gift of Charlotte Petersen. SC99.176.

1027. Rural Landscape

Watercolor on paper, 13 3/4 x 10 1/2 (34.9 x 26.7)
Probably the countryside near the Iowa State campus or the City of Ames.
Charlotte Petersen; Mary Petersen; CPC, Purchased by the Christian Petersen Memorial Fund. UM92.190b.

1028. Saints among Savages

Colored pencil on paper, 16 3/4 x 13 3/4 (42.5 x 34.9)
Three sketches of groupings, each with three religious figures on pedestals.
Inscription: Saints among savages
CPC, Purchased from Mary Petersen with funds from the Christian Petersen Memorial Fund. UM92.256.

1029. Sculpture Sketch

Pencil or conté on paper, 14 x 7 (35.6 x 17.8)
Charlotte Petersen; Mary Petersen; CPC, Purchased by the Christian Petersen Memorial Fund. UM92.377.

1030. Sculpture Sketch

Charcoal on paper, 8 1/2 x 11 (21.6 x 27.9)
Seated figure with a figure below on each side, and reliefs on columns extending outward from the center figures.
Charlotte Petersen; Mary Petersen; CPC, Purchased by the Christian Petersen Memorial Fund. UM92.10.

1031. Seated Figures

Charcoal on paper, 8 1/2 x 11 (21.6 x 27.9)
Seated and robed figure with two figures below on each side.
Charlotte Petersen; Mary Petersen; CPC, Purchased by the Christian Petersen Memorial Fund. UM92.9.

1032. Seated Woman

Pencil or conté on paper, 13 3/4 x 16 3/4 (34.9 x 42.5)
Detailed sketch of a seated woman with ankles crossed.
Charlotte Petersen; Mary Petersen; CPC, Purchased by the Christian Petersen Memorial Fund. UM92.213.

1033. Seated Woman

Pencil and conté on paper, 13 3/4 x 16 3/4 (34.9 x 42.5)
Figure drawing of seated woman in profile.
Charlotte Petersen; Mary Petersen; CPC, Purchased by the Christian Petersen Memorial Fund. UM92.393.

1034. Seated Woman

Pencil or conté on paper, 12 x 18 (30.5 x 45.7)
Nude woman sitting, with turned torso, on a pedestal base.
Charlotte Petersen; Mary Petersen; CPC, Purchased by the Christian Petersen Memorial Fund. UM92.327.

1035. Seated Woman

Pencil or conté on paper, 8 3/4 x 11 3/4 (22.2 x 29.8)
Seated nude woman, leaning forward with arm stretched over her head.
Charlotte Petersen; Mary Petersen; CPC, Purchased by the Christian Petersen Memorial Fund. UM92.163.

1036. Self-portrait

Watercolor and crayon on paper, 8 1/2 x 11 (21.6 x 27.9);
Image: 7 1/2 x 4 1/2 (19.1 x 11.4)
One of few known self-portraits. Shows the artist in profile with a moustache.
Charlotte Petersen; SC, Gift of Charlotte Petersen. SC99.175.

1037. Single Figure Drawing

Colored pencil on paper, 8 1/2 x 11 (21.6 x 27.9)
Rectangle with a figure stretching inside.
Charlotte Petersen; Mary Petersen; CPC, Purchased by the Christian Petersen Memorial Fund. UM92.16.

1038. Structure

Pencil on paper, 11 x 8 1/2 (27.9 x 21.6)
Rough sketch of a vertical structure, possibly a cabinet with shelves. Inscription at top: Dans K. Sambirke, Kristianagade 8, Kobenhaun 0, A. Kamp–Director for Dans K. Sambirke, Pedaktor–for Denmarks Poster.
Charlotte Petersen; SC, Gift of Charlotte Petersen. SC99.187.

1039. Teacher and a Student

Pencil or conté on paper, 4 3/8 x 6 7/8 (11.1 x 14.5)
Sketch of two people, suggestive of a teacher and a student.
Charlotte Petersen; Mary Petersen; CPC, Purchased by the Christian Petersen Memorial Fund. UM92.54.

1040. Three Figures

Pencil or conté on paper, 5 3/4 x 7 3/4 (14.6 x 19.7)
Sketch of three figures, one with arms extended upward.
Charlotte Petersen; Mary Petersen; CPC, Purchased by the Christian Petersen Memorial Fund. UM92.106.

1041. Trees and a Stream

Pencil or conté on paper, 14 x 10 (35.6 x 25.4)
Charlotte Petersen; Mary Petersen; CPC, Purchased by the Christian Petersen Memorial Fund. UM92.149.

1042. Vegetation

Pencil and purple colored pencil on paper, 11 7/8 x 8 3/4 (30.2 x 22.2)
Study of barren tree branches and other plant life.
Charlotte Petersen; SC, Gift of Charlotte Petersen. SC99.202.

1043. Virgin Mary and Jesus

Ink, colored pencil, and conté on paper, 11 7/8 x 8 3/4 (30.2 x 22.2);
Images: 6 x 6 1/4 (15.2 x 15.9) and 4 x 3 (10.2 x 7.6)
Recto: Five sketches of variations of Virgin Mary and Jesus in different poses and one of Madonna praying with a halo.
Verso: Top: Madonna with a halo and three kneeling figures in robes in front of her. Bottom: Small Madonna in profile holding Jesus.
Charlotte Petersen; SC, Gift of Charlotte Petersen. SC99.206ab.

1044. Virgin Mary Holding Jesus

Pencil on paper, 11 7/8 x 8 3/4 (30.2 x 22.2)
Sketch for an engraving of Virgin Mary standing holding an infant Jesus in front of her. Three bearded kneeling male figures in robes are in front of them, looking at Jesus.
Charlotte Petersen; SC, Gift of Charlotte Petersen. SC99.201.

1045. Virgin Mary Holding Jesus

Pencil or conté on paper, 5 3/4 x 9 (14.6 x 22.7)
Profile sketch of Virgin Mary holding infant Jesus with her shawl draped around him.
Charlotte Petersen; Mary Petersen; CPC, Purchased by the Christian Petersen Memorial Fund. UM92.114.

1046. Winged Figure

Pencil on paper, 13 7/8 x 7 3/8 (35.2 x 18.7);
Main image: 7 1/4 x 2 3/8 (18.4 x 6)
Three sketches. Small one unknown. Two larger ones of a standing winged male on a pedestal holding a sword in his right hand.
Charlotte Petersen; SC, Gift of Charlotte Petersen. SC99.204.

1047. Woman

Pencil and colored pencil on paper, 11 3/4 x 8 3/4 (29.8 x 22.2)
Two sketches. Top is a study of a bust of a woman with her hair up. Bottom is a plan for a bas-relief with a border around it. The bas-relief has a bust in the upper half and an empty box for an inscription in the bottom.
Charlotte Petersen; SC, Gift of Charlotte Petersen. SC99.171.

1048. Woman

Pencil or conté on paper, 13 3/4 x 16 3/4 (34.9 x 42.5)
Sketch of a woman.
Charlotte Petersen; Mary Petersen; CPC, Purchased by the Christian Petersen Memorial Fund. UM92.214.

1049. Woman

Colored pencil on paper, 13 3/4 x 16 3/4 (34.9 x 42.5)
Sketch of a sculpture of a woman with a figure on each side of her, and a detail of the woman's head.
Charlotte Petersen; Mary Petersen; CPC, Purchased by the Christian Petersen Memorial Fund. UM92.216.

1050. Woman

Pencil or conté on paper, 13 3/4 x 16 3/4 (34.9 x 42.5)
Profile of a woman.
Charlotte Petersen; Mary Petersen; CPC, Purchased by the Christian Petersen Memorial Fund. UM92.283a.

1051. Woman

Pencil or conté on paper, 12 x 18 (30.5 x 45.7)
A woman in profile in a circle.
Charlotte Petersen; Mary Petersen; CPC, Purchased by the Christian Petersen Memorial Fund. UM92.284a.

1052. Woman

Pencil or conté on paper, 13 3/4 x 16 3/4 (34.9 x 42.5)
Profile of a woman in a circle.
Charlotte Petersen; Mary Petersen; CPC, Purchased by the Christian Petersen Memorial Fund. UM92.284b.

1053. Woman

Pencil or conté on paper, 13 3/4 x 16 3/4 (34.9 x 42.5)
Profile of a woman.
CPC, Purchased from Mary Petersen with funds from the Christian Petersen Memorial Fund. UM92.284c.

1054. Woman

Red pencil on paper, 14 x 17 (35.6 x 43.2)
Sketch of a woman.
Charlotte Petersen; Mary Petersen; CPC, Purchased by the Christian Petersen Memorial Fund. UM92.289.

1055. Woman and Child

Pencil or conté on paper, 12 x 18 (30.5 x 45.7)
Charlotte Petersen; Mary Petersen; CPC, Purchased by the Christian Petersen Memorial Fund. UM92.307.

1056. Woman with Child

Colored pencil on paper, 12 x 18 (30.5 x 45.7)
Six sketches of a woman holding a baby.
Charlotte Petersen; Mary Petersen; CPC, Purchased by the Christian Petersen Memorial Fund. UM92.322.

1057. Woman in a Cloak

Charcoal on paper, 12 x 18 (30.5 x 45.7)
Three sketches, including a sketch of a woman in a cloak, one woman and a child.
Charlotte Petersen; Mary Petersen; CPC, Purchased by the Christian Petersen Memorial Fund. UM92.319a.

1058. Woman in Profile

Pencil or conté on paper, 13 3/4 x 16 3/4 (34.9 x 42.5)
Charlotte Petersen; Mary Petersen; CPC, Purchased by the Christian Petersen Memorial Fund. UM92.394.

1059. Woman Releasing a Bird

Brown pencil and paper, 8 1/2 x 11 (21.6 x 27.9)
Charlotte Petersen; Mary Petersen; CPC, Purchased by the Christian Petersen Memorial Fund. UM92.118.

1060. Woman and Sculpture Site

Pencil on paper, 11 7/8 x 8 3/4 (30.2 x 22.2)
Five sketches. Recto: Study of a woman in a dress, facing forward and wearing heels. Verso: Four views of walls, probably proposed settings for sculptures. Three aerial views, one frontal with measurements.
Charlotte Petersen; SC, Gift of Charlotte Petersen. SC99.211ab.

1061. Woman's Face

Colored pencil on paper, 13 3/4 x 16 3/4 (34.9 x 42.5)
Outline of woman's face.
Charlotte Petersen; Mary Petersen; CPC, Purchased by the Christian Petersen Memorial Fund. UM92.202b.

1062. Woman's Face

Pencil or conté on paper, 13 3/4 x 16 3/4 (34.9 x 42.5)
Sketch of a woman's face in profile.
CPC, Purchased from Mary Petersen with funds from the Christian Petersen Memorial Fund. UM92.206.

1063. Woman's Face

Pencil or conté on paper, 16 3/4 x 13 3/4 (42.5 x 34.9)
Sketch.
Charlotte Petersen; Mary Petersen; CPC, Purchased by the Christian Petersen Memorial Fund. UM92.240.

1064. Woman's Face

Colored pencil on paper, 16 3/4 x 13 3/4 (42.5 x 34.9)
Charlotte Petersen; Mary Petersen; CPC, Purchased by the Christian Petersen Memorial Fund. UM92.246.

1065. Woman's Legs

Violet pencil on paper, 4 x 6 (10.2 x 15.2)
Sketch.
Charlotte Petersen; Mary Petersen; CPC, Purchased by the Christian Petersen Memorial Fund. UM92.49.

1066. Woman Washing Dishes

Pencil on paper, 11 7/8 x 8 3/4 (30.2 x 22.2)
Woman in profile, standing and washing dishes in a sink.
Charlotte Petersen; SC, Gift of Charlotte Petersen. SC99.196.

1067. Women

Pencil on paper, 12 x 8 3/4 (30.5 x 22.2)
Seven sketches of seated, kneeling and standing females. Some are on bases, two have frameworks behind them, and one holds a branch.
Charlotte Petersen; SC, Gift of Charlotte Petersen. SC99.179.

1068. Women

Pencil on paper, 9 1/2 x 7 1/4 (24.1 x 18.4)

An older female in profile within a box in the upper right corner, as a bas-relief looking at the other sketch of a young nude woman arching her back with her right leg bent.

Charlotte Petersen; SC, Gift of Charlotte Petersen. SC99.198.

1069. Women

Pencil or conté on paper, 13 3/4 x 16 3/4 (34.9 x 42.5)

Two sketches, one of a woman with two figures at her side, the other of two women.

Charlotte Petersen; Mary Petersen; CPC, Purchased by the Christian Petersen Memorial Fund. UM92.205.

1070. Women

Colored pencil on paper, 12 x 18 (30.5 x 45.7)

Ten sketches of nude, single, and group figures.

Charlotte Petersen; Mary Petersen; CPC, Purchased by the Christian Petersen Memorial Fund. UM92.321.

1071. Young Girl's Face

Brown pencil on paper, 16 3/4 x 13 3/4 (42.5 x 34.9)

Sketch.

Charlotte Petersen; Mary Petersen; CPC, Purchased by the Christian Petersen Memorial Fund. UM92.237.

APPENDIX A: WORKS OF ART BY PETERSEN KNOWN TO HAVE BEEN DESTROYED

1072. Ruth Holden and Alice Illingworth Haskell, 1919

Bronze, approximately 24 (61) [height]

Memorial plaque may have been executed by Petersen from a design by George Nerney. Melted during a World War II scrap metal drive, according to photograph caption in CPP.

Inscription: A TRIBUTE / FROM THE WOMEN OF ATTLEBORO / NINETEEN HUNDRED AND NINETEEN

Originally in Sturdy Memorial Hospital, Attleboro, Massachusetts.

1073. Fountain of the Blue Herons, 1930

Bedford limestone

Fountain and reflecting pool. Destroyed 1950.

Formerly A.E. Staley Manufacturing Company, Decatur, Illinois.

1074. Grant Wood, 1934

Painted clay, 19 3/4 x 22 3/4 x 15 1/2 (50.2 x 57.8 x 39.4)

This portrait bust was a gift of Christian Petersen to the students of William McKinley School in Cedar Rapids. It was removed for an unauthorized bronze casting that is located at the Cedar Rapids Museum of Art. The original portrait bust was likely destroyed during the bronze casting process.

Presented in 1934 to Cedar Rapids Community Schools.

1075. Helen Cunningham, 1935

Plaster

Bas-relief portrait of the daughter of J.C. Cunningham.

Marjorie C. Shrigley.

1076. Bud and Bill Ryan, 1940

Plaster

Life-size bust portraits of the sons of Dr. and Mrs. Charles Ryan.

Dr. and Mrs. Charles Ryan; Charles J. Ryan, M.D., Naples. Florida.

1077. Ethel Cessna Morgan, ca. 1941

Unfired clay

Clay bust of the Petersens' friend and neighbor.

Ethel Cessna Morgan; Margaret Morgan Hauptman, Harrisburg, Illinois.

1078. The Rising Christ (Resurrection)

Plaster

Charlotte Petersen; Purchased at 1964 sale by Donald W. Gade, Bakersfield, California.

APPENDIX B: WORKS OF ART CREATED BY PETERSEN IN COLLABORATION WITH HIS STUDENTS

1079. Nativity Scene
Special Collections in the Iowa State University Library, ISU, has a photograph of this approximately life-size nativity scene that was erected on campus at Christmas. It included a kneeling Mary, standing Joseph, an infant Jesus in a wooden manger, and relief murals of animals in the background.

APPENDIX C: CASTS AND REPRODUCTIONS OF WORKS OF ART CREATED BY CHRISTIAN PETERSEN

DATED WORKS

1080. A Dedication to the Future, 1961
Bronze, 18 (45.7) [height]
Nude man standing and holding a nude male child in his upraised hands.
Original sculpture commissioned by J.W. Fisher for the Fisher Community Center, Marshalltown, Iowa. Bronze reproductions of the model for this work of art were distributed in Marshalltown, Iowa, by J.W. "Bill" Fisher.

1081. Christ with Bound Hands
(Christ before Pilate with Bound Hands), 1960
Plaster, 25 x 6 1/4 x 6 1/2 (63.5 x 15.9 x 16.5)
Three casts of this figure are believed to have been made, one of which was given to Archbishop Rohlman of Dubuque, Iowa, in 1950. Copies were produced and sold at Saint Thomas Aquinas Church and Catholic Student Center in Ames, Iowa, in 1960.

1082. Saint Christopher, early 1960s
Plaster, 10 1/2 x 1/2 (26.7 x 1.3) [diameter x depth]
This medallion features an adult Saint Christopher with a child Jesus on his shoulder. The medallion was reproduced for sale by Saint Cecilia Church in the 1960s.
CPC, Gift of Saint Cecilia Church, Ames, Iowa.UM95.83.

1083. Two Children, ca. 1960–1964
Plaster, Boy: 12 1/2 x 5 1/4 x 4 (31.8 x 13.3. x 10.2);
Girl: 12 1/2 x 4 3/4 x 5 1/4 (31.8 x 12.1 x 13.3)
One piece depicts Mary Petersen, the artist's daughter, holding her rag doll in dejection and the other depicts her playmate — a neighborhood boy — holding his new puppy after bragging about it and telling her, "You can't play with it." Five plaster castings sold at the 1964 sale. Permastone castings were made in 1986.

1084. The Gentle Doctor, 1976
Cast bronze, 80 x 24 1/2 x 23 (203.2 x 62.2 x 58.4)
Cast reproduction of the original. Cast by Paul Shao.
Commissioned by the College of Veterinary Medicine. Permanent installation at College of Veterinary Medicine courtyard. CPC/AOC, Gift of Dr. and Mrs. J.E. Salsbury U88.70.

1085. The Gentle Doctor, 1980
Cast resin on wood base
From 1960 until 1980, the Iowa State Veterinary College sold eighteen-inch plaster castings of *The Gentle Doctor* as a fundraiser for the Christian Petersen Scholarship Fund, with royalties to Charlotte Petersen for every piece purchased. Her husband had created the piece for his veterinary friends in 1959. In 1980, the original mold had deteriorated and The Veterinary College commissioned a new copyrighted resin casting of the piece, which is currently sold by the College with proceeds to the continuing scholarship fund for the Christian and Charlotte Petersen Scholarship Fund.

1086. Pegasus, 1984

Bronze

Three casts made of a 1938 Petersen spoof of a draft horse getting a pair of wings. Casting done by George-Ann Neudeck Tognoni, a student of Christian Petersen's in the 1940s. The reproductions were produced by Pegasus Productions, through royalty arrangements with Charlotte and Mary Petersen.

Casting 1: College of Veterinary Medicine, ISU. Casting 2: Patricia L. Bliss, Sedona, Arizona. Casting 3: Private collection.

1087. Mask of Lincoln, 1986

Bronze, 8 1/2 (21.6) [height]

Fifteen bronzes of a 1936 original cast by Pegasus Productions with royalties to Charlotte Petersen. Ten of them given to the Octagon Center for the Arts, Ames, Iowa, in 1986 for an annual volunteer of the year award in memory of Christian and Charlotte Petersen.

1088. Two Children, 1986

Permastone, Boy: 12 1/2 x 5 1/4 x 4 (31.8 x 13.3. x 10.2); Girl: 12 1/2 x 4 3/4 x 5 1/4 (31.8 x 12.1 x 13.3)

Thirty-six pairs of castings of the originals were done by Pegasus Productions in 1986, by royalty arrangement with Charlotte and Mary Petersen.

1089. Marriage Ring (Wedding Ring, Ring of Life), 1992

Plaster reproduction, 6 x 21 1/2 x 7 (15.2 x 54.6 x 17.8)

Forty-two reproductions of the 1943 original were made by Foster Willey of Minneapolis, Minnesota. One was purchased for the Brunnier Art Museum, one for Museum education program, and forty were given as gifts to donors to the Family and Consumer Sciences Department of Iowa State University.

1090. Marriage Ring (Wedding Ring, Ring of Life), 1994

Concrete reproduction of children from the 1942 original.

Terra cotta sculpture group, 37 x 117 x 16 1/2 (94 x 297.2 x 41.9), with pool, 17' (5.18 m) [diameter including outside capstone of pool] Concrete pigmented to terra cotta color. Casting commissioned by University Museums, Iowa State University, Ames, Iowa. Casting done by Mayda Jensen Conservation, Omaha, Nebraska. Inscription on end block: Christian Petersen

Commissioned by University Museums, Iowa State University. Permanent installation at MacKay Hall. CPC/AOC, U94.13.

1091. George Washington Carver, 1999

Bronze, 43 x 13 1/2 x 11 (109.2 x 34.3 x 27.9)

This bronze sculpture was cast by J.A.M. Studio from the original plaster sculpture created by Christian Petersen in 1942. The sculpture is a full length figure of Carver who holds a peanut in his raised left hand. Three castings were made.

Commissioned by University Museums. Casting 1: Permanent installation in the Carver Hall Courtyard. CPC/AOC, Gift of John and Linda Dasher. U99.18. Casting 2: CPC. UM99.29. Casting 3: Pioneer Hi-Bred International, Des Moines, Iowa.

UNDATED WORK

1092. Mother and Father

Porcelain, 5 x 4 (12.7 x 10.2)

Reproduced by Mrs. C. Edward Christians, Des Moines, Iowa, from 1910 bronze bas-relief of Petersen's parents, Helene and Peter Petersen.

SC, Gift of Mrs. C. Edward Christians and Mrs. Athena Harley.

The following people and organizations lent works of art to the exhibition Christian Petersen, Sculptor.

Mary (Mrs. Bertrand) Adams
Eleanor and William Butler
Ms. Carol Mae Campbell
Central Iowa Art Association, Marshalltown
M. Burton Drexler
Maridee Hegstrom
Margaret Hunziker
Iowa State University:
    Art on Campus Collection, University Museums
    Botany Department
    Brunnier Art Museum, University Museums
    College of Veterinary Medicine
    Department of Landscape Architecture
    Memorial Union
    Special Collections, Iowa State University Library
Joan Lange Kaas
Robin Krueger
Lynn Sollenberger Lucido
Helene Petersen Male
Joan and Robert Mannheimer
Isabel Matterson
Helen and Keith McRoberts
Wayne Moore
The Newark Museum, New Jersey
Mary Petersen
Saint Cecilia Church
Marjorie Shloss Spevak and Frances M. Shloss
Virginia Slater
Scott Sollenberger
State Historical Society of Iowa
Reece Stuart III
Helen (Mrs. J. William) Uhrig

University Museums would like to express its deep appreciation and gratitude to the donors who provided major gifts to support this project.

Roberta and Robert W. Boeke, Ames, Iowa
The Coppola Family in honor of Joseph M. Coppola, Sr., Des Moines, Iowa
Iowa State University Foundation, Ames, Iowa
Estate of William R. Merrill
National Endowment for the Arts, Washington, D.C.
Mary Petersen, Beverly Hills, Florida
Mary Alice and Bill Reinhardt, Centralia, Missouri
John and Doris Salsbury, Bozeman, Montana
Helen Sebek, Fort Dodge, Iowa
Stockman Family Foundation, Albuquerque, New Mexico
Target Stores, Inc., Ames, Iowa
College of Veterinary Medicine, Iowa State University, Ames, Iowa

Patricia Lounsbury Bliss is a 1950 journalism graduate of the University of Iowa. Shortly after graduation, she became the first woman copy desk editor for *The Des Moines Tribune.* From 1952 until 1986, she was a freelance writer-editor for Iowa State University. For three years she researched the Christian Petersen papers and conducted extensive interviews with the artist's widow, Charlotte. This research formed the basis for her book, *Christian Petersen Remembered* (ISU Press, 1986). Bliss was the first to identify and organize Petersen's photographs and sketches, and she successfully nominated Petersen's dairy industry murals to the National Register of Historic Places.

Lea Rosson DeLong received her B.A. from the University of Oklahoma and her master's and Ph.D. from the University of Kansas. Concentrating on American art of the Depression era, she has curated exhibitions and written on the Southwestern painter Alexandre Hogue and on New Deal art of the Midwest. With Gregg Narber, she co-authored a catalogue of New Deal murals in the state of Iowa. She has also curated exhibitions and written on contemporary art. She is currently research curator at the Des Moines Art Center, where her most recent publication was the exhibition catalogue *Shifting Visions: O'Keefe, Guston, Richter.*

Dr. Charles C. Eldredge, presently the Hall Distinguished Professor of American Art and Culture at the University of Kansas, was formerly director of the Smithsonian's National Museum of American Art. He has published and lectured widely on topics relating to the American art, especially of the late nineteenth and early twentieth centuries, ranging from fin-de-siècle symbolists to 1930s regionalists.

Linda Merk-Gould is a Fellow of the American Institute for Conservation and a Fellow of the International Institute for Conservation. She received an Art History degree from Wellesley College and her M.A. in sculpture conservation at The Queen's University in Kingston, Ontario. She worked at several museums before becoming the head of conservation at Harvard University's Peabody Museum. In 1982 she started Fine Objects Conservation, Inc., which was re-incorporated in Connecticut in 1995 as Conservation Technical Associates LLC.

Dana L. Michels received a B.A. from Drake University and an M.A. with a focus on twentieth-century American art from the University of Iowa. She has worked for the University of Iowa Museum of Art in Iowa City, Iowa; the Charles H. MacNider Museum in Mason City, Iowa; the Des Moines Art Center in Des Moines, Iowa; and the Museum of Kyoto in Kyoto, Japan. She is currently curatorial assistant for the Brunnier Art Museum, University Museums, Iowa State University.

Lynette L. Pohlman has been the director of the University Museums at Iowa State University since 1981. She administers and is chief curator of the Brunnier Art Museum and the Farm House Museum, and she heads the Art on Campus Program at ISU. Lynette has a personal and professional commitment to museums and their responsibility to acquire, preserve, educate, and interpret the visual and cultural arts. She is also an authority in the areas of public art, campus museum management, the decorative arts, and nineteenth-century architecture.

INTRODUCTION

Figure I.1 — University Museums archives
Figure I.2 — National Academy of Design
Figure I.3 — The Historical Society of Washington, D.C., David Blume, photographer
Figure I.4 — Photo courtesy of Katherine Crum; photographer, Christopher A. Johnson
Figure I.5 — Coe College, Cedar Rapids, Iowa; George T. Henry, photographer

CHAPTER 1

Figure 1.1–1.2 — University Museums archives
Figure 1.3 — City of Lexington, Massachusetts
Figure 1.4 — Lea Rosson DeLong, Des Moines Art Center
Figure 1.5 — U.S. Department of the Interior
Figure 1.6–1.7 — Special Collections, ISU Library
Figure 1.8–1.9 — University Museums Archives
Figure 1.10 — City of New York, New York
Figure 1.11 — Special Collections, ISU Library
Figure 1.12 — Collection of the Newark Museum, gift of Whitehead and Hoag, 1929
Figure 1.13 — University Museums archives

CHAPTER 2

Figure 2.1–2.13 — University Museums archives
Figure 2.14–2.15 — Greg Narber
Figure 2.16–2.25 — University Museums archives

CHAPTER 3

Figure 3.1–3.2 — University Museums archives
Figure 3.3 — University Photo Services
Figure 3.4 — Special Collections, ISU Library
Figure 3.5–3.6 — University Museums archives
Figure 3.7 — Family collection of Mrs. L.M. Forland
Figure 3.8 — University Museums archives
Figure 3.9 — College of Veterinary Medicine archives

CHAPTER 4

Figure 4.1–4.8 — University Museums archives
Figure 4.9 — Special Collections, ISU Library
Figure 4.10–4.14 — University Photo Services

Figure 4.15 — Special Collections, ISU Library
Figure 4.16 — University Photo Services
Figure 4.17 — University Museums Archives
Figure 4.18 — University Photo Services
Figure 4.19–4.22 — University Museums archives
Figure 4.23–4.24 — University Photo Services
Figure 4.25 — Special Collections, ISU Library
Figure 4.26–4.29 — University Photo Services

CHAPTER 5

Figure 5.1 — University Museums archives
Figure 5.2 — Doug Smith
Figure 5.3 — University Museums archives
Figure 5.4–5.5 — Doug Smith
Figure 5.6–5.7 — University Photo Services

CHAPTER 6

Figure 6.1 — University Museums archives
Figure 6.2–6.5 — University Photo Services
Figure 6.6 — Jan Morgan (previously published in *Christian Petersen Remembered*, ISU Press, 1962)
Figure 6.7 — Special Collections, ISU Library
Figure 6.8 — University Museums archives
Figure 6.9 — University Photo Services
Figure 6.10–6.11 — University Museums archives
Figure 6.12 — Bob Baum
Figure 6.13 — St. Bernard's Church, Breda, Iowa
Figure 6.14 — University Photo Services
Figure 6.15 — University Museums archives
Figure 6.16–6.17 — University Photo Services
Figure 6.18 — Special Collections, ISU Library

CHARLOTTE PETERSEN

Figure 1–2 — University Museums archives
Figure 3–4 — Special Collections, ISU Library
Figure 5 — Family collection of Mary Petersen

CONSERVATION INSIGHTS

Figure 1–2 — Conservation Technical Associates
Figure 3–4 — University Museums archives
Figure 4–19 — Conservation Technical Associates

Lynette L. Pohlman
Director and Chief Curator

Mary Atherly
Collections Manager
Farm House Museum Curator

Stacy Brothers
Administrative Assistant

Matthew DeLay
Curator of Education and Interpretation

Terri Hasselman
Development Director

Dana L. Michels
Curatorial Assistant

Susan Olson
Development Secretary

Eleanor Ostendorf
Collections and Curatorial Program Assistant

Marilyn Vaughan
Public Relations Coordinator

Jackie Wilson
Educational Assistant and Security Officer

Molly Wong
Museum Store Manager

INDEX